STOLNE AND SURREPTITIOUS COPIES

PUBLISHED BY ARRANGEMENT WITH THE COMMONWEALTH LITERARY FUND

STOLNE AND
SURREPTITIOUS COPIES

A COMPARATIVE STUDY
OF
SHAKESPEARE'S BAD QUARTOS

BY

ALFRED HART

FOLCROFT LIBRARY EDITIONS 1970

Limited to 150 Copies

STOLNE AND SURREPTITIOUS COPIES

A COMPARATIVE STUDY
OF
SHAKESPEARE'S BAD QUARTOS

BY

ALFRED HART

MELBOURNE UNIVERSITY PRESS
IN ASSOCIATION WITH
OXFORD UNIVERSITY PRESS
MELBOURNE AND LONDON
1942

REGISTERED AT THE G.P.O., MELBOURNE, FOR TRANSMISSION
THROUGH THE POST AS A BOOK

WHOLLY SET UP AND PRINTED IN AUSTRALIA FOR THE BOARD OF
MANAGEMENT OF THE MELBOURNE UNIVERSITY PRESS, THE
UNIVERSITY OF MELBOURNE, CARLTON, N.3, VICTORIA, BY BROWN,
PRIOR, ANDERSON PTY. LTD., 430 LIT. BOURKE ST., MELBOURNE, C.1

FOREWORD

THIS volume is, to the best of my knowledge, the first book devoted entirely to an investigation of the many problems associated with the relation between the 'stolne and surreptitious copies' of which Heminge and Condell complain in their address 'To the great Variety of Readers,' and the corresponding plays of Shakespeare printed by them in the first folio. For nearly two and a half centuries prior to the publication of the important Cambridge Shakespeare of 1863-6, many editors and commentators held firmly to the opinion that these words condemned all the quarto editions published in the life-time of the poet. They preferred to rely on the folio version for the text of a play although careful collation had previously proved that the folio text of this play had been set up from one of the earlier quarto editions. Such deep-rooted and widely spread errors of belief are hardy weeds difficult to eradicate from the literary field, and it was not until 1909 that Professor A. W. Pollard in his *Shakespeare Folios and Quartos* proved beyond possibility of future doubt that the damnatory words of Shakespeare's friends applied only to *Contention, True Tragedy* and the first quartos of *Romeo and Juliet, Henry V, Merry Wives* and *Hamlet;* this group of texts he aptly termed 'Bad Quartos.'

During the past one hundred and fifty years each of these bad quartos has been the theme of numerous monographs from the pens of noted editors and scholars; Malone's *Dissertation on Henry VI* (1787) was the first and is the most famous. His reputation rests on the solid foundation of wide learning, good judgment, industry and honesty, but certain defects of his dissertation have deprived it of any but historical importance. He gave enduring currency to many erroneous statements about the versification of these plays, and trustful editors and copying commentators still perpetuate his incorrect assertion that the plays on Henry VI contain an excessive number of classical similes and allusions. Moreover by mixing together two separate problems, the problem of authorship and the problem of priority of composition, he started a brace of hares which five generations of literary sportsmen have coursed with more zeal than success. To the great influence of this dissertation is due the unfortunate twist given to most of the subsequent criticism of *Contention* and *True Tragedy*. Most illogically and in total disregard of all the evidence many essayists have excluded these plays from the list of 'stolne and surreptitious copies' of the master's plays; they have thus lost their status as his illegitimate and rather disreputable offspring, the deformed heirs of his invention, and have been reduced to keep company with such nameless waifs as *Jack Straw*, *George-a-Greene* and *The Famous Victories*. In accepting *2 Henry VI* and *3 Henry VI* as Shakespeare's, Malone dishonoured the god of his idolatry by imputing to him wholesale plagiarism from *Contention* and *True Tragedy*, which he magisterially declared were the work of Marlowe, Greene and Peele. For these and other reasons I agree with the considered judgment of Professor Alexander:

The dissertation on these plays is infected throughout by hasty observation, imperfect reasoning, and ill-established conclusions.[1]

I shall break with past custom and not offer any explanation of my inclusion of these two plays in the list of bad quartos; my reasons will appear at large in almost every chapter of this work. I agree with Professor Alexander that, if they can be proved corrupt derivatives of *2 Henry VI* and *3 Henry VI,* the controversy is over, and those critics who take upon them to attack the authenticity of two plays printed in the first folio of Shakespeare have no other or better arguments than their own subjective impressions.

My reading of Malone's essay led me to examine the text of the two early bad quartos in detail. Subsequently I perused with a steadily decreasing interest all the essays written on the bad quartos prior to 1908; it seemed to me that many of the authors preferred conjecture to fact and the patient drudgery imposed on any one who would undertake what was really a scientific investigation. Copies of some theses were not available in Australia, but most of these discuss the relation between one pair only of the six parallel texts. Sir Edmund Chambers recognized the importance of the bad quartos by treating them as a group and discussing their defects in *William Shakespeare*;[2] later he briefly analyzed each of

---

1. *Shakespeare's Henry VI and Richard III*, p. 214, (1929).
2. Vol. i, pp. 155-162.

them and its connection with the corresponding play of Shakespeare in chapter IX of that well-documented book.

Literary controversy is wearisome to readers and does not always help to the truth, and, with the exception of what has been said of Malone's *Dissertation*, I have refrained from criticizing in any detail the work of any one not now alive. In my chapter on 'Repeated Lines' and elsewhere I have briefly examined, and, I think, have refuted Professor Tucker Brooke's statement that Marlowe was unusually prone to repetition of lines that had captured his fancy. Much more space has been given to testing the ingenious theory of partial or double revision which Professors Pollard and Dover Wilson propounded some twenty years ago as their solution of the origination of the bad quartos. My reasons for rejecting their theory are set out at considerable length, because it is, in essence, the older 'first sketch' theory in disguise. They have pressed into their service the new 'science' of bibliography; upon the value of this recent aid to learning and literary research I am not competent to offer an opinion. Yet I venture to suggest that bibliography does not provide all the props necessary to support the extensive superstructure which their theory requires.

Dr. W. W. Greg's *Two Elizabethan Abridgments* (1923) is a model hand-book of the principles and practice of investigating play-pathology. It represented a long-overdue revolt against the sterile warfare of theory-mongers, and cleared the air with an invigorating breeze of good sense. He kept to the narrow path of the scientific method, and obtained all his results concerning the genesis of *Orlando Furioso Q1* from his closely reasoned analysis of the materials in that play and in the Dulwich MS. of Orlando's part. His deductions are such and so many as the facts will support. Up to the present no one has questioned his facts, methods or conclusions; he has definitely proved that all the forms assumed by corruption in this play were beyond question the work of actors and reporters. My own debt to his book is everywhere manifest, and several of my chapters, notably those on abridgment, verse structure, blunders, repetition and stage directions begin with some evidence, extracted from the texts of the Dulwich MS. and *Orlando Furioso Q1,* that into this quarto some persons, almost certainly actors or reporters or both, have introduced much the same kind of corruption as exists in the bad quartos. This conclusion is of the greatest importance to my inquiry. It suggests that a bad quarto version of a lost play written by Greene, of which only Orlando's part is now extant, was in existence almost thirty years before the editors of Shakespeare's plays protested against the publication of 'stolne and surreptitious copies.' It suggests also that at least a dozen plays of this period, including Marlowe's *Doctor Faustus* and *Massacre at Paris,* Peele's *Old Wive's Tale* and *Battle of Alcazar,* and such anonymous plays as *Jack Straw, A Shrew, George-a-Greene,* etc., are all bad quartos of non-extant plays. Unfortunately not a fragment remains of the authentic texts; all that time has left is a mutilated 'plat' or skeleton outline of the *Battle of Alcazar.*

One fortunate circumstance separates the six bad quartos of Shakespeare from the rest of the ragged company to which they naturally belong—an authentic text of each was printed in the folio or in a 'good' quarto. Study of Dr. Greg's book convinced me that all the problems arising from the interrelation of the first quarto and the second quarto of *Romeo and Juliet* or *Hamlet* could be completely solved by collecting and classifying all the relevant facts obtainable from each pair of parallel texts, and then deducing such inferences as the facts justified. With this end in view I collected, wherever possible, and classified the respective vocabularies of each pair of parallel texts, made a line-for-line collation of the two texts, noting all variations of importance, examined the verse in detail, collecting all deviations from that of the authentic text, gathered words, phrases, lines and passages of Q1, which were without meaning except in the light thrown upon them from the parallel passages of the poet's play, made lists of lines belonging to the authentic text which were repeated or anticipated in Q1, and put my results in a compact table wherever possible. Only a small selection of my abundant material is incorporated in this volume; the amount used may seem excessive but is necessary, in my opinion, for a complete proof, especially in an investigation in which premediæval standards of inquiry have been prevalent for more than a century, and facts have been less plentiful than guesses.

When I began my investigation, my intention was to limit my work to a study of the problems arising from the relationship between *True Tragedy* and *3 Henry VI,* but I found myself compelled to include *Contention.* Reflection and more research convinced me that the problem of priority of composition was almost identically the same for each of the six pairs of parallel texts. Each bad quarto suffers from the same disease and exhibits, in the main, similar symptoms, but *True Tragedy, Romeo and Juliet Q1* and *Henry V Q1* have the disease in a milder form, and the ravages of corruption have not spread so widely and have not penetrated so deeply as in *Contention, Merry Wives Q1* and *Hamlet Q1.* All my work is directed to one end—to prove that the six bad quartos are derivative texts and take their origin from the corruption of the respective six plays written by Shakespeare. For the rest any one may conjecture what he pleases. Whether Shakespeare used non-existent early plays as raw material for his own, how the reported plays came to the press, who were the pirates and reporters, and why such a well-managed company as the Chamberlain's men came to suffer the piracy of four popular plays within six years are, in comparison with the major problem of priority, matters of small importance. I have ventured to hazard a wide solution of one or two such riddles; did not Sir Thomas Browne admit that such a puzzling question as 'what Song the Syrens sang' is 'not beyond all conjecture'?

Much of my matter appears in print for the first time. Some of my conclusions have been obtained by using methods not often applied to the solution of literary problems, and consequently may fail to win ready acceptance. I regret that it has been necessary to crowd so much tabular detail into the first hundred pages, but no other method is so concise and so effective. So wide is the range of topics incident to a complete investigation of this subject that the observance of any logical sequence in successive chapters is very difficult; occasionally the sole link that binds chapter to chapter is the theme of the book, that the bad quartos are garbled abridgments of the acting versions made by order of the company from Shakespeare's manuscripts. For this reason the book ends with a short summary, to which I refer readers who may find my tests based on play-vocabularies and word-groups hard to follow. My note on the authorship of *2 Henry VI* and *3 Henry VI* has been placed in an appendix.

It may seem presumptuous for an unknown scholar living in Australia to compile a bulky volume on the bad quartos and omit mention of almost all the notable scholars who have written in the aggregate so many thousand pages on this still-vexed question; but what was the alternative? A complete bibliography would go back nearly two hundred years and would fill perhaps twenty octavo pages; even historians of Shakespearean study would boggle at writing a detailed account of the various opinions held by two or three hundred critics and editors. I decided to pass over what had been written prior to 1912, begin afresh, treat the relation between the bad quartos and Shakespeare's plays as a problem in detection, and base my solution on a critical survey of all the facts. Where conjecture was necessary I have tried to keep on the lee side of probability. I was encouraged to proceed by the kindly reception given in England and Germany to my work on play abridgment and to my book, *Shakespeare and the Homilies.*

My obligations to living authors and to my friends must not be left unacknowledged. To Dr. Greg's book I owe the inspiration that original work always gives; any elaborate treatment of *Merry Wives Q1* was, I felt, superfluous, after I had read his edition of that play. Professor Pollard's *Shakespeare Folios and Quartos* is an earlier milestone on the road to truth; it provides a solid background to any criticism of the bad quartos because he has proved that it is against them and them only that Heminge and Condell directed their censure. Professor Alexander's *Henry VI* and *Richard III,* though written on different lines, has been very helpful. My indebtedness to *The Elizabethan Stage* and *William Shakespeare,* those admirable and encyclopaedic works of Sir Edmund Chambers, is very great, though in some small points it may not be acknowledged. My lists of repeated and borrowed lines have been gathered from multifarious sources. Some have been gleaned from *The Elizabethan Stage,* others from editions of Kyd's works by Professor Boas, of Greene's plays by Churton Collins, of Marlowe's plays by Dyce, Tancock, Briggs and Professor Tucker Brooke, of *Arden of Feversham* by Professor Tucker Brooke, (*The Shakespeare Apocrypha*), and from a collection of parallel passages in the latter's monograph on the *Authorship of the Second and Third parts of Henry VI.* Many other borrowings, especially those in *Romeo and Juliet Q1* and *Hamlet Q1* come from my own reading; I trust that any omission to name my source will be ascribed to ignorance or forgetfulness.

To my friend, the late E. H. C. Oliphant, I owe some suggestions arising from discussions, and to Professor G. H. Cowling and Dr. W. V. Aughterson some criticism on various points. I owe a heavy debt of gratitude to Dr. Greta Hort, principal of Melbourne University Women's College, for her kindness in giving many hours of her time to the task of reading this book in typescript, and I have benefited from her advice and encouragement. I must thank Miss Marie E. Monckton and Mr. H. G. Seccombe, senior lecturer in English, Melbourne University, for undertaking the laborious task of correcting the proof sheets, the officers of the Melbourne Public Library and Mr. Leigh Scott, the University librarian, for their uniform courtesy and helpful assistance in the provision of books, and Mr. Frank Wilmot for his never-failing care in seeing this book through the University Press. Finally, I must express my thanks to the members of the Literary and Parliamentary Committees in control of the Commonwealth Literary Fund for their support.

A.H.

South Yarra, Melbourne,
July 1939.

CONTENTS

CHAPTER I

BIBLIOGRAPHY OF THE PARALLEL TEXTS

I PROPOSE to attempt the solution of the problem concerning the relationship between two groups of play-texts; the first group consists of the so-called 'bad' quartos, and the second of the corresponding good texts, written by or attributed to Shakespeare and first printed in quarto or in the first folio. Detailed literary discussion began with Malone in his *Dissertation on Henry VI* (1787), and this famous essay has had an influence in the formation of opinion far beyond what its merits deserve. He arbitrarily assumed that *Contention* and *True Tragedy* were original plays written by Marlowe, Greene and others, and that Shakespeare had used them as his sources for the parallel texts of *2 Henry VI* and *3 Henry VI*. He thus confused two separate problems. With the texts of *2 Henry VI* and *Contention* or those of *3 Henry VI* and *True Tragedy* before him, a critic has, in my opinion, all that is necessary for him to decide the main question, that of priority of composition; the question of authorship is a second and independent problem. To provide an adequate basis for criticism and judgment the main facts will be set out as briefly as possible.

I have included *Contention* and *True Tragedy* among the bad quartos, and do not understand why they have been excluded from this group. If, as I firmly believe, these two surreptitious plays are corrupt abridgments derived from the acting versions of plays printed in the first folio, the problem of the authorship of these bad quartos ceases to exist. Critics who refuse to accept *2 Henry VI* or *3 Henry VI* as authentic plays of Shakespeare must furnish arguments against including them in the canon strong and plentiful enough to prevail over the cumulative evidence provided by Greene, Shakespeare himself in the epilogue to *Henry V*, the entry on the Stationers' Register of 19 April 1602, the title-page of the *Whole Contention* printed in 1619, and his friends and fellow-actors, Heminge and Condell, in the first folio.

Each of the bad quartos preceded in publication the correspond-

1

ing play attributed by the editors of the first folio to Shakespeare. Greene's allusion to 'Shake-scene' suggests that *3 Henry VI* took its present form and was therefore written by Shakespeare at least three years before *True Tragedy* was published. Since the opening line of *3 Henry VI* was obviously written by the author of *2 Henry VI,* to which play it is the sequel, both these plays were probably in existence at least two years before *Contention* was entered on the Stationers' Register. Again, the title-page of *Romeo and Juliet Q1* (printed 1597) makes it certain that Shakespeare's play was acted between the end of July 1596 and March 1597; the comparatively good condition of the first quarto text suggests that it was printed soon afterwards. We have the allusion to Essex in the opening chorus of *Henry V,* which proves that Shakespeare had written this play more than a year before the entry in the Stationers' Register referring to the 'staied' publication. No evidence exists to prove that *Romeo and Juliet Q1* or *Merry Wives Q1* or *Hamlet Q1* was in print before Shakespeare's play of the same title had been written or acted. On the other hand definite proof can be given that matter found in one or other of these plays of Shakespeare but not in the corresponding first quarto must have been in existence before this quarto had been entered on the Stationers' Register. Some bibliographical facts concerning the early editions of each pair of parallel texts are set out below.

I CONTENTION

Entered on Stationers' Register, 12 March 1594.

Title-Pages:

The First part of the Contention betwixt the two famous Houses of Yorke and Lancaster, with the death of the good Duke Humphrey: And the banishment and death of the Duke of Suffolke, and the Tragicall end of the proud Cardinall of Winchester, with the notable Rebellion of Iacke Cade: And the Duke of Yorkes first claime vnto the Crowne. London. Printed by Thomas Creed, for Thomas Millington, and are to be sold at his shop vnder Saint Peters Church in Cornwall. 1594.

Second Edition. Title-page identical with above except for minor variations. It is dated 1600, and was printed by Valentine Simmes.

II TRUE TRAGEDY

No entry on Stationers' Register.

Title-Pages:

The true Tragedie of Richard Duke of Yorke, and the death of good King Henrie the Sixt, with the whole contention betweene the two Houses Lancaster and Yorke, as it was sundrie times acted by the Right Honourable the Earle of Pembrooke his seruants. Printed at London by P(eter) S(hort) for Thomas Millington, and are to be sold at his shoppe vnder Saint Peters Church in Cornwal. 1595.

This edition was in octavo, not quarto.

Second Edition has title-page identical with that of the first except for small changes. It is dated 1600, and was printed by W(illiam) W(hite).

The third edition of these two plays was printed by Thomas Pavier to whom Millington had assigned his copyright 19 April 1602; they were entered as 'The firste and Second parte of Henry the vj ij bookes.' The title-page runs:

The Whole Contention betweene the two Famous Houses, Lancaster and Yorke. With the Tragicall ends of the good Duke Humfrey, Richard Duke of Yorke and King Henrie the sixt. Diuided into two Parts: And newly corrected and enlarged. Written by William Shakespeare, Gent. Printed at London, for T(homas) P(avier).

These plays have an undated title-page, but the signatures are continued in *Pericles* dated 1619. The printer was Jaggard who issued these plays with five others of Shakespeare's including *Henry V Q3* and *Merry Wives Q2* as a first instalment of what may have have been intended for a complete edition of the plays. Some errors of the earlier editions are corrected but fresh errors and misprints appear in the text. The extra matter consists of a few lines and passages of no great importance.

III ROMEO AND JULIET

No entry on Stationers' Register.

Title-Page:

An Excellent conceited Tragedie of Romeo and Juliet. As it hath been often (with great applause) plaid publiquely, by the right Honourable the L. of Hunsdon his Seruants. London. Printed by Iohn Danter. 1597.

B

This edition was not reprinted, most probably because two years later the authentic text came to press. Below is the title-page:

The Most Excellent and lamentable Tragedie, of Romeo and Iuliet. Newly corrected, augmented, and amended: As it hath bene sundry times publiquely acted, by the right Honourable the Lord Chamberlaine his Seruants. London Printed by Thomas Creede, for Cuthbert Burby, and are sold at his shop neare the Exchange. 1599.

It will be noted that Shakespeare's name does not appear on either title-page or on that of the quarto dated 1609, and that the name of the company has been changed to that borne by it in 1599.

IV HENRY V

No entry on Stationers' Register.

An undated memorandum appears on a spare page of the Stationers' Register to the following effect:

$$\left.\begin{array}{l} \text{4 Augusti} \\ \text{Henry the ffift, a booke} \end{array}\right\} \text{to be staied.}$$

Title-Pages:

The Chronicle History of Henry the fift, With his battel fought at Agin Court in France. Togither with Auntient Pistoll. As it hath bene sundry times playd by the Right honourable the Lord Chamberlaine his seruants. London. Printed by Thomas Creede, for Tho. Millington, and Iohn Busby. And are to be sold at his house in Carter Lane, next the Powle head. 1600.

Second Edition. On 14 August 1600 the copyright was transferred from Millington to Thomas Pavier who published the second edition in 1602. Copies 'are to be sold at his shop in Cornhill, at the signe of the Cat and Parrets neare the Exchange'.

Third Edition has a title-page identical with that of 1602 except for the words 'printed for T(homas) P(avier) 1608.'

This is a false date, and should be 1619.

V THE MERRY WIVES OF WINDSOR

Entered on Stationers' Register 18 January 1602 by John Busby.

Title-Pages:

A Most pleasaunt and excellent conceited Comedie, of Syr Iohn Falstaffe, and the merrie Wiues of Windsor Entermixed with sundrie variable and pleasing humors, of Syr Hugh the Welch Knight, Iustice Shallow, and his wise Cousin M. Slender. With the swaggering vaine of Auncient Pistoll, and Corporal Nym. By William Shakespeare. As it hath bene divers times Acted by the right Honourable my Lord Chamberlaines seruants. Both before her Maiestie, and else-where. London. Printed by T(homas) C(reede) for Arthur Iohnson, and are to be sold at his shop in Powles Church-yard at the signe of the Flower de Leuse and the Crowne. 1602.

Second Edition

A Most pleasant and excellent conceited Comedy, of Sir Iohn Falstaffe, and the merry Wiues of Windsor. With the swaggering vaine of Ancient Pistoll, and Corporall Nym. Written by W. Shakespeare. Printed for Arthur Iohnson, 1619.

This is the first surreptitious quarto to bear Shakespeare's name as author.

VI Hamlet

Entered on the Stationers' Register, 26 July 1602.

Title-Pages:

The Tragicall Historie of Hamlet Prince of Denmarke By William Shake-speare. As it hath beene diuerse times acted by his Highnesse seruants in the Cittie of London: as also in the two Vniuersities of Cambridge and Oxford, and else-where. At London printed (by Valentine Simmes) for N(icholas) L(ing) and John Trundell. 1603.

This edition was not reprinted because the authentic text was printed the following year. The title-page runs:

The Tragicall Historie of Hamlet, Prince of Denmarke. By William Shakespeare. Newly imprinted and enlarged to almost as much againe as it was, according to the true and perfect Coppie. At London, Printed by I(ames) R(oberts) for N(icholas) L(ing) and are to be sold at his shoppe vnder Saint Dunstons Church in Fleet-Street. 1604.

The title-page of some copies is dated 1605.

The words 'his Highnesse seruants' prove that *Q1* was printed after 19 May 1603.

No argument of any strength for or against the Shakespearean authorship of the bad quartos can be inferred from the absence or presence of his name on the title-pages. All the editions published during the poet's life-time of the four earlier surreptitious plays were anonymous; *Merry Wives Q1* and *Hamlet Q1,* though by far the most corrupt and mutilated, were publicly fathered on him, imperfections and all. One reason for this piece of imposture is not far to seek. Buyers and readers of plays recognized the merits of *Richard III, Richard II, Romeo and Juliet, Henry IV* and the comedies, and by the year 1602 the poet's name on a title-page meant a ready sale; hence came about the piracy of *Merry Wives Q1* (1602) and *Hamlet Q1* (1603), and the false ascription of a play such as *London Prodigal* (1605) to William Shakespeare, and of *Cromwell* (1602) and *Puritan* (1607) to W.S. Up to the year 1600, two-thirds of all the printed plays written for the public theatres or acted between the years 1587 and 1600 did not have the authors' names on their title-pages, though the names of the authors of many of these plays were certainly known to the play-going, and perhaps to many of the play-reading public. Lyly, Peele, Greene, Kyd, Marlowe, Shakespeare, Heywood, Drayton and others contributed to the long list of nameless plays. It is correct to state that anonymity was the rule rather than the exception. Jonson, Chapman, Marston, Middleton, Dekker and others began the custom of placing their names on the title-pages of plays written for the public stage, and edited them with some amount of care. Shakespeare varied his practice with the times, though it is more than possible that his fellow-actors and the publishers were more jealous of his reputation than the author himself. His name does not appear on the title-pages of the first editions of *Richard III* (1597), *Richard II* (1597) and *1 Henry IV* (1598), but does appear on the title-page of what may be the second edition of *Loue's Labour's Lost* (1598) and on the title-pages of the second editions of *Richard III* (1598), *Richard II* (1598) and *1 Henry IV* (1599). It is remarkable that neither the second quarto (1599) nor the third quarto (1609) of *Romeo and Juliet* bears the author's name, though its publication was probably due to the desire of the author or his fellow-actors to give the public a correct copy of a very popular play. References to it were made by Francis Meres and Marston prior to the issue of the second quarto. Some critics object to the authenticity of *Titus Andronicus* that Shakespeare's name was omitted on the title-pages of three editions printed in the poet's life-time; they accept *Romeo and Juliet* as Shakespeare's, though the second and third quartos, and many copies of the fourth quarto are anonymous.

It must not be forgotten that the piracy of each of the four longer surreptitious quartos most probably took place during periods when the theatres were closed, and that these plays were printed either during the period of restraint or shortly afterwards.

During nearly two years from June 1592 to June 1594 the London theatres were open for only seventy days, mainly in January 1593 and January 1594. *Contention* was entered on the Stationers' Register three months before the theatres reopened for continuous playing and was printed later in 1594. *True Tragedy* was one of the plays belonging to the unfortunate Pembroke's men, and was not printed till 1595, though it may have been sold at the same time as *Contention*.

Romeo and Juliet Q1 was probably printed early in 1597, if we may accept the implications of the statement on the title-page,

as it hath been often (with great applause) plaid publiquely by the right Honourable the L. of Hunsdon his Seruants.

This fixes definite limits between 22 July 1596 when Lord Hunsdon succeeded his father as second baron and 17 March 1597 when he became Lord Chamberlain, as his father had been till his death. Sir Edmund Chambers says:

The title-page and other preliminaries . . . were generally printed, at any rate in first editions, after the body of the book. . . . It is of the nature of an advertisement, and separate copies were struck off as hand-bills.[1]

Usually the name of the company mentioned was that of the one which had performed it last. Accordingly if the title-page was printed later than 17 March 1597 we should most probably have on it 'the Lord Chamberlain his Seruants' as in the second edition (1599), and in *Richard II* (1597) and *Richard III* (1597). Henslowe records that the London theatres were closed for fourteen weeks after the Lord Chamberlain's death in July 1596; perhaps the death of the company's patron, the appointment of Lord Cobham, something of a Puritan, as his successor, and the outbreak of plague after the restraint for the offence caused by the *Isle of Dogs*, all combined to help Danter to his last and most

1. *William Shakespeare*, vol. I, p. 174.

important success as a pirate of plays. Two distinct founts of type were used in printing the first quarto, a fact which suggests that Danter may have died during the printing.

Hamlet Q1 was entered on the Stationers' Register 26 July 1602 by James Roberts; the entry concludes:

as yt was latelie Acted by the Lord Chamberleyne his servantes.

When *Q1* appeared in 1603, the title-page added,

By William Shake-speare. As it hath beene diuerse times acted by his Highnesse seruants in the Cittie of London: as also in the two Vniuersities of Cambridge and Oxford, and else-where. At London printed (by Valentine Simmes) etc.

Roberts, who entered it, was a printer; he printed the authentic text of *Q2* in 1604, but not that of *Q1*, and probably had nothing to do with its publication. Shakespeare and his fellows became His Majesty's servants on 19 May 1603; this is the earliest possible date for the publication of *Q1*, and by this time the appalling plague of this year had begun to rage in London. The theatres had then been closed for two months and remained closed till the beginning of the next year.

The title-pages of two of the parallel authentic texts, viz., *Romeo and Juliet Q2* and *Hamlet Q2*, have already been transcribed. The folio version of *Romeo and Juliet* was printed from Q3 which was itself printed from Q2; the folio version of *Hamlet* is ultimately derived from the manuscript that was the source of the second quarto, with some variant readings and additions and omissions of text. All the other plays, viz., *2 Henry VI, 3 Henry VI, Henry V* and *Merry Wives* made their first appearance in the first folio (1623). Their head-titles are

The second Part of Henry the Sixt, with the death of the Good Duke Humfrey.
The third Part of Henry the Sixt, with the death of the Duke of Yorke.
The Life of Henry the Fift.
The Merry Wiues of Windsor.

There is no evidence that the editors of the quarto editions of *Contention, True Tragedy, Henry V* and *Merry Wives,* printed in 1619, had access to any portion of the manuscripts from which the folio texts of *2 Henry VI, 3 Henry VI, Henry V* and *Merry*

Wives were printed four years later. Textually these four editions differ very little from the original 'stolne and surreptitious copies.' Much the smallest amount of change was made in *Merry Wives Q1;* the second quarto of 1619 is a reprint of Q1 with about fifty verbal alterations of little or no importance and affecting about forty lines of text.

Each of the two later editions of *Contention, True Tragedy* and *Henry V Q1* differs from the one that preceded it. Q2 corrected some obvious misprints and errors of Q1, and introduced some of its own; some of the latter changes Q3 corrects by reinserting the readings of Q1, and contributes, in its turn, its own quota of 'improvements,' variations and blunders. Most of the changes involve alteration of spelling, punctuation and lining of speeches, though the majority of such defects was left uncorrected; grammar and metre receive a little attention here and there, but it is doubtful whether these corrections are related in any definite instance to the folio text. Except in a few places nothing has been done to alter the numerous inversions of order, to restore omissions, to excise the enclitics that mar the verse, or to correct blunders. Needless to say, actors' gags and catchwords, lines that repeat or anticipate folio lines, passages in disorder, borrowings from other plays and non-Shakespearean lines of unknown origin remain untouched. In all these plays except *Merry Wives Q2,* the editions of 1619 include lines not in Q1 or omit lines that were in Q1, but except in *Contention Q3* no passages of any length have been added. Even in this play the total length of new passages is smaller than we find in any of the parallel texts of Shakespeare for which we have a good quarto and the folio version, each derived from an independent manuscript.

Contention Q1 and Q3

One correction made in the stage directions of Q2 removed all the barbarous Latinity of Q1; the compiler of Q3 changed, however, *'exeunt'* wherever used in Q2 to *Exit,* and thus we have *exit murtherers, exit omnes, ex. om.,* etc. As in *True Tragedy Q3* he disliked Shakespeare's habit of inverting subject and verb; he frequently emended the folio reading of Q1, e.g., in i, 52, 53, 63, 139 of the first scene, whilst in only one instance in this scene,

the change of a plural to a singular, does he revert to the folio
text. His changes are erratic; the armourer calls York 'my master'
instead of 'my Lord' as in Q1 and Fo, and refers to the King as
'your worship' instead of 'Your Maiestie' as in the rest of the
texts. He changes 'erst' (Q1 and Fo) to 'ere,' which was then
obsolete as an adverb, and yet uses the obsolescent 'for to fight'
in place of Shakespeare's 'to fight' (iii.131). The poet's 'angry
Hiue of Bees' he turns into 'an hungry hiue of bees.' One folio
line (1.3.78), not in Q1,

> She beares a Dukes (whole) reuenewes on her backe,

appears in Q3, but is defective metrically owing to the interpolation
of 'whole.'

Three passages of Q3 have had additions made to the corresponding portions of Q1; the latter are ii.16-19; ii.44-7 and vi.11-27.

In the first quarto (ii.15-19) Gloster relates a dream of the
previous night:

> This night when I was laid in bed, I dreampt that
> This my staffe mine Office badge in Court,
> Was broke in two, and on the ends were plac'd,
> The heads of the Cardinall of Winchester,
> And William de la Poule first Duke of Suffolke.

Except for the mislineation in the first line, this passage makes
good sense, and an elision makes the fourth line metrical. In the
third quarto we read:

> This night when I was laid in bed, I dreampt
> That this my staffe mine Office badge in Court
> Was broke in twaine, by whom I cannot gesse;
> But as I thinke by the Cardinall.
> What it bodes God knows; and on the ends were plac'd
> The heads of Edmund Duke of Somerset,
> And William de la Pole, first Duke of Suffolke.

This passage is found in *2 Henry VI* (1.2.25-31) as follows:

> Me thought this staffe mine Office-badge in Court
> Was broke in twaine: by whom, I haue forgot,
> But as I thinke, it was by 'th Cardinall,
> And on the peeces of the broken Wand
> Were plac'd the heads of Edmond Duke of Somerset,
> And William de la Pole first Duke of Suffolke.
> This was my dreame, what it doth bode God knowes.

These passages of Q1 and Q3 manifestly represent different reports of the same original text made by different persons. Each begins with the same interpolated line which renders superfluous retention of half the last folio line, and each has the second and the last lines practically identical with the first and sixth lines of the folio version. Q1 crushes five lines of the authentic text into two, yet if for the words 'the Cardinall of Winchester' was substituted 'Edmund Duke of Somerset,' the five lines would give the sense of the genuine text in tolerable verse. Apart from the interpolated line at the beginning this passage of Q3 bears several distinctive marks of a badly reported text; two lines cannot be scanned, one line and most of another are omitted, and part of the last folio line has been changed and transposed. Though nearer to what Shakespeare wrote, this passage does not come from any authentic manuscript.

Eleanor speaks the next passage (ii.44-7) immediately after her husband leaves the stage. He asks her to join the royal hawking party with him, and she says:

> Ile come after you, for I cannot go before,
> But ere it be long, Ile go before them all,
> Despite of all that seeke to crosse me thus,
> Who is within there?

This is expanded in Q3 as follows:

Ile come after you, for I cannot go before,
As long as Gloster beares this base and humble minde:
Were I a man, and Protector as he is,
I'de reach to 'th Crowne, or make some hop headlesse.
And being but a woman, Ile not behinde
For playing of my part, in spite of all that seek to cross me thus.
Who is within there?

Her speech in the authentic version (1.2.61-9) runs:

> Follow I must, I cannot go before
> While Gloster beares this base and humble minde.
> Were I a Man, a Duke, and next of blood,
> I would remoue these tedious stumbling blockes,
> And smooth my way vpon their headlesse neckes.
> And being a woman, I will not be slacke
> To play my part in Fortunes Pageant.
> Where are you there?

As in the first example the passage of Q3 is a mixture of the extracts from Q1 and Folio; it begins with the first line of Eleanor's speech in Q1 and ends with the last two lines of this speech. All her speech except half the first line is not in the authentic version. Instead of the line,

> But ere it be long, Ile go before them all,

Q3 has inserted four and a half lines, partly from the folio text and partly from other sources, but all irregular in versification. All these defects point to a report of Shakespeare's text.

The third passage replaces the earlier portion of York's pedigree which is discussed later (pp. 207-13). In the edition of 1619 this is altered so much from what is found in *Contention* vi.11-27 that the editor of Q3 must have read the chronicle. His version reads:

> The second was William of Hatfield
> Who dyed young.
> The third was Lyonell, Duke of Clarence.
> The fourth was Iohn of Gaunt,
> The Duke of Lancaster.
> The fift was Edmund of Langley,
> Duke of Yorke.
> The sixt was William of Windsore,
> Who dyed young.
> The seauenth and last was Sir Thomas of Woodstocke, Duke of Yorke.
> Now Edward the blacke Prince dyed before his Father, leauing behinde him two sonnes, Edward borne at Angolesme, who died young, and Richard that was after crowned King, by the name of Richard the second, who dyed without an heyre
>> Lyonell Duke of Clarence dyed, and left him one only daughter, named Phillip, who was married to Edmund Mortimer earle of March and Vlster: and so by her I claime the Crowne, as the true heire to Lyonell Duke of Clarence, third sonne to Edward the third.

If this account be compared with the folio pedigree, two mistakes will be discovered; first, the order of birth of the sixth and the seventh sons is reversed, and second, the fifth son and the seventh son are each styled Duke of Yorke. Another unimportant error is in terming the seventh son 'Sir Thomas of Woodstocke'; this comes from Q1. Though free from most of the nonsense and ridiculous blunders of Q1, York's account of his pedigree in Q3 omits essential details of his descent from 'Phillip, only daughter of Lyonell Duke of Clarence.' Every one of the genealogical facts narrated in *2 Henry VI* must be stated. York must trace his own descent from Phillip, and prove also that no other descendant of hers was alive who had a better title. In Q3 he asserts that he is 'true heire to Lyonell Duke of Clarence,' but leaves a complete gap in his pedigree between his great-grandmother and himself. Thus in trying to clear up the muddle in Q1, the editor of Q3 left the story half told.

Comparison makes it clear that Q3 retains the set-out of Q1, corrects some of the blunders in the catalogue of Edward's sons but introduces two new errors. The reference to 'Edward borne at Angolesme' comes from the chronicle, not from the folio version; it erroneously asserts that the Black Prince, who died in 1376, left 'behinde him two sonnes' though his son Edward had died five years before his father. Q3 includes all the other mistakes of Q1 contained in the successive speeches of Salisbury and York. Apparently some one had informed Pavier that the pedigree in Q1 was full of blunders, and what we find in Q3 may be the work of a printer.

True Tragedy Q1 and Q3

Many of the usual small changes were made by the editor of Q3 in the text of Q1, but no passage of any length is found in Q3 that is not in Q1. One line (5.6.79) of Gloster's folio speech, not in Q1,

King Henry, and the Prince his Son are gone,

is in Q3; it may represent, however, the editor's expansion of the part-line 'Henry and his sonne are gone' (Q1. xxii.79), as the next two lines of Q3 are clearly an editorial enlargement of what follows in Q1, and are not derived from the folio version. Q3 inserts a line of unknown origin and little to the purpose,

Vnder pretence of outward seeming ill,

after a line (xxii.76) common to Q1 and folio,

For I will buz abroad such prophesies.

This editor omits xxii.55 and xxiii.36 of Q1; the second of these is verbatim in the folio. Another line (Q1. xxiii.26), also verbatim in folio,

Clarence and Gloster, loue my louely Queene,

has been expanded into two lines in Q3, both metrically defective,

> Brothers of Clarence and of Gloster,
> Pray loue my louely queene,

The first line is borrowed from the opening line of scenes ten and twelve of Q1. Except for the doubtful example above, no line or emendation of Q1 present in Q3 can be proved to come from the folio text. Mislineation is unusually prevalent in *True Tragedy*, probably because the first edition was printed in small octavo, though for the sake of uniformity it is frequently referred to as a quarto; on account of the narrowness of the page the compositor seems to have carried the final word or words of a long line into the line that followed, with the inevitable result of metrical confusion. Attempts in Q3 to mend the metre of Q1 are not based on what is in the folio text; the editor uses elisions occasionally, and we find here and there such aphetic forms as 'gainst and 'mongst, but additions to lines of verse are very rarely removed. Thus *crooke-backe* of the folio becomes successively *crook-backt* (Q1), *crooke-backt* (Q2) and finally *crookt-backt* (Q3); later for *crookt-backe* (xxi.69) Q3 has *crooke-backe*. Unusual words are sometimes altered: a stage direction or two have been inserted, but most of the changes made in Q3 spring from an editor of little competence.

Henry V Q1 and Q3

Three quarto editions of the much abridged *Henry V* were published before the appearance of the authentic text in the first folio, and Q3, though published in 1619, bears the false date, 1608. It is a reprint of Q1 and where it differs from it, differs generally for the worse. Corrections were made to regularize defective metre, but the words introduced rarely come from the folio version. Whoever edited Q3 seems to have objected to Shakespeare's inversions, especially of subject and predicate, and made a number of lines unmetrical by changing the poet's order. Thus the second (3.6.142) of two folio lines,

> I thought, vpon one payre of English Legges
> Did march three Frenchmen. Yet forgiue me God,

becomes in Q3,

> Did march three Frenchmens. Yet God forgiue me.

Sense as well as metre suffers from these changes. Q1 retained the inversion but introduced 'Frenchmens' into the text, a blunder retained in Q3. Another example (Q1, xiv.83), of this bungling occurs in a line found identically in the folio,

But by the mas, our hearts are in the trim,

which the stupid editor of Q3 printed,

But by the mas, our hearts within are trim.

Ludicrous blunders result from his meddlesome ignorance. The Dauphin jeeringly refers to England as if king and country,

Were busied with a Whitson Morris dance,

a line retained in Q1,v.10 except for the omission of 'Whitson.' Q3 has

Were troubled with a Morisdance,

as though it was some form of disease. Q2 adds one delightful touch. When Pistol patches up his quarrel with Nym he says (ii.84-5) as in the folio except for 'accrue,'

for I shall Sutler be
Vnto the Campe, and profits will occrue.

In Q2 Pistol is 'Butler vnto the Campe'! Q3 restores Pistol to his 'sutlery.' One line (iii.20) is omitted to the destruction of the sense; this may be a printer's error. In the scene of Pistol's final discomfiture, Q3 introduces an unnecessary stage direction after (xx.35),

He makes ancient Pistoll bite of the Leeke.

Romeo and Juliet Q1

Romeo and Juliet Q1 is interesting bibliographically, and exhibits two unusual peculiarities in its make-up. In the Praetorius facsimile, sheets A3-D4 (pp. 3-30), containing the prologue and Acts I-II, iii, 81, are printed in a larger type than sheets E1-K4 (pp. 31-77) which contain the rest of the play. The first part has 32 lines to the printed page of $5\frac{3}{4}$ inches, whilst the second part has 36 lines to the page of 5 9/16 inches. No generally acceptable reason has been offered for the use of a smaller fount of type when little more than a third of the play had been printed. Halliwell suggested that to save time Danter may have used two presses simultaneously, but many of the master printers had only one press; perhaps Danter by his flagrant disregard of trade custom had incurred the censure of the powerful Company of Stationers, and transferred his half-completed play to another printing office.

Another noticeable difference between the two parts is that the first four sheets are printed so closely that scarcely a line of space is wasted; the last line of one scene is separated from the opening line of the next scene by a one-line entry or other stage direction. In the second part an amount of space equal to three lines of text is allotted to each entry or short stage direction; in addition, after the end of act three, scene four, a printer's ornament, $3\frac{1}{4}$ inches in width, is placed at the end of each scene, and precedes certain stage directions in long scenes. Hence it results that, instead of having 36 lines of text to the printed page, many pages contain eight, ten or even fourteen lines less. This prodigal waste of space was probably deliberate. If Danter or the second printer had continued to use the larger type found in the first four sheets, he would have been compelled to use seven sheets to complete the play, and would have increased the cost of the paper by ten per cent. and his other costs considerably. By printing 36 lines to the page he reduced the number of sheets required to six, but soon discovered that if he did not allot more space to entries and the numerous stage directions, he would disfigure his book by having two or even three blank leaves at the end instead of the customary blank leaf. This may be the explanation of the change in the set-out of the play in the final thirty pages.

Whatever may be the origin of the typographical anomalies associated with *Romeo and Juliet Q1,* variation in the spelling of the proper names in the two parts ought not to need much comment. Professors Pollard and Wilson[2] have made one of these variations a main prop of their theory that *Romeo and Juliet Q1* is a mixture of two corrupt texts. To this theory of double revision I shall refer later. Here it is sufficient to say that they claim that Act I and Act II, scenes i-v, represent Shakespeare's first revision of an *Ur-Romeo and Juliet,* and that the unrevised remainder of this old play was touched up here and there by Shakespeare and was padded out with memorized scraps of Shakespeare's authentic text of the other acts. They assert that in the old play the spelling

2. *Times Literary Supplement,* 14/8/1919.

was 'Cap*o*let' and that Shakespeare during his rewriting of the first two acts changed this to 'Capulet.' Dr. Greta Hort[3] has shown that the spelling 'Capulet' is found in sheets A_3-D_4 only, except for the first entry of the play, where it appears as 'Cap*o*let,' a spelling found uniformly in sheets E_1-K_4. 'Cap*o*let' is found in viii.5, a scene which Professors Pollard and Wilson admit is Shakespeare's. She contends that the difference in spelling is due to the circumstance that one compositor set up the first four sheets and a second compositor the rest of the play. The facts, in my opinion, support her contentions. Exactly the same explanation may be offered for the spelling 'La*u*rence' in Q1 and the variant 'La*w*rence' in Q2; in *Two Gentlemen of Verona* the compositor preferred 'La*u*rence.' Elizabethan spelling had in it something of chance medley, and inferences based on it have such endurance and solidity as a house built on quicksands; Montague's line (xi.112) in Q1,

O Tibalt, O Tybalt, O my brothers child,

tells its story in epitome.

Another bibliographical point of some interest may be discussed here. In their article in *The Times Literary Supplement,* these critics made it clear from a comparison of capital letters, italics, punctuation and spelling in certain passages common to Q1 and Q2, e.g. 2.4.40-6 and 3.5.27-32, that some definite bibliographical connection existed between the two texts. I do not regard the evidence offered for the first example chosen as very convincing, and think that a better example is to be found in 1.2.84-106, beginning with the words 'the great rich Capulet' and continuing to the end of the scene. Dr. Hort cites twenty lines of the third scene (1.3.13-32), which exhibit the most exact correspondence of spelling, punctuation, italics, etc., between the two quartos, and, by close reasoning from the facts, demonstrates that some parts of Q2 were set up from pages of Q1, corrected by reference to the author's manuscript. Acceptance of her conclusion involves rejection of the theory put forward by Professors Pollard and Wilson that Q1 was 'derived from' the same revised MS. as Q2, but at an 'earlier stage of its development.'

---

3. *The Good and Bad Quartos of Romeo and Juliet* and *Love's Labour's Lost,* 1926, *Modern Language Review* xxi, pp. 140 *et seq.*

CHAPTER II

LENGTH

AS a group the bad quartos differ from all the equally corrupt plays in Elizabeth's reign in their much greater length. In the following lists are set out separately the lengths of the bad quartos and of certain corrupt plays written by other authors known and unknown.

1 Length in Lines of Bad Quartos

Contention	1,972	Henry V Q1	1,623
True Tragedy	2,124	Merry Wives Q1 ..	1,419
Romeo and Juliet Q1	2,215	Hamlet Q1	2,154

Average length, 1918 lines

2 Length in Lines of other Corrupt Plays

A Shrew	1,483	Doctor Faustus ..	1,485
Famous Victories ..	1,580	Massacre at Paris ..	1,263
Pinner of Wakefield	1,224	Jack Straw	1,050
Orlando Furioso ..	1,488	Old Wives' Tale ..	964
Battle of Alcazar ..	1,486		

Average length, 1,333 lines

Average length of 7 longer, 1,425 lines

Four of the longer bad quartos average 600 lines a play more than the two shorter; the two latter in length and other characteristics are much nearer to the second group of corrupt plays than are *Hamlet Q1* and the three earlier bad quartos. Critical examination of the two early issues of *Doctor Faustus,* i.e., those dated 1604 and 1616, the *Battle of Alcazar* and the extant 'plat,' and *Orlando Furioso Q1* and Orlando's part in manuscript has proved that these corrupt plays are what the actors and reporters have left of much longer originals, and that the loss of the author's texts due to official abridgment and the subsequent manipulation of the actors may, in some plays, amount to many hundreds of lines. Little doubt exists that each of the other plays named in the second group has suffered similar abridgment and garbling.

In the following list[1] the average lengths in lines of certain groups of Elizabethan plays are given:

	Lines
31 plays with sound texts (1590-1594) .. .. (Shakespeare's omitted)	2,157
12 corrupt plays (1590-1594)	1,479
3 bad quartos (1594-1597)	2,104
64 plays with sound texts (1590-1603) .. .. .. (Shakespeare's and Jonson's omitted)	2,297
14 corrupt plays (1590-1603)	1,476
4 long bad quartos (1594-1603)	2,116

The bad quartos are not included in the totals of corrupt plays.

The average length of the three early bad quartos is about the same as that of the uncorrupted play acted before 1595. *Hamlet Q1* is about three hundred lines shorter than the average play of the year 1603, but it is not exceptionally short. At least fifteen plays now extant, including some written by Lyly, Shakespeare, Dekker, Chapman, Marston, Middleton and others, have each fewer lines than the first quarto of *Hamlet*. Most of these plays were carefully edited by their authors and would contain all that they wrote and probably more than the actors played. Each of the longer bad quartos was full of action, and would, in representation, require not much less than 'the two howres' spoken of in the garbled prologue of *Romeo and Juliet Q1* as the amount of time usually allotted by the actors for that purpose. All the corrupt plays of Shakespeare's chief predecessors belong to the period of *Contention* and *True Tragedy*. How many lines had been removed from the original text of such a play as the *Massacre at Paris* before it was reduced to its present condition can not be estimated with any approach to certitude. Five accepted plays of Marlowe which have good texts vary in length from 1,736 lines (*Dido*) to 2,676 lines (*Edward II*), and average 2,297 lines a-piece, or a little more than the average length of plays written and acted at this time. These facts suggest that not less than six hundred and perhaps a thousand lines of the *Massacre at Paris* have disappeared and about seven hundred lines of *Faustus Q1*. Four extant plays of Greene's having sound texts show a narrower range of length. They vary from the 1,941 lines of *Alphonsus* to the 2,430 lines of

---

1. Taken from the author's book, *Shakespeare and the Homilies* (1934), p. 85.

C

James IV, and average 2,197 lines each. Judged by these figures *Orlando Furioso Q1* must have lost at least five hundred lines; but as a considerable portion of the extant text consists of interpolations made by the actors, and as only 351 lines remain in Q1 of the 522 lines written for Orlando's part by Greene, the omissions of what the author wrote may amount to seven or eight hundred lines. Only two of Peele's plays, written for the public stage and with good texts, now survive, but their length and Dr. Greg's investigations make it certain that the *Battle of Alcazar* was drastically abridged.

CHAPTER III

VOCABULARIES OF THE BAD QUARTOS

COMPLETION of that monument of English scholarship, the *Oxford English Dictionary,* has made it possible, by adopting some systematic method, to obtain from any play or long poem adequate material for studying the vocabulary. Comparison of the full vocabularies of two or more plays may now be made with some exactness, and the results are likely to prove helpful to students of our drama. In recent years tests dependent on verbal comparisons have fallen into some disrepute, mainly because they have been misused in support of preconceived hypotheses. Such critics as Robertson and Sykes made great play with a parade of their so-called verbal 'clues.' During a reading of the plays, poems and translations of Marlowe and Chapman, Robertson noted that some twenty, thirty, forty or even sixty words used rather frequently by these dramatists were also present in one or more plays of Shakespeare. He labelled these words 'Marlowe' words or 'Chapman' words, thus suggesting that these poets had acquired some proprietorial right to their exclusive use; he commented on their infrequency in Shakespeare, and, buttressing them with some parallel passages, inferred that Marlowe or Chapman was the author of the play of Shakespeare under investigation. This quest of verbal clues was a main part of his critical apparatus to which he gave the grandiloquent title of the scientific method applied to literature; actually such a critical method was in vogue during the dark ages, and his inferences were propounded in a spirit of confident dogmatism far surpassing even mediæval standards.

Such critics either were ignorant of or ignored several relevant facts. First, several of the plays of Shakespeare which Robertson proposed to extrude from the canon contain each 3,000 words or more; the total vocabulary of Marlowe's works, plays, poems and translations, amounts to about 7,200 words of which 6,200 at least are found also in the Shakespeare concordance. Is it reasonable or scientific to select arbitrarily from 6,200 words common to Marlowe and Shakespeare sixty words and then christen them 'Marlowe' words? Such a proceeding smacks of hocus-pocus. Secondly, Robertson does not seem to have known that Shakespeare was a life-long and insatiable word-collector; even Mr. Bernard Shaw stumbled on this truth in *The Dark Lady of the Sonnets*. Shakespeare's unmistakable sign-manual in a play is the presence of plenty of words peculiar to it alone. Thus in *Hamlet, Lear, Troilus and Cressida, 1 Henry IV, 2 Henry IV* or *Love's Labour's Lost* more than eight per cent. of the vocabulary consists of words not found in any other play. Robertson dogmatically asserted that too many of such words in a play of Shakespeare's indicated the hand of two or more authors, and was unlucky enough to pick on Chapman as part author of *Troilus and Cressida; Hamlet* and *Lear* between them contain as many such 'peculiar' words as are to be found in any five of Chapman's plays. Thirdly, this critic was unaware that Shakespeare was a far more prolific word-maker than Chapman whom he termed 'the supreme neologist' of his age; *Troilus and Cressida* has more words used in our literature for the first time than are to be found in any three of 'the supreme neologist's' plays.

Comparative tests which take into account the full vocabularies of two or more plays or large groups of words present in each of these plays are not difficult to make, and the results derived from using them may be accepted with confidence rather than distrust. My vocabulary totals have been compiled from the Shakespeare concordance, and from Crawford's concordances to the works of Marlowe and Kyd. Crawford included in his Marlowe concordance the vocabularies of *Contention* and *True Tragedy* and those of the three plays on Henry VI, *Selimus, Locrine,* and *Edward III;* to the concordance to Kyd's works he added the vocabularies of *Arden of Feversham, Soliman and Perseda, Jeronimo, Hamlet* (Q2 and Fo.) and *Hamlet Q1.* Non-existence of concordances to the plays and poems of any other contemporary dramatists limits the employment of such tests as depend on our having complete vocabularies; useful word-lists can be gathered from any play or group of plays without excessive drudgery. Fortunately Shakespeare's plays and poems cover the period from 1592 to 1613, and the great size of his vocabulary enables the concordance to his works to be used as a standard word-book for any play of these prolific years. By collecting and classifying the vocabularies of Shakespeare's, Marlowe's and Kyd's plays certain tests of a general nature can be applied to the diction of the bad quartos.

Before attempting to analyze or contrast the respective vocabularies of two intimately related plays such as *3 Henry VI* and *True Tragedy* or *Hamlet Q2* and *Hamlet Q1*, it seems desirable to get some knowledge concerning the vocabularies of two plays written by Shakespeare in close sequence, e.g., *2 Henry VI* and *3 Henry VI*, and *1 Henry IV* and *2 Henry IV*, and to set down such conclusions as a study of the facts suggests. Again, the many differences between the diction of a source-play, such as *Troublesome Raigne*, and that of the daughter-play, *King John*, will serve to make clear how Shakespeare's rewriting affected the vocabulary of his source. With the aid of some generalizations logically deduced from the vocabularies of these two groups of plays, a student will be able to offer a considered opinion upon the still widely accepted belief that the bad quartos are wholly or in part Shakespeare's source-plays or first sketches, which were subsequently revised or rewritten by him. Below is set out a table with certain details of the distribution of the vocabularies of paired plays; each play has a sound text and is reasonably comparable to the other play of the pair in length. The capital letters at the head of the columns give:—

A Names of the paired plays.

B Number of lines in each play.

C Number of words in the vocabulary of each play. For *Troublesome Raigne* and *King Leir* estimates only are given.

D Number of words common to each pair of plays.

E Percentage of totals under D based on the corresponding totals under C.

F Number of words peculiar to each play of each pair, i.e., not found in the other play paired with it.

TABLE I

VOCABULARY DISTRIBUTION OF PAIRED PLAYS

	A	B	C	D	E	F
I	*Troublesome Raigne*	2,972	2,600 (est.)	1,290	50%	1,310
	King John	2,570	2,901		44%	1,611
II	*King Leir*	2,567	2,400 (est.)	1,377	61%	1,023
	King Lear	3,205	3,339		41%	1,962
III	*2 Henry VI*	3,075	3,146	1,649	52%	1,497
	3 Henry VI	2,902	2,790		59%	1,141
IV	*1 Henry IV*	2,968	3,028	1,591	52%	1,437
	2 Henry IV	3,180	3,130		51%	1,539
V	*Spanish Tragedy* ..	2,736	2,547	1,211	47%	1,336
	Arden of Feversham	2,469	2,302		53%	1,091
VI	*Edward II*	2,670	2,373	1,352	57%	1,021
	Edward III	2,498	2,943		46%	1,591
VII	*Othello*	3,229	3,075	1,546	50%	1,529
	King Lear	3,205	3,339		46%	1,793

From the results set down above there may be drawn certain important conclusions with respect to the vocabularies of two plays each of which complies with the conditions previously prescribed, that plays must have sound texts, and pairs of plays must have lengths as nearly equal as may be.

(i) The number of words common to any pair of plays will rarely fall below forty per cent. of the larger vocabulary.

(ii) The number of words peculiar to that one of two paired plays which has the larger vocabulary rarely exceeds sixty per cent. of this vocabulary.

(iii) No substantial difference is observable between the percentages of words common to a source-play and Shakespeare's derived play and the percentages of words common to any other pairs of plays. Shakespeare was able to forget almost completely the vocabulary of the play which he was using as raw material.

I shall now compare the vocabularies of the parallel texts, subdividing each of them into the words common to the two texts and the words peculiar to each play of each pair; another column has been included in this table in which the percentage of the vocabulary that is peculiar to each play of each pair of parallel texts is given. For all the plays of Shakespeare and the first three bad quartos, the totals of the vocabularies have been compiled from the concordances and are as accurate as such a tedious count

may be; the totals for the first quartos of *Romeo and Juliet,
Henry V* and *Merry Wives* are estimates only, based on the length
of the plays, the known size of the vocabularies belonging to other
corrupt plays, the state of the text, the number of what I call the
'rarer' words and the compound words—the latter two totals are
accurate—and other groups of words. Errors of a hundred words
will not affect the validity of the inferences made.

TABLE II

VOCABULARY DISTRIBUTION OF PARALLEL TEXTS

Names of Plays	A No. of Lines in Play	B No. of Words in Vocabu- lary	C Words Common to Two Plays	D Percent- age of C on B	E No. of Words Peculiar to Play	F Percent- age of E on B
I *2 Henry VI*	3,075	3,146	1,757	55·9	1,389	44·1
Contention	1,972	2,027		86·6	270	13·4
II *3 Henry VI*	2,902	2,790	2,036	73·0	754	27·0
True Tragedy	2,124	2,182		93·3	146	6·7
III *Hamlet Q2 + Fo.* . .	3,762	3,882	1,956	50·4	1,926	49·6
Hamlet Q1	2,154	2,251		86·9	295	13·1
IV *Romeo and Juliet Q2*	2,986	2,949	2,093	71·0	856	29·0
Romeo and Juliet Q1	2,215	2,300 (est.)		91·0	207	9·0
V *Henry V Fo.*	3,166	3,180	1,669	52·5	1,511	47·5
Henry V Q1	1,623	1,800 (est.)		92·7	131	7·3
VI *Merry Wives Fo.* . .	2,634	2,560	1,384	54·0	1,176	46·0
Merry Wives Q1 . .	1,419	1,600 (est.)		86·5	216	13·5

If these totals are compared with those obtained for *Troublesome
Raigne* and *King Leir* and the derived folio plays which are set
out in the previous table giving the 'Vocabulary Distribution of
Paired Plays' two main points of difference are noticeable:

(a) The number of words 'peculiar' to any bad quarto is very
small.

(b) The number of words common to each pair of the parallel
texts, except to the first quarto and folio texts of *Merry
Wives*, is unusually large.

If these first quartos are accepted as corrupt abridgments of
Shakespeare's authentic plays, no explanation of these anomalies
is needed beyond the statement that the unofficial abridgers must
be responsible for the introduction of the comparatively small

number of words peculiar to the quarto. If the quartos, however, predate the fuller versions and are thus source-plays worked over by Shakespeare in whole or in part, there are many difficulties to explain. First, the words peculiar to the quartos must be assumed to be those which Shakespeare rejected. The greatest number of words rejected by him in any of these supposedly rewritten quartos was 295 out of a total of 2,251, or little more than 13 per cent. of the full vocabulary of *Hamlet Q1*. The lowest proportion was 146 of a total of 2,182 or 6·7 per cent. of the full vocabulary of *True Tragedy*. During his rewriting of the *Troublesome Raigne* he rejected 1,310 words, or 50 per cent., of a vocabulary estimated at 2,600 words; he omitted 547 words or 34 per cent. of the vocabulary of *A Shrew*, estimated at 1,600 words, and over 40 per cent. of the words in *King Leir*. If the term *rewriting* appropriately describes the process which removed nearly half the vocabulary of the *Troublesome Raigne* and left scarcely a dozen lines of this play in *King John,* some other term would more accurately describe the method by which Shakespeare retained fourteen-fifteenths of the vocabulary of *True Tragedy* untouched, and more than two-thirds of the lines either verbatim or with no more than two words altered per line. *Revision* might seem a more suitable term for such a change, but an increase of length which added more than a third to *True Tragedy* and *Romeo and Juliet Q1* and almost doubled the length of *Henry V Q1* scarcely comes within the definition of revision.

Secondly, my table shows that the words of each bad quarto have been subdivided into those peculiar to it and those which are found also in the corresponding canonical play. Consequently the exceedingly high number of words common to each pair of these parallel texts serves to differentiate them from every other pair of plays by any authors. The highest total (known to me) of words common to a pair of plays each not less than 2,300 lines in length, is 1,679; these are the totals for *2 Henry VI* and *Edward III;* the highest percentage of common words is 61 per cent. in *1 Tamburlaine* and *2 Tamburlaine,* the percentage being calculated on the play with the smaller vocabulary. Reference to the table setting out the 'Vocabulary Distribution of Paired Plays' shows that the number of words common to any pair does not invariably increase with the increase of vocabulary. High totals and the higher percentages of words in common are found only in pairs of plays written in rapid sequence by one author on similar themes during an era when dramatic diction had become somewhat fixed. The number of words common to a bad quarto over 2,100 lines in length and the corresponding parallel text ranges from 1,956 to 2,093, and the percentage of such words in common varies from slightly less than 87 per cent. to over 93 per cent. of the full vocabulary of the bad quartos. Contrast these results with the 1,290 words—equal to 50 per cent. of the vocabulary of *Troublesome Raigne*—common to this source-play and its derivative *King John,* and also with the 1,377 words (equal to 57 per cent. of the vocabulary of *King Leir*) common to *King Lear* and its source-play.

I cannot insist too strongly that the relation between the vocabularies of such known source-plays as *Troublesome Raigne, A Shrew* and *King Leir* and Shakespeare's respective derivative plays, *King John, The Shrew* and *King Lear* differs in not the slightest respect from the relationship between the vocabularies of *The Spanish Tragedy* and *Arden of Feversham;* it duplicates in every important detail the relationship between the vocabularies of *1 Henry IV* and *2 Henry IV.* Each play was conceived and written independently, and the vocabulary is also independent. The peculiar interrelation of the vocabularies of *Hamlet Q1* and *Hamlet Q2* suggests dependence. Either the official play-cutter and the persons who gave the copy for Q1 to the press are responsible for the abridgment and corruption of Q2, or Shakespeare, after omitting 400 lines, corrected syntax, diction, sense, verse and order of what was left of Q1 with minute exactitude and fidelity; he then inserted nearly two thousand lines of poetry, unnecessary to the story or action and of little dramatic value. This method of mending old plays was not used by any known dramatist, least of all by the author of *The Shrew, King John* and *King Lear.* Certainly the poet who, his fellows said, 'never blotted out line' does not fit the picture of dull and patient drudgery which such line-by-line revision suggests.

Chapter IV

THE RARER WORDS OF SHAKESPEARE'S PLAYS

BY far the most important and interesting group of words belonging to a play of Shakespeare consists of those that I term his 'rarer' words; by this epithet I denote words peculiar to the play and in addition all those which are found also in not more than three other plays of his. However arbitrarily chosen and named this group may seem to be, it includes almost all the words coined by the poet, all the main-words and compound adjectives and nouns that he was the first to use in our literature and most of the many other words that give colour, freshness, imagination and distinction to his diction; they amount in all to nearly two-thirds of the poet's entire vocabulary. It may seem ludicrous to term nearly 12,000 words 'rare,' yet an author who is credited by the compilers of the *Oxford English Dictionary* with being the first user of about 3,200 words and who has six thousand other words each in not more than two plays or long poems has verbal riches compelling the employment of superlatives in describing them. Plays written by other authors invariably have a number of words not in the Shakespeare concordance, as well as many of the words found in not more than four of his plays.

Below I set out in tabular form subdivided lists showing the distribution of the rarer words present in certain pairs of named plays. These are arranged in such order that Shakespeare's treatment of this important group of words in a source-play during the process of transforming it into his play in the canon may be studied. I have also added similar details in order to explain what happened to such a group of words in a play to which he wrote a sequel; the last example refers to the 'rarer' words of *Hamlet* and *Othello*.

The columns designated respectively A, B, C, D, E, F give in each row for source-play and its derivative, or for each of Shakespeare's two authentic plays the following totals of words:—

A The number of words not in the Shakespeare concordance.
B The number of concordance words peculiar to the play named.

C The number of concordance words found in the play named and *one* other play or long poem written by Shakespeare.
D The number of concordance words found in the play named and *two* other plays or long poems written by Shakespeare.
E The number of concordance words found in the play named and *three* other plays or long poems written by Shakespeare.
F The total number of words included in groups A-E.

TABLE III

SUBDIVIDED TABLE OF RARER WORDS I

SOURCE-PLAYS AND PLAYS IN SEQUENCE

Group-Changes in Paired Plays	A	B	C	D	E	F
I *Troublesome Raigne* and *King John*						
Rare Words in *Troublesome Raigne* ..	136	94	88	100	92	510
Not used by Shakespeare in *King John*	136	88	81	86	78	469
Retained in *King John*	0	6	7	14	14	41
Added to *King John*		134	93	82	82	391
Rare Words in *King John*		140	100	96	96	432
II *King Leir* and *King Lear*						
Rare Words in *King Leir*	82	74	67	60	57	340
Not used by Shakespeare in *King Lear*	82	70	62	55	53	322
Retained in *King Lear*	0	4	5	5	4	18
Added to *King Lear*		342	129	135	118	724
Rare words in *King Lear*		346	134	140	122	742
III *2 Henry VI* and *3 Henry VI*						
Rare Words in *2 Henry VI*		157	102	115	123	497
Not used by Shakespeare in *3 Henry VI*		157	93	104	96	450
Retained in *3 Henry VI*		0	9	11	27	47
Added to *3 Henry VI*		115	70	63	55	303
Rare Words in *3 Henry VI*		115	79	74	82	350
IV *1 Henry IV* and *2 Henry IV*						
Rare Words in *1 Henry IV*		269	136	133	122	660
Not used by Shakespeare in *2 Henry IV*		269	126	121	104	620
Retained in *2 Henry IV*		0	10	12	18	40
Added to *2 Henry IV*		245	125	130	85	585
Rare Words in *2 Henry IV*		245	135	142	103	625
V *Hamlet* and *Othello*						
Rare Words in *Hamlet*		401	240	190	165	996
Not used by Shakespeare in *Othello* ..		401	227	165	142	935
Retained in *Othello*		0	13	25	23	50
Added to *Othello*		222	132	107	67	528
Rare Words in *Othello*		222	145	132	90	589

Certain verbs, viz., 'rejected,' 'retained' and 'added' used in this and the following tables may seem to suggest that when Shakespeare was writing a play he consciously or deliberately rejected or retained rare words present in the vocabulary of his source-play or in that of a play of his own written a few weeks, months or even a year or two previously. I do not intend any such meaning in my use of these words, which express what happened rather than any conscious act on the part of the poet. I believe that with a slight change of scene, character, plot, circumstance or emotion, came fresh thought, difference in the mode of expressing that thought, and fresh words in plenty. Moreover in this neological age when almost every writer coined some words and the tyranny of the dictionary had not atrophied invention, a writer was rarely gravelled for want of a word to express the slightest shade of difference in meaning; he either invented a new word, usually from Latin, or employed some well-known word in a new sense.

On the table itself some remarks may fitly be made, and some comments will be made on the results. For each pair of plays numbered respectively I-V, the first row gives for the first-named play of the pair the number of the rarer words found in each of the subdivisions classified under the headings A-F, whilst in the column under the heading F is given the total number of the rarer words in the play; in the second row we have in the same order of subdivision the number of the rarer words belonging to the first play which are not in the second play. Totals of rarer words common to the two plays, i.e., those of the first play which are in the second are set out in their subdivisions in the third row with the totals at the extreme right. The fourth row contains for each subdivision the numbers of the rarer words which Shakespeare inserted in his second play, whilst the fifth row repeats for the second play what the first row did for the first play. A glance makes it evident that for any subdivision B-E, the sum of the rare words common to both plays and the words peculiar to one play gives the total number of the rarer words in that subdivision of that play.

Several important results may be deduced from the totals given in this table:—

(i) 'Rarer' words represent from a fourth to a tenth of the vocabulary of each of Shakespeare's plays.

(ii) Reference to the previous table shows that Shakespeare did not use 469 of the rare words of *Troublesome Raigne* in writing *King John;* this total equals 36 per cent. of the 1310 unused words of this source-play. Similarly the 322 'rare' words of *King Leir* not used by Shakespeare represent 36 per cent. of all the words rejected by him during the composition of *King Lear*. Results for plays of Shakespeare written in rapid sequence are in excellent agreement. Thus the 450 'rare' words in *2 Henry VI* but not in *3 Henry VI* equal 30 per cent. of 1,497 words discarded by Shakespeare when he wrote the sequel to *2 Henry VI*. Similarly during the writing of *2 Henry IV* he omitted 620 'rare' words present in the first part, or 43 per cent. of the 1,437 words in the first part not used by him.

(iii) The small totals of 'rare' words common to both plays offer a most striking contrast to the very large totals of the rare words peculiar to each play. Every pair of plays of comparable lengths and with sound texts exhibits this contrast. Rare words common to *Troublesome Raigne* and *King John* provided Shakespeare with less than ten per cent. of the rare words found in the latter play and represent little over three per cent. of the 1,290 words common to the two plays. Similarly *Othello* has ten per cent. of its rare words in common with *Hamlet*.

THE RARER WORDS OF THE BAD QUARTOS

Totals of the rarer words present in the six pairs of parallel texts are given in table IV on page 32. These words will be classified in exactly the same way as in the previous table entitled 'Subdivided Table of Rarer Words'; a new column under the heading G gives the total number of words in the vocabularies of the plays named; estimates only can be given for the number of words in the vocabularies of *Romeo and Juliet Q1, Henry V Q1,* and *Merry Wives Q1*. In general the explanatory remarks that precede and follow the earlier table apply to table IV on page 32.

Comparison of the two tables of Rarer Words reveals several important differences.

(a) In table III the total number of rare words in the first play of a pair may be greater or less than that in the second play; in table IV the number of rare words in each first quarto is very much smaller than, and in three pairs not a third of, the number of such words present in the authentic play of Shakespeare. Though each bad quarto is very much shorter than the corresponding parallel play, the number of rare words does not depend entirely on the number of lines. Thus there are as

STOLNE AND SURREPTITIOUS COPIES

TABLE IV

SUBDIVIDED TABLE OF RARER WORDS II

THE PARALLEL TEXTS

Changes in Groups of Words	A	B	C	D	E	F	G
I *Contention* and *2 Henry VI*							
i Total in *Contention*	25	75	60	48	51	259	2,027
ii Rejected by Shakespeare in *2 Henry VI*	25	14	22	11	9	81	
iii Retained by Shakespeare in *2 Henry VI*	0	61	38	37	42	178	
iv Added by Shakespeare in *2 Henry VI* ..		96	64	78	81	319	
v Total in *2 Henry VI*		157	102	115	123	497	3,146
II *True Tragedy* and *3 Henry VI*							
i Total in *True Tragedy*	16	63	47	45	49	220	2,182
ii Rejected by Shakespeare in *3 Henry VI*	16	9	5	1	4	35	
iii Retained by Shakespeare in *3 Henry VI*	0	54	42	44	45	185	
iv Added by Shakespeare in *3 Henry VI*		61	37	30	37	165	
v Total in *3 Henry VI*		115	79	74	82	350	2,790
III *Romeo and Juliet Q1* and *Q2*							
i Total in *Romeo and Juliet Q1*	23	119	72	53	52	319	2,300 (est.)
ii Rejected by Shakespeare in *Q2*	23	10	6	8	12	59	
iii Retained by Shakespeare in *Q2*		109	66	45	40	260	
iv Added by Shakespeare in *Q2*		90	39	42	48	219	
v Total in *Romeo and Juliet Q2*		199	105	87	88	479	2,916
IV *Henry V Q1* and *Henry V Fo*							
i Total in *Henry V Q1*	15	71	51	43	40	220	1,800 (est.)
ii Rejected by Shakespeare in *Fo*	15	8	7	6	3	39	
iii Retained by Shakespeare in *Fo*	0	63	44	37	37	181	
iv Added by Shakespeare in *Fo*		183	101	94	93	181	
v Total in *Henry V Fo*		246	145	131	130	653	3,130
V *Merry Wives Q1* and *Merry Wives Fo*							
i Total in *Merry Wives Q1*	28	88	59	40	23	238	1,600 (est.)
ii Rejected by Shakespeare in *Fo*	28	22	12	13	11	86	
iii Retained by Shakespeare in *Fo*	0	66	47	27	12	152	
iv Added by Shakespeare in *Fo*		163	73	51	71	358	
v Total in *Merry Wives Fo*		229	120	78	83	510	2,527
VI *Hamlet Q1* and *Hamlet Q2*							
i Total in *Hamlet Q1*	24	107	90	67	60	348	2,251
ii Rejected by Shakespeare in *Q2* and *Fo*	24	13	18	15	9	79	
iii Retained by Shakespeare in *Q2* and *Fo*	0	94	72	52	51	269	
iv Added by Shakespeare in *Q2* and *Fo* ..		307	168	138	114	269	
v Total in *Hamlet Q2* and *Fo*		398	240	190	163	991	3,882

In the arrangement of this table it is assumed that each bad quarto predates in composition the corresponding play written by Shakespeare, i.e., that each bad quarto was treated by him as raw material.

many rare words in the 2,084 lines of *Macbeth* as in the 2,986 lines of *Romeo and Juliet Q2*, as many in the 2,015 lines of *Tempest* as in 3,600 lines of *Richard III*, and *Love's Labour's Lost* has more than *Cymbeline*, which is over 600 lines longer. *King Leir,* an undoubted source-play with a sound text, has a smaller number of rare words than the very corrupt *Hamlet Q1* which is 400 lines shorter.

(b) In table III the number of rare words of the first play not used by Shakespeare is many times greater than those retained by him. In table IV the number of words rejected by Shakespeare is much smaller than those retained by him. On combining the separate totals for each pair in table IV we find that he rejected less than a fourth of the rarer words present in the first quartos, and used the remaining three-fourths in his own plays. Moreover, he usually gave each word the same relative position in his own text as it had occupied in the text of the bad quarto. He added, on the average, five rare words of his own for every three borrowed from his source. Thus three-eighths of the rarer words in Shakespeare's six parallel texts come from what are assumed to be six source-plays, and the remaining five-eighths from his own inexhaustible stock. Contrast this procedure with his method of rewriting *Troublesome Raigne* and *King Leir.* He discarded all but seven per cent. of the rarer words present in these plays, and in *King John* and *King Lear* the rare words from the sources represent a twentieth of their total. Similarly only seven per cent. of the rare words present in *2 Henry VI, 1 Henry IV* and *Hamlet* find a place in *3 Henry VI, 2 Henry IV* and *Othello* respectively in which plays they amount to less than a tenth of the rarer words.

(c) Perhaps the most important and instructive portion of the two tables is column A, which exhibits the excessive difference in the numbers of non-concordance words in table III and table IV. Every non-Shakespearean play contains such words, which vary from not less than three per cent. to about seven per cent. of the full vocabulary. I have examined the vocabularies of over 50 plays written by authors other than Shakespeare, and have not found any play of 2,100 or more lines with less than 70 non-concordance words. Each bad quarto has some non-concordance words; the shortest and most corrupt, *Merry Wives Q1,* has the most, and the play with the least is *Henry V Q1,* the only bad quarto which has no borrowings from other plays. The vocabularies of the bad quartos, taken together, average a trifle over one per cent. of non-concordance words, a fact which suggests that these plays must be put in a class by themselves. The following list gives some particulars of the content of non-concordance words for certain short plays some sound, some corrupt, written by various known and unknown authors.

Name of Play	No. of non-concordance words	Name of Play	No. of non-concordance words
Tamburlaine I	112	Faustus Q1	88
Tamburlaine II	113	Massacre at Paris ..	45
Dido	69	Old Wive's Tale	63
Soliman and Perseda	70	Orlando Furioso Q1 ..	76
Locrine	150	Battle of Alcazar	78
Humorous Day's Mirth	70	Taming of a Shrew ..	61
All Fools	148	Jeronimo	60

This list gives the totals of non-concordance words in plays that vary from 2,300 to less than 1,000 lines. The group of seven plays in the second column consists of corrupt abridgments of plays written mainly in verse; all are less than 1,500 lines in length, yet the non-concordance words must average about four per cent. of the full vocabularies— Jeronimo and Marlowe's two fragments contain 193 such words in 3,935 lines of text or nearly 5 per cent. My conclusion must be that the number of non-Shakespearean words in each bad quarto is small because the author was Shakespeare himself.

(d) Another important though obvious fact must be mentioned. Non-concordance words form by far the smallest group of rare words in each bad quarto, but in the three undoubted source-plays and in fifty non-Shakespearean plays (including about a dozen corrupt ones) this group is invariably the largest of the five groups of rare words; the reason is not far to seek. This group draws upon all the words of the English language except the seventeen thousand that Shakespeare used, and thus offers an author almost limitless choice; these words therefore ought to be and are far more numerous than any of the other four groups of words each of which must comply with the arbitrary restriction that it must be in one or more plays of Shakespeare. If I were classifying the vocabulary of True Tragedy and were unaware of its relation to 3 Henry VI, my experience would suggest that in a play of its length there should be from seventy to one hundred or more words not in the Shakespeare concordance. If I found that these numbered only sixteen I would be mystified until I discovered that no fewer than 185 of 229 rare words were in *3 Henry VI*, and would exclaim 'Shakespeare aut diabolus.'

(e) Another remarkable difference between the vocabularies of the undoubted source-plays and those of the bad quartos is that the latter contain a number of unintelligible words and some variants and perversions of words present in the corresponding parallel texts. Not many are printers' errors; most of them are good English words which either do not suit the context or vulgarize the passages in which they appear. These are more common in the three later surreptitious quartos than in the earlier group. Some examples chosen from *Henry V* and *Hamlet* are given below; a few may be mishearings of what appear in the folios and second quartos. Those that are below are from *Henry V Q1;* by the side appear the relevant words of the corresponding passages in the folio text.

After *the function* i.45	After *defunction* . . . 1.2.60
To guard your *England* .. i.85	to defend our *in-land* 1.2.144
The coursing *sneakers* .. i.86	the coursing *snatchers* 1.2.145
examplified by her selfe i.95	*exampl'd* by her selfe 1.2.158
Thy *messful* mouth ii.40	thy *nastie* mouth 2.1.47
profit will *occrue* ii.85	profits will *accrue* .. 2.1.102
A burning *tashan* *contigian* feuer ii.91	A burning quotidian Tertian 2.1.108-9
A *crysombd* childe iv.5	Any *Christome* Child 2.3.11-12
Cophetua be thy counsel-lor iv.41	*Caueto* be thy Coun-sailor 2.3.49
Wombely vaultes of France v.72	*Wombie Vaultages* of France 2.4.130
Short nooke ile of England ix.8	*nooke-shotten* Isle of Albion 3.5.14
A few *spranes* of vs .. ix.2	a few *sprayes* of vs 3.5.5
The Kings a *bago* xii.10	The King's a *Bawcock* 4.1.45
the *apposed* multitudes xiii.3	th' *opposed* number 4.1.291
I haue built two *chanceries* xiii.14	I haue built two *Chauntries* 4.1.301
daughter is *con-tamuracke* xv.13	daughter is *contam-inated* 4.5.17
Yorke all *hasted* ore .. xvii.11	Yorke all *hagled* over 4.6.11

D

A few examples from *Hamlet Q1* are added:

Shrill crowing throate ..	i.116	*shrill sounding* throat .	1.1.151
impudent and bed-rid ..	ii.2-3	*impotent* and bed-red ..	1.2.29
those *related* articles . ..	ii.9	these *delated* articles ..	1.2.38
new *vnfleg'd* courage ..	iii.31	new hatcht *vnflegd* courage	1.3.65
burst their *ceremonies* ..	iv.26	burst their *cerements* ..	1.4.48
That *beckles* ore his base	iv.44	That *bettles* ore his base	1.4.70
Now is he totall *guise* ..	vii.152	Now is he totall *Gules* .	2.2.479
in *calagulate* gore	vii.154	with *coagulate* gore ..	2.2.484
with tongue *inuenom'd* speech	vii.173	with tongue in *venom* steept	2.2.533
a *towne bull* bellow ..	ix.4	the *Towne crier* spoke my lines	3.2.3
if he doe not *bleech*	ix.62	if a doe *blench*	2.2.626
ergo	xvi.11	*argall*	5.1.54
Wilt drinke vp *vessels*	xvi.154	Woo't drinke vp *Esill* .	5.1.299
The worde had been more *Cosin german* to the phrase	xviii.21-2	The phrase would bee more *Ierman* to the matter	5.2.299

Detailed comment is unnecessary. Nearly all the passages from *Henry V Q1* would be without meaning were it not that the folio text is available for comparison. *Occrue* for *accrue, apposed* for *opposed, spranes* for *sprayes* may be the printer's contribution to the muddle. Change of '*defunction*' to a meaningless '*the function*' suggests that the stage arch-bishop suspected that *defunction* was a mispronunciation of *the function* very much as Alice speaks of 'the neck' as 'de nick.' *England* for *in-land, chanceries* for *chauntries* and other mistakes come perhaps at second hand from the reporter or person who provided the 'copy' of Q1. *Cophetua* for *Caueto* seems a reminiscence of Falstaff's mocking bombastic line,

Let King Coueta know the truth thereof,

addressed (*2 Henry IV*, 5.3.101) to Pistol. Other blunders such as *contigian, tashan, bago, hasted, wombely, contamuracke*, etc., resemble those of *Hamlet Q1*, e.g. *related, ceremonies, beckles, guise, calagulate, vessels*; they represent the bungling efforts of ignorant, ill-educated mummers to pronounce the unusual words used by the company's poet. Many of their perversions would baffle the most ingenious and erudite of our tribe of emendators. I can never sufficiently admire the confidence in their judgment of critics who declare that Shakespeare emended the lines of the first quarto (vii.173-4) :

> Who this had seene with tongue inuenom'd speech
> Would treason haue pronounced,

into the well known text of Q2 (2.2.533-4) :

> Who this had seene, with tongue in venom steept
> Gainst fortunes state would treason haue pronounst.

I shall refer later to the numerous blunders in sense and fact; they are of decisive importance in determining the priority of composition between the bad quartos and the corresponding plays of Shakespeare.

I find it impossible to believe that Shakespeare almost simultaneously used two widely divergent and mutually exclusive methods of rewriting source plays. In transforming the first quarto of *Romeo and Juliet* into the second quarto he must have deliberately retained more than 80 per cent. of the rarer words in his source-play, and transferred them to his own play with the result that 57 per cent. of all such words in Q2 were borrowed from an old play. When rewriting *Troublesome Raigne* perhaps a year later he retained barely 8 per cent. of the rarer words, and in *King John* they amount to less than 10 per cent. of the total used. That the mature Shakespeare should have employed these two self-contradictory methods of rewriting the so-called *Ur-Hamlet* and *King Leir* seems to me as incredible as absurd.

So far the results presented in the various tables have been interpreted on the assumption that the bad quartos were source-plays used by Shakespeare. If the priority of the poet's plays is assumed, and the bad quartos are accepted as the mutilated and corrupt abridgments of acting versions made officially for the company from his manuscripts, a rearrangement of the statistics given for each pair of parallel plays will be requisite. Thus the heading of the columns will remain and have each the same meaning, but the order of the rows will be completely reversed, because the change will be from a play of Shakespeare to the corresponding bad quarto. Consequently the fifth row will become the first, and the first the fifth in the new table. I shall recast the portion of the previous table which gives the results for *Contention* and *2 Henry VI,* and leave the reader to make similar changes for the five remaining pairs of parallel texts.

TABLE V

SUBDIVIDED TABLE OF RARE WORDS

Names of Plays	A	B	C	D	E	F	G
2 Henry VI and *Contention*							
i Rare Words in *2 Henry VI*		157	102	115	123	497	3,146
ii Number omitted in *Contention* ..		96	64	78	81	319	
iii Number retained in *Contention* ..		61	38	37	42	178	
iv Number added to *Contention*	25	14	22	11	9	81	
v Rare Words in *Contention*	25	75	60	48	51	259	2,027

If the bad quartos were sound abridgments of the original plays, the combined losses of peculiar and other scarce words for each play and for all the plays as a whole should be roughly proportional to the reduction in length due to abridgment. Accordingly the reduction of the 3,762 lines of *Hamlet* (received text) to an acting version of 2,154 lines (the number of lines of *Hamlet Q1*) should carry with it a corresponding reduction of 401 words peculiar to it to 230. This total for an abridged *Hamlet* of 2,154 lines is in fair agreement with the 197 words peculiar to the 2,084 lines of *Macbeth* or the 202 such words in the 2,015 lines of *Tempest.* We may judge of the ravages committed by the reporter and his accomplices upon this non-extant acting version of *Hamlet* by their reduction of the hypothetical 230 words peculiar to it to the beggarly remnant of 94 words left in Q1, a loss of more than 59 per cent.

Taken together, the six bad quartos retain 447 only of the 1,270 words peculiar to one or other of the six corresponding plays of Shakespeare. This loss occurred in two stages. Reduction of the texts of his plays to acting versions of lengths equal to those of the extant bad quartos means a reduction of 38 per cent. in length and in words peculiar to them; consequently 789 words should remain of the original 1,270. These 789 words the reporter and his assistant pirates reduced to 447 words, or a loss of 43 per cent. of what the official play-cutter had left.   Official and unofficial abridgers between them eliminated 65 per cent. or nearly two-thirds of the most important words inserted by Shakespeare. Of 3,484 rarer words in these six plays the bad quartos keep 1,225 or thirty-five per cent. of the total. This loss of over two thousand vital words, two thousand 'drops of that immortal man', has been, in my opinion, a main reason for the low estimation and neglect of the bad quartos, so customary among Shakespearian students.   This excessive omission of the rare words in comparison with the much smaller loss of the remainder of the vocabulary will be easily perceived on examining the following table in which are given particulars for the three pairs of parallel texts for which exact information is available.

TABLE VI

COMPARATIVE TABLE OF WORD-LOSSES

Name of Plays	No. of Words in Vocabulary	Total Loss and Loss per cent.	No. of Rare Words	Loss and Loss per cent.	Rest of Vocabulary	Loss and Loss per cent.
I *2 Henry VI*	3,146		497		2,649	
Contention	2,027		178		1,849	
		1,119 (36%)		319 (64%)		800 (30%)
II *3 Henry VI*	2,790		350		2,440	
True Tragedy	2,182		185		1,997	
		608 (21·8%)		165 (47%)		443 (18%)
III *Hamlet* (received text)	3,882		996		2,886	
Hamlet Q1	2,251		269		1,982	
		1,631 (42%)		727 (73%)		904 (31%)
Three Shakespeare Plays	9,818		1,843		7,975	
3 Bad Quartos	6,460		632		5,828	
		3,358 (34%)		1,211 (66%)		2,147 (27%)

More than a third of the total vocabularies was lost during the complex series of changes which reduced Shakespeare's plays to the degraded state of the bad quartos. By far the heaviest losses proportionately were of those forceful and figurative words to which his plays owe so much of their distinction and perennial vitality; instead of a cluster of

Jewels five-words-long
That on the stretch'd forefinger of all Time
Sparkle for ever,

one or two survive, a little damaged, to cast a fitful light upon the dull and lifeless lines of the quarto. Causes other than the official abridgment of over-long plays account for most of this denudation of the poet's work. When the actors cut down a play as a preliminary to stage representation they did not expunge a word beyond those in the omitted passages. We have two independent texts of *King Lear,* both sound though differing considerably in length; not one word, common or uncommon, has been struck out of any passage common to the first quarto and the folio versions. Similarly in plays that remained in manuscript up to our own days, e.g., *Edmund Ironside, Thomas of Woodstock, The Captives, Dick of Devonshire,* etc., the actors marked numerous passages for omission, but very rarely struck out or changed a word of the text that was retained. Under such conditions the number of peculiar or rare words that disappeared during the making of the acting version would, as was said above, vary more or less directly as the number of lines of text excised by the play-adapter. Reporters and their assistants managed to print an amount of text equal in length to five-sixths of the genuine text known to them, but in it they preserved less than half of the 'peculiar' words and one-half of the 'rarer' words which the official play-adapters had left in the acting versions.

CHAPTER V

COMPOUND WORDS

N O group of words serves to differentiate one play from another more markedly than the number and type of compound words present in each. Resourceful authors of our own time invent a few compounds as a gesture of personal defiance to the dictionary, but during the last years of Elizabeth's reign poets and dramatists revelled in the newly discovered power of enriching their writings and the language with expressive and concise double-words. They form a large and important part of Shakespeare's vocabulary and number over 3,000. Nearly two-thirds are of his own coining and are rarely used more than once except in the one play; Elizabethan poets rarely borrowed compounds coined by others. Thus, as the following table shows, Shakespeare rejected practically all the compound words when he was redramatizing his source-plays, retaining 14 only of 232; seven of the fourteen used by him, e.g., *Ascension Day*, *birth-right* and *mother-queen* in *King John* and *loose-bodied*, *trunk-sleeve*, *taming-school* and *wedding-day* in *The Shrew* are necessary to the subject-matter and have no synonyms. Further he increased the proportion of adjectives, especially of those ending in a past or present participle. Shakespeare had a tendency to repeat in the second of two plays written in rapid sequence some of the compounds used in the first play. Thus of 135 compounds in *2 Henry VI* he used twenty in *3 Henry VI*, and in *2 Henry IV* he used 24 of 236 compounds in *1 Henry IV*. In general, however, the compounds used in one play, except for such dubious examples as *afternoon*, *good-man*, *good-morrow*, *nobleman*, *sixpence*, *to-day*, *to-night*, etc., are not found in other plays. Thus only two of those in *Hamlet* and eight of those in *Othello* are found among the 156 compounds of *King Lear*; three only of 167 in *Romeo and Juliet* are in *King John*.

The following table sets out the distribution of the compound words present in each bad quarto and the corresponding play of Shakespeare; similar details are tabulated for each of the source-plays and the derived play of Shakespeare:

41

TABLE VII

DISTRIBUTION OF COMPOUNDS

Name of Play	No. of compounds in Quarto or Source	No. not in Shakespeare's Play	No. used by Shakespeare	No. added by Shakespeare	No. of compounds in Shakespeare's Play
I Contention	81	25			
2 Henry VI			56	79	135
II True Tragedy	76	13			
3 Henry VI			63	46	109
III Romeo and Juliet Q1	125	18			
Romeo and Juliet Q2			107	60	167
IV Henry V Q1	66	12			
Henry V Fo.			54	94	148
V Merry Wives Q1	73	22			
Merry Wives Fo.			51	95	146
VI Hamlet Q1	73	25			
Hamlet Q2 Fo.			48	82	130
Totals	494	115	379	456	835
VII A Shrew	56	50			
The Shrew			6	97	103
VIII Troublesome Raigne	98	94			
King John			4	110	114
IX King Leir	78	74			
King Lear			4	152	156
Totals	232	218	14	359	373

N.B. The arrangement adopted in setting out the facts presented in the above table assumes that the bad quartos are source-plays rewritten by Shakespeare. On the contrary assumption of the priority of Shakespeare's plays, if the order of the columns was reversed, the various headings suitably altered, and the table read from right to left, the same set of facts would serve to exhibit the distribution and losses of the compounds present in the bad quartos after play-adapter, reporter and actors had done their worst with the author's play. Reference to the above table and my preliminary remarks make it evident that:

(i) Shakespeare retained less than seven per cent. of the compound words present in the source-plays, and those retained represent less than four per cent. of the number in Shakespeare's derived plays.

(ii) He retained in the parallel texts over three-fourths of the compounds in the bad quartos which represent over forty-five per cent. of the compounds in his corresponding plays.

(iii) He does not repeat in any of his authentic plays many of the compounds used in an earlier play.

Some of the compounds found in the bad quartos seem to be variants of compounds in the corresponding plays of Shakespeare. Thus *thrice-famous, bare-head, rope-ripe, bridal-bed, trundle-bed, short-nooke, cain-colour, crookt-backe or crook-backt, far-fetched, stand-bag* are compounds in the bad quartos which in the authentic plays appear respectively as *thrice-famed, bare-headed, roperie, bride-bed, truckle-bed, nooke-shotten, cain-coloured, crook-back, far-fet, sand-bag.* In other examples a change is made in one or other of the two words forming the compound. Thus the quartos have *barne-door, new-borne-babe, laughing-stock, well-foretelling, begger-wench, best-seeming, flattering-true, lazie-pacing, mariage-bed, kitchin-drudg, capon-cramm'd, shrill-crowing, town-bull, winding-sheete, honour-dying, never-ending, hie-master, old-vanisht, sweet-heart,* etc. These appear respectively in Shakespeare's plays as *Church-doore, cradle-babe, pointing-stock, well-forewarning, begger-maid, well-seeing* (seeming), *flattering-sweet, lazie-puffing, bridal-bed, kitchen-wench, promise-cramd, shrill-sounding, town-cryer, shrowding-sheete, honour-owing, noble-ending, Grand-master, long-vanisht, honey-sweet,* etc. I refuse to believe that Shakespeare was responsible for making so many petty corrections of another man's work; the man who invented neary nineteen hundred compound words and discarded nearly ninety-five per cent. of the compounds present in his undoubted source-plays was not a petty pedant.

All the vocabulary tests tell the same tale; the bad quartos are not old plays used by Shakespeare as raw material. Distribution of the full vocabularies, of 'peculiar' words, of the 'rarer' words and of compound words between each pair of parallel texts gives results entirely different from those obtained for the undoubted source-plays and Shakespeare's daughter-plays, or for two plays written by him on similar themes in rapid sequence.

Some brief summary of the results obtained during this survey of the vocabularies of certain play-groups seems worth making. Shakespeare's methods of using the fable and plot of an old play changed as the years went on, but his treatment of his predecessor's language seems to have been always the same. His vocabulary in *King John* shows no sign that he had read *Troublesome Raigne*, and differs as much from that of his source-play as the vocabulary of *Winter's Tale* from that of *Tempest*. My examination shows that the main differences observable between the vocabularies of two textually sound Elizabethan plays written largely in verse and not less than two thousand lines in length are:

(i) Any two such plays have in common a number of words varying from forty to sixty per cent. of the total number present in the play with the smaller vocabulary.

(ii) Each play of any such pair has from sixty to forty per cent. of its vocabulary peculiar to itself.

(iii) Each play or long poem of Shakespeare's has from 70 to 396 words not found in any other of his plays or long poems; and each play of any other author, textually sound and not less than 1,600 lines in length, has not less than 60 words not in the concordance to Shakespeare's works. This second statement is true also of nearly all the corrupt plays.

(iv) 'Rare' words common to any pair of plays, textually sound and of average length, do not exceed ten per cent. of those in the play with the smaller vocabulary. I define a 'rare' word as one that is found in not more than four plays or long poems of Shakespeare.

(v) Except for words in common use for centuries, very few of the compound words present in one play are found in the other play of the pair compared.

These results are true of any two plays of average length chosen at random from those of Kyd, Greene, Peele, Marlowe, Shakespeare, Chapman, and the many plays of unknown authorship. What is more important for my present purpose, these results are, within limits, true for all pairs of corrupt plays except the bad quartos, and true also for Shakespeare's source-plays and the plays which he based upon them.

During my examination of the vocabularies of the bad quartos and the parallel texts of Shakespeare the following facts were established:

(i) The number of words common to a bad quarto and the corresponding parallel text written by Shakespeare ranged from a minimum of 86·5 per cent. to a maximum of over 93 per cent. of the vocabulary of the bad quarto.

(ii) Words peculiar to the bad quarto but not in the corresponding play of Shakespeare range from a maximum of 13·5 per cent. to a minimum of under 7 per cent. of the vocabulary of the quarto.

(iii) Non-concordance words present in the bad quartos range from 28 to 16. Those totals are far smaller than those for corrupt plays very much shorter than the bad quartos.

(iv) If the non-concordance words are deducted in each instance, my results show that 75 per cent. of the compound words and 85 per cent. of the 'rare' words in the bad quartos are found also in the corresponding plays of Shakespeare.

These vocabulary tests are, in my opinion, sufficient in themselves to make untenable the theory that the bad quartos were, either wholly or in part, Shakespearean source-plays on which he based his own plays.

CHAPTER VI

VOCABULARY AND THE THEORY OF DOUBLE
REVISION

PROFESSOR Dover Wilson has revived the first sketch theory
in a modified form. He believes that Shakespeare rewrote the
MSS. of four old plays by unknown authors on the same themes as
those of *Romeo and Juliet, Henry V, Merry Wives* and *Hamlet,*
and that he worked over each play twice, rewriting the one portion
in 1593 and the other part in some later year. Sir Edmund
Chambers summarizes this theory:

The theory is that the plays existed in non-Shakespearean versions
before 1593; that by that year Shakespeare had made a beginning
with the revision of them all; that from the manuscripts in this
condition abridged transcripts were 'hastily' taken for the provincial tour of 'Strange's' men which began in May 1593; that
Shakespeare subsequently retouched and completed his revisions on
the original manuscripts; and that when these were performed, the
bad quartos were printed from the transcripts, which had been
brought by the pirate actor, into 'some kind of conformity' with
the final versions.[1]

Professors Wilson and Pollard are more definite and explicit in
their papers on *Romeo and Juliet* and *Hamlet.* Of *Romeo and
Juliet* they hold:

Q1 contains 'pre-Shakespearian' passages 'of the Greene-Lodge
school.' The MS. was twice handled by Shakespeare. At a first
revision he brought Acts i and ii very nearly to their final state,
but only rewrote iii-v here and there. At a second revision he
altered iii-v less thoroughly, omitting to prefix sonnets, as he had
done for i and ii, and leaving the spelling 'Capolet' in place of
'Capulet.' Q1 represents 'an abridged version of Shakespeare's
first revision of an older play eked out by what a pirate could
remember of the later version.'[2]

We know that about 1589-1590 there existed an earlier play,
not now extant, on the fable treated in *Hamlet,* and Professor
Wilson uses this fact as the starting point for his theory of the
origin of *Hamlet Q1*:

---

1. Chambers, *William Shakespeare,* Vol. i, p. 226.   2. Ibid., Vol. i, p. 343.

He thinks that the reporter did no more than make additions to an early *Hamlet* text. This was an abridged transcript for provincial use from the old play as partly revised by Shakespeare. The revision 'had not extended much beyond the Ghost-scenes.' The original manuscript remained available for a subsequent further revision by Shakespeare into the *Hamlet* of Q2 and F. In this the reporter acted not only Voltimand and Marcellus, but also other small parts, perhaps a Player, the Second Grave-digger, Reynaldo, the Priest, Fortinbras's Captain, and the English Ambassador; and from his memories of the scenes in which these occur and such other fragments as he could pick up at the stage-door, he attempted to supply the gaps left by abridgement in the manuscript. Of other scenes he knew nothing, and here we get in Q1 bits of the old play not reached by Shakespeare's first revision.[3]

This theory of the origin of Q2 and Q1 dates back to 1918 and is still maintained by its propounder except for a change of a date In his introduction to his edition of *Hamlet* for the Clarendon Press he says:

It looks, therefore, as if Shakespeare may first have handled the play sometime after Lodge's reference of 1596, and then revised it in 1601.[4]

His theory of double or partial revision has the great merit of making definite criticism possible. Vague as many parts of it are, the outlines are quite simple. Shakespeare's hasty revision of the three old plays in 1593 and *Hamlet* in 1596 was followed by second revisions between 1594 and 1601. The first rewriting of the old *Romeo and Juliet* was limited to Acts I-II, and that of *Hamlet* to the Ghost-scenes. Before discussing these statements, something must be said on the state of the bad quarto texts.

All critics agree that the bad quartos are not and, in the present state of the texts, cannot be the untouched work of educated dramatists; they admit that corruption is present in every scene, but usually fail to recognize that this corruption has undermined the foundations on which sound literary judgment must rest. If all the distinctive marks of an author's style have disappeared, the critic's occupation is gone. Unlike most of the earlier and some modern commentators, Professor Dover Wilson never forgets that every bad quarto is a mutilated abridgment of a sound text. He insists that a manuscript, free from corruption, must be the

---

3. Ibid., Vol. i, p. 420.   4. J. Dover Wilson, *Hamlet* (1934), p. xxii.

ultimate source of each printed text, and that the mutilation and perversion of the text of this manuscript must have generated the 'copy' for this printed text.   His study of these plays led him to the opinion that the variation from act to act in the amount and kind of garbling and corruption, and the presence of much non-Shakespearean matter in the later acts, were inconsistent with the theory that the bad quartos were the direct, if degenerate, offshoots of Shakspeare's plays.   He formulated a theory which, in his opinion, accounted for the many peculiar characteristics of these quartos.   His theory postulates the existence of a manuscript of an anonymous play, part of which had been rewritten by Shakespeare, and the other part left almost unrevised except 'here and there'.   This manuscript would be free from any but accidental corruption, and an acting version made from it would be on the acting list of Strange's men during their provincial tour and perhaps later in London.   Subsequently the poet rewrote the unrevised part, and the company put on the boards an acting version of the play as it now exists.   Shortly afterwards the old play as first revised by Shakespeare came surreptitiously to press. The printed play was a 'report' based on the poet's first revision, 'eked out' by what a pirate could remember of the final revision.

I propose to discuss the merits of this theory.   Can each bad quarto be divided into two portions, one the corrupt work of Shakespeare, the other the corrupt remainder of the source-play upon which Shakespeare worked?   What are we to understand by the vague phrase, 'eked out by what a pirate could remember of the later version'?

Corruption assumes as many shapes as Proteus, and its incidence is variable and unexpected.   In his *Two Elizabethan Stage Abridgments* Dr. W. W. Greg has given students an adequate notion of the depths to which a play might sink under the debasing activities of actors and pirates.   Examination of the words foisted by them into that portion of Orlando's part for which the Dulwich MS. provides a check leads to some illuminating results.   This portion of *Orlando Furioso Q1* amounts to 407 lines of which 303 correspond more or less to lines of the MS.   The remaining 104 lines are divisible into two sections; the first contains 48 genuine lines from the pen of Greene, comprising two roundelays (10 lines), an English paraphrase of Italian verses of Ariosto (14 lines), 3 lines illegible in MS., and 21 lines of what in Q1 is Orlando's last speech. The second section contains 56 spurious lines, found in spurious scenes, and is the work of the actors.

I find in the 407 lines of Q1 no fewer than 118 words which are not in the manuscript version of Orlando's part. Of these 34 are to be found in the 48 genuine lines omitted in MS. and 48 in Orlando's interpolated speeches. Altogether 82 of the alien words of Q1 occur either in passages absent in the Dulwich MS. or in speeches not written by Greene. Thus after these necessary deductions have been made, the corruption present in 303 lines common to MS. and Q1 resulted in the introduction into Q1 of 36 words not in Greene's authentic play. This total is, proportionately, slightly less than the number found in *Contention* or *Hamlet Q1*.

I have set out in the appropriate section of the table below the number of words present in each act of each bad quarto but not in the corresponding act of the parallel play written by Shakespeare. I call these 'alien' words. These totals will enable some estimate to be made of the variation in the amount of corruption present in each play and in each act of each play. For purpose of comparison I have added the totals for the known source-plays, these being subdivided into suitable groups of scenes. The results for the six parallel texts are arranged in six separate groups. Three rows give for each pair of parallel texts comparative results under separate headings:

(i) In the first row of each group are set out for Shakespeare's play the total number of lines, the number of lines in each of the five acts, and the total number of words in the vocabulary.

(ii) In the second row of each group are set out for the corresponding bad quarto the total number of lines, the number of lines in the group of scenes equivalent to each act of the corresponding play of Shakespeare, and the total number of words in the bad quarto. For three of them, viz., *Romeo and Juliet Q1*, *Henry V Q1* and *Merry Wives Q1*, the totals given for the vocabularies are estimates.

(iii) The third row gives for the bad quarto named the number of 'alien' words present in each act or group of scenes, i.e., the number of words not in the vocabulary of the corresponding play of Shakespeare; in the last column is the total number of words in the bad quarto which are not in the authentic text of the corresponding play. Each total in the six third rows of table VIII consists partly of words interpolated in corrupted lines of one or other of Shakespeare's plays, and partly of words found in non-Shakespearean lines and passages present in the bad quartos.

For the sake of simplicity the term 'act' will be used for the group of quarto scenes which corresponds to an act of Shakespeare's parallel play. For purpose of comparison I add a table giving the distribution of the non-concordance words in the source-plays rewritten by Shakespeare.

TABLE VIII

DISTRIBUTION OF WORDS OF Q1 NOT IN THE PARALLEL TEXT

| Plays and No. of Words | No. of Lines | Number of Lines in | | | | | No. of Words |
		Act I	Act II	Act III	Act IV	Act V	
2 Henry VI	3,075	659	494	828	755	339	3,146
Contention	1,973	469	394	434	449	227	2,027
Words of Contention not in Folio		61	51	53	67	38	270
3 Henry VI	2,902	580	704	561	559	498	2,790
True Tragedy	2,124	499	568	342	320	395	2,182
Words of True Tragedy not in Folio ..		25	43	13	26	36	143
Romeo and Juliet Q2	2,986	713	621	827	400	425	2,916
Romeo and Juliet Q1	2,215	527	503	603	271	311	2,300 (est.)
Words of Q1 not in Q2		23	22	66	51	45	207
Henry V Fo.	3,166	442	564	690	969	501	3,147
Henry V Q1	1,623	220	340	313	548	202	1,800 (est.)
Words of Q1 not in Fo.		27	30	24	32	18	131
Merry Wives Fo. ..	2,634	543	584	653	551	303	2,527
Merry Wives Q1 ..	1,419	261	356	377	258	167	1,600 (est.)
Words of Q1 not in Fo.		42	50	45	39	40	216
Hamlet (Cambridge text)	3,762	850	701	885	649	677	3,882
Hamlet Q1	2,154	633	407	511	288	315	2,251
Words of Q1 not in Received Text		53	66	87	48	41	295

TABLE IX

DISTRIBUTION IN SOURCE PLAYS OF WORDS NOT IN DERIVATIVE PLAYS

1 *Troublesome Raigne*

	Prologue Pt. I sc. i-ii	Pt. I sc. iii-ix	Pt. I sc. x-xiii	Prologue Pt. II sc. i-iii	Pt. II sc. iv-ix	Totals
Number of Lines	642	475	647	646	562	2,972
Number of Words .. .. *not* in *King John*	344	244	300	262	160	1,310

2 *King Leir*

	sc. i-vi	sc. vii-xiv	sc. xv-xx	sc. xxi-xxv	sc. xxvi-xxxi	Totals
Number of Lines	562	559	605	555	286	2,567
Number of Words .. .. *not* in *King Lear*	301	228	206	188	100	1,023

3 *A Shrew*

	Act I	Act II	Act III	Act IV	Act V	Totals
Number of Lines	480	292	338	188	185	1,483
Number of Words .. .. *not* in *The Shrew*	157	129	143	80	38	547

NOTES ON TABLES

1 I have included in Act III of *Romeo and Juliet Q2* the sixth scene of the second act which corresponds to the tenth scene of Q1. My reason is that, in fairness to Professor Wilson, it must be supposed that this scene of Q1, which differs entirely in language from Act II, sc. vi of Q2, was rewritten by Shakespeare during his suggested second revision.

2 In *Hamlet Q1* the order in which certain episodes are found differs from the order of their occurrence in Q2. For the purpose of exact comparison of the vocabularies, I have regrouped certain scenes and portions of scenes of Q1 to bring them into exact conformity with the position of these episodes in Q2. This does not affect in any way the division of the play postulated for the theory of double revision.

3 I estimate the vocabulary of *Troublesome Raigne* at 2,600-2,700 words, and that of *King Leir* at 2,400-2,500 words; my preference favours the lower limits. The vocabulary of 'A Shrew' would not exceed by much 1,600 words.

Some notes follow on the various totals given in the table:

(i) I find the vocabulary of *Contention* consists of 1,757 words also in *2 Henry VI* and 270 alien words, or words not in the

E

parallel text; in that of *True Tragedy* are 2,036 words belonging to 3 *Henry VI* and 148 alien words; whilst *Hamlet Q1* has 1,956 words in common with the received text of *Hamlet* and 295 alien words. Hence follows the inevitable inference that the vocabularies of these three bad quartos are overwhelmingly Shakespearean; for each alien word they average eight words in common with the vocabulary of the corresponding parallel text.

(ii) In contrast are the vocabularies of Shakespeare's two source-plays which have good texts. For each nine words common to them and to Shakespeare's two derivative plays there are seven words peculiar to the source-plays. This characteristic of source-plays serves to differentiate them very sharply from the bad quartos.

(iii) Not one act of the thirty acts in the six bad quartos has more than 87 alien words; each of the ten acts in the two longer source-plays has from 100 to 344 words peculiar to it. From these figures I infer that not one act of any bad quarto is entirely or even mainly of non-Shakespearean origin.

(iv) Variations in the number of alien words present in successive acts of the bad quartos are not in any way abnormal, if such important factors as the lengths of the acts, changes of themes, amount and character of abridgment, presence or absence of non-Shakespearean matter, etc., are taken into account. Variations within such narrow limits as are exhibited in the table do not warrant any suggestion of difference in authorship.

(v) Much of the variation observable in the number of alien words present in consecutive acts of certain bad quartos is largely due to the fortuitous occurrence of short passages of non-Shakespearean verse or prose; each of these contains some words not in the parallel text. Below I give a list of such words .as occur in non-Shakespearean passages of not less than five lines each for *Contention, Romeo and Juliet Q1* and *Hamlet Q1*. For *True Tragedy* I give totals only. Seven-eighths of *Merry Wives* is in prose, and *Henry V Q1* has no spurious verse or prose.

I CONTENTION

i. 24-29	excessive, lavish, beseem	3
iv. 14-19	mask, hellish, pierce, bowels, centric, twinkling	6
31-37	pool, fiery, waggon, amidst, singe, parched, smoke (n), road, river, spell (n)	10

vi. 53-62	aid (vb), invenomed, presage (vb), maugre	4
vii. 4-9	heinous, barefoot, taper, white	4
ix.133-143	Irish, plant (vb), pale (n), redress (n), fortunate, far-fetcht, uncontrolled	7
xviii. 17-21	lustily, petticoat, kirtle, smock	4
75-84	rest (arrest), paper-house, common-place, whoreson, sergeant, cogging, hough	7
87-97	countryman, mutinous, rebellion, mildly, over-throw (n), whereat	6
xxi. 52-6	curled, lock, deep-trenched, furrow	4
xxiii. 40-51	sinew, shrink, smear, welter, luke-warm, immortal, secure, furiously	8
68-88	faint-heart, buckle, thick, throng, weary, prop, remainder, increase (vb), boldest-spirited	9

This gives a total of 72 words not in *2 Henry VI* in 9 passages containing 110 lines of non-Shakespearean origin.

II TRUE TRAGEDY

iii. 50-4	..	4 words;	vi.1-48	..	14 words
xv. 1-20	..	4 words;	xxi.1-20	..	10 words

Thus the *True Tragedy* has 32 words not in *3 Henry VI* in 4 passages containing 93 lines not written by Shakespeare.

III ROMEO AND JULIET Q1

x. 1-30	Grant (n), consist, pointed, consummate, band, never-parting, witness, guess, mist, frolic, fairness, defer, embracement, linger, hinderer, cross-way	16
xi. 67-77	mount, shoulder, peasantly, sexton, base, epitaph, guts	7
xvii. 28-35	closet, requisite, tyre, rebato, chain	5
xix. 44-79	nip, unjust, impartial, destiny, sad-faced, map, wholly, partaker, charity, otherwise, mate, tombed, together, prodigy, forlorn, destitute, remediless, absented, sumptuous	19
xxii. 8-13	Bridal-bed, circuit, model, eternity, adorn, remain, praise (n)	7

These five passages of *Romeo and Juliet Q1* have 54 alien words in 91 lines not written by Shakespeare.

IV Hamlet Q1

Hamlet Q1 has 94 alien words in twelve non-Shakespearean passages containing 146 lines.

In these four longer quartos there are, in all, thirty non-Shakespearean passages, each not less than five lines in length; they amount to 440 lines in which are 252 alien words. If the minimum length of the non-Shakespearean passages included in the above list had been reduced to three lines, the total of 252 words would have been considerably increased. In *Hamlet Q1* the last four lines of the hero's first speech contain four words—italicized —not in Q2:

> Nor all together *mixt* with outward *semblance,*
> Is equall to the *sorrow* of my heart,
> Him haue I lost I must of force forgoe,
> These but the *ornaments* and sutes of woe,

It may be noted that the fourth line of this fustian is identical with the last line of the corresponding speech in Q2 except that *ornaments* replaces 'trappings.' This speech is, in Q1, a reply to one of the King's in which four non-Shakespearean lines, separated into two pairs by a corrupted line of Q2, contain four alien words more. Three lines, addressed to Ophelia by her father at the end of the next scene,

> For louers lines are *snares* to *intrap* the heart;
> *Refuse* his tokens, both of them are keyes
> To *vnlocke Chastitie* vnto Desire,

contain five more such words. Five lines taken from the conversation between Osric and Hamlet are responsible for another five alien words not in Q2:

> *Ham.* And you sir: foh, how the *muske-cod* smels!
> *Gen.* I come with an *embassage* from his maiesty to you.
> *Ham.* I shall sir giue you attention:
> By my *troth* me thinkes t'is very colde.
> *Gent.* It is indeed very *rawish* colde.

The first three lines are not in Q2; the two lines following are adaptations of lines in Q2, and serve to illustrate the manner in which almost half the alien words were foisted into Q1.

Examination of table VIII reveals the fact that no definite or uniform relation exists between the lengths of consecutive acts of a bad quarto and the respective numbers of the alien words present in them. If the longer passages of non-Shakespearean verse and prose were removed from a bad quarto only a small decrease—about five per cent.—of length would result, but such a removal of text would necessarily involve deduction of the numbers of the alien words present in the passages excised. Below will be found a revised table showing the distribution of the alien words in the acts of the four longer bad quartos. The first row of the previous table is omitted as unnecessary; the new first row of the revised table gives for each of the four quartos the reduced totals of lengths of acts and of the play, after the longer non-Shakespearean passages have been removed, and the new second row gives the correspondingly reduced numbers of alien words after the deduction of those present in the omitted passages. Deductions of lines and of words have been made in each act of *Contention* and *True Tragedy,* but only in Acts III-V of *Romeo and Juliet Q1* and Acts II-V of *Hamlet Q1.* Reasons for this difference will be given later.

TABLE X

REVISED TABLE: DISTRIBUTION OF ALIEN WORDS IN QUARTOS

	Act I	Act II	Act III	Act IV	Act V	Totals
Contention						
Lines	450	378	423	423	189	1,863
Words	42	43	46	50	17	198
True Tragedy						
Lines	494	520	342	300	375	2,031
Words	21	29	13	22	26	111
Romeo and Juliet Q1						
Lines	527	503	562	227	305	2,124
Words	23	22	43	27	38	153
Hamlet Q1						
Lines	632	384	462	226	303	2,007
Words	53	47	50	21	30	201
Four Bad Quartos						
Lines						8,025
Words						663

Removal of these thirty clumps of non-Shakespearean prose and verse reduces the length of the four bad quartos by very little; 8,465 lines become 8,025, a loss of about five per cent. The consequential reduction of the number of the alien words from 915 to 663 is far greater, with the result of a more even distribution of these words among the acts of each bad quarto. Variation in consecutive acts still exists, but the most resolved revisionist would scarcely suggest that it is sufficient support for a theory. Comparison of the totals in the two tables for the 'Distribution of Alien Words' in the acts of the quartos is illuminating. First, we have 252 alien words in 440 lines of non-Shakespearean matter; these totals are of the same order as and tally with the results set down for the first two scenes of *Troublesome Raigne* and the first six scenes of *King Leir*. Hence five per cent. of the text of these four bad quartos is in the condition that experience suggests an unrevised source play should be. Secondly, the total of 663 alien words in the remaining 8,025 lines of these bad quartos is in excellent agreement with the 53 alien words present in 633 lines in the first act of *Hamlet Q1*. Shakespeare's first revision, says Professor Wilson, did not extend much beyond the Ghost-scenes, that is, the first act. He puts the abridgment and corruption found in this act to the account of reporter and actors, an explanation which I accept but extend without any reservation to all the corrupt passages of each bad quarto.

I now propose to discuss briefly Professor Wilson's theory of double revision with special reference to *Romeo and Juliet* and *Hamlet*. He suggests that scenes i-ix, or 1,030 lines, of *Romeo and Juliet Q1*, which correspond to the first act and five scenes of the second act of Q2, are substantially Shakespeare's, except for some contamination due to the reporter; further, he maintains that the 1,185 lines of scenes x-xxii of Q1, which correspond to the sixth scene of the second act and the remaining acts of Q2, are the work of another author, excepting for a little rewriting 'here and there' and some additions bunglingly foisted into the text of Q1 from the reporter's recollections of the poet's fully revised play. My subdivision of the words of Q1 which are not in Q2 indicates that the reporter inserted 45 words of his own into the first part which Professor Wilson admits is 'very nearly in its final state,' and that Shakespeare a year or more after his supposed first revision rejected 162 words of Q1 during his second revision which covered 1,185 lines written by some other author than Shakespeare. Certainly the difference between the two parts is noticeable, yet is the theory of two revisions necessary to explain this difference? Some points of importance are worth a little consideration.

First, I submit that the two parts differ in their literary make-up. A quarter of the first part consists of heroic couplets and there is almost as much prose; the actors always retain either rhyming couplets or prose better than blank verse of which the larger part of the second portion of the play consists. Secondly, if the Shakespeare who transformed *Troublesome Raigne* into *King John* had rewritten 1,185 lines of an old play, he would have rejected not 162 words but more than five hundred, had all of these lines been un-Shakespearean as were the 91 lines which have been excluded from the revised table X. In consequence the theory of a Shakespearean rewriting as drastic as that which turned *A Shrew* into *The Shrew* is not tenable. Thirdly, I have shown that 54 of the 162 alien words are found in five passages amounting in all to 91 lines of non-Shakespearean verse. These 91 lines are almost exactly a thirteenth of the 1,185 lines in the second part, and their omission or exclusion leaves untouched twelve-thirteenths of what Professor Wilson terms the unrevised portion of the old play used by Shakespeare as his raw material. Disappearance from the play of these 91 lines ought not to affect the validity of the theory to any extent, or destroy the strength of the arguments used to establish it any more than the omission to use five hundred lines of *Troublesome Raigne* affects its claim to be Shakespeare's source-play. Reference to the revised table informs us that 108 alien words remain in 1,094 lines of an old play unrevised except 'here and there.' This result is not in agreement with the result for the rewriting of *A Shrew;* Shakespeare omitted 547 words of the vocabulary of a play 1,483 lines in length. We know that the actors inserted 36 words in 303 lines of Orlando's part, and Professor Wilson admits that the reporter and his assistants are responsible for the presence of 53 alien words in the 633 lines of the first act of *Hamlet Q1.* These results are in very good agreement with the figures quoted for the twelve-thirteenths of the second part of *Romeo and Juliet Q1,* viz., 108 alien words in 1,094 lines, and I conclude logically that the actors and reporters who gave the 'copy' of this quarto to the printer inserted them in its text.

Professor Wilson thinks that Shakespeare's first revision of the *Ur-Hamlet* about 1596 'had not extended much beyond the Ghost scenes,' and that the second revision covered the other four acts of the play. This means that the extant *Hamlet Q1* contains 633 lines of Shakespeare's, many of them garbled, and 1,521 lines of an earlier text which the reporter patched with such scraps as he could remember of the acting version of Q2 or could pick up at the stage door. In the 633 lines of the poet's first revision there are 53 words not in Q2, and in the remaining 1,521 lines of the unrevised portion of Q1 there are 242 such words. In twelve non-Shakespearean passages belonging to the unrevised part of Q1 there are 147 lines in which are 94 words not in Q2 or Fo. I shall treat the unrevised part of *Hamlet Q1* exactly as I did that of *Romeo and Juliet Q1,* and deduct from the total length of the second part 147 lines or less than a tenth of the whole. Omission of a tenth of the unrevised portion leaves nine-tenths of it still unrevised. When the deductions of lines and words have been made, there are found in 1,375 lines, supposedly by another author, not the six hundred alien words that should be expected in a source-play but 148 alien words only—a result in very good agreement with the totals given for the first or revised part of Q1. If the pirate, as Professor Wilson admits, inserted 53 words in Shakespeare's first act, why should we not debit the 148 words in 1,375 lines of the rest of the play to the same agency?

Another test that I shall make of Professor Wilson's theory depends on the distribution in the two bad quartos of certain word-groups found in the two parallel texts. These consist of words peculiar to *Hamlet Q2* or *Romeo and Juliet Q2* and of words found in one of these plays and also in some other play of Shakespeare. Below are particulars for the parallel texts of these two named plays, of the totals and distribution of these words; for the purpose of discussing the double revision theory each had been divided into the two parts which acceptance of the theory postulates.

TABLE XI

WORD-GROUPS IN PARTS OF TWO PARALLEL TEXTS

Name of Plays	Number of Lines	Number of Words	Calculated Totals
Romeo and Juliet			
Part I Q2	1,334	152	118
Q1	1,030	114	114
Part II Q2	1,652	138	99
Q1	1,185	61	61
Hamlet			
Part I Q2	850	147	109
Q1	633	55	55
Part II Q2	2,912	474	242
Q1	1,521	111	111

N.B. I have calculated for each part of the two authentic texts the proportional number of these words that would be present if the number of lines was reduced to the number present in the corresponding part of Q1. For example, the calculated total of 118 represents the number of the 152 words in the first part of *Romeo and Juliet Q2* which would probably be present in 1,030 lines of this part.

From the column of the 'Calculated Totals' for *Hamlet* it will be seen that the combined efforts of the official abridger of plays and the unofficial corrupter of acting versions have produced almost an equal amount of havoc in the respective vocabularies of Part I and Part II. If Part I of *Hamlet Q1* is Shakespeare's, more than a little scratched and tattered, we may reasonably deduce from this test that Part II of *Hamlet Q1* is also derivative Shakespeare in somewhat more serious disrepair. Part I of *Romeo and Juliet Q1* was reported exceedingly well, and is undoubtedly Shakespeare's; Part II, though much inferior to the first part, is superior to the first part of *Hamlet Q1* and is therefore debased Shakespeare.

Professor Wilson offers, in my opinion, two contradictory explanations of two similar sets of facts. My vocabulary tests confirm his opinion that the first act of *Hamlet Q1* and the first two acts of *Romeo and Juliet Q1* are abridged and corrupt derivatives of the corresponding portions of the respective second quartos, but the same tests prove that the remaining portions of these quartos are not Shakespearean source-plays, i.e., they give results quite inconsistent with those derived from undoubted source-plays. On the contrary my tests indicate that Acts II-V of *Hamlet Q1* and Acts III-V of *Romeo and Juliet* are the more severely abridged and more deeply corrupt derivatives of the corresponding acts of the respective second quartos. Abridgment, official and unofficial, is the core of the interrelationship between the parallel texts.

This critic does not make clear what readers are to understand by his use of the terms 'revision' and 'rewriting.' No one would say that Shakespeare 'revised' *Troublesome Raigne*, because he left practically nothing of its text in *King John*. Professor Wilson states that Shakespeare had the manuscript of an early play on the theme of Romeo and Juliet to work upon, and suggests that he developed from the first part of it the first two acts of *Romeo and Juliet Q2* very much as they exist now, and rewrote the rest of his original 'here and there.' These words vaguely describe what may be something or nothing, but can scarcely be applied to Act III and Act IV, scene i, of Q1, which, taken together, contain 665 of the 1,155 lines in the last three acts. Apart from fourteen lines that may be part of the old play and 77 lines of prose, the recognizably Shakespearean verse in this act and scene amounts to 574 lines or half the last three acts. Of these lines 248 are identical with lines of Q2, 100 lines differ from the corresponding lines of Q2 by one word in a line, and 44 other lines differ from those of Q2 by two words only in each line. Thus 392 lines of the total verse in Act III and Act IV, scene i, of Q1, are substantially identical with lines of Q2. If for comparative purposes the alien lines and the prose are omitted, this portion of *Romeo and Juliet Q1* is almost as well preserved as the first act of *Hamlet Q1*, which has 29 non-Shakespearean lines and 425 verse-lines substantially identical with lines of *Hamlet Q2*. This result will serve to explain my reason for saying that Professor Wilson draws two contradictory inferences from two similar sets of facts; if he ascribes the corruption of the first act of *Hamlet Q1* to the blunders of an illiterate pirate, no other agent need be sought for the garbling of the above scenes of *Romeo and Juliet Q1*. I certainly prefer this explanation to relying upon sporadic rewriting and the happy-go-lucky recollections of the pirate. In spite of the progressive degeneration of the text from the second scene of the fourth act to the end of the play, three-fourths of the verse in this part of Q1 are derived from lines of Shakespeare. Only one scene of Q1, the tenth, could be termed the 'source' of Shakespeare's corresponding scene, and only in two other scenes do the non-Shakespearean lines equal as much as thirty per cent. of the length.

How much 'a pirate could remember' of the second quarto which was on the acting list but unprinted when Q1 came to the press, Professor Wilson does not say and I do not know. If he is responsible for the present text of scenes xi-xvi of Q1, then he was the person guilty of garbling the first two acts of Q2. There is nothing surprising in his being capable of reproducing twelve per cent. more of the verse in scenes i-ix than of that in scenes xi-xvi; according to the theory of double revision he had been familiar with the earlier scenes for two years before the later scenes were written. This explanation is not necessary, however, to account for a comparatively slight difference in the proportion retained well; most persons remember longer and more accurately the first part of a poem committed to memory than the middle or the end.

My comments on the other arguments used by Professors Pollard and Wilson will be brief. Underlying their theory of double revision—the foundation, indeed, on which the whole structure is built—is a settled belief that Shakespeare began and ended his career of dramatist as a patcher of other men's plays. These critics conjecture that early in 1593 he was engaged in patching up a miscellaneous group of four old plays for Strange's men. Apparently this versatile young man was oddly original in his working methods; as soon as he had vamped up an act of the *Ur-Hamlet,* he put it aside and cobbled away at a couple of acts of the *Ur-Romeo and Juliet,* and so for the other two derelict plays. When each of the four was less than half-finished, the company took them on their country tour. Shakespeare may have stayed near London, as some commentators conjecture, to correct the proofs of *Venus and Adonis* which had been entered on the Stationers' Register 18 April, 1593. Eighteen months later we find him a prominent member of the Chamberlain's men, and Professors Pollard and Wilson suggest that he resumed his old trade as play-dresser, and between July 1594 and 1601 completed the interrupted revision of the four plays. In 1601 he completed that piece of cobblery, *Hamlet Q2.*

My only objection to this pretty piece of fanciful theorising is that there is not a tittle of evidence in favour of it. Of the play-patcher I may say in those 'memorable and tremendous words' of Betsey Prig, 'I don't believe there's no sich person.' We know something of Henslowe's play-factory and of the various chares performed by his ill-paid hacks, but there is no record of payments for tasks such as play-patching. 'Fanciful' adequately describes the suggestion that Shakespeare simultaneousy repaired four plays, an act or two of each at a time; nor can I reason myself into believing that Strange's men, driven by plague and poverty to make a provincial tour, would pay Shakespeare £10 to £15 for his work and the Master of the Revels his fees for licensing the plays, would buy new properties, prepare new parts for the actors, conduct a series of rehearsals and then produce these plays for the first time in some small country towns. I do not think that the first act of *Hamlet Q2* was written eight or even five years before the other acts; the style of this play, so greatly planned and universal in its appeal, is as homogeneous as the wide range of its characters, representative of all intimate human relations and ranks of society, permits. Whatever diversity of style and thought may appear in the first scene is found throughout the play, because varying moods, the flow and ebb of emotion correspondent to the continuous change of theme and circumstance, and the clash of character instinctively suggest to the master variant modes of expression. There are as many styles as characters, and if a 'Centinel' talks in the early or simpler style and the scholar and Prince's friend in the more mature style we are thankful to the poet for such infinite variety.

Professors Pollard and Wilson suggest that Shakespeare wrote his new plays on the margins of the manuscripts of the old plays which he was treating as raw material. Economically it was penny wise and pound foolish; it was a wanton waste of property. Enough paper for the manuscript of *Hamlet Q2* could be bought for sixpence, and the company might get a pound or thirty shillings for the old *Hamlet* from a reputable stationer. Again, the manuscript of such a revised play with its text, now horizontal, now vertical, full of minutely written interlineations, with lines partly or wholly scored out, with stage directions anywhere or nowhere, would be a perennial source of annoyance and inconvenience to producer, play-adapter and prompter whenever it was revived. My third reason is that Shakespeare could not do it, unless he had an honest method for rewriting plays already in print and a dishonest method for the so-called 'revising' of plays in manuscript. Compare *Troublesome Raigne* and *King John*, *A Shrew* and *The Shrew*, *Famous Victories* and *Henry V*, *King Leir* and *King Lear*, and we perceive that he left exceedingly few lines of his originals in a recognizable state; large portions of the source-plays are unused and all the characters feel, think and talk differently. This is Shakespeare's known and honest way of revising old plays in print. Obviously Professors Pollard and Wilson have in mind such a type of revision as would turn the less corrupt parts of *Romeo and Juliet Q1* into the full version of Q2. This would mean deletion in the manuscript of Q1 of many words, phrases and lines, and a considerable amount of interlineation often difficult to read correctly. Additions of five or six lines might be placed cross-wise in the left-hand margins; longer passages would necessarily be written on blank paper and

thus become part of the manuscript. This method of revision
implies that more than nine-tenths of *Romeo and Juliet Q1* would
be retained in Q2.

We know nothing of *Ur-Hamlet* except that such a play was in
existence about 1590 and was acted in June, 1594, probably by
Strange's men. What was its length? We must remember that
31 textually sound plays written between 1587 and 1594 by authors
other than Shakespeare average 2,157 lines a-piece, the two
longest being *Troublesome Raigne* (a play in two parts and so
acted), and *Spanish Tragedy,* which has 2,736 lines. I suggest
that this early *Hamlet* did not exceed 2,500 lines in length. When
Shakespeare undertook its revision or rewriting, he would sketch
out a short plot but would not know how many lines he would
write. If he preserved as little of this play as he did of his
acknowledged source-plays not many more than ten or twenty
lines would survive; only the margins of the manuscript would be
available for writing his own play, unless he struck out every line
of the play and wrote interlineations between each pair. Even
then he would find it necessary to use thirteen or fourteen sheets
of blank paper to complete it. Such a suggestion may seem
ridiculous but what is the alternative? Certainly he could have
written *Hamlet Q2* on sheets of unused paper; if so, exit the
double revision theory. On the other hand he could have adopted
or adapted, in plain English, stolen, most of the lines of his first
act from *Ur-Hamlet,* making such minor corrections as I have
suggested above for the supposed revision of *Romeo and Juliet Q1;*
to these he must have added two or three hundreds of lines of his
own, some on the margins, but the majority on fresh sheets. This
is the dishonest method which Shakespeare did not use; but if
Shakespeare rewrote his first act on the manuscript of *Ur-Hamlet,*
he must have been the most reckless plagiary of his day.

My criticism of the double revision theory has been made
difficult because Professors Pollard and Wilson have not made
definite and clear what was in the manuscript of the semi-revised
Romeo and Juliet upon which Shakespeare worked during his
second revision. They state that the first two acts were practically
as they were in Q2, but what was in the rest of the manuscript?
Writing in general terms of all the bad quartos they tell us that

'the [first] revision had in no case proceeded much beyond Act II,'[1] and that the non-Shakespearian 'material . . . is, on our theory, the production of the dramatists whose manuscripts came into Shakespeare's hands.'[2]

I gather from these two statements that, except for a little rewriting 'here and there,' Acts III-V of the transcript made from Shakespeare's first revision in 1593 were almost entirely the work of the anonymous author. They sum up by saying that Q1 represents,

an abridged version of Shakespeare's first revision of an older play eked out by what a pirate could remember of the later version.[3]

After careful examination I find in Acts III-V of *Romeo and Juliet Q1* 1,185 lines, of which 103 are prose, 145 are non-Shakespearean verse, and 937 are Shakespeare's verse; the last comprise 323 lines identical with lines of Q2, 210 lines differing from those of Q2 by no more than two words in corresponding lines, and 404 lines deviating more considerably from lines of Q2 but recognizably Shakespeare's. Thus it would seem that 937 lines of Shakespeare's verse have, in the unrevised third, fourth and fifth acts of the transcript, taken the place of what may have been as many verses by the unknown author; only 145 of the latter's verses have survived. His prose, also, disappears almost as completely; of 103 lines of prose all but about a dozen are Shakespeare's.

What an extraordinary person this pirate must have been! He has had the good luck to pick up an abridged transcript of perhaps the most popular play of the day; half of it is Shakespeare's. Instead of hurrying to Danter's house at once with his loot and receiving his thirty pieces of silver, what does this queer rascal do? He buys some paper, discards the unrevised part except for reference when his memory fails him, and spends many a laborious night in rewriting Acts III-V from his recollections of what he had heard on the stage or behind the scenes. Except for three scenes his work is not badly done, and the first half of it is not much below the standard of the first two acts in Q1, but why did he put himself to such trouble? Danter was himself a pirate-printer

1. *Times Literary Supplement*, 16 January, 1919.
2. *Ibid.*
3. *Times Literary Supplement*, 14 August, 1919.

and publisher, and his editions of *Jack Straw, Orlando Furioso* and *Old Wive's Tale* prove his willingness to print as little or as much as his brother-pirates, the actors, were able to steal for him; a play was the thing he wanted. I admire the elaborate ingenuity of this theory and am prepared to believe that Shakespeare may have rewritten an old play on this theme very much as he did perhaps a year later for *King John;* for the rest a pirate actor who may have had a part in this old play would account for everything in Q1.

CHAPTER VII

STATE OF THE QUARTO TEXTS

WE possess in Dulwich MS. and *Orlando Furioso Q1* a pair of parallel texts for about two-thirds of Orlando's part, and a comparison of the two versions reveals the havoc made by the actors in Greene's verse. Lines or part-lines in MS. number 474, of which 441 are lines of verse or fragments of verse-lines and 33 lines are prose. Of the poetry the pirates kept 296 lines, and 7 lines only of the prose; they added to Orlando's part 56 lines of their own. Included in Q1 are 48 lines omitted in MS., half of which are certainly genuine, viz., the two roundelays and Greene's paraphrase of the extract from Ariosto. If these 48 lines are added to the 474 lines of the MS., Orlando's part (from line 596 of Q1 to the end) equals 522 lines, of which Q1 keeps 351 or 67 per cent., or a little more proportionately than *Contention* keeps of *2 Henry VI*. Of these 351 lines common to the two versions Q1 has 96 lines of MS. verbatim, and 168 lines differ from Greene's text by not more than two words a line; each of the remaining 87 lines of Q1 differs from the corresponding line of MS. by more than two words, but all are certainly derived from Greene's manuscript. Dr. W. W. Greg has shown that there are extensive omissions comprising whole scenes and episodes, and interpolations, mainly comic, have been introduced into Q1. These interpolations introduce episodes in some of which Orlando takes a part, and thus give a comic turn to portions of the genuine text. Omissions, apart from those due to defects of MS., are of scenes and episodes in which the hero has no share, and consequently no trace of them is found in MS. These parallel texts of Orlando's part exhibit in many respects precisely the same relationship as *3 Henry VI* and *True Tragedy;* consequently this resemblance suggests that study of the interrelation of Dulwich MS. and Orlando's part in Q1 is likely to help to a sound understanding of the large group of Shakespeare's parallel texts.

Most of the problems awaiting solution in the parallel texts of Shakespeare are practically the same as those which Dr. Greg

has solved in *Orlando Furioso Q1* and *Dulwich MS.   Henry V Q1*
and *Merry Wives Q1,* each of which is of about the same length
as Greene's play, omit several scenes, but neither has much
interpolated matter.   *Merry Wives Q1* shows some changes from
the folio version in the order of incidents, but as it is nearly all
prose I shall not discuss here what it adds or omits.   *Henry V Q1*
retains a much greater proportion of the prose than of the poetry,
but it is the only bad quarto that has no borrowings from other
plays.

The most important and most characteristic difference between
the authentic play and the corresponding surreptitious quarto is
that of length, and this difference extends to almost every pair
of corresponding scenes.   Each scene of *Romeo and Juliet Q1* is
shorter than the corresponding scene of the second quarto.   Except
for the two shortest of the Cade scenes, two short scenes, the
seventh and the twenty-third, of *True Tragedy,* which are identical
in length with those of *3 Henry VI,* and the interpolated fourteenth
scene of *Hamlet Q1,* each of the remaining 120 scenes of the six
bad quartos is shorter than the corresponding scene of Shakespeare's
parallel plays.   In each bad quarto the same theme, plot and
episodes, and the same characters, are treated in the same manner,
and for the most part in the same order as in the parallel text.
Much the same is true of each pair of corresponding scenes; the
same actions occur, and the same characters appear in the same
order and make the same speeches in language largely identical.

Some of this uniform similarity will be manifest on studying the
tables set out below.   They give details of the subdivision of each
pair of texts into acts and scenes.   Most of the headings above
the columns sufficiently explain what the numbers in the columns
below each heading mean, but some account of the meaning
intended in styling various columns A, B, C, D, E will be necessary.

In the column with the heading A is given for each scene and
act the number of lines of prose or verse or both present in
the bad quarto named, and found also, substantially, in the
corresponding scene and act of Shakespeare's parallel play.

To the right of the column headed A are three columns which
bear in order the headings B, C and D respectively; these columns

give separate sets of totals for each scene and act of the bad quarto named. Details are as follow :—

(i) Under the heading B is given in the same row as A the number of verse-lines in the same scene or act of the bad quarto named, each line of which is verbally identical with the corresponding line of Shakespeare's parallel play.

(ii) Under the heading C is given in the same row as A and B the number of verse-lines in the same scene or act of the bad quarto named, each line of which is, except for a change in *one* word, verbally identical with the corresponding line of Shakespeare's parallel play.

(iii) Under the heading D, exactly as for C, except that there are changes in *two* words of a line.

(iv) The thirteenth column headed 'Totals' gives for a row the sum of the totals in the same row under the headings B, C and D; in other words, it gives for each scene and act of the bad quarto named the total number of lines, each of which differs by not more than two words from the corresponding line of Shakespeare's parallel text.

(v) In the column under the heading E is given for each act of the bad quarto the percentage which the total given for that act in the thirteenth column is of the total given for the same act in the ninth column. Otherwise, column E states for each act the percentage of lines common to the two versions which the first quarto retains with no more than two changes in a line. It follows, therefore, that the difference between the two totals for each scene or act of any bad quarto under columns numbered IX and XIII represents the total number of lines of this bad quarto, each of which differs from the corresponding line of Shakespeare's play by more than two words. Throughout these pairs of parallel plays Shakespeare's prose remains prose in the first quartos though it may be printed as verse, and his verse remains verse in spite of the vagaries of pirate and printer.

TABLE XII A

2 Henry VI and Contention

I	II	III	IV	V	VI	VII	VIII	IX	X	XI	XII	XIII	XIV
Fo.	Scene	No. of Lines	Cont. Scene	No. of Lines	Verse Lines not in Fo.	A	Cont. Prose	Cont. Verse in Fo.	B	C	D	Total	E

Act

I	i	254	i	166	26	140	13	127	52	21	12	85	
	ii	107	ii	80	29	51	—	51	7	5	3	15	
	iii	218	iii	169	31	138	40	98	17	7	15	39	
	iv	80	iv	54	26	28	5	23	7	2	—	9	
Totals		659		469	112	357	58	299	83	35	30	148	50%

II	i	200	v	170	18	152	—	152	41	12	7	60	
	ii	82	vi	65	14	51	—	51	6	8	6	20	
	iii	102	vii	78	11	67	33	34	10	1	3	14	
	iv	110	viii	81	12	69	—	69	15	9	9	33	
Totals		494		394	55	339	33	306	72	30	25	127	42%

III	i	383	ix	192	54	138	—	138	23	19	16	58	
	ii	412	x	221	14	207	—	207	72	49	22	143	
	iii	33	xi	21	7	14	—	14	1	—	2	3	
Totals		828		434	75	359	—	359	96	68	40	204	57%

IV	i	147	xii	78	11	67	—	67	10	11	6	27	
	ii	183	xiii	128	5	123	110	13	1	—	3	4	
	iii	17	xiv	6	—	6	6	—	—	—	—	—	
	iv	60	xv	26	6	20	—	20	5	1	2	8	
	v	12	xvi	13	—	13	6	7	6	1	—	7	
	vi	15	xvii	15	—	15	15	—	—	—	—	—	
	vii	124 }	xviii	121 { 86 / 35	26	95	88	7	1	3	—	4	
	viii	66 }											
	ix	49	xix	26	21	5	2	3	1	—	—	1	
	x	82	xx	36	6	30	16	14	1	3	1	5	
Totals		755		449	75	374	243	131	25	19	12	56	43%

V	i	216 {	xxi	89	37	52	—	52	1	5	2	8	
		{	xxii	41	3	38	—	38	14	8	4	26	
	ii	90 }	xxiii	97	63	34	—	34	16	4	3	23	
	iii	33 }											
Totals		339		227	103	124	—	124	31	17	9	57	46%
Play Totals		3,075		1,973	420	1,553	334	1,219	307	169	116	592	48·6%

TABLE XII B

3 *Henry VI* and *True Tragedy*

I	II	III	IV	V	VI	VII	X	XI	XII	XIII	XIV
Fo.	Fo. Scene	No. of Lines	T.T. Scene	No. of Lines	Lines of verse not in Fo.	A	B	C	D	Total	E

Act

I	i	273	i	230	10	220	124	53	17	194	
	ii	75	ii	55	18	37	5	6	5	16	
	iii	52 }	iii	214	10	204	117	48	15	180	
	iv	180 }									
Totals		580		499	38	461	246	107	37	390	84·6%
II	i	209	iv	172	13	159	86	31	8	125	
	ii	177	v	170	4	166	84	39	24	147	
	iii	56	vi	48	27	21	9	4	2	15	
	iv	13	vii	13	6	7	6	0	1	7	
	v	139 }	viii	165	20	145	51	32	25	108	
	vi	110 }									
Totals		704		568	70	498	236	106	60	402	80·8%
III	i	101	ix	41	2	39	11	6	4	21	
	ii	195	x	132	3	129	41	30	15	86	
	iii	265	xi	169	12	157	88	27	11	126	
Totals		561		342	17	325	140	63	30	233	71·6%
IV	i	149	xii	109	15	94	15	17	13	45	
	ii	29 }	xiii	55	8	47	25	9	6	40	
	iii	64 }									
	iv	35	xv	23	14	9	1	1	0	2	
	v	29	xiv	23	9	14	2	0	2	4	
	vi	102	xvii	22	4	18	4	1	0	5	
	vii	87	xvi	58	8	50	10	4	4	18	
	viii	64	xvii	25 }	2	28	10	9	4	23	
			xviii	5 }							
Totals		559		320	60	260	67	41	29	137	52·8%
V	i	113	xix	79	5	74	27	20	12	59	
	ii	50 }	xx	65	18	47	23	7	8	38	
	iii	24 }									
	iv	82 }	xxi	122	18	104	40	18	13	71	
	v	90 }									
	vi	93	xxii	83	2	81	39	18	7	64	
	vii	46	xxiii	46	0	46	36	9	0	45	
Totals		498		395	43	352	165	72	40	277	78·7%
Play Totals		2,902		2,124	228	1,896	854	389	196	1,439	75·9%

TABLE XII C

Romeo and Juliet Q2 and *Romeo and Juliet Q1*

I	II	III	IV	V	VI	VII	VIII	IX	X	XI	XII	XIII	XIV
Q2 Act	Q2 Scene	Q2 No. of Lines	Q1 Scene	Q1 No. of Lines	Verse Lines of Q1 not in Q2	A	Q1 Prose	Verse Lines of Q1 in Q2	B	C	D	Total	E
Prologue		14	Prol.	12	—	12	—	12	4	2	1	7	
I	i	236	i	141	—	141	42	99	59	21	9	89	
	ii	101	ii	94	—	94	—	94	69	8	6	83	
	iii	106	iii	65	—	65	—	65	45	3	2	50	
	iv	114	iv	94	2	92	—	92	46	15	12	73	
	v	142	v	121	1	120	—	120	54	37	6	97	
Totals		713		527	3	524	42	482	277	86	36	399	82·6%
Prologue		14		—	—	—	—	—	—	—	—	—	
II	i	42⎫	vi	208	—	208	—	208	108	53	17	178	
	ii	190⎬											
	iii	94	vii	88	—	88	—	88	60	17	6	83	
	iv	204	viii	163	1	162	154	8	1	2	1	4	
	v	77	ix	44	8	36	7	29	5	2	2	9	
	vi	37	x	30	29	1	—	1	—	—	1	1	
Totals		658		533	38	495	161	334	174	74	27	275	82·3%
III	i	193	xi	150	1	149	77	72	24	12	5	41	
	ii	143	xii	60	6	54	—	54	18	9	5	32	
	iii	175	xiii	143	2	141	—	141	82	33	4	119	
	iv	36	xiv	27	1	26	—	26	9	4	3	16	
	v	243	xv	193	2	191	—	191	65	27	17	109	
Totals		790		573	12	561	77	484	198	85	34	317	63·7%
IV	i	126	xvi	92	2	90	—	90	50	15	10	75	
	ii	47	xvii	44	12	32	—	32	6	6	4	16	
	iii	58	xviii	28	3	25	—	25	2	2	1	5	
	iv	28⎫	xix	107	29	78	26	52	6	5	1	12	
	v	141⎬											
Totals		400		271	46	225	26	199	64	28	16	108	54·2%
V	i	86	xx	63	4	59	—	59	13	6	9	28	
	ii	30	xxi	20	3	17	—	17	4	1	1	6	
	iii	309	xxii	228	51	177	—	177	44	17	13	74	
Totals		425		311	58	253	—	253	61	24	23	108	42·7%
Play Totals		2,986		2,215	157	2,058	306	1,752	774	297	136	1,207	68·8%

TABLE XII D

Henry V Fo and *Henry V Q1*

I	II	III	IV	V	VI	VII	VIII	IX	X	XI	XII	XIII	XIV
Fo. Act	Fo. Scene	No. of Lines	Q1 Scene	Q1 No. of Lines	Verse Lines of Q1 not in Fo.	A	Q1 Prose	Verse Lines of Q1 in Fo.	B	C	D	Total	E
Chorus		34	—										
I i		98	—	—	—	—	—	—	—	—	—	—	
ii		310	i	220	—	220	—	220	86	66	40	192	
Totals		**442**		220	—	220	—	220	86	66	40	192	87·3%
Chorus		42	—	—	—	—	—	—	—	—	—	—	
II i		123	ii	92	—	92	92	—	—	—	—	—	
ii		193	iii	112	—	112	—	112	60	30	10	100	
iii		60	iv	46	—	46	46	—	—	—	—	—	
iv		146	v	90	—	90	—	90	34	24	6	64	
Totals		**564**		340	—	340	138	202	94	54	16	164	81·2%
Chorus		35	—	—	—	—	—	—	—	—	—	—	
III i		34	—	—	—	—	—	—	—	—	—	—	
ii		129	vi	31	—	31	31	—	—	—	—	—	
iii		58	vii	18	—	18	—	18	11	5	2	18	
iv		56	viii	31	—	31	31	—	—	—	—	—	
v		68	ix	23	—	23	—	23	4	4	5	13	
vi		164	x	148	—	148	116	32	17	6	4	27	
vii		146	xi	62	—	62	62	—	—	—	—	—	
Totals		**690**		313	—	313	240	73	32	15	11	58	80%
Chorus		53	—	—	—	—	—	—	—	—	—	—	
IV i		293 {	xii	114	—	114 }	114	20	6	4	4	14	
			xiii	20	—	20 }							
ii		63	—	—	—	—	—	—	—	—	—	—	
iii		132	xiv	99	—	99	—	99	32	19	14	65	
iv		75	xvi	31	—	31	31	—	—	—	—	—	
v		23	xv	18	—	18	—	18	3	4	2	9	
vi		38	xvii	35	—	35	—	35	11	10	4	25	
vii		172	xviii	138	—	138	105	33	11	5	5	21	
viii		120	xix	93	—	93	57	36	16	7	4	27	
Totals		**969**		548	—	548	307	241	79	49	33	161	66·6%
Chorus		45	—	—	—	—	—	—	—	—	—	—	
V i		82	xx	60	—	60	60	—	—	—	—	—	
ii		360	xxi	142	—	142	101	41	4	3	3	10	
Epilogue		14											
Totals		**501**		202	—	202	161	41	4	3	3	10	20%
Play Totals		**3,166**		1,623	—	1,623	846	777	295	187	103	585	75·3%

TABLE XII E

Merry Wives Fo. and *Merry Wives Q1*

Fo. Act	Scene	*Fo.* No. of Lines	*Q1* Scene	*Q1* No. of Lines
I	i	286	i	103
	ii	11	ii	9
	iii	97	iii	85
	iv	149	iv	64
Totals		543		261
II	i	215	v	137
	ii	280	vi	165
	iii	89	vii	54
Totals		584		356
III	i	115	viii	73
	ii	79	ix	36
	iii	217	x	106
	iv	108	xi	101
	v	134	xii	61
Totals		653		377
IV	i	78	—	—
	ii	200	xiii	76
	iii	11	xiv	10
	iv	89	xv	51
	v	118	xvi	87
	vi	55	xvii	34
Totals		551		258
V	i	28	—	—
	ii	14	—	—
	iii	24	—	—
	iv	4	—	—
	v	233	xviii	167
Totals		303		167
Play Totals		2,634		1,419

TABLE XII F

Hamlet Q2 + Fo. and *Hamlet Q1*

I	II	III	IV	V	VI	VII	VIII	IX	X	XI	XII	XIII	XIV
Q2 Act	Q2 Scene	Q2+Fo. No. of Lines	Q1 Scene	Q1 No. of Lines	Verse not in Q2 or Fo.	A	Q1 Prose	Verse Lines of Q2 or Fo. in Q1	B	C	D	Total	E
I	i	175	i	140	—	140	—	140	71	35	14	120	
	ii	257	ii	188	12	176	—	176	59	44	9	112	
	iii	136	iii	71	16	55	—	55	17	7	4	28	
	iv	91 }	iv	234	1	233	—	233	101	44	20	165	
	v	191 }											
Totals		850		633	29	604	—	604	248	130	47	425	70·4%
II	i	120	v	66	24	42	—	42	17	7	4	28	
	ii	581	vi (to l.110)	110	29	81	—	81	25	18	13	56	
			vii	237	12	225	167	58	14	10	6	30	
Totals		701		413	65	348	167	181	56	35	23	114	63%
III	i	188	viii	40	37	3	—	3	—	—	—	—	
			vi (ll.111-204)	94	12	82	58	24	1	5	2	8	
	ii	382 (to l.210 and ll.224-39)	ix	226	21	205	143	62	22	8	3	33	
	iii	98	x	31	16	15	—	15	3	2	—	5	
	iv	217	xi (to l.110)	110	48	62	—	62	7	7	4	18	
Totals		885		501	134	367	201	166	33	22	9	64	38·6%
IV	i	45	xi (ll.111-131)	21	14	7	—	7	1	—	—	1	
	ii	30	ix (ll.211-223)	13	—	13	13	—	—	—	—	—	
	iii	67	xi (ll.132-174)	43	11	32	32	—	—	—	—	—	
	iv	66	xii	6	—	6	—	6	—	—	—	—	
	v	214	xiii	127	35	92	22	70	27	12	1	40	
	vi	31	xiv	36	36	—	—	—	—	—	—	—	
	vii	196	xv	55	34	21	—	21	—	2	—	2	
Totals		649		301	130	171	67	104	28	14	1	43	41·7%
V	i	287	xvi	165	11	154	114	40	8	6	4	18	
			xvii	11	11	—	—	—	—	—	—	—	
	ii	390	xviii	130	27	103	39	64	1	10	6	17	
Totals		677		306	49	257	153	104	9	16	10	35	33%
Play Totals		3,762		2,154	407	1,747	586	1,161	374	217	90	681	58·7%

TABLE XIII

Summary of Previous Tables for Parallel Texts

I	II	III	IV	V	VI	VII	VIII	IX	X	XI	XII
Play	In Play	Verse	Prose	Play	In Play	Verse	Verse of Shake-speare	Inter-polated Verse	Total Prose Prose Non-S.		Total
2 H.VI	3,075	2,602	473	Cont.	1,973	1,639	1,219	420	334	21	1,532
3 H.VI	2,902	2,902	—	T.T.	2,124	2,124	1,896	228	—	—	1,896
R.J.Q2	2,986	2,585	401	R.J.Q1	2,215	1,909	1,752	157	306	7	2,051
Ham.Q2	3,762	2,715	1,047	Ham.Q1	2,154	1,568	1,161	407	586	12	1,735
Totals	12,725	10,804	1,921		8,466	7,240	6,028	1,212	1,226	40	7,214
H5 (fo.)	3,166	1,931	1,235	H.5Q1	1,623	777	777	—	846	—	1,623

Numbers give totals of lines of verse and prose.

The totals in column XII give the number of Shakespearean lines in the bad quarto named.

Modern editors are responsible for the division of the six plays of Shakespeare, except *Merry Wives,* into acts, and the subdivision of each act into scenes. *Merry Wives* has each act and scene of the folio text clearly marked. *Henry V* is, in the folio text, divided into five acts, of which only the last corresponds to the fifth act of modern editions; only one scene is marked, the first of the first act. Each of the two plays on Henry VI begins with 'Actus Primus, Scaena Prima,' and has no other act or scene marked. *Romeo and Juliet Q2* and *Hamlet Q2,* like most of our early play-texts, have no stage directions for either acts or scenes.

Whether all plays written during the reign of Elizabeth for the popular stage had act-intervals is still unsettled; poets may have used the term 'Act' for a portion of a play usually extending to several scenes, but in the unroofed theatres the actors certainly could not have allotted an appreciable amount of time to mark the end of one act and the beginning of the next. For most purposes the scene seems to have been the unit of dramatic action, and modern editors usually regard the retirement of all the characters from the stage as fixing the end of a scene. From the tables it may be perceived that each bad quarto has a smaller number of scenes than Shakespeare's corresponding play; the deficiency ranges from one scene in *Contention* to five scenes in *True Tragedy* and *Merry Wives Q1.*

Up to the end of act four, scene six of *2 Henry VI,* each of Shakespeare's scenes has one closely correspondent to it in *Contention*; the pirate's eighteenth scene is an amalgam of the last two scenes of the fourth act.. On the other hand, he split up without much reason the first scene of the fifth act of *2 Henry VI* into two *Contention* scenes, and balanced this increase by combining the last two scenes of *2 Henry VI,* referring to the first battle of St. Albans, to form the twenty-third scene of *Contention.*

True Tragedy has twenty-three scenes only in place of the twenty-eight present in *3 Henry VI,* but no scene of the latter is unrepresented in the surreptitious text. Battle scenes, of which there are six in *3 Henry VI* and *True Tragedy,* seem to have offered difficulties to editors in prescribing limits to consecutive scenes. Convention assumed that the main battle went on 'within'; at intervals a single combat, a capture or a rescue in which some important character figured, would be exhibited on the stage. After the tumult and the shouting were over, the victors would appear with their forces. In each of the battles of Wakefield, Towton, Barnet and Tewkesbury, editors divide into two scenes a part of the play which the pirate told in one; in addition, the two scenes in which is told the story of Edward's capture by Warwick and Clarence become one scene, the thirteenth, in *True Tragedy.* The sixth and eighth scenes of the fourth act of *3 Henry VI* recount the temporary restoration of Henry to his throne; they have been reduced to one in *True Tragedy,* much to the injury of the plot; on the other hand, a snippet of the concluding scene of the fourth act, describing the seizure of Henry by Edward, is counted as a separate scene in *True Tragedy.*

Romeo and Juliet Q1 lacks the chorus prefixed to the second act of Q2, but treats, as does Q2, the first and second scenes of this act as a continuous scene. Romeo has hidden himself from Benvolio and Mercutio, but is in sight of the audience whilst his friends are cracking jokes. His line,

> He ieasts at scarres that neuer felt a wound,

carries one scene into the next. Only one other change occurs; in Q1 the fourth and fifth scenes of the fourth act are treated as one.

Henry V Q1 omits all the choruses, the first scenes of the first and third acts, and all but the last line and a half of the second scene of the fourth act; in addition, the order of the fourth and fifth scenes of this latter act is reversed.

Merry Wives Q1 omits five scenes, one at the beginning of the fourth act, and the four short scenes at the beginning of the fifth act.

Hamlet Q1 exhibits almost every type of change. Two scenes of Q2, the fourth and fifth of the first act, form the fourth scene of Q1. Eight scenes of Q2, which include all the play from the beginning of the second scene of the second act to the end of the third scene of the fourth act, are huddled into six scenes, viz., the sixth to the eleventh, of Q1, with considerable change in the order of the various episodes common to the two versions. The sixth scene of Q1 is made up from the second scene (part only) of the second act and a part taken from the first scene of the third act. Scene nine of Q1 represents part of the second scene of the third act and the whole of the first scene of the fourth act; whilst the eleventh scene of Q1 comprises the whole of the fourth scene of the third act and both the first and third scenes of the fourth act of Q2. In addition *Hamlet Q1* has an interpolated scene—the fourteenth— which replaces a Shakespearean scene of slightly less length.

If the reader will consult the table, together with the summary, he will see that each bad quarto, except *Henry V Q1,* has a considerable amount of non-Shakespearean matter; this varies from a little over 7 per cent. of the total length of *Romeo and Juliet Q1* to over 22 per cent. of the total length of *Contention.* Nearly all the interpolations are in verse, and all told they equal a seventh of the total length of the four corrupt plays. Numerical losses of Shakespeare's text, i.e., of verse and prose in the four authentic texts but not in the four bad quartos, amount to the enormous total of 5,511 lines or more than 43 per cent. of his received text. Separate totals range from a minimum of 935 lines or about 31 per cent. of *Romeo and Juliet Q2* to a maximum of 2,027 lines or 54 per cent. of the received text of *Hamlet.* About one half of the text of *2 Henry VI* is not in *Contention,* and the transformation of *3 Henry VI* into *True Tragedy* was done with the loss of over a thousand lines of the original. These losses of the authentic text are not spread evenly throughout the play but grow greater from act to act. On collecting the respective totals for each act of both the authentic text and the bad quarto, I find that the percentage of the authentic text retained in the corresponding act of Q1 falls from an average of 69 per cent. for the group of first acts to an average of less than 44 per cent. for the group of fourth acts. Losses of Shakespeare's text increase, therefore, from an average loss of 31 per cent. for the four first acts to an average loss of 56 per cent. for the combined fourth acts of the grouped bad quartos. The group of fifth acts average about 51 per cent. of the total lines in the corresponding acts of the authentic plays. *True Tragedy* keeps about 80 per cent. of the text in the first act of *3 Henry VI*; this is the highest percentage in any bad quarto. On the other hand, the fourth act of *Hamlet Q1* has only 28 per cent. of the fourth act of Q2.

So far the results have been based not merely on first quarto lines substantially the same as the corresponding lines of Shakespeare's plays, but also on all other lines which have something in them sufficiently in common with lines of the authentic plays to justify their inclusion in the ninth column of the above tables. Reference to the column headed B in the tables for pairs of parallel texts shows that *Contention* has 307 lines of 2,602 verse-lines of *2 Henry VI* identical with those of the fuller version; in other words *Contention* retains verbatim 12 per cent. only of the verse of *2 Henry VI*. Further, the least corrupt of the bad quartos, viz., *Romeo and Juliet Q1,* preserves without alteration only 30 per cent. of the verse in Q2. Taken as a whole, the four bad quartos retain little more than a fifth of the verse in the four corresponding plays, exactly as Shakespeare wrote them. Even if the standard is lowered, and we accept as substantially identical verses of a bad quarto which differ from the corresponding verses of the authentic text by no more than two words in a line, we discover that *True Tragedy* has barely half its lines of this reduced standard, whilst one line only of four verse-lines in *Hamlet Q1* reaches this lower standard of verbal accuracy.

Study of the tables enables me to test the validity of Professor Wilson's theory of double revision. Acts III-V of *Romeo and Juliet Q1,* which, on his hypothesis, should be part of an old play rewritten 'here and there' and 'eked out by what a pirate could remember of the later version,' contain 1,155 lines. Prose amounts to 103 lines; of these it is enough to say that except for seven lines spoken by Mercutio the others are Shakespeare's, or, if they belong to the old play, were left untouched when he gave the play his second revision. On deducting this prose 1,052 lines of verse remain; of these 116 are not Shakespeare's and should be part of the source-play. Strangely enough, five of these non-Shakespearean lines are adapted or echoed from early plays of Shakespeare, an inveterate habit of the pirates responsible for the printing of the surreptitious quartos These 116 lines not in Q2 represent almost exactly a ninth of the total verse in this portion of Q1; their distribution, especially in nine of the twelve scenes, suggests that they found their way into the text very much as casual weeds whose seeds have been blown by the winds of chance into an ill-kept garden and have taken root among the flowers. Four-fifths of these alien verses are clustered in three scenes; even there Shakespeare's lines outnumber them three to one. Thus, outside of prose, the verse of Acts III-V is eight-ninths Shakespeare's, and one-ninth from the pen of someone else; verses of Q1 substantially identical with those of Q2 are nearly five times as numerous as non-Shakespearean lines. Does Professor Wilson wish us to believe that some rewriting 'here and there' together with the pirate's gleanings from the later version could effect such an extraordinary metamorphosis? Some trifle more of such rewriting in five scenes, and a shade more 'eking' of the pirate's recollections would have rid the play of almost all its foreign matter and deprived Professor Wilson of his 'evidence of revision.'

Hamlet Q1 shares with *Contention* the demerit of being the most corrupt of the five bad quartos written mainly in verse. Professor Wilson thinks that Shakespeare's first revision of his source-play did not extend 'much beyond the Ghost-scenes,' i.e., ended with the first act. Acts II-V must be, therefore, mainly un-Shakespearean with the exception of what a many-parted reporter could remember of the scenes in which he had acted a succession of small parts; actually these four acts contain 586 lines of prose, most of them Shakespeare's or with a pronounced Shakespearean flavour, and 935 lines of verse of which 378 are not the poet's. Thus Shakespeare's hand or finger is present in at least two-thirds of this portion of Q1, which the theory of double revision asserts is the untouched work of the old playwright save for some scattered recollections of the reporter. This result remains true although 1,800 lines of the received text have disappeared from Acts II-V without leaving any traces in Q1; in consequence of this enormous loss the first act of Q1 contains 47 lines more of Shakespearean verse than the rest of the play. Professor Wilson accepts the proseless first act of Q1 as Shakespeare's; it keeps 70 per cent. of the verse common to the two texts substantially identical. The second act of Q1 has a considerable amount of prose and double the amount of alien verse present in the first act, yet it retains 63 per cent. of the verse common to the two versions substantially identical; this act, he declares, is part of the old play of which the first act only was revised by Shakespeare. I cannot logically reconcile these two opinions. In my opinion, the groundwork of *Hamlet Q1* is a drastically abridged text of Q2, with many flaws, some gaps and an overlay, thin here, thicker there, of interpolations.

Chapter VIII

THE PLOTS OF THE BAD QUARTOS

ALL critics must allow that the plot of each bad quarto is, except for minor variations of small importance, identical with that of the corresponding play of Shakespeare. *2 Henry VI, 3 Henry VI* and *Henry V* are based on raw material chosen mainly from the second and enlarged edition of Holinshed's *Chronicle.* This author copied very largely from Halle for this portion of his subject-matter and added a little from other writers. All the characters of *2 Henry VI* and *3 Henry VI* except Simpcox, some of Cade's rabble and three watchmen, figure in Halle and Holinshed. Both these plays bristle with anachronisms and historically impossible events, but Shakespeare prefers a coherent and picturesque drama to historic truth. He was making plays concerning men and their actions of nearly a century and a half ago for the pleasure of an uncritical audience, which learnt all they knew of English and Roman history as they stood in the pit.

Anachronisms cluster in the first scene of *2 Henry VI.* The play opens with the coronation of Queen Margaret in 1445. As a reward for making the match, Henry creates Suffolk a duke, a belated marriage-present not received by Suffolk till 1448. Warwick, not then an Earl, was only seventeen years of age, and, though he might have wept for the loss of Anjou and Maine, could not boast of Maine 'which by maine force Warwicke did winne.' York did not go to Ireland as regent till 1448, and therefore Salisbury could not in 1445 truthfully praise York's

> Acts in Ireland
> In bringing them to ciuill Discipline.

Eleanor Cobham, Duke Humphrey's wife, had been banished to the Isle of Man nearly four years before the royal marriage; thus all her plots, quarrels, ambitions and vanities were forgotten before the action of this play begins. She did dabble, and suffered for dabbling, in mediæval sorcery, but she did not receive a box on the ear from Queen Margaret whom most probably she never saw. Nor was the middle-aged Suffolk the girlish queen's lover; their strongest bond was their common hatred of Duke Humphrey, who remained in power for five years after his wife's disgrace, and lost his protectorship and his life as a result of some obscure court intrigue. York did not leave for Ireland till two years after Gloucester's death, and Beaufort died three years before Suffolk was banished. Many of the incidents of the Peasant Revolt in 1381 were incorporated in the account of Cade's rebellion in 1450, yet the poet's picture of mob rule will fit any year. In the last five scenes of the play the events of the six years 1450-55 are in 'most admired disorder'; we may say of this portion of 2 Henry VI what Cade says of his rabble, 'Then are we in order when we are most out of order.' The dramatist represents Cade as alive when York returns from Ireland; he had then been dead a year. Buckingham went as envoy to meet York with the news that Somerset was imprisoned in the Tower; the latter reached the Tower four years after. When York offers his sons Edward and Richard as their 'Fathers baile,' Richard was unborn. Civil war broke out three years afterwards, and three-year-old Richard did not kill Somerset 'vnderneath an Ale-house paltry signe,' nor did his father York kill the elder Clifford.

3 Henry VI continues the blunders, anachronisms and perversions of 2 Henry VI exactly as the third volume of a three-volume novel takes up the fiction where the second volume ends. Warwick and other Yorkist leaders celebrate their victory, and the valiant three-year-old prodigy triumphantly shakes the gory head of Somerset in the presence of peers and princes. Between the twentieth and twenty-first lines of the play five years pass silently, and the succession to the throne is settled in such a way that the continuance of the brutal civil war becomes inevitable. Richard has grown apace, and at eight is logician and casuist, able to persuade his father to break his oath,

> neyther by Treason nor Hostilitie,
> To seeke to put me downe, and reign thy selfe.

Rutland was not an 'innocent child,' but over seventeen years of age, old enough to lead armies. He fought at Wakefield and was killed by Clifford after surrendering; the chronicles relate that his father York was killed in the same battle, and not, as in the play, stabbed by Clifford and Margaret. Neither Richard nor Clarence

G

fought at Towton. Henry's capture followed instead of preceding the courtship and marriage of Lady Grey to King Edward. In the third scene of the third act many events of eight years are huddled indiscriminately. Margaret sought aid from King Louis of France as early as 1462, Warwick's embassy to arrange a marriage between King Edward and Bona, sister-in-law of Louis, occurred in 1464, and the marriage between Prince Edward and Warwick's second daughter was celebrated during Warwick's second visit to France in 1470, a year after Clarence had married the elder sister. Historical events of 1469, 1470 and 1471 are mixed in a bewildering muddle from early in the fourth act; the sixth scene provides an excellent example. Henry had been restored to his title and throne and had surrendered his regal powers to Warwick and his son-in-law Clarence, naming them joint protectors; a post enters and announces:

> That Edward is escaped from your Brother,
> And fled (as hee heares since) to Burgundie.

Time speeds apace from line to line in this scene; the first line alludes to events of October 1469, the second to those of September 1470. During the interval between these two seemingly successive happenings, Edward had been reconciled to Warwick and Clarence, who afterwards fomented a rebellion against him. On this being suppressed they fled to France where they arranged the marriage spoken of above, invaded England and took Edward by surprise; he (as said above) fled to Burgundy. According to the order of events in *3 Henry VI,* Queen Elizabeth decides to take sanctuary to preserve the life of her unborn child—born nearly twelve months later! Edward's return from Burgundy brings the story back to 1471, and thenceforward the play keeps to the sequence of events found in the chronicle.

True Tragedy retains every event and, excepting five, every character of *3 Henry VI.* From the fourth to the eighth scene of act four, the order of events in *True Tragedy* has been re-arranged, and two scenes, the sixth and the eighth have been squeezed into one; this compression results in much confusion, and dramatic illusion almost disappears or is carried beyond the limits of credibility. Shakespeare may represent as almost simultaneous events separated by years in the chronicles but his story is simple straightforward and coherent. In the third scene of the fourth act of *3 Henry VI* Edward is captured and left a prisoner in charge of George Nevil, Archbishop of York, and in the next scene his queen takes sanctuary. Then follows Edward's escape and he gallops to the nearest seaport. Meanwhile Warwick and Clarence have reached London, liberated and crowned Henry, and have become protectors. Their satisfaction is short-lived for news arrives that Edward has escaped and is off to Burgundy. Warwick leaves London to provide for the safety of the realm. In the next scene Edward returns to England; in the eighth Warwick and the Lancastrians prepare for war, and the act ends with the recapture of Henry.

Transposition of the fourth and fifth scenes of *True Tragedy* and combination of the sixth and eighth have turned logical order into confusion. Warwick ends the third scene with a line not in the folio text,

Ile post to Yorke, and see how Edward fares.

As soon as his captors have turned their horses' heads towards London, Edward escapes from captivity, and, a stage minute after his escape, his queen laments his imprisonment and takes sanctuary. Immediately she has left the stage, her husband enters 'with a troope of Hollanders' and informs the amazed audience,

Thus far from Belgia haue we past the seas.

He then begins his march on London which Warwick and Clarence have just reached in time to release and crown Henry. Apparently no one has heard of Edward's escape, flight to Burgundy, return to England and capture of York city. Suddenly there enters 'one with a letter to Warwike.' Thereafter except for unimportant details, the account given in *True Tragedy* corresponds closely to what is related in *3 Henry VI*.

Romeo and Juliet Q1 contains practically everything present in the second quarto. Action is better than words even on the stage, so the pirates described in a stage direction the brawl between the rival houses which the audience saw; some brisk dialogue between the servants prior to the entry of the maskers is omitted.

My table shows that *Hamlet Q1* retains not half of what Shakespeare wrote in Q2. Most of this loss is due to official abridgment, but almost two-thirds of what the play-abridger left in the acting version is very much the worse for the actors' wear and tear. Q1 contains more than four hundred lines of non-Shakespearean matter; most of these express in halting verse what the reporter took to be the sense of vaguely remembered passages, half understood. One might suppose that this butchery meant the disappearance of episodes or scenes as it has done in modern stage abridgments of this play, yet more than skeleton outlines remained of even the most poorly preserved portions. I have referred elsewhere to changes in Q1 of the order in which certain scenes and portions of scenes occur in Q2.

Two changes require some detailed criticism. Scene fourteen of Q1 replaces the sixth scene of the fourth act of Q2, and lines 1-74 of the final scene of Q2 are not represented in Q1. This omitted scene of Q2 narrates the interview between Horatio and some sailors who have brought him a letter from Hamlet addressed to the king. Horatio thus learns of Hamlet's return to Denmark, and shrewdly devises means of forwarding the prince's letter to the king without bringing the sailors or himself into danger; in this way the presence of the prince remains unknown to the court till he can appear in public with safety. Q1 also omits the long passage (5.1. 1-74) giving a vivid account of Hamlet's discovery of the fate awaiting him in England; from it the audience learns how he turned the tables on his treacherous schoolfellows, and realizes the determined resolve of the king to destroy his step-son. Scene fourteen of Q1 describes an interview between Horatio and the queen; we do not learn how Hamlet made his way back to Denmark, but otherwise this scene gives briefly the same facts as in the portions of Q2 omitted. Something is missing before and after the fifth line of Horatio's first speech,

> Being crossed by the contention of the windes;

it is not connected with the context, and seems an echo of Cassio's words to Desdemona,

> The great Contention of Sea, and Skies
> Parted our fellowship.

Abridgment and corruption mar Horatio's last speech in answer to the queen's question,

> But what became of Gilderstone and Rossencraft?

He replies,

> He being set ashore, they went for England,
> And in the Packet there writ down that doome
> To be perform'd on them poynted for him:
> And by great chance he had his fathers Seale,
> So all was done without discouerie.

What these five lines mean can be discovered only from Q2 (5.1.1-74) of which it seems a muddled remembrance.

Some critics have stressed the fact that in Q1 the queen turns against her husband. Certainly she says,

> Then I perceiue there's treason in his lookes
> That seem'd to sugar o're his villanie;

but she qualifies this outburst in her next line,

> But I will soothe and please him for a time.

Even in Q2 she promises to be neutral, 'not to breathe what you haue said to me.'

Much has been written on the alteration of the names 'Polonius' and 'Reynaldo' to 'Corambis' and 'Montano' respectively, or, is it vice versa? Metrically these pairs of names are interchangeable, though not one line of verse in Q2 which contains either of the first pair of names has been retained in Q1. Except for the name Corambus in *Bestrafte Bruder-mord* no reason can be given for the assumption that Corambis and Montano were names of characters in the *Ur-Hamlet*. Censorship, as Sir E. K. Chambers suggests, may be behind these changes. English history from 1599 to 1602 was a period of domestic unrest and trouble abroad. From the date of Essex's unauthorized return from Ireland in the autumn of 1599 to the end of 1601, the vigilance of the censor would not sleep a moment; the play-licensers would not forget how Harsnett, one of their number, had suffered, for not anticipating that John Hayward's dedication to Essex of his book on the first year of Henry the Fourth's reign would become an act of constructive treason when Essex fell out of Elizabeth's favour. Poland was then a large and important country; her ambassadors and the envoys from the independent Hanse towns had strongly protested against the rights of search claimed and exercised by the captains of the queen's ships and their actions in confiscating contraband goods, especially 'munityon and Victual' intended for Spain, with which country England had been at war for many years. Such a name as Polonius associated in a popular play with a meddlesome, pragmatic and foolish wiseacre might be regarded by the all-powerful Privy Council as likely to be offensive to a nation with which there were already more than enough commercial and political disputes. When the second quarto was printed the Spanish war was over and official vigilance was relaxed.

The plots of *Henry V Q1* and *Merry Wives Q1* differ from those of the respective folio plays much less than the great reduction of length would suggest. Shakespeare keeps closely to Holinshed for the main story of his play. Omission of the five choruses and the epilogue deprives Q1 of some fine description and poetry; these attempts to fill gaps in action due to lapse of time were not successful, and their disappearance from Q1 does not create any breach of continuity. Three folio scenes were omitted in Q1. As neither archbishop nor bishop appears after the end of the first act, the first scene of the play is not necessary to the main story. Burbage would enjoy declaiming that fine piece of royal rhetoric, Henry's speech to his soldiers before Harfleur, but Elizabethan companies had no need to pander to the vanity of their star-actors. At least a quarter of *Henry V* must be omitted to reduce it to a play lasting two hours, and the Harfleur speech may be omitted without injury to the plot. The disappearance of the second French camp scene is of more importance, because the staging of Q1 becomes difficult. Darkness changes to daylight in the interval between two long scenes in both of which the king plays the principal part; he has half a minute—the time necessary for speaking ten lines of text—to remove his disguise and to put on his armour for the battle. The order of the fourth and fifth scenes of the fourth act in the folio has been changed in Q1, but whether Pistol brags and blusters before or after the appearance of the panic-stricken French noblemen is of no importance. Eleven speaking actors drop out of a very large cast, and some speeches are transferred from one character to another as in other bad quartos and even in some folio texts. All the comic scenes are represented in Q1, though there is no trace of the episode in which Captain Gower and three captains belonging to the minor British tribes boast, strut and quarrel. Those scenes in which Fluellen figures are closer to the folio text than those in which Pistol is the principal 'irregular humorist.' *Henry V Q1* is the only bad quarto in which passages from other plays do not occur.

Merry Wives Q1 is the shortest and most corrupt of the six bad quartos. Q1 omits the scene in which William Page on 'a playing-day' suffers an oral examination in Latin, conducted by a Welsh parson to an obligato of obscenity provided by Mistress Quickly; omitted also are the four short scenes that precede the last scene of the play, but the text of Q1 supplies evidence that portions at least of these scenes were spoken on the stage. Two characters, William Page and Robin, do not speak in Q1. The order of certain passages is varied, and the hours at which Falstaff visits Mistress Ford differ in the two texts; gags, non-Shakespearean verse and lines interpolated from other plays are present, but the plots of the two versions are practically identical.

Q1 was derived from some transcript of the poet's manuscript at a time when the disguised Ford assumed the name of Brooke not Broome as in the folio text. I do not think this change was made to avoid offending the Brooke family of which Lord Cobham was the head. Sufficient and better reasons for this change may be found in the ruin of the Brookes in 1603 for their share in the mysterious conspiracy to put Arabella Stuart on the throne. George Brooke was executed, and his brother Henry Brooke, Lord Cobham, was condemned, attainted, and reprieved only when his head was on the block; all their goods and lands were confiscated and bestowed on court favourites. Cobham was Raleigh's only accuser, retracted his evidence, and, as Hume says, 'retracted his retraction.' *Merry Wives* was, according to the Revels Accounts, now accepted as genuine, acted before King James on 4 November 1604, or less than a year after the downfall of the Brookes; without doubt the managers of the company would change 'Brooke' to 'Broome' in order not to revive unpleasant memories. Shakespeare's carelessness over trifles cannot be better exemplified than in his retention of Falstaff's quip, when he was informed that Master Brooke had sent him 'a mornings draught of Sacke,' 'Call him in,' says the Knight, 'such Brookes are welcome to mee,

that ore' flowes such liquor'—a pointless saying when Brooke was
altered to Broome, but it still remained in the text. How much
learned ingenuity would have been spent on this folio passage, were
the quarto not available to explain what the original text was!

Some commentators maintain that Falstaff was called Oldcastle
in an early form of the play. Enough evidence exists to prove
that Oldcastle was the original name of Falstaff in *1 Henry IV*
and perhaps in *2 Henry IV*. Dr. Greg in a note upon the host's
words (Q1, xv.4), 'Sir John, theres his Castle' says: 'I suggest
though nobody seems to have noticed it before, that here is an
allusion to the original name of the character we know as Falstaff.'
This suggestion Robertson develops in characteristically reckless
fashion. He asserts that the substitution of 'Oldcastle' for 'Falstaff'
in several quarto verse-lines would make them metrical. I have
examined all the lines of quarto verse or doggerel in which the
name 'Falstaff' is used; they are all metrical except one and the
substitution favoured by Robertson would make them all unmetrical. Dr. Greg's suggestion merits consideration.

Here follows the passage (4.5.3-8) in the folio:—

> *Simp.* Marry Sir, I come to speake with Sir Iohn Falstaffe
> from M. Slender.
> *Host.* There's his Chamber, his House, his Castle, his stand-
> ing-bed and truckle-bed; 'tis painted about with the
> story of the Prodigall, fresh and new:

Dr. Greg has proved that the folio text precedes in composition
that of the quarto. No one, certainly not Dr. Greg, will maintain
that the word 'Castle' in the folio text conceals a guarded reference
to 'Oldcastle'; such an allusion would be so smothered in the
context that it could reach neither ear nor eye. It is not difficult
to make good sense of the host's seemingly inconsequential
garrulity if a scrap of law knowledge is assumed. A guest's
'chamber' is legally his 'house' as long as the landlord is content
to accept payment from his guest, and the legal maxim that a
man's 'house' is his 'castle' was even then a century-old proverb.
So far an Elizabethan audience would follow the speaker with
understanding. Then, with cheery irrelevance, he adds 'his stand-
ing-bed, his truckle-bed,' and next, with a sly hit at his guest,
describes to the badgered Simple the chamber's decorations. Dr.

Greg declares that the pirate-actor played the part of the host; if so, he becomes in Q1 as confused as his butt, Simple:

Sim. Sir, I am sent from my M. to sir Iohn Falstaffe.
Host. Sir Iohn, theres his Castle, his standing bed, his trundle bed, his chamber is painted about with the story of the prodigall, fresh and new.

If the quarto version is a report of what we find in the folio text, the reference to Oldcastle in Q1 must come from the reporter not from Shakespeare. By itself the phrase 'Theres his Castle' lends some colour to Dr. Greg's suggestion; but taken with its context it seems a muddled recollection of what the host could remember, the word 'chamber' being transferred to keep company with the description of it.

Stevens and some modern commentators assert that the term 'bully-rook' used by the host, conceals an oblique allusion to Oldcastle. This opinion does not seem tenable. First, the host addresses Ford, Page, Shallow as well as Falstaff as 'bully-rook.' Secondly the use of 'castle' as a synonym of 'rook' in the game of chess is not found in our language till at least half a century later. Beale, translator of Biochimo's treatise on chess, speaks in 1656 of the 'Rooke, Rock, or Duke, who is sometimes fashioned with a round head, sometimes like a Castle,' and nowhere in his dedication or poem or description of the pieces or Gambits, used 'Castle' as a synonym for 'Rook.' Hoyle (1760) uses the term 'rook' only.

Throughout any discussion of the relationship existing between any pair of these parallel texts certain fundamental facts must be always kept in mind. In each of the two plays the same selected incidents are dramatized in the same order, and the same characters describe the same actions in identical or similar language. That two dramatists should independently select the same incidents from the lengthy chronicles of Halle or Holinshed would be an extraordinary but not incredible coincidence; that each should pervert a number of facts and make a number of blunders in relating what appeared in the chronicles would be most remarkable. That each should pervert the same facts and commit the same blunders in their respective narrations of the same set of facts would be incredible. But that both dramatists should so write their plays, that each of the characters common to the two plays performed the same acts in precisely corresponding parts of each play, had identical motives for doing these acts and should describe acts, motives and emotions in language largely identical, is preposterous, incredible and impossible. We are forced to conclude that one man selected the incidents and characters from the chronicles, perverted facts wherever he thought perversion more dramatic than truth, committed the blunders consciously or carelessly, planned the common plot, divided each play into scenes, and wrote verse or prose as he thought best fitted for his themes and characters.

Many writers on this subject have completely forgotten this essential identity of such parallel texts as the first and the second quartos of *Romeo and Juliet* or of *3 Henry VI* and *True Tragedy*; they have rated what are really unimportant differences of plot, fact or text so highly that some have suggested different authors for each play. Anyone can test such a suggestion very easily by making a simple experiment. If an acting version of *Romeo and Juliet Q2* or of *3 Henry VI* is prepared by striking out of the authentic text all lines not in the corresponding bad quarto, and including such lines of Shakespeare as are replaced in the bad quarto by non-Shakespearean lines, the reader would have an abridgment of Shakespeare's play about 2,200 lines in length. If he will then read in conjunction, scene by scene, this abridgment and the bad quarto, he will be convinced that the bad quarto is a garbled and corrupt abridgment of some such acting version made by the company's play-adapter from the poet's manuscript. If he will subsequently read by themselves the lines excised from the authentic text, he will discover that they contain very little, if anything, necessary to the plot or dramatic development.

CHAPTER IX

STYLE OF THE BAD QUARTOS

ONE difference that forces itself upon the attention of any reader of a bad quarto such as *True Tragedy* or *Romeo and Juliet Q1* is the extraordinary variation in style, diction, verse and thought, not merely in successive scenes but in portions of one and the same scene. For a few minutes he is reading with some pleasure what seems a slightly imperfect version of Shakespeare's work, when suddenly he comes upon a long passage written in jog-trot, halting metre, debased in language, amorphous in style, and vulgarized in tone and thought. In general, the earlier scenes are best; this is true of *Romeo and Juliet Q1, True Tragedy, Hamlet Q1* and even *Henry V Q1,* whilst *Contention* and *Merry Wives Q1* are more uniformly corrupt.

Some examples will illustrate the various defects.

CONTENTION

(i) Duke Humphrey, the Protector, has left the Council Chamber angry and indignant over the terms of the marriage-treaty made by Suffolk with France, and Cardinal Beaufort attacks him (i. 93-104). Compare *2 Henry VI*, 1.1. 142-159.

> There goes our Protector in a rage,
> My Lords you know he is my great enemy,
> And though he be Protector of the land,
> And thereby couers his deceitful thoughts,
> For well you see, if he but walke the streets,
> The common people swarme about him straight,
> Crying Iesus blesse your royall excellence,
> With God preserue the good Duke Humphrey.
> And many things besides that are not knowne,
> Which time will bring to light in smooth Duke Humphrey.
> But I will after him, and if I can
> Ile laie a plot to heaue him from his seate.

Only five of these rambling, disconnected lines are recognizable in the corresponding speech of *2 Henry VI;* three others are inserted from later scenes of Shakespeare's play and one is borrowed from *3 Henry VI.*

(ii) Suffolk, who is accompanied by the Queen, dismisses with threats certain persons who mistook him for Duke Humphrey, and tears up their petitions. Queen Margaret declares (iii. 44-54) her contempt of her husband, her distrust of Humphrey, and her hatred of his Duchess. Compare *2 Henry VI*, 1.3. 40-85.

> My Lord of Suffolke, you may see by this,
> The Commons loues vnto that haughtie Duke,
> That seekes to him more then to King Henry:
> Whose eyes are alwaies poring on his booke,
> And nere regards the honour of his name,
> But still must be protected like a childe,
> And gouerned by that ambitious Duke,
> That scarse will moue his cap nor speake to vs,
> And his proud wife, high minded Elanor,
> That ruffles it with such a troupe of Ladies
> As strangers in the Court takes her for the Queene.

These lines represent portions of two separated speeches in the parallel text. Only three lines of the above passage, and scraps of two others are in Shakespeare's authentic text; the fifth line echoes a line of *Edward II,* and four others are in later scenes of *Contention.*

(iii) York and Old Clifford meet on the battlefield and fight. Clifford is killed (xxiii. 32-41):

> *Yorke.* Now Clifford, since we are singled here alone,
> Be this the day of doome to one of vs,
> For now my heart hath sworne immortal hate
> To thee, and all the house of Lancaster.
> *Clifford.* And here I stand, and pitch my foot to thine,
> Vowing neuer to stir, till thou or I be slaine.
> For neuer shall my heart be safe at rest,
> Till I haue spoyld the hateful house of Yorke.
>
> *Alarmes, and they fight, and Yorke kils Clifford.*
>
> *Yorke.* Now Lancaster sit sure, thy sinowes shrinke,
> Come fearefull Henry grouelling on thy face,
> Yeeld vp thy Crowne vnto the Prince of Yorke.

Not one line of this passage agrees with the version of *2 Henry VI;* it is a conglomerate of fragments. The first line comes from *3 Henry VI* or *George-a-Greene* (l. 651), the next echoes a line in *Titus Andronicus,* the third is substantially line 57 of Clifford's speech and the fourth occurs frequently in the plays of *Henry VI.* York's second speech contains a phrase from *Massacre at Paris;*

'grouelling on thy face' is part of *2 Henry VI*, 1.2.9, and the last line echoes lines of *3 Henry VI*.

Other shorter passages of *Contention* may be quoted. Humphrey decides that there shall be a trial by combat between the apprentice and the armourer, his master, who was charged with treason (iii.124-9) :

> (iv) The law my Lord is this by case, it rests suspitious,
> That a day of combat be appointed,
> And there to trie each others right or wrong,
> Which shall be on the thirtith of this month,
> With Eben staues, and Standbags combatting
> In Smythfield, before your Royall Maiestie.

Compare *2 Henry VI*, 1.3. 202-8. The last two lines of the above quotation form part of a stage direction following *2 Henry VI*, 2.3.58; the passage in the folio text corresponds to iii.153-7.

(v) Duchess Eleanor is persuaded by Sir John Hume to hire witches and conjurors to assist her plot against the King and Queen.

> *Witch.* Then Roger Bullinbrooke about thy taske,
> And frame a Cirkle here vpon the earth,
> Whilst I thereon all prostrate on my face,
> Do talke and whisper with the diuels be low,
> And coniure them for to obey my will.
>
> *She lies downe vpon her face*
> *Bullenbrooke makes a Cirkle*

Reference to the folio version shows that this passage describes actions on the stage, some of which are given as portion of stage directions.

For other passages see vi. 53-62; xviii. 87-97; xxiii. 43-52.

True Tragedy

(vi) Four lines (i. 116-9), peculiar to this play, are addressed by the King to his rival:

> Ah Plantagenet, why seekest thou to depose me?
> Are we not both (both) Plantagenets by birth,
> And from two brothers lineallie discent?
> Suppose by right and equitie thou be King, etc.

Then follow eight lines (i.120-7) almost verbatim in *3 Henry VI*.

(vii) Edward and Richard have escaped from the battle-field of

Wakefield, and are discussing the phenomenon of 'three glorious suns' shining in the firmament at once, when a messenger tells (v.29-44) the story of their father's capture and death:

> When as the noble Duke was put to flight,
> And then pursu'de by Clifford and the Queene,
> And manie souldiers moe, who all at once
> Let driue at him and forst the Duke to yeeld:
> And then they set him on a molehill there,
> And crownd the gratious Duke in high despite,
> Who then with teares began to waile his fall.
> The ruthlesse Queene perceiuing he did weepe,
> Gaue him a handkercher to wipe his eies,
> Dipt in the bloud of sweet young Rutland
> By rough Clifford slaine: who weeping tooke it vp.
> Then through his brest they thrust their bloudy swordes,
> Who like a lambe fell at the butchers feete.
> Then on the gates of Yorke they set his head,
> And there it doth remaine the piteous spectacle
> That ere mine eies beheld.

Compare *3 Henry VI*, 2.1. 50-67, which gives the same facts. This speech of *True Tragedy* has only eight of the folio lines in substantially the same form; most of the others are descriptive of what took place in the fourth scene. One of Shakespeare's lines (2.1.53),

> But Hercules himselfe must yeeld to oddes;

is spoken later by Warwick when dying on the field of battle (xx.24), though it should have been part of the messenger's speech.

(viii) Being repulsed at Towton the Yorkist leaders meet, and Richard describes (vi.15-25) to Warwick the death of his father, the Earl of Salisbury:

> Ah Warwike, why haste thou withdrawne thy selfe?
> Thy noble father in the thickest thronges,
> Cride still for Warwike his thrise valiant son,
> Vntill with thousand swords he was beset,
> And manie wounds made in his aged brest,
> And as he tottring sate vpon his steede,
> He waft his hand to me and cride aloud:
> Richard, commend me to my valiant sonne,
> And still he cride Warwike reuenge my death,
> And with those words he tumbled off his horse,
> And so the noble Salsbury gaue vp the ghost.

Of this speech the folio has the first and last lines; it was not Salisbury but his illegitimate son and Warwick's half-brother who was killed. Shakespeare does not tell us when Salisbury died; actually he was taken prisoner and beheaded after the battle of Wakefield.

(ix) On learning that Warwick had renounced his allegiance to Edward, Clarence and Somerset desert the King, who asks Gloster (xii.92-102):

> What saie you brother Richard, will you stand to vs?
> *Glos.* I my Lord, in despight of all that shall
> Withstand you. For why hath Nature
> Made me halt downe right, but that I
> Should be valiant and stand to it, for if
> I would, I cannot runne awaie.
> *Edw.* Penbrooke, go raise an armie presentlie,
> Pitch vp my tent, for in the field this night
> I meane to rest, and on the morrow morne,
> Ile march to meet proud Warwike ere he land
> Those stragling troopes which he hath got in France.

Gloster's speech is in verse with the lines ending at 'you' — — 'right' — — 'it' — — 'awaie'; the interpolation of 'My Lord' has made a 'thirteener' of what in the folio version is a line with a double ending. Edward's speech in *True Tragedy* is necessary to the plot because these five lines prepare the audience for his capture in the following scene. Shakespeare makes two scenes of what is one in the quarto. In his second scene he exhibits Warwick and Oxford, later joined by Clarence and Somerset, marching with their army to take Edward by surprise. They leave the stage and three watchmen who are guarding the king's tent open the third scene with talk about him; Warwick enters and captures the king. In the *True Tragedy* the watchmen are unnecessary because the audience knows that Edward has ordered Pembroke to 'pitch vp my tent.'

(x) Warwick has been mortally wounded, and when Oxford bids him 'cheere vp thy self and liue' replies (xx.23-6):

> Whie then I would not flie, nor haue I now,
> But Hercules himselfe must yeeld to ods,
> For manie wounds receiu'd, and manie moe repaid,
> Hath robd my strong knit sinews of their strength,
> And spite of spites needs must I yeeld to death.

This speech, except for part of the opening line, is a piece of patchwork, mainly of lines spoken by Warwick in the sixth scene of this play. The second line comes, as was said above, from the messenger's speech (*3 Henry VI*, 2.1.53); the first line is in part an echo of Warwick's words (vi.27),

> Ile kill my horse because I will not flie,

which is identical with the folio line. Lines three to five are adapted from Warwick's speech in *True Tragedy* (vi.3-5); the fifth line keeps closer to the folio line (2.3.5),

> And spight of spight, needs must I rest a-while,

than to the corresponding line of the bad quarto.

Other passages of *True Tragedy* worth some study are vi.40-7; viii.1-13; xv.1-13.

Romeo and Juliet Q1

This play has almost all its non-Shakespearean verse in the last three acts.

(xi) After the deaths of Mercutio and Tybalt, the nurse arrives with the ladder of cords, and gives Juliet so confused an account of the duel that the young bride thinks her husband is dead:

> Ah Romeo, Romeo, what disaster hap
> Hath seuerd thee from thy true Iuliet?
> Ah why should Heauen so much conspire with Woe,
> Or Fate enuie our happie Marriage,
> So soone to sunder vs by timelesse Death?

Not one of these lines is in Q2.

(xii) After the supposed death of Juliet the wedding-guests indulge in a threnody. Paris begins (xix. 44-70):

> Haue I thought long to see this mornings face,
> And doth it now present such prodegies?
> Accurst, vnhappy, miserable man,
> Forlorne, forsaken, destitute I am:
> Borne to the world to be a slaue in it.
> Distrest, remediles, and vnfortunate
> O heauens, O nature, wherefore did you make me,
> To liue so vile, so wretched as I shall.
> *Cap*: O heere she lies that was our hope, our ioy,
> And being dead, dead sorrow nips vs all.
>
>   *All at once cry out and wring their hands.*

All cry: And all our ioy, and all our hope is dead,
Dead, lost, vndone, absented, wholy fled.
Cap: Cruel, vniust, impartiall destinies,
Why to this day haue you preseru'd my life?
To see my hope, my stay, my ioy, my life,
Depriude of sence, of life, of all by death,
Cruell, vniust, impartiall destinies.
Cap: O sad fac'd sorrow map of misery,
Why this sad time haue I desired to see.
This day, this vniust, this impartiall day
Wherein I hop'd to see my comfort full,
To be depriude by suddaine destinie.
Moth. O woe, alacke, distrest, why should I liue?
To see this day, this miserable day.
Alacke the time that euer I was borne.
To be partaker of this destinie.
Alacke the day, alacke and welladay.

Opinion is divided whether Shakespeare was burlesquing such pitiful bathos as this funeral lament; certainly the nurse's lines savour of mockery, and mother, father and lover make their grief mechanically. Only one line, the first quoted, is in the corresponding part of Q2. Another line (4.5.15) spoken by the nurse,

Oh welladay that euer I was borne,

is echoed in the third line of the mother's lament. 'Impartiall' in the sense of 'partial' is not Shakespearean.

(xiii) Paris visits the family vault of the Capulets to scatter flowers over Juliet's tomb. This speech (xxii. 7-13) is preceded by a stage direction as stupid as it is unnecessary:

Paris strewes the Tomb with flowers.

Sweete Flower, with flowers I strew thy Bridale bed:
Sweete Tombe that in thy circuite dost containe,
The perfect modell of eternitie:
Faire Iuliet that with Angells dost remaine,
Accept this latest fauour at my hands,
That liuing honourd thee, and being dead
With funerall praises doo adorne thy Tombe.

Again the first line is Shakespeare's only one; the rest is artificial in sentiment and might have been written for a sister, friend or mother. Two lines, the fifth and the last, are borrowed from *Richard III* and *Titus Andronicus* respectively.

H

58348

(xiv) Friar Laurence relates (xxii. 174-187) to Prince Escalus the chain of mischances that involved the lovers in tragedy.

> Then did I giue her (tutored by mine arte)
> A potion that should make her seeme as dead:
> And told her that I would with all post speed
> Send hence to Mantua for her Romeo,
> That he might come and take her from the Toombe.
> But he that had my Letters (Frier John)
> Seeking a Brother to associate him,
> Whereas the sicke infection remaind,
> Was stayed by the Searchers of the Towne,
> But Romeo vnderstanding by his man,
> That Iuliet was deceasde, returnde in post
> Vnto Verona for to see his loue.
> What after happened touching Paris death,
> Or Romeos is to me vnknowne at all.

These lines are typical of the poor verse in the bad quartos. Much of this passage consists of repetition; thus the fourth and fifth lines are little more than a recast of xvi. 90-1, and the next four lines represent xxi. 4-8. Obviously the eighth and ninth lines are misplaced.

MERRY WIVES Q1

There is not much verse in this play, but the reporter has done his worst with what was retained. Fenton tries to persuade the Host to help him to carry off and marry Ann Page (xvi. 6-18):

> (xv) Then thus my host. Tis not vnknown to you,
> The feruent loue I beare to young Anne Page,
> And mutally her loue againe to mee:
> But her father still against her choise,
> Doth seeke to marrie her to foolish Slender,
> And in a robe of white this night disguised,
> Wherein fat Falstaffe had a mightie scare,
> Must Slender take her and carrie her to Catlen,
> And there vnknowne to any, marrie her.
> Now her mother still against that match,
> And firme for Doctor Cayus, in a robe of red
> By her deuice, the Doctor must steale her thence,
> And she hath giuen consent to goe with him.

Fenton tells the host (who knows nothing of the plot to shame Falstaff or of the diverse intentions of Mistress Page and her husband regarding the marriage of Anne) enough to make the reference to Falstaff intelligible; he also explains why 'Nan' will 'present the Fairie-Queene.' Though the audience knows what is intended, the host does not, and this is a serious defect in the plot.

Another passage similar to that quoted is xiv. 16-30.

HAMLET Q1

This play was reported by the most illiterate of all the pirates, and contains numerous short passages little better than nonsense.

(xvi) Ophelia describes (v. 33-42) the strange behaviour of Hamlet:

> O my deare father, such a change in nature,
> So great an alteration in a Prince,
> So pitifull to him, fearefull to mee,
> A maidens eye ne're looked on.
> *Cor.* Why what's the matter my Ofelia?
> *Of.* O yong Prince Hamlet, the only floure of Denmark,
> Hee is bereft of all the wealth he had,
> The Iewell that ador'nd his feature most
> Is filcht and stolne away, his wit's bereft him.

This is an excellent specimen of the reporter's muse: the one line spoken by Corambis comes from Q2.

(xvii) Claudius begins the sixth scene with three lines (vi. 1-3) that mean not but blunder round a meaning:

> Right noble friends, that our deere cosin Hamlet
> Hath lost the very heart of all his sence,
> It is most right, and we most sory for him:

(xviii) After her interview with Hamlet Ophelia bewails (vi. 201-4) the decay of his mind; and the hidden auditors comment (vii. 1-7) upon what they have heard.

> *Ofe.* Great God of heauen, what a quick change is this?
> The Courtier, Scholler, Souldier, all in him,
> All dasht and splinterd thence, O woe is me,
> To a seene what I haue seene, see what I see.   *Exit.*
> *King.* Loue? No, no, that's not the cause,   *Enter King*
> Some deeper thing it is that troubles him.   *and Corambis.*
> *Cor.* Wel, something it is: my Lord, content you a while,
> I will my selfe goe feele him: let me worke,
> Ile try him euery way: see where he comes,
> Send you those Gentlemen, let me alone
> To finde the depth of this, away, be gone.   *Exit King.*

With this compare Q2. 3.1.150-188. Ophelia begins with an adjuration taken from *Richard III*, keeps three words of the second line in Q2 and ends with a line and a half of Shakespeare's text verbatim. All that remains is the reporter's fustian. What is most odd is the abrupt and dictatorial tone of the order, 'away, be gone' addressed by a subject to his king.

(xix) Another piece of such nonsense occurs in the next scene, when Corambis begins to outline (viii. 24-29) his plan for espionage:

> Madame, I pray be ruled by me:
> And my good Soueraigne, give me leaue to speake,
> We cannot yet finde out the very ground
> Of his distemperance, therefore
> I hold it meete, if so it please you,
> Else they shall not meete, and thus it is.

No wonder Claudius stands amazed and gasps 'What i'st Corambis?'

(xx) The famous speech beginning,

> Looke heere vpon this Picture, and on this,

has suffered more than a 'sad sea-change'; it is vulgarized beyond description (x. 28-42):

> Why this I meane, see here, behold this picture,
> It is the portraiture, of your deceased husband,
> See here a face, to outface Mars himselfe,
> An eye, at which his foes did tremble at,
> A front wherin all vertues are set downe
> For to adorne a King, and guild his crowne,
> Whose heart went hand in hand euen with that vow,
> He made to you in marriage, and he is dead.
> Murdred, damnably murdred, this was your husband,
> Looke you now, here is your husband,
> With a face like Vulcan.
> A looke fit for a murder and a rape,
> A dull dead hanging looke, and a hell-bred eie,
> To affright children and amaze the world:
> And this same haue you left to change with this.

Compare Q2, 3.4.53-76; lines 71-6 are omitted in the folio version and probably in representation. Lines 34-5 of Q1 come from the ghost's speech, bits of Shakespeare's speech appear here and there. The paronomasia of 'face to outface' is found in *Comedy of Errors*,

Richard II and *Love's Labour's Lost;* 'Mars' and 'Vulcan' are both mentioned in *Hamlet Q2.*

(xxi) Gertrude asks Horatio 'what became of Gilderstone and Rossencraft?'; his reply (xiv. 28-32) has a meaning if we read Q2:

> He being set ashore, they went for England,
> And in the Packet there writ down that doome
> To be perform'd on them poynted for him:
> And by great chance he had his fathers Seale,
> So all was done without discouerie.

Q1 gives no explanation why Hamlet was 'set ashore,' and all the details must come from Shakespeare's play.

(xxii) Another example of the pirate's inability to write plain English appears in the King's conversation (xv. 9-13) with Laertes:

> Nay but Leartes, marke the plot I haue layde,
> I haue heard him often with a greedy wish,
> Vpon some praise that he hath heard of you
> Touching your weapon, which with all his heart,
> He might be once tasked for to try your cunning.

Other passages in Q1 bearing the debasing marks of the pirate are ii. 33-9; iii. 3-20, 65-70; vi. 87-95, 120-133; viii. 1-16; ix. 100-112; xi. 90-5, 104-7, 113-17; xiii. 65-8; xiv. 1-9; xv. 40-50; xvi. 129-134; xviii. 117-122.

(xxiii) Excellent instances of the reporter's incompetence are to be found in the versions of Hamlet's soliloquies; the last fared best in being omitted. I quote the first soliloquy, and at the left hand side of each line put the line of Q2 which corresponds to that in Q1 most nearly.

129	O that this too much grieu'd and sallied flesh
130	Would melt to nothing, or that the vniuersall
	Globe of heauen would turne al to a Chaos!
132, 138	O God, within two moneths; no not two: maried,
151, 146	Mine vncle: O let me not thinke of it,
152–6	My fathers brother: but no more like
	My father, then I to Hercules.
	Within two months, ere yet the salt of most
	Vnrighteous teates had left their flushing
150–1	In her galled eyes: she married, O God, a beast
	Deuoyd of reason would not haue made
146	Such speede: Frailtie, thy name is Woman,

143–4   Why she would hang on him, as if increase
        Of appetite had growne by what it looked on.
156–7   O wicked wicked speede, to make such
        Dexteritie to incestuous sheetes,
147–9   Ere yet the shooes were olde,
        The which she followed my dead fathers corse
158   Like Nyobe, all teares; married, well it is not,
        Not it cannot come to good:
159   But breake my heart, for I must holde my tongue.

Another such example will be found by comparing *Contention* xii. 20-40 with *2 Henry VI* 4.1.15-116; similarly lines 16-39 of the tenth scene of *True Tragedy* represent lines 18-20, 33-5, 26-32, 42-5, 21-25, 52 of the second scene of the third act of *3 Henry VI*.

Who wrote the passages quoted above from the bad quartos? Certainly not any contemporary dramatist known to us. There exist enough specimens of authentic plays with sound texts written by Lyly, Greene, Peele, Marlowe, Kyd, Lodge, Heywood, Dekker, Chapman and others, and we are forced to the conclusion that even the best of the bad quartos cannot, in their existing condition, be fathered upon any one of these dramatists. Each one of them was an educated man, some of them men of genius, and all of them could and did write correct prose and verse.

Most of these passages share certain characteristics in common— little elevation of thought, a certain coarseness verging on vulgarity, almost complete lack of fancy or imagination, dull, pedestrian and irregular verse, poor and overworked vocabulary, frequent errors in grammar and syntax, and a primitive type of sentence-con- struction. King, queen, cardinal, duchess, peer, soldier, lover, courtier, artisan, peasant, servant and child all speak alike. Cardinal Beaufort's attack on Duke Humphrey is a typical example of a rambling and seemingly interminable anacoluthon, winding along with straggling relatival and conditional clauses and par- ticiples pendent; Margaret's conversation with Suffolk and the messenger's report to the sons of the Duke of York are of similar character. Essentially each of these and many other speeches exhibit all the marks of garrulous illiteracy struggling amidst a maze of words to express what had been learnt or heard or recited or seen on the stage; they remind us of the vulgar gossiping of the immortal Sairey Gamp or the chattering irrelevancy of the inane Mrs. Nickleby.

Our early actors seem to have loved a lord as well as the most snobbish Georgian of our day; they gave men of rank or position their titles on every possible occasion, and 'your Grace,' 'Prince Hamlet,' or 'Yong Prince Hamlet,' 'my Lord,' 'Sir John' (Falstaffe) 'Duke Humphrey,' 'Uncle Gloster,' etc., were thrust into a line of verse without a thought whether the metre was spoiled or not. Falstaff must sign his letter to the wives 'Syr Iohn Falstaff,' and Hamlet ends his love-rhymes with the signature, 'Prince Hamlet.'

Each bad quarto has a surplusage of such gags and catch-words as 'let me alone,' 'with all my heart,' 'I warrant you (him)' 'see where he comes,' 'go thy ways,' 'Ile tell you,' 'it likes me,' etc. Each play has certain phrases repeated ad nauseam, e.g. 'so farewell,' 'monstrous rebel,' 'cold news to me,' 'the score and the tally,' 'revenge my death,' in *Contention*; 'come let's go,' 'let us march away,' 'away with him,' 'hear him speake,' in *True Tragedy;* 'ancient Pistoll,' 'looke you' or 'looke you now,' in *Henry V Q1;* 'dinner stays for you,' 'so kad vdge me,' 'Ifaith sir,' 'cuckally knave,' 'God blesse me,' 'Jeshu blesse me,' in *Merry Wives Q1;* 'contents me not,' 'content my selfe,' 'sonne Hamlet,' 'I prithee' (*Hamlet Q1*).

Another infallible mark of the reporter and his associates is their inveterate habit of inserting 'and,' 'but,' 'why,' 'what,' 'for,' 'tell him,' 'tell me,' etc., wherever and whenever a phrase or a sentence seemed to need linking to the previous context. This habit results in many unmetrical lines which I shall discuss later. Another phase of this habit is that in *Contention* and *True Tragedy* there are many passages of which two, three or even four consecutive lines begin with 'and'; see examples numbered vii and viii. Compare also *Contention* iv. 1-8; x. 186-190; xxiii. 76-81, and *True Tragedy* ii. 27-33 and xx. 28-33. In consequence there results a style of narration more like that of a child than that of a playwright. Such passages as those numbered i, ii, iv, vii, xv, and xvii-xxiii cannot be the work of any man of ordinary education.

I have explained that Cardinal Beaufort's speech (example one) consists mainly of lines borrowed from other parts of *2 Henry VI*; the abrupt breaks in sense and syntax at the ends of the fourth and the eighth lines indicate that the stupid thief could not cover up his pilferings or fit them into the few lines of the authentic speech. Queen Margaret in the second passage rambles on from comments on the people's affection for Duke Humphrey to contemptuous criticism of her husband, the duke and his duchess; each portion is tagged to what went before by a relative pronoun. Humphrey's judgment (example four) seems and is a very odd one; the irrelevant words 'it rests suspitious' refer to the omitted portion of the 'judgment' or 'doome' (*2 Henry VI.* 1.3.203-4):

> Let Somerset be Regent o're the French,
> Because in Yorke this breedes suspition.

These lines appear substantially later in *Contention* (iii. 153-7). If they are removed, the third line partly rewritten and placed at the end, we have tolerable sense. In some respects the messenger's report (example seven) resembles the speeches of Beaufort and Margaret. He begins with a cluster of dependent clauses, and, neglecting to provide a principal sentence, leaves the first four lines in the air; later he compels the reader to search the context for the antecedents of two relative pronouns. Fenton's speech (example fourteen) is ambiguous, inconsistent with the folio version, defective metrically in several lines, and amounts to a continuous perversion of Shakespeare's text. His language with its accumulation of 'hers' leaves the hearers in doubt whether Doctor Caius is to steal Anne or her mother. *Hamlet Q1* has many pieces bordering on nonsense. To discuss which character, Polonius, Claudius or Laertes, reaches the lowest depth of inanity is not worth while.

Revisionists would have us believe that the poet selected some lines from such speeches as these, and rewrote his own speeches around the few lines retained. To such critics I commend a comparative study of Hamlet's soliloquies in Q1 and Q2. I have quoted the first quarto version of the first soliloquy because it contains little non-Shakespearean matter. Does any one seriously believe that the Shakespeare who wrote four of the world's greatest tragedies used what he found in Q1 with such reverence? He must have sedulously re-arranged the words, phrases, half-lines and lines in order, corrected the grammar, set the broken lines to his own music, and added to this renovated thing of shreds and patches, that is, to another man's work, half as much again. No more fantastic thought ever entered the mind of man.

CHAPTER X

NON-SHAKESPEAREAN LINES

DR. Greg has demonstrated that the actors responsible for the copy of *Orlando Furioso Q1* introduced into it scenes and episodes mainly of a comic nature, and also many lines here and there. My comparative tables show that each bad quarto has a large number of non-Shakespearean lines; in the four longer plays such lines represent nearly a sixth of the total verse. The percentage varies widely. *Henry V Q1* has none but lines found in the folio text, while *Merry Wives Q1* has very little verse, much of it interpolated. For each scene of each bad quarto the total number of verses not in the parallel text is set out; in *Contention* and *Hamlet Q1* they represent 26 per cent. of the total verse, in *Romeo and Juliet Q1* 8 per cent., and in *True Tragedy* a little over 11 per cent. If scenes wholly or mainly in prose are excluded, every other scene of *Contention* and *True Tragedy* except the very short sixteenth scene of *Contention* and the twenty-third scene of *True Tragedy* contains some non-Shakespearean verse; this is true also of *Hamlet Q1* except for the first and twelfth scenes. *Romeo and Juliet Q1* has only four lines of interpolated verse in the first eight scenes which contain 788 lines of verse; in the third act, which in Q1 equals 496 verse lines, non-Shakespearean lines number a dozen. Sixteen scenes are practically free from contamination, having only twenty-two non-Shakespearean lines; about two-thirds of such lines in Q1 are massed in the tenth, nineteenth and twenty-second scenes.

Usually if a quarto scene has a large proportion of non-Shakespearean verses, those derived from the parallel text will be badly preserved and the percentage of lines substantially identical with those of Shakespeare's play will be low; this is true in the main of *Contention* and *Hamlet Q1*. In *True Tragedy* the amount of interpolation seems to vary with the presence or the absence of the actors who played the parts of Clifford and Warwick; this is noticeable in the third, fourth, eighth, eleventh and twentieth scenes. The actor of Suffolk does not exercise such an influence on the text of *Contention,* but Warwick in the final scene, two-thirds of which consists of interpolated verse, alone keeps fast to the text of *2 Henry VI.*

One, two or three lines of non-Shakespearean matter are found sporadically in the majority of the quarto scenes, but longer passages ranging up to forty lines are not very frequent. As stated above, one scene of Shakespeare's is, in *True Tragedy* and *Romeo and Juliet Q1,* replaced by one in which the same characters discuss the same topics but in much inferior diction and verse; in *Hamlet Q1,* the fourteenth scene between Horatio and the queen takes the place of the scene in Q2 between Horatio and the sailors, and refers also to Hamlet's description of his escape from the ship bound for England. These interpolated scenes are short, and may, in *Romeo and Juliet Q1,* represent reported portions of pre-existing plays bearing the same title and on the same theme. Below I give illustrative details of the haphazard occurrence of such non-Shakespearean matter in several scenes chosen from each of the four longer quartos.

CONTENTION

  i. ll. 24-9, 31-2, 75, 82-7, 90, 95-8, 103-4, 109, 112, 126-7.
  ii. ll. 6-7, 9, 11, 13, 22-3, 37-8, 41-2, 45-6, 59-67, 70, 74, 76-80.
 xxiii. ll. 2-5, 16-19, 23-4, 26, 32-61, 63-71, 73-7, 80-1, 83, 85-6.

TRUE TRAGEDY

  i. ll. 116-119, 168-9, 211, 228-30.
  ii. ll. 8-9, 13-16, 21-3, 31-5, 39-40, 42.
  vi. ll. 7-13, 16-25, 30, 34-5, 37-41, 46-7.
  viii. ll. 1-8, 12-13, 17, 22, 46, 51, 54, 57-8, 60, 72, 158.

ROMEO AND JULIET Q1

 xxii. ll. 5-14, 22, 64-5, 70, 85, 96, 103, 107-8, 112, 122-3, 128, 138, 140-1, 148-9, 154-5, 157-9, 161-2, 166-7, 172, 176-7, 180-7, 193, 206-7, 209.

HAMLET Q1

  iii. ll. 2-6, 10-11, 17, 19-20, 50, 66-70.
  x. ll. 1-13, 17-18, 31.
  xiii. ll. 1-14, 26, 41-5, 55-6, 58-9, 63-4, 66-9, 72-3, 114-27.

I have chosen the scenes from *True Tragedy* because the second, sixth and eighth scenes have the highest totals of interpolated lines; the first scene is included because some of the interpolated lines occur unexpectedly in a part of the play much of which is nearly verbatim from the folio version. In the eighth scene all but two of the introduced lines are found in the early portion which editors of the folio version usually treat as a separate scene. Apart from the interpolated scene—the tenth—*Romeo and Juliet Q1* has only one scene, the last, that deserves attention; in three scenes are congregated seventy per cent. of the foreign matter. Reviewing each scene of each of these two bad quartos, a critic cannot but conclude that the numerous rents and small holes in Shakespeare's garments have been patched by unskilful botchers with scraps of shoddy cloth of divers colours, but the plays are Shakespeare's in tattered disarray. *Contention* and *Hamlet Q1* are in much worse disrepair; yet three-fourths of the total verse is Shakespeare's, though many lines are barely recognizable in the ruins.

Three facts, or rather opinions commonly accepted as facts, have, in the past, helped to sway the judgment of many commentators. They made no allowance for the official abridgment which reduced plays varying in length from 2,900 to 3,760 lines to acting versions not much exceeding 2,300 lines in length; in other words, they did not realize that the actors could not speak much more than 2,300 lines in the two hours allotted for representation, and must remove from 600 to 1,400 lines from their originals. Secondly, many critics have stressed difference rather than likeness; interpolations amount to slightly less than a fifth part of the very corrupt *Contention* and barely a fourteenth part of *Romeo and Juliet Q1*. Thirdly, they have greatly overstated the losses of Shakespeare's text due to piracy in their explicit or implicit assumption that the actors staged 2,902 lines of *3 Henry VI*, 2,986 lines of *Romeo and Juliet Q2*, 3,075 lines of *2 Henry VI* and—wonderful to relate— 3,762 lines of *Hamlet*. By combining thus losses due to omissions, official and unofficial, and interpolations, they attributed to the reporters the removal from Shakespeare's plays of text varying from a thousand to two thousand lines.

Some specimens are given below of the twelve hundred lines of non-Shakespearean verse in the four longer quartos.

CONTENTION

(i) Three petitioners await the arrival of Duke Humphrey. By mistake they give their petitions to Suffolk who is with the queen. He reads the petitions and tears them into pieces, and dismisses the men from the court (iii. 41-3) :—

> *Suffolke.* So now show your petitions to Duke Humphrey.
> Villaines get you gone and come not neare the Court,
> Dare these pesants write against me thus.
> *Exet Petitioners.*

(ii) Duke Humphrey learns that his wife has been guilty of sorcery and replies (v. 157-61) to Beaufort :—

> Forbeare ambitious Prelate to vrge my griefe,
> And pardon me my gratious Soueraigne,
> For here I sweare vnto your Maiestie,
> That I am guiltlesse of these hainous crimes
> Which my ambitious wife hath falsly done.

(iii) His wife is sentenced to imprisonment for life, and he asks permission (vii. 15-19) to retire :—

> Oh gratious Henry, giue me leaue awhile,
> To leaue your grace, and to depart away,
> For sorrowes teares hath gripte my aged heart,
> And makes the fountaines of mine eyes to swell,
> And therefore good my lord, let me depart.

(iv) Humphrey has been arrested, and his enemies decide to murder him. A messenger enters with news (ix. 131-9) of rebellion :—

> *Queene.* How now sirrha, what newes?
> *Messen.* Madame I bring you newes from Ireland,
> The wilde Onele my Lords, is vp in Armes,
> With troupes of Irish Kernes that vncontrold,
> Doth plant themselues within the English pale.
>
> - - - - - - - - - -
>
> And burnes and spoiles the Country as they goe.

The last line is out of place, being in *Contention* part of York's speech.

(v) Iden presents Henry with the head of Cade, and the King replies (xxi. 52-56) :—

A visage sterne, cole blacke his curled locks,
Deepe trenched furrowes in his frowning brow,
Presageth warlike humors in his life.
Here take it hence and thou for thy reward,
Shalt be immediatly created Knight.

(vi) Young Clifford finds his father dead (xxii. 43-52) and vows vengeance on the house of York :—

Young Clifford. Father of Comberland,
Where may I seeke my aged father forth?
O! dismall sight, see where he breathlesse lies,
All smeard and weltred in his luke-warme blood,
Ah, aged pillar of all Comberlands true house,
Sweete father, to thy murthred ghoast I sweare,
Immortall hate vnto the house of Yorke,
Nor neuer shall I sleepe secure one night,
Till I haue furiously reuengde thy death,
And left not one of them to breath on earth.

TRUE TRAGEDY

(i) York decides to make war upon Henry (ii. 23-25) :—
I, saist thou so boie? why then it shall be so,
I am resolude to win the crowne, or die.
{Edward, thou shalt to Edmund Brooke Lord Cobham, }
{With whom the Kentishmen will willinglie rise: }
Thou cosen Montague, shalt to Norffolke straight,
And bid the Duke to muster vppe his souldiers,
And come to me to Wakefield presentlie.
And Richard thou to London strait shalt post,
And bid Richard Neuill Earle of Warwike
To leaue the cittie, and with his men of warre,
To meete me at Saint Albons ten daies hence.
My selfe heere in Sandall castell will prouide
Both men and monie to furder our attempts.

The two lines enclosed in brackets are in *3 Henry VI.*

(ii) York, defeated at Wakefield, is a fugitive (iii. 50-3) :—

Ah Yorke, post to thy castell, saue thy life,
The goale is lost thou house of Lancaster,
Thrise happie chance is it for thee and thine,
That heauen abridgde my daies and cals me hence.

Three of these lines are found in Peele's *Battle of Alcazar.*

(iii) During the battle of Towton the Yorkists suffer a temporary reverse. This scene contains a greater number of introduced lines than any other in this play.

> *Edw.* Smile gentle heauens or strike vngentle death,
> That we maie die vnlesse we gaine the daie ;
> What fatall starre malignant frownes from heauen
> Vpon the harmlesse line of Yorkes true house? *Enter George.*
> *George.* Come brother, come, lets to the field againe,
> For yet theres hope inough to win the daie :
> Then let vs backe to cheere our fainting Troupes,
> Lest they retire now we haue left the field.
> *War.* How now my lords : what hap, what hope of good?

(iv) Richard and Clifford exchange defiances (vii. 1-6) :—

> *Rich.* A Clifford a Clifford.
> *Clif.* A Richard a Richard.
> *Rich.* Now Clifford, for Yorke & young Rutlands death,
> This thirsty sword that longs to drinke thy bloud,
> Shall lop thy limmes, and slise thy cursed hart,
> For to reuenge the murders thou hast made.

(v) Margaret asks (xi. 3-9) aid of King Lewis who promises to give her help before he knows why she has come and what she needs of him ; she thanks him :—

> *Lewes.*   And here I vow to thee,
> Thou shalt haue aide to repossesse thy right,
> And beat proud Edward from his vsurped seat.
> And place King Henry in his former rule.
> *Queen.* I humblie thanke your royall maiestie.
> And pray the God of heauen to blesse thy state,
> Great King of France, that thus regards our wrongs.

(vi) Edward has been captured by Warwick, and Clarence tells (xiii. 47-50) his fellow-conspirator what should be done :—

> What followes now, all hithertoo goes well,
> But we must dispatch some letters to France,
> To tell the Queene of our happy fortune,
> And bid hir come with speed to ioine with vs.

(vii) Richard accompanied by Hastings and Stanley rescues (xiv. 1-9) Edward from captivity :—

> Lord Hastings, and sir William Stanly,
> Know that the cause I sent for you is this.
> I looke my brother with a slender traine,

Should come a hunting in this forrest heere,
The Bishop of Yorke befriends him much,
And lets him vse his pleasure in the chase,
Now I haue priuilie sent him word,
How I am come with you to rescue him,
And see where the huntsman and he doth come.

(viii) Young Prince Edward rallies his troops (xxi. 17-20) before the battle of Tewkesbury :—

I will not stand aloofe and bid you fight,
But with my sword presse in the thickest thronges,
And single Edward from his strongest guard,
And hand to hand enforce him for to yeeld,
Or leaue my bodie as witnesse of my thoughts.

ROMEO AND JULIET Q1

(i) After much delay Juliet learns from the nurse that her marriage to Romeo is arranged. The scene concludes (ix. 41-4) :—

Nur: Doth this newes please you now?
Iul: How doth her latter words reuiue my hart.
Thankes gentle Nurse, dispatch thy busines,
And Ile not faile to meete my Romeo.

(ii) Lady Capulet, her daughter and the nurse prepare (xvii. 31-5) for Juliet's marriage to Paris :—

Moth: I pree thee doo, good Nurse goe in with her,
Helpe her to sort Tyres, Rebatoes, Chaines,
And I will come vnto you presently.
Nur: Come sweet hart, shall we goe:
Iul: I pree thee let vs.

(iii) Friar Laurence's long speech (xxii. ll. 157-197) is full of interpolations :—

But her Soule
(Loathing a second Contract) did refuse
To giue consent; and therefore did she vrge me
Either to find a meanes she might auoyd
What so her Father sought to force her too;
Or els all desperately she threatned
Euen in my presence to dispatch her selfe.   ll. 167-173.

And told her that I would with all post speed
Send hence to Mantua for her Romeo,
That he might come and take her from the Toombe.
                                                  ll. 176-8.

But Romeo vnderstanding by his man,
That Iuliet was deceasde, returnde in post
Vnto Verona for to see his loue.
What after happened touching Paris death,
Or Romeos is to me vnknowne at all.   ll. 183-7.

Hamlet Q1

(i) Laertes' long opening speech in the third scene has been reduced to eleven lines in Q1; seven of these are not in Q2.

But ere I part, marke what I say to thee:
I see Prince Hamlet makes a shew of loue
Beware Ofelia, do not trust his vowes,
Perhaps he loues you now, and now his tongue,
Speakes from his heart, but yet take heed my sister,
⎧The Chariest maide is prodigall enough,   ⎫
⎨If she vnmaske hir beautie to the Moone.   ⎬
⎩Vertue it selfe scapes not calumnious thoughts,⎭
Belieu't Ofelia, therefore keepe a loofe
Lest that he trip thy honor and thy fame.

(ii) Polonius concludes the third scene with five more interpolated lines (iii. 66-70) not in the original; in Q1 he is styled Corambis.

"For louers lines are snares to intrap the heart;
"Refuse his tokens, both of them are keyes
To vnlocke Chastitie vnto Desire:
Come in Ofelia, such men often proue,
"Great in their wordes, but little in their loue.

(iii) Polonius and his family are outdone by Claudius and his two courtier-spies in talking near-nonsense. Claudius opens the sixth scene with the following sorry stuff (vi. 4-8) :—

Therefore we doe desire, euen as you tender
Our care to him, and our great loue to you,
That you will labour but to wring from him
The cause and ground of his distemperancie.
Doe this, the King of Denmarke shal be thankefull.

(iv) Much of the famous soliloquy 'To be or not to be' is omitted, and the gaps partly stopped with rhythmless rubbish in hopeless disorder (vi. 120-131) :—

(For in that dreame of death, when wee awake,)
And borne before an euerlasting Iudge,

⎛From whence no passenger euer retur'nd, ⎞
⎝The vndiscouered country, at whose sight ⎠
  The happy smile, and the accursed damn'd.
  But for this, the ioyfull hope of this,
(Whol'd beare the scornes and flattery of the world,)
  Scorned by the right rich, the rich curssed of the poore?
  The widow being oppressed, the orphan wrong'd,
  The taste of hunger, or a tirants raigne,
⎛And thousand more calamities besides, ⎞
⎝To grunt and sweate vnder this weary life, etc. ⎠

(v) Claudius' soliloquy which opens the tenth scene retains not one line of Shakespeare:—

  O that this wet that falles vpon my face
  Would wash the crime cleere from my conscience!
  When I looke vp to heauen, I see my trespasse,
  The earth doth still crie out vpon my fact,
  Pay me the murder of a brother and a king,
  And the adulterous fault I haue committed:
  O these are sinnes that are vnpardonable:
  Why say thy sinnes were blacker then is ieat,
  Yet may contrition make them as white as snowe:
  I but still to perseuer in a sinne,
  It is an act against the vniuersall power,
  Most wretched man, stoope, bend thee to thy prayer,
  Aske grace of heauen to keepe thee from despaire.

(vi) Even the ghost's speech (x. 71-7) slips into disconnected platitude:—

  Hamlet, I once againe appeare to thee,
  To put thee in remembrance of my death;
  Doe not neglect, nor long time put it off.
  But I perceive by thy distracted lookes,
  Thy mother's fearefull, and she stands amazde;
  Speake to her Hamlet, for her sex is weake,
  Comfort thy mother, Hamlet, thinke on me.

(vii) Horatio's last speech fitly ends (xviii. 117-122) this long string of mock-verse wanting in metre, music and sense.

  Content your selues, Ile shew to all, the ground,
  The first beginning of this Tragedy:
  Let there a scaffold be rearde vp in the market place,
  And let the State of the world be there:
  Where you shall heare such a sad story tolde,
  That neuer mortall man could more vnfolde.

J

How did the twelve hundred lines of verse not derived from the parallel texts come into being and find a place in one or other of the bad quartos? *Contention, True Tragedy* and *Hamlet Q1* have each about fifty such lines, consisting of repetitions or borrowings from other plays. Several of the latter are present in the quotations given above; but this group and its importance in this enquiry will be discussed later. It is not unreasonable to suggest that at least an equal number of lines were borrowed from other contemporary plays no longer extant; it must be kept in mind that barely a seventh of the plays acted by the Admiral's men reached the press.

It is easier to say what these non-Shakespearean lines are not than what they are. They are not the comminuted débris of lines written by Shakespeare or any other contemporary dramatist of repute, nor the poor work of some hack poet—if such existed in those days—for he would at least write correct English, nor may they be debited to the account of the Elizabethan printer. They cannot be part of a stenographic paraphrase of what was heard on the stage; only an educated man could learn and practise the primitive shorthand of this period, and his report, however far from being verbatim, would certainly be intelligible. Whatever be their origin, they were beyond all doubt born in corruption, and my own count shows that those present in *True Tragedy* have a greater proportion of defective verse than the rest of the play. They abound in repetition of expletives, cant phrases, catch-words and vulgarisms; the verse is defective in scansion, halting and lacks music. Imagination, fancy, metaphor and figurative expressions, each of them hall-marks of Shakespeare's work, are wanting; most of the longer passages are lifeless, tame and dull. In general they represent the barren flats and morasses of the play, whilst the garbled and mutilated portions of the author's text are its fertile plains, highlands and peaks, clouded over with the mists of misunderstanding.

Various reasons have been propounded for the presence in each of the longer bad quartos of so large a number of non-Shakespearean verse-lines. I have already referred to Professor Wilson's revival of the 'first-sketch' theory in his suggestion that Shakespeare recast old plays on the same themes in two instalments with two years or more between his rewriting of each instalment. I have shown that vocabulary tests tell strongly against the acceptance of this theory. An equally strong if not decisive argument against its validity is furnished by comparing the total of un-Shakespearean lines in the alleged unrevised portion of *Romeo and Juliet Q1* with the number of lines derived from the parallel text of Q2. All told there are in the thirteen unrevised scenes of Q1 143 interpolated lines of verse, i.e., 143 lines of the old play which the theory claims Shakespeare partly revised, and 936 lines which correspond more or less exactly to lines of Q2. Actually the number of lines in this portion of Q1 which are found verbatim in Q2 is considerably more than double the total number of non-Shakespearean lines in the play. These totals should be reversed if we are to accept Professor Wilson's theory that Q1 is 'an abridged version of Shakespeare's first revision of an older play eked out by what a pirate could remember of the later version.' Similar criticism applies to any theory of double revision which attempts to account for the non-Shakespearean verse in *True Tragedy;* it represents little more than a tenth of the play, is well distributed throughout each act and only in three short scenes does it equal or surpass the amount of verse present which is found in the corresponding scene of *3 Henry VI*. Probably an older play on the same period of English history existed, and some passages of this may have been used by forgetful actors or reporters to fill gaps.

Hamlet Q1 is a more difficult problem. Prose is absent in the first act which, Professor Wilson thinks, was the limit of Shakespeare's first revision. Acts II-V of Q2 contain 1,047 lines of prose and 1,771 lines of verse; in the corresponding portion of Q1 are 586 lines of prose and 935 lines of verse. Except for omissions, most of them probably cuts, and an interpolation of 14 lines, the prose of Q1 is reported rather well; the 935 verse-lines consist of 557 lines corresponding to lines of Q2 and 378 not by Shakespeare. Rewriting here and there, the recollections of the pirate with eight parts, and what he could pick up at the stage door might credibly amount to 557 of 1,771 lines of Shakespeare's verse. But the 3,668 lines of Q2 would certainly be cut down to about 2,300 lines— *Macbeth* has only 2,084 lines—and with 633 lines retained in Q1 of the 850 lines in the first act of Q2, the 2,818 lines left in Acts II-V of Q2 would necessarily be reduced to not more than 1,700 lines in the acting version. If we allow for the retaining of 630 lines of prose, 1,070 lines of Shakespeare's verse would be spoken on the stage during the performance of Acts II-V of the acting version made from Q2; Professor Wilson makes his reporter responsible for recovering 557 lines, not of the 1,771 written by the poet, but of these 1,070 lines of verse. This versatile actor would have six parts still to play, but while he was on the stage he would speak or hear spoken 222 lines only of the acting version of Q2; of these he seems to have preserved 150 lines, and filled the gaps with 54 lines presumably drawn from the old play. What a falling-off from his admirable piece of work as Marcellus! There would remain in the acting version of Q2 848 lines, and of these Reynaldo—ambassadors Danish and English—player—captain— priest—assistant grave-digger would neither speak nor hear spoken one line. Yet he managed to gather 407 verse-lines, more or less damaged, of the revised versions of Acts II-V, and even more prose in a much better state of preservation, and padded it out with 322 lines of verse and 14 lines of prose from the old play.

Professor Wilson's theory of double revision insists that the reporter did not have access to any portion of Shakespeare's revised text, except for the passages in which he had a part or depended on the recollections of the other actors. Would he get any help from the chief actors, Burbage, Heminge, Pope, Phillips, Condell or the poet, all of them men of property and keen to keep what hard work had earned? The propounder of this ingenious theory has, in my opinion, hedged it round with such unnecessary restrictions as make it certain that the facts shall not fit in with his theory. No one expects a pirate, manacled, leg-ironed and rigid in a strait-jacket, to practise his profession with success.

CHAPTER XI

ABRIDGMENT—OFFICIAL AND UNOFFICIAL

FOR many years one group of critics has supported the theory that the very great losses of Shakespeare's original text were, except for some small amount of official abridgment, almost entirely due to corruption, the result either of inefficient stenography or of the defective memories of dishonest actors and reporters desirous of 'faking copy' for a printer. Another group of critics has, however, preferred the simple and attractive theory that Shakespeare revised or rewrote the whole or a part of an old play, either his own or that of another dramtist. Neither theory has won its way to sole acceptance. Most editors have discussed the relationship between each pair of these parallel texts as an isolated phenomenon or special problem affecting one play of Shakespeare, and have lost sight of the fact that some broad principle must condition the sixfold repetition of this phenomenon or problem. Further, the separation of *Contention* and *True Tragedy* from the other bad quartos has been based on insufficient and illogical reasons; the detailed investigation of the relationship between them and the parallel plays on the reign of Henry VI has been subordinated to pre-conceived impressions, mainly subjective and aesthetic, on the authorship of *2 Henry VI* and *3 Henry VI*— a question that has nothing or very little to do with the relationship between *Contention* and *2 Henry VI* or *True Tragedy* and *3 Henry VI*.

Dr. Greg's study of the two versions of Orlando's part in Dulwich MS. and *Orlando Furioso Q1* suggests that students of the bad quartos should rely on facts and not on subjective impressions. It was stated above that 441 lines of verse present in Dulwich MS. were reduced to 296 lines in *Orlando Furioso Q1,* a loss slightly greater proportionally than that which reduced the verse of *Romeo and Juliet Q2* to what is left in Q1. On collating the two texts, MS. and Q1, it is noticeable that several long passages, e.g., ll. 225-242, 262-288, 349-375, 444-456, and 509-24, or 97 lines altogether, have been omitted without leaving much trace of their existence in Q1. In addition, certain shorter passages of MS., e.g., ll. 181-6, 211-15, 256-9, 295-300, 410-413, 464-7, 476-482, and 496-8 are not in Q1. Dr. Greg thinks, and I agree with him, that most of the longer passages and some of the shorter were official cuts made by the play-adapter and were not careless omissions made by the actors who furnished the 'copy' for Q1. All these passages are packed with classical allusions, and many of the latter must have meant nothing, even to educated Elizabethans. Even famous Ned Alleyn would scarcely have been permitted to declaim much of what Greene wrote for him. Melissa has cured Orlando of madness and explains to him how Sacrepant had contrived to make him believe that Angelina was false. Orlando replies (MS. 349-358) as follows :—

> Hast then the frenzy of Alcumenas child
> ledd fourth my thoughts, with far more egar rage
> then wrasteld in the brayne of phillips sonne
> when madd with wyne, he practised Clytus fall
> break from the cloudes, you burning bronds of jre
> that styrre within ye thunderers wrathful fistes
> and fixe your hideous fyers on Sacrapant
> from out your fatall tresoryes of wrath
> you wastfull furyes, draw those eben bowles
> that bosted lukewarme bloud at Centawres feast,
> etc., etc.

What could the ordinary listener make of this, or the phantasmagoria of muddled classical embroidery that followed in which Clymene, Hebe, the nymphs, Etna, Cyclops, Pindus, Venus in Erycinne, the vale of Colchos, Nemesis and the phoenix pass in bewildering procession? Evidently the actors knew the temper of their audience; they struck out the lot and replaced this foolish rigmarole by two lines (Q1 1340-1) of plain English :

> Thanks sacred Goddes for thy helping hand
> Thether will I hie to be revengd.

I think that they excised four lines (MS. 410-413) a little later :

> Extinguish proud tesyphone those brandes
> fetch dark Alecto, from black phlegeton
> or Lethe waters, to appease those flames
> that wrathful Nemesis hath sett on fire.

These lines are a piece of jargon, most absurdly put into the mouth of Orlando immediately after the dying Sacrepant confesses his crime. Much of this play could not be understood by the modern student of English literature unless he had at hand a dictionary of classical mythology, and most of the passages in MS. but not in Q1 would probably be omitted by the actors as unintelligible to any audience, London or provincial. Why was such sad stuff permitted to remain in Orlando's part? These embroideries of learning were a novelty in 1589, and were probably to the liking of scholars and members of the Inns of Court. Moreover the actors were compelled to keep a large share of them if they wished to have any lines left and get back the money which they had paid Greene for his play. It was, perhaps, too short to allow of drastic abridgment; had all the mythology been excised, Orlando and the other characters would have had very few lines for declamation. Whatever we may think of the interpolated clowning scenes and episodes, they had the merit of raising a laugh, and were made amusing by the company's low comedians. Alleyn's part contained many of these non-dramatic and almost pointless speeches, but the disappearance in Q1 even in comparatively well-retained scenes of such similes as MS. 395-8:

> As Lampethusa's brother from his coach
> prauncing, and . . . . one went his course
> and tombled from Apollos chariott
> So shall thy fortunes, and thy honor fall,

suggests that many of the passages of MS. not present in Q1 were not spoken on the stage. Is it possible to estimate how many lines the actors cut out of this play? They reduced the lines of their best actor by at least a third, and probably the parts of less important persons would suffer at least an equal reduction. If the existing play represents two-thirds of what Greene wrote, the loss of original text would be about 750 lines.

That Elizabethan plays were abridged by some official of the company before the representation of the plays is admitted by all competent editors and critics, but writers on the bad quartos have largely ignored official abridgment as a factor of importance. Recognition of the fact that such abridgment was the customary practice of Elizabethan companies and an indispensable portion of the preliminary work preceding the staging of every play is, in my opinion, vital to an understanding of the relationship between each pair of parallel texts. For an account of my own views on 'Play

Abridgment' the reader is referred to three essays[1] with this title (pp. 77-153) in my book, *Shakespeare and the Homilies* (1934). A very brief summary must suffice here; it forms the opening paragraph (p. 119) of Part III :—

The following facts have been established during the present investigation:

1 Jonson and Shakespeare wrote three-fourths of all extant plays containing more than 3,000 lines a-piece; plays of this length are about one-eighth of the total number, and therefore are the exception and not the rule.
2 The average length of all extant plays (exclusive of Jonson's) with sound texts, written between 1587 and 1616, does not much exceed 2,400 lines.
3 Dramatists and actors concur in stating that in all the important London theatres two hours were allotted for the representation of a play.
4 Not more than 2,400 lines—this number is, in my opinion, over-stated by about 100 lines—could possibly be acted in two hours.
5 The plays presented in the summer months seem to have been no longer than those acted during the winter.
6 The time spent on the whole entertainment either in winter or in summer, at the unroofed theatres, inclusive of play, jig, dances, songs, etc., rarely exceeded the two hours and a half between two o'clock, the hour of commencement, and half-past four o'clock when daylight was failing in winter.

From the facts thus set out was deduced a most important conclusion (p. 120) that :—

if the actors adhered rigidly to the limit of two hours for the representation, all plays exceeding 2,300 to 2,400 lines in length would be liable to abridgment and usually would be abridged.

Accordingly, plays such as *2 Henry VI, 3 Henry VI, Romeo and Juliet Q2*, and *Hamlet Q2* would be reduced by the play-adapter to acting versions not much exceeding 2,300-2,400 lines in length before the actors' parts were transcribed and distributed. Acceptance of this conclusion helps to explain how the plays of Shakespeare were subsequently reduced to the condition of the bad quartos. Between the manuscript of *3 Henry VI* and the printed text of *True Tragedy* there once existed an acting version of about 2,300-2,400 lines, and similarly for each of these parallel texts.

1. Previously printed in *The Review of English Studies*, April, October 1932, January, 1934.

How the progressive destruction of Shakespeare's text may have occurred is set out in tabular form below.

TABLE XIV

PROGRESSIVE DESTRUCTION OF SHAKESPEARE'S TEXT

Name of Play	Number of Lines in		Name of Bad Quarto	Number of Lines in Quarto	Number of Lines of Shakespeare's Play in Quarto
	Play	Acting Version			
2 Henry VI	3,075	2,400	Contention	1,973	1,532
3 Henry VI	2,902	2,400	True Tragedy	2,124	1,896
Romeo and Juliet Q2	2,986	2,400	Romeo and Juliet Q1	2,215	2,051
Hamlet Q2 + Fo. ..	3,762	2,400	Hamlet Q1	2,154	1,735
Totals	12,725	9,600		8,466	7,214

First, 12,725 lines written by the poet were, for purpose of representation, reduced by order of the company to at most 9,600 lines, probably less; the 3,125 lines thus jettisoned amount to nearly three-fourths of the difference between the combined length of the four authentic plays and that of the four 'stolne and surreptitious copies' of which Heminge and Condell speak. Not one line of these official omissions would usually be included in the parts prepared from the acting versions for the players or would be spoken on the stage. Thus nearly a fourth of Shakespeare's best poetry would be unknown to players or play-goers prior to the publication of the first folio or the authentic quartos. Subsequent reduction of the 9,600 lines included in the four hypothetical acting versions to the 8,466 lines printed in the first quartos must be debited to the account of the various reporters and their assistants; if the acting versions were less than the suggested 2,400 lines, the loss due to official abridgment would be increased and that due to corruption lessened. This loss of 1,134 lines is not the half of the pirates' destructive work; the total in the last column shows that they replaced an additional 1,252 lines of what Shakespeare wrote with an equal number of fustian lines of their own. Consequently corruption is responsible for the disappearance of 2,386 lines from these four plays. All told, 5,511 lines, or more than three-sevenths of the authentic texts, have disappeared, and scarcely half of what remains is even moderately preserved. Of the verse the quartos keep in some recognizable form an average of five verses out of nine in the authentic texts, but only two of each five are verbatim.

Hamlet Q1 has suffered the most severe abridgment, mainly because the full text is 600 lines longer than that of any other of these plays. Removal of 1,360 lines from Shakespeare's longest and most famous play in order to reduce it to standard size may seem sacrilege to the arm-chair idolators of the play and the poet, but the stage history of the play is one long chronicle of increasing abridgment. I have tabulated the amount of text left in the various acting versions prepared for the most celebrated tragedian then alive at intervals of about half a century and find a tendency for the play to dwindle to the postulated length of the Elizabethan acting version.

Act	Burbage (1602)	Betterton (1676)	Wilks (1723)	Garrick (1770)	Kean (1820)
I	633		596	560	564
II	413		409	422	442
III	501		687	624	604
IV	301		423	385	358
V	306		540	478	475
	2,154	2,827	2,655	2,469	2,443

Most probably Burbage did not play in an acting version of the play only as long as *Hamlet Q1*, but I do not believe it exceeded 2,400 lines. No copy of the Players' Quarto (1676) is available in Australia, and I have followed Odell in fixing the length of the *Hamlet* in which Betterton played at 2,827 lines. This length is, I think, considerably overstated. No original play of the early Restoration period much exceeds 2,600 lines; moreover, the customary time allotted for the representation of a play was still two hours as in the Carolean period before the civil war. Davenant in his prologue to *Playhouse to be Let,* acted about 1662-3, says his audience may come,

> And join your heads together in one room,
> Where, for your money, you may sit at ease,
> Two hours a day, till Christmas if you please.

My other totals have been carefully checked. Abridgment, as marked in the edition of 1723, the cast for which dates back to about 1715, is well distributed through the five acts; 56 passages are excised from the first act, 41 from the second, 50 from the third, 48 from the fourth and 44 from the fifth, or 239 cuts in all, ranging from half a line to 74 lines in length. Later acting versions of Garrick and Kean added a little to Act II, but decreased each of the others.

Hamlet has been on the acting list of some English company since the play was written, and is one of the few plays whose stage history has been continuous, except for the years of the Commonwealth, to the present day. Three great actors cover the period from 1601 to 1710. Richard Burbage and Joseph Taylor take us to the closing of the theatres in 1642. Almost as soon as his theatre was built in Lincoln's Inn Fields, Sir William Davenant staged *Hamlet* with Thomas Betterton in the name part, and till 1710 two generations of the theatre-going public remained faithful to the *Hamlet* of Betterton. Davenant had written plays during the early years of the reign of Charles I; he must have known how much of the play was acted, and probably explained to the young Betterton how the famous Joseph Taylor played the part of the hero. If the acting time was limited to two hours, at least four hundred lines more than Odell states must have been omitted from the acting edition played by Betterton. In the days of Garrick the play, then 2,450 lines in length, began at six and ended at nine o'clock, and was followed by a farce. After allowing for each of four act-intervals, seven minutes, the actors from 1750 to 1840 took two hours and a half to play an acting version of *Hamlet* not much longer than was customary in Shakespeare's time. This increase in the time taken in representation may be put down to the use of scenery and a more stately and measured method of speaking.

I do not insist that the lengths of the various abridgments made of *Hamlet Q2* from 1661 onwards offer reliable evidence that it was abridged to the same extent and in the same way some sixty years before. Yet the time limit remained unaltered for some years at least, and with the introduction of scenery some increase in the time beyond the customary two hours would be essential if the acting version remained of the same length. Probably Davenant, and Caroline actors such as Hart, Clun, Burt and Mohun maintained the traditions and methods of the pre-restoration stage. Davenant had written many plays for the King's Men, the actors named except Mohun had been members of that company, and it is reasonable to suppose that they staged *Hamlet* as if the gap of twenty years had not existed. Perhaps the acting version of Burbage and Taylor was played by Betterton and his fellows.

Something has been said on the methods of abridgment used by the actors. They were responsible for the numerous cuts that reduced Orlando's part in Dulwich MS. to what we find in Q1, but how many of them are official and how many due to the later activities of the reporter cannot be estimated with any certainty. I have shown in *Shakespeare and the Homilies* (pp. 121-3) that nearly all plays left in manuscript show substantial amounts marked for omission, and that the number of lines so marked does not seem to bear much relation to the length of the play. *Edmund Ironside,* a chronicle play that forms part of the Egerton MS., offers perhaps the best and most instructive example of the methods of abridgment practised by Elizabethan and Jacobean actors. A reprint of this play published by the Malone Society extends to 2,061 lines, but this total included 106 lines of stage directions, etc., and the full amount of text is 1,955 lines. This amount would scarcely take up the full time of two hours for representation, yet 67 passages containing 196 lines are marked for omission; the acting version would be 1,759 lines in length. The passages so marked range in length from one to thirteen lines, and are distributed rather uniformly throughout; half of the omissions are found in the middle third of the play. These cuts consist almost wholly of complete lines or groups of lines, and do not usually involve injury to the sense or breach of continuity or defect of syntax and grammar. Lines are removable so easily partly because the majority of the cuts do not exceed two lines, and partly because the entire play, apart from odd patches of rhyming couplets, is written in the end-stopped decasyllabic blank verse prevalent for some years after 1587. Long speeches suffer most abridgment; the play contains sixty speeches each of ten lines or more, amounting in all to 1,126 lines, equal to sixty per cent. of the full length. From these speeches 178 lines were struck out, whilst 18 only of the remaining 829 lines were marked for omission. This principle of curtailing long speeches more drastically than the dialogue was adopted by the play-adapters of the various companies. Cutting improved the play, ridding it of surplus similes, irrelevant learning, bits of mythology, repetition and over-amplification of common-place thoughts. Comic passages do not lose a line.

Some examples chosen from *Edmund Ironside* will illustrate how, and to some extent why, the players made their cuts. I have expanded the contractions of spelling used in the manuscript, but keep the original spelling and punctuation. Omissions are marked with a vertical line at the side.

Canute holds a council and discusses (ll. 121-7) English disaffection under Danish rule:—

> They all rebell and with conioyned force
> Assault vs manly and from euery parte
> of this perturbed Iland banish vs
> | wee are not able to resist theire powers
> | but fall like leaues before the Northen winde
> | huge heapes of vs lie dead in euery place
> And wee vnles you helpe shall all bee slaine.

Such an amount of amplification invited some pruning, and the simile shared the usual fate of poetic ornament.

Uskataulf counsels moderation (ll. 170-4):—

> I am a Daine renowned Soueraigne
> | You haue experience of my loyaltie
> | And that my Councell is not mercinary
> Yf I weare wise enough to giue aduice
> You should not proue a tyrant but a kinge.

Self-praise was no recommendation to the actors. Canute is impressed by his advice and promises (ll. 210-17) to follow it:—

> I will indeuor to suppresse my rage
> and quench the burninge choller of my harte
> | Which sometimes soe inflames my inward partes
> | as I fall out with my best loued frinds
> | I will therefore so moderate my self
> | As Englishmen shall thinke mee English borne
> I wilbee mild and gentle to my foes
> Yf gentlenes cann winn their stobborne hartes.

Very little is added to the sense by the omitted lines, and the context is not affected by their absence; prolixity was not a royal prerogative on the stage.

Edricus, the villain of the play, has a foot in each camp, and in a long soliloquy explains (ll. 290-2) his scoundrelly arts:—

> They cannot so desemble as I can
> Cloake Cosen Cogge and flatter with the kinge
> | Crouch and seeme Courtious promise and protest,

Even the actors objected to this surplusage of alliterative words; the third line merely expounds the second.

In the next passage the lines omitted (ll. 323-5) injure the sense of what remains:—

> For Edmunds father first did raise mee vppe
> To be a duke for all my villainie
> | And so as oft as I doe looke on him
> | I must remember what hee did for mee
> | And whence I did descend, and what I am
> Which thoughts abace my state most abiectly.

The last line cannot be linked-up with the second; this type of cut is unusual in early plays.

Edricus orders his 'chamberlaine' Stich to beat his master's parents out of his palace, and describes (ll. 524-34) why 'he favours fooles':—

> we must suppresse good witts
> And keepe them vnder, we must fauor fooles
> And with promotions winn their shallow pates
> | A Redie witt would quickly wind vs out
> | And prie into our secrett trecharies
> | And wade as deepe in pollecy as wee
> | But such loose braind and windy headed slaues
> | Such blockheades doltes fooles dunces idiotts
> | Such logger headed rogues are best for vs
> | for wee may worke theire wills to what wee will
> And winn their hartes with gold to anie thinge.

Not a sign indicates that seven lines have been omitted; actors did not like such philosophic reflections as did not assist the progress of the plot.

Canute, incensed at the defection of Turkiellus and Leofricke, orders the mutilation of their sons whom he held as hostages:—

> Therefore I meane to make you worthie men
> Such as the world will afterward reporte
> did suffer torments for theire Countries good
> | Come on I saye prepare your visadges
> | To beare the tokens of eternitie
> prepaire your noses, bid your hands adue.

Repetition is unnecessary especially as Canute and Edric had discussed at length the respective merits of mutilation and of death as punishment. Both these punishments were not uncommon in Elizabeth's days.

Classical platitudes about Fortune were disliked by the actors as will appear in the following extract (ll. 769-76) :—

> dispaire not noble kinge tyme comes in tyme
> Know yee nott tis a deede of pollecye
> in fickell Chaunce to Crosse your mightienesse
> | for elce in Tyme you might dismounte the Queene
> | And throw her headlonge from her rowlinge stone
> | And take her whirlinge wheele into your hand
> I tell your grace Chaunce euer enuies wise men
> and fauors fooles promoting them aloft.

Two archbishops engage in a battle of abuse. York thus addresses (ll. 833-8) Canterbury who demands homage from a 'proud, irreligious Prelate' :—

> Noe, Canterbury, noe
> I humble me to God and not to thee
> A traytor a betrayor of his kinge
> | A rebell, a prophane preist, a Pharesie,
> | A parrasite, an enemie to peace
> A foe to trewth and to religion.

This excision omits abuse for which the rest of the text of the play gives little or no excuse. In the Elizabethan drama priest does not insult priest; it was the peculiar province and privilege of the laity.

Another example comes from the speech of a messenger who reports to Edmund the invasion of the Danes :—

> They swarme along thy costs like little gnates
> Ouer a riuer in a Summers night,
> | or like to bees when they begine to flight
> | Soe Comes theis Daines prepared to fitt to fight
> Theire Battaile mane of Three score Thowsand men
> with bristle poynted speeres vpright stand
> | shewes like a shred groues of Ashes tall
> | or elce a wood of pines and ceaders small

Three similes in six lines of a messenger's speech! Figures of speech were rarely retained by the actors, certainly not three in eight lines.

In the final scene Edric proposes that the war shall be ended by a duel between Canute and Edmund (ll. 1886-1897) :—

What then is thend of this your en(d)les grudge?
None other but when all your men bee slaine,
You then must fight alone or els accord,
| And hee that then is kinge shall rule noe men,
| Nor gouerne nations, for consuminge warr
| Will quite devoure this solatary Ile,
| Not leauinge anie ouer whome to rule,
| (Nor) to resist forraine inuacions.
| Yf loue of kingedomes bee the cause of this
| Suppresse the boyleinge of your haughtie mindes
You haue approued your souldiers forwardnesse
Then now at last shake hands and ioyne in league.

The seven lines omitted only expand the second and third, and are unneeded train-bearers to a simple thought.

These examples help us to understand how the play-adapter went about his necessary task. He knew his audience loved an interesting story, packed with plenty of action and told in simple language, and rid the play of similes, amplificatory passages, platitudes, philosophic reflections, repetition, classical common-places, and literary ornament, wherever they could be spared without injury to the context.

Shakespeare was the first dramatist to tell us the amount of time allotted by the actors for the performance of a play in the public unroofed theatres. His reference to 'the two howres traffique of our Stage' in *Romeo and Juliet Q1* is not later than 1596, and his second reference to the 'two short houres' in *Henry VIII* came in 1613. He wrote only seven plays with less than the maximum number of lines that could be played in two hours, and thirty longer plays that would need, each of them, some abridgment. Abridged they were in his own days, and they have been abridged for more than three centuries since. (See p. 122.)

When the author had read his play to the company, the partners would allocate parts according to the known ability of the various members of the company—sharers or hired actors. In some plays the important characters might be assumed by the sharers. Thus in *True Tragedy* nine characters (including Margaret and Elizabeth) speak all but 390 lines, in *Romeo and Juliet Q1* eleven characters (inclusive of Juliet, Lady Capulet and the Nurse) speak more than nine-tenths of the play, and in *Hamlet Q1* ten characters (including Ophelia and the Queen) account for seven-eighths of speeches and dialogue. Thus seven sharers in *True Tragedy,* and eight in *Romeo and Juliet Q1* and *Hamlet Q1* together with their apprentices could take almost the whole of these plays. Moreover, by doubling or even trebling parts, the expense of hiring actors could be lessened. In *Contention* Duke Humphrey is murdered before the end of Act III, scene i, Cardinal Beaufort dies at the end of the third act, and Suffolk at the end of the following scene; thus three actors would be available for parts such as Jack Cade, Iden and Young Clifford. In *True Tragedy* York dies at the end of the first act, Clifford dies at the beginning of the last scene of the second act; the same actors could be used to take the parts of Oxford and Hastings. So in *Romeo and Juliet Q1* the player of Mercutio or Tybalt could double the part of the apothecary. Probably at the first reading certain passages might be marked for omission.

Next the play would be sent to the Master of the Revels, and might be returned with a conditional allowance, dependent on the excision of certain passages or, less usually, scenes. Ordinarily his markings were neither numerous nor important, for such a company as that of Shakespeare's kept on the blind side of authority. Then the play would be handed over to the play-adapter to prepare it for representation.

OFFICIAL ABRIDGMENT—THE ACTING VERSION

Prompt making of the acting version was desirable for several reasons. First the number of actors and hired men must be fixed, and this could not be done till the play-adapter had done his work; then the plot or 'plat,' i.e., the outline of the play divided into scenes and acts, and containing the names of the actors and the parts taken by them in order of entry, with the various exits and entrances must be prepared and hung up in the play-house; next, properties and costumes must be bought or refurbished for use, and finally the scribe must write out and check thoroughly with the author's manuscript each part before rehearsals could begin.

How would the play-adapter set about his task? His main concern would be to preserve a coherent, intelligible story or, as Fletcher puts it, 'a good tale Told in two hours.' Purple patches

K

meant nothing to him. He would keep the main plot untouched and would carefully retain all scenes and episodes essential to development and understanding. Shakespeare's bad quartos such as *Henry V Q1* and *Merry Wives Q1* suggest that scenes were omitted. *True Tragedy and Hamlet Q1* have each two non-consecutive scenes of Shakespeare's play combined in one; but these plays are not acting versions of the authentic plays but rather the garbled remains of acting versions which have been wrecked by the actors. Examination of fourteen manuscript plays bearing the customary marks of official abridgment reveals that not one scene has been deleted in any play. Three of Shakespeare's parallel good texts have each a scene present in one text and missing in the other. *Titus Andronicus* has a scene (III, ii) in the folio version which is not found in any of the quartos; style, versification, diction and tone alike suggest that it belongs to a period not later than the date of the first quarto. *2 Henry IV Q2* has a scene not found in Q1. Critics think that it was omitted by accident; I have endeavoured to prove (*Shakespeare and the Homilies*, pp. 154-218) that this play, and especially this scene, was drastically censored. *King Lear Q1* contains a scene (IV, iii) not in the first folio version; this scene, unlike those in the two plays above, is of importance to the plot in that it prepares the spectators for the entrance of Cordelia in the next scene. This omission may be part of an official abridgment, but the folio text is not an acting version, because this abridged version would be five hundred lines longer than the maximum length of a two-hour play.

Of methods adopted by Restoration and modern abridgers no trace exists in any play belonging to the Elizabethan or Jacobean periods. Such perversions as Dryden's *Tempest*, Colley Cibber's *Richard III* and *King John*, Tate's *Lear* and *Coriolanus*, Garrick's *Hamlet* and *Winter's Tale*, Kemble's *Coriolanus* and Irving's *Merchant of Venice* were impossible in the great age of our drama. Henslowe records a number of payments for 'mending' or making additions to plays, but wherever the two editions are extant, as in *Spanish Tragedy* or *Malcontent* or *Fair Quarrel*, we find the text of the original edition remains practically untouched and the 'additions' take the form of increasing the length of scenes that had proved popular. Two new scenes and an Induction are found in the third edition of *Malcontent* besides additions to several other scenes, but no additional characters, costumes, properties or parts would be necessary.

In making an acting version passages would be struck out mainly because they were, in the opinion of the play-adapter, unlikely to prove interesting to the audience or would not lend themselves to a display of effective recitation. In general, he omitted excursions into the arid realms of philosophy, sage reflections on life, conduct and character, over-much moralizing, unnecessary displays of learning and classical allusions, for the good reason that such topics were not concerned with the action and were of little interest to the majority of the auditors. For the same reasons similes, elaborated comparisons, over-worked metaphors, excessive word-play, out-of-date topical references, iteration and amplification of ideas previously expressed were always in danger of suppression. A line or two in one place, a short passage in another, a long speech or even an episode might disappear, and not a sign of their existence remain. Continual practice would make an intelligent play-cutter very skilful in his choice of what might be left out without injury to the plot; he usually planned his omissions so that no noticeable hiatus occurred in the immediate context. Almost invariably he left sense and metre to look after themselves and adjustments are very rare. Professor Wilson suggests[2] that the making of an abridged version 'would of necessity involve a certain amount of adaptation since after a rent had been made in the text it would generally be necessary to stitch the ends together.' Later he elaborated this statement: 'The adapter's whole object was to cut the play down and his stitch work would take the form of one or at most two lines composed of the material he had thrown overboard.' How far do these statements square with the known facts? Excellent examples of the methods adopted by the official adapter or abbreviator exist in the parallel good texts of Shakespeare. The references below are to the various volumes of the Cambridge *Shakespeare* in which the plays named are found.

Richard II

Ten passages of the version of the first quarto are missing in the Folio text, and in each instance the gap has been closed by bringing

2. *Times Literary Supplement*, 9 January, 1919, p. 18.

the broken ends together. One of these (1.3.129-133) has the sense and grammar of the context destroyed; two others (3.1.32 and 5.3.99) affect metre and rhyme respectively, and another (3.2.29-32) leaves Aumerle's comment on Carlisle's speech without much point. No attempt has been made to 'stitch' the rent. Only one piece of 'stitchery' is found in this play. When the abdication scene (4.1.154-317) was censored, some one, perhaps not Shakespeare, repaired the torn text quite well, but by retaining ll. 321-3 made it clear that something had been omitted.

2 HENRY IV Q1

Seven of fourteen omissions in Q1 of text found in the folio version require no adjustment, but of the remainder one (1.1.189-209) leaves the preceding two lines of Morton's speech in Q1 without any meaning or connection with the context; two others (1.3.85-108; 2.3.23-45) affect the verse, whilst the sense, verse or context is injured by omissions in such passages as 4.1.55-79; 4.1.103-139; 4.2.117 and 4.5.76. The folio version of 4.2.101-2 emends the verse of the quarto passage, and it emends the quarto text (3.1.53-6 and 4.1.93, 95) apparently to restore verse and sense.

RICHARD III

At least sixty omissions of text present in the folio version occur in Q1; they affect plot, sense, context and verse. Most of them need no surgery because lines or groups of lines could be excised from all our early plays without disorder in the verse. In one passage only was any mending done, viz., 4.1.2-6.

HAMLET

Twenty-seven part-lines, lines or longer passages present in Q2 are omitted in the folio version; on the other hand twenty-six such portions of text present in the folio are not in Q2. Many of these occur in prose, but neither these nor most of those in verse interfere much with sense, context, grammar or metre. I note among the folio excisions seven that affect metre or sense. One instance only (4.7.69-82) provides an example of the adapter's patchwork; he prefixed the word 'some' to the words 'two months since' (l. 82) and thus filled out the words 'And call it accident' of line 68 into a metrical line.

OTHELLO

Q1 omits forty passages of text found in the folio version; the folio omits seven passages present in Q1. Of those omitted in the first quarto fourteen injure metre, sense or context. They are 1.2.20, 1.2.72-7, 1.3.63, 1.1.118, 2.1.39-40, 2.1.82, 2.1.156, 3.1.55, 3.3.387-394, 3.3.457-464, 3.4.196-7, 4.2.152-165, 4.3.58-61 and 5.2.249-51. Not one of these shows any sign of the adapter's 'stitchery.'

KING LEAR

This play has seventy-three cuts, more than half of them in the folio text. Almost a third of them involves verse disorder, defects in sense or difficulty in the immediate context. Four passages show some evidence of mending, viz., 1.1.38-43, 1.1.80-4, 2.2.136-142 and 4.1.6-9.

I have examined also the texts of such plays preserved in manuscript as have passages marked for abridgment, and have come to the conclusion that the adapter struck out as much as he thought fit, and did not take upon him the task of healing or even bandaging the wounds made in the author's text. He was satisfied if he avoided injury to the story or plot, or did not create too noticeable a gap in sense or action; limping lines he left to the actors whose job it was to declaim them. Let it not be forgotten that neither actors nor audience in the theatre nor readers of our early quarto texts were likely to discover metrical excess or defect; many of our more sophisticated readers would scarcely notice many of these shortcomings were they not forced upon their notice by the commentators.

We are not without knowledge of the methods adopted by the abridger of plays acted by the company for which Shakespeare wrote plays. Some of his plays, viz., *Richard III, Richard II, 2 Henry IV, Hamlet, Othello, King Lear* and *Troilus and Cressida*, have passages in the folio version of 1623 which are not in one or other of the earlier-dated quartos, and likewise passages in these quartos which are not in the first folio. Editors usually make up a composite text for each of these plays from the two parallel texts, each supplying passages wanting in the other. They reasonably assume that this composite text represents all that Shakespeare wrote, and are entitled, except perhaps in *Richard III,* to the opinion expressed by them that all the additions found in the folio were written simultaneously with what appears in the earliest quartos. They explain these differences between each pair of parallel texts of this type by suggesting that each is derived from a manuscript of the play shortened, but each version shortened differently, for the purpose of staging. I agree that these omissions were made for abridgment, but think it most improbable that either the quarto text or the folio text of any of these seven plays was itself an acting version. Even if the sum of the passages abridged in both versions is deducted from the length of the received text, the total amount of curtailment is far too small to justify us in terming the resulting abridged play an acting version.

If *Richard II* be excluded, these parallel texts include the three longest of Shakespeare's plays; the length of the received text of the shortest, *2 Henry IV,* is 3,180 lines and that of the longest, *Hamlet,* is 3,762 lines. Not much reduction is to be noted in the early quartos; their lengths range from 3,009 lines (*2 Henry IV Q1*) to 3,668 lines (*Hamlet Q2*), whilst the lengths of the first folio texts vary from 2,926 lines (*King Lear*) to 3,568 lines (*Richard III*). All these first or second quartos exceed 3,000 lines a-piece and cannot be acting versions. From 1614 the average length of plays declined and about 1620 it was about 2,250 lines, at which length it remained steady for over twenty years. Yet the average length of the six folio plays named above is nearly a thousand lines longer than that of the plays written in 1623. It seems nonsense to suggest that the folio texts of *Richard III, 2 Henry IV, Othello* and *Troilus and Cressida,* which have lost respectively 32, 40, 8 and 7 lines of the full received text, are acting versions—they average 3,314 lines each, and the shortest is 3,140 lines or nearly 900 lines longer than the usual length of plays then being written for the public stage. I can offer no explanation why the folio texts of these four plays should be greater than those of the respective quarto texts, except that Heminge and Condell tried to offer them to the readers 'cur'd, and perfect of their limbes'; nor do I attempt to explain why the folio *Hamlet* and *King Lear* should have omitted so many lines already published. Any explanation is a guess.

Abridgment in three of the early quartos seems a haphazard affair; cuts made in *Hamlet Q2* and *King Lear Q1* affect only a few scenes of each play. In *Hamlet Q2* only the second scene of the second act and the last scene of the play lose any substantial number of lines; all told, 35 lines only were struck out from nearly 2,120 lines in Acts III-V, and from fifteen of the twenty scenes abridgment took a total of six lines of text. So in *King Lear Q1* two-thirds of the omitted lines come from the first half of the play and 28 lines only from the second half; fourteen scenes of the quarto contribute three lines only to the abridgment. Five scenes only of *2 Henry IV Q1* can be described as abridged, for losses of one, two or three lines may be put down to other causes. *Richard III* and *Othello Q1* each show some short excisions in the majority of the scenes, but in six scenes only does the abridgment exceed ten lines a scene. The largest amount struck out of *Richard III Q1* is 81 lines in the very long fourth scene of the fourth act; in *Othello Q1* the third scene of the fourth act loses 47 lines.

One remarkable feature of the abridgment in *2 Henry IV* is that verse scenes are abridged and prose scenes unabridged in Q1, whilst poetic scenes are unabridged and prose scenes abridged in the folio version. After the first scene of the fourth act no abridgment except of two or three lines occurs to the end of the play in either version.

Abridgment of the folio texts of *Hamlet* and *King Lear* is heaviest in the second halves of these plays; if we include in this portion Act III, scene iv of *Hamlet,* and Act III, scenes vi and vii of *King Lear,* we find that four-fifths of the total abridgment occur here. On the other hand, the second half of *Othello Q1* contains about 70 per cent. of the total abridgment. This contrasts oddly with the result already given for *2 Henry IV*. In *Richard III Q1* cuts are distributed evenly throughout the play, whilst in *Troilus and Cressida Q1* the total amount is almost negligible. I have said that not one of these parallel texts is an acting version. Further, if the number of lines omitted in the Quarto is added to the number omitted in the folio and the total deducted from the number in the received text there will remain a *Hamlet* of 3,444 lines, a *Richard III* of 3,355 lines, a *Troilus and Cressida* of 3,253 an *Othello* of 2,974 lines and a *King Lear* of 2,814 lines; the shortest of these would require at least two hours and a half to be acted, and the two longest a full three hours. Yet the passages excised from these parallel texts were undoubtedly portions not spoken on the public stage, and serve to illustrate the manner in which the adapter got rid of play-surplusage. To save space the passages discussed will not be quoted in full; references are to the lining in the Cambridge Shakespeare (1863-66).

RICHARD III

Few critics will maintain that *Richard III Q1* is an early acting version; to represent nearly 3,400 lines of a play so full of action would occupy three hours even under the primitive stage conditions then existent. Only a few more lines are missing in Q1 than were marked for omission in the manuscript of *Edmund Ironside,* an English history play of scarcely half the full length of *Richard III.* Not many passages of any size have been struck out of Q1 and only one is missing in the folio text. Heminge and Condell were not altogether unmindful of their promise to give as complete a text of their 'fellow' Shakespeare's plays as they could.

(i) This play kept the stage for forty years; the plays on Henry VI 'which oft our Stage hath showne' were probably off the acting list before 1599. Accordingly, it would be necessary to cut out references to events such as are referred to in 1.2.156-167, where Gloster alludes to the deaths of his father and his brother Rutland described in the first act of *3 Henry VI.*

(ii) Clarence's pathetic prayer (1.4.69-72) for his wife and children has been excised without injury to sense or verse. Other passages could be better spared.

(iii) Two omissions, 2.2.89-100 and 2.2.123-140, were apparently made to reduce the number of actors present in this scene. Dorset, Rivers and Hastings have no entry in Q1; their parts are omitted and with them two speeches of Buckingham's and Gloster's. Nothing is lost by striking out the prosy platitudes uttered by Dorset and Rivers before the entrance of Gloster and other lords, nor do the speeches of Rivers, Hastings, etc., contain anything necessary or important. With nearly fifty speaking parts to provide for, much doubling and trebling of the minor parts would be necessary; three citizens were required for the following scene, and these cuts would release three actors for these parts.

(iv) Four lines have been removed (3.4.104-7) from the end of the scene prior to the execution of Hastings; they repeat what has been said in the earlier part of the concluding episode.

(v) Three lines spoken by Gloster (3.5.103-5)

> Goe Louell with all speed to Doctor Shaw,
> Goe thou to Fryer Penker, bid them both
> Meet me within this houre at Baynards Castle,

are not in Q1, probably because neither Shaw nor Penker takes any part or appears in the play. Shakespeare seems to have written these lines because Holinshed gives them prominence as supporters of Richard's claims, and forgot to use them afterwards.

(vi) Ten lines (3.7.144-153) of Gloster's speech in reply to Buckingham's formal offer of the throne have been cut out. They do little more than elaborate the thought contained in the preceding three lines, and delay rather than advance the action; they are unnecessary because the royal orator knew all the tricks of the orator's trade.

(vii) Elizabeth's farewell to the Tower (4.1.98-104) is omitted in Q1. This omission does not injure the plot, verse or context, but illustrates the indifference, if not the active distaste, of the actors for poetry. It can be spared, but so can most of the scene after the entrance of Lord Stanley.

(viii) Nearly seventy lines (4.4.221-234, 288-342) of the long scene in which Richard seems to succeed in winning the consent of Queen Elizabeth to his marriage with his own niece have been omitted in Q1; we may well wonder why the actors did not strike out all this lifeless imitation of the lively scene between Richard and Anne. Not a scrap of action breaks the monotonous spate of false rhetoric, falser emotions, specious pleading and verbal quibbles. Perhaps this episode is an early 'addition' made to the play by Shakespeare on a revival; curiously enough, Richard's previous references to this projected marriage occur in two short soliloquies, one in each of the two previous scenes.

(ix) One only of the folio's omissions (4.2.103-120) is of any length. It is the famous 'clock' passage. Why it was omitted in the enlarged version I cannot suggest, but even Cibber's butchery preserved this episode, so characteristic of Shakespeare's Richard.

RICHARD II

Q1 omits the abdication scene (4.1.154-318) but little else; the folio version, following Q4, restores this but leaves out several passages amounting in all to fifty lines.

(i) Richard's speech could without disadvantage lose such a rhetorical and non-dramatic flourish as the ten lines (1.3.129-138) beginning with 'And for we thinke etc.,' and still retain all that is necessary to the sense. Of these lines the second group of five is adjectivally dependent on the first group, and may be omitted without doing any harm to the context; the folio version omits lines 129-133 and retains lines 134-138 beginning with 'Which so rouz'd up etc.,' making the passage unintelligible.

(ii) Gaunt had advocated in council the banishment of his son, the Duke of Hereford, and then made three speeches in palliation of the acceptance of his own advice. Four lines (1.3.239-242) beginning 'O had it been etc.,' are omitted in the folio version probably because they repeat what he had said before.

(iii) Nearly half (1.3.268-293) of the leave-taking between father and son was struck out in the folio. Each loses a speech which the actor would have found tiresome to recite; the audience would have thought this prattle to be tedious. The cut is excellent. The parting is too long and too fantastically expressed, and harps monotonously on the one theme. How contrary to nature it is will be perceived at once by one who reads the similar scene of *Coriolanus*.

(iv) Carlisle briefly expounds, bishop-like, the theory of divine right (3.2.27-8), and adds four lines to the effect that providence is on the side of the big battalions. In the folio these four lines are omitted, and Aumerle's reply to them is left in the air.

(v) Eight lines (4.1.52-9) have been excised from the quarrel between the wolvish peers. The adapter did well to rid the play of such useless repetition; the folio did not provide an entry for 'another Lord' who challenges Aumerle, and it may be that a reduction of the cast explains this omission.

2 HENRY IV Q1

Elsewhere[3] I have given reasons for my opinion that certain passages excised from Q1 were marked for omission by the censor.

3. *Shakespeare and the Homilies* (1934), pp. 154-218.

This criticism does not apply to four passages discussed below.

(i) Fourteen lines (1.1.166-179) beginning 'You cast th' euent of Warre, etc.,' represent Morton's musings on the death of Harry Percy; perhaps they were struck out because Lord Bardolph says much the same in half the number of lines.

(ii) Morton's next speech (1.1.189-209) was, I think, censored though some of it ought to have been retained. As it stands the cut is a very bad one; the two lines of it remaining (ll. 187-188) are meaningless. If the first and last lines of the omitted passage were retained, some meaning would be given to the opening two lines.

(iii) Lord Bardolph is the principal speaker in the first part of the third scene. He loses four lines (1.3.21-4) in the folio version; these merely expand the thought in his opening lines:—

> But if without him we be thought to feeble,
> My iudgement is, we should not step too farre.

(iv) Most of his next speech (ll. 36-55) is missing in the folio. This passage (1.3.36-55) contains a simile extending to four lines and a long drawn-out comparison between building a house and planning a conspiracy and rebellion. Such figurative speeches always fared badly.

(v) Kate Percy's praise of her dead husband (2.3.9-45) was heavily retrenched partly because no woman was allowed to speak thirty-seven consecutive lines on the Elizabethan stage, but mainly because the eulogy of Hotspur by whose light,

> Did all the Cheualrie of England moue
> To do braue Acts. He was (indeed) the Glasse
> Wherein the Noble-Youth did dresse themselues,

might recall thoughts of Essex, the Elizabethan Hotspur, then in disgrace.

HAMLET

Of the two good texts the quarto is the longer abridgment, but nearly twelve hundred lines more must be struck out of the shorter folio version to provide such an acting version as could be played in two hours upon the stage of an Elizabethan theatre. Q1 is very corrupt, but preserves some lines of Q2 that are not in the folio and some lines of the folio which are not in Q2.

(i) Barnardo's comment on Horatio's story of Fortinbras and Hamlet's father, and Horatio's reminiscences of Julius Caesar and his dissertation on astrology fill the time between the first and the second appearances of the ghost, but do not develop the action or story. This passage (1.1.108-125) beginning,

I think it be no other but ee'n so,

has never been spoken on the public stage until recently, if acting versions are reliable. Shakespeare wrote sufficient to provide for a four-minute interval between the successive appearances of the apparition; in Q1 the interval would be two and a half minutes; in 1829 it was reduced to a minute, because Fortinbras and all references to him were omitted from the cast.

(ii) Polonius' first speech (1.2.58-61) in Q2 is reduced to a line and a half in the folio. This is enough of his circumlocutory chatter, but Q1 retains the first and the last of the four lines; this suggests that the earliest acting version kept these two lines at least.

(iii) Another long passage (1.4.17-38) of Q2, which is omitted in the folio, includes all of Hamlet's long speech prior to the entrance of the ghost. His last line in the folio is,

More honour'd in the breach, then the obseruance.

Such philosophic reflections as follow this line rarely survived.

(iv) Another small snippet (1.4.75-8) omitted in folio comes from the last four lines of Horatio's speech, beginning 'The very place puts toyes etc.,' and describing the dizziness due to looking downwards from a height. This fragment of reflective comment is non-dramatic.

(v) Q2 has not lost 100 lines by abridgment, but a long passage (2.2.235-263), beginning 'Let me question more in particular,' in which Hamlet describes Denmark as 'a prison,' and the spies arouse his suspicion by harping on the word 'ambition,' has been excised. Perhaps the censor is responsible for the disappearance of that portion which referred to the native land of Queen Anne, but the plot seems to demand a reason for Hamlet's attitude to his old school-fellows.

(vi) Q2 loses also the sentence 'The Clowne shall make those laugh whose lungs are tickled a' th' sere.' This is in Q1, the line was spoken on the stage, and therefore Q2 was not an acting version.

(vii) Another long omission in Q2 comes from the same scene; these lines (2.2.325-345) refer to what the folio styles 'an ayrie of Children, little Yases.' Enough of this passage, e.g., 'noueltie carries it away,' 'priuate playes,' and 'the humour of children' is found in Q1 to make it certain that some lines at least were spoken on the stage. What is extraordinary is that Q2 omitted topical matter when it was comparatively fresh and would be appreciated by readers, whilst the folio included it twenty years later when it was so stale that it could scarcely be understood. Perhaps the company did not wish to offend the queen, who was in 1604 a patroness of one company of children but had died four years before the publication of the folio.

(viii) Several passages found in Q2 were omitted in the folio version of the long scene between Hamlet and his mother. The first (3.4.71-6), beginning with 'sence sure youe haue, etc.,' is a neat cut, which injures neither sense, verse nor context; it is a semi-philosophic reflection well-suited to the character of the prince but not likely to satisfy public taste; this criticism applies equally well to the omission of ll. 78-81, beginning with 'Eyes without feeling, etc.' Both of these occur in the one speech. Another two such omissions of Hamlet's musing on life, habit and customs occur in 3.4.161-5, 167-70. The first passage, beginning with 'That monster custome etc.,' ends in the middle of line 165, with the result that the line preceding the omitted passage,

Assume a vertue if you haue it not,

has become a 'fourteener' in the folio, the end of line 165 'refraine to night' being added to it. Here the omission removes non-dramatic matter as it does in the second passage.

(ix) This scene in the folio version loses nine more lines (3.4.202-210). They begin 'Ther's letters sealed etc.,' and explain Hamlet's distrust of his schoolfellows and prepare the spectators for the events to come. They are not necessary to the story, and were treated as a piece of repetition by the adapter.

(x) Four lines (4.1.41-4) of the king's speech, beginning with the line, 'Whose whisper ore the worlds dyameter,' are omitted in the folio. Some words have dropped out of the preceding line with the result that these lines are not in syntactical connection with it. This sententious passage, tagged with a simile, would certainly have been struck out by the adapter.

(xi) Q1 and Q2 both preserve a prose passage (4.3.26-8) which is missing in folio, but necessary to the sense of what follows.

(xii) Hamlet's conversation with the captain and his final soliloquy beginning 'How all occasions doe informe against me' (4.4.9-56) are found only in Q2. Not a line of this omitted passage is in Q1 or the folio or in any acting version since Shakespeare's day. Modern critics make much of the dramatic contrast between the man of action and the man of thought, but neither the conversation nor the incident itself nor the soliloquy has any dramatic importance; on the stage the soliloquy would be 'caviare to the general.'

(xiii) Several omissions occur in the folio text of Act IV, scene vii. Three passages (4.7.69-82, 101-103, 115-124) have been removed without much loss to plot, action or sense. Claudius subtly comments on Laertes' skill in fencing, 'A very riband in the cap of youth,' on 'the Scrimoures' of the French nation, and on the gradual decay of filial affection as time goes on; however artistic and philosophic these reflections may be, on the stage they are superfluous and dramatically nought.

(xiv) Q2 omits one passage (5.2.68-81) only in the last scene; of this half a line, 'To quit him with this arme?' is needed to complete the sense of what preceded. Perhaps the vertical line, placed by the adapter at the left hand side of the lines to be excised, extended further upward than was intended. Most of the rest could be omitted, but the presence in Q1 (xviii. 1-2) of almost two lines,

> beleeue mee, it greeues me much Horatio,
> That to Leartes I forgot my selfe,

substantially identical with two folio lines, proves that portion of this omitted passage was spoken on the Elizabethan stage.

(xv) Much the longest passage (5.2.104-136) omitted in the folio comes from the 'roasting' of the fop Osric by Hamlet. This passage—and very much else—is not in Q1, and has suffered the same fate in almost all acting versions. Probably the fashionable jargon here satirized was out of date in a few years. So also Horatio's aside (5.2.147-8) which breaks the dialogue between Osric and Hamlet has disappeared in the folio. Q2 retains the short dialogue between 'A Lord' and Hamlet after Osric leaves the stage; the folio omits it and provides no entrance for such a lord. In Q1 the 'Bragart Gentleman,' that is, Osric, gives Hamlet the message which 'A Lord' gives to Hamlet in Q2. Perhaps the cut in the folio text was made to save the expense of the actor needed to take the part of 'A Lord.'

OTHELLO Q1

Q1 is 3,066 lines in length, the folio version 3,222 lines, but each text is far too long to be an acting version. All the passages of any length omitted by the play-adapter come from Q1.

(i) After his first line, most of Roderigo's long answer (1.1.121-137) to Brabantio's questions has been struck out as a piece of repetition by the adapter who supposed, probably correctly, that Iago's malicious and licentious insults have told the Senator and the audience the story of Desdemona's elopement; the sense of the four lines left in Q1 of Roderigo's speech suffers a little, but on the stage it would pass.

(ii) When Brabantio finds his daughter with Othello he charges his newly-made son-in-law with enchanting Desdemona and binding her 'in Chaines of Magick,' and continues in like strain (1.2.72-7); this passage the adapter of Q1 omits as unneeded repetition. The last line thus omitted,

I therefore apprehend and do attach thee,

is requisite for the sense of the lines that follow.

(iii) Perhaps the part of *Othello* that could be best spared is the opening portion of the third scene up to the entrance of a messenger bringing accurate news of the numbers and destination of the Turkish fleet. Seven lines (1.3.24-30) of this scene are omitted in Q1. Whether this fleet was making for Rhodes or Cyprus is of little importance—the story would be unchanged.

(iv) Two short passages have been excised from the exceedingly long third scene of the third act. The first (3.3.387-394) beginning 'By the world, etc.,' exhibits the self-tortured inquietude of Othello's mind, of which this and other scenes have enough and to spare; while the second is the famous passage (3.3.457-464) 'Like to the Pontic Sea, etc.' Such similes rarely escaped the adapter's pen-stroke of omission.

(v) Probably the heavy cut (4.2.152-165) of Desdemona's speech beginning 'Heere I kneele etc.,' is due largely to the fact

that the lines written for female characters were more severely cut
down than those for men.

(vi) In Q1 the 'willow' song and nearly all references to it have
been excised, perhaps because the boy that played the part of
Desdemona could not sing. Hence not only this passage (4.3.30-51)
beginning 'I have much to do etc.,' has disappeared, but certain
consequential cuts (4.3.53-55) and (5.2.249-251) were made.

(vii) Emilia's long lecture (4.3.83-100) on the duties of
husbands to wives, commencing 'But I do thinke etc.,' would not be
popular with an audience almost entirely masculine.

(viii) Omission of the passage (5.2.188-196), which follows
Emilia's startling statement in the presence of Othello, Iago,
Montano and Gratiano,

> My Mistris heere lyes murthered in her bed,

can scarcely be due to the actors. Before their entrance she had
shrieked (5.2.169-170), in spite of Othello's threats,

> Helpe, helpe, hoe, helpe,
> The Moore hath kill'd my Mistris, Murther, Murther.

Evidently the new-comers had not heard these words spoken from
within, for immediately after line 188 comes from all present 'O
Heavens, forefend' (l. 189). The comments of Montano and
Gratiano (also omitted) prove that these persons hear of the
murder not before but after they enter the bed-room.

(ix) From Othello's speech after he had obtained 'a Sword of
Spaine, the Ice-brookes temper,' seven lines (5.2.269-275) are
missing in Q1. This cut is not a good one and extends a line too
far ; the last line,

> Now : how dost thou looke now ? Oh ill-Starr'd wench,

is required to ease the excessive abruptness in the change of subject
due to the excision.

King Lear

If the omissions from quarto and folio are added this play has
lost more than any other of the seven that are being reviewed ; if
this total is deducted from that of the received text a play of 2,800
lines remains or about 500-600 lines too much for the two hours
allotted for playing. Some of the early omissions in Q1 improve
the play for intelligent auditors by removing passages in which the

same thought is expressed in different words. Thus Lear's 'fast intent' (1.1.37),

To shake all Cares and Businesse from our Age,

is repeated subtantially ten lines lower in the folio, but is omitted in Q1, and the same is true of ll. 43-5, which reappear in different words in ll. 81-3 of the folio but not in Q1. Similarly in the second scene Q1 omits ll. 103-8 and the folio ll. 137-143. Both passages expand or elaborate what Gloucester says in ll. 98-103. In the next scene the folio version leaves out ll. 17-21 and 25-6, each of which repeats in different words what Goneril said earlier in the same scene. Very heavy toll has been taken of the fool's part probably because he 'is not altogether fool,' though the taste for crude clowning never dies in the groundlings; thus it came about that the adapter struck out 2.4.45-53 and 3.2.79-95 in Q1 and in the folio 1.4.135-150 and 3.6.17-54. Twelve omitted lines (1.4.317-328) of dialogue between Goneril and Albany beginning 'This man hath good Counsell,' etc., seem necessary to the plot in that they present Goneril's reasons for her behaviour to Lear. Three lines in the folio (2.1.10-12) alluding to 'likely Warres' between Albany and Cornwall are omitted in Q1, but later this news appears in both texts. In the folio version eight lines (3.1.7-15) of 'a Gentleman's' description of Lear in the storm are omitted, probably because Lear will be on the stage two or three minutes later.

Censorship probably played a part throughout King Lear. Q1 cuts out (3.1.22-9) a reference to 'Servants,'

Which are to France the Spies and Speculations
Intelligent of our State,

and the folio removes the next thirteen lines (3.1.30-42) referring to 'a power' that is coming from France. Nearly half of Act III, scene vi is omitted in folio; perhaps it did not play too well on the stage.

Madness was popular then as a dramatic theme and spectacle, but Goneril's arraignment (3.6.17-54) was a trial with a phantom in the dock. Lear was mad, but the audience knew that Edgar was shamming, and the fool was no clown. The natural end of this scene comes at line 95; Kent's speech and Edgar's platitudes were deservedly excised as superfluous.

In the next scene we sup full with horrors, and Shakespeare wrote some servants' chatter (3.7.98-106) to soothe our feelings;

L

this has been omitted in the folio; on the other hand Q1 omits three lines of Edgar's wisdom which open the next scene. Edgar's catalogue of fiends (4.1.59-63) may have been preserved in Q1 out of compliment to King James whose *Daemonologie* had been reissued in London during the plague year, 1603. James and his queen agreed little better than Albany and Goneril; the quarrel (4.2.31-50; 53-59, 62-8) between the latter may have been a politic omission because Albany bore a Scottish title. Perhaps, too, some members of the audience may have had their enjoyment spoilt by such recollections of their domestic life. No difficulty follows the removal of the third scene of the fourth act—a conversation between Kent and a 'Gentleman' without a scrap of action. Omission of the opening eight lines concerning the invading French army would have satisfied the censor; the rest relates to the reappearance of Cordelia in England—and may be omitted because she is on the stage in the next scene.

Once more a small gossiping episode (4.7.86-98) is well left out by the adapter; it spoils the natural close of this scene which should end on the reconciliation of father and daughter. Another short incident (5.3.205-222) disappears without much loss when the actors struck out Edgar's story of his meeting with Kent; were the Jacobean actors and audiences becoming too sophisticated to accept the dramatic convention of a double disguise?

While it is difficult to explain convincingly why a certain passage present in the quarto was omitted in the folio, or conversely why a passage not in the quarto was inserted later in the folio, some sufficient reason or purpose must lie behind most of such changes in the texts. No copy of *Hamlet Q1* was known to any editor of *Hamlet* for more than a century after Rowe had published his edition of the plays, yet many passages, long and short, omitted in the numerous acting versions published in the eighteenth and nineteenth centuries are missing also in Q1. Reference to the totals given for each act of various stage versions of this play shows that for Acts I-III Q1 retains within sixty lines as much of *Hamlet* as the versions used by Garrick (1770) or Kean (1820). On scrutinizing those portions of *Hamlet* well preserved in Q1, it is found that the main omissions in Q1 correspond rather closely to those in the editions of 1723 and 1820, if allowance is made for the fact that these versions cut out nearly all those passages which refer in any way to Fortinbras. Thus Horatio's speech (1.1.112-125) beginning 'A moth it is etc.,' is missing in Q1 and the editions of 1723 and 1820; so, too, the passages referring to Denmark and the boy companies and Hamlet's last soliloquy are missing in the three versions, except that three or four lines remain in Q1 on the boy actors. Claudius' opening speech (39 lines) is cut down to 10 lines in Q1, 12 in edition 1723 and 14 in edition 1820; his next long speech (21 lines), beginning 'Tis sweet and commendable,' is reduced to 13, 12 and 14 lines respectively in the editions named. Of Hamlet's first soliloquy (31 lines) there remain 21 lines in Q1, 20 in the edition of 1723 and 25 in that of 1820. Polonius has a family gathering in the third scene; of the 136 lines Q1 retains 71, the edition of 1723 the same number, and that of 1820 only 62. Laertes' long piece (35 lines) of brotherly advice is cut down to 11, 10 and 12 lines respectively; Polonius' advice to Laertes (27 lines) is reduced to 20 lines in Q1, and three only in the other two editions, and of his long rebuke (21 lines) addressed to Ophelia, 5 lines are left in Q1, and 7 in each of the others. The passage (22 lines) in the next scene beginning 'This heauy headed reveale etc.,' is lacking in each of the three texts, as are the lines on the dizziness produced from looking down from the edge of a cliff. Of the next scene in the household of Polonius Q1 keeps 66 lines of 120, whilst the other two have 34 only, largely because both cut out the whole of the conversation between Polonius and Reynaldo. Very heavy toll has been taken of the 80 lines included in the scene played before the king; Q1 has 32 lines, the edition of 1723 one more line, and there are 36 lines in the edition of 1820.

Corruption and interpolation have made far too heavy inroads in the text of Q1 to make any more such comparisons of texts worth while; yet the close agreement of acting versions made at intervals of a century in the choice of many passages to be excised from this play—of which at least 1,300 lines were bound to be struck out—needs little explanation. Q1 preserves the skeleton outline of a good acting version; if we insert the original text of Q2 in place of the four hundred lines of interpolations and also restore the correct text in other passages that have been garbled in the reporting, the play would reproduce most of that in which Burbage and Taylor pleased.

CHAPTER XII

THE FIRST SKETCH THEORY

SOME critics still term the bad quartos 'first sketches' of the corresponding parallel texts written by Shakespeare. This must be a mis-statement; verse, grammar and diction sufficiently prove that even *True Tragedy* or *Romeo and Juliet Q1* are corrupt, garbled and probably abridged versions of non-extant plays with sound texts. These lost originals would be long enough to require no more than the two hours allotted by the actors for representation, and if abridgment of all over-long plays is accepted as the customary practice of Elizabethan companies, there is no need to look for any other originals of these so-called 'first sketches' than the acting versions made by the actors from *3 Henry VI* and *Romeo and Juliet Q2*. Those who prefer century-old opinion to contemporary facts attested by Elizabethan dramatists and actors, and take their stand on a literary sentimentalism which refuses to believe that the lengthy plays of Shakespeare were abridged by his fellows exactly as were those of every other dramatist, will remain firm in their acceptance of what seems the easiest explanation of the relationship between the bad quartos and the corresponding parallel texts.

Pre-existence of the play of Shakespeare, and prior representation of it on the stage before the copy for the text of any of the bad quartos corresponding to the parallel texts was in the hands of the printer, may be proved by cumulative evidence of a kind which would be accepted by a judge in a court of law. My discussions of the numerous passages present in each bad quarto which can be explained only by reference to and comparison with the corresponding portions of the parallel text written by Shakespeare will provide plenty of such irrefutable evidence. Such doubting Thomases as ask for more will find it in blunders in the relation of necessary facts, in mistakes due to mishearing, in defective verse, in composite lines, etc.

Let us examine Shakespeare's supposed methods of rewriting *True Tragedy*. According to some critics of last century he rejected

228 lines of the 2,124 lines, left 854 untouched, altered, added or removed one word in each of 389 lines, changed, added or removed one or two words in each of another 196 lines, and made more extensive variations in each of the remaining 457 lines. He transferred lines and passages from one scene of the play to another, and broke up each of a number of lines into two lines. He distributed over a thousand new lines in every page of his text of 1,900 lines in passages ranging from a line or even part of a line to thirty-five lines—his praise of a shepherd's life. This addition of more than half the original length left it essentially unchanged in plot, in the number and order of scenes and even episodes (except for some minor variations), in the names and the number of the characters. *3 Henry VI,* the new play, is *True Tragedy* writ large, more subtly conceived, plentifully decorated with the poetic ornament then in fashion, freer from blunders, more dignified, but a poorer acting play.

Certain of these additions deserve some discussion, especially allusions to classical mythology and history, similes, and, in the two plays on Henry VI, the many references to natural history. If the advocates of the 'first sketch' theory are right, Shakespeare must have increased each of these groups of allusions out of all proportion to the increase in the length of these plays. This will be. evident from the following table.

TABLE XV

NUMBER OF ALLUSIONS IN PLAY NAMED

Play	Classical Allusions		Similes		References to Natural History	
Contention	9		14		23	
2 Henry VI Fo.		25		51		38
True Tragedy	16		15		24	
3 Henry VI Fo.		29		45		40
Romeo and Juliet Q1 ..	9		14			
Romeo and Juliet Q2 ..		12		28		
Henry V Q1	7		8			
Henry V Fo.		28		23		
Hamlet Q1	15		19			
Hamlet Q2 + Fo.		28		54		
Totals	56	122	70	201	47	78

Supporters of the 'first sketch' theory contend that Shakespeare used two entirely different methods of re-writing old plays. He treated some plays with sound texts, such as *Troublesome Raigne* and *King Leir,* and a corrupt abridgment such as *A Shrew* as raw material, varied the plot and characters, decreased or increased the length of some scenes, rejected others, added new episodes or even sub-plots, retained barely two dozen lines of the three plays, cut out nearly all the compound words, classical allusions, similes, figurative expressions, etc., and inserted his own. His method of re-writing the bad quartos was almost the opposite, and remained unchanged during the decade or so that elapsed between the composition of *2 Henry VI* and *Hamlet Q2.* His second method best appears in transforming *True Tragedy* into *3 Henry VI* and the first quarto of *Romeo and Juliet* into the second. Plot, scenes, episodes, and characters are practically unchanged, and he used up every scrap of these corrupt plays except about a tenth of *True Tragedy* and a fourteenth of *Romeo and Juliet Q1,* with superstitious reverence making over two thousand petty corrections and changes in each play to preserve the text as exactly as possible. In his maturity he continued to employ the poetic devices and ornament prevalent in his prentice years. He more than doubled the classical allusions that were growing unfashionable in 1600-1, and trebled the number of similes. One change he did make; the numerous similes and comparisons drawn from his observation of animals, birds, insects, etc., were substantially reduced.

Dr. Greg has shown that the players struck out long passages of Orlando's part which was stuffed with similes and classical allusions; but of 108 such passages in this part alone, necessity compelled them to keep 51 if they were to have any play left. Even after this severe pruning of poetic exuberance and a plentiful dilution of comic interpolation to make Greene's classical bombast palatable to their audience, they were compelled to present a play one-fourth of which consisted of mythological embroidery. *Orlando Furioso* probably predates any extant play of Shakespeare's; and this excessive addiction to non-dramatic stuff caviare to the general was perhaps a main reason of the disfavour of which Greene complained. Kempe's famous remark to Burbage is usually dated c.1601 :

Few of the vniuersity pen plaies well, they smell too much of
that writer Ouid, and that writer *Metamorphosis,* and talke too
much of Proserpina & Iuppiter. Why heres our fellow Shakespeare puts them all downe, I and Ben Ionson too.[1]

Kempe had left the Chamberlain's men nearly two years before the
anonymous Cambridge writer made this reference, but it indicates
clearly enough that Shakespeare's fellow-actors disliked too much
talk 'of Proserpina & Iuppiter' and consequently removed many of
these allusions from the acting versions. Both of these celebrated
actors were prominent on the stage when Marlowe and the other
University dramatists began to write literary plays for the London
theatres, and in this passage expressed the opinions of their
audiences.

From the beginning of his career Shakespeare was sparing in his
use of such poetical ornament. Marlowe has more than twice the
number of classical allusions in *Edward II* than are in *1 Henry VI,*
a play which Malone mistakenly asserted had an excessive number
for Shakespeare. Greene is far more profuse than Marlowe, and
crammed many more into the 474 lines of Orlando's part in the
Dulwich MS. than are to be found in the 12,000 lines of the York
and Lancaster tetralogy. Peele uses them about as freely as
Marlowe. Shakespeare's supposed additions to *True Tragedy*
include some Latin words, phrases and sentences, all of which are
rare in the bad quartos; he must have put them in in order that
his friends might have something to strike out. The classical
allusions present in *True Tragedy,* e.g.,

> No bending knee will call thee Caesar now,

or,

> Farewell my Hector and my Troyes true hope,

or,

> Thou are no Atlas for so great a weight,

would be understood by most Elizabethan theatre-goers, but some
of those which according to the 'first sketch' theory were added to
Contention and *True Tragedy* would mean little or nothing to
any but classical scholars. Thus York's

> Me thinkes the Realmes of England, France, & Ireland,
> Beare that proportion to my flesh and blood,
> As did the fatall brand Althæa burnt,
> Vnto the Princes heart of Calidon,   *2 Henry VI,* 1.1.227-30.

1. *3. Parnassus,* 4.3.1806-11.

and Warwick's long simile,

> That as Vlysses, and stout Diomede,
> With sleight and manhood stole to Rhesus Tents,
> And brought from thence the Thracian fatall Steeds;
> So wee, well couer'd with the Nights black Mantle,
> At vnawares may beat downe Edwards Guard,
> And seize himselfe;   *3 Henry VI.* 4.2.19-24.

may have been a literary challenge to Marlowe and Greene. His actor-partners certainly did not speak these lines; what were Althæa or Diomede to them or the groundlings? Dramatically such comparisons are bad art; Shakespeare soon learnt to use his mythology with a difference, and few theatre-goers, readers or critics realize that *Merchant of Venice, Henry V* or *Hamlet* contains as many allusions to mythology and ancient history as either *2 Henry VI* or *3 Henry VI*.

Another series of additions to the first sketches or bad quartos consists of similes, some short and others long and elaborate enough to figure in an epic poem; the best are drawn from the poet's minute observation of nature, the worst, such as those quoted above, from mythology. Thus York's description of his defeat at Wakefield,

> With this we charg'd againe: but out alas,
> We bodg'd againe, as I haue seene a Swan
> With bootlesse labour swimme against the Tyde,
> And spend her strength with ouer-matching Waues.
>   *3 Henry VI,* 1.4.28-31.

suggests that Shakespeare, like Spenser, had watched the swans swimming in the Thames. Another description involves a simile drawn from coursing,

> Edward and Richard like a brace of Grey-hounds,
> Hauing the fearfull flying Hare in sight,
> With fiery eyes, sparkling for very wrath,
> And bloody steele graspt in their yrefull hands
> Are at our backes, and therefore hence amaine.
>   *3 Henry VI,* 2.5.129-33.

is admirable and reminds us of *Venus and Adonis,* but the actors rightly excised it, and also the Prince's line,

> For Warwicke rages like a chafed Bull,

as unsuited to the hurry, disorder and panic incident to a flight

from the battle-field after a crushing defeat. On the other hand
two very tedious and over-elaborate similes in Gloster's long
soliloquy (*3 Henry VI*, 3.2.134-143, 174-179) are not in any
sense dramatic. If Shakespeare added them to please himself, the
actors excised them because they lived by pleasing their auditors.

Such additions as these increase the length of *Contention* by 162
lines and of *True Tragedy* by 115 lines without adding anything
dramatically worth-while to these plays; they detract from and
delay rather than help the action. Most of the passages which the
'first sketch' theory suggests were inserted by the poet are
amplificatory of something preceding them and unnecessary to sense
or context. I propose to take one well-preserved scene of each bad
quarto and compare it briefly with the corresponding scene in the
longer version; I assume that Shakespeare added the passages to
the bad quarto.

CONTENTION. Scene x = Act III, scene ii of *2 Henry VI*.

Shakespeare rejected 14 lines of the original (ll. 3-6, 32, 50-1,
70, 185, 193, 211-3), transferred ll. 11, 14-15 to the previous
scene (3.1.140, 69, 71) and added 205 lines. Among the more
important are:—

> 3.2.1-5 (murder not committed on stage as in *Contention*).
> 23-6, 29-32 (Margaret's and Beaufort's hypocrisy).
> 34-7 (attempts to revive the King who has swooned). ·
> 58-65, 68-71, 76-81, 86-121 (Margaret's defence, reproaches
> and complaints).
> 136-148 (Henry's grief at his uncle's death, and self-pity).
> 163-170 (Details of the murdered Gloster's appearance).
> 230-9 (brawl in court).
> 250-269 (Salisbury's speech).
> 301-6 (Margaret's anger at Suffolk's exile).
> 330-2 (a simile).
> 339-342, 351-6 (Margaret's grief).
> 359-366 (Suffolk's grief).
> 381-385, 403-5 (Margaret's farewell).

TRUE TRAGEDY. Scene ix = Act III, scene i of *3 Henry VI*.

The poet rejected two lines, retained 39 and added 62.

> 3.1.4-11 (talk of the two keepers before entrance of Henry).
> 24-27, 35-41, 47-54 (amplification of King's soliloquy).
> 70-91 (sermon on oath of allegiance with long simile).
> 94-6, 100-101 (implied in *t.t.* ix, 38-9).

ROMEO AND JULIET Q1. Scene xv = Act III, scene v of Q2.

Two lines rejected, ll. 23, 157 of Q1 repeat ll. 6, 191 of Q2, one line of Q1 anticipated from the fifth scene of the fourth act of Q2.

3.5.60-4 (Juliet moralises on Fortune).
    67-8 (an aside of Juliet's).
    72-4 (maternal platitude).
    76-9, 83-8, 93-4, 97-103 (pieces of dialogue between mother and daughter carrying double meanings).
    111, 119-121, 125, 127-8, 133-4, 136 (word-play and figurative speech of Capulet).
    141, 144-5, 169, 174 (Capulet's anger).
    207-214 (Juliet's request to the nurse for help).
    222-3 (Nurse's praise of Paris's eyes).

HENRY V Q1. Scene iii = Act II, scene ii of *Henry V Fo.*

Eighty-one lines added.

2.2.3-7 (comments of nobles before entry of King and conspirators).
    17-18, 20-4, 26-8 (amplification of what has been expressed).
    72-3 (expansion of previous thought).
    105-142 (Henry's denunciation of conspirators—not needed).
    155-165 (in Q1 Masham alone speaks. Shakespeare gives each culprit a speech).
    170-3 (are necessary to what follows).
    187-191 (expressed before in different words).

HAMLET Q1. Scene iv = Act I, scene iv and v.

One line rejected, 2 repeated, 2 transferred to a later scene (ll. 49-50). 229 lines retained, 56 lines added.

1.4.5-6 (are necessary).
    17-38 (general reflections, in Q2 but not in Folio).
    75-8 (effect of looking down from a height).
    89, 91 (repetition of a line before or after).
sc.5.3-4 (details of hell).
    6-8 (unnecessary).
    34, 43.
    47-52 (Ghost's comment on Gertrude's infidelity).
    68, 72.
    76-7 (expansion of idea already expressed 82-3; perhaps censored).
    87-8 (amplificatory of previous line).
    93-5 (added detail).
    103, 108.

If a stage manager excised from *3 Henry VI* all the passages not present in any form in *True Tragedy,* and retained also such other portions of Shakespeare's play as were necessary to the story but were differently expressed in the quarto, he would have an excellent acting version of about 2,200 to 2,300 lines. On the other hand if he collected all the seven or eight hundred lines excised, he would discover that story and plot had entirely disappeared; there would remain a heterogeneous assortment of disconnected extracts such as are found in a dictionary of quotations, e.g., excursions into practical philosophy and wisdom, general reflections on life, character and conduct, moralising and ethics, similes, overworked metaphors, comments, asides, out-of-date topical matter, at times short episodes, some parade of learning, classical allusions, amplificatory detail, repetition of what is stated in the context, etc. However admirably they may read, most of them carry little reference directly to fable, plot or action, and many could be fitted almost equally well in a suitable portion of another play. Cibber did this in his *Richard III,* which for more than two centuries usurped the place of Shakespeare's play in our theatre; much of the early portion is a mingle-mangle of scraps lifted from *1 Henry VI, 2 Henry VI, 3 Henry VI, Richard II, 1 Henry IV, 2 Henry IV, Henry V* and other plays, cemented together with Colley's own fustian.

Such purple passages rank high as poetry or rhetoric; dramatically they are nought, and are fitter for the study than the stage. The fourth act of *2 Henry VI* opens with the famous lines beginning,

> The gaudy blabbing and remorsefull day,
> Is crept into the bosome of the Sea, etc.,

a passage quite irrelevant to what follows. Iden's defiance of Cade,

> Oppose thy stedfast gazing eyes to mine, etc.,

might well figure as a prelude to any single combat in any play. Fourteen lines of Young Clifford's speech on war, commencing with,

> Shame and Confusion all is on the rout,

have little to do with the battle of St. Albans, and would not be out of place in any play in which warfare is the theme. Henry's pleasing

description in *3 Henry VI* of the placid happiness of a shepherd's
life might be fitted into *As You Like It* or *Winter's Tale*. No
audience of apprentices could endure Lady Capulet's over-elaborate
comparison of County Paris to a richly bound book, or Juliet's
tiresome quibbling on 'I,' or too much of the Friar's rebuke of
Romeo's conduct, or Queen Margaret's dreary, drawn-out, meta-
phorical speech in *3 Henry VI* before the battle of Tewkesbury, or
Gloster's first soliloquy, packed with similes. Many of the long
speeches of *Henry V* shout for abridgment. Henry, the theme of
many others' rhetoric, wallows in rhetoric himself; the conspirators
suffered more than one death whilst the voluble monarch pronounced their doom, and his monologue on the vexations incident
to kingship obstructs the action of the play.

Did such a shrewd and intelligent master of stage-craft as
William Shakespeare insert these passages into plays which freed
from corruption were quite long enough for the two hours' traffic
of his stage? His complete knowledge of stage custom, his common
sense, and all that is known of Shakespeare the man and poet tell
very strongly against such a suggestion.

Heminge and Condell's oft-repeated diatribe against

diuerse stolne, and surreptitious copies, maimed, and deformed by
the frauds and stealthes of iniurious impostors, that expos'd them:
euen those, are now offer'd to your view cur'd, and perfect of their
limbes; and all the rest, absolute in their numbers, as he conceiued
them,

was almost certainly directed against Jaggard's re-publication in
1619 of four bad quartos, *Contention Q3, True Tragedy Q3,
Henry V Q3, Merry Wives Q2,* together with reprints of four
good quartos, *Midsummer Night's Dream Q2, Merchant of Venice
Q2, King Lear Q2, Pericles Q4* and two plays, *Yorkshire Tragedy*
and *Sir John Oldcastle* not written by Shakespeare, but ascribed to
him by unscrupulous booksellers. Heminge had known Shakespeare as actor, partner, poet and friend from not later than 1594
to his death in 1616. While inveighing against the 'iniurious
impostors' whose 'frauds and stealthes' had 'maimed and deformed'
his fellow's plays, he implicitly affirms that the 'stolne and surreptitious copies' thus printed were being sold as Shakespeare's works
because they were to a large extent derived from his authentic

plays, and not vice versa. If Marlowe, Greene, Peele, Kyd, Heywood, singly or grouped in any kind of combination, had written the *Contention* and *True Tragedy,* why all this indignation and pother? The editors could have expressly disavowed Shakespeare's authorship. Heminge was not much over sixty years of age when, with Condell, he edited the first folio—a volume which three hundred years afterwards some critics insist was cradled in deceit and ignorance—and his memory could be trusted in speaking of happenings less than thirty years before. I prefer the testimony of two life-long friends to the theories of modern iconoclasts.

The commendation of their friend's genius:

His mind and hand went together: And what he thought, he vttered with that easinesse, that wee haue scarse receiued from him a blot in his papers,

agrees with what his more critical friend, Ben Jonson, says in *Discoveries*:

Hee was (indeed) honest, and of an open, and free nature: had an excellent Phantsie; brave notions, and gentle expressions: wherein hee flow'd with that facility, that sometime it was necessary he should be stop'd.

It is impossible to reconcile this 'easinesse,' this facile flow of 'Phantsie, brave notions and gentle expressions' with patient endurance of the tiresome drudgery required for rewriting the bad quartos, six literary chares more intolerable than the tasks imposed on a teacher of Latin in correcting the exercises of his dullest pupils. I calculate that in this alleged tinkering with about a thousand lines of verse in *True Tragedy* Shakespeare must have made more than 2,500 literal and verbal changes, and have mended many hundreds of verses; in addition he must have rejected 228 lines of his original, and have composed over a thousand new verses, not such as his imagination would body forth but such as suited the text of the quarto. Such rewriting of an old play would be infinitely more tedious than the retelling of a hundred thrice-told tales.

No contemporary evidence warrants the assumption so popular with many theory-mongers that in his nonage Shakespeare was what Jonson contemptuously styles his enemy Dekker, a 'play-dresser'; certainly the myriad-minded author of the plays on *Henry IV, Twelfth Night* and *Hamlet Q2* had poetry and self-confidence enough to dispense with every line of any old play which was being used as raw material. I refuse to fasten Pegasus to the shafts of a rubbish cart.

I have discussed in the third section of my third essay on 'Play Abridgment'[2] the methods of play revision practised during Shakespeare's life as a working dramatist. I have nothing to add to what I wrote there except this—the length of each of the other bad quartos was increased precisely as was the length of *Romeo and Juliet Q1*. Table XVI on page 161 sets out for each pair of the parallel plays the number of speeches and of lines added to the bad quartos on the assumption that Shakespeare began his dramatic career as a play-dresser, and continued the practice of play-dressing, with plagiarism unlimited as a side-line, even when he was writing the great tragedies.

If the 104 lines interpolated by the actors in Orlando's part as it appears in Q1 are excluded, the hero speaks 171 lines less than Greene wrote for him. The totals set out in the table (p. 161) suggest that 136 lines of the amount struck out by the actors came from the long speeches. This conclusion is not warranted because it does not take into account the fact that if any speech in MS. was reduced to less than ten lines, the residue would not be included in any speech-total given for *Orlando Furioso Q1*. The result given in the table is very important because it demonstrates conclusively that the actors disliked too many long speeches and lessened them both in number and in length.

In their early plays written for the public stage the University dramatists wrote too many long speeches; probably they followed the methods customary in University plays and the so-called 'closet' drama. Daniel's *Cleopatra* (1594) is an excellent example of this type. It is in quatrains, is provided with choruses, and, apart from three short passages of stichomythia totalling about forty lines, is almost devoid of dialogue. Speeches average 45 lines each; Cleopatra opens with a monologue of 196 lines, and a messenger concludes the play, except for the inevitable chorus, with a description of Cleopatra's death extending to 253 lines. Nothing

2. *Shakespeare and the Homilies* (1934), pp. 137-148.

happens. Marlowe, Peele, Kyd and Greene reduced this overdose of long speeches by introducing a considerable amount of dialogue. Speeches average eight lines each in Greene's *Alphonsus* and Peele's *Battle of Alcazar* and nearly ten lines a-piece for the first three

TABLE XVI

NUMBER OF SPEECHES AND OF LINES IN PLAYS NAMED

Name of Play	Play	Number of Lines in					
		A Speeches of 30+Lines	B Speeches between 20–29 Lines	C Speeches between 10–19 Lines	D All Speeches in A+B+C	Rest of Play	Percentage of Speeches in Play
Orlando's Part.							
(a) Dulwich MS.	474	—	81 (3)	155 (12)	236 (15)	238	49·8
(b) *Orlando Furioso Q1* ..	303	—	26 (1)	74 (5)	100 (6)	203	33·0
Contention ..	1,973	—	95 (4)	308 (22)	403 (26)	1,570	20·4
2 *Henry VI.*	3,075	315 (8)	233 (10)	650 (49)	1,198 (67)	1,877	39·1
True Tragedy	2,124	215 (6)	89 (4)	312 (24)	616 (34)	1,508	29·0
3 *Henry VI.*	2,902	378 (9)	218 (9)	494 (36)	1,090 (54)	1,812	37·4
Romeo and Juliet Q1	2,215	76 (2)	204 (9)	279 (22)	559 (33)	1,656	25·3
Romeo and Juliet Q2	2,986	385 (10)	188 (8)	468 (38)	1,041 (56)	1,945	36·3
Henry V. Q1	1,623	177 (5)	140 (6)	325 (25)	642 (36)	981	39·7
Henry V. Fo	3,166	780 (18)	246 (10)	550 (44)	1,576 (72)	1,590	49·8
Hamlet Q1 ..	2,154	61 (2)	162 (7)	386 (30)	609 (39)	1,545	28·4
Hamlet Q2+Fo	3,762	517 (14)	306 (13)	786 (58)	1,609 (85)	2,153	42·7
1. Total lines in Bad Quartos	10,089	529 (15)	690 (30)	1,610 (123)	2,829 (168)	7,260	28·0
2. Total lines in Plays of Shakespeare	15,891	2,375 (59)	1,191 (50)	2,948 (225)	6,514 (334)	9,377	41·0
Increase of lines	5,802	1,846	501	1,338	3,685	2,117	
Percentage increase based on totals in 1	57·7	347	72·6	83·1	130·3	30·0	

N.B.—The digits enclosed in brackets give the number of speeches which contain the number of lines set down in the same row immediately to the left.

hundred lines of *Orlando Furioso Q1*. *Tamburlaine* has 54 per cent., *Alphonsus* 58 per cent., *David and Bethsabe* 54·5 per cent., *Spanish Tragedy* 48 per cent., and *Locrine* 64·4 per cent. of speeches ten lines or more in length. In the plays usually accepted as their latest, Marlowe, Greene and even Peele heavily reduced the proportion of long speeches. Thus *Edward II* has but two speeches of over thirty lines, and little more than 23 per cent. consists of speeches ten lines or longer; *James IV* has three thirty-line speeches and 29 per cent. of speeches of at least ten lines, and *Friar Bacon* one speech of thirty lines and 31 per cent. of long speeches of ten lines or more. Apparently each of these dramatists was making an effort to give the actors a larger proportion of dialogue.

On the other hand such corrupt plays of these dramatists and of anonymous authors as *Old Wive's Tale, Massacre at Paris, A Shrew, George-a-Greene,* if taken together, have only one speech as long as thirty lines and eight speeches exceeding twenty lines. Almost every page of these plays offers ample evidence that some illiterate persons, probably actors, have been garbling, mutilating or abridging the text. The almost complete disappearance of speeches more than twenty lines in length from the plays named above at a time when nearly every play in verse with a sound text contained from a dozen to twenty of them carries with it a strong presumption that the long speeches, originally present in these plays before they became corrupt, underwent the same kind of abridgment as actually occurred in *Orlando Furioso Q1.*

Shakespeare the actor knew that his fellows cut down oversize plays and severely abridged long speeches, yet Shakespeare the playwright began by writing longer plays than any of his predecessors, continued to write longer plays than any of his contemporaries except Jonson, and ended as he began. Almost twenty years separated the composition of *2 Henry VI* from that of *Cymbeline;* each play would require nearer three than two hours for representation, and each has about two-fifths of its length in speeches that any play-adapter worth his salt would abridge on sight. Long speeches in his plays touch a maximum of slightly over fifty per cent. in *Richard II.* Yet *Henry V Fo.* is the outstanding example of his fondness for writing Gargantuan lengths of rhetorical poetry; no less than two-thirds of the verse consists of speeches of not less than ten lines each, and speeches of over thirty lines represent a fourth of the whole play. Even more remarkable is the fact that of 777 lines of verse in *Henry V Q1* 482 lines, or

about five-eighths of the poetry, consist of speeches ten lines or
more in length—an extraordinary result for any play intended for
the public theatre, and unique in one which is a continuous perversion of a longer play.

Shakespeare's supposed methods of adding to the length of a
bad quarto are easily discovered from an examination of the table.
Apart from 1,212 lines of verse which he inserted to replace an
equal number of lines rejected by him during his supposed rewriting
—these do not appear in the table—he added 5,802 lines divisible
into 3,685 lines of speeches, each of at least ten lines, and 2,117
other lines of verse and prose; the latter may be termed dialogue.
No one knew better than Shakespeare that brisk dialogue was, and
is, the quintessence and life of drama, and this most unusually large
increase of long speeches during this revision of the bad quartos is
very difficult to understand or explain.

These five plays of Shakespeare contain 59 speeches which
average forty lines a-piece; fifteen of them are in the bad quartos
and average five lines less. Thirty-line speeches are scarce in all
the bad quartos except *True Tragedy* and *Henry V Q1;* there are
two each in *Romeo and Juliet Q1* and *Hamlet Q1* and none in
Contention. *True Tragedy* has six such speeches, and if Shakespeare rewrote it he retained with only trifling changes practically
every line of five, adding three lines to the forty spoken by
Margaret, not a line to those of York (39 lines), Warwick (38
lines), or Clifford (34 lines), and rejecting a line of Gloster's final
soliloquy (34 lines); thus 185 lines of *True Tragedy* became 187
in *3 Henry VI.* One substantial addition of forty-two lines was
made to Gloster's first soliloquy, and the result is Shakespeare's
longest speech. *Henry V Q1* has five speeches of at least thirty
lines; all but one were considerably increased in the folio version,
and thirteen others were added. Seven of these are entirely new,
not a line coming from the quarto. They include the five choruses,
Henry's address to his soldiers before the walls of Harfleur, and
his grumbling soliloquy on ceremony and the troubles of kingship.
Burgundy speaks four lines in Q1 which Shakespeare has enclosed
in a speech of forty-five lines, mainly descriptive of the devastated
condition of France; this is not from Holinshed, and may be
adapted from some contemporary account of the desolation resulting

M

from civil war between the Catholic League and the Huguenots, which came to an end when Henry of Navarre abjured his religion. Other remarkable instances of expansion occur in *2 Henry VI*. Margaret's seven-line speech in *Contention* after the murder of Gloster is discovered is enlarged by the poet to a most unnecessary forty-nine lines, and the six-line outburst of the captain of the ship who captured Suffolk is increased in *2 Henry VI* to thirty-four lines of abuse and denunciation. Henry's pious musings, while seated on a mole-hill during the battle of Towton, are limited to thirteen doleful lines, which in *3 Henry VI* develop into fifty-five lines of fine pastoral verse of little dramatic value; whilst his queen's thirteen-line address to her soldiers in *True Tragedy* before Tewkesbury fight grows into a tortuous, figurative comparison depressing enough to account for their defeat. Juliet's famous soliloquy after her marriage beginning,

Gallop apace, you fierie footed steedes,

ends at the fourth line in Q1, but continues for another thirty in Q2. Hamlet's last soliloquy of thirty-six lines is missing in Q1; several other speeches of about ten lines each in Q1, notably two of the King's, one of the player-King's, and one of Laertes', have each been increased to nearly forty lines.

If Shakespeare rewrote the bad quartos, some of his additions suggest that he was rather capricious in his choice of the characters whose parts he increased. After allowance has been made for lines of the quartos rejected and replaced by him, he added over fifty per cent. to the remainder of *True Tragedy* and about seventy-five per cent. to that of *Contention*. In *True Tragedy* his additions to Clifford's part comprise three lines; he increased Warwick's part by a little over a fifth, and York's by thirty per cent. On the other hand Henry and his queen have their parts more than doubled. In *Contention* the rather short part of Warwick receives less than a quarter extra, and those of Cade and Suffolk an increment of fifty per cent. Elinor speaks twice as much in *2 Henry VI*, and the parts of Henry, York, and Margaret in *Contention* are each nearly trebled in Shakespeare's play. If no attention is paid to the small number of lines rejected by Shakespeare during his supposed revision of *Romeo and Juliet Q1* he increased the play by a third, the men's parts receiving an average addition of a quarter and those of the women a half. In *Henry V Q1*, the shortest of these five plays, the increase made by Shakespeare amounts to 95 per cent., or, if the choruses and three scenes—all omitted in Q1—are excluded from the count, to 70 per cent. Exeter is the historical character to whose part the least amount, viz., a sixth, has been added. The comic characters also receive much less than the average proportion of additions, the parts of Pistol, Nym, Mrs. Quickly and Fluellen being increased in the aggregate by little more than a fourth. This treatment is the direct opposite of what occurred in additions made to other plays by the actors themselves and by other authors. Dr. Greg has offered what almost amounts to proof that the comic interpolations in *Orlando Furioso Q1* and the excisions from the rest of the play are the work of the actors; most probably the 'adicyones in doctor fostes' for which Henslowe paid two actors, William Bird and Samuel Rowley, in 1602 were the comic passages that appear first in the text of 1616. So also the additions made by Marston or Webster to *Malcontent* consist, except for the Induction, of new scenes or additions to scenes in which Bilioso, Passarello, Maquerelle and Malevole play the fool, whilst the new passages added to Middleton's *Faire Quarrell* gave the audience more of 'Mr. Chaughs and Trimtrams Roaring.' In the quarto version of *Henry V* the French characters do not fare too well, though Shakespeare was as fair-minded as any Elizabethan could be. He trebled the aggregate number of lines allotted in Q1 to the French king, the Dauphin, Mountjoy, Katharine and Burgundy, though the parts of most of the important English characters gain little more than seventy per cent. To *Hamlet Q1* the poet added altogether seventy-five per cent. of text, if no allowance is made for lines rejected and replaced by him. Of the chief characters Ophelia received the smallest amount of additions, whilst the Ghost, Horatio and the Grave-digger in the order named had less than the average proportion of new lines received by Hamlet, Polonius and Gertrude. The player-king speaks nine lines in Q2 for every four in Q1, and Claudius eight lines for every three.

One does not expect to find any exact uniformity in making increments to the parts of the various characters if Shakespeare adopted this rather odd method of increasing the length of the bad quartos. Yet what reasons can be suggested for increasing the 507 lines spoken by Warwick and Clifford in *True Tragedy* to 574 lines in *3 Henry VI,* an increase of 13 per cent., and simultaneously raising the 350 lines given to Henry and Margaret to 611 lines, an increase of 76 per cent.? Similar problems present themselves for solution in each of the other bad quartos. Thus in *Contention* Margaret and York together speak 332 lines and 674 in *2 Henry VI,* whilst the 323 lines in the parts of Suffolk and Warwick become 421 lines in the fuller version. Again in *Hamlet Q1* Horatio and the Ghost speak 252 lines which are expanded to 360 lines in Q2, whilst the 252 lines of Claudius and the player-king rise to 650 lines.

These remarkable anomalies of distribution seem to depend partly upon the length and condition of the quarto, partly upon the relative excellence or inferiority of the various parts, and partly on the rank and sex of the characters represented. He added least to the least corrupt portions of the bad quartos. Apparently if he did not reject many lines of a part spoken by the actor playing a certain character, and altered comparatively few lines of the remaining text of that part, he made correspondingly small additions to it in his own play. This peculiarity is exemplified in the relatively small increase made to the parts of Suffolk and Warwick in *Contention* and to those of Warwick and Clifford in *True Tragedy.* Six characters in *Contention* speak more lines than Warwick whose share of *2 Henry VI* could have been doubled without destroying the balance or increasing unduly the length of the play. Similarly six characters in *True Tragedy* have longer parts than Clifford's, which remains almost unaltered in *3 Henry VI.*

Shakespeare's treatment of women's parts is interesting. He increased them in *True Tragedy* and *Romeo and Juliet,* the two best preserved of the bad quartos, by nearly sixty per cent., whilst to the parts of the male characters he added thirty per cent. Queens and princesses received double tribute, receiving the honours of royalty and the respect due to women; in the aggregate he almost doubled the parts of Queen Margaret in *Contention* and *True Tragedy,* of Lady Grey in *True Tragedy* and of Queen Gertrude in

Hamlet Q1. These large increments of women's parts, spoken in those days by boys, were much greater proportionally than the additions made to the various parts played by the far more competent actor-sharers and hired actors. This method of giving the worst speakers and actors more to do may be an empty flourish of gallantry, but lacks the practical wisdom of the playwright grown old in the traditions of the theatre; it is not in agreement with his expressed opinions of the competence of boy-actors. Hamlet's comment on hearing of the arrival at Court of the players,

> the Lady shall say her minde freely: or the black (blank) verse shall hault for't,

indicates that the boys who played women's parts had their lines abridged and spoke blank verse badly. His subsequent criticism:

> But there is Sir an ayrie of Children, little Yases, that crye out on the top of question; and are most tyrannically clap't for't: these are now the fashion, and so be-ratled the common Stages (so they call them) that many wearing Rapiers, are affraide of Goose-quils, and dare scarse come thither,

is clearly contemptuous, and Hamlet's query 'Do the Boyes carry it away?' strikes a note of astonishment that theatre-goers of our own days can understand when our press informs the world that seven-year-old Shirley Temple is a great actress. Cleopatra feels, too, that the cup of degradation, filled for fallen majesty, will be most bitter when she shall see,

> Some squeaking Cleopatra Boy my greatnesse
> I'th' posture of a Whore.

Actors personating kings, queens and princesses wore the richest costumes, came upon the stage to a flourish of trumpets, and received bowings and obeisance from every character, but in the bad quartos the parts of royalty have not the length consistent with their rank, and, sad to relate, their lines abound in nonsense and gross blunders of diction, grammar, and metre. The parts of Henry VI in *Contention* and *True Tragedy* together with the part of Claudius in *Hamlet Q1* amount to 602 lines; Shakespeare is said to have increased them to 1,232 lines, or more than doubled their parts. Again in *Henry V Q1* the part of the English king received an addition slightly more than the proportionate increase to the whole play; the French royal family, father, mother, son and daughter speak 123 lines which Shakespeare almost trebled in his own play.

There is ample evidence to be derived from the vocabulary, defective verse, blunders, anticipation of lines, repetition, and borrowings from other dramatists, that each bad quarto was a corrupt abridgment of some short version of the extant authentic text. Of this short version a manuscript was probably in existence, and if Shakespeare did not write this, he had the longest and most successful career as a literary thief and impostor of which history keeps record. If Shakespeare was the author of this abbreviated manuscript, his literary conduct, judged by any standard based on reason, seems inconsistent, inexplicable and most strangely devoid of good sense. I cannot believe that he would or could have expanded his own first sketch by using the extraordinary methods described above. To suggest that he undertook the distasteful and purposeless task of play-dressing, and could at will 'recapture the first fine careless rapture' of writing *Romeo and Juliet* or *Hamlet* is to rank him in that lower order of poets, who, after a day devoted to meditating "the thankles Muse," retire to rest content with changing the place of a comma. His supposed additions come from the poet and rhetorician rather than from the dramatist, and most of them would have been struck out by the play-adapter on sight. When the poet took charge, and his brain was seething with imaginative thought and on fire with passion and emotions, he may have filled *Hamlet* with 1,600 lines of long speeches; later, when the dramatist heard them read, he would have shaken his head in critical disapproval and accepted the decision of his fellows to declaim less than a half of these speeches on the stage. Nor do I think any man of the theatre, least of all an actor-author, would have distributed so capriciously such additions among the characters of the play. He would know the capacity of each member of the company, and would not have provided dull actors, always listening for the prompter's whisper, or boys incapable of understanding the words they were parrotting, with more lines to mispronounce or mangle. Finally, why should a dramatist so indifferent to literary fame as Shakespeare seems to have been, add fifteen hundred lines to *Hamlet,* and then not trouble himself to see the revised edition through the press? Not one of the revision theories will stand investigation; each raises more doubts and difficulties than it explains.

CHAPTER XIII

BLUNDERS THAT BEAR WITNESS

CRITICS rightly insist on proof that *Romeo and Juliet Q2* preceded *Romeo and Juliet Q1* in composition, though the latter was printed two years before the former; many will, however, refuse to accept any proof that the *True Tragedy,* which was published 28 years before *3 Henry VI,* is a surreptitious abridgment of the folio play. It must be admitted that some of the inferences deduced from differences in the texts of the *True Tragedy* and *3 Henry VI* are of little importance in deciding whether the *True Tragedy* was the source play of *3 Henry VI* or no. On the other hand, conclusions drawn from the fact that a meaningless passage of the *True Tragedy* takes a meaning only after comparison with the text of the corresponding passage of *3 Henry VI* must have a very high if not decisive importance in solving the problem of priority. Such blunders occur in all the bad quartos, and I have collected from each of them some passages in which the text is defective or without meaning or suggests some omission of matter relevant to the context or even the plot. I have discussed each passage separately, and have shown that after reading the text of the corresponding passage of the folio or good quarto, the text of the bad quarto passage may be restored, the sense made good, and the relation of the passage to the rest of the context satisfactorily explained.

These blunders generally occur in those parts of the bad quarto in which the two texts approximate most nearly; in fact, unless the text of Q1, both before and after the passage in which the defective line or lines occur, is in close agreement verbally with that of the corresponding folio or good quarto, little reliance can be placed upon the conclusion. Perhaps some of these defects result from injudicious cuts made by the company's play adapter, but such omissions are good evidence of a pre-existing text of Shakespeare's. Sometimes a word or a phrase is changed with disastrous results to the meaning of what was before or came after, but if the rest of the passage takes a meaning only after the substitution of

170

Shakespeare's word or phrase, judgment must pass in favour of the priority of Shakespeare's text. In certain examples chosen from the *Contention, True Tragedy* and *Henry V Q1* mistakes of fact are found which cannot be those of any competent dramatist, and here again the verdict must be that the compilers of these bad quartos were guilty of garbling the original texts. Moreover, some misused or unintelligible words found in these plays seem to be perversions of words in the corresponding passages of the authentic plays.

Such blunders will occur in any play, the text of which is based mainly on what the actors could recollect of their parts. *Orlando Furioso Q1* retains barely three hundred lines of the version of Orlando's part which appears in the Dulwich MS. but the mistakes made by the actors offer proof that Q1 is surreptitious. I shall discuss a few passages.

(i) Orlando rhapsodizes (Q1. 604-6) on Angelica:

> Faire Flora make her couch amidst thy flowres,
> Sweet Christall springs, wash ye with roses,
> When she longs to drinke. Ah, thought my heauen;

These lines are defective metrically and in sense. What does the second line mean? Why does such a monotonously regular metrist as Greene write two irregular lines of verse? These questions are answered on turning to the MS. (ll. 10-12):

> kinde Clora make her couch, fair cristall springs
> washe you her Roses, yf she long to drinck
> oh thought, my heauen, etc.

Interpolation of the words 'amidst thy flowers' caused the metrical disorder; the defective sense is due to stupidity and the insertion of 'with' for 'her.'

(ii) Another example occurs in the same scene when Orlando has learnt of Angelica's supposed faithlessness. The passage in both versions is sorry stuff. In Q1. 712-4 it runs:

> And Titans Neeces gather all in one
> Those fluent springs of your lamenting teares,
> And let them flow alongst my faintfull lookes.

What the second line means I cannot say. Greene's fanciful use of classical mythology gives the modern reader pause, but the second line would make him stare and gasp. The MS. version (ll. 85-7) is:

proud Titans neces gather all in one
those fluent springs of your lamenting eyes
and let them streame along my [faithfull] looks.

    faintfull

If for 'in one' he had written 'your teares' and deleted the second
line the sense would have been retained; in the quarto passage
'Titans Neeces' are bidden to gather 'all in one' their eyes and let
them flow,' etc. Reference to the MS. is necessary to find a
meaning for a line of Q1.

(iii) Orlando 'enters like a poet'—whatever this may mean—and
plunges into a morass of mythology. He asks (Q1. 1172-3) his
page:

    Is not her face siluerd like that milke-white shape,
    When Ioue came dauncing downe to Semele.

These lines are difficult to understand; once more the MS. must be
consulted, and we read (MS. 222-3) what Greene wrote:

    her face siluered like to the milkewhite shape
    yt Ioue came dauncing in to Cemele.

Greene makes us understand that Jove assumed the milk-white
shape; this is not clear in Q1.

(iv) My last instance from Q1 resembles one passage that will
be discussed among those in *True Tragedy*. Orlando has defeated
two of the Peers of France in single fight, and the play proceeds
(Q1. 1530-4):

    Og: Oh Oger how canst thou stand & see a slaue
    Disgrace the house of France: Syrra prepare you,
    For angry Nemesis sits on my sword to be reuenged.
    Orl: Well saide Frenchman, you haue made a goodly oration:

As the MS. gives the cues only of all speeches except those of
Orlando this passage appears thus in MS. (ll. 459-460):

    by my side - - - - - - - - - - - - - - You - - - - - - - - -
    Orl: So sir you haue made a goodly oration.

Orlando's cues differ in the two texts. This suggests text is
missing or altered. Ogier in Q1 speaks three lines, certainly not
'a goodly oration' for the chief of the twelve peers, the best
swordsman of France. Several lines of his speech must be missing
in Q1.

These examples are of great importance. *Orlando Furioso Q1*
is a corrupt abridgment of a play written by Greene, and from his

manuscript a scribe prepared the Dulwich MS. of Orlando's part. Obscure and unintelligible passages of this part as they appear in Q1 become clear and intelligible on comparing them with the corresponding passages of the MS. which was in existence before Q1 was compiled or printed. If obscure and meaningless passages of a bad quarto gain clarity and meaning only after consulting the parallel text of Shakespeare, analogically the priority of the latter text is established.

Numerous examples may be chosen from the bad quartos; I shall discuss those in the better preserved texts first, and subsequently consider those in the more corrupt *Contention* and *Hamlet Q1*. Mistakes in relating historical facts common to a pair of parallel texts will be treated with a fulness commensurate with their importance. References to the bad quartos are to scenes and lines, and those to Shakespeare's plays are to act, scene and lines, as they appear in the text of the Cambridge Shakespeare (1863-66).

True Tragedy and 3 Henry VI

(i) After the battle of Wakefield the captured Duke of York is bidden to yield to the mercy of the victors, and Clifford, whose father York had killed, jeeringly says (iii. 69-70) :

> I, to such mercie as his ruthfull arme
> With downe right paiment lent vnto my father.

'Ruthfull' may be defended as a piece of bitter irony, but this subtlety is not in character with the brutal directness and instinctive savagery of Clifford, so consistently presented by the poet. I confess I cannot explain the meaning of the passage; the folio text (1.4.31-2) must and does interpret the meaning of the quarto :—

> I, to such mercy, as his ruthlesse Arme
> With downe-right payment, shew'd vnto my Father.

(ii) 'Tygers of Arcadia' (iii. 189) must be a blundering recollection of the folio's 'Tygers of Hyrcania.' Topsell does not include 'Arcadian' among his long list of 'Epithites' for this beast. Marlowe in *Dido* refers to 'Tygers of Hyrcania,' and *Hamlet Q1* turns 'Th' ircanian beast' of Q2 into 'th' arganian beast.'

(iii) The changes made in the line of the quarto (iii. 200),

> As now I reape at thy two cruell hands,

from the folio's

> As now I reape at thy too cruell hand,

are not uncommon in these texts; it may be a printer's error, but the double change makes this doubtful.

(iv) Halle mentions (p. 251) an incident said to have occurred before the battle of Mortimer's Cross,

at which tyme the sunne (as some write) appered to the erle of March, like iii sunnes, and sodainly ioined all togither in one.

This incident is described in both texts, and the effect of this phenomenon on Edward is described (iv. 19-23) in *True Tragedy*:

> I thinke it cites vs brother to the field,
> That we the sonnes of braue Plantagenet,
> Alreadie each one shining by his meed,
> May ioine in one and ouerpeere the world,
> As this the earth.

'World' here is used in its literal sense of 'universe' and thus includes the 'earth.' Edward out-Tamburlaines Tamburlaine in bombastic extravagance by transposing 'world' and 'earth.' He desires that the three 'sonnes of braue Plantagenet' may 'ouerpeere the world' or universe, as that inferior luminary, the sun, does 'the earth.' On turning to the folio text (2.1.34-8) we read:

> I think it cites vs (Brother) to the field,
> That wee, the Sonnes of braue Plantagenet,
> Each one alreadie blazing by our meedes,
> Should notwithstanding ioyne our Lights together,
> And ouer-shine the Earth, as this the World.

Here, and elsewhere in the bad quartos, metaphors and other figures of speech fare badly; with the collapse of the comparison the sense disappeared.

(v) Misuse of personal pronouns, such as employing singular for plural, or the feminine form instead of the masculine, is very common in the bad quartos. Two lines of Clifford's (v. 12-13),

> Whose hand is that the sauage Beare doth licke?
> Not his that spoiles his young before his face.

make the reader uncertain whether it is the young of the bear or the young of the man that is being 'spoiled.' These lines read in *3 Henry VI* (2.2.13-14) thus:

> Whose hand is that the Forrest Beare doth licke?
> Not his that spoyles her yong before her face.

The reporter has changed the sex of the hand-licking bear, though bears were plentiful enough on the streets or at the Bear Garden. Another instance of this misuse occurs toward the end of the play. Warwick standing on the walls of Coventry, sees King Edward approach instead of his son-in-law Clarence, and exclaims (xix. 13-15):

> O vnbid spight, is spotfull Edward come?
> Where slept our scouts or how are they seduste,
> That we could haue no newes of their repaire?

'Their repaire' or their arrival must, in strict grammar, refer to 'our scouts'; the sense of the passage makes it certain that Warwick is speaking of Edward. This passage is almost identical in the folio text (5.1.18-20) except that the last line reads,

> That we could heare no newes of his repayre.

(vi) The Yorkists have been repulsed at Towton. Richard enters and describes (vi. 15-27) the death of Warwick's father; I omit lines not relevant to my subject.

> *Rich.* Ah Warwike, why haste thou withdrawn thy selfe?
> Thy noble father in the thickest thronges,
> Cride still for Warwike his thrise valiant son,
> ....
> ....
> Richard, commend me to my valiant sonne,
> And still he cride Warwike reuenge my death,
> And with those words he tumbled off his horse,
> And so the noble Salsbury gaue vp the ghost.
> *War.* Then let the earth be drunken with his bloud,
> Ile kill my horse because I will not flie:

This account of Salisbury's death is a piece of fiction, not an error. Halle narrates (p. 251):

After this victorie [at Wakefield] by the queene, the earle of Salisburie and all the prisoners were sent to Pomfret and there beheaded; whose heads (togither with the duke of Yorkes head) were conueied to Yorke, and there set on poles ouer the gate of the citie.

This occurred three months before Towton. The day before Towton, Halle tells us (p. 255) was slain

the bastard of Salisburie, brother to the earle of Warwike, a valiant young gentleman, and of great audacitie.

Salisbury had played a prominent part in *Contention,* and the reporter, not knowing what had become of him describes his death here. Apart from this mis-statement, what is the meaning of Warwick's extraordinary opening line,

> Then let the earth be drunken with his bloud,

which cannot be referred to anything before or after? The folio text restores us to the realms of history and good sense (2.3.14-22) :

> Ah Warwicke, why hast thou withdrawn thy selfe?
> Thy Brothers blood the thirsty earth hath drunk.
> . . . .
> . . . .
> So vnderneath the belly of their Steeds,
> That stain'd their Fetlockes in his smoaking blood,
> The Noble Gentleman gaue vp the ghost.
> *War.* Then let the earth be drunken with our blood :
> Ile kill my Horse, because I will not flye.

The puzzle is solved. Warwick's opening line in the folio version springs naturally from the context ; it picks up and echoes the second line of Richard's preceding speech (omitted in the quarto), the speaker's memory being revived by the words 'his smoaking blood' in the second last line. The absurd change of the folio's 'our blood' to the quarto's 'his bloud' makes it impossible to give any meaning to Warwick's first line in *True Tragedy,* and its presence can only be explained by reference to the authentic text.

(vii) Another line (vi. 32) of the same scene,

> And in that vow now ioine my soule to thee,

is obviously a blundering remembrance of the folio line (2.3.34),

> And in this vow do chaine my soule to thine.

Edward could not 'ioine' or 'chaine' his soul to Warwick.

(viii) An unmetrical triplet (viii. 47-9) deserves notice. The lines run,

> *1. Sould.* Was euer son so rude his fathers bloud to spil?
> *2. Sould.* Was euer father so unnaturall his son to kill?
> *King.* Was euer King thus greeud and vexed still?

Though the sense is satisfactory why are an alexandrine, a four-teener and a decasyllabic line joined in rhyme? Reference to the folio text (2.5.109-110) explains what has happened.

Son. Was euer sonne, so rew'd a Fathers death?
Fath. Was euer Father so bemoan'd his Sonne?
Hen. Was euer King so greeu'd for Subiects woe?

These three lines in each version occur in a passage of sticho-myth-like dialogue in which father, son and King, each in turn, speak a line or a pair of lines, concluding with rhyming couplets. In the folio text Shakespeare omits in characteristic fashion the relative 'who' or 'that' before 'rew'd,' 'bemoan'd' and 'greeu'd'—a trick of style that proved a pitfall for the reporting pirate. He remembered and tried to achieve the antithetic point of the original, and did it at the expense of his verse. The frame-work and sense of the three lines are the same in both versions. He took 'rew'd' to be an adjective, was forced to jettison 'his father's death' because it did not seem to make sense, and eked out the line with the phrase 'his father's bloud to spil,' stolen from *Edward II*, which belonged to the Pembroke repertoire. Continuing his constructive work, he remodelled the second line to match the first, and topped off the line by rhyming 'kill' and 'spil'; the third line was less altered. To convert the version of the *True Tragedy* into that of *3 Henry VI* suggests a semi-reverential care for his original on the part of Shakespeare not more ridiculous than incredible.

(ix) After the victory at Towton, Warwick counsels Edward to march to London, and urges an alliance with France to render the defeated Lancastrians helpless. He wisely says (viii. 149-152):

And hauing France thy friend thou needst not dread,
The scattered foe that hopes to rise againe.
And though they cannot greatly sting to hurt,
Yet looke to haue them busie to offend thine eares.

The sense of the fourth line is imperfect. Why 'thine eares'? On turning to the folio text the last line (2.6.95) reads,

Yet looke to haue them buz to offend thine eares.

Actors did not like elisions such as 't' offend,' and preferred a needless Alexandrine at the expense of the meaning.

(x) Shakespeare wrote an admirable piece of brisk and natural dialogue in the first portion of Act III, scene two, of *3 Henry VI*. King Edward enters with his brothers, and explains to them that Lady Grey is urging him to restore to her the lands of her deceased husband. Up to the end of the thirty-second line Clarence and

Gloster hear what the King and the lady are saying, and pass mocking gibes on his questions and her answers. Evidently the King became annoyed by his brothers' bad manners, and, turning towards them, says (3.2.33):

> Lords giue vs leaue, Ile trye this Widowes wit.

They obey what is a royal command, walk away and hear no more, but keep up a running fire of sarcastic comments on the blushes, knitting of brows, anger and sadness mirrored successively on the tell-tale face of Lady Grey, as she listens perforce to the dishonourable suggestions of the King.

The version of the *True Tragedy* puts the King's order to the brothers much earlier in the scene, i.e., after x. 18, and thus arises the absurdity that they continue to break their wit and comment on a conversation which stage convention assumes that they cannot hear. This portion of the scene could not be acted unless the asides of the brothers, viz., x. 23-4, 26, 33-8, were deleted from *True Tragedy*. How did such a text come to exist? It was not a transcript of an acting version or a prompter's book; it could not have been compiled from a careful collation of the four actors' parts because the cues would have prevented each of them from being faulty in precisely the same place. Certainly the much-abused Elizabethan printer was not responsible for this complicated type of error. If the copy for the *True Tragedy* came from those who had acted in it, the assembling of the parts must have been done by persons ignorant of the elementary principles of stage-craft. The text of *3 Henry VI* must be read to understand the text of *True Tragedy*.

(xi) Warwick visits the French court to ask the hand of Lady Bona for King Edward. Margaret is present and exclaims in despair (xi. 22):

> And if this go forward all our hope is done.

Such eleven-syllable lines with an extra initial syllable are very frequent in *True Tragedy* but unknown in *3 Henry VI*. Her corresponding line (3.2.58) of *3 Henry VI*

> If that goe forward, Henries hope is done,

is no closer to the first line than an earlier folio line (3.2.32):

> And if thou faile vs, all our hope is done.

The make-up of the line in *True Tragedy* suggests its composite character, and that parts of ll. 1-43 of the folio scene were spoken on the stage. Up to the entrance of Warwick only a line and a half of this scene of *3 Henry VI* are present in the bad quarto.

(xii) Margaret has few lines to speak in the eleventh scene of *True Tragedy*. After Warwick has delivered to Lady Bona an affectionate greeting from King Edward, Margaret exclaims (xi. 29-31):

> King Lewes and Lady Bona heare me speake,
> Before you answere Warwike or his words,
> For hee it is hath done vs all these wrongs.

The last line is Margaret's complete speech on her own and her husband's behalf; she remains silent till the arrival of the English post with the news of Edward's marriage to Lady Grey turns the tide in her favour. The audience would expect to hear a defence of her husband's rights, and an attack upon Edward and Warwick; she says nothing. Reference to the folio text proves that she did speak sufficiently for her purpose. Before Warwick arrives she explains (3.3.21-37) what 'all these wrongs' are, and the three lines above are extended to thirteen lines (3.3.65-77), in which she vigorously charges Edward with usurpation and tyranny. Much the same thing occurs (p. 172) in *Orlando Furioso Q1*. Here is presumptive evidence of the suppression in *True Tragedy* of a speech present in the folio version, and the existence of which is implied in the language used above in the quotation.

(xiii) In the Parliament scene which opens *3 Henry VI* Warwick urges (1.1.25-7) York to claim the crown:

> This is the Pallace of the fearefull King,
> And this the Regall Seat: possesse it Yorke,
> For this is thine, and not King Henries heires.

These lines in *True Tragedy* (i. 23-4) run:

> This is the pallace of that fearefull King,
> And that *the regall chaire?* Possesse it Yorke:
> For this is thine and not King Henries heires.

Holinshed (iii. 655), copying Halle, speaks

of an oration, which the duke of Yorke vttered, sitting in *the regall seat,* there in the chamber of peeres.

Since the phrase italicized is Holinshed's not Halle's, Shake-

N

speare borrowed it from him; the words, 'the regall chaire,' found in *True Tragedy* are therefore an alteration of Shakespeare's text.

(xiv) When King Edward made dishonourable proposals to Lady Grey she answered (*3 Henry VI*, 3.2.97-8):

> I know, I am too meane to be your Queene,
> And yet too good to be your Concubine.

In *True Tragedy* (x. 75-6) her words are:

> I know I am too bad to be your Queene,
> And yet too good to be your Concubine.

Shakespeare took his account from Holinshed (iii. 726):

> And in conclusion she shewed him plain, that, as
> she wist hir selfe too simple to be his wife, so
> thought she hir selfe too good to be his concubine.

Here again the version in *True Tragedy* is a stupid alteration of the lines in *3 Henry VI*.

(xv) Professor Alexander in his *Shakespeare's Henry VI and Richard III* has stressed (pp. 63-4) the importance of the following example in discussing the relationship of these two parallel texts. Edward's marriage to Lady Grey may have been impolitic, but he seized the opportunity of creating a new nobility dependent on his favour, and enriched his wife's relatives by marrying them to the heiresses of nobles who had fallen in the civil wars. In the opening scene of the fourth act of *3 Henry VI* Shakespeare describes a violent quarrel between the King's brothers and Edward over the honours heaped upon men who had been Lancastrians. Halle refers to this subject several times. After Lady Grey's marriage

she was with great solempnitie crouned quene at Westmynster. Her father also was created erle Ryuers, and made high Constable of Englande: *her brother lorde Anthony, was maried to the sole heyre of Thomas Lord Scales, and by her he was lord Scales.* Syr Thomas Grey, sonne to syr Ihon Grey, the quenes fyrst husband, was created Marques Dorset, and maried to Cicilie, heyre to the lord Bonuile. (p. 264).

He again refers to this cause of discord in relating the intrigues of Clarence and Warwick against Edward:

The erle had not halfe told his tale, but the duke in a greate fury answered, why my lorde, thynke you to haue hym kynd to you, that is vnkynd, and vnnatural to me beynge his awne brother, thynke you that frendship will make hym kepe promise, where neither nature nor kynred, in any wise can prouoke or moue hym, to fauor his awne bloud? Thynke you that he will exalte and promote his cosin or alie, *whiche litle careth for the fall or confusion of his awne line and lignage*: This you knowe well enough, *that the heire of the Lord Scales he hath maried to his wifes brother, the heire also of the lorde Bonuile and Haryngton, he hath geuen to his wifes sonne, and theire of the lorde Hungerford, he hath graunted to the Lorde Hastynges: thre mariages more meter for his twoo brethren and kynne then for suche newe foundlynges as he hath bestowed theim on*: But by swete saincte George I sweare, if my brother of Gloucester would ioyne with me, we would make hym knowe, that we were all three one mannes sonnes, of one mother and one lignage discended, whiche should be more preferred and promoted then straungers of his wifes bloud. (p. 271).

The King's policy is apparent in the attitude of the earl of Pembroke, whom the King, says Halle, 'of a meane gentleman had promoted hym to the estate of an erle.' He became an enemy of Warwick, because the latter was

the sole obstacle (as he thought) why he obteined not the wardship of the Lorde Bonuiles daughter and heire, for his eldest sonne. (p. 273).

Shakespeare follows (4.1.47-58) Halle's account of Clarence's complaint given above very closely:

> *Clar.* For this one speech, Lord Hastings well deserues
> To have the Heire of the Lord Hungerford.
> *King.* I, what of that? it was my will, and graunt,
> And for this once, my Will shall stand for Law.
> *Rich.* And yet me thinks, your Grace hath not done well,
> To give the Heire and Daughter of Lord Scales
> Vnto the Brother of your louing Bride;
> Shee better would haue fitted me, or Clarence:
> But in your Bride you burie Brotherhood.
> *Clar.* Or else you would not haue bestow'd the Heire
> Of the Lord Bonuill on your new Wiues Sonne
> And leaue your Brothers to goe speede elsewhere.

The version (xii. 33-40) of the *True Tragedy* is muddled:

> *Cla.* For this one speech the Lord Hastings wel deserues
> To haue the daughter and heire of the Lord Hungerford.
> *Edw.* And what then? It was our will it should be so?
> *Cla.* I, and for such a thing too the Lord Scales
> Did well deserue at your hands, to haue the

> Daughter of the Lord Bonfield, and left your
> Brothers to go seeke elsewhere, but in
> Your madnes, you burie brotherhood.

Shakespeare's lines are an excellent versified transcript of Clarence's conversation with Warwick; the facts are correctly stated, and the complaints against the King's policy of enriching and ennobling his wife's kinsfolk are admirably summed up in the line,

> But in your Bride you burie Brotherhood.

The version in *True Tragedy* bristles with purposeless blunders, for not one fact is correctly given. No mention is made of the grievance that Lady Grey's father, brother and son are being enriched whilst the King's brothers must 'go speede elsewhere.' The errors in the facts are worth examination.

(a) Mary Hungerford was the grand-daughter, not daughter, of the Lancastrian Lord Hungerford who was attainted and executed in 1463. Her father was Sir Thomas Hungerford (executed in 1469), and his daughter was 'heir' to her grandfather. She was probably a small girl, and was contracted, not to Lord Hastings, but to his four-year-old son and heir, Edward Hastings.

(b) Cecily Bonvile was the great-grand-daughter, not the daughter of Lord Bonvile, and was his heiress. He was a Yorkist, executed by the Lancastrians, and survived both son and grandson; the latter had become Lord Harington in right of his mother and his small daughter inherited the vast estates of Bonvile and Harington. Halle himself blunders in styling her 'Lord Bonvile's daughter and heir' (p. 273) but this was not the source of the blunder in *True Tragedy*.

(c) Three blunders are crowded by the reporter into the statement that 'Lord Scales' had 'the Daughter of the Lord Bonfield.' Anthony Wydville, the queen's brother, became Lord Scales in right of his wife, and he could not marry a second wife in her life-time, even one so richly dowered as Cecily, great-grand-daughter, and not daughter, of Lord Bonvile. The actors may have confused him with his father-in-law, the famous Lord Scales, who appears in *Contention*.

(d) Gloster does not, in *True Tragedy*, associate himself as in *3 Henry VI* with the charges made by Clarence against the king of neglecting his brothers and enriching his wife's relatives. Clarence speaks the last line of Gloster's speech in the folio version; the presence of this line and the blundering mention of 'Lord Scales' offer sufficient proof of the pre-existence of Gloster's folio speech before the copy for *True Tragedy* was prepared.

Any dramatist of the period who had used this portion of Halle's chronicle would have stated the facts very much as Shakespeare did, and certainly could not have been guilty of so many senseless mistakes. This passage of *True Tragedy* is in precisely the same relation to Shakespeare's account in *3 Henry VI* and the relevant passages of Halle and Holinshed, as the ridiculous and muddled details of York's pedigree bear to the succinct statements in *2 Henry VI* and the fuller account of the chronicles. Shakespeare blunders in company with the chroniclers; the reporter blunders because he was ignorant, forgetful and incapable.

(xvi) Gloster has come 'to make a bloudie supper in the Tower,' and with deliberate brutality tells (xxii. 25) the father,

> Thy sonne I kild for his presumption.

The account of his death given in the previous scene (xxi. 76),

> *Edw.* Take that, the litnes of this railer heere.
> *Queen.* Oh kill me too.

suggests that King Edward alone struck and killed the prince, and that Gloster took no part in the murder.

Gloster's line in *3 Henry VI* (5.6.34) is identical with the above,

> Thy Son I kill'd for his presumption.

The folio version of the murder (5.5.38-41) is:

> *Edw.* Take that, the likenesse of this Rayler here. *Stabs him.*
> *Rich.* Sprawl'st thou? take that, to end thy agonie.
> > *Rich. stabs him.*
> *Clar.* And ther's for twitting me with periurie. *Clar. stabs*
> *Qu.* Oh, kill me too. > *him.*

Gloster's assertion that he had killed Prince Edward proves the omission in *True Tragedy* of lines necessary to the sense which are present in *3 Henry VI;* accordingly the latter text must have been in existence before the copy for the *True Tragedy* was compiled.

(xvii) The final scene of *True Tragedy* is very close to that of

3 Henry VI, but an odd blunder has crept into Gloster's lines (xxii. 28-9) when he gives the kiss of peace to his infant nephew:

> And that I loue the fruit from whence thou
> Sprangst, witnesse the louing kisse I giue the child.

Once more the folio version must be consulted, and the two lines (5.7.28-9) are explained:

> And that I loue the tree from whence thou sprang'st:
> Witnesse the louing kisse I giue the Fruite.

Metaphor once more proved a pitfall for the unimaginative actor.

Eighteen passages in ten scenes of *True Tragedy* are obscure or meaningless unless the corresponding passages of *3 Henry VI* are consulted. These results prove the priority of *3 Henry VI* for these ten scenes, and inferentially for all the scenes.

Romeo and Juliet Q1 and Q2

Blunders in the text of *Romeo and Juliet Q1* provide some proof that it is the derivative and not the source of Q2. Ten difficult or obscure passages which neither audience nor reader could understand are made intelligible with the assistance of the second quarto; in other words Q2 preceded Q1 in composition. These passages occur in one or other of nine scenes, and are relatively as frequent in Part II as in Part I. They offer irrefutable evidence that Acts III-V were in existence before the copy for Q1 was in the hands of the printer, and that the actors' parts prepared from the author's manuscript of Q2 were in use before the pirate compiled Q1. Half the passages occur in four scenes which Professor Wilson asserts are the unrevised work of another author except for rewriting 'here and there.'

(i) After the fray between Montagues and Capulets, Montague talks with Benvolio and, on seeing Romeo approach, leaves the stage. The following dialogue (i. 82-7) ensues between the young men:

> *Benuo:* Good morrow Cosen.
> *Romeo:* Is the day so young?
> *Ben.* But new stroke nine.
> *Romeo:* Ay me, sad hopes seeme long.
> Was that my Father that went hence so fast?
> *Ben.* It was, what sorrow lengthens Romeo's houres?

What does Romeo mean by his 'sad hopes seeme long'? and how is it related to Benvolio's reply? The version of Q2 explains the difficulty. 'Hopes' should be 'houres,' and 'sorrow' should be 'sadnesse'; otherwise the two texts are identical.

(ii) Capulet and Paris enter, and Paris opens (ii. 1-3) the second scene:

> Of honorable reckoning are they both,
> And pittie tis they liue at ods so long:
> But leauing that, what say you to my sute?

Nothing is said in the text to explain who are 'they' that are 'of honorable reckoning' and 'liue at ods.' From the first scene the audience and reader know that the reference is to the Montagues and Capulets, but why does Paris in the third line ask Capulet for his daughter's hand in marriage, after referring in the two previous lines to his father-in-law elect as if he were absent? On reading the version of Q2 the difficulty vanishes (1.2.1-6):

> *Capu*: But Montague is bound as well as I,
> In penaltie alike, and tis not hard I thinke,
> For men so old as we to keepe the peace.
> *Par*. Of honourable reckoning are you both,
> And pittie tis, you liu'd at ods so long:
> But now my Lord, what say you to my sute?

I suggest that the company's play-abridger struck out Capulet's speech; if Paris spoke what Shakespeare wrote for him, he could begin the scene almost as effectively as Capulet. The stupidity of a forgetful reporter is the only explanation of the obscurity necessary.

(iii) Two lines (iv. 49-50) of the Queen Mab speech deserve notice; the lines that precede and follow them are practically the same in both versions:

> The traces are the Moone-shine watrie beames,
> The collers crickets bones, the lash of filmes.

Queen Mab's coach comes from fairy-land, but 'the lash of filmes' implies a whip in the hands of the coachman. I put the three lines of Q2 into verse (1.4.61-3) for purpose of comparison:

> Her traces of the smallest spider web,
> Her collors of the moonshines watry beams
> Her whip of Crickets bone, the lash of Philome.

All the authentic quartos and folios print this speech as prose; Q1 has all it retains in verse. I suggest that the error occurred when a scribe was making a fair copy of the actor's recollections of this speech. His original probably contained the three lines of Q2 with such small changes as 'the' for 'her' at the beginning, 'are' for 'of' in the first and second lines, and 'is' for 'of' in the third line. After transcribing 'the traces' his eye unconsciously shifted to the line below, and he completed the first line as we find it in Q1. Repeating this process he produced the second line of Q1. He then began with 'Her waggoner' etc., and continued for three lines which substantially are those of Q2. These lines of Q1 imply the pre-existence of the lines in Q2.

(iv) Friar Laurence has reached the thirtieth line of a soliloquy when his pupil Romeo greets him (vii. 25-6):

> *Rom*: Good morrow to my Ghostly Confessor.
> *Fri*: Benedicite, what earlie tongue so soone saluteth me?

This scene is one of the best preserved of Q1. Except for this pair of lines, the rest of the verses are rhymed couplets. Here a decasyllabic line is followed by a 'fifteener,' and the pair do not rhyme. In our early plays metrical disorder means mislineation or corruption. On turning to Q2 the corresponding lines (2.3.31-2) are:

> *Ro.* Good morrow father.
> *Fri.* Benedicitie.
> What early tongue so sweete saluteth me?

The explanation is that in Q2 the word 'benedicite' completes the verse which Romeo begins; in Q1 a line borrowed and adapted from Juliet's greeting (2.6.21) to the Friar,

> Good euen to my ghostly confessor,

fills the line completely with the result that 'Benedicite' overflows into the next line. Thus the presence in Q1 of a line, adapted from a line in a later scene of Q2, proves that this scene which is not in Q1 had been spoken on the stage before John Danter had received the MS. of Q1.

(v) Romeo has met his friend Mercutio, and a battle of wits proceeds. These lines (viii. 45-9) are part of the word-play:

> *Rom.* I cry you mercy my busines was great, and in such a case as mine, a man may straine curtesie.
> *Mer.* Oh thats as much to say as such a case as yours wil constraine a man to bow in the hams.
> *Rom.* A most curteous exposition.

Puns and double meanings fill the air when Mercutio is on the stage, but Romeo's last comment has no apparent connection with the two previous speeches. The version of Q2 (2.4.47-53) explains all:

> *Ro.* Pardon good Mercutio, my businesse was great, and in such a case as mine, a man may straine curtesie.
> *Mer.* Thats as much as to say, such a case as yours, constrains a man to bow in the hams.
> *Ro.* Meaning to cursie.
> *Mer.* Thou has most kindly hit it.
> *Ro.* A most curtuous exposition.

The two omitted speeches of Q1 are necessary to explain Mercutio's intentionally ambiguous phrase 'to bow in the hams.'

(vi) Juliet has learnt that Romeo has killed her cousin Tybalt, and has, in consequence, been banished. She talks wildly in her grief and asks (xii. 52-6) her nurse:

> *Iul:* Where are my Father and my Mother Nurse?
> *Nur:* Weeping and wayling ouer Tybalts coarse.
> Will you goe to them?
> *Iul:* I, I, when theirs are spent,
> Mine shall be shed for Romeos banishment.

Where is the noun to which 'theirs' and 'mine' refer? Though the context and scene suggest 'tears,' this is but a guess, and something is missing which the second quarto (3.2.127-131) supplies:

> *Iu:* Where is my father and my mother Nurse?
> *Nur.* Weeping and wayling ouer Tybalts course,
> Will you go to them? I will bring you thither.
> *Iu.* Wash they his wounds with teares? mine shall be spent,
> When theirs are drie, for Romeos banishment.

Once more the evidence favours the priority of Q2.

(vii) The nurse visits Friar Laurence at his cell, and Romeo asks her (xiii. 95-99) for news of Juliet; she replies:

> *Nur*: Oh she saith nothing, but weepes and pules,
> And now fals on her bed, now on the ground,
> And Tybalt cryes, and then on Romeo calles.
> *Rom*: As if that name, shot from the deadly leuel of a gun
> Did murder her.

The nurse's account is unintentionally comic. Juliet weeps, falls on her bed, rolls from it to the ground, and then shrieks out the names of Tybalt and Romeo. To which of these names does Romeo refer? According to Q1, Juliet is on the ground before she names either; consequently the text of the first quarto gives no support for Romeo's suggestion that the mention of his name has made her fall to the ground as if shot. Reference to the text of the second quarto (3.3.99-104) clears up the difficulty:

> *Nur.* Oh she sayes nothing sir, but weeps and weeps,
> And now falls on her bed, and then starts vp,
> And Tybalt calls, and then on Romeo cries,
> And then downe falls againe.
> *Ro.* As if that name shot from the deadly leuel of a gun,
> Did murther her.

The reason for Romeo's outburst is clear; Juliet falls on her bed, starts up again, calls on Tybalt, then on Romeo and then falls down again; this partly justifies Romeo's extravagant simile. Omission of a sentence 'and then starts vp' present in Q2 but necessary to the sense of Q1, is responsible for the nonsense in Q1. The verse also suggests disorder as a result of omission.

(viii) Another example of the reporter's bungling occurs in the same scene. As befits a man of the church, Friar Laurence sternly rebukes Romeo for threatening to commit suicide. He opens his long speech with the following lines (xiii. 105-9):

> Hold, stay thy hand: art thou a man? thy forme
> Cryes out thou art, but thy wild acts denote
> The vnresonable furyes of a beast.
> Vnseemely woman in a seeming man,
> Or ill beseeming beast in seeming both.

The last two lines are not related to the three lines above. Why does the friar call Romeo an 'Vnseemely woman,' and an 'ill-beseeming beast' in seeming both man and woman? Some reference to a woman is missing. The speech (3.3.108-113) in Q2 is as follows:

Hold thy desperate hand:
Art thou a man? thy forme cries out thou art:
Thy teares are womanish, thy wild acts denote
The vnreasonable furie of a beast,
Vnseemely woman in a seeming man,
And ilbeseeming beast in seeming both.

Omission of 'Thy teares are womanish' in Q1 leaves the fourth line of the passage in the air and almost meaningless, and renders the concluding line obscure and less forceful.

(ix) After the supposed death of Juliet, Peter asks the musicians assembled to celebrate the marriage, to 'play me some merie dump'; they refuse because 'tis no time to play now.' He begins to banter them (xix. 88-92):

Ser: Then will I giue it you, and soundly to.
1. What will you giue vs?
Ser. The fidler, Ile re you, Ile fa you, Ile sol you.
1. If you re vs and fa vs, we will note you.
Ser. I will put vp my Iron dagger, and beate you with my wodden wit. Come on Simon sound Pot, Ile pose you.

Peter's last speech is so abrupt and disconnected with what went before that it is inexplicable to a reader, though stage 'business' may have enabled the audience to understand it. We must read Q2 (4.5.109-121) to clear up the difficulty:

Peter. I will then giue it you soundly.
Minst. What will you giue vs?
Peter. No money on my faith, but the gleeke.
I will giue you the Minstrell.
Minstrel. Then will I giue you the Seruing-creature.
Peter. Then will I lay the seruing-creatures dagger on your pate. I will cary no Crochets, Ile re you, Ile fa you, do you note me?
Minst. And you re vs, and fa vs, you note vs.
2 M. Pray you put vp your dagger, and put out your wit. Then haue at you with my wit.
Peter. I will dry-beate with an yron wit, and put vp my yron dagger. Answere me like men.

Peter, alias Will Kemp, did not 'pose' his audience as in Q1.

(x) Her unhappy parents have discovered 'Iuliet dead before Warme and new kild' in the tomb. Capulet exclaims (xxii. 142-4):

See Wife, this dagger hath mistooke:
For (loe) the backe is empty of yong Mountague,
And it is sheathed in our Daughters breast.

We cannot take the words, 'the backe is empty of yong Mountague'
to mean the 'sheath' or 'house' of the dagger that Montague wore
on his back is empty. We must refer to Q2 (5.3.201-4):

O heauens! O wife looke how our daughter bleeds!
This dagger hath mistane, for loe his house
Is emptie on the back of Mountague,
And it missheathd in my daughters bosome.

HENRY V Q1 AND HENRY V FO.

(i) Over sixty years ago Daniel pointed out, in his introduction
to the edition of the 'Parallel Texts of the Quarto and Folio' of
this play, published by the New Shakespeare Society, certain
remarkable peculiarities of the Archbishop's speech as it appears
in Q1. With the texts of both versions of this speech arranged
on opposite pages the deficiencies of Q1 become manifest. Any
reader must be convinced that the two versions have a common
origin; four-fifths of the lines of Q1 are either the same as the
corresponding lines of the folio or differ from the folio lines in
one word or two only per line. More than a third of the folio
speech is missing, and included among the folio lines that are
omitted in Q1 are some which are necessary to the sense of lines
present in Q1. As Daniel puts it, the quarto 'in itself contains
evidence of *omission* of passages found in the fuller version.'
From the evidence afforded in this speech and in a later scene he
infers the priority of the folio text. Of Q1 he says,

instead of regarding it as the author's first sketch, we can only
look on it as an imperfect copy of his work.

I have followed Daniel's example in placing the two versions
of the Archbishop's speech on opposite pages; I have also prefixed
Holinshed's version, italicizing the portions, even the words, that
Shakespeare inserted from it in his metrical paraphrase. This I
have borrowed from W. G. Boswell-Stone's *Shakespeare's Holinshed,* pp. 169-171.

Archbishop Chichele inveighed 'against the surmised and false fained law Salike, which the Frenchmen alledge euer *against* the kings of England in *barre* of their iust title *to* the crowne of *France.* The verie words of that supposed law are these: *"In terram Salicam mulieres ne succedant"*; that is to saie, "Into the *Salike land* let not women *succeed." Which the French* glossers expound *to be the realme of France, and* that *this law* was made by King *Pharamond*; whereas *yet their owne authors affirme, that the land Salike is in Germanie, betweene the* riuers *of Elbe and Sala;* and that when *Charles the great* had ouercome *the Saxons,* he placed there *certeine French*men, which hauing in *disdaine the dishonest maners of the Germane women,* made a *law* that the *females should* not succeed to any inheritance with*in* that *lond, which at this daie is called Meisen;* so that, if this is true, this law *was not* made *for the realme of France, nor the French* men *possessed* the *land Salike, till foure hundred* and *one and twentie yeares after* the death *of Pharamond,* the *supposed* maker *of this* Salike *law;* for this Pharamond deceassed *in the yeare* 426, and *Charles the great subdued the Saxons, and* placed *the French*men in those parts *beyond the riuer of Sala, in the yeare* 805.

'Moreover, it appeareth by *their* owne *writers,* that *King Pepine, which deposed Childericke,* claimed *the crowne of France as heire generall,* for that he was *descended of Blithild, daughter to King Clothair* the first. *Hugh Capet* also *(who usurped the crowne* vpon *Charles Duke of Loraine,* the *sole heire male of the line and stocke of Charles the Great) to* make *his* title seeme true, and appeare good *(though* indeed *it was* starke *naught) conueied him selfe* as *heire to the Ladie Lingard, daughter to* King *Charlemaine, sonne to Lewes, the emperour,* that was *son to Charles the great.* King *Lewes* also, *the tenth* (otherwise called saint Lewes) being verie *heire to the* said *vsurper* Hugh *Capet, could* neuer be *satisfied in his conscience* how he might iustlie keepe and possesse *the crowne of France, till* he was persuaded and fullie instructed *that queene Isabell his grandmother was lineallie* descended *of the ladie Ermengard, daughter* and heire *to the* aboue named *Charles duke of Loraine; by the which marriage, the* bloud and *line of Charles the great was* againe *vnited* and restored *to the crowne* and scepter *of France: so that* more *cleere* than *the sunne* it openlie *appeareth,* that *the title of King Pepin, the claime of Hugh Capet,* the possession *of Lewes;* yea, and *the* French *Kings to this daie* are deriued and conueied from *the* heire *female;* though *they would,* vnder the colour of such a fained *law, barre* the kings and princes of this realme of England of their right and lawfull inheritance.'

HENRY V (FOLIO)

                              There is no *barre*
To make *against* your Highnesse Clayme *to France*,
But this which they produce from Pharamond,
40 *In terram Salicam Mulieres ne succedant,*
No Woman shall *succeed in Salike Land*:
Which Salike Land, *the French* vniustly gloze
To be the Realme of France, and Pharamond
44 The founder of *this Law,* and Female Barre.
Yet their owne Authors faithfully *affirme,*
That the Land Salike is in Germanie,
Betweene the Flouds *of Sala and of Elue*:
48 Where *Charles the Great* hauing subdu'd *the Saxons,*
There left behind and settled *certaine French*:
Who holding *in disdaine the German Women,*
For some *dishonest manners of* their life,
52 Establisht then this Law; to wit, No Female
Should be Inheritrix *in* Salike *Land*:
Which Salike (as I said) 'twixt Elue and Sala
Is at this day in Germanie, *call'd Meisen.*
56 Then doth it well appeare, the Salike *Law*
Was not deuised *for the Realme of France*:
Nor did *the French possesse the Salike Land,*
Vntill foure hundred one and twentie yeeres
60 *After* defunction of King *Pharamond,*
Idly *suppos'd* the founder *of this Law,*
Who died with*in the yeere* of our Redemption
Foure hundred twentie six: and *Charles the Great*
64 *Subdu'd the Saxons, and* did seat *the French*
Beyond the Riuer Sala, in the yeere
Eight hundred fiue. Besides, their *Writers* say,
King Pepin, which deposed Childerike,
68 Did *as Heire Generall,* being *descended*
Of Blithild, which was *daughter* to *King Clothair,*
Make Clayme and Title to *the Crowne of France.*
Hugh Capet also, who vsurpt the Crowne
72 *Of Charles* the Duke of *Loraine, sole Heire male*
Of the true *Line and Stock of Charles* the *Great*:
To find *his Title* with some shewes of truth,
Though in pure truth *it was* corrupt and *naught,*
76 *Conuey'd himselfe as* th'*Heire to* th'*Lady Lingare,*
Daughter to Charlemaine, who was the *Sonne*
To *Lewes the Emperour,* and Lewes the *Sonne*
Of Charles the Great: also *King Lewes the Tenth,*

HENRY V (QUARTO)

There is no bar to stay your highnesse claime to France 24
But *one,* which they produce from Faramount

No *female* shall succeed in salicke land,
Which salicke land the French vniustly gloze
To be the realme of France:
And Faramont the founder of this law and female barre: 28
Yet their owne *writers* faithfully affirme
That the land salicke *lyes* in Germany
Betweene the flouds of *Sabeck* and of *Elme,*
Where Charles the *fift* hauing subdude the Saxons, 32
There left behind, and setled certaine French,
Who holding in disdaine the Germaine women,
For some dishonest maners of their liues,
Establisht there this lawe. To wit, 36
No female shall *succeed* in salicke land:
Which salicke land as I said before,
Is at this *time* in Germany called Mesene:
Thus doth it well appeare the salicke lawe 40
Was not deuised for the realme of France,
Nor did the French possesse the salicke land,
Vntill 400. one and twentie yeares
After *the* function of King Faramont,
Godly supposed the founder of this lawe:

Hugh Capet also *that* vsurpt the crowne,

To fine his title with some showe of truth, 48
When in pure truth it was corrupt and naught:
Conuaid himselfe as heire to the Lady *Inger,*

80 Who was sole *Heire to the Vsurper Capet,*
   Could not keepe quiet *in his conscience,*
   Wearing *the Crowne of France,* 'till satisfied,
   That faire *Queene Isabel, his Grandmother,*
84 *Was Lineall of the Lady Ermengare,*
   Daughter to Charles the foresaid *Duke of Loraine*:
   By the which Marriage, the Lyne of Charles the Great
   Was re-*vnited to the Crowne of France.*
88 *So, that* as *cleare* as is *the* Summers *Sunne,*
   King *Pepins Title,* and *Hugh Capets Clayme,*
   King *Lewes* his satisfaction, all *appeare*
   To hold in Right and Title of *the Female*:
92 So doe the Kings of France vn*to this day.*
   Howbeit, *they would* hold vp this Salique *Law,*
   To *barre* your Highnesse clayming from the Female,
   And rather chuse to hide them in a Net,
92 Then amply to imbarre their crooked Titles
   Vsurpt from you and your Progenitors.

Daughter to Charles, the foresaid Duke of Lorain,

So that as cleare as is the sommers Sun,   52
King Pippins title and Hugh Capets claime,
King Charles his satisfaction all appeare,
To hold in right and title of the female:
So do the *Lords* of France vnt*il* this day.   56
Howbeit they would hold vp this salick lawe
To bar your highnesse claiming from the female,
And rather choose to hide them in a net,
Then amply to imbace their crooked causes,   60
Vsurpt from you and your progenitors.

o

Comparison of the three texts will convince any reader of the following facts:—

(i) That Holinshed's chronicle was here the common and only source of both folio and quarto versions. Shakespeare preserves the incorrect arithmetic, the mis-spelt names, the blunders of fact of his source; the quarto merely adds a blunder or two of its own to those taken over from Holinshed by Shakespeare.

(ii) That the corresponding portions of folio and quarto agree in choosing from Holinshed's account almost precisely the same words, phrases and sentences—a circumstance which by itself makes it certain that one man's work was the basis of both versions. Moreover, the verses in which these borrowings from Holinshed are placed either are verbally identical or differ by not more than one or two words in a line. Which of these two versions is the earlier?

(iii) That the folio version keeps closer to Holinshed's language and facts than Q1, and gives a logical and accurate paraphrase of the Archbishop's oration; the author of Q1, by changing a word or two in some lines and omitting more than a third of his original, presents a version, incomplete, illogical and not even consistent with itself. This suggests that Shakespeare wrote the folio speech with his eye on the text of the chronicle, and that Q1 is a garbled abbreviation of the poet's work made by some incompetent muddler. Why should any man, capable of the work done in the folio, have the stupid blunders of Q1 fathered upon him as a first sketch?

(iv) That the version of the Archbishop's speech in Q1 is the derivative not of Holinshed's chronicle but of Shakespeare's text. In each of a dozen or more lines common to the two texts where the quarto line differs from the corresponding folio line in one word only, the word used in the folio comes from the source-line of Holinshed. I have italicized all the words of the quarto text which vary in this way from the corresponding lines of the folio and the chronicle. These variations are the work of the person responsible for the other changes found in the text of Q1; the insertion of several such words in quarto lines, e.g. 'fift,' 'Inger,' 'Charles' and 'Lords' results in mis-statements of facts given in the chronicle but correctly stated in the folio. Shakespeare's mistakes of fact come from following the chronicle; the additional mistakes of fact in Q1 do not arise from misreading Holinshed but from a defective memory of what Shakespeare wrote. The relation of the two versions to each other and to their source compels us to infer that Shakespeare wrote the folio text first, and that Q1 is derived directly from the folio.

These inferences are confirmed when the five lines of Q1, viz., ll. 47-51, which are all that remain of lines 62-87 of the folio text, are examined as Daniel did. The crop of blunders which sprang from the omission of twenty-one lines of the folio, would have been impossible if the compiler of Q1 had been working from his sources.

(a) The line (Q1, i, l. 47)

Hugh Capet also that vsurpt the crowne,

is common to both versions. The word 'also' points to some omission in Q1. Reference to the folio text or Holinshed explains what is omitted. King Pepin was the first of the kings of France to claim the crown in 'right and title of the female,' thus setting aside the supposed bar created by the Salic law. His was the first case quoted, which accounts for the word 'also' here. The text of Q1 proves that the above explanation is correct, for the Archbishop in his summary (Q1, ll. 53-55) names 'King Pippins title' before 'Hugh Capets claime.'

(b) The omission of the two lines immediately following the mention of Hugh Capet results in another gap in the sense. 'The Lady Inger' (a blunder for the folio 'Lingare') is wrongly styled,

Daughter to Charles, the foresaid Duke of Lorain.

No mention has been made previously in Q1 of any 'Duke of Lorain.' We must peruse Holinshed or the folio text to learn that this was the king whose throne Hugh Capet usurped.

(c) Another amazing blunder results from the omission of eight lines of text. Ermengare, the daughter of Charles of Loraine, is confused with 'Inger,' daughter of Charlemaine (really Charles the Bald). The quarto text makes Hugh Capet base his claim to the French crown on his being descended from the daughter of the man whom he had deposed and murdered. Once more the blunder of Q1 results from omission of lines present in the folio.

(d) The summary of the Archbishop's speech is almost identical in the two versions, except that 'Charles' in Q1 replaces 'Lewes' of the folio. Q1 names, as does the folio, three French Kings who claimed the crown 'in Right and Title of the Female,' but neither Pepin nor Lewes has been mentioned before in Q1. Once again there is proof of the omission of passages present in the folio which are necessary to the understanding of portion of Q1.

The series of blunders discussed above is exactly parallel to the bungling in the pedigree of York which is found in the *Contention,* and the mistakes concerning the marriages of the heiresses in *True Tragedy.*

(ii) Other passages may be cited in support of the opinion that the text of Q1 is derived from the folio rather than directly from the chronicles. Thus Holinshed reports (iii. 526) the sentence of death passed by King Henry upon the conspirators against his life as follows:

Get ye *hence therefore,* ye *poore miserable wretches,* to the
receiving of *your* iust reward; wherein *Gods* maiestie *giue*
you grace *of his mercie, and repentance of your* heinous *offences.*

Shakspeare inserts (2.1.177-181) much of this almost verbatim:

> *Get* you *therefore hence,*
> (*Poore miserable wretches*) to *your* death:
> The taste whereof, *God of his mercy giue*
> *You* patience to indure, *and* true *Repentance*
> *Of* all *your* deare *offences.* Beare them hence.

Q1 keeps close to what Shakespeare wrote, but deviates far more from the exact words of Holinshed (iii. 104-7),

> *Get ye therefore hence: poore miserable* creatures to *your*
> death,
> The taste whereof, *God* in *his mercy giue you*
> Patience to endure, *and* true *repentance* of all *your* deeds
> amisse;
> Beare them hence.

(iii) Henry proclaims (i. 154-7) in full council his resolve to conquer and rule France or die:

> Eyther our Chronicles shall with full mouth speak
> Freely of our acts,
> Or else like toonglesse mutes
> Not worshipt with a paper Epitaph.

The third and fourth lines are without logical or grammatical connection with the previous lines and are void of meaning. Two lines are metrically defective and some words have been lost. On consulting the folio version (i.2.230-3) sense is restored:

> Either our History shall with full mouth
> Speake freely of our Acts, or else our graue
> Like Turkish mute, shall haue a tonguelesse mouth,
> Not worshipt with a waxen Epitaph.

The omission of the essential words 'or else our graue' and the crushing together of the words in the third line of the folio text have caused the muddle in Q1.

(iv) Henry has been insulted by a gift of tennis balls which he rightly takes as a taunt directed at his 'wilder days,' and he explains (i. 190-2) the thoughts of his youth:

> We neuer valued this poor seate of England.
> And therefore gaue our selues to barbarous licence:
> As tis common seene that men are merriest
> When they are from home.

As in the previous example little connection exists between the first two lines and what follows, though here both portions are quite intelligible. Referring to the folio (i.2.269-72) we read:

> We neuer valew'd this poor seate of England,
> And therefore liuing hence, did giue our selfe
> To barbarous license: As 'tis euer common,
> That men are merriest, when they are from home.

Omission of the words 'liuing hence,' i.e., away from the court— 'this poor seate of England'—is the key to the true sense of the third and fourth lines. The folio must explain Q1 as it did in the previous example.

(v) Henry has taken Harfleur. The French King and Council discuss defence and the characters of their enemies, and the Constable refers (ix. 2-4) to the Norman conquerors of England:

> Mordeu ma via: Shall a few spranes of vs,
> The emptying of our fathers luxerie,
> Outgrow their grafters.

What does this mean? 'Sprane' is unknown to lexicographers, and even a misprint for 'sprayes' does not explain 'outgrow their grafters.' On reference to the folio text (3.5.5-9) we read:

> *Dolph.* O Dieu viuant: Shall a few Sprayes of vs,
> The emptying of our Fathers Luxurie,
> Our Syens, put in wilde and sauage Stock,
> Spirt vp so suddenly into the Clouds,
> And ouer-looke their Grafters?

The Constable's oath is not his own but Britaine's or Bourbon's, and the speech is the Dolphin's in the folio version, but the cause of the confusion in Q1 is the omission of the third and fourth folio lines, which are necessary to the sense of what is left in Q1.

(vi) Mountjoy, the French Herald, bids (x. 110-2) Henry 'consider of his ransome,' demands satisfaction and to this adds defiance:

> England shall repent her folly: see her rashnesse,
> And admire our sufferance. Which to raunsome,
> His pettinesse would bow vnder.

He confuses 'England' the country with 'England' as an abbreviation for King of England; he speaks of *her* folly, *her* rashnesse, and *his* pettinesse; why *his*? To what antecedent does 'which' refer? It can not be 'folly' or 'rashnesse' or 'sufferance.' For an explanation of this muddle the folio speech (3.6.116-21) must be consulted:

> England shall repent his folly, see his weakenesse, and
> admire our sufferance. Bid him therefore consider of his
> ransome, which must proportion the losses we haue
> borne, the subiects we haue lost, the disgrace we haue digested;
> which in weight to re-answer, his pettinesse would bow vnder.

This passage serves to fill up the blanks left in the text of Q1. The antecedents of 'which' are 'losses,' 'subjects' and 'disgrace'; in addition, the King's ransom is expressly mentioned for the first time.

(vii) Henry's long soliloquy on ceremony at the end of the first scene of the fourth act is omitted in Q1, and the corresponding scene of Q1 closes with a line spoken by the King,

> For to morrow the King himselfe wil be a clipper.
> *Exit the souldiers.*

Dramatic convention requires that Henry should remain on the stage, but he must have left it if we accept the implication in the centred stage direction, that immediately follows the line quoted.

> *Enter the King, Gloster, Epingam, and Attendants.*

At once Henry falls on his knees in their presence and confesses publicly that he, the King of England, who had invaded France as rightful heir to the French throne, is himself a usurper, and the son of a usurper who had deposed and murdered Richard, and that he is neither rightful King of England nor true heir to the throne of France. This confession is astonishing enough, but the next stage direction is 'Enter Gloster,' who is or should be on the stage. He calls 'My Lord,' and the King recognizes his brother's voice—it is night—and leaves the stage with him. These absurd mistakes must be the result of an attempt to reconstruct stage directions from memory. The actors remembered that Henry, Erpingham and Gloster in that order were on the stage towards the end of the scene; Erpingham does not speak a line in Q1, but the entry here is a proof that his part was not cut out of the acting version.

On consulting the folio text we find that Henry was interrupted at the fifty-sixth line of his soliloquy by the entrance of Erpingham, who tells him that the nobles are seeking him. The King orders him to collect them at his tent, and Erpingham leaves the royal presence; then follows the battle prayer, and afterwards Gloster's arrival and departure with the King.

(viii) Another significant blunder involves the almost complete disappearance of a scene. Shakespeare wrote two sets of contrasting scenes; first, he gives us night-scenes in the French camp and in the English camp, and secondly, morning-scenes in the French army and in the English army before the battle. Q1 omits the morning-scene in the French army, except that the concluding line and a half are tagged as the conclusion of the French camp-scene of the previous night. This in Q1 is very short. At line 26 Burbon exclaims 'Will it neuer be morning?' and six lines later Gebon remarks, 'The Duke of Burbon longs for morning.' Yet at the sixtieth line the Constable most inappropriately concludes the scene with the words,

Come, come away:
The sun is hie, and we weare out the day.

With this line and a half, except that 'out-weare' replaces 'weare out' the Constable concludes in the folio text the subsequent morning-scene in the French camp; they are all that remain of it in Q1. They give evidence that the folio version was spoken on the stage before the copy for the quarto was entered on the Stationers' Register. Possibly the two scenes were amalgamated and the person charged with this duty forgot that the sun does not rise in France at two o'clock in the morning.

This omission of the French morning-piece has thrown the stage directions of Q1 into chaos. In my previous example I showed that if the actors produced the play as the stage directions required, they would have committed a ridiculous blunder; further, an entry was provided for a person already on the stage. Scene thirteen of Q1, corresponding to the end of Act four, scene one, concludes as does the folio text with the King's words (4.1.292-3) to Gloster,

> I will goe with thee:
> The day my friends, and all things stayes for me.

In the folio the French morning-scene follows which Q1 omits. When the King and Gloster conclude the above quarto scene, no 'exeunt' was marked for them; and immediately after the words 'stayes with me' follows

> *'Enter Clarence, Gloster, Exeter and Salisburie.'*

Gloster must have left the stage by one door and immediately entered by the same or another door, exactly as the King did twenty lines previously; in the quarto versions, his opening line (4.3.1) in the folio,

> Where is the King?

is omitted, fortunately for readers of this text.

(ix) Exeter describes the deaths of Suffolk and York on the battle-field. Suffolk was dead when York, mortally wounded, reaches him (xvii. 15-20):

> And cryde aloud, tary deare cousin Suffolke:
> My soule shall thine keep company in heauen:
> Tary deare soule awhile, then flie to rest:
> And in this glorious and well foughten field,
> We kept togither in our chiualdry.
> Vpon these words I came and cheerd them vp.

The passage lacks cohesion; the fourth and fifth lines seem a meaningless interpolation, and, as Exeter knew that Suffolk was dead, he could not cheer *them* up. Difficulties and blunders vanish on reading this passage (4.6.15-20) in the folio text:

> He cryes aloud, Tarry my Cosin Suffolke,
> My soule shall thine keepe company to heauen:
> Tarry (sweet soule) for mine, then flye a-brest:
> As in this glorious and well-foughten field
> We kept together in our Chiualrie.
> Vpon these words I came, and cheer'd him vp.

Petty alterations such as 'in' for 'to,' 'awhile' for 'for mine,' 'to rest' for 'a-breast,' 'them' for 'him' have completely destroyed the sense of Q1.

CONTENTION AND 2 HENRY VI

Of the five quartos written mainly in verse *Contention* is the worst preserved. Consequently the two parallel texts are not so close in language as the other pairs, and a smaller number of passages throw light upon the question of priority.

(i) Shakespeare depicts in the hawking scene a quarrel between Duke Humphrey and his political opponents, Suffolk and Cardinal Beaufort. Part of this appears in *Contention* (v. 17-24) as follows:

> *Card.* Proude Protector dangerous Peere, to smooth it thus
> with King and common-wealth.
> *Humphrey.* How now my Lord, why this is more then needs,
> Church-men so hote. Good vnckle can you doate.
> *Suffolke.* Why not Hauing so good a quarrell & so bad
> a cause.
> *Humphrey.* As how, my Lord?
> *Suffolke.* As you, my Lord. And it like your Lordly
> Lords Protectorship.

What is this all about? The passage from 'Good vnckle' to the end is as difficult of understanding as a modern imagist poem; the dialogue moves from speech to speech without logical connection of ideas. To find its meaning *2 Henry VI* must be read. In 2.1.21-30 we have:

> *Card.* Pernitious Protector, dangerous Peere,
> That smooth'st it so with King and Common-weale.
> *Glost.* What, Cardinall?
> Is your Priest-hood growne peremptorie?
> Tantae ne animis Coelestibus irae, Church-men so hot?
> Good Vnckle hide such mallice:
> With such Holynesse can you doe it?
> *Suff.* No mallice Sir, no more then well becomes
> So good a Quarrell, and so bad a Peere.
> *Glost.* As who, my Lord?
> *Suff.* Why, as you, my Lord.
> An't like your Lordly Lords Protectorship.

Compression of the last two lines of Gloster's first speech in the folio to 'Good vnckle can you doate,' hides all reference to the word 'mallice,' which is the text of Suffolk's reply. 'Doate,' a common spelling of 'dote' may be intended for 'doot' or doo't, but this is doubtful, and 'how' may be a misprint for 'who'; in either instance the folio text is giving a meaning to what is not intelligible in *Contention.* However, the omission of 'peere' and the insertion of 'cause' is the main reason for the difficulty in understanding the last three lines of the first quotation.

(ii) The line in *Contention* (viii. 49) spoken by Elinor,

And impious Yorke and Bewford that false Priest,

is obviously an error for the line (2.4.53) in *2 Henry VI,*

And Yorke, and impious Beauford, that false Priest.

No Protestant dramatist would waste 'impious' upon 'Yorke' when he could hang this epithet upon Cardinal Beaufort.

(iii) Cade's sentence (xiii. 68-9) on the 'Clarke of Chatham,'

Oh hes confest, go hang him with his
penny-inckhorne about his necke,

represents a compression of two speeches (4.2.100-3) in *3 Henry VI,*

All. He hath confest: away with him: he's a Villaine
and a Traitor.
Cade. Away with him I say: Hang him with his Pen
and Inke-horne about his necke.

Holinshed (iii. 436) in his account of the peasant rebellion of 1381 says:

It was dangerous among them to be known for one that
was lerned, and more dangerous if any man were found
with a *penner and inkhorne* at his side: for such
seldome or neuer escaped from them with life.

The 'penny-inckhorne' of *Contention* is a blunder due to mis-hearing.

(iv) Any spectator who was witnessing a representation of the *Contention* would find the early portion of the twenty-first scene difficult to follow. In the previous scene Iden kills Cade, and the twenty-first scene continues the main story from the point when the nineteenth scene ended; in it Somerset is in attendance on the King and Queen, and Buckingham with Clifford has brought 'the rebels, with halters about their necks,' to receive the royal pardon. No mention is made of York, who has been absent from England since the conclusion of the ninth scene. He opens the twenty-first scene with the words,

In Armes from Ireland comes Yorke amaine,

and tells the audience he has invaded England to claim the crown. Suddenly Buckingham enters and demands (xxi. 10),

To know the reason of these Armes in peace,

and why 'with colours spred' he comes so near the court. York is taken aback, dissembles, delays an answer and finally says (xxi. 21-3):

> I came to remoue that monstrous Rebell Cade,
> And heaue proud Somerset from out the Court,
> That basely yeelded vp the Townes in France.

Buckingham returns (xxi. 24-7) this astonishing reply:

> Why that was presumption on thy behalfe,
> But if it be no otherwise but so,
> The King doth pardon thee, and granst to thy request,
> And Somerset is sent vnto the Tower.

First we are not informed why Buckingham tells (xxi. 9) York,

> I come as a Messenger from our dread Lord and soueraign, Henry.

Then how comes it that Buckingham meets York at all, so confidently assumes regal functions, pardons York for his invasion, and is able to inform him that Somerset is in the Tower? Something essential to the understanding of the *Contention* text is missing. The riddles are solved on reading ll. 23-49 of the ninth scene of the fourth act in the folio version. Henry has learnt of York's invasion and of his intention to remove Somerset from his place in the King's Council; he has sent Buckingham to ask York 'the reason of these Armes' and instructs his envoy not to be 'rough in termes.' Somerset is sent to the Tower and goes there willingly. Here we have proof of matter, omitted in *Contention* but present in *2 Henry VI*, which is necessary to the sense of passages in *Contention*.

(v) Proof of the priority of *2 Henry VI* is to be found in a passage taken from the twenty-second scene of *Contention*. York has renounced his allegiance to King Henry and been arrested by Somerset; he summons his sons, Edward and Richard, 'to be my baile,' and the Queen calls for Clifford. Finally, after many recriminations, York says (xxii. 15-22):

l. 144. *Yorke.* Call hither to the stake, my two rough beares,
l. 192. *King.* Call Buckingham, and bid him Arme himselfe.
l. 193. *Yorke.* Call Buckingham and all the friends thou hast,
[Both thou and they, shall curse this fatall houre.]

After *Enter at one doore, the Earles of Salsbury and Warwicke,*
l. 147. *with Drumme and souldiers. [And at the other, the Duke of Buckingham, with Drumme and souldiers.]*

l. 148. *Cliff.* Are these thy beares? weele bayte them soone,
      [Dispight of thee, and all the friends thou hast.]
l. 196. *War.* You had best go dreame againe,
l. 197. To keep you from the tempest of the field.

I have placed opposite to each line the numbered line of the corresponding passage in the folio scene, and have enclosed within square
brackets two lines of text and the second portion of the stage
direction because they are not Shakespeare's. These eight lines
represent what is left of fifty-four lines of Shakespeare's text.
Only the relevant portions of the folio version (5.1.144-197) are
set out below:

    Yorke. Call hither to the stake my two braue Beares,
    That with the very shaking of their Chaines,
    They may astonish these fell-lurking Curres,
    Bid Salsbury and Warwicke come to me.

    Enter the Earles of Warwicke, and Salisbury.

    Clif. Are these thy Beares? Wee'l bate thy Bears to death,
    And manacle the Berard in their Chaines,
    If thou dar'st bring them to the bayting place.
           Omit 5.1.151-191.
    King. Call Buckingham, and bid him arme himselfe.
    Yorke. Call Buckingham, and all the friends thou hast,
    I am resolu'd for death *and* dignitie.
    Old Clif. The first I warrant thee, if dreames proue true.
    War. You were best to go to bed, and dreame againe,
    To keepe thee from the Tempest of the field.

Warwick's speech in *Contention*, if intended to be a reply to the
preceding speech made by Clifford, is completely meaningless.
Why 'dreame' or 'dreame againe'? and how can dreaming serve to
keep Clifford 'from the tempest of the field'? Comparison of the
two versions makes it clear that the actors heavily abridged Shakespeare's text and rearranged the staging and order of the little that
was left. They seem to have planned a simultaneous and spectacular
entrance of the two opposing factions, drums beating, banners
flying, the Yorkists with white roses, the Lancastrians with red
roses in helmets and caps. Staging such a procession made it
necessary to vary the order of the remnant of folio lines. They
wished to retain Clifford's biting retort to York's first line, but
were forced to defer it until the two armies were on the stage.
Consequently Clifford in *Contention* really replies to two speeches
of York's separated from one another in the folio by fifty lines of

text, for Clifford's second line, obviously an interpolation, echoes the first line of York's second speech.

Each of the two folio lines (ll. 194-5) missing in *Contention* is necessary to the sense of this passage. York's second line,

> I am resolu'd for death (and) or dignitie,

evokes Clifford's apt rejoinder,

> The first I warrant thee, if dreames proue true.

The word 'dreames' is taken up by Warwick,

> You were best to go to bed, and dreame againe.

Each part of this last line is needed in the folio. Warwick roughly bids the elder Clifford 'to go to bed' and thus avoid 'the tempest' of fierce fighting for which his age unfitted him; he adds 'and dreame againe' to answer Clifford's last words 'if dreames come true.' Warwick's first line in *Contention*,

> You had best go dreame againe,

is clearly a compression of the folio line; it is unmetrical, contains the vulgarism 'had best,' omits the words 'to bed' which would have given the next line some meaning, and concludes with 'and dreame againe' words which nothing before or after explains.

Here we have definite proof of omission in *Contention* of a line found in the folio text, necessary to the sense of the passage in this bad quarto.

(vi) Pedigrees figure prominently in the York and Lancaster series of plays, and the accurate detail necessary proves a pitfall to pirates and reporters of the surreptitious versions. In each of *Contention, True Tragedy* and *Henry V Q1* a garbled and absurd account of what is plainly set out in both the chronicles and Shakespeare's plays exhibits the incompetent muddling of the persons who provided the copy for these quartos. These accounts are demonstrably not derived at first hand from the chronicles and they represent the work of persons who relied solely on months-old memories of what they or others had spoken on the stage. In *Contention* they were unable to state correctly the names and the right order of birth of Edward the Third's seven sons, and hopelessly confused the relationship of his descendants belonging to the fourth, fifth and sixth generations. This fact will be understood if the reader will compare the genealogies of Richard, Duke of York, given in *2 Henry VI* and in *Contention* respectively with Holinshed's account.

HOLINSHED, P. 657

Edward the third had issue, *Edward prince
of Wales; William of Hatfield,* his *second sonne;
Lionell the third, duke of Clarence; Iohn of
Gant,* fourth, *duke of Lancaster; Edmund of
Langleie, fift, duke of Yorke; Thomas of
Woodstoke, sixt, duke of Glocester;* and *William
of Windsor, seauenth.*

The said *Edward* prince of Wales, which *died*
in the life time of *his father,* had issue *Richard,*
which succeeded *Edward the third* his grandsire.

Richard died without issue: *William of Hatfield,*
the second sonne of Edward the third, *died without*
issue. Lionell the *third sonne* of Edward the third,
duke of Clarence, had issue Philip his *daughter*
and heire, which was coupled in matrimonie vnto
Edmund Mortimer, earle of March, and *had issue Roger*
Mortimer *earle of March,* hir sonne and heire, which *Roger
had issue Edmund,* erle of March, Roger Mortimer,
Anne, Elianor; which Edmund, Roger, and Elianor
died without issue.

And the said *Anne* coupled in matrimonie to
Richard earle of Cambridge, the *sonne* of *Edmund*
of *Langleie,* the *fift sonne* of Henrie (*Edward*) *the
third,* and had issue Richard Plantagenet,
commonlie called Duke of Yorke; . . . . To the which
Richard duke of Yorke, as sonne to Anne,
daughter *to Roger* Mortimer *earle of March, sonne*
and heire of the said *Philip, daughter* and
heire of the said *Lionell,* the third sonne of
king Edward the third, the right, title, dignitie
roiall, and estate of the crownes of the realmes
of England and France, and the lordship of Ireland,
perteineth and belongeth afore anie issue of the
said Iohn of Gant, the fourth sonne of the
same King Edward.

2 Henry VI, 2.2.10-58

Yorke. *Edward the third,* my Lords, had seuen Sonnes,
The first, *Edward* the Black-Prince, *Prince of Wales;*
The *second, William of Hatfield*; and *the third,*
Lionel, Duke of Clarence; next to whom,
Was *Iohn of Gaunt,* the *Duke of Lancaster;*
The *fift,* was *Edmond Langley, Duke of Yorke;*
The *sixt,* was *Thomas of Woodstock, Duke of Gloster;*
William of Windsor was the *seuenth* and last.
Edward the Black-Prince *dyed* before *His Father,*
And left behinde him *Richard,* his onely Sonne,
Who after *Edward the third's* death, raign'd as King,
Till Henry Bullingbrooke, Duke of Lancaster,
The eldest Sonne and Heire of Iohn of Gaunt,
Crown'd by the Name of Henry the Fourth,
Seiz'd on the Realme, depos'd the rightfull King,
Sent his poore Queen to France, from whence she came,
And him to Pumfret; where, as all you know,
Harmlesse Richard was murthered traiterously.

Warw. Father, the Duke hath told the truth;
Thus got the House of Lancaster the Crowne.

Yorke. Which now they hold by force, and not by right:
For Richard, the first Sonnes Heire, being dead,
The Issue of the next Sonne should haue reign'd.

Salisb. But *William of Hatfield dyed without* an Heire.

Yorke. *The third Sonne, Duke of Clarence,* From whose Line
I clayme the Crowne, *had Issue Phillip,* a *Daughter,*
Who marryed *Edmond Mortimer, Earle of March*:
Edmond *had Issue, Roger, Earle of March;*
Roger had Issue, Edmond, Anne and Elianor.

Salisb. This Edmond, in the Reigne of Bullingbrooke,
As I haue read, layd clayme vnto the Crowne,
And but for Owen Glendour, had beene King;
Who kept him in Captiuitie, till he dyed.
But to the rest.

Yorke.   His eldest Sister, *Anne,*
My Mother, being Heire vnto the Crowne,
Marryed *Richard, Earle of Cambridge,* who was (*sonne*)
To *Edmond Langley, Edward the Thirds fift* (*sonnes*)
                          sonne;
By her I clayme the Kingdome; she was Heire
To Roger, Earle of March, who was the *Sonne*
of Edmond Mortimer, who marryed *Phillip,*
Sole *Daughter* vnto *Lionel,* Duke of Clarence.
So, if the Issue of the elder Sonne
Succeed before the younger, I am King.

Warw. What plaine proceedings is more plain then this?
Henry doth clayme the Crowne from Iohn of Gaunt,
The fourth Sonne, Yorke claymes it from the third;
Till Lionels Issue fayles, his should not reigne.
It fayles not yet, but flourishes in thee,
And in thy Sonnes, faire slippes of such a Stock.

The Contention. vi. ll. 7-52.

Yorke. Then thus my Lords.
Edward the third had seuen sonnes,
The first was Edward the blacke Prince,
Prince of Wales.
The second was Edmund of Langly,
Duke of Yorke.
The third was Lyonell Duke of Clarence.
The fourth was Iohn of Gaunt,
The Duke of Lancaster.
The fifth was Roger Mortemor, Earle of March.
The sixt was Sir Thomas of Woodstocke.
William of Winsore was the seuenth and last.
Now, Edward the blacke Prince he died before his father,
And left behind him Richard, that afterwards was King,
Crownde by the name of Richard the second, and he died
without an heire.
Edmund of Langly Duke of Yorke died, and left be-
hind him two daughters, Anne and Elinor.
Lyonell Duke of Clarence died, and left behind Alice,
Anne, and Elinor, that was after married to my father,
And by her I claime the Crowne, as the true heire to
Lyonell Duke of Clarence, the third sonne to Edward
the third. Now sir. In the time of Richard's raigne,
Henry of Bullingbrooke, sonne and heire to Iohn of
Gaunt, the Duke of Lancaster fourth sonne to Edward
the third, he claimde the Crowne, deposde the Merth-
full King, and as both you know, in Pomphret Castle
harmlesse Richard was shamefully murthered, and so
by Richards death came the house of Lancaster vnto
the Crowne.

Sals. Sauing your tale my Lord, as I haue heard, in
the raigne of Bullenbrooke, the Duke of Yorke did
claime the Crowne, and but for Owen Glendor had
bene King.

Yorke. True. But so it fortuned then, by meanes of
that monstrous rebel Glendor, the noble Duke of York
was done to death, and so euer since the heires of Iohn
of Gaunt have possessed the Crowne. But if the issue
of the elder should sucseed before the issue of the yonger,
then am I lawfull heire vnto the Kingdome.

War. What plaine proceedings can be more plaine, hee
claimes it from Lyonel Duke of Clarence, the third sonne to
Edward the third, and Henry from Iohn of Gaunt the fourth
sonne So that till Lyonels issue failes, his should not
raigne. It failes not yet, but florisheth in thee & in
thy sons, braue slips of such a stock.

The errors made in *Contention* may be taken in order. They arise mainly because the author forgot the name of the second son of Edward the Third. He knew accurately the names of the first, third, fourth, sixth and seventh sons, could remember that Edmund Langley, Duke of York, was a son, and had heard mention of Roger Mortimer, Earl of March, three times in the pedigree.

(i) Edmund of Langley, Duke of York, was the fifth not the second son. The absurdity of the statement in *Contention* is manifest, because, if it was true, the rest of the pedigree except that concerning the Black Prince and John of Gaunt was unnecessary surplusage. It was not a slip, but was repeated elsewhere.

(ii) The reporter in recounting the names of the children of Edward III puts Edmund of Langley in the second place immediately after the Black Prince, and bestows on him two daughters, Anne and Elinor. We are told nothing more of these two presumptive heirs of the childless Richard II or of their descendants, if any. Oddly enough, Warwick, one of York's two guests, had married the grand-daughter of Constance, only daughter of Edmund Langley, Duke of York. The Christian names of the latter's two non-existent daughters, Anne and Elinor, are the same as those of two of Lionel's three non-existent daughters. This pair of names comes from a hazy recollection of a folio line, omitted in *Contention*,

Roger had issue, Edmund, Anne and Elinor.

(iii) The historical Edmund of Langley, Duke of York, had one daughter, Constance, and two sons; the elder was Edward, the Aumerle of *Richard II,* who left no heirs and was killed at Agincourt (see *Henry the Fifth*). The younger was Richard, Earl of Cambridge, who was executed for treason (see *Henry the Fifth*) ; his son, Richard Plantagenet, lost all his estates and titles (see *1 Henry VI*) until the regent restored him to his Dukedom. This is the Duke of York of the play. Neither Edmund Langley (died 1402) nor his son Edward 'claimed the crowne in the raigne of Bullenbrooke' for the excellent reason that the reigning House of Lancaster had a superior title. The mention of the 'Duke of Yorke' twice, once by Salisbury and once by York, in two consecutive paragraphs of *Contention* suggests that the reporter in his own queer way was supporting his earlier statement that Edmund of Langley, Duke of York, was the second son.

P

(iv) 'Lyonell Duke of Clarence died,' says the reporter, 'and left behinde Alice, Anne, and Elinor, that was after married to my father, and by her I claime the crowne, as the true heire to Lyonell Duke of Clarence, the third sonne to Edward the third.' What was the name of 'my father'? Which of the three daughters did he marry? What became of the other two? This maze of blunders in *Contention* has no outlet. York's father married not a daughter, but a great-grand-daughter of Lionel Duke of Clarence, and thus York himself was the great-grandson not the son of Edward the Third's grand-daughter, Phillippa.

(v) 'The fifth' (son), says the author of *Contention*, 'was Roger Mortimer, Earle of March.' On his mother's side he was the great-grandson of Edward III, and he was therefore the maternal grandfather of York. The reporter knew that he must name seven sons, and filled the gap in his memory with the name of a man mentioned twice on the stage.

The story of *Contention* is grossly inconsistent with itself. It begins with the assertion that Edmund Langley, Duke of York, was the second son, and refers to a Duke of York that claimed the crown fifty years before. It assumes implicitly that the claimant Duke of York was a descendant of Edmund Langley, and then bases the right and title of this descendant to the crown on his descent from the third son. Very strangely, Warwick's summary of York's claim, which is identical in both versions, says 'hee claimes it from Lyonel Duke of Clarence,' and is silent on a title that would have been incontestable.

While the origin of *Contention* version must depend on an attempt to reconstruct the folio account from memory, the insertion of York's last folio speech, beginning 'His eldest Sister Anne' is necessary to the sense of Warwick's speech that follows.

Shakespeare faithfully versified Holinshed's account of York's pedigree, but added considerably to the length by inserting in suitable places portions of a speech which Halle states was delivered in 1460 by the Duke of York from 'the trone royall (under the clothe of estate).' He thus introduced an account of the usurpation of Henry Bolingbroke and the deposition of King Richard, and repeated the blunder made by Halle elsewhere in confusing Sir Edmund Mortimer with his nephew, Edmund fifth Earl of March. Shakespeare's reason for the insertion of extraneous matter probably was to turn part of what threatened to be a very long and dull speech into dialogue.

Comparisons of the extracts from Holinshed and the corresponding texts of the two versions prove:

(i) That Holinshed's Chronicle was the source used by Shakespeare in his account of York's pedigree and the other matter included therein; he kept close to the details given there.

(ii) That Holinshed's Chronicle was not the primary source of the corresponding version in *Contention*. No dramatist of the time who had read the Chronicle carefully and had subsequently written the pedigree from memory could have produced such an erroneous, inconsistent and stupidly pointless narrative. It is true that the language of *Contention* is not so close to that of Holinshed as is that of *2 Henry VI*, but a man possessing a memory sufficiently retentive to remember many of the words of Holinshed ought to have been capable of giving the essential facts more accurately than in *Contention*.

(iii) The two additions mixed up in the story of York's descent are, except for change of names, concerned with the same set of facts in both versions. Further, the language of both versions up to the end of line 20 of *2 Henry VI* is very close throughout; some lines are verbatim, others vary in a word or two. The two scenes must have a common origin, because two dramatists would not pick out the same two additions from the large number available in the Chronicle.

(iv) Shakespeare could not have written up his account of York's pedigree from what he found in *Contention,* but must have corrected it by consulting Holinshed. My study of Shakespeare's methods in rewriting *The Troublesome Raigne* convinces me that he took his facts directly from Holinshed, and that *Contention* is a debased copy of *2 Henry VI*.

HAMLET Q2 AND HAMLET Q1.

(i) The ghost has appeared a second time to Horatio, Marcellus and Barnardo. Horatio again adjures it to speak (i. 105-111), but it remains silent and is stalking away:

> *Hor.* Speake to me, stay and speake, speake, stoppe it Mar-
> cellus.
> *Exit Ghost.*

2. Tis heere.
Hor. Tis heere.
Marc. Tis gone, O we doe it wrong, being so maiesti-
call, to offer it the shew of violence,
For it is as the ayre invelmorable,
And our vaine blowes malitious mockery.

If we assume that Marcellus obeyed Horatio and offered to stop it
with 'the shew of violence,' the 'vaine blowes' are still without
explanation. This passage in Q2 reads (1.1.139-45) as follows:

Hor. Speake of it, stay and speake, stop it Marcellus.
Mar. Shall I strike it with my partizan?
Hor. Doe if it will not stand.
Bar. Tis heere.
Hor. Tis heere.
Mar. Tis gone.
We doe it wrong being so Maiesticall
To offer it the showe of violence,
For it is as the ayre invulnerable,
And our vaine blowes malicious mockery.

Thus lines omitted in Q1 are necessary to explain the words 'vaine
blowes,' referring to the attempts of the guards to strike it with
their partizans.

(ii) In Q1 the opening speech of Claudius (ii. 1-7) is obscure;
he does not inform his Council what the purpose of Fortinbras is,
nor tell us why he is sending ambassadors to 'olde Norway':

Lordes, we here haue writ to Fortenbrasse,
Nephew to olde Norway, who impudent
And bed-rid, scarcely heares of this his
Nephews purpose: and Wee heere dispatch
Yong good Cornelia, and you Voltemar
For bearers of these greetings to olde
Norway.

Claudius, king of Denmark, has done a most extraordinary thing.
He has written to Fortinbras, a subject of the King of Norway,
and, at the same time, has sent two ambassadors to carry 'these
greetings,' whatever they may be, to 'olde Norway' who is described
as 'impudent and bed-rid.' Reference to what is said of Fortinbras
in the first scene of Q1 does not help very much; all we learn is
that he has been gathering an army for some unstated purpose. For
an explanation we must read the version (1.2.27-35) in Q2:

                                    we haue heere writ
To Norway Vncle of young Fortenbrasse
Who impotent and bedred scarcely heares
Of this his Nephewes purpose; to suppresse
His further gate heerein, in that the leuies,
The lists, and full proportions are all made
Out of his subiect, and we heere dispatch
You good Cornelius, and you Voltemand,
For bearers of this greeting to old Norway.

This passage is necessary to clear up the blunders and obscurity of the extract from Q1, and make it more intelligible. Claudius wrote not to Fortinbras but to Norway, and requires him to put an end to his nephew's hostile activities; further, he sends ambassadors to bear his letter and insist on compliance with his demands. The purpose of Fortinbras is fully explained in 1.1.96-105, and in ll. 17-27 preceding the above extract from the King's speech. Omissions in Q1 of passages in Q2 necessary to the sense of portions of Q1 are here explainable only upon the assumption that these omissions were known to the actors before Q1 was sent to the press.

(iii) The ghost beckons Hamlet to follow it, but his companions endeavour (iv. 43-5) to deter him:

Hor. What if it tempt you toward the flood my Lord.
That beckles ore his bace, into the sea,
And there assume some other horrible shape.

Words descriptive of something 'that beckles ore his base' are necessary to the sense of this passage. Q2 enlightens us (1.4.69-72):

Hor. What if it tempt you toward the flood my (Lord).
Or to the dreadfull somnet of the cleefe
That bettles ore his base into the sea,
And there assume some other horrable forme.

Q2 supplies the missing line which must have been left in Horatio's part; the rest of his speech except line 74 is not in Q1, being probably a 'cut.'

(iv) The ghost has revealed to Hamlet that his father was murdered and continues (iv. 93-5):

O I find thee apt, and duller shouldst thou be
Then the fat weede which rootes it selfe in ease
On Lethe wharffe: briefe let me be.

Some conditional clause necessary to the completion of the sense is missing after 'wharffe'; this appears (1.5.31-4) in Q2:

> I find thee apt,
> And duller should'st thou be then the fat weede
> That rootes it selfe in ease on Lethe wharffe,
> Would'st thou not sturre in this; now Hamlet heare.

Apart from the defective sense of the passage in Q1 which requires the words of Q2 omitted in Q1, this clause would have made the verse normal. The sentence 'briefe let me be' is an anticipation of line 110 in Q1 or line 59 in Q2; the initial 'O' is the sign-manual of the pirate.

(v) Polonius describes to Hamlet the versatility of the actors who had come to play at court, concluding (vii. 104-5) with this eulogy:

> Seneca cannot be too heauy, nor Plato too light:
> For the law hath writ those are the onely men.

Skilful emendators might guess that 'Plato' was a blunder for 'Plautus,' but what can any guesser make of the second line? Q2 must solve the puzzle (2.2.381-3):

> Seneca cannot be too heauy, nor Plautus too light for
> the lawe of writ, and the liberty: these are the only men.

Modern editors differ on the exact meaning of the phrase 'the lawe of writ and the liberty,' but it must be the source of the meaningless line of Q1.

(vi) After Hamlet has declaimed a dozen lines of blank verse, he asks the player to proceed; he recites thirty lines, and Polonius remarks, 'This is too long' (2.2.476). In Q1 the speech is reduced to six lines (vii. 158-164):

> *Play.* Anone he finds him striking too short at Greeks,
> His antike sword rebellious to his Arme,
> Lies where it falles, vnable to resist.
> Pyrrus at Pryam driues, but all in rage,
> Strikes wide, but with the whiffe and winde
> Of his fell sword, th'unnerued father falles.
> *Cor.* Enough my friend, t'is too long.

Various changes have been made in the text of Q2 retained, but the comment of Corambis makes it certain that a drastic 'cut' has reduced the player's speech so heavily that Corambis seems to be talking nonsense. Compare *3 Henry VI,* example xii, and the similar example in *Orlando Furioso Q1.*

(vii) Two lines of the first player's speech (vii. 173-4) referring to Hecuba,

> Who this had seene with tongue inuenom'd speech,
> Would treason haue pronounced,

have little meaning with or without their context. What is the meaning of 'tongue inuenom'd speech'? Why should any one cry treason because the chances of war had pulled Queen Hecuba from her high estate? The corresponding passage (2.2.488-9) runs:

> Who this had seene, with tongue in venom steept,
> Gainst fortunes state would treason haue pronounst.

Q2 makes good an omission and explains an ingenious mishearing of the text of Q1.

(viii) Hamlet has given his advice to the players, to which in Q1 the pirate has tagged ten lines of specimen jests always in the mouth of the clown; the following dialogue (ix. 43-6) ensues:

> *Ham.* Maisters tell him of it.
> *players.* We will my Lord.
> *Ham.* Well, goe make you ready.   *exeunt players.*
> *Horatio.* Heere my Lord.
> *Ham.* Horatio, thou are euen as just a man, etc.

No entry has been provided for Horatio, nor does Hamlet summon him; his appearance is unexpected, and his words 'Heere my Lord' suggest that he is 'Heere' because he has been called. Considerable difference exists between the two versions at this point as the passage (3.2.41-9) of Q2 explains:

> *Ham.* Goe make you readie. How now my Lord, will
> the King heare this peece of worke?
>   *Enter Polonius, Guyldensterne, & Rosencrans.*
> *Pol.* And the Queene to, and that presently.
> *Ham.* Bid the Players make hast. Will you two help to hasten
>   them.
> *Ros.* I my Lord.   *Exeunt they two.*
> *Ham.* What howe, Horatio.   *Enter Horatio.*
> *Hora.* Heere sweet Lord, at your seruice.
> *Ham.* Horatio, thou art een as iust a man, etc.

No exits have been inserted in Q2 for the players or Polonius, but Hamlet's words addressed to them are equivalent to a dismissal. At the moment of the players' departure, Polonius and his fellow spies, who have probably been eavesdropping at one door, enter. Hamlet at once puts a question to Polonius 'How now my Lord, etc.?' to which Polonius makes the reply in the text. Hamlet then curtly says to him, 'Bid the Players make hast,' and Polonius, who has charge of them, leaves at once to do the prince's bidding. Turning to the spies, Hamlet dismisses them more politely with 'Will you two help to hasten them'; Rosencrantz replies 'I my Lord,' and the stage direction of Q2 marks their exit. Hamlet is now freed from espionage, and his call to Horatio takes the form of a friendly 'What howe, Horatio,' and his friend, who has been at the other door, immediately enters as the stage direction in Q2 indicates. Omission in Q1 of lines 42-7 of Q2, and especially of Hamlet's summons 'What howe, Horatio,' present in Q2 and necessary to the understanding of both versions, affords clear evidence of the priority of what we read in the second quarto.

(ix) After paying a tribute to his friend's sincerity and disinterestedness and telling him some details of the play about to be acted before the king, queen and court, he asks Horatio to keep a vigilant eye upon the king's face. Their conversation is broken off by the entrance of the royal party, and the scene (ix. 68-72) continues thus:

> *Ham.* Harke they come.
>   *Enter King, Queene, Corambis, and other Lords.*
> *King.* How now son Hamlet, how fare you, shall we haue a
>   play?
> *Ham.* Yfaith the Camelions dish, not capon cramm'd,
> feede a the ayre.
> I father: My Lord, you playd in the Vniuersitie.
> *Cor.* That I did my L: and I was counted a good actor.

Claudius in Q1 asks Hamlet not one question as in Q2 but two, and receives a reply to each of them in proper order. Hamlet's answer to the first question involves a whimsical play upon two possible meanings of the King's 'how fare you'; his terse and disconnected references to 'the Camelion's dish,' 'capon-cramm'd' and 'feede a the ayre' would mystify the audience far more than the King, and leave in the minds of all a doubt of Hamlet's sanity. His answer 'I father' to the second question is entirely out of character and is too blunt to be polite; without another word he turns to the more congenial pastime of badgering Polonius.

What Hamlet did say is found (3.2.85-93) in Q2 and clears up the confusion:

> *Enter Trumpets and Kettle Drummes, King, Queene,*
> *Polonius, Ophelia.*
>
> *Ham.* They are coming to the play. I must be idle.
> Get you a place.
> *King.* How fares our cosin Hamlet?
> *Ham.* Excellent yfaith,
> Of the Camelions dish, I eate the ayre.
> Promis-cram'd, you cannot feede Capons so.
> *King.* I haue nothing with this aunswer Hamlet,
> These words are not mine.
> *Ham.* No, nor mine now my Lord.
> You playd once i'th' Vniuersitie you say,
> *Pol.* That did I my Lord and was accounted a good Actor.

On reading the above passage all the difficulties due to the muddle of camelions and capons disappear. Hamlet was not rudely abrupt in closing his conversation with Claudius, but the 'I father' of Q1 definitely marks the presence of the pirate. Throughout Q2 Hamlet does not address Claudius as 'father,' nor does he permit him, without some aside or demur, to call him 'son.'

(x) In the early part of the grave-digging scene the thirsty clown sends his assistant for 'a stope of drinke,' and continues thus (xvi. 18-31):

> *Clowne.*   but before thou
> Goest, tell me one thing, who buildes *strongest,*
> Of a Mason, a Shipwright, or a Carpenter?
> *2.* Why a Mason, for he buildes all of stone,
> And will indure long.
> *Clowne.* That's prety, too't agen, too't agen.
> *2.* Why then a Carpenter, for he builds the gallowes,
> And that brings many a one to his long home.
> *Clowne.* Prety agen, the gallowes doth well, mary howe
> dooes it well? the gallowes dooes well to them that doe ill,
> goe get thee gone:
> And if any one aske thee hereafter, say,
> A Graue-maker, for the houses he buildes
> Last till Doomes-day. Fetch me a stope of beere, goe.

This riddle in Q1 cannot be in the correct form, because the second grave-digger must choose one of the three artisans named; he has been adjudged wrong in naming the 'Mason' and the 'Carpenter,' and the correct answer should be the 'Shipwright.' In Q1 the clown does not solve his own riddle, and would be in danger of being hissed off the stage before he drank his share of the beer. Reference to the parallel text shows that the riddle in Q2 (5.1.46-8) was:

> What is he that buildes *stronger* then eyther the Mason, the Shypwright, or the Carpenter.
> *Other.* The gallowes maker, for that out-liues a thousand ten-
> ants.

The clown banters his companion much as in Q1, propounds his riddle again, as riddle-mongers do, and, when his butt confesses 'Masse I cannot tell,' gives the same answer (5.1.62-3) as in Q1:

> Say a graue-maker, the houses hee makes last till Doomesday.

In Q2 the clown solves his own riddle as a shrewd and successful stage-clown must always do. *Strongest* in Q1 should be *stronger,* though this change would mean that the first guess of the assistant must be struck out and the second guess emended.

(xi) When the queen has been poisoned and the dying Laertes reveals to Hamlet the king's plot against him, Hamlet stabs Claudius (xviii. 93-5) exclaiming:

> The poysned Instrument within my hand?
> Then venome to thy venome, die damn'd villaine:
> Come drinke, here lies thy vnion here.   *The King dies.*

This passage is largely a jumble of earlier lines of Q2, but the word 'vnion' cannot be explained because there has been no previous reference to a 'vnion' or fine pearl in Q1. Before the fencing-match begins, the king addresses (5.2.254-261) the spectators:

> Set me the stoopes of wine vpon that table
> If Hamlet giue the first or second hit,
> Or quit in answere of the third exchange,
> Let all the battlements their ordnance fire.
> The King shall drink to Hamlets better breath,
> And in the cup an Vnice shall he throwe,
> Richer then that which foure successiue Kings
> In Denmarkes Crowne haue worne: giue me the cups.

Hamlet gives Laertes 'a hit, a very palpable hit' and the king calls (5.2.269-270) for a brief pause in the bout:

> Stay, giue me drinke, Hamlet this pearle is thine.
> Heeres to thy health: giue him the cup.

Probably, as some critic has suggested, the King holds up for all to see a glazed pellet of poison modelled like a pearl, and drops it into the wine. When treachery and poison have done their work, Hamlet cries (5.2.312-3) to Claudius whom he has stabbed:

> Heare thou incestious damned Dane,
> Drinke of this potion, is the Onixe heere?

Folios and the first quarto agree in terming the gem said to be dropped by Claudius into the cup of wine a 'vnion'; all the good quartos and the folios use the phrase 'this pearle is thine.' Omission of the two earlier passages of Q2 referring to the onyx or pearl makes this passage of Q1 unintelligible.

These obscure or meaningless passages of *Hamlet Q1* offer enough evidence to suggest that this abridged and very corrupt play is the illegitimate offshoot of Q2. Eleven such passages of Q1 occur in eight scenes, four being in the first act, and six in the remainder of the play.

Chapter XIV

VERSE STRUCTURE OF THE BAD QUARTOS

DURING the discussion of the remarkable blunders that prove the derivation of the bad quartos and their dependence upon the corresponding plays of Shakespeare, some allusions were made to the defective verse which frequently resulted from the changes made by reporters. Examination of the metrical structure of these verses proves that the deviations from normal ten and eleven-syllable lines are far more numerous than in contemporary plays with sound texts. I propose to show that more than five-sixths of these deviations from normality are almost invariably associated with corruption of Shakespeare's text, and that examples of every possible type of broken-down blank verse are plentiful.

Shakespeare commenced his dramatic career by using a blank verse very much like that of his contemporaries and predecessors, and it will be necessary to glance at the kind of blank verse then fashionable. For a study of the versification of Greene, Peele and Marlowe we have extant for each author sound, if not perfect, texts of their generally accepted plays written at different periods of their short dramatic careers. Their blank verse was almost uniformly decasyllabic, prevailingly end-stopped, and with the stress customarily on the second syllable of each foot. The number of short lines is usually small, and the percentage of lines with an extra syllable at the end of the line varies from nothing to about four per cent. of the total blank verse. Some critics assert that nine-syllable lines are due to printers' errors, but in *Tamburlaine* and *Edward II* this conclusion is doubtfully valid. In table XVII on page 223 are some details of the versification of the first part of *Tamburlaine* and *Edward II*.

Verse alone being counted *1 Tamburlaine* has 40 short lines and 55 feminine endings compared with 151 short lines and 108 feminine endings in *Edward II*. This change in this poet's versification is more apparent than real. *Edward II* contains few long speeches and much dialogue; question and answer, and the thrust and parry incident to dialogue are responsible for the rise in the number of split lines. The percentage of feminine endings grew slightly during the four or five years that may have elapsed between the performance of *1 Tamburlaine* and the writing of *Edward II,* but even the percentage for the latter play is not a half of that for *True Tragedy,* and is less than a third of the percentage for *2 Henry VI* or *3 Henry VI.* Run-on lines are relatively less in number in *Edward II* than in any of Shakespeare's early plays; this may be due to the large amount of dialogue in Marlowe's

TABLE XVII

MARLOWE'S VERSIFICATION

Number of Syllables in each Line, etc.	Number of Lines in *1 Tamburlaine*	Number of Lines in *Edward II*
Under 8 syllables	17	101
8 syllables	6	15
9 syllables		
A Wanting syllable at beginning	8	17
B Wanting syllable in middle	6	12
C With unstressed final syllable	3	6
10 syllables—unmetrical	7	10
11 syllables		
A With extra syllable at beginning	0	2
B With extra medial syllable	3	18
C With unstressed final syllable	55	108
12 syllables	20	13
More than 12 syllables	5	0
Number of Lines of Prose	78	24
Number of Blank Verse Lines	2,079	2,418
(Includes feminine endings)		
Number of Lines of Rhymed Verse	94	64
Number of Split Lines	4	30
Number of Run-on-Lines or Overflow	332	225
Number of Lines in Play	2,316	2,670

drama. He has far more nine-syllable lines than are found in early dramas of Shakespeare; some of these lines become normal if monosyllables such as 'fire,' 'sure,' 'earl,' 'sworn,' etc., are pronounced as dissyllables, and if words such as 'secret,' 'monstrous,' 'chaplain,' etc., are treated as trisyllabic. Thus in *1 Tamburlaine* (2.3.59-60) we have,

    Tamb. And kill as sure as it swiftly flies.
    Cos. Thy words assure me of kind success,

two examples of this metrical device or liberty in consecutive lines. Twelve-syllable lines or Alexandrines are almost as rare in Marlowe's uncorrupted plays as in Shakespeare's until the period of *Hamlet*. Rhymes show a tendency to decrease, but some of those included in my count may be accidental or unintended. Verse other than the normal decasyllabic does not equal an eighth of the total in *Edward II;* in *2 Henry VI* and *3 Henry VI* it amounts to a fifth and in *Richard III* to a fourth of the verse. Marlowe's mighty line breathed poetry into our drama, but Shakespeare was the chief innovator.

Our early corrupt quartos are mainly in blank verse; the one exception is *Famous Victories,* which most probably predates *Tamburlaine.* Greene and Peele used prose freely in comic scenes, but it is very scarce in Marlowe's good texts. Dr. Greg has shown that the prose scenes of *Orlando Furioso Q1* are interpolations, and it is likely that the texts of *Faustus* and *Jew of Malta,* popular plays that remained unpublished for many years after the author's death, suffered similar contamination. Critics with good reason doubt the authenticity of the prose found in *Tamburlaine* and *Edward II,* and I do not think that a line of *Massacre at Paris,* perhaps the most corrupt play of this period, was originally in prose. Two prose passages, viz., ll. 487-498 and ll. 816-829, begin scenes otherwise wholly in verse, and if unnecessary connectives, so plentifully used by the players, are removed from them, they make passable verses, not much inferior to what follows.

Thus the speech of the soldier hired by Guise to assassinate Mugeroun may be recast as verse, except the second line, without making any but the most trivial changes. If the first word 'sir' be omitted, and also the word 'and' in the third line, there follow eight consecutive lines of blank verse. If after the word 'question' the word 'and' be struck out, three more lines of blank verse conclude this episode.

> (Sir) To you sir, that dares make the Duke a cuckolde
> And vse a counterfeite key to his priuie (Chamber) doore:
> (And) although you take out nothing but your owne,
> Yet you put in that which displeaseth him,
> And so forestall his market, and set vp
> Your standing where you should not, and whereas

Hee is your Land lord you will take vpon
You to be his, and till the ground that he him selfe
Should occupy, which is his own free land.
If it be not too free, theres the question:
(And) though I come not to take possession,
(As I would I might) yet I mean to keepe
You out, which I will if this geare holde;
What are you come so soone? haue at ye sir.

Except for the second line, not a word need be changed, and the
four omissions are of words unnecessary to the sense; the whole
passage would certainly pass muster in the rather tattered regiment
of verse that surrounds it. The earlier passage contains three
complete blank verses at the beginning and two at the end.
Dialogue is difficult to memorize, but the rest of the scene is in
verse. Both passages relate episodes complete in themselves, and
the fragmentary character of this corrupt play throws suspicion
on prose that may become verse with such trifling changes.
Probably Marlowe thought prose unsuited to tragedy; except in
2 Henry VI and Richard III Shakespeare used none in his early
plays on English history.

Regularity and monotony of rhythm and stress hall-mark the
blank verse of Peele and Greene. Alphonsus is probably the
earliest of Greene's extant plays, and its verse lacks distinction of
any kind. Of its nineteen hundred lines thirty only deviate from
the normal; six lines are short, two or three have an extra syllable
at the end of the line, and there is a doubtful Alexandrine.
Some lines lack a syllable in the middle; these may be scribal slips
or printer's errors. Others may be explained by counting 'fire,'
'sure,' etc., as dissyllables. Slurring helps to normalize a dozen
verses which appear to have an extra medial syllable; occasional
rhyming couplets relieve decasyllabic regularity. Friar Bacon is
longer and more mature, but the amount of prose reduces the verse
to sixteen hundred lines including some doggerel. Short lines
number sixty, of which nearly half are octosyllabic; undoubted
feminine endings are rare as in all Greene's plays. I count about a
dozen, but this total would be more than doubled if terminal words
such as 'heaven,' 'friar,' 'power,' etc., are taken as dissyllables.
Alexandrines are used rather freely—I find twenty-four—and just
as in Alphonsus some verses lack a syllable at the beginning or in

mid-line. Three or four verses have an extra mid-line syllable. All told, eight per cent. of the verse deviate from the normal.

Both of these plays have sound texts, but *Orlando Furioso Q1* is exceedingly corrupt. Plot, style and versification alike suggest that it was written very soon after *Alphonsus,* but its special importance to students of our drama depends on the lucky accident which preserved first-hand or contemporary evidence to prove how such corrupt texts came into existence. Dr. W. W. Greg's study of the Dulwich MS. of Orlando's part and of the same part in *Orlando Furioso Q1* has shown that in the process of reporting and transmitting to paper three or four hundred lines of Greene's verse, the actors made fantastic blunders of every kind, and thus produced a text similar in every detail to the texts of the bad quartos. Some detailed discussion of the changes made by them in the verse of Orlando's part as it appears in the Dulwich MS. is vital to my inquiry.

References are to the Malone Society's reprint of *Orlando Furioso Q1* and to Dr. Greg's reprint of the Dulwich MS. in *Henslowe Papers.*

(i) My first example comes from the MS. where it begins to give the complete text of the hero's speeches (MS. 8-12):

> (Tread) she thes lawndes sweet flora bost thy flowers
> seek she for shade, spred cedars for her sake
> kinde Clora make her couch, fair cristall springs
> washe you her Roses, yf she long to drinck
> oh thought, my heauen oh heauen that knowes my thought.

This passage appears in Q1. 602-7 thus:

> Tread she these lawnds, kinde Flora boast thy pride;
> Seeke she for shades, spread Cedars for her sake,
> Fair Flora make her couch amidst thy flowres,
> Sweet Christall springs, wash ye with Roses,
> When she longs to drinke. Ah, thought my heauen;
> Ah heauen that knowes my thought.

Five metrically good lines of MS. have grown into six lines of Q1, with the help of an interpolation 'amidst thy flowres' in the middle of the third line. Hence result a nine-syllable line with the last syllable unstressed, an unscannable nine or ten-syllable line, and a short line with three stresses. One line only of the five quoted from MS. is unchanged in Q1.

(ii) Orlando's next speech of four lines in MS. has ten changes in Q1 which do not affect the metre, but line 22 of MS.,

> this gordyon knott together covnites,

is printed in Q1. 610 as an Alexandrine:

> But soft this Gordion knot together co-unites.

(iii) Three lines later (MS. 25), the line,

> hir name hir writing, foolishe and vnkind,

becomes (Q1. 613) by the addition of an unnecessary enclitic,

> Her name, her writing? Ah foolish and vnkinde,

an eleven-syllable line with an extra mid-line syllable.

(iv) The following passage (ll. 48-49) of the MS.,

> dare Medor court my Venus, can hir eyes
> bayte any looks, but suche as must admyre,

has been reduced (Q1. 660) to the following:

> What dares Medor court my Venus?

This fragment cannot be scanned as verse because the actors inserted their enclitic 'what.'

(v) A short line (MS. 59),

> What thinkst thou of it,

has become octosyllabic by the omission of the last two words and by the addition of some actor's gags:

> Now tell me boy, what dost thou thinke? (Q1 670).

(vi) Orlando's reply (MS. 68) to the shepherd,

> As follow loue, darest thou disprayse my heauen,

suffers the same corruption as in example three above:

> As follow love? why darest thou dispraise my heauen,

This line (Q1. 685) may be scanned as an Alexandrine.

(vii) Mislineation of two lines (ll. 72-3) of the MS.,

> she is, then speak thou peasant what he is
> that dare attempt, or court my quene of loue,

results in metrical variety in Q1 (691-3);

> She is.
> Then speake thou peasant, what is he that dares
> Attempt to court my Queene of loue.

Q

Two normal lines of MS. give rise to a line of two syllables, a normal line and an octosyllabic line.

(viii) Changes in lines (MS. 107-8) made by the actors,

> I must to hell to fight with Cerberus
> and find out medor ther, you Vilaynes or Ile dye,

are interesting. The quarto version (ll. 762-3) runs:

> I must to hell, to seeke for Medor and Angelica,
> Or else I dye

Q1 retains the beginning and the end of the original lines, and has filled the gap with a line (l. 116) found later in MS. and (l. 769) in Q1. The complete line of Q1 is repeated in an interpolated scene (ll. 888-9) of Q1. Thus the normal line and Alexandrine of MS. become a fourteener and a four-syllable line in Q1.

(ix) Much verse is mislined in Alleyn's MS. Probably 'sir' at the end of line 165, which is metrically complete without it, belongs to l. 166.

> Sir, spare no cost, run me to Charlemayne.

Omission and inversion create from this (Q1. 1013) a non-metrical line,

> Run to Charlemaine, spare for no cost.

(x) Green wrote some Alexandrines; perhaps the exclamatory 'ah, ah' of MS. 169,

> ah, ah as though that Sagitarr in all his pride,

may not be his. Any student will be astonished to read the version (l. 1017) of Q1,

> As though that Sagittarius in his pride.

The reporter omits the two enclitics, gives the god his classical name, and writes a normal line.

(xi) Another Alexandrine (l. 178) of the MS.,

> And see yf I dare combat for Angelica,

is metrically mangled by the intrusion of 'not' in Q1. 1026:

> and see if I dare not combat for Angelica.

Result is a 'thirteener.'

(xii) Octosyllabic lines are not very common in Greene's plays and perhaps the following line (MS. 190) has lost a word or two,

> Art thou not fayre Angelica.

With the help of the enclitic 'why' and an interpolated 'that' this line (Q1. 1047) has become normal:

> Why art thou not that same Angelica.

(xiii) Having restored to normality the above two lines, the actors left l. 194 of the MS. limping. The original is,

> Why are not these, those ruddy coulered cheeks.

This became an irregular seven-syllable line (Q1. 1051),

> Art not these the beauteous cheekes.

(xiv) Much more change has been made in line 198 of MS.,

> Are not my sweet, thes eyes those sparkling lampes,

which has been reduced (Q1. 1054) to the first line of the pair below:

> Are not my dere those radient eyes,
> Whereout proud Phoebus flasheth out his beames?

The result is that the second line which makes good sense with the line of MS. becomes nonsense in Q1.

(xv) Orlando in MS. begins his next scene (ll. 220-1) with a rhetorical question:

> Sirha is she not like those purple coulered swannes
> that gallopp by the coache of Cynthia.

Greene's Alexandrine has been transformed in Q1 (ll. 1168-9) into a 'fifteener' that cannot be scanned:

> Orgalio, is not my loue like those purple coloured swans
> That gallop by the Coache of Cynthia.

While 'Orgalio' could be treated as a short line, the change of 'she' in MS. to 'my loue' in Q1 has destroyed the metre of this line.

(xvi) In MS. Orgalio does not reply to the question addressed to him by Orlando, and the next two lines continue with the second question:

> her face siluered like to the milkwhite shape
> that Ioue came dauncing in to Cemele.

In Q1 Orgalio replies to his master's first question,

> Yes marry is shee my Lord,

and in consequence Orlando's second question takes exactly the same form as his first:

> Is not her face siluerd like that milke-white shape,
> When Ioue came dauncing downe to Semele.

Unless 'siluerd' is expanded to three syllables and stressed wrongly. the first line is metrically hopeless; the second line is so changed that it wants sense.

(xvii) Addition of a connective to the first line (MS. 246) has resulted in changing the next to a twelve-syllable line. Thus the lines,

> yf he denye to send me downe the shirt
> that Deianyra sent to Hercules,

were transformed (Q1. 1178-9) to,

> And if he doo denie to send me downe
> The shirt which Deianyra sent to Hercules.

(xviii) Another line (MS. 249),

> Ile vp the Alpes, and post to Meroe,

is turned, by prefixing an actors' catchword, to an Alexandrine (Q1. 1182):

> Tell him Ile passe the Alpes, and vp to Meroe.

(xix) Melissa undertakes the cure of the hero's madness by giving him a potion and charming him with a magic wand. His blank verse, somewhat uncertain before, improved with his restoration to semi-sanity, but the actors could not make sense of the passage (MS. 309-11):

> what heauenly sights of pleasaunce filles my eyes
> that feed their pride, with vew of such regard
> as heauen admyres, to see my slombring dreames.

They cut their difficulties, and gave us (Q1. 1260-2) the following:

> What shewes are these that fill mine eies
> With view of such regard as heauen admires,
> To see my slumbring dreames.

These lines have the merit of scanning, but two are short as a result of omissions, and the first is a piece of patchwork.

(xx) Greene wrote line 334 of MS. as an Alexandrine:

> with that mounted, vpon hir party coulered coach.

By cutting down 'vpon' to 'on,' the line of Q1 (l. 1296) reads:

> With that mounted on her parti-coulered coach.

Thus a non-metrical eleven-syllable line came into being.

(xxi) Orlando's first speech after he has regained his senses concludes thus (MS. 337-8):

> wher in what woodes, what vncouth groue is this
> how thus disguysd? wher is Argalio, Argalio.

The second 'Argalio' summons his page and is no part of the second line. The actors made short work of Greene's attempt to portray the hero's bewilderment; their version (1301-2) runs,

> What desert groue is this? How thus disguisde?
> Where is Orgalio?

(xxii) Orlando again questions (MS. 340) his page:

> say me sir boy, how cam I thus disguysd,

which the actors turned into an octosyllable (Q1. 1304),

> Sirah, how came I thus disguisde,

(xxiii) Argalio answers his master's question in the previous example by informing him that he had been out of his senses; Orlando asks (MS. 344) him,

> tell me what furye, hath inchaunted me?

Orlando's reply (Q1. 1309-10) became an Alexandrine:

> What was I mad? What furie hath inchanted me?

(xxiv) Orlando disguised as 'a slauishe Indian mercenary' interposes (MS. 377-82) when Sacrepant is pursuing Marsillus and Mandricard:

> Princes for shame, vnto your royall campes
> base not your selues, to combatt such a dogg
> follow the chase, mount on your coursers straight
> manage your spears, and lett your slaughtring swords
> be taynted, with the bloud, of them that flee
> from him passe ye, he shall be combated.

By omitting portions of three lines, the actors cut out two lines and their version (Q1. 1332-5) is:

> Stay Princes, base not your selues to cumbat such a dog.
> Mount on your coursers, follow those that flie,
> And let your conquering swoordes be tainted in their blouds
> Passe ye, for him he shall be combatted.

Here a 'thirteener' and an Alexandrine are made from the débris of four lines of Greene.

(xxv) The first two lines (MS. 384-5) of Orlando's next speech,

> I am thou seest, a cuntry seruile swayne
> homely attired, but of so hawty thoughts,

have been altered by the actors, and the two lines (Q1. 1361-2) that take their place,

> I am thou seest a mercenarie souldier
> Homely, yet of such haughtie thoughts,

consist of eleven and eight syllables respectively.

(xxvi) Quotations from the Dulwich MS. contain the speeches of Orlando, a few stage directions and little else. In the following example (MS. 401-2) I assume that the quarto gives one of Sacrepant's speeches accurately; the cue, 'thy name,' is the same in both texts.

> *Sacr.* (Then freely tell me whats) *thy name*
> *Orl.* - ffirst thyne.

Orlando's two words in this split line are expanded to six (Q1. 1382): and thus two short lines in Q1 replace one normal line of MS.

> *Sacr.* Then freely tell me whats thy name
> *Orl.* Nay first let me know thine?

(xxvii) Our early dramatists often used a rhetorical trick of repeating the last word, part-line, or line uttered by the preceding speaker. Thus it comes about that the line (MS. 405),

> Then lett me, at thy dying day intreat,

has swollen in Q1 (l. 1385) to a 'thirteener,'

> Sacrepant. Then let me at thy dying day intreate.

'Sacrepant' is the last word of the preceding quarto line, and is the 'cue' for the above line in MS.

(xxviii) Sacrepant confesses the trick that he had played on Orlando. The actors, being public entertainers with an eye to the main chance, jettisoned the first four lines of Orlando's outburst in which he babbled of 'tesyphone,' 'Alecto,' 'phlegeton,' 'Lethe' and 'Nemesis'; the next two lines are good examples of Greene's work (MS. 414-5):

> dead is the fatall author of my yll
> vassall, base vilayne, worthlesse of a crowne.

Both these lines the actors turned into unmetrical eleven-syllable lines (Q1. 1400-1), beginning the first with 'then,' and inserting in the second a superfluous mid-line syllable:

> Then dead is the fatall authour of my ill,
> Base villaine, vassall, vnworthie of a crowne.

(xxix) Repetition and anticipation of lines and phrases are an infallible sign of corruption. Thus Greene's line (MS. 431),

> I am a slavishe Indian mercenary,

becomes in line 1490 of Q1,

> I am a common mercenary souldier.

This line with a feminine ending is modelled on line 1360 of Q1.

(xxx) The scribe who wrote out Orlando's part seems to have dropped out some letters or a word or two from lines 437-8 of MS., though 'spoke' may be 'spokē,' i.e., spoken:

> Twelue peres of fraunce, twelue divylles, whats that
> what I haue spoke, ther I pawne my sword.

The actors have made three lines (Q1. 1521-3) out of the above:

> How Madam, the twelue Peeres of France?
> Why let them be twelue diuels of hell:
> What I haue said Ile pawne my sword.

'How Madam' is an actor's interpolation; the 'cue' is the same in both versions, and Greene, in his usual way, repeated the words 'Twelue Peeres of France' from the previous line spoken by Angelica. Expansion of the second half of Orlando's first line in MS. has resulted in two octosyllabic lines in place of a normal blank verse line.

(xxxi) Orlando's next speech in MS. (ll. 442-4),

> You that so proudly bid him fight
> out with your blade, for why your turne is next
> tis not this champion, can discorage me,

is badly reported in Q1 (1521-5):

> Heare you sir. You that so peremptorily bad him fight,
> Prepare your weapons for your turne is next,
> Tis not one Champion that can discourage me,
> Come are yee ready.

'Peremptorily' for 'proudly' may be the correct reading in MS., otherwise the verse is regular. Verse and text of Q1 are in serious disorder. Lines of thirteen, ten, eleven and five syllables occur in succession, largely as the result of adding two gags.

(xxxii) Whoever played or reported the stage Orlando seems to have insisted on introducing something of his own at the beginning of each line. Thus line 457 of MS.,

> hold madam, and yf my life but last it out,

begins in Q1 (l. 1528) with a contemptuous 'so stand aside'
addressed to the defeated Oliver,

> So stand aside, and Maddam if my fortune last it out.

The result is a 'fourteener.'

(xxxiii) Similar additions are made (MS. 460-2) to Orlando's
speech,

> So sir you haue made a goodly oration
> but vse your sword better, lest I well
> beswindg you.

These lines offer some difficulty in scansion, but by making a
couple of elisions, will pass muster. An addition at the beginning
and subsequent changes turn the quarto version (Q1. 1533-5) into
prose, and as prose it is printed:

> Well saide Frenchman, you have made a goodly
> oration: But you had best to vse your sword
> better, lest I beswinge you.

(xxxiv) Orlando's first line (MS. 472) after he had been
discovered by the 'Peers of France,'

> So was I Lordes, but geue me leaue a while

became eleven syllables in Q1 (l. 1550), with the intruded syllable
in the middle,

> So was I Lordinges: but giue mee leaue a while.

(xxxv) What must in MS. (l. 485) be an Alexandrine,

> grew by suspition to causlesse Lunacye,

still remained a twelve-syllable line in Q1 (l. 1555),

> grew by suspition to a causeles lunacie,

in spite of the addition of an extra syllable.

(xxxvi) Greene's six-syllable line (l. 487),

> Thanks sweet Angelica,

loses a foot in Q1,

> Thankes my sweet loue.

Critics think that *Orlando Furioso* was written between 1588
and 1591; the abridged version, i.e., the extant text, was entered
on the Stationers' Register on 7 December 1593. It was acted at
Court before the end of 1591, and, not as a new play, on 21

February 1592; we have no record of later performances. Nothing is known of the date of the Dulwich MS. Dr. Greg thinks it most likely represents the play in its original form, containing corrections and insertions in Alleyn's hand, and must therefore have belonged to one of his companies. It need not necessarily have been made for the revival recorded in the Diary, which was unsuccessful.

With this opinion I agree, and I have assumed throughout that the text of the corrupt quarto must have been derived ultimately, though not directly, from a manuscript which was the immediate source of Orlando's part as it appears in the Dulwich MS.

Orlando Furioso Q1 retains, as was said above, 303 of the 474 lines of Orlando's part present in this MS.; the 36 examples cited above prove that 56 lines of what was retained suffered a metrical change. Only 72 of the 303 lines are word and verse perfect, and consequently Q1 keeps not more than 15 per cent. of Orlando's part as Greene wrote it, or about as much as *Henry V Q1* preserves, without defect, of the folio text. Undoubtedly the Dulwich MS. must be accepted as a literal transcript made by some scribe from Greene's manuscript, and Dr. Greg's investigations make it certain that the changes observable in Q1 involve some kind of what he happily terms 'memorial reconstruction,' due to the agency of the reporter and actors. Abnormal verses of similar character are to be found in every scene of the play, including those in which Orlando had no share. His conclusion is not merely reasonable but irrefutable, that nearly all the remainder of the verse abnormality in Q1 must be ascribed to the same agents as have been proved responsible for the defects of Orlando's part in the printed text. No limit can be fixed to the damage that such illiterate muddlers could do to an author's play; yet of all dramas produced at this period Greene's end-stopped decasyllabic verse would present the least difficulty to an intelligent pirate.

I have collected and classified in groups, based on the number of syllables in a line, all the abnormal verses of *Orlando Furioso Q1;* certain groups have been subdivided according to the type of anomaly involved. For purpose of comparison I have added two similar classified sets of abnormal verse present in two other corrupt plays, *Massacre at Paris* and *A Shrew,* for which corresponding sound texts are not extant.

TABLE XVIII

VERSE ABNORMALITY

Number of Syllables in Line	Number of Lines in Plays Named		
	Orlando Q1	Massacre at Paris	A Shrew
Eight-Syllable Lines	38	43	14
Nine-Syllable Lines			
A Initial Monosyllabic Foot	11	14	10
B Mid-line Syllable Missing	9	13	15
C Final Syllable Unstressed	9	5	6
Unmetrical Decasyllabic Lines	15	9	23
Eleven-Syllable Lines			
A Extra Syllable at Beginning	7	35	32
B Extra Mid-line Syllable	22	39	32
C Final Syllable Unstressed	15	14	33
(Feminine Ending)			
Twelve-Syllable Lines	44	50	26
Lines over Twelve Syllables	19	7	5
Totals	189	229	196

Short lines of less than eight syllables have not been included. They are plentiful in *Orlando Furioso Q1,* and many are in scenes written in verse. Some are regular in metre; others are indistinguishable from prose, and cannot be scanned or combined with lines that precede or follow them. If the interpolated prose is omitted from the count, the actors must have replaced at least 250 decasyllabics of Greene's, equal to nearly a fifth of the extant verse, with a ragged detachment of verse and prose ranging from two to fifteen syllables in length. *Massacre at Paris* fared worse, because, being a popular play, it was on the acting list and remained unprinted for years after the author's death; it is, perhaps, the most corrupt play of the period. If repeated and borrowed lines are excluded, not much less than thirty per cent. of the verse is irregular, and, in my opinion, not one line in ten remains as Marlowe wrote it.

On the title page of the undated first quarto is printed the statement that Christopher Marlowe was the author; this ascription contains almost precisely the same amount of truth as the assertions on the title-pages of *Merry Wives Q1* and *Hamlet Q1* that William Shakespeare wrote what we find in these texts. Unfortunately many critics have forgotten that the extant *Massacre at Paris* is not printed from Marlowe's manuscript, and they use for the purpose of quotation and comparative criticism the text of this play as though it had authority equal to the texts of *Tamburlaine* and *Edward II*. No critic would venture quoting a line of *Hamlet Q1* as Shakespeare's unless it was found in Q2 as well, yet commentators still glean, without critical disapproval, support for their theories on the authorship of the plays on Henry VI from such a rubbish heap as the *Massacre at Paris*.

Each of the bad quartos exhibits the same types and, proportionally, an equal amount of irregular verses such as are found in *Orlando Furioso Q1*. As far as my knowledge extends, no one has disputed Dr. Greg's conclusions respecting the relationship between the two versions of Orlando's part, nor has any one yet undertaken the task of proving that the Dulwich MS. is a portion of Greene's revision of an old play, *Orlando Furioso Q1*. Reasoning back from results to the causes, we are logically entitled to assume that there must have pre-existed for each bad quarto a manuscript at least as good as is the Dulwich MS. of Orlando's part. Sound texts such as are suggested exist for each of the bad quartos in the folio versions of *2 Henry VI*, *3 Henry VI*, *Henry V* and *Merry Wives* and in the second quartos of *Romeo and Juliet* and *Hamlet*. If the critics of to-day would put aside all that had been written on the problems of the bad quartos prior to the past twenty years, they would shake off their bondage to criticism based on subjective and pre-conceived opinions. If they approached these problems in the liberalising spirit of inquiry that is the soul of the scientific method, and based their conclusions on facts, analogy and the balance of probabilities, an almost unanimous verdict would follow. The high court of literary appeal would unanimously reverse previous judgments, and find that the bad quartos are debased abridgments of Shakespeare's corresponding plays, which have passed through a cycle of changes similar to those which transformed the Dulwich MS. into the travesty of it in *Orlando Furioso Q1*.

Below is a table in which the irregular verse of each bad quarto is classified exactly as in the preceding table. Some additional rows of data are set out for each quarto. In preparing the results each line of each bad quarto has been compared with the corresponding line, if it exists, of the parallel text. Wherever the very frequent mislineation, accompanied by or arising from omissions or additions, has culminated in verse disorder, the necessary allowance for the changes, if any, made in each line has been made. Much time and thought have been spent on details of doubtful scansion, and perhaps another investigator, who may devote himself to a like task, may obtain slightly different results. Full criticism of each of more than two thousand irregular verses would fill several volumes, but the origin or development of almost every kind of defective verse has been already explained and criticized in the examples cited from *Orlando Furioso Q1*.

TABLE XIX

ABNORMAL VERSE OF BAD QUARTOS

Number of Syllables in Line	Cont.	Number of Lines in Play Named						
		True Tragedy Play	Non-S. Part	*R. & J. Q1* Play	Acts 1–2	*Henry V Q1*	*Hamlet Q1* Play	Act 1
1. Under eight syllables	39	48	11	55	20	64	154	67
2. Eight syllables ..	48	41	6	42	14	26	42	14
3. Nine syllables								
A Initial monosyllabic foot	21	23	2	10 ⎫		5	18	6
B Mid-line syllable missing	21	25	4	20 ⎬ 11		11	16	6
C Final syllables unstressed	23	19	2	10 ⎭		17	18	2
4. Unmetrical Decasyllables	47	12	7	23	7	7	24	9
5. Eleven syllables								
A Extra syllable at beginning ..	40	41	4	8 ⎫		5	18	10
B Extra mid-line syllable	61	53	14	25 ⎭ 19		9	21	6
C Final syllable unstressed	61	167	8	91	26	87	162	71
6. Twelve syllables ..	67	80	10	47	15	15	70	27
7. More than twelve syllables	31	15	1	25	9	22	28	7
Totals	459	524	69	356	121	268	571	225
8. Total lines of verse	1,652	2,124	228	1,909	855	777	1,568	633
9. Rhymes	50	81	4	333	269	28	149	12
10. Blank verse (includes totals in 4 and 5 (c))	1,602	2,043	224	1,576	586	749	1,419	621
11. Blank verse, after deduction of totals in rows numbered 1, 2, 3, 6, 7, 9 ..	1,352	1,792	188	1,367	517	589	1,073	492

NOTES ON THE TABLE

In general arrangement this table corresponds to the previous one. Totals under the heading 'Play' give for each named bad quarto the number of lines that correspond to the description given of the group in the row. For each of *True Tragedy, Romeo and Juliet Q1* and *Hamlet Q1* an additional list has been provided under a separate heading. This subsidiary list of totals for the *True Tragedy* applies to the non-Shakespearean portions of the play; for *Romeo and Juliet Q1* to Acts I-II and for *Hamlet Q1* to Act I. Appended are some other particulars for each play or part of a play; these will enable some important comparisons to be made.

(i) *Contention* and *True Tragedy,* the two early bad quartos, display three peculiarities. First, each has an unusually large number of eleven-syllable lines with the superfluous syllable, usually a word, at the beginning of the line, a type of verse very rare in Shakespeare's work. Secondly, an even larger number of eleven-syllable lines has the extra syllable in the interior of the line. This type of verse was used sparingly at first, but from 1596 onwards such lines gradually increase in number, and in plays from *Hamlet* onwards are a very important feature of his metrical system. Thirdly, these two plays contain many twelve-syllable lines, some metrically regular, others sheer perversions of verse, beginning with an accented syllable and ending with an unstressed one. Sir E. K. Chambers finds nine alexandrines in *3 Henry VI; True Tragedy* has no less than 80 lines of twelve syllables. It is true that *Hamlet Q1* has 70 such lines, but *Hamlet Q2* has 43 and some of these were transferred to Q1; the rest are the pirate's.

(ii) Reference to the totals makes it evident that the portions of *True Tragedy* not derived from *3 Henry VI* contain examples of every kind of defective verse to an even greater extent proportionately than the rest of the play. If feminine endings are included as blank verse, the Shakespearean portion of *True Tragedy* contains less than 16 per cent. of irregular verse compared with 27 per cent. of such verse in the non-Shakespearean portion. No good reason can be assigned for this difference if each part of the play was textually sound before the pirate began his garbling and mutilation. Perhaps the only satisfactory explanation is that the lines of *True Tragedy* not derived from *3 Henry VI* are, with all their defects, as good as the pirate could write unaided, whilst the percentage for the bulk of the play depended solely on the memories of himself and his fellow-actors. I shall prove later that the reporter of *3 Henry VI* did not like declaiming verse which was studded here and there with clumps of feminine endings.

(iii) If the sixth scene of the second act is omitted, the rest of the first two acts of *Romeo and Juliet Q1* contains 1,030 lines. From this total 255 lines of rhymed verse and 205 lines of prose must be deducted, and there remain 570 lines of blank verse; in this total are 119 non-decasyllabic verses, or 93 such verses if feminine endings are accepted as regular blank verse. Accordingly those two acts have a little more than 16 per cent. of irregular verse. With Acts III-V is included the last scene of the second act, and the total length is 1,185 lines. After subtracting 103 lines of prose and 78 lines of rhymed verse, 1,004 lines of blank verse are left; non-decasyllabic verses number 237 or 172 without the verses with feminine endings. Thus in the second part of *Romeo and Juliet Q1* irregular verses represent 17 per cent. of the total verse exclusive of rhyming couplets.

These verse tests show that the first two acts of *Romeo and Juliet Q1* are in about the same state of preservation as the Shakespearean portion of *True Tragedy*. Furthermore the remarkably close agreement between the results for the two parts into which Professor Wilson has divided this play tells against the existence of such a subdivision, which is the fundamental postulate necessary to his theory of double revision. If the garbling and muddling of the reporter have affected 16 per cent. of Shakespeare's blank verse in Part I, is it not logical to suggest that the same agency is entirely responsible for 17 per cent. of similar mutilation in Part II? Certainly this part contains about twelve per cent. of alien matter, but the remaining seven-eighths are Shakespeare's.

(iv) Results for *Hamlet Q1* as for *Romeo and Juliet Q1* have been set out in two divisions to enable me to test the double revision theory. Act I of Q1 contains 633 lines of which 12 are rhymed. The 621 lines of blank verse have 225 lines that deviate from the decasyllabic type, or 154 such lines after the verses with feminine endings are deducted. Irregular verses, therefore, equal 25 per cent. or almost a fourth of the first act. There are 1,521 lines in Acts II-V, which are reduced to 798 blank verse-lines, when 586 lines of prose and 137 rhymed lines have been removed from the total. Irregular verses in Part II total 346 which become 255 after subtracting the number of lines with feminine endings. Thus Part II contains 798 lines of blank verse of which 255 are irregular in their versification, or 32 per cent. Included in the blank verse of Part II are 378 lines from the pen of the pirate, and this large amount of non-Shakespearean verse accounts to some extent for the high proportion of irregular verse. From consideration of the percentages it would seem that the first act of *Hamlet Q1* was much more corrupted than the first and second acts of *Romeo and Juliet Q1,* but nearly all the increase of the irregular verse in the first play arises from the much greater number of lines with feminine endings and of those under eight syllables in length. The numerous short lines originate in Shakespeare's growing habit of concluding a speech with a broken line, which was usually completed by the next speaker. Abridgment, official or unofficial, might retain one broken end or both or neither, with the result that *Hamlet Q1* and *Henry V Q1* keep fragments of these broken ends as short lines. Moreover, the pirate of *Hamlet Q1* was a less competent thief, and hammered out a more ungainly and tuneless line of blank verse than his thievish predecessors of 1595 or 1597.

(v) Lines with feminine endings found in the portions of *True Tragedy* derived from *3 Henry VI,* if calculated as in the tables appended to Sir E. K. Chambers's *William Shakespeare* (vol. II, p. 400) on all verses of ten and eleven syllables except those in rhyme, amount to the high value of 9·9 per cent. of the total, whilst those in the non-Shakespearean portions amount to 4·4 per cent. of such verse. For the first two acts of *Romeo and Juliet Q1* the percentage is about 5 per cent., for the second part 7·6 per cent. of blank verse of ten or eleven syllables. In *Hamlet Q1* feminine endings constitute 14·4 per cent. of blank verse in Part I, and 15·6 per cent. of that in Part II; the latter percentage far exceeds that of any dramatist other than Shakespeare known to be writing in 1593 or even in 1596. Chambers gives the corresponding percentages of feminine endings for *3 Henry VI* as 14 per cent., for *Romeo and Juliet Q2* as 8 per cent., and for *Hamlet* (received text) as 23 per cent. I count 22 per cent. in the first act of *Hamlet,* and therefore the remaining acts must exceed 23 per cent. a little.

(vi) If the totals for the rhymed lines and double endings are deducted from those for the verse of the play and from those for the irregular verse, the results are that *Contention* has 26 per cent., *True Tragedy* 19 per cent., *Romeo and Juliet Q1* 18 per cent., and *Hamlet Q1* 32 per cent. of irregular verse.

I have selected some hundreds of examples illustrative of the various types of irregular verse tabulated above, including some of each group from each bad quarto. My purpose is to make clear the metrical interrelations of each pair of parallel texts and the essential sameness of the metrical changes and verse disorder in this group of corrupt texts. Such examples will be chosen as will exhibit the variety of the alterations made by the reporters, and study of these should satisfy any reader that Shakespeare did not meticulously correct the corrupt text of the bad quartos in the manner which the 'first sketch' theory demands.

The text of Shakespeare's plays as it appears in *Romeo and Juliet Q2* and *Hamlet Q2* and in the first folio versions of *2 Henry VI, 3 Henry VI* and *Henry V* will be used as authentic, that of the first quartos being treated as derivative. Those who accept the 'first sketch' theory will find the examples of some interest. Omissions of words belonging to Shakespeare's text will be indicated by enclosing the omitted words within square brackets; changes of words in a line by enclosing these words within round brackets and placing immediately above them the words used in Q1; addition of words to the authentic version by a caret and by placing the added words above the line in smaller type. Whenever a line of Q1 represents the result of compressing two lines of Shakespeare's text, the portions omitted will be enclosed within square brackets, and what is left together with the words, if any, printed above will be the corresponding line of Q1. Whenever the amount of change made in a line or lines of Shakespeare's text is excessive or involves rearrangement in Q1, the corresponding line of Q1 will be placed immediately above the corresponding quotation from Shakespeare's text. A subsequent chapter of this volume will explain the origin of what I term a 'composite' line. Quotations come from the Praetorius facsimile of *Romeo and Juliet Q2,* the Griggs facsimile of *Hamlet Q2,* Booth's facsimile of the first folio, and the texts of the bad quartos as printed in the Cambridge Shakespeare (1863-6). Quotations from the named text of Shakespeare will be indicated by giving act, scene and line, those from the bad quartos by scene and line only.

Octosyllabic Lines

Octosyllabic verse precedes blank verse in our literature, and lends itself to rhythmic speaking, but it is rare in our early dramas except in those that are corrupt. No fewer than thirty-eight such lines occur in *Orlando Furioso Q1*; wherever the Dulwich MS. is available for comparison, these lines prove themselves a corruption of Greene's text. Usually they correspond to decasyllabic lines of the parallel text, of which two syllables at the beginning or end or in the middle have been omitted, but other examples represent loss of half or more of Shakespeare's line and insertion of less than the portion lost. Mislineation and some small omissions account for the presence of others. Occasionally an eleven-syllable line has suffered truncation of three syllables at the end or the beginning. Others originate in the fusion of parts of two consecutive lines belonging to the parallel text. Some are peculiar to the bad quartos, but no examples will be given of these.

2 Henry VI and Contention

Iesus preserue your [Royall] Maiesty.	1.2.70
How now Suffolke, where's our unkle?	x.16
Where is our Vnckle? what's the matter Suffolke?	3.2.25
Yet doe not goe [away] : come Basiliske.	3.2.52
call And (cry out) for thee to close [vp] mine eyes.	3.2.395
How now, whither goes Vawse so fast?	x.182
Whether goes Vaux so fast? [What newes I prethee?]	3.2.367
defence. This hand [of mine] hath writ in thy (behalfe).	4.1.63

R

     will
[For I] my selfe (must) hunt this Deere to death. 5.2.15

  Braue Lord
(Then nobly Yorke), 'tis for a Crown thou fightst. 5.2.16

3 HENRY VI and TRUE TRAGEDY

My Title's [good, and] better farre then his. 1.1.130

  could   chuse
I (should) not (for my Life) but weep with him. 1.4.170

  What,
(Why how now) long-tongu'd Warwicke, dare you speak?
                  2.2.33

      faints
And when thou (failst) [as God forbid the houre]
Must Edward fall.   2.1.191-2

[Look here,] I throw my infamie at thee. 5.1.82

       thinkest
And set vp Lancaster. [Why,] (trowest) thou, [Warwicke]
                 5.1.85

Why what a [peeuish] Foole was that of Creet. 5.6.21

ROMEO AND JULIET Q2 and ROMEO AND JULIET Q1

Rom. Farewell [my] Coze.
        Nay Ile
Ben.   (Soft I will) go along. 1.1.193

        vp and downe
She could haue [run and] wadled (all about). 1.3.38

[What man] tis not so much, tis not so much. 1.5.32

This field-bed is too cold for me [to sleepe]. 2.1.40

      Now
Rom. (What shall I sweare) by?
      Nay
Iul.   ∧ Do not sweare at all. 2.2.112

You are to blame [my Lord] to rate her so. 3.5.169

         to
[Looke sir,] here comes the Lady (toward) my Cell. 4.1.17

  What Frier Lawrence
(Holy Franciscan Frier), brother, ho. 5.2.1

HENRY V Fo. and HENRY V Q1

      The
(They of those) Marches, gracious Soueraign.   1.2.142

           controlles
Th'aduised head (defends) [it selfe] at home.   1.2.180

                      your Prince.
So get you hence [in peace] : And tell (the Dolphin).   1.2.298

           reward
Sooner then (quittance of desert) and merit.   2.2.34

Of him
∧Breed [by his sufferance] more of such a kind.   2.2.46

Were busied with a [Whitson] Morris-dance.   2.4.26

                wombely vaultes
That Caues and (Wombie Vaultages) of France.   2.4.130

       short-nooke   England
In that (nooke-shotten) Ile of (Albion).   3.5.14

    in truth
And yet∧I doe thee wrong, [to mind thee of it].   4.3.12

    Gods will
(How now), what meanes this [Herald] ? Know'st thou not.
                           4.7.66

HAMLET Q2 and HAMLET Q1

Appeares before them, walkes.   ii.120
[Goes slowe and stately by them;] thrice he (walkt). 1.2.201-2

                        prince
[So please you,] something touching the (Lord) Hamlet. 1.3.89

    He
                            heart
(The Serpent) that did sting thy fathers (life).   1.5.39

[And curde] like eager droppings into milke.   1.5.69

O horrible, [o horrible] most horrible.   1.5.80

     I
(How now) a Rat, dead for a Duckat, [dead.]   3.4.23

          cleaues
[O] Hamlet thou (hast cleft) my hart in twaine.   3.4.156

Come   here lies thy Vnion
∧Drinke [of this potion] (is the Onixe) heere.   5.2.312

NINE-SYLLABLE LINES

Many of the octosyllabic lines would pass muster on the stage but verses of nine syllables have no place in our blank verse drama; they can neither be recited nor be scanned except by making a pause or using some other artifice. This irregularity of stress makes them harsh or unmusical. They are most uncommon in our early verse plays, and very rare in the authentic plays of Shakespeare and his contemporaries. There are next to none in the good texts of Peele or Greene. Three examples are to be found in Orlando's part in the quarto, viz., those numbered i, ix and x in what precedes, and it is proven that each of these is the work of the reporter. I have previously noted that a number of nine-syllable lines are present in *Tamburlaine* and *Edward II;* most of them have a monosyllabic foot at the beginning, but in *Edward II* the metre of some lines is defective elsewhere in the line. Perhaps the text of this play is not above suspicion; it is significant that three such lines which are faulty in the text of 1598 are metrically correct in that of 1594. Editors make various suggestions to explain them, but possibly Marlowe assumed the right of a poet to deviate from the normal at his pleasure.

Those present in the bad quartos are divisible into three groups according as a syllable is missing at the beginning, in the middle, or at the end of the line. Many of these lines are, except for the missing word or words, identical with lines in the corresponding parallel texts of Shakespeare; a monosyllable may have dropped out or replaced a dissyllable. Pause or elision usually covers the defect. Some arise from the inversion of parts of a line, or from the linking up of two halves of successive lines. Some of the third group, those with the last syllable unstressed, represent remnants of lines of the parallel texts with double endings. Examples set out below have been selected from over 260 examples of nine-syllable verses to illustrate the relation between each pair of parallel texts.

2 HENRY VI and CONTENTION

(A) ∧ The very trayne of her worst [wearing] Gowne.   1.3.82

∧ My Lord, ('tis) but a base [ignoble] minde.   2.1.13

Do   claime   house
(How they) affect the (House) and (Clayme) of Yorke.

3.1.375

I,   Duke   that
(Iacke Cade), the D. of York hath taught you (this).   4.2.143

meane   so
Yorke, if thou (meanest) wel, I greete thee (well).   5.1.14

(B) What, worse then naught? [nay], then a Shame take all.

3.1.307

villaine
Stay (Whitmore), [for] thy Prisoner is a Prince.   4.1.44

Poull
I∧Kennell, puddle, sinke, [whose filth] and dirt.   4.1.71

my
I feare (me) Loue, if [that] I had beene dead.   4.3.33

England
(C) Euen as I haue of fertile (Englands) [soile].   1.1.233

Of ashy semblance, [meager,] pale, and bloodlesse.   3.2.162

our   swords
And if∧words will not, [then] our (Weapons) shal.   5.1.143

What is he mad? to Bedlam with him.   xxii.6
To Bedlem with him, is the man growne mad?   5.1.131

3 HENRY VI and TRUE TRAGEDY

to
(A) And I (vnto) the Sea, from whence I came.   1.1.209

friendlie
[If] Friend or Foe, let him be (gently) vsed.   2.6.48

[Say,] what art thou that talk'st of Kings and Queens.   3.1.55

[Why] then mine Honestie shall be my Dower.   3.2.73

And [not] bewray thy Treason with a Blush.   3.3.97

[Why,] what is Pompe, Rule, Reigne, but Earth and Dust?

5.2.27

(B) Till our [King] Henry had shooke hands with Death.   1.4.102

makes
'Tis Beautie that [doth] oft (make) Women prowd.   1.4.128

full of ioie
Mine such, as fill my heart (with vnhop'd ioyes).   3.3.172

Farewell my Hector, [and] my Troyes true hope.   4.8.25

                    he
Yes Warwicke, (Edward) dares, and leads the way.   5.1.112

The women wept and the widwife cried.   xxii.63
The Midwife wonder'd and the Women cri'de,   5.6.74

                    indurate
(C) Thou, sterne, (obdurate), [flintie,] rough, remorselesse.
                                                1.4.142

Well, ieast on Brothers; I can tell you [both].   3.2.116

                        England.
From worthy Edward, King of (Albion)   3.3.49

All that, [which] Henry the Fift had gotten.   3.3.90

                Souldiers
Courage my (Masters) : [Honor] now, or neuer.   4.3.24

                                me
And Richard, doe not frowne vpon (my) [faults].   5.1.100

ROMEO AND JULIET Q2 and ROMEO AND JULIET Q1

(A) *Rom.* [I] would I were thy bird.
    Iu.   Sweete so would I.   2.2.183

    Speake
   ∧ Benuolio, who began this [bloudie] fray?   3.1.156

                        Sicamoure
(B) Where vnderneath the groue [of] Syramour.   1.1.119

I should haue bene [more] strange, I must confesse.   2.2.102

            Tybalt
Tybalt, (my Cozin), O my brothers child   3.1.142

                                pules
Oh she sayes nothing [sir], but weeps and (weeps.)   3.3.99

            wrong   that
That is no (slaunder) sir, (which) is a truth.   4.1.333

                    knife
[No, no,] this shall forbid it, ∧ lie thou there.   4.3.23

Well Ile   you.
∧ (I will) be gone [sir], and not trouble (ye).   5.3.40

            Kinsman   Ah
(C) Hath bene my (Cozen), (O) [sweete] Iuliet.   3.1.109

Is father, mother, Tybalt, (Romeo,) Iuliet.   3.2.123

haue   thankes ye
I (sir), but she will none, she (giues you thankes).   3.5.139

What   not   thanke
(How) will she (none)? doth she not (giue) vs [thankes]?
        3.5.142

HENRY V Fo. and HENRY V Q1

    Constable dispatch, send Montioy forth.   ix.19
(A) Therefore Lord Constable, hast on Montioy.   3.5.62

                                    such
(B) We will [in France] by Gods grace play ∧a set.   1.2.266

        we   vs
When (I) do rowse (me) in [my] Throne of France.   1.2.279

        deeds   amisse
Of all your (deare) (offences). Bear them hence.   2.2.181

                        are
The Gates of Mercy (shall be) all shut vp.   3.3.10

                        blood
Comes to him, where in (gore) he lay [in]steeped.   4.6.12

    To whom   spirit
(C) (Vnto whose) [grace] our (passion) is as subiect.   1.2.244

                        service
To do your Grace incessant (services).   2.2.38

                    we were to grace him.
You know how apt (our loue was, to accord).   2.2.86

Braue Clarence, and my Lord of Gloster.   xiv.5
My deare Lord Gloucester, and my good Lord Exeter. 4.3.9

                    day   Cryspin
This day is call'd the (Feast) of (Crispian).   4.3.42

    Go
(Follow), [and] see there be no harme betweene them. 4.7.181

        men
What (Prisoners) of [good] sort are taken Vnkle.   4.8.76

HAMLET Q2 and HAMLET Q1

            Lordes,   here haue
(A)   ∧ We (haue heere) writ
    To [Norway Vncle of young] Fortenbrasse.
                                    1.2.27-8

[O] day and night, but this is wondrous strange.   1.5.164

       O   Hamlet, the drinke.
(No, no) the drinke, the drinke, (O my deare Hamlet). 5.2.296

(B) We doubt [it] nothing, hartely farwell.   1.2.41

                        your grace
Haue I my Lord? I assure (my good Liege).   2.2.43

Here Hamlet, thy mother drinkes to thee.   xviii.75
The Queene carowses to thy fortune Hamlet.   5.2.276

Leartes come. you dally with me.   xviii.77
Come for the third Laertes, you doe but dally.   5.2.284

                      Leartes
(C) Haue you your fathers leaue∧. [What saies Polonius?]
                                         1.2.57

                devoyd
O God, a beast (that wants discourse) of reason.   1.2.150

   No,   it   my deere Ofelia.
(O) feare (me) not. ∧   ∧   ∧   1.3.51

Laer.   O thou vile King
Giue me my father.
Quee.   [Calmely good Laertes.]   4.5.111-2

ELEVEN-SYLLABLE LINES

(A) *First Syllable Hypermetrical*

Lines of eleven syllables are normal lines with an extra syllable; this may be found at the beginning, in the middle or at the end of the line. Lines with the redundant syllable at the beginning of the line, like nine-syllable lines, have no place in our blank verse drama. Neither Greene nor Peele nor Marlowe used them; I find none in *1 Tamburlaine* and two only in *Edward II*. They are the result of prefixing a monosyllabic enclitic such as 'and,' 'then,' 'what,' 'why,' etc., to a normal line; wherever editors find such a line in a sound text they usually emend it out of existence. Nothing more definitely proves the derivative character of *True Tragedy* than the very large number—it amounts to two per cent. of the total length—of such lines present in scenes very close to those of *3 Henry VI*. No dramatist known to us employed this type of verse, which must be the work of reporter or pirate. Reference to the Table shows that this type of unmetrical line is exceedingly common in the very corrupt texts of *Massacre at Paris* and *A Shrew*. The sudden fall in the number found in *Romeo and Juliet Q1* and *Henry V Q1* suggests that in the two years between the publication of *True Tragedy* and the first of the succeeding bad quartos, the managers of the theatre had succeeded in reducing the amount of this type of gagging; it reappears to some extent in *Hamlet Q1*.

2 HENRY VI and CONTENTION

I
∧ But by the grace of god, and Humes aduice.   1.2.72

As   the   takes
∧ Strangers in ∧ Court, [doe] (take) her for the Queene.   1.3.75

And
∧ Warwicke may liue to be the best of all   1.3.110

I   speake.
∧ But I can giue the loser leaue to (chide).   3.1.182

The   false   here
∧ Vnlesse (Lord) Suffolke (straight) be done to death.   3.2.244

For
∧ I haue great matters to impart to thee.   3.2.299

Sirs,   fields.
∧ Meet me to morrow in S. Georges (Field).   5.1.46

3 HENRY VI and TRUE TRAGEDY

And
∧ If I be not, Heauens be reueng'd on me.   1.1.57

Why
∧ Henry the Fourth by Conquest got the Crowne.   1.1.133

And   doubt of
∧ Why should I [not] now (haue) ∧ the like successe?   1.2.75

I
∧ Such pitty as my Rapiers point affords.   1.3.37

Harke, what   this   that   his
∧ (Whose) soule is (that) (which) takes (hir) heauy leaue?
                                                          2.6.42

Why
∧ Hee is the bluntest Wooer in Christendome.   3.2.83

And so
∧ (Now) for a-while farewell good Duke of Yorke.　　　4.3.57

And　　　　　　　　passe
∧ In euery Countie as we (goe) along.　　　　　　　5.3.33

ROMEO AND JULIET Q2 and ROMEO AND JULIET Q1

And
∧ Then he dreams of an other Benefice.　　　　　　1.4.79

Tut　　　　　　　　marrie if one
∧ This cannot anger him, ('twould anger him).　　　2.1.23

I　　　gaue
∧ He (lent) me counsell, and I lent him eyes.　　　　2.2.81

What
∧ Euermore weeping for your Cozens death.　　　　3.5.69

I　　　　　　or
∧ And from my soule (too), else beshrew them both.　3.5.228

HENRY V Fo. and HENRY V Q1

Why
∧ All things be ready if our minds be so.　　　　　4.3.72

HAMLET Q2 and HAMLET Q1

O　　　　　　　　　　watch
∧ You come most carefully vpon your (houre).　　　1.1.6

Well
∧ It is not, nor it cannot come to good.　　　　　　1.2.158

O　　　　your loues,
∧ Your loues, ∧ ∧ as mine to you, farwell.　　　　1.2.253

O
∧ The King doth wake to night and takes his rowse.　1.4.8

It
∧ Would have made milch the burning eyes of heauen.　2.2.495

And
△ Out of my weakenes, and my melancholy.　　　　2.2.577

No　　　　　　　　　　Mary there it goes.
∧ To sleepe, (perchance) to dreame, I (there's the rub.)　3.1.65

And thinke
∧ (That) I haue shot my arrowe ore the house.　　　5.2.230

ELEVEN-SYLLABLE LINES

(B) *Extra Mid-line Syllable*

Lines with an extra syllable in the middle of the verse form the second group of eleven-syllable lines. Such verses are present in all Shakespeare's plays except the early comedies, but with *Hamlet* they become an important and very effective element in the poet's scheme of versification. Surrey does not use this line, and Peele, Greene and Marlowe have very few in their plays with sound texts; but *Massacre at Paris* has more than all Marlowe's other plays put together. From Orlando's part comes evidence of the manner in which the pirates introduced them into the play—see examples numbered iii, xx, xxviii, and xxxiv. Many of these lines found in the bad quartos are identical, except for a slight change, with lines in the corresponding parallel texts. In some a monosyllable, frequently a conjunction, is inserted, in others a dissyllable replaces a monosyllable with the result that Shakespeare's line becomes unmetrical. Of special interest are those in which the intrusive word is a relative pronoun, omitted in Shakespeare's way even when it is subject of a sentence. Sometimes a redundant syllable arises from the reduction of two lines of Shakespeare's work to one in the bad quarto. Occasionally inversion of two half-lines leaves a superfluous syllable in the middle. Some of the examples below may become normal by elision or slurring, but most of them are past such surgery. They are five times as numerous in *Contention* and *True Tragedy* as in the parallel texts of *Henry VI*.

2 HENRY VI and CONTENTION

So will I In England worke your [Graces] full content.	1.3.64-5
greater matters But (mightier Crimes) are lay'd vnto your charge.	3.1.134
Tell them we all ∧ ∧ (I) thanke them ∧ for their [tender] louing care.	3.2.280
thus their meanes. And had I not beene cited (so) by (them) ∧	3.2.381
Ransome it shal (Rate) me at what thou wilt, (thou shalt) be payed.	4.1.30

I,∧ but these ragges are no part of the Duke.   4.1.47

(sir above ∧)

Hold Warwick:∧ seek thee out some other chace.   5.2.14

(and above ∧)

3 HENRY VI and TRUE TRAGEDY

Wee'le all assist you:∧ he that flyes, shall dye.   1.1.30

(and above ∧)

Thinke you ('twere) preiudiciall to (his) Crowne?   1.1.144

(that were above 'twere; the above his)

Write vp his Title with ∧ vsurping blood.   1.1.169

(thy above ∧)

And learne this Lesson:∧ Draw thy Sword in right.   2.2.62

(boy above ∧)

'Twas not your valor Clifford ∧ droue me thence.   2.2.107

(that above ∧)

Thou pittied'st Rutland, ∧ I will pitty thee.   2.6.74

(and above ∧)

His (Land) then ∧ seiz'd on by the Conqueror.   3.2.3

(lands above Land; were above ∧)

Be pittifull, ∧ dread Lord, and graunt it (then).   3.2.32

(then above ∧; them above then)

At my (depart), these were his very words.   4.1.92

(departure above depart)

(Nay) this way (man), See where the (Huntsmen) stand.   4.5.15

(No above Nay; huntsman above man; keepers above Huntsmen)

ROMEO AND JULIET Q2 and ROMEO AND JULIET Q1

(And on) my life ∧ hath stolne him home to bed.   2.1.4

(Vpon above And on; he above ∧)

When ∧ King Cophetua lou'd the begger (mayd).   2.1.14

(young above ∧; wench above mayd)

I would not for the world they ∧ (saw) thee here.   2.2.74

(should find above ∧ saw)

Doest thou loue me? ∧ I know thou wilt say I.   2.2.90

(Nay above ∧)

For this being smelt ∧ with that part, cheares each (part).   2.3.25

(too above ∧; hart above part)

       lazie
Oh she is (lame), loues heraulds should be thoughts.   2.5.4

So in that sense your worship
∧ (Your worship in that sense) may call him man.   3.1.56

          saye ye
On Thursday (sir) : the time is very short.   4.1.1

HENRY V Fo. and HENRY V Q1

          vs   against
We must not onely arme ∧ (t'inuade) the French.   1.2.138

         examplified
For heare her but (exampl'd) by her selfe.   1.2.158

                gracious father
          [Good] my ∧ (Soueraigne),
   cut   this
(Take) vp (the) English short.   2.4.75-6

[Dying like men], though buryed in your Dunghills.   4.3.101-2
(We) shall be fam'd.

               into
I was not angry since I came (to) France.   4.7.53
    See also 2.2.54 ; 4.3.26.

HAMLET Q2 and HAMLET Q1

   mine   beastly
But (this) most foule, (strange) and vnnaturall.   1.5.28

Ham. May sweepe to my reuenge.
                    O
Ghost.   ∧ I finde thee apt.   1.5.31

         nay
Hic et ubique, ∧ then weele shift our ground.   1.5.156

ELEVEN-SYLLABLE LINES

(C) *Feminine Endings*

Our first extant specimen of blank verse appeared some forty years before the production of *Tamburlaine;* twenty-five years later Shakespeare had written the blank verse of *Tempest.* Surrey seems to have been content to pack ten syllables into a line without overmuch discord; he rarely used less, and about as rare are lines with an extra unaccented syllable at the end, the so-called feminine or double ending. Not one such ending is discoverable in the third act of *Ferrex and Porrex*. Peele wrote one hundred and fifty lines of blank verse in *Arraignment of Paris;* not one double ending is to be found in the Prologue, the oration of Paris or Diana's eulogy of the nymph Eliza. He is sparing in such deviations from the normal decasyllable in *Alcazar* and *David and Bethsabe,* but a little freer in *Edward I.* His dated poems in blank verse, *The Honour of the Garter* (1593) and *Anglorum Feriae* (1595), have few, if any, verses of eleven syllables. Greene has some poems in blank verse scattered in his novels from *Morando* (1584) to *Perimedes* (1589); he has no feminine endings in these, only two or three in *Alphonsus of Arragon,* fifteen in *Orlando Furioso Q1,* and from one to three per cent. in *Friar Bacon, Looking Glass* and *James IV.*

Marlowe did not employ this form of verse very much in his plays; my table shows a small increase in the interval between *1 Tamburlaine* and *Edward II.* Certain critics, notably Robertson, have drawn unwarrantable conclusions from the fifteen per cent. of feminine endings found in this poet's translation of Lucan's *Pharsalia, Book I,* into blank verse, or more than three times the highest percentage of such endings present in any of his accepted plays. This translation seems to have been a self-imposed task, made the more difficult because the author undertook to give a line-for-line rendering of Lucan's hexameters in English blank verse. He must cram the literal meaning of fourteen to sixteen syllables of a highly inflected language into ten syllables of an almost uninflected speech; the result was elision, slurring, clipping proper names, awkward inversions, unusual compounds, paraphrasing, etc. No one with any knowledge of the difficulties confronting the translator will be surprised that Marlowe was compelled to use an extra syllable rather frequently; so also, when he made a line-for-line rhymed translation of Ovid's *Amores* he was forced to employ many double rhymes. In Lucan lines with an additional syllable occur in clumps of two, three or even four, and are distributed sporadically; thus there are nine in ll. 20-43, two in the next forty lines, nine in the succeeding twenty lines and another nine in the next eighty lines, and so on. Probably because the poet was not expressing his own thoughts he voluntarily wore a metrical strait-jacket; in his plays he wrote what he thought as pleased him best. This rigid bondage may have taught him economy in the use of words, but his translation of Lucan's *Pharsalia,* unprinted till 1600, had no influence upon the versification of its author or of any other author.

For some years after Shakespeare's arrival in London the end-stopped verse of *Tamburlaine* dominated our drama, and must have become monotonous for audiences to hear and for actors to recite. Intelligent auditors would realize that they were listening to language unlike anything spoken by any persons of their work-a-day world. Each of the sixty opening lines of *Looking Glass* has a pause at the end of the line, and the sense of almost every one of the 126 lines spoken in the famous abdication scene of *Edward II* ends with the line. Under such conditions even the best actors would tend to an over-stressing of each fifth foot, and this recurrent emphasis preceding an almost compulsory, if slight, pause would afflict a sensitive ear. How could the actor-sharer Shakespeare break his fellows of this ingrained habit, and banish from the theatre this drumming beat on each tenth syllable?

Shakespeare was to spend many years in writing dramatic poetry before he achieved an ideal blank verse, one which preserved the rhythm and music of poetry and which persuaded listeners that they were hearing the speech of an ordinary man lifted by emotion a little above himself. His first efforts were designed to prevent in part the monotonous iteration of the stressed final syllable; accordingly he introduced into the verse of *2 Henry VI* and *3 Henry VI* about one line in every seven with an extra eleventh syllable which was unstressed. The effect was to separate stress and pause at the end of that line. Some short lines, some rhyming couplets, and about ten per cent. of 'line-overflows' would help to vary regularity of pausation at the end of the line. All told, the number of lines in which the terminal pause either disappeared or was varied amounted in *3 Henry VI* to about twenty-eight lines in a hundred, and rose to forty per cent. in *Richard III.* As happens with many reformers, he did not count on human dislike of change and the strength of habit in man. Plenty of evidence is obtainable from *Contention* and *True Tragedy* to show that the actors did not like feminine endings, apparently because they were a hindrance to the uniformity of their rhetorical goose-step. The strength of this objection is not so noticeable in *Romeo and Juliet Q1,* and had much weakened when *Hamlet Q1* was entered on the Stationers' Register; the pirate had begun to mix his own double endings with his own decasyllables.

True Tragedy is divisible into two unequal parts; the smaller consists of 228 non-Shakespearean lines and of these eight only have feminine endings. All the remaining 1896 lines of the play correspond more or less exactly to lines of *3 Henry VI,* and should, on the assumption of even subdivision, contain 240 feminine endings; 159 is the number present. This loss of a third suggests that the actors somewhat disliked what was to them a new kind of verse; it disturbed the comfortable jog-trot of the ever-recurrent decasyllable, and made the task of memorizing more difficult. Small changes smoothed some into normal lines, an extra word at the end turned others into Alexandrines, omissions reduced others to nine-syllable lines, whilst additions at the beginning turned a few into 'thirteeners' or 'fourteeners.' Calculating the percentage on the total number of lines of ten or eleven syllables, I find that *True Tragedy* contains 9·3 per cent. of feminine endings, or double the percentage present in any other play of the period written by authors other than Shakespeare. If the non-Shakespearean lines are removed from the count, the portion of the play derived from *3 Henry VI* has nearly ten per cent. of double endings, or 4 per cent. less than is found in the parallel text. Feminine endings of *Romeo and Juliet Q1* represent 6·6 per cent. of the text as compared with 8 per cent. in Q2. When the actors prepared their perversion of *Henry V Q1* three years later, they had lost much of their objection to the line with a double ending. *Hamlet Q1* has 407 lines of alien verse in which are embedded several clumps of feminine endings. Below are the opening lines of the fourteenth scene:

> Madame, your sonne is safe arriv'de in Denmarke,
> This letter I euen now receiv'd of him,
> Where as he writes how he escap't the danger,
> And subtle treason that the king had plotted,
> Being crossed by the contention of the windes,
> He found the Packet sent to the king of England.

Q1 contains 15 per cent. of these lines compared with 23 per cent. in Q2; what Professor Wilson terms the lines from the old play have no less than 18 per cent. Does the theory of double revision require that the old *Hamlet,* which probably goes back to 1589, contained what would be then a unique proportion of double endings?

I have stated that the actors who compiled *Contention* and *True Tragedy* avoided double endings; numerous examples may be chosen from the latter play in each of which the sole change made in the corresponding line of *3 Henry VI* involves the final word or words:

<pre>
                    breakes   speake
My heart for anger (burnes), I cannot (brooke it).   1.1.60

                              in warres
And tenne to one, is no impeach (of Valour).   1.4.60

                                    much
Alas poore Yorke, but that I hate thee (deadly).   1.4.84

                                      content
Your Crowne Content, and you, must be (contented).   3.1.67

                                  world
Whose Wisdome was a Mirror to the (wisest).   3.3.84

                          is   heir
To linke with him, that (were) not lawful (chosen).   3.3.115

                          these wrongs
But what said Lady Bona to (my Marriage)?   4.1.97
</pre>

To the danger of his royall person then.   xv.12
No, but the losse of his owne Royall person.   4.4.5

<pre>
                                resolue
Women and Children of so high (a courage).   5.4.50

                                death
Nor I, but stoupe with patience to my (fortune).   5.5.6

                        tyrant
What's worse then (Murtherer), that I may name [it]?   5.5.58

                        remaine in thee
If any sparke of Life (be yet remaining).   5.6.65
</pre>

Twenty more examples could be cited from *True Tragedy* of this reduction of lines with feminine endings to normal lines, though other changes occur in some examples.

s

Addition of a word to some eleven-syllable lines of this type turns them into twelve-syllable lines, some of which are difficult to scan; sometimes more extensive changes produce similar results.

hurt   wherefore   kill
I neuer did thee (harme) : (why) wilt thou (slay) me? 1.3.40

me
The Foe is mercilesse, and will not pitty∧. 2.6.24

grant it
What seruice wilt thou doe me, if I (giue) ∧them? 3.2.44

euen vpon thy honor tell me true
Now Warwicke, (tell me euen vpon thy conscience). 3.3.113

your   state
You haue a Father able to maintaine (you). ∧ 3.3.154

Edw. Thou call'dst me King.

now
War.   I, but the case is alter'd. ∧ 4.3.31

Additions made to portions of a line with a feminine ending other than at the end are worth noting to illustrate how *3 Henry VI* was converted into such a corrupt text as is that of *True Tragedy*. Most of these twelve-syllable lines cannot be scanned.

amongst
Or (with) the rest, where is your Darling, Rutland? 1.4.87

hand
He on his right∧, asking a wife for Edward. 3.1.41

Come hither widdow, howe many children haste thou? x.22
How many Children hast thou, Widow? tell me. 3.2.26

would be loath
['Twill grieue] your Grace,∧my Sonnes should call you Father.
3.2.100

hinder
To (crosse) me from the Golden time I looke for. 3.2.127

Then
∧Draw neere, Queene Margaret, and be a witnesse. 3.3.138

Some such eleven-syllable lines are reduced to unmetrical decasyllabic lines:

breasts
I cannot weepe: for all my (bodies) moisture. 2.1.79

Tell me What said Lewis to our letters.   xii.62
What answer makes King Lewis vnto our Letters?   4.1.91

I my good Lord: [my] Lord I should say rather.   5.6.2

Some such lines lose two syllables from re-arrangement and omission:

                               here.
[Intend here] to besiege you in your Castle. ∧   1.2.50

   Till   doe talke a word
(While) I (vse further conference) with Warwicke.   3.3.111

Subdivision (C) (p. 248) gives two examples of nine-syllable lines in *True Tragedy* formed from lines with feminine endings in *3 Henry VI*, viz., 1.4.142 and 4.3.24. Reduction of lines with double endings to octosyllables occurs in *3 Henry VI,* 5.1.85 quoted above. In addition we have:

                  of thee
And thus I prophesie,∧ [that many a thousand].   5.6.37

I have preferred to discuss the feminine endings of *True Tragedy* somewhat fully for various reasons. Excepting this play, each bad quarto has a considerable amount of prose, and when this is removed from the count, *Romeo and Juliet Q1* is the only other quarto in which the total verse is comparable to that of *True Tragedy*. Each has some rhymed verse and some non-Shakespearean lines, and after making all such deductions *True Tragedy* has 1,819 lines of blank verse, *Romeo and Juliet Q1* 1,419 lines, *Contention* 1,182 lines, *Hamlet Q1* 1,018 lines and *Henry V Q1* 749 lines. Both *Contention* and *Hamlet Q1* are in too advanced stages of disintegration for the results obtained from their texts to have much evidential value. Apart from the greater amount of blank verse, *True Tragedy* has a text much closer to that of *3 Henry VI* than is the text of the first quarto of *Romeo and Juliet* to that of the second quarto. The percentage of blank verse lines that differ from the corresponding lines of Shakespeare's text by not more than two changes in the line is seven per cent. greater in *True Tragedy* than in *Romeo and Juliet Q1*. The latter play has few feminine endings in the well-preserved first and second acts; I count only 26 or a little over four per cent. of the blank verse.

They are more plentiful in the remainder of the play which consists mainly of blank verse.

In all these surreptitious plays occur lines with feminine endings which are normal in the parallel texts; usually they are the result of continued mislineation or of omission of text. They are infrequent in *Contention* or *True Tragedy;* a few examples will be chosen from the later quartos.

ROMEO AND JULIET Q2 and ROMEO AND JULIET Q1

        quickly bring   thether
As Phaetan would ∧ [whip] you (to the west).   3.2.3

     is   Sir that   bad
Here (sir) a Ring ∧ she (bid) me giue you [sir];   3.3.163

     meanes   weapons
What (meane) these maisterlesse and goarie (swords). 5.3.142

HENRY V Fo. and HENRY V Q1

             defences.
That England being emptie of (defence).   1.2.155

                   gaue   selues
And therefore [liuing hence did] (giue) our (selfe)
To barbarous license.   1.2.274-5

                         it.
That if requiring faile, he will compell. ∧   2.4.106

                           body.
My Ransome, is this frayle and worthlesse (Trunke). 3.6.150

                    all too litle.
Though all that I can doe, is (nothing worth).   4.1.304

HAMLET Q2 and HAMLET Q1

                 morning
The Cock that is the trumpet to the (morne).   1.1.150

Ophe. Tis in my memory lockt.
Lear. I humbly take my leaue, farewell Ofelia,
And remember well what I haue said to you.
Ofel. It is already lock't within my hart.   iii.43-5

Laer. Most humbly doe I take my leaue my Lord.
Pol. The time inuests you goe, your seruants tend.
Laer. Farewell Ophelia, and remember well
What I haue sayd to you.   1.3.82-5

This last passage of Q1 is an excellent example of the manner in which two eleven-syllable lines, one with a feminine ending, the second with an unnecessary first syllable were developed from the text of Shakespeare.

Twelve-Syllable Lines

Metrists disagree on the precise meaning to be attached to the term 'Alexandrine.' Some mean by it a line of six feet with six accents or stresses; others use it more loosely for any line of twelve syllables independent of the number of stresses; even the normal decasyllabic line has often fewer than five strongly stressed syllables. Reference to the table shows *Orlando Furioso Q1* and *Massacre at Paris* have each a considerable number of Alexandrines—I use this term for the sake of brevity; relatively to length, the latter play has eight times as many as *Edward II,* and the compilers of *Orlando Furioso Q1* inserted seven in about three hundred lines of Orlando's part. Twice only did Shakespeare exceed twenty in even his longest plays before he wrote *Hamlet Q2;* with it began a freer use of this verse-form, a recognition of the variety it brought into his versification. Some year or two previously he had begun to experiment with the eleven-syllable line with the extra syllable in the middle of the line, the so-called feminine section, and developed a type of verse pleasing to the ear and giving freedom from end-stopped rigidity.

Contention and *True Tragedy,* abridgments though they are, contain six times as many as the two parallel texts; when one notes that ten Alexandrines occur in 228 alien lines of *True Tragedy,* it is evident that the pirates must be debited with the excessive number present in that play.

2 Henry VI and Contention

```
For          he
∧ Suffolke, ∧ the new-made Duke that rules the rost.          1.1.106
                    dainty visage
        Could I come neere your (Beautie) with my Nayles.     1.3.138
                  I      it
        Faith holy Vnckle, ∧ would't ∧ were come to that.     2.1.35
                      can          will entangle
        And flye thou how thou (canst) they ('le tangle) thee. 2.4.55
```

         bleeding heart
Witnesse my ∧ (teares), I cannot stay to speake.   2.4.86

Had   bene there   fetcht pollices
∧ [If] Yorke, ∧ with all his far-(fet) (pollicie),
[Had beene the Regent there].   3.1.293-4

My Lord,
∧ ∧ The Commons like an angry Hiue of Bees.   3.2.125

Indeed
∧ 'Tis like the Commons, rude vnpolisht Hindes.   3.2.271

                diest assured of heauenly
Lord Card'nall, if thou ∧ (think'st on heauens) blisse.   3.3.37

3 HENRY VI and TRUE TRAGEDY

                and   out
Ile plant Plantagenet, ∧ root him (vp) who dares.   1.1.48

                              my lord
They seeke reuenge, and therefore will not yeeld ∧ ∧.   1.1.179

  Reuenged   accursed
(Reueng'd) may she be on that (hatefull) Duke.   1.1.266

              and   reuenge
Richard, I beare thy name, ∧ Ile (venge) thy death.   2.1.89

Thy husbands
∧ (His) Father reuel'd in the heart of France.   2.2.150

                rude his fathers bloud   to spil?
Was euer sonne, so (rew'd a Fathers death) ∧ ∧   2.5.109

                      is   awaie
But thinke you [Lords] that Clifford ∧ fled ∧ with them? 2.6.38

                busie
Yet looke to have them (buz) to offend thine eares.   2.6.95

   Wer it not
('Twere) ∧ pittie they should lose their Fathers Lands.   3.2.31

           we meane to
Lords giue vs leaue, ∧ (Ile) ∧ trye this Widowes wit.   3.2.33

I will   go clad
∧ ∧ (And decke) my Body in gay Ornaments.   3.2.149

Then
∧ Draw neere, Queene Margaret, and be a witnesse.   3.3.138

What saie you   to
∧ (Now), ∧ Brother Richard, will you stand (by) vs?   4.1.145

Except you presently
(If you'le not here) proclaime your selfe our King.   4.7.49

        rosiate
I Seale vpon the ∧ lips of this sweet Babe.   5.7.29

ROMEO AND JULIET Q2 and ROMEO AND JULIET Q1

            Iuliet   by the
For then [she] could ∧ stand hylone, nay (by th) roode.   1.3.37

      is it   you
How long (ist) [now] since [last] (your) [selfe] and I
Were in a maske?
                      1.5.30-1

                    I heare some comming
Ere one can say, it lightens, (sweete good night).   2.2.120

I   that   of
∧ Would ∧ I were sleepe and peace (so) sweet to rest.   2.2.188

      to all   murdrers   none
Mercie ∧ ∧ but (murders), pardoning (those) that kill.   3.1.193

          —Window,
Ascend her chamber, ∧ hence and comfort her.   3.3.147

And not the   See
∧ (No) ∧ Nightingale, (looke) Loue what enuious streakes.   3.5.7

   Out you greene sicknesse [carrion, out you] baggage,
Out
∧ You tallow face.
                      3.5.156-7

           Princely
[A Gentleman] of (noble) parentage,

                      trainde.
[Of faire demeanes,] youthfull and nobly (liand).   3.5.180-1

HENRY V Fo. and HENRY V Q1

                 yonger
Betweene [the promise of] his (greener) dayes,
         musters
And these he (masters) now.   2.4.142-3

             I must repent :
Goe [therefore] tell thy Master, heere I am.   3.6.148-9
My Liege,
∧ ∧ I hope they will not come vpon vs now.   3.6.164

For yet a many of your [horsemen peere,]
  French do keep
(And gallop ore) the field.   4.7.85-6

Hᴀᴍʟᴇᴛ Q2 and Hᴀᴍʟᴇᴛ Q1

Mar. Who ist that can informe mee?

Mary
Hora.   ∧ That can I.   1.1.79

Who   was
(Was) as you knowe ∧ by Fortinbrasse of Norway.   1.1.82

sir
Against your selfe, ∧ I knowe you are no truant.   1.2.173

good
My ∧ Lord, I came to see your fathers funerall.   1.2.176

O
∧ I pre thee doe not mocke me fellowe studient.   1.2.177

attentive
With an (attent) eare till I may deliver   1.2.193

wonder
Hora. This (maruile) to you.
                                              it.
Ham.   For Gods loue let me heare ∧   1.2.194

triumphes
Ham. The (triumph) of his pledge.
                                        here?
Hora.   Is it a custome ∧ ?   1.4.12

Hamlet
∧ Adiew, adiew, adiew, remember me.   1.5.91

news with you?
Farewell. How now Ophelia, whats the (matter) ? ∧   2.1.74

allowances
On such regards of safety and (allowance).   2.2.79

Pirrus   but all
Pirrhus at Priam driues, ∧ ∧ in rage strikes wide.   2.2.450

Why   Hecuba
∧ What's Hecuba to him or he to (her) ?   2.2.532

Ham. And hurt my brother.
Sir
Laer.   ∧ I am satisfied in nature.   5.2.231

Hamlet, thou hast not in thee halfe an houre of life.   xviii.89
In thee there is not halfe an houres life.   5.2.302

CHAPTER XV

RHYMED LINES

ELIZABETHAN actors memorized rhyming lines more easily than blank verse or prose, and retained word perfect a higher proportion of the rhyming verse common to two parallel texts than of the blank verse. Of 332 lines of rhymed verse common to the two earliest versions of *Romeo and Juliet,* no fewer than 196 or nearly 60 per cent. of those in Q1 are word perfect, whilst of 1,419 blank-verse lines common to these two texts 578 or forty per cent. of those in Q1 are verbally identical. Much the same result holds for a more corrupt text such as *Hamlet Q1* which, outside of the players' scene, contains incidental pairs only of heroic couplets at the ends of certain speeches and scenes. Fifty per cent. of rhymed lines common to Q2 and Q1 are word perfect in Q1 compared with thirty per cent. of blank verse common to the two versions. However, if all rhyming lines, five-foot, short and doggerel, are included, the proportion of that which is word-perfect in *Hamlet Q1* almost equals that in *Romeo and Juliet Q1.*

Romeo and Juliet Q1 has the best material for studying the changes made by the pirates in passages of rhymed verse. Five-sixths of the heroic couplets or quatrains common to the two earliest versions are either identical or the same except for a change in one word; many lines of the remainder, however mutilated otherwise, keep the full number of the syllables present in the corresponding lines of Q2 and retain each the same rhyming word at the end. All the alterations in Q1, either of the number of syllables in the line or of the terminal rhyme found in the version of Q2, suggest the presence of a reporter and, therefore the priority of Q2.

(i) *Romeo and Juliet Q2* opens with a Prologue, spoken by 'Corus,' a typical Shakespearean sonnet consisting of three quatrains and a final heroic couplet. Six lines (ll. 7-12) are:

Whose misaduentur'd pittious ouerthrowes,
Doth with their death burie their Parents strife.

The fearfull passage of their death-markt loue,
And the continuance of their Parents rage:
Which but their childrens end nought could remoue:
Is now the two houres trafficque of our Stage.

These lines are reduced (Q1 7-10) to four:

Whose misaduentures, piteous ouerthrowes,
(Through the continuing of their Fathers strife,
And death-markt passage of their Parents rage)
Is now the two houres trafficque of our Stage.

Loss of the third and fifth lines belonging to the quotation from the sonnet in Q2 has reduced the third quatrain to a pair of rhymed lines in Q1. Consequently the sonnet of Q2 has become in Q1 a poem of twelve lines, made up of two quatrains and two heroic couplets, an unusual but possible verse form. The first line (except for a letter) and the last line of each quotation are the same in each text. How have four lines of Q2 become two lines in Q1? No trace of the fifth line of the extract from Q2 is recognizable in Q1, but its omission meant the disappearance of its rhyming mate, the third line of the quotation from Q2. The second line of the quotation from Q1 is made up of snippets from the fourth and the second lines of the extract from Q2. Two words of the omitted third line in the extract from Q2, viz., 'passage' and the unusual compound word 'death-markt,' have been introduced instead of the words 'the continuance' into the fourth line of the quotation from Q2, and this remodelled line forms the third line of the extract from Q1. Obviously the omitted third line of the quotation from Q2 was used by the compiler of the 'copy' for Q1, and must have been spoken on the stage before this 'copy' was prepared. Logically it may be insisted that the missing fifth line of the sonnet in Q2 was also spoken on the stage. The twelve lines of Q1 represent not a new verse form but what the reporter left of Shakespeare's sonnet.

(ii) Two lines (1.1.124-5) of Q2,

Griefes of mine owne lie heauie in my breast,
Which thou wilt propagate to haue it preast,

have been changed in Q1 (i. 112-3):

Griefes of mine owne lie heauie at my hart,
Which thou wouldst propagate to haue them prest.

Sense and grammar have been altered, but the presence of two unrhymed lines in a passage which is preceded and followed by rhymed couplets is more than suspicious.

(iii) A split line (1.1.193-4) of verse in Q2,

> *Rom.* Farewell my Coze.
> *Ben.*   Soft I will go along:
> And if you leaue me so, you do me wrong.

is probably responsible for the mislineation and metrical faults of the passage (i. 120-2) in Q1:

> *Rom.* Farewell Cose.
> *Ben.*   Nay Ile go along
> And if you hinder me you doo me wrong.

Here the reporter rhymes an octosyllabic line with a normal line.

(iv) Similar blunders occur in a number of places. Thus a little later (1.1.206-7) we read:

> Well in that hit you misse, sheel not be hit
> With Cupids arrow, she hath Dians wit:

The second line of this couplet (i. 135) is thus in Q1:

> With Cupids arrow, she hath Dianaes wit.

This is an obvious mistake: here an unrhythmical eleven-syllable line is linked with a normal line as a couplet.

(v) More changes are made in the following lines (1.2.34-5) of Q2:

> Come go with me, go sirrah trudge about,
> Through faire Verona, find those persons out.

Q1 omits Capulet's last words to Paris and begins (ii. 27-8) in Q1:

> Where are you sirra, goe trudge about
> Through faire Verona streets, and seeke them out:

Here the pirate couples in metrical matrimony a nine-syllable line and a decasyllable.

(vi) Changes made by the actors in their version of Q2 (1.4.48-9) are indicated in the usual way:

>   So   by
> *Rom.* (And) we meane well (in) going to this Mask.
> But tis no wit to go.
>
>   Romeo
> *Mer.*   Why. ∧ may one aske?

Shakespeare's habit of dividing a line between two speakers even in a scene largely in rhyming couplets was a stumbling-block to the pirates. Here the normal line rhymes with an Alexandrine.

(vii) Such rhyming as 'delights' with 'night' (ii. 21-2), 'meeting' with 'greetings' (v. 65-6), 'how' with 'vowes' (vii. 55-6) and 'bring' with 'things' (xxii. 223-5) may be credited, very doubtfully, to the printer.

(viii) The evidential value of the change made in Q2 (2.3.31-2), which produced the text of Q1 (vii. 25-6), has been previously discussed (iv, p. 186). The interpolation not merely breaks the continuity of the rhyming couplets, but gives evidence that the scene of which it was a part had been spoken on the stage before the copy for Q1 was prepared.

(ix) Romeo has killed Tybalt and fled. Benvolio has been arrested and the Prince asks (3.1.146-7):

> *Prin.* Benvolio, who began this bloudie fray?
> *Ben.* Tybalt here slain, whom Romeos hand did slay.

This is the last of five couplets; in Q1 (xi. 107) we read:

> Speake Benuolio who began this fray?

The next line is verbatim as in Q2. This limping line comes from the reporter.

(x) Two speeches in the same scene (3.1.178-81) are not in Q1; thus Capulet's half line, 'The life of Tybalt,' is omitted. The relevant part of Q2 (3.1.182-3) runs:—

> *Cap.* The life of Tybalt.
> *Prin.*   And for that offence,
> Immediately we do exile him hence.

This omission in Q1 of Capulet's half-line makes this broken rhyme very conspicuous in a passage wholly in rhymed couplets.

(xi) The final couplet of this scene differs in the two versions. The lines of Q2 (3.1.192-3) are:

> Beare hence this body, and attend our will,
> Mercie but murders, pardoning those that kill.

Both lines are changed (xi. 149-150) in Q1:

> Pittie shall dwell and gouerne with vs still:
> Mercie to all but murdrers, pardoning none that kill.

This rhyming of a normal line with an Alexandrine is of a piece with all this 'very false gallop of verses,' and is excellent evidence of the pirates' presence. The framework of the last line and most of the words have been retained; the thought is the same but more awkwardly expressed.

(xii) I have previously (vi, p. 187) commented on the various mistakes that have transformed Q2 (3.2.129-131) to Q1 (xii. 54-6). Here the reporter rhymes an eleven-syllable line divided between two speakers with a decasyllabic line.

(xiii) *Romeo and Juliet* Q2 ends with a speech of six rhyming lines spoken by Prince Escalus; two rhyming couplets had preceded them.

> A glooming peace this morning with it brings.
> The Sun for sorrow will not shew his head:
> Go hence to haue more talke of these sad things,
> Some shall be pardoned, and some punished.
> For neuer was a Storie of more wo,
> Then this of Iuliet and her Romeo.

Q1 is poorly preserved towards the end especially in the last act, and the first three lines are very much the worse for wear. They are in Q1:

> A gloomie peace this day doth with it bring.
> Come, let vs hence,
> To haue more talke of these sad things.
> Some shall be pardoned and some punished:
> For neare was heard a Storie of more woe,
> Than this of Iuliet and her Romeo.

In Q2 the play ends with ten rhyming lines, concluding with a quatrain and a rhyming couplet; in the first quarto the verse of the last six lines is in disorder except for the final couplet. Alteration of 'brings' to 'doth bring' in the first line destroys the rhyme with 'things' in the third line. Omission of the second line left the fourth a line of blank verse. The third line of Q2 has been expanded by the pirate and broken into two short lines, one of four, the other of eight syllables. This speech in Q1 is nothing but a perversion of what Shakespeare wrote.

3 Henry VI and True Tragedy

About one half of the rhymed lines in the folio play are found in *True Tragedy*, and some of them bear witness against the reporter. I shall not discuss all the variations in detail, and shall set out examples of the changes made in the folio text in the usual way.

> Edward Plantagenet, arise a Knight
> And learne this Lesson ∧ ; Draw thy Sword in right.   2.2.61-2

where ∧ marks *boy*

> [Why] What is Pompe, Rule, Reigne, but Earth and Dust
> And liue we how we can, yet dye we must.   5.2.27-8

> Sound Drums and Trumpets, farwell ∧ sowre annoy,
> For heere I hope begins our lasting ioy.   5.7.45-6

where ∧ marks *to*

Other examples exhibit other changes than the simple ones above. The changes that turned three blank verse lines (2.5.109-11) of the folio text into three irregular rhyming lines have been fully discussed in an earlier portion of my inquiry (viii, pp. 176-7).

HENRY V Fo. and HENRY V Q1

Outside of Pistol's bombast, this play has not many heroic couplets. I have discussed elsewhere (viii, pp. 201-2) the transfer of the rhyming couplet (4.2.62-3) spoken by the Constable:

> [And vse it for my haste.] Come, come away,
> The Sunne is high, and we out-weare the day.

to an earlier scene in Q1 (xi. 61-2), in which the first portion of the first line is omitted. Were no parallel text in existence, the disparate rhyming lines would indicate corruption.

Another such pair of short and long lines ends the misplaced quarto version of the fourth scene of the fourth act; the whole quarto scene is in as confused disorder as the French army. The folio ends with Bourbon's despairing words (4.5.24-5):

> The diuell take Order now, Ile to the throng;
> Let life be short, else shame will be too long.

Speakers and the words spoken vary much in the two versions; the Constable in Q1 speaks two of his own lines, and concludes with an adaptation (xv. 17-18) of the above lines spoken by Burbon:

> Come, come along,
> Lets dye with honour, our shame doth last too long.

HAMLET Q2 and HAMLET Q1

If the rhyming lines spoken in the play acted before the King are omitted, *Hamlet Q2* contains a smaller number of heroic couplets than any other of the four great tragedies. Q1 retains about one half of these verses and adds a dozen couplets not in Q2; in addition the opening twelve lines of the players' scene are not those in Q2. Thus the pirate wrote or stole 36 lines of rhymed verse, and each line is metrically correct and rhymes well enough with its partner. Defective rhymes in Q1 represent the best that memory could supply of verses spoken on the stage from the second quarto.

(i) In concluding his fatherly reproof of Ophelia's affection for Hamlet, Corambis adapts (iii. 69-70) a line and a half from Viola's speech (2.4.108-9) in *Twelfth Night*:

> Come in Ofelia, such men often proue,
> 'Great in their wordes, but little in their loue.'

The stolen lines are:

> Our shewes are more then will: for still we proue
> Much in our vowes, but little in our loue.

This petty larceny from an unprinted play most probably on the acting list in 1601 is almost in itself proof that this couplet was patched up by some man of the theatre.

(ii) The next scene between Ophelia and her father concludes in Q2 (2.1.118-9) with a rhyming couplet:

> Come, goe we to the King,
> This must be knowne, which beeing kept close, might moue
> More griefe to hide, then hate to utter loue.

Not much sense is apparent in the two lines (v. 65-6) of the corresponding scene of Q1:

> Lets to the King, this madnesse may prooue,
> Though wilde a while, yet more true to thy loue.

His poor memory had left Corambis little to work up, the phrase 'to the King,' the knowledge that there was a rhyming couplet, and the last word 'loue'; result, an unmetrical nine-syllable line rhymes with a meaningless decasyllabic line.

(iii) Ophelia ends the speech in which she returns to Hamlet's 'remembrances of yours' with two rhyming lines (Q2. 3.1.100-1):

> Take these againe, for to the noble mind
> Rich gifts wax poore when giuers prooue vnkind.

Her speech in Q1 keeps the first and last lines well enough, but the three lines between them have suffered an eclipse; the first of her two rhyming lines (vi. 160-1) is two feet short:

> But now too true I finde,
> Rich giftes waxe poore, when giuers grow vnkinde.

The pirate had the second line of what he knew was a rhyming couplet firmly fixed in his 'ignoble mind,' but could not recollect the first line. He wrote six words, ending with a rhyme to 'vnkinde,' and being like Hamlet, 'ill at these numbers,' left it at that.

(iv) Ophelia did better with her next couplet (3.1.160-1):

> Blasted with extacie, o woe is mee
> T'haue seene what I haue seene, see what I see.

For 'blasted with extacie' she substituted 'All dasht and splintered thence,' which sounds well but means nothing; it fills up the line.

After reading these plays a critic may seem justified in asserting that no person with the most rudimentary knowledge of verse could have written many of the lines quoted above from the bad quartos. Such an assertion does not take into account all the facts. Each of the four longer bad quartos has a number of rhymed couplets stolen from some play or manufactured by the reporter and not representative of anything in the parallel text; nearly all are sound in metre and rhyme. *Hamlet Q1* has twelve such non-Shakespearean rhyming couplets, all technically complete, viz., iii. 69-70; x. 12-13; xi. 32-3, 171-4; xiii. 43-4, 120-1, 124-7; xiv. 15-16; xv. 54-5; xviii. 121-2; of poetry or sense the less said the better. To these may be added xi. 100-111, spoken by the 'Duke and Dutchesse' in the play acted before the king; they may possibly be part of the old play. We may test the remainder of the rhyming couplets in Q1 by comparing them with what Shakespeare wrote in Q2; those that are defective in metre or rhyme equal half of those common to the two versions. Probably the reporters who garbled the bad quartos varied in their ability to bombast out blank or rhymed verse, but even the least literate of these pirates knew how many syllables and feet ought to be present in a line and what rhyming meant. Each bad quarto except *Henry V Q1* has some rhyming couplets from the pen of its reporter, and most of those in *Romeo and Juliet Q1* are free from

defect. It seems anomalous that a person able to compose, as in
Hamlet Q1, a dozen rhyming couplets and to set them down
correctly, could have been guilty of inserting in the text elsewhere
couplets which had one or more syllables less in one line than in
the other. The explanation, perhaps, is that a person may be
capable of writing passable rhymes if he is at liberty to choose
his subject and mode of expression, but may fail in satisfying
simultaneously the demands of memory, subject, metre and rhyme.
If his defective memory has left a gap equal to half a line or more,
and he must satisfy the demands both of the context before and
after and of the rhythm, and fill the gap with a fixed number,
four, five or six rhythmical syllables, he may find the difficulty too
hard to overcome, and cut the knot by leaving the gap unfilled or
bridging it incompletely.

Any reader who takes a comprehensive survey of the irregular
verse of a bad quarto will realize how corrupt and garbled the
play is. Not one scene, scarcely a passage of twenty lines in *True
Tragedy* or *Romeo and Juliet Q1* but has at least one or two lines
defective or changed, if the standard is to be the corresponding
play of Shakespeare. Short lines, or lines of verse with less than
five feet, are proportionately over three times as numerous as in
the parallel texts. Lines of eight or nine syllables are so rare
in the authentic texts as to be, for purpose of comparison, almost
non-existent; they equal almost a twelfth part of the blank verse
in the three earlier bad quartos. Eleven-syllable verses other than
those with double endings number 34 and Alexandrines 33 in
2 Henry VI, 3 Henry VI and *Romeo and Juliet Q2* taken together;
in the corresponding bad quartos, *Contention, True Tragedy* and
Romeo and Juliet Q1 these lines with eleven syllables total 228
and Alexandrines 194. Relatively to total length, such irregular
verses are more than eight times as numerous in the bad quartos.
Each group of abnormal verses in *True Tragedy* is divided in
the Table into two sub-groups, and one of these, the non-
Shakespearean sub-group, contains a much higher proportion of
irregular verse than the remainder of the play.

Octosyllabic verses average about forty a play in each of the
five bad quartos; but relatively to length, *Orlando Furioso Q1* and
Massacre at Paris have each a larger proportion than any bad

T

quarto. Probably the explanation is that neither Greene nor Marlowe uses many double endings, and thus the incidence of corruption falls more heavily on the normal line, which is the main source of this introduced octosyllabic verse. *True Tragedy* contains as many as the two parts of *Tamburlaine, Dido,* and *Edward II* put together. Comparison of Orlando's part in the Dulwich MS. and in Q1 proves that the compilers of the latter text manipulated by omission or rearrangement many lines of Greene's blank verse so that it was reduced to eight syllables. Similar examples set out above indicate how frequently omission of a word or two or some rearrangement altered the normal line of Shakespeare's text exactly as in *Orlando Furioso,* with the result that an octosyllabic line appears in the bad quarto. I am of opinion that such is the full explanation and all that is necessary.

Lines of nine syllables included in the first sub-group cannot be metrical because the beat or stress must fall on the odd instead of on the even syllables. In certain examples an initial monosyllable such as 'I,' 'Yorke,' 'friend' or 'Lordes' may carry an initial stress if followed by a slight pause, and thus in recitation an escape is provided from the false or jolting rhythm almost inevitable in examples belonging to this sub-group. Disappearance of a syllable in the interior of a line results in harshness, and this can rarely be softened unless a medial pause is possible. Marlowe has a number of such lines in *Edward II,* some of which have crept somehow into the later editions of this play. Possibly Marlowe wrote carelessly, or took the liberty of being a pioneer in writing blank verse drama for the public theatres. All lines of nine syllables ending with an unstressed syllable are treated by editors as textual blunders in texts otherwise sound. They are far too numerous in each bad quarto to be the work of scribe or printer; such a verse is the child of illiteracy and poor memory.

Eleven-syllable verses with the superfluous syllable at the beginning of the line offer, I think, the strongest possible evidence of interpolation. Six or seven of those in *Contention* may be explained otherwise; one is in the folio text, but the rest have become unmetrical during the process of reporting. Those in *True Tragedy* are most plentiful in scenes where the text is closest to that of *3 Henry VI,* and one at the beginning comes from the folio text. Four result from the formation of composite lines; five, viz., i. 128; xv. 6, 8 and 16; xxi. 33 belong to the non-Shakespearean portion of the play (the group in the fifteenth scene is instructive), while most of the others betray their origin at once. Initial enclitics vary in popularity; 'and,' 'why,' 'but,' 'ay,' 'tut' being the most common. Many consist of a normal line of *3 Henry VI* with the addition of some such prefix; in others an alteration is found in one or two words of the folio line; occasionally the insertion of a dissyllable or two enclitics produces an Alexandrine. They occur most commonly in the snip-snap of dialogue; a continuative 'and' or 'ay,' a disjunctive 'but,' a rhetorical 'why,' an exclamatory 'what,' etc., are and were customary in dramatic conversation. If the author used these sparingly, the actors made good what they took to be needful links between line and line or sentence and sentence. The examples quoted from *Hamlet Q1* offer proof that this type of gagging was almost as rife as ten years before when *Orlando Furioso* and *3 Henry VI* were being acted.

Twelve-syllable lines are present in unusually large numbers in *Orlando Furioso Q1, Massacre at Paris, Contention* and *True Tragedy* at a time when Marlowe, Greene and Shakespeare were using this type of verse very little. This fact suggests that most of these lines represent a by-product of the all-pervading corruption that marks each of these plays. I have shown that nearly all the Alexandrines found in Orlando's part were inserted by the actors who compiled the text of the play; the twelve hundred lines of *Massacre at Paris* contain more Alexandrines than are in the nine thousand lines of the two parts of *Tamburlaine, Edward II* and *Dido*. No less than ten are present in the 228 lines of non-Shakespearean verse of *True Tragedy*. Reference to the examples quoted from *True Tragedy* will exemplify the various methods of forming the 80 examples of twelve-syllable lines found in it. Some are exactly as in *3 Henry VI*, a dozen or more represent normal lines of the parallel text with the addition of such unnecessary words as 'indeed,' 'nearly,' 'my lord,' 'ay but,' etc., or the name of a person; others expand a line of the folio play in which a vowel has been elided or lightly sounded, and fill out the line with a more or less suitable enclitic; others represent a line with a feminine ending, which was turned into a twelve-syllable line by adding a monosyllable to the end or into an unscannable monstrosity by prefixing an enclitic to the beginning; others are composite lines, whilst a few have passed through more complex changes but are clearly derived from lines of the folio text.

We know that the author of *King Lear* did not keep a line of his source-play *King Leir,* and I cannot believe that the author of *Hamlet Q2* patched a single line of the old play. Nor can I believe the author of *Venus and Adonis, Lucrece* and the *Sonnets* took over the rhyming couplets and the sonnets that some critics declare were in *Romeo and Juliet Q1* when he write Q2. Such persons suggest that he was as careful of his predecessor's text as if the author was Melpomene's son, and that he mended broken verses as carefully as a poor woman does her one black silk dress. Certain defective lines of rhymed verse, viz., those in examples numbered i, viii, x and xiii offer in themselves evidence that Q2 preceded Q1, in that Q1 omits words of Q2 necessary to the sense of the passage in Q1. Logically it follows that the other defective rhymed verses spring from the corruption of corresponding verses in Q2.

CHAPTER XVI

COMPOSITE LINES

DURING the preceding examination of the verse structure of the bad quartos several references have been made to what were termed 'composite' lines. This type of verse is peculiar to these texts, and some detailed account is relevant and necessary. Many years ago I noted the presence in *True Tragedy* of certain lines of blank verse, each of which represented an amalgamation of portions of two lines, generally but not invariably consecutive, of *3 Henry VI*. Two explanations of this phenomenon were possible. If *True Tragedy* was the source-play of *3 Henry VI*, Shakespeare must have expanded one line of his supposed original into two; if *True Tragedy* was a corrupt abridgment of *3 Henry VI*, the play-adapter or the actors must have made a composite line out of two lines belonging to the poet's play by combining portion (usually one or two words) of the first line and a second portion (usually the latter part) of the second line. In what follows I assume that the second explanation is correct, and shall offer what seem sufficient reasons for this assumption. Further investigation showed that such composite lines are present in each of the other bad quartos, and, in my opinion, they must be accepted as examples of a more or less unconscious abridgment, exemplifying what Dr. Greg terms the 'memorial reconstruction' of these texts. This peculiarity seems to have escaped the notice of commentators, and examples chosen from each surreptitious text are worth quoting.

For the purpose of illustrating the various ways in which composite lines may have originated, I shall begin with instances chosen from the comparatively good texts of *True Tragedy* and *Romeo and Juliet Q1*. They afford some excellent specimens of lines, each reconstructed by memory from two lines of an author's text; in some not a word is added, altered or transposed, though the metre may become irregular. The other bad quartos are more seriously corrupted and in part disintegrated; in consequence they have preserved a smaller number of lines verbally identical with the retained portions of the corresponding parallel text. Many other such vamped-up lines of each bad quarto omit, transpose or vary words belonging to one or both lines of the original text.

3 HENRY VI and TRUE TRAGEDY

(i) Edward and Richard suggest to their father a breach of the pact recently made with King Henry. Edward declares (1.2.16-17):

> But for a Kingdome any Oath may be broken:
> I would breake a thousand Oathes, to reigne one yeare.

A metrical composite line, an Alexandrine, (ii. 11-12) replaces these lines:

> But I would breake an hundred othes to raigne
> One yeare.

The sense of the first folio line is implicit in the second; the actor kept 'But' of the first line, and added the second with a slight change.

(ii) Before the battle of Towton, King Henry deplores the outbreak of civil war, and is reproved (2.2.56-7) by the queen:

> My Lord cheere vp your spirits, our foes are nye,
> And this soft courage makes your Followers faint.

In *True Tragedy* (v. 55) this reduces to,

> My Lord, this harmefull pittie makes your followers faint.

Clifford had used the words 'harmefull pittie' (l. 10); the reporters seem to have interpolated them with a view to preserving the rhythm of the line.

(iii) The son, who has killed his father, explains (2.5.65-6) how they came to be on opposite sides:

> My Father, being the Earle of Warwickes man,
> Came on the part of Yorke, prest by his Master.

Faulty memory reduced to one (viii. 21) these two lines:

> My father, he came on the part of Yorke.

In this example the composite line consists of the earlier pieces of the two lines, and is made good metrically by introducing a grammatically superfluous 'he.'

(iv) Clifford's body is discovered by the leaders of the victorious Yorkists on the battle-field. King Edward speaks (2.6.58-9) in triumph:

> Now death shall stop his dismall threatning sound,
> And his ill-boading tongue, no more shall speake.

This composite line (viii. 116) is of the simplest pattern:

Now his euill boding tongue no more shall speake.

In the folio version Warwick, Edward, Warwick and Richard, each in turn, speak four lines of text. This artificial symmetry, so very common in Elizabethan plays, is lost owing to the forgetfulness of the actor who played Edward's part. The significance of this change is that the reporter, not the official play-abridger, must be responsible for it.

(v) King Edward makes trial (3.2.16-17) of Lady Gray:

Widow, we will consider of your suit,
And come some other time to know our minde.

The composite line (x. 15), with the extra syllable at the beginning of the line, will remind the reader of the first example above:

Widow come some other time to know our mind.

(vi) Edward answers (4.1.14-15) his brother's sarcastic objection that Warwick and Lewis will not be offended at his marriage:

Suppose they take offence without a cause:
They are but Lewis and Warwicke, I am Edward,
Your King and Warwickes.

In the quarto version this speech (xii. 6-7) is compressed:

Suppose they doe, they are but Lewes and Warwike,
And I am your king and Warwickes.

Mislineation in Q1 puts 'Warwike' in the second line; the change gives the full sense of the original.

(vii) King Henry has been released by Warwick from the Tower. He acknowledges himself unfit for royal power and creates Clarence and Warwick joint protectors of England (4.6.38-44):

Warwick and Clarence...............
....
I make you both Protectors of this Land,
While I my selfe will lead a priuate Life,
And in deuotion spend my latter dayes,
To sinnes rebuke, and my Creators prayse.

This scene is in disorder in *True Tragedy,* and this passage (xvii. 3-7) has been rewritten in four metrical lines:

Clarence and Warwike doe you Keepe the crowne,
And gouerne and protect My realme in peace,
And I will spend the Remnant of my dayes,
to sinnes rebuke And my Creators praise.

The second last line of the lower passage represents what the
actor remembered of two original lines. The interpolation of the
words 'in peace' and the alteration of the phrase 'my latter dayes'
seems to be due to a hazy recollection of line 1666 of *Selimus*,

> And liue in peace the remnant of our days.

(viii) King Edward tricks the mayor and aldermen of York
into a surrender of the city (4.7.35-8):

> So, Master Maior: these Gates must not be shut,
> But in the Night, or in the time of Warre.
> What, feare not man, but yeeld me vp the Keyes,
>   *Takes his Keyes.*
> For Edward will defend the Towne, and thee.

The quarto version (xvi. 20-3) exhibits a curious change, due
perhaps to defective memory; one part of the third line keeps the
same relative position:

> So my Lord Maire, these gates must not be shut,
> But in the time of warre, giue me the keies.
> What, feare not man for Edward will defend
> the towne and you.

In this example the composite lines are formed from the two ends
of successive lines of the folio text.

(ix) King Edward, returning from exile, pretends (4.7.45-7)
that he abandons his claim to the throne:

>   Thankes good Mountgomerie;
> But we now forget our Title to the Crowne,
> And onely clayme our Dukedome.

Bad memory has reduced the quarto version (xvi. 29-30) to two
lines:

>   Thankes braue Mountgommery,
> But I onlie claime my Dukedom.

The regal 'we' and 'our' of the folio version subtly suggest the
claim to the throne which he pretends to renounce; the quarto
sentence is a literal abdication.

(x) Edward unexpectedly appears at Coventry when Warwick
is unprepared, and taunts him (5.1.21-4) with rebellion:

> Now Warwicke, wilt thou ope the Citie Gates,
> Speake gentle words, and humbly bend thy Knee,
> Call Edward King, and at his hands begge Mercy,
> And he shall pardon thee these Outrages?

Here the change is a double one, and two composite lines (xix. 16-17) remain:

> Now Warwike wilt thou be sorrie for thy faults,
> And call Edward king and he will pardon thee.

Both lines are unmetrical. The first composite line keeps the sense but changes the words. Warwick's three lines (ll. 18-20) spoken before Edward's speech, and his four-line reply (ll. 25-28) to Edward is reproduced in the quarto with changes in four words only. Most probably the last two lines of Warwick's speech in the folio were spoken on the stage; in an interpolated speech of *Contention* (xiii. 119-121) Stafford asks Cade:

> 'Wilt thou yeeld thy selfe vnto the Kings mercy, and he will pardon thee and these, their outrages and rèbellious deeds?'

Other examples in *True Tragedy,* some of which exhibit various freaks of mummers' memories will be recognized on comparing

> 1.1.211-2   with i. 199.
> 3.2.58-61   and x. 45-6.
> 3.3.199-200 and xi. 135.
> 3.3.219-222 and xi. 134-6.
> 4.1.108-110 and xii. 78-9.
> 5.3.20-1   and xx. 60.

ROMEO AND JULIET Q2 and ROMEO AND JULIET Q1

(i) My first example of a composite line comes from the first quarto version of the sonnet-prologue which has already been quoted to prove the priority of Q2. Two lines of the authentic version,

> The fearfull passage of their death-markt loue,
> And the continuance of their Parents rage,

appear in Q1 as a mangled composite line,

> And death-markt passage of their Parents rage.

Unless the first line of the two quoted had been spoken on the stage the pirate could not have included two fragments of it in his composite line. What is unusual is the pirate's preference of the compound epithet 'death-markt' of the poet's own making to the every-day adjective 'fearfull.'

(ii) What may be looked upon as two consecutive composite

lines occur in the portion of the Queen Mab speech already quoted from Q1 (see pp. 185-6). I have suggested a scribal error as a possible explanation, but these two blunders in consecutive lines may be composite lines due to the muddled recollections of the actors. Each explanation implies the priority of Q2.

(iii) Tybalt has been killed, and the nurse informs (3.2.55-6) Juliet that she has seen the body:

> Pale, pale as ashes, all bedawbde in bloud,
> All in goare bloud, I sounded at the sight.

The construction of the composite line (xii. 17) needs no explanation:

> All pale as ashes, I swounded at the sight.

(iv) Romeo bewails (3.3.20-2) his banishment from Verona:

> And worlds exile is death. Then banished,
> Is death, mistermd, calling death banished,
> Thou cutst my head off with a golden axe.

These lines occur in a speech almost perfectly retained in Q1 except for the composite line (xiii. 21-2):

> And world exilde is death. Calling death banishment,
> Thou cutst my head off with a golden axe.

The alteration of 'banished' to 'banishment' does not affect metre or sense.

(v) Capulet scolds Juliet (3.5.129-130) for her tears:

> How now a Conduit girle, what still in tears,
> Euermore showring.

Evidently the actor remembered the beginning of each line, and eked his own line out with a favourite enclitic:

> Why how now, euermore showring?

(vi) Juliet implores her father (3.5.158-9) to hear her plea:

> Good Father, I beseech you on my knees,
> Heare me with patience, but to speake a word.

The first quarto composite line (xv. 118) is very short:

> Good father, heare me speake?

Q1 has a centred stage direction 'She kneeles downe,' which, in anticipation of the methods of modern playwrights, explains the obvious.

(vii) Paris parts from Juliet (4.1.42-3) at the friar's cell:

Iuliet, on Thursday early will I rowse yee,
Till then adue, and keepe this holy kisse.

Except that 'farwell' replaces 'adue,' the composite line (xvi. 43) is of the customary type:

Iuliet farwell, and keep this holy kisse.

(viii) Before drinking the sleeping draught, Juliet's imagination pictures some gruesome details on her awakening in the family vault (4.3.55-7):

O looke, me thinks I see my Cozins Ghost,
Seeking out Romeo that did spit his body
Vpon a Rapiers poynt; stay, Tybalt, stay:

Except in the two love-scenes with Romeo, her speeches are badly preserved throughout the play. The sense of the composite line (xviii. 27) is at odds with that of the previous lines:

Me thinkes I see
My Cosin Tybalt weltering in his bloud,
Seeking for Romeo: stay Tybalt stay.

Shakespeare does not use the verb 'welter'; Greene in *Orlando Furioso Q1* and Marlowe in *1 Tamburlaine* and *Edward II* (a Pembroke play) refer to persons 'weltering' or lying prostrate 'in their blood.' Clifford in *Contention* discovers his father 'weltred in his luke-warme blood'; here it seems ludicrous for the heroine to describe Tybalt, prostrate in his blood, 'seeking for Romeo.'

(ix) Juliet has been discovered apparently dead in her bed; the nurse bids (4.5.97-8) the hired musicians leave a house of mourning:

Honest good fellowes, ah put vp, put vp,
For well you know, this is a pitifull case.

The composite line (xix. 80) changes an epithet and loses the jest:

Put vp, put vp, this is a wofull case.

(x) Romeo takes poison, and addresses (5.3.116-8) Death:

Come bitter conduct, come vnsauoury guide,
Thou desperate Pilot, now at once run on
The dashing Rocks, thy seasick weary barke.

This composite line (xxii. 76) is of the simplest form,

Come desperate Pilot now at once runne on
The dashing rockes thy sea-sicke weary barge.

Other examples worth some attention will be recognized on comparing:

$$
\begin{aligned}
&1.5.84\text{-}5 \quad \text{and v. 63;} \\
&3.2.127\text{-}131 \text{ and xii. 52-6:} \\
&5.3.49\text{-}53 \quad \text{and xxii. 39-40.}
\end{aligned}
$$

2 HENRY VI and CONTENTION

In *Contention* corruption has penetrated more deeply and spread more widely over the various scenes, with the result that composite lines chosen from this play exhibit far more changes than in the two pairs of parallel texts just considered.

(i) The quarrel between Duke Humphrey and his political opponents comes to a head, when the Cardinal interposes by charging the Protector with opposing the King. Duke Humphrey retorts (1.1.134-6):

> My Lord of Winchester I know your minde.
> 'Tis not my speeches that you do mislike;
> But 'tis my presence that doth trouble ye.

This composite line is unusually complex, consisting of the beginnings of the first and second lines and the end of the third line, prefixed by a metre-marring enclitic; the sense is retained (i. 88) well enough:

> Nay my Lord tis not my words that troubles you,
> But my presence.

(ii) Gloster reproves (2.1.25-6) Cardinal Beaufort for his unchristian anger and malice:

> Church-men so hot? Good Vnckle hide such mallice:
> With such Holynesse can you doe it?

One composite line (v. 20) replaces these:

> Church-men so hote. Good vnckle can you doate.

'Doate' may be a mis-spelling of 'do't' often written 'doot,' but more likely is intended for 'dote.'

(iii) Suffolk has contrived the murder of Duke Humphrey. On the day when the latter should be tried, the King asks Suffolk to bring the prisoner into court, and when Suffolk returns without him the King demands (3.2.27-8):

> How now? why look'st thou pale? why tremblest thou?
> Where is our Vnckle? what's the matter Suffolke?

This brisk battery of questions was too much for the actor who played the King's part; the best he could do (x. 16) was to retain one of the questions and portion of the last:

How now Suffolke, where's our unkle?

(iv) Suffolk has been banished, and the queen reproaches him (3.2.307-8) for his want of spirit:

Fye Coward woman, and soft harted wretch,
Hast thou not spirit to curse thine enemy.

One line (x. 145) takes the place of these two; the words differ but the sense is kept:

Fie womanish man, canst thou not curse thy enemies?

(v) Suffolk, the queen's lover, declares (3.2.394-8) his readiness to die in her presence, but if away from her, he protests:

Where from thy sight, I should be raging mad,
And cry out for thee to close vp mine eyes:
To haue thee with thy lippes to stop my mouth:
So should'st thou eyther turne my flying soule,
Or I should breathe it so into thy body.

Except that the third and fourth lines are reduced to one, the quarto version (xi. 203-6) keeps close to the authentic text:

Where from thy sight I should be raging madde,
And call for thee to close mine eyes,
Or with thy lips to stop my dying soule,
That I might breathe it so into thy bodie.

The memory of the actor was not equal to the strain of giving exact utterance to this quaint mediæval notion.

(vi) Suffolk is seized by pirates and disdainfully reminds them (4.1.56-8) of their low birth and menial station:

How often hast thou waited at my cup,
Fed from my Trencher, kneel'd downe at the boord,
When I haue feasted with Queene Margaret?

Faulty recollection produced a composite line of nine syllables (xii. 55) made from parts of the first and second lines:

Hast thou not waited at my Trencher,
When we haue feasted with Queene Margret?

(vii) Iden replies (4.10.29-30) to Cade's abuse and threats:

Why rude Companion, whatsoere thou be,
I know thee not, why then should I betray thee?

The composite line is non-metrical (xx. 10) :

Why sawcy companion, why should I betray thee?

Other examples, not so clear cut on account of the corrupt condition of the text may be studied in:

> 1.3.48-51 and iii. 59-61 ;
> 1.3.120-1 and iii. 90.
> 2.1.40-3   and v. 60-1.
> 4.2.100-8 and xiii. 68-9.
> 4.1.121-2 and xii. 67-8.

MERRY WIVES Fo. and MERRY WIVES Q1

Seven-eighths at least of this play is in prose, and the corruption pervading every scene of Q1 has left little of the verse unspared. One instance I have noted. Falstaff's last speech but one (5.5.221-2) is printed as prose in the Folio text, but may easily be scanned as verse:

I am glad, though you haue tane a special stand
To strike at me that your Arrow hath glanc'd.

These two lines form a composite line (xvii. 147) in Q1 :

I am glad yet that your arrow hath glanced.

Compare also 4.6.3-5 and xvi. 3-4.

HENRY V Fo. and HENRY V Q1

(i) Henry is reminded (1.2.163-7) by the Archbishop that the King of Scots was taken prisoner whilst Edward III was in France:

whom shee did send to France,
To fill King Edwards fame with prisoner Kings,
And make their Chronicle as rich with prayse,
As is the Owse and bottome of the Sea
With sunken Wrack, and sum-lesse Treasuries.

This appears except for one line in i. 100-103; the composite line keeps the sense of the two lines but adds and alters some words:

Whom like a caytiffe she did leade to France,
Filling your Chronicles as rich with praise
As is the owse and bottome of the sea
With sunken wrack and shiplesse treasurie.

(ii) Exeter points out (1.2.177-8) the safeguards against border raids:

Since we haue lockes to safegard necessaries,
And pretty traps to catch the petty theeues.

The reporter's version (i. 113) proves that he remembered the concrete but forgot the abstract:

Since we haue trappes to catch the petty thieues.

(iii) Henry prays that God will pardon him for his father's faults and promises (4.1.285-7) redress and penitence:

And I haue built
Two Chauntries, where the sad and solemne Priests
Sing still for Richards Soule. More will I doe.

These two and a half lines of the poet's have become a twelve-syllable line (xiii. 15) in Q1:

And I haue built two chanceries, more wil I do.

(iv) Exeter describes (4.6.21-2) the deaths of York and Suffolk on the battle-field of Agincourt:

He smil'd me in the face, raught me his hand,
And with a feeble gripe, sayes: Deere my Lord.

This composite line (xvii. 21) consists of the initial word 'he' and the two ends of the lines:

He tooke me by the hand, said deare my Lord.

'Raught,' an archaic preterite of 'reach,' was used in 2 *Henry VI* and 3 *Henry VI,* but disappeared from both plays as from *Henry V.*

(v) Henry, on his entrance, greets (5.2.1-3) the King and Queen of France:

Peace to this meeting, wherefore we are met;
Vnto our brother France, and to our Sister
Health and faire time of day.

In the first quarto there is no entry, speech or reference to the Queene of France, but there is an entry for 'Queene' Katharine. The composite line (xxi. 1-2) may have been written to suit this change in the cast, but is probably a consequence of it:

Peace to this meeting, wherefore we are met.
And to our brother France, Faire time of day.

For other examples compare:

1.2.3-6   and i. 1-3 ;
1.2.181-4 and i. 116-7 ;
1.2.232-5 and i. 154-7 ;
2.2.71-5   and iii. 54-5.
3.6.24-5   and x. 21-2 ;
4.7.171-3 and xviii. 132.

HAMLET Q2 and HAMLET Q1

More than sixteen hundred lines of Q2 are missing in Q1, and of those retained many are sadly garbled or paraphrased. Composite lines similar to those in *True Tragedy* are less common, and most of the examples quoted come from the first act.

(i) At the suggestion of Marcellus, Horatio asks (1.1.46-9) the Ghost:

> What art thou that vsurpst this time of night,
> Together with that faire and warlike forme,
> In which the Maiestie of buried Denmarke
> Did sometimes march.

This passage (i. 41-3) in Q1 hobbles unmetrically thus:

> What art thou that thus vsurps the state in
> Which the Maiestie of buried Denmarke did sometimes
> Walke?

Two lines of Q2 have been crushed together by dropping three words of the first line and all the second. The sense has been preserved by changing 'this' to 'the' and 'forme' to 'state.' The interpolation of 'thus' destroys the metre.

(ii) Horatio informs his companions, Barnardo and Marcellus, why such elaborate preparations for war are on foot (1.1.80-4):

> our last King
> Whose image euen but now appear'd to vs,
> Was as you knowe by Fortinbrasse of Norway,
> Thereto prickt on by a most emulate pride
> Dar'd to the combat:

This passage (i. 77-80) of Q1 runs as follows:

> Our late King, who as you know was by Forten-
> Brasse of Norway,
> Thereto prickt on by a most emulous cause, dared to
> The combate.

Horatio's speech in Q2 rambles on for 28 lines before it reaches a full stop, though a suitable pause is possible in the middle of the sixteenth line. The reporter was quickly in trouble. He changed 'whose' to 'who,' omitted the rest of the second line of the speech, and thus began with a composite line. Confusion was the consequence, and the anacoluthon ended only after twelve lines.

(iii) Horatio thus concludes (1.1.104-7) the story which the previous quotation began:

> and this I take it,
> Is the maine motiue of our preparations
> The source of this our watch, and the chiefe head
> Of this post hast and Romadge in the land.

The last line of this passage is not in Q1, and the second and third lines of Q2 are reduced to a mislineated composite line, most of which consists of a rearrangement of the third line. The result of these varied changes (i. 93-4) is:

> And this (I take it) is the
> Chiefe head and ground of this our watch,

(iv) Hamlet asks (1.2.169-173) Horatio why he has left Wittenberg:

> *Hora.* A truant disposition good my Lord.
> *Ham.* I would not heare your enimie say so,
> Nor shall you doe my eare that violence
> To make it truster of your owne report
> Against your selfe, I knowe you are no truant.

Of these five lines the first is slightly changed, the second omitted, and a composite line has been made of the third and fourth. There remains (ii. 87-90) in Q1 this verse mixture:

> *Hora.* A trowant disposition, my good Lord.
> *Ham.* Nor shall you make mee truster
> Of your owne report against your selfe:
> Sir, I know you are no trowant.

The abrupt 'Nor' at the beginning of Hamlet's speech makes it almost certain that something has been omitted. The reporter has made sense of his twelve-syllable composite line by changing 'it' to 'mee,' but his habit of prefixing unnecessary enclitics to what the poet wrote has spoilt the metre of the next line. Three such enclitics were introduced into the dozen lines that followed.

(v) Horatio describes (1.2.199-203) the appearance of the ghost to Hamlet:

> A figure like your father
> Armed at poynt, exactly Capapea
> Appeares before them, and with solemne march,
> Goes slowe and stately by them; thrice he walkt
> By their opprest and feare surprised eyes.

This passage has been made ungrammatical in Q1 (ii. 118-121) by the interpolation of 'by' before the beginning; the composite line

U

is a foot short, and is followed by a piece of blundering characteristic of the bad quartos.

> by a figure like your father,
> Armed to poynt, exactly Capapea
> Appeeres before them thrise, he walkes
> Before their weake and feare oppressed eies.

(vi) The ghost has revealed to Hamlet the story of his uncle's
crime and his mother's shame, and urges him to punish his uncle
but spare his mother (1.5.84-6):

> But howsomever thou pursues this Act,
> Tain't not thy minde; nor let thy soule contriue
> Against thy mother aught, leaue her to heauen.

Whilst the metre of this passage (iv. 130-2) in Q1 is confused, the
composite line which ends with 'conspire' is a good specimen:

> But howsoeuer, let not thy heart
> Conspire against thy mother aught,
> Leaue her to heauen.

(vii) Hamlet has asked his companions to swear never to make
known what they had seen that night. Their replies seem
ambiguous, and he asks them to swear upon the cross of his sword.
The ghost from beneath the stage cries 'sweare.' Hamlet (1.5.
150-152) proceeds:

> Ha, ha, boy, say'st thou so, art thou there trupenny?
> Come on, you heare this fellowe in the Sellerige,
> Consent to sweare.

These lines in Q1 (iv. 196-7) are reduced to:

> Ha, ha, come you here, this fellow in the sellerige,
> Here consent to sweare.

The metre of the composite line is spoilt by the unnecessary 'come.'

(viii) Polonius teaches his retainer (2.1.66-8) some of the tricks
of the spy's trade:

> By indirections find directions out,
> So by my former lecture and aduise
> Shall you my sonne; you haue me, haue you not?

Two lines (v. 25-6) of Q1 replace these:

> By indirections, finde directions forth,
> And so shall you my sonne; you ha me, ha you not?

Interpolation of 'And' has filled out the composite line and made it a metrical Alexandrine.

(ix) Laertes has attacked Hamlet at the funeral of Ophelia; they struggle and Hamlet addresses (5.1.248-250) his assailant:

> I prethee take thy fingers from my throat
> For though I am not spleenatiue rash,
> Yet haue I in me something dangerous.

Some variations occur in the wording of the composite line (xvi. 148-9):

> I prethee take thy hand from off my throate,
> For there is something in me dangerous.

Hamlet Q1 provides some other examples. Compare:

> 1.2.216-7 and ii. 141-2.
> 1.4.5-7   and iv. 5.
> 1.5.45-6   and iv. 104.
> 1.5.92-5   and iv. 137-8.
> 1.5.147-8 and iv. 194.
> 5.2.303-6 and xviii. 90-1.

Before suggesting an explanation of this peculiar method of abridgment I shall discuss a few examples present in *Orlando Furioso Q1*.

(i) Orlando has been restored to sanity by Melissa's potions and magic, and on his recovery relates some of his dreams, which most absurdly centre round gods, goddesses and legends associated with classical mythology. The passage (MS. ll. 327-333) runs:

> Iuno methought sent from the heauen by Joue
> cam sweeping swiftly thorow the glomye ayre
> and calling Iris, sent hir straight abrode
> to sommon fawnes, ye satyres, and the nimphes
> the dryades, and all the demygodes,
> to secret counsayle, wher some parle past
> she gaue them violles, full of heauenly dew.

From the version of Q1 (ll. 1291-5) three lines have gone:

> Iuno mee thought sent downe from heauen by Ioue.
> Came swiftly sweeping through the gloomy aire
> And calling Fame the Satyres and the nymphs,
> She gaue them viols full of heauenly dew.

Except that 'Fame,' perhaps by misreading, replaces the author's 'fawnes,' the composite line is well made; the two missing lines that follow it in MS. may have been an original cut.

(ii) One of Greene's worse than useless classical similes is excised in the next example. Orlando has mortally wounded Sacrepant who tells his conqueror that he has killed a King. Orlando replies (MS. 391-3) :

> Then mayst thou deme, some second mars from heauen
> is sent, as was Amphitrios foster sonne
> to vale thy plumes, and heave the from a crowne.

Q1 reduces these three lines to two (Q1. 1372-4) :

> Then maist thou think that Mars himself
> Came down to vaile thy plumes, and heaue thee
> from thy pompe.

Greene's stupid reference to Hercules is cut out; 'second Mars' becomes 'Mars himself' and 'came down' neatly replaces 'from heauen is sent.'

(iii) Orlando requests the princes to leave Sacrepant to his own just vengeance (MS. 377-8) :

> Princes for shame, vnto your royall campes
> base not your selues, to combatt such a dogg.

In Q1 one long line (ll. 1352-3) replaces these :

> Stay Princes, base not your selues to cum-
> bat such a dog.

Except for the intrusive 'stay,' this is an excellent composite line.

(iv) Orlando explains (MS. 495-9) how he had taken his revenge on Sacrepant :

> I am the man, that did the slaue to death
> who falsely wronged Angelica and me
> for when I stabd the traytor to the hart
> and he lay breathing on his latest gaspe
> he frankly made confession at his death,

Three lines drop out of Q1. 1568-9 :

> I am the man that did the slaue to death
> Who frankely there did make confession.

This is perhaps a piece of neat abridgment; the change at the end of the second line of Q1 is requisite to avoid ending two consecutive lines with the same word.

Inferences of much importance may be drawn from the presence of four composite lines in about three hundred lines or a fifth of *Orlando Furioso Q1*. Dr. Greg has shown that the

Dulwich MS. of Orlando's part differs from Greene's autograph manuscript of *Orlando Furioso* by no more than scribal errors, and that corrections have been made in this MS. by Alleyn himself; it is the primary source for the text of Orlando's part. Critics agree with Dr. Greg's opinion that the actors and their accomplices are responsible for all deviations from Greene's text. Such composite lines as occur in *Orlando Furioso Q1* must be the work of the actors or their agents, as are all other variants and corruption of the author's text. Composite lines are thus associated with corruption of text.

How are the composite lines of the bad quartos to be explained in terms of the relationship between the parallel texts? Some examples present in such a comparatively good text as that of *True Tragedy* suggest certain conclusions. Seven of the ten examples quoted from the text of that play come from the part of Edward; not one composite line occurs in the equally long but less corrupt part of Warwick or in the not much shorter but almost equally corrupt part of Richard. This irregularity of distribution points to a cause that affected mainly the part of Edward; probably the actor speaking this part had neither an exact nor a retentive memory. Such a defect would explain why the percentage of Edward's lines kept perfect in *True Tragedy* is lower than that for any other important character common to the versions. If *True Tragedy* is derived from *3 Henry VI,* most of the difference in length is due to cuts made by the play-adapter during his preparation of the acting version. Why should he use this method of abridgment only for Edward's part and not apply it to the reduction of parts written for Warwick, Richard, Clifford, York, Clarence and others? Such partial and haphazard treatment of one actor's lines seems improbable and even absurd. Moreover, we know something of the methods adopted by the official play-cutter from a study of extant Elizabethan and Jacobean plays still in manuscript. Some of these have passages marked for omission. *Edmund Ironside* is shorter than either *True Tragedy* or *Romeo and Juliet Q1* yet it has 67 passages ranging from one to ten lines and amounting in all to 196 lines marked for omission. Though the monotonously end-stopped lines would have made the formation of composite lines very easy, not one is to be found. Nor have I noted one line made out of two or more in any other contemporary play in manuscript, which has been prepared for stage use.

The company's official cannot be responsible for the composite lines of *True Tragedy,* and is not to blame for those present in the other bad quartos. This phenomenon is associated with defective verse and other kinds of corruption. Thus most of the examples present in *Hamlet Q1* are found in the well-preserved first act and not in passages defective in metre and grammar. Conversely, all but two of the examples occurring in *Romeo and Juliet Q1* are found in the third, fourth and fifth acts which are textually inferior to the first and second.

If, on the other hand, *True Tragedy* is the source-play used by Shakespeare when writing *3 Henry VI,* it may seem reasonable to suggest that he may have expanded in this way a line of his original here and there, but on what principle of logic or good sense are we to explain the poet's differential treatment of Edward's part? He would be rewriting, not the extant *True Tragedy,* but a manuscript of this play free from all its corruption; he would add to Edward's part 108 lines of which ten would be the result of expanding one line into two or more. To the parts of the remaining characters of the play he must add 670 lines, of which no more than five or six would result from this type of expansion. Mathematically, the odds against his choosing fortuitously twice as many lines from Edward's part for such expansion as from the rest of the play are very great. Moreover the extra lines thus introduced into the folio text do not exhibit such superiority in vigour, poetic quality or dramatic suitability over the lines of the old version as might have been expected from the rewriting by Shakespeare of another man's verse. He did not employ this device in turning *Troublesome Raigne* into *King John* three or four years later. Careful examination of those plays which exist in parallel good texts, e.g., the folio and the quarto versions of *King Lear* or *Hamlet,* does not reveal any examples of this method of shortening or expansion. Neither Jonson in his elaborate revision of *Every Man in His Humour* nor Chapman in his rewriting of *Bussy D'Ambois* expanded or compressed the earlier version in this way. Finally, Shakespeare's facility of expressing his thoughts was such that he would find it an easier and more congenial task to rewrite a play than to emend, patch, and fill in the play of any dramatist.

Any teacher who asked a class of schoolboys to write out from memory a long poem, learnt and repeated some months previously and since unread, would find many gaps in the answers of his pupils. Mistakes made would involve such variants from the text of the poem as inversions in the order of words, phrases and lines, broken lines and metre, mislineation, mis-spellings, composite lines, etc.; in fact he would have examples of all such textual errors and omissions as changed the acting version of *3 Henry VI* into *True Tragedy*. Every new Elizabethan play was put on the boards not for daily performances over a period of some weeks or months, as is our modern custom, but once every four or five days for a few weeks, and subsequently at widening intervals of seven, ten or fourteen days; usually it was taken off the acting list before the end of a year after the first performance. As one result of such infrequent representation of a play actors would be less perfect in their parts than now. Many allusions were made to the 'dull' actor who was 'out' of his part; perhaps the hired men were the worst offenders. Actors, who were endeavouring to repeat a part indifferently learnt some months earlier, and who forgot all but a word or two of one line though nearly word-perfect in the next line, must have been not uncommon in this era of a daily change of play. Such persons took part in the reconstruction of *Orlando Furioso Q1* towards the end of 1593, and one or more of them may have had a finger in the making of *Contention* a few months later. It is not probable that the same person or persons, members of the Chamberlain's company, should have been able to repeat piracies of Shakespeare's plays in 1595, 1597, 1600, 1601 and 1602. When *Contention* was entered on the Stationers' Register, the city theatres had been shut up for nearly a year and three-quarters; probably it had not been acted for many months, and the result was a very corrupt and garbled text. *True Tragedy, Romeo and Juliet Q1* and *Henry V Q1* appeared in years when the theatres had been open almost continuously with consequent improvement in the pirated texts. Composite lines, depending as they do upon a mental process involving a lapse of memory, occur in each bad quarto, but are most plainly outlined and definite in the plays named above.

CHAPTER XVII

EMENDATIONS OF SHAKESPEARE'S TEXT FROM THE BAD QUARTOS

WHEN Daniel was discussing the inter-relation of *Henry V Q1* and the folio version he declared:

Without the aid afforded us by comparison with the folio edition, it would, I admit, be a matter of extreme difficulty to determine the position of the Qo; with it, however, a reasonably certain decision may, I think, be arrived at.

The opinion I have formed from a careful examination, line for line, of both texts is, that the play of 1599 (the Fo.) was shortened for stage representation; the abridgement done with little care, and printed in the Qo edition with less: probably from an imperfect manuscript surreptitiously obtained and vamped up from notes taken during the performance, as we know was frequently done.[1]

He gives briefly his reasons for this opinion, referring in turn to 'the more stately scenes of the play,' and 'the comic scenes' and concludes,

to me, bearing in mind the general condition of the Qo text, however difficult it may be to prove the point, the most reasonable verdict must be—imperfect representation on the part of Qo; not, after elaboration, in Fo.[2]

He considers that it would be 'a needless labour' to discuss every point and adds:

I shall therefore only adduce two instances in support of my opinion. These being, I think, indisputable, will also, I presume, be considered sufficient; for if in a single case it can be clearly proved, not that Qo is merely deficient in, but that it actually *omits* any portion of the Fo. version, judgment may be allowed to pass on other places where the evidence is not of so convincing a character.[3]

His two instances are those under the heading '*Henry V Q1* and *Henry V Fo.*' (pp. 190-202), numbered (i) and (viii) by me. I agree with him that two such instances ought to be sufficient to convince critics who have no preconceived opinions, are capable of

---

1. Daniel, G., *Introduction to the Parallel Texts of Henry V* (New Shakespeare Society), p. x.
2. *Ibid.*, p. xi.
3. *Ibid.*, p. xi.

weighing evidence, and are willing to base their judgment on facts and such reasonable inferences as the facts will bear. Let it not be forgotten that, in fixing the date of *Henry V*, most critics accept the reference in the last chorus to Essex as a sufficient proof not that the chorus alone but the entire play was written and produced not later than August, 1599. Unfortunately an age addicted to the delights of theory-monging disregards inconvenient facts and brushes aside other evidence as negligible.

I have therefore deliberately multiplied the number of examples which exhibit this particular relation between each pair of parallel texts, and have shown that in ten scenes of *True Tragedy*, nine scenes of *Romeo and Juliet Q1*, eight scenes of *Hamlet Q1*, six scenes of *Contention* and six scenes of *Henry V* there occur in all over fifty passages, each of which provides definite proof that the bad quarto has *omitted* some necessary portion of text present in the parallel text of Shakespeare. Thus eighteen lines or passages of *True Tragedy* are obscure or irrelevant or difficult to understand or without meaning until the corresponding portions of *3 Henry VI* have been read; the only possible explanation is that Shakespeare's play had been acted before the quarto was in existence.

In seemingly direct contradiction of this important truth we have the fact that almost all editors of Shakespeare's plays have occasionally found themselves compelled to borrow a word, a phrase, or even a line from the text of a surreptitious quarto, in order to emend the defective text of the corresponding portion of Shakespeare's authentic version. Some little reflection suggests that this occasional use of a quarto text to correct the text of the play from which it was derived might reasonably be anticipated as not improbable, if we keep in mind the circumstances connected with the compiling and printing of a surreptitious play. The latter was not the corrupt abridgment of Shakespeare's complete text, but was a report of what had been spoken on the stage; its immediate source was the official acting version, which may or may not have been specially prepared from the author's manuscript for the use of the prompter. From this acting version the parts of the players would be written out by the scribe, who would have the advantage of being able to consult Shakespeare if a letter or word was illegible or if he thought that a phrase or a line had dropped out of the manuscript. Carefully transcribed parts made by a man, accustomed to read the poet's handwriting and in a position to have a doubtful word or a line verified, may at times have provided a more accurate text for the actors than a modern stage-manager could get from the second quarto of *Hamlet* or *Romeo and Juliet*. Accordingly there is nothing surprising or paradoxical in the fact that a report based on memorization of actors' parts, which were portions of the acting version, should occasionally preserve, amongst its two or three thousand deviations from the poet's text, some variants or an odd omitted line or two, which serve to emend an obviously defective passage of the author's play or to give a few better readings. We have no reason for believing that the printer took less care in setting up the type for the copy provided by the pirate than for the manuscripts sponsored by the poet or the company. We may, I think, fairly attribute the occasional superiority of the surreptitious text to an actor's accurate memory of what was spoken on the stage, supplemented perhaps by such scraps of manuscripts or fragments of parts as a snapper-up of unconsidered trifles might obtain.

Editors of Shakespeare's plays have always differed in the valuation placed upon the bad quartos for the purpose of emending the texts of the good quartos or the folio versions. Pope undoubtedly made far too much use of *Romeo and Juliet Q1;* the folio version is a reprint of the third quarto and therefore contains the errors of both second and third. Concurrence of Q1 and the first folio in readings is very rare, and usually signifies agreement in error. The Cambridge Editors (1865) say:

A careful study of the text of *Romeo and Juliet* will show how little we can rely upon having the true text as Shakespeare wrote it, in those plays for which the Folio is our earliest authority.[4]

I find about fifty lines of Q2 for each of which Q1 supplies missing words or makes better sense or restores the metre or otherwise suggests some marked or necessary improvement. *Hamlet* has two parallel yet independent sound texts, and nearly all those lines of Q2 which Q1 serves to emend could be just as well emended by using the text of the folio. Of the two early plays on Henry VI, *True Tragedy,* being much less corrupt than *Contention,* is more helpful in solving some textual problems of the two folio versions.

4. Clark and Wright, *The Works of Shakespeare,* vol. vii, p. xi.

Henry V Q1 contains barely half the folio text, but not much use can be made of it except to correct some obvious blunders of the printer in the folio.

From his study of the five quartos of *Richard II* Professor Pollard has made it clear that each successive edition of a quarto, usually printed from the text of the preceding one, corrected very few of the errors in the quarto used as copy, and added a much larger crop of fresh errors to keep those left uncorrected company. Thus the first quarto of *Richard II* has 69 printing slips; in the fifth quarto 44 of these still remained, and 214 others had been added, making in all 258 or nearly four times the number in the first quarto. Professor Dover Wilson analyzed the folio variants made during the reprint of *Much Ado About Nothing Q1;* they totalled 141. Of these the printer inserted 17 in his own text; omissions, pronominal changes, spellings and contractions, and substitutions of one word for another account for more than two-thirds of the remaining 124.[5]

The above totals give some adequate notion of the substantial contribution made by the printers to textual confusion. Many of the examples discussed below come from the comparatively well preserved *True Tragedy* and *Romeo and Juliet Q1* or from *Hamlet Q1* of which two independent parallel texts exist.

Lines of the bad quarto, not found in the corresponding passage of Shakespeare's play but necessary to the sense of the immediate context, are not common. Thus in *Contention* the dialogue (xii. 30-33) runs as follows:

> *Cap.* The Duke of Suffolke folded vp in rags.
> *Suf.* I sir, but these rags are no part of the Duke,
> Ioue sometime went disguisde, and why not I?
> *Cap.* I but Ioue was neuer slaine as thou shalt be.

In the folio version (4.1.46-8) we read:

> *Whit.* The Duke of Suffolke, muffled vp in ragges?
> *Suf.* I, but these ragges are no part of the Duke.
> *Lieu.* But Ioue was neuer slaine as thou shalt be.

Speech-prefixes, order of lines, versification and length of speeches differ much in the two versions, but the sense requires the insertion in the folio version of the second line of Suffolk's speech

5. The New Shakespeare, *Much Ado About Nothing,* pp. 154-7.

in *Contention*. Somehow this line dropped out of the authentic text, but it was spoken on the stage and must have been in Suffolk's part.

Three lines of *True Tragedy*, viz., iv. 80, viii. 72, and xxii. 69 are usually inserted by editors in their editions of *3 Henry VI*. Each of them has the right Shakespearean flavour, but only the second seems necessary to the sense of the folio version. Portion of Clifford's dying speech (viii. 72-4) begins a new paragraph with a new metaphor:

> The common people swarme like summer flies,
> And whither flies the Gnats but to the sun?
> And who shines now, but Henries Enemies?

In the folio version (2.6.9-10) the first line of the above speech is omitted:

> And whether flye the Gnats, but to the Sunne?
> And who shines now, but Henries enemies?

There is a break in continuity which the insertion of the first line of the quotation from *True Tragedy* covers up.

Most modern editions of *Romeo and Juliet* include as part of Benvolio's speech after the line (Q2.1.4.6),

> Skaring the Ladies like a Crowkeeper,

two lines found only in Q1 (iv. 7-8):

> Nor no withoutbooke Prologue faintly spoke
> After the Prompter, for our entrance.

They are characteristically Shakespearean, but may be omitted or included at an editor's pleasure.

On the other hand one line of Q1, not present in Q2 or the folio, is always added to the received text. Peter's doggerel verses (xix. 94-6),

> When griping griefe the heart doth wound,
> And dolefull dumps the minde oppresse:
> Then musique with her siluer sound,
> Why siluer sound?

have the second line which is not in Q2 and Folio, yet when he has given his insulting answer to the question 'Why siluer sound?' he completes (Q2. 4.5.137-8) his broken quatrain:

> Then Musique with her siluer sound with speedy help doth lend redresse.

Here we must read Q1 if we would understand why this last line is inserted.

In *Henry V Q1* Bardolph tries to make Nym and Pistol friends, but Nym, before consenting to be friends, asks (ii. 72) for an assurance that Pistol will pay him a debt of honour.

> *Nym.* I shal haue my eight shillings I woon of you at beating,

to which come pat Pistol's immortal words,

> Base is the slaue that pays.

Brawling is resumed. Once more Bardolph restores peace, and Nym repeats his former question to which Pistol replies:

> A noble shalt thou haue and readie pay.

Nym does not repeat his question in the folio version, and thus there results the ridiculous absurdity that Pistol offers to pay a debt without being asked for the money more than once.

One line is usually added from the quarto text to the folio version of the King's speech on St. Crispian's day. After the line (4.3.49),

> Then will he strip his sleeue, and shew his skarres,

most editors usually add the line,

> And say, these wounds I had on Crispines day,

which follows the first line in Q1 and seems necessary to complete the sense.

Many editors insert a number of lines from *Merry Wives Q1* in their editions of the folio text; perhaps the one (viii. 60) that has had the most general acceptance for more than a century is the host's

> Giue me thy hand terestiall.

Only the next line,

> So giue me thy hand celestiall,

is found in the folio.

One line of *Hamlet Q1* (ix. 176),

> What, frighted with false fires?

is omitted in Q2 but is in the folio text, where it is spoken perhaps as an aside, during the presence of the king and queen. In Q1 Hamlet speaks it immediately after the stage direction, *Exeunt King and Lordes.* All editors accept it.

Speech-prefixes are occasionally assigned in the good quartos and the folio version to the wrong characters. Such misplacing is far more frequent in the bad quartos, but here and there reference to Q1 corrects a blunder in the later printed text. Thus at the meeting of the rival house before the battle of Towton, the lines (v. 130-1) of *True Tragedy,*

> Whosoeuer got thee, there thy mother stands,
> For well I wot thou hast thy mothers tongue,

are assigned to Richard, but in the folio text to Warwick. That Richard spoke them is certain because Queen Margaret undoubtedly addresses her reply (v. 132-4), or (2.2.135-8),

> But thou are neyther like thy Sire nor Damme,
> But like a foule mishapen Stygmaticke, etc.,

to Crookback Richard.

In *Romeo and Juliet Q2* Romeo, who is not on the stage, asks (2.4.19) Mercutio,

> Why what is Tybalt?

In Q1 this speech is properly given to Mercutio's companion, Benvolio. Later in this scene Romeo is, in Q2, debited with a jeering 'a sayle, a sayle,' when he catches sight of the nurse and her man. This speech is spoken in Q1 by Mercutio. Juliet had promised to send a messenger to Romeo, who knew and had spoken to the nurse and certainly would not insult her. Both the folio and second quarto texts in the last scene call Romeo's servant 'Peter' instead of 'Balthazar,' though two scenes earlier in Q2 his master had addressed him by the latter name.

Another example of an incorrect speech-prefix is to be found in the opening scene of *Hamlet.* Francisco has been relieved, and Barnardo greets 'the riualls of my watch,'

> Welcome Horatio, welcome good Marcellus.

To this speech the reply (1.1.21) is a question:

> What, ha's this thing appeard againe to night?

Marcellus asks this in Q1, Horatio in Q2. Marcellus certainly asked this question; he was a sentinel, had seen the apparition twice before, and had asked Horatio, a friend of the prince, to accompany him. Horatio was a sceptical visitor with a disbelief in ghosts.

So many speeches of the very corrupt *Merry Wives Q1* are in confusion and wrongly assigned that discussion is not worth while; in *Henry V Q1* a dozen characters are omitted, and some of their speeches are put in the mouths of other characters.

Since the text of a bad quarto was compiled mainly from recollections of the actors' parts, we might anticipate that a report of a scene made by one or more of those that had played in it would occasionally be sufficiently accurate to correct careless mistakes in the use of speech-prefixes in the authentic text.

Many defects of the verse in Shakespeare's play are due to the omission of words or syllables; some of these are supplied to the parallel texts by the corresponding bad quartos.

In the tenth line of *True Tragedy* we read that the Duke of Buckingham,

> Is either slaine or wounded dangerouslie.

This line (1.1.11) in *3 Henry VI* ends with 'dangerous' which may be defended; most editors adopt the quarto reading. Warwick's line (iv. 150),

> Why via, To London will we march amaine,

has lost (2.1.182) the last word in the folio version, and is short a foot.

Romeo and Juliet Q2 provides more instances of metrically defective lines which become normal, if a correction suggested by the corresponding line of Q1 is inserted. Something has dropped out of the text (1.1.198-200) of the second line in all versions:

> *Ro.* What shall I grone and tell thee?
> *Ben.* Grone, why no: but sadly tell me who?
> *Ro.* A sicke man in sadness makes his will:

Q1 omits 'Grone' in the second line, but apart from punctuation the first and second lines are identical with those of Q2. Romeo's third line (i. 128) in Q1 runs:

> Bid a sickman in sadnes make his will.

This gives better sense and is metrically sound.

Other examples in which the defective verse of Q2 may be adjusted with the help of Q1 are to be found in Q2 (2.2.99):

> And therefore thou maiest think my behauior light,

which becomes regular on substituting for 'behauior' the truncated 'hauiour' of Q1. Again later in this scene Juliet's line (2.2.181),

> And with a silken threed, plucks it backe againe,

loses its jolting rhythm in Q1, which writes 'silke' for silken. Similarly Capulet's line (xiv. 26) in Q1,

> Afore me it is so very late,

has lost a 'very' in Q2, and is reduced to an octosyllable. On the other hand Lady Capulet's line (5.3.190) in Q2,

> O the people in the street crie Romeo,

is hypermetrical; the opening enclitic 'O' is not in the first quarto where lines of this type are common. So in Romeo's questions (5.1.14-15) addressed to Balthazar,

> How doth my Lady, is my Father well:
> How doth my Lady Iuliet? that I aske againe,

the second line (xx. 12) is expressed in Q1 thus,

> How fares my Iuliet? that I aske againe.

The last line probably represents what was in the actor's part; apparently the scribe who prepared the copy for the second quarto carelessly repeated the first half of the preceding line, looked at his manuscript a second time and added 'Juliet' before penning the mark of interrogation. The result is an Alexandrine in Q2.

In the folio version of *Henry V* Pistol's challenge (2.1.68) addressed to Nym, 'I defie thee agen' has been rejected by nearly all modern editors in favour of 'I thee defie agen' Q1 (ii. 57) which is right Pistolese. Twice in one scene (2.4.75,115) the French king spoils the verse by referring to 'our brother of England'; in Q1 (v. 30,90) the intrusive 'of' disappears, and the phrase, 'our brother England,' restores the metre. Modern editors adopt the readings of Q1.

Examples of lines metrically faulty in Q2 but normal in Q1 and the folio text are rather numerous in *Hamlet*. In the first scene of Q2 the last line (1.1.175) is,

> Where we shall find him most conuenient;

in Q1 and the folio the line ends with 'conueniently' which is less harsh. Hamlet's remark (ii. 94) to Horatio in Q1,

> I thinke it was to (see) my mothers wedding,

lacks 'see' in Q2, and is thus defective in sense as well as metre. Later in the same scene his line (ii. 146) in Q1,

> Indeed, indeed sirs, but this troubles me,

is a foot short in Q2 (1.2.224) owing to the omission of an 'indeed.' Similar omissions of 'my Lord' in Q2 (1.5.122):

> *Ham.* But you'le be secret.
> *Both.*   I by heauen (my Lord),

and 'of vs all' in the line Q2 (3.1.83),

> Thus conscience dooes make cowards (of vs all),

leave these lines metrically incomplete, and have forced editors to fill the gaps with what is found in the first quarto and the folio.

Q1 does not preserve the third scene of the first act very well, but retains a word or two to enable us to emend lines of Q2. Thus Polonius says (1.3.115) to his daughter,

> I, springs to catch wood-cockes, I doe knowe,

a nine-syllable line exceedingly rare in Shakespeare. Q1 has '*Springes* to catch wood-cocks,' which restores the metre.

In other verses Q2 has a syllable too much in a line. Thus the famous line spoken by Polonius (1.3.63),

> Grapple them vnto thy soule with hoopes of steele,

becomes much smoother if we accept 'to,' the reading of Q1 and Fo, instead of 'vnto.' Another line (2.2.73),

> Giues him threescore thousand crownes in anuall fee,

is metrically unsound; on referring to the line in Q1 'three' replaces 'threescore' as it does in the folio.

Some examples are concerned with deviations from normal grammar. Use of the wrong tense occurs in Edward's line (2.2.173) in *3 Henry VI,*

> Since thou denied'st the gentle king to speake,

where *True Tragedy* has 'deniest'; the refusal to permit Henry to speak takes place during the scene. King Edward has announced his intention to 'marry her,' i.e., Lady Elizabeth Grey, and the ensuing dialogue (x. 90-1) is as follows:

> *Cla.*   Marrie her my Lord, to whom?
> *K. Edw.* Why Clarence to my selfe.

v

In the folio version (3.2.112) we read,

> *Clarence.* To who, my Lord?
> *King.*   Why Clarence, to my selfe.

Another example is found in *Romeo and Juliet Q2*. Friar Laurence reproves Romeo for inconstancy, and his pupil replies (2.3.85-6) :

> I pray thee chide me not, her I loue now,
> Doth grace for grace, and loue for loue allow.

This couplet appears in Q1 (viii. 80-1) :

> I pree thee chide not, she whom I loue now
> Doth grace for grace, and loue for loue allow.

Even in the folio edition of *Henry V* we have (1.2.243),

> As *is* our wretches fettred in our prisons,

a mistake which the quarto did not make. Evidently the parts written out from Shakespeare's manuscript or the acting version made from it did not contain some of the solecisms which are present in the authentic texts.

Most of the remaining examples affect the sense of the passage, or give a better or more precise meaning to it; I discuss some only of those changes which nearly all editors make.

In *3 Henry VI* King Henry says (1.1.105) most absurdly,

> *My* Father was as thou art, Duke of Yorke,

a blunder that remained uncorrected in all the succeeding folios. Had Heminge and Condell consulted *True Tragedy* they would have changed '*My*' to '*Thy*.' Later in the same scene Prince Edward tells (i.223) his father,

> When I returne with victorie *from* the field
> Ile see your Grace.

In the folio version he talks the nonsense of returning 'with victorie *to* the field.'

Romeo and Juliet Q2 has many lines which modern editors emend from the corresponding lines of Q1. Thus Capulet's line (Q2, 1.2.29), informs Paris that,

> Among fresh fennell buds shall you this night
> Inherit at my house,

a piece of absurdity repeated in the other quartos and the first folio; evidently the editor of the second folio took the trouble of

consulting Q1 or the parts and changed 'fennel' to 'female.'
Mercutio's line (Q2, 2.1.10),

> Cry but ay me, prouaunt but loue and day,

is meaningless; reference to Q1 suggests that 'pronounce but Loue
and Doue' has suffered a sad word-change. So also 'the lazie
puffing Cloudes' of Q2 would be more difficult to 'bestride' than
'the lasie pacing cloudes' of Q1. Most persons who quote the
famous passage,

> That which we call a Rose
> By any other name would smell as sweet,

are unaware that up to the time of Pope 'word' of Q2 and the
folios replaced 'name' of Q1. Friar Laurence reminds (Q1, vii. 68)
his pupil Romeo that

> Thy old grones ring yet in my ancient eares;

in the second quarto the line is:

> Thy old grones yet ringing in thine auncient eares.

Sense, grammar and metre are all at odds in these few words.

Much has been written on the four lines with which Friar
Laurence opens the seventh scene of the play. From the beginning
of last century the version of Q1 has been accepted by editors as
substantially that written by Shakespeare, and it is now part of
the received text. It is:

> The gray ey'd morne smiles on the frowning night,
> Checkring the Easterne clouds with streakes of light,
> And flecked darkenes like a drunkard reeles,
> From forth daies path, and Titans fierie wheeles.

This passage, with several textual variations, appears twice in the
texts of Q2, Q3 and the first folio; first, as part of Romeo's last
speech in the balcony scene, it precedes his final couplet. The seven
lines (2.2.184-190) are:

> Would I were sleepe and peace so sweet to rest
> The grey eyde morne smiles on the frowning night,
> Checkring the Eastern Clouds with streaks of light,
> And darknesse fleckted like a drunkard reeles,
> From forth daies pathway, made by Tytans wheeles.
> Hence will I to my ghostly Friers close cell,
> His helpe to craue, and my deare hap to tell.

These four lines make their second appearance as the opening lines
of Friar Laurence's speech in the next scene (2.3.1-4):

> The grey-eyed morne smiles on the frowning night,
> Checking the Easterne clowdes with streaks of light:
> And fleckeld darknesse like a drunkard reeles,
> From forth daies path, and Titans burning wheeles:

How any printer could have duplicated these lines with only
Romeo's concluding couplet between them passes understanding,
and it is even more difficult to offer any reasonable explanation of
the textual variations. No scribe could have inserted so many
changes in his copy had they not been there, unless he transcribed
it whilst reeling in 'flecked darkness like a drunkard.' Perhaps
Sir Edmund Chambers has hit the mark in his suggestion that
Shakespeare made a false start. He may have originally intended
to close the sixth scene with Romeo's line (2.2.184),

> Would I were sleepe and peace so sweet to rest,

and have commenced to write the friar's speech, when he realized
that he was making a dramatic slip. No mention had been made of
this botanizing clerical chemist, and the audience would be wonder-
ing who he was and why he was on the stage, filling his 'osier cage'
with 'balefull weedes' and discoursing learnedly of poisons.
Accordingly Shakespeare abruptly ceased writing the friar's speech
and ended the sixth scene with Romeo's resolve to visit his
'ghostly Father's cell' as in Q1. He forgot to delete the four lines
already written, and with the careless prodigality of genius partly
rewrote the last line of the four. Pope's adoption in his text of
Shakespeare's first draft with its mixture of the abstract and the
concrete in the line,

> From forth daies pathway made by Tytans wheeles,

reveals the limitation of this editor's imaginative faculties.

Reference to the context makes it clear that 'Fantasticoes'
(viii. 26) of Q1 is preferable to the abstract 'phantacies' of Q2;
'His aged arme' (Q2, 3.1.171), in referring to Romeo, is an
obvious blunder for 'his agill arme' (xi. 124) of Q1. When
Tybalt returns to the place where he killed Mercutio, Romeo
exclaims (Q2, 3.1.118-120):

> He gan in triumph and Mercutio slaine,
> Away to heauen, respectiue lenitie,
> And fier and furie, be my conduct now.

Almost all editors prefer the version (xi. 91-3) of Q1:

> A liue in tryumph and Mercutio slaine?
> Away to heauen respectiue lenity:
> And fier-eyed fury be my conduct now.

Numerous other changes in words, some of them perhaps misprints, make it necessary to correct the text of Q2 with the aid of that of Q1. Thus:

Q1	Q2
past cure (xvi. 50)	past care (4.1.40);
slay (xvi. 62)	stay (4.1.72);
Pretie (xix. 99, 101)	Prates (4.5.139, 141);
pay (xx. 53)	pray (5.1.75);
ew-trees (xxii. 2)	yong Trees (5.3.5);
more early downe (xxii. 144)	now earling downe (5.3.209).

Q1 provides at least sixty necessary emendations of the text of Q2, and there are many more which competent editors accept. The reporter seems to have been more intelligent than any of those concerned with the 'faking' of the other bad quartos, with the possible exception of the person who provided the copy of *True Tragedy*.

Perhaps the printer is responsible for three defects of *Henry V Fo* which affect the sense. Thus the passage (1.2.211-2):

> So may a thousand actions once a foote
> *And* in one purpose,

is made intelligible by the reading of Q1, viz., *'end'* for 'and'; Pistol's advice to his wife (2.3.47),

> The *world* is, Pitch and pay,

takes a meaning when 'world' is changed as in Q1 to *'word.'* Nym affirms (2.1.22-3) oracularly if nonsensically,

> though patience be a tyred *name*, yet she will plodde,

and achieves some sense in Q1 (ii. 10-11) where *mare* replaces *name*. Other such examples occur in x. 5, 100.

Hamlet Q1 is, except for the first act, poorly preserved. No one could make much of the lines (1.5.56-74) of Q2:

> So but though to a radiant Angle linckt
> Will sort it selfe in a celestiall bed.

In Q1 (iv. 107-8) we make some progress towards understanding:

> So Lust, though to a radiant angle linckt,
> Would fate it selfe from a celestiall bedde,

but the folio version (1.5.56-7) probably gives us what Shakespeare wrote:

> So Lust, though to a radiant Angell link'd,
> Will sate it selfe in a Celestiall bed.

Another good example of the help given by Q1 to the formation of a standard text occurs in Q2 (2.2.410) where we read,

> Weele ento't like friendly Fankners; fly at any thing we see.

On turning to Q1 (vii. 125) we find the riddle solved:

> Weele euen too't, like French Falconers,
> Flie at any thing we see.

So Hamlet's famous line,

> What's Hecuba to him, or he to Hecuba,

is found in Q1; the later quartos read:

> What's Hecuba to him, or he to her.

Nor do I think that Hamlet said (3.2.2-3) to the players,

> But if you mouth it as many of our Players do;

Shakespeare almost certainly wrote 'your players' as in the first quarto and the folio. Shakespeare's fellows were pleasantly conscious of the other fellows' shortcomings. There is general agreement among editors in accepting the reading of Q1 for the following passage (ix. 163-4):

> *Oph.* Still better and worse.
> *Ham.* So you must take your husband.

Q1 makes Hamlet's quip personal rather than general; the other quartos and the folios unite in reading,

> So you mistake your husbands.

Similarly the first word of Lucianus' line (ix. 168),

> Confederate season else no creature seeing,

has replaced 'considerat,' the reading of the second quarto.

CHAPTER XVIII

REPETITION OF LINES, ETC.

AMONG the marked characteristics of corrupt Elizabethan plays
is repetition; in *Massacre at Paris* and *Orlanao Furioso Q1*
such additions to the text represent more than two per cent. of the
total length. What share is due to author and reporter respectively?
For an answer some examination of the dramatic style and
technique used in plays with sound texts by Shakespeare's predecessors is necessary.

Lines repeated in a play with a good text may be divided into
three main groups according as the repetition is,

(i) A rhetorical or dramatic device employed by the author
for a poetic or dramatic purpose, or

(ii) Some formula of leave-taking or welcome, entry or
departure, or

(iii) Subconscious, the result of accident or laziness.

Each of the three main groups will be discussed in turn.

(i) Rhetorical repetition takes two forms:—

(a) Two or more characters may each conclude their
speeches with an identical line or, it may be, lines.

(b) A line, usually one that concludes a speech, may be
picked up as the opening line of the next speech.

Some examples will be given of each type.

(i) (a) Peele in *The Arraignment of Paris* (printed 1584)
used this device three times. After Ate had 'trundled the ball into
place' each of the three goddesses claims it, saying in conclusion,

Let this vnto the fairest giuen be,
The fairest of the three—and I am she.

Immediately afterwards each states her reasons for this claim,
and concludes her speech with the lines,

If then this prize be but bequeath'd to beauty,
The only she that wins this prize am I.

313

Diana is finally chosen as umpire, and each goddess speaks in turn, ending her speech with the following six lines:—

> That whereso'er this ball of purest gold,
> That chaste Diana here in hand doth hold,
> Vnpartially her wisdom shall bestow,
> Without mislike or quarrel any mo,
> *Pallas* shall rest content and satisfied,
> And say the best desert doth there abide.

In the two other speeches the names of 'Juno' and 'Venus' respectively appear instead of 'Pallas.'

Peele did not abandon this primitive method of attracting attention; it is found in *Alcazar, David and Bethsabe* and *Edward I.* Greene also uses this type of repeated line in *Orlando Furioso.* Two lines,

> But leauing these such glories as they be,
> I loue my Lord, let that suffize for me,

conclude the speech of each of the four suitors (ll.39-40, 58-9, 79-80, 97-8), and Orlando retains the first line changing the second. Rasni ends his opening speech in '*A Looking Glass*' with the line,

> Rasni is god on earth and none but he. (l.27).

The Kings of Cilicia and Crete follow him with shorter speeches, which close with this couplet (ll.34-5, 43-4):

> May make a King match with the gods in gree,
> Rasni is god on earth, and none but he.

This same rhetorical figure is found in *Locrine, Edward III, Troublesome Raigne* and other anonymous plays of this period.

Professor C. F. T. Brooke in a dissertation on *The Authorship of 2, 3 Henry VI,* published in the seventeenth volume of the *Transactions of Connecticut Academy,* discusses at length the repeated lines present in certain plays of Marlowe, and states his opinion that

a striking line or expression which has already been used once in the play lingers in the poet's mind and repeats itself later either from carelessness or a conscious rhetorical device.

Marlowe's use of the particular 'rhetorical device' which is being discussed is practically confined to *2 Tamburlaine;* I know no example in any other play of his which has a good text. Two examples will sufficiently illustrate how he used this trick of rhetoric:

> *Tam.* These words assure me boy, thou art my sonne,
> When I am old and cannot mannage armes,
> Be thou the scourge and terrour of the world.
> *Amy.* Why may not I my Lord, as wel as he,
> Be tearm'd the scourge and terrour of the world?
> *Tam.* Be al a scourge and terror to the world,
> Or els you are not sons of Tamburlaine.   ll.303-9

In this example words are changed to suit the context of the passage in which it appears. In the following example the line is unchanged:

> *Orc.* So from Arabia desart, and the bounds
> Of that sweet land, whose braue Metropolis
> Reedified the faire Semyramis,
> Came forty thousand warlike foot and horse,
> Since last we numbred to your Maiesty.
> *Treb.* From Trebizon in Asia the lesse,
> Naturalized Turks and stout Bythinians
> Came to my bands full fifty thousand more,
> That fighting, knowes not what retreat doth meane,
> Nor ere returne but with the victory,
> Since last we numbred to your maiesty.
> *Sor.* Of Sorians from Halla is repair'd
> And neighbor cities of your highnesse land,
> Ten thousand horse, and thirty thousand foot,
> Since last we numbred to your maiestie.   ll.1212-26

The other examples found in *2 Tamburlaine* are given below. The word enclosed in brackets replaces in the second line the word that precedes it in the first.

> Where (with) Sigismond the King of Hungary.   ll.9,54
> Sclauonians, Almans, Rutters, Muffes and Danes.   ll.22,58
> All Asia (Affrike) is in Armes with Tamburlaine.   ll.72,76
> Is (all) Barbary vnpeopled for thy sake.   ll.379,394
> With that accursed traitor Almeda   1.1,018
> That curst and damned Traitor Almeda   1.1,022
> And shall I die, and this vnconquered.   ll.2,219,2,227

A study of the various passages in which these lines occur will convince any reader that this type of repetition in this play is deliberate and purposeful, not accidental or careless. Some instances are tiresome and inartistic; the trick becomes stale with

too much use. Marlowe did not invent it. The poet rather than the
rhetorician is responsible for one most admirable use of this
figure. That famous line,

> To entertaine divine Zenocrate,

found five times as the refrain of the magic blank verse quatrains
in which Tamburlaine chants his swan song of love for his dying
queen shows with what superb mastery Marlowe could use the
device of the repeated line. Such is the great manner of the Bible,
Homer, Virgil, Spenser, Milton and Shakespeare. Zenocrate's
dirge spoken over the dead bodies of Bajazeth and Zabina in
1 Tamburlaine with its measured iteration of

> Behold the Turke and his great Emperesse,

is an earlier and less successful essay in the same manner.

(i) (b) This second type of repetition is somewhat frequent in
our early plays. Peele has examples in three of his plays. One
line spoken by King Sebastian (1.773), in the *Battle of Alcazar,*

> To aide Mahamet King of Barbarie,

is repeated exactly by the Bishop as the next line. So, too, another
line (1.829) of Sebastian's,

> To propagate the fame of Portugall,

is echoed by the Spanish ambassador. I have noted three such
repeated lines in *David and Bethsabe,* and two in *Edward I.* The
first pair in the earlier of these two plays is:

> *Cu.* Where is Lord Ioab, leader of the host?
> *Joab.* Here is Lord Ioab, leader of the host.

Another such primitive repetition occurs in the third Act. Apart
from the examples of this type of repetition given in my list of the
repeated lines found in *Orlando Furioso Q1,* there are two in
Alphonsus of Aragon. One of these is of an unusual kind.
Belinus, King of Naples, terms Alphonsus (ll.168-171 of Act II):

> That runnagate, that rachell, yea, that theefe?
> For well I wot, he hath robd me of a Crowne.
> If euer he had sprung from gentle blood,
> He would not thus misuse his fauorer.

Albinius is incensed at this coarse abuse of his sovereign, and
begins his rebuke by repeating the line,

> That runnagate, that rachell, yea, that theef?

Marlowe does not affect this kind of repetition overmuch. The best example occurs in *1 Tamburlaine*. Cosroe has been crowned by Tamburlaine as King of Persia, and Menander says:

> Your Maiestie shall shortly haue your wish,
> And ride in triumph through Persepolis.   *Exeunt.*

> *Manent Tamb. Tech. Ther. Vsum.*

> *Tam.* And ride in triumph through Persepolis?
> Is it not braue to be a King, Techelles?
> Vsumcasane and Theridimas,
> Is it not passing braue to be a King,
> And ride in triumph through Persepolis?

Perhaps the poet repeated this line from sheer delight in its beauty and rippling melody; the sound of the word 'Persepolis' seems to have charmed his ear, for he ends five lines with it. Marlowe was almost the first of our great poets to perceive that the variety of the vowels in such sonorous names as Persepolis, Usumcasane, and Theridamas gives flexibility, melody and rapidity to a language so stiff with monosyllables and doubled consonants as is our English. More than a hundred lines in these two plays end on a thundering 'Tamburlaine.' Several scenes of the second part contain long catalogues of resounding and harmonious names of countries, towns and peoples. A simpler piece of repetition is that of the line,

> Vnlesse they haue a wiser king than you;

which Mycetes helplessly repeats after his insulting brother. Shakespeare did not disdain to use this rhetorical trick in *King John* (4.3.57-60). His nobles have discovered the dead body of Prince Arthur, and the Bastard says,

> It is a damned, and a bloody worke,
> The gracelesse action of a heauy hand,
> If that it be the worke of any hand.

Salisbury is astonished that any defence should be offered for what he takes to be a deliberate murder, and cries out

> If that it be the worke of any hand?

(ii) Such dramatically conventional lines or sentences as 'giue me leaue to speake,' 'I thanke your maiestie,' 'I take my leaue,' and

the customary variants are common in most plays of the Elizabethan era. They are stage formulae and cannot be included
among the repeated lines considered above. Questions addressed
to messengers, such as 'how now sirra, what newes?' or 'how now,
what's the newes with you?' are part of the dramatic machinery of
a play. Excessive use of such sentences as 'See where he comes'
or 'Come, let vs go' is a characteristic of corrupt texts; the pirates
were always in trouble when it was necessary to get characters
on or off the stage.

(iii) Sub-conscious or accidental repetition of lines is not very
common in our early plays if free from corruption. I note three
such lines in *Alphonsus of Arragon,*

> I do not doubt but ere the time be long;
> For to reuenge his death on thee again;
> Nay then I see tis time to looke about.

Each of these lines appears later in a different scene. Most of the
examples in *Orlando Furioso Q1* are probably due to the actors or
reporter rather than the author. Marlowe's textually sound plays
do not contain many unintentionally repeated lines. In *1 Tamburlaine* I find:

> Or plead for mercie at your highnesse feet.   1.81
> Must plead for mercie at his kingly feet.   1.1,272

and in the second part,

> To sue for mercie at your highnesse feete.   1.2,058

In *2 Tamburlaine* the final lines of the second and sixth scenes are:

> Come banquet and carouse with vs a while.   1.174
> Come let vs banquet and carouse the whiles.   1.474

Apart from lines concerned with leave-taking and news-bringing,
I find three instances of seemingly accidental repetition in
Edward I:

> Will be the ruine of the realme and vs.   1.239
> Will be the ruine of the realme and you.   1.1,009

> Forbeare to leuie armes against the king.   1.289
> And leuie armes against your lawfull king.   1.1,516

> My vncles taken prisoner by the Scots.   1.917
> Mine vncles taken prisoner by the Scots.   1.944

Such casually repeated lines are hard to find; they recur unexpectedly and with some small variation in words.

This brief study enables some conclusions to be deduced concerning the occurrence of repeated lines in our early drama.

(i) Rhetorical repetition is not uncommon in early plays with good texts; this device was in use before Marlowe or Shakespeare had written a line for the public stage. Peele, Greene and Marlowe seem to have employed it to produce dramatic emphasis or as a poetical ornament, and it is found also in anonymous plays.

(ii) Nearly all Marlowe's examples are found in the two parts of *Tamburlaine;* they are rare in his later work.

(iii) Repeated lines other than those inserted intentionally for some poetic or artistic reason are not plentiful in plays printed from the author's manuscript or some copy of it.

(iv) Repeated lines occur sporadically in *1 Tamburlaine* and *Edward II* and taken together number very few all told; the very corrupt *Massacre at Paris,* which is scarcely a quarter of the combined length of these two plays, has no less than 24 such repeated lines. *Alphonsus of Arragon* furnishes eight lines thus repeated, *Orlando Furioso Q1* no less than seventeen. Seven are proved by Dr. Greg to occur in that portion of Orlando's part for which the Dulwich MS. provides us a check; for the insertion of these lines the actors or reporter are responsible, and we may assume that they have introduced nearly all the repeated lines that are so abundant in corrupt plays. Those present in *Orlando Furioso Q1* are ll.27,32,106; 39-40, 58-9, 79-80, 97-8,134; 184,202; 346,351; 804,816; 825,1,565; 114,116,118,120,122; 703,704; 762,768,889; 468,1,045; 1,360,1,499; 1,394-7, 1,570-3. The last five examples we know are the work of the actors or the reporter, and we are entitled logically to the inference that all lines and phrases, used a second time or oftener without any stylistic or dramatic reason, and for which the check provided by the Dulwich MS. does not exist, are also the work of the same agents. This inference has the support of style, vocabulary, diction, versification, etc.

(v) Repeated lines that subserve no artistic or dramatic purpose are more numerous in *Massacre at Paris;* they are ll.2,27; 12,76; 171,277; 246,729; 198,569; 202-3,445; 289,317; 281,451-2; 305,

356; 340-1,539; 349,504; 510,514; 524,1,149; 526,906; 534,1,141; 647,829; 660,791-2; 717-9,735-6; 938-9,956-7; 966-8,1,168-1,171; 1,142,1,168-9; 56,582; 1,192,1,201; 527,657. In addition, this play has many repeated phrases, an inordinate number of titles of address, e.g., 'my Lord,' 'my good Lord,' 'your Maiesty,' 'the Lord Admiral,' etc., and a large number of short lines. When due allowance has been made for repetition, for the borrowing of about forty lines from other plays, for other excrescences and for short lines, the length of this play cannot much exceed eleven hundred lines of blank verse; probably about a hundred lines are exactly as the poet wrote them. Considered as a specimen of our early poetic drama, the extant *Massacre at Paris* bears much the same relation to the lost play of Marlowe as *Hamlet Q1* to *Hamlet Q2*. In my opinion, Professor Brooke is not entitled to prop up his theory that Marlowe was prone to repetition by putting in as evidence the above twenty-four lines repeated in this corrupt play; the two parts of *Tamburlaine, Edward II, Dido,* and the earlier acts of *Jew of Malta* provide ample material for the formation of a considered judgment of his language, style and literary peculiarities, if such exist. I hold the opinion that Marlowe is no more responsible for the numerous repeated and borrowed lines and phrases so abundant in *Massacre at Paris* than is Shakespeare for the even greater amount of repetition and borrowing in *Hamlet Q1*.

Repetition of lines, phrases and words is, as stated above, a specific mark of that omnipresent corruption which has half destroyed the text of the bad quartos; the amount of repetition is, in itself, almost a measure of the depth to which corruption has penetrated the play. This feature is especially noticeable in *Contention* and *Hamlet Q1,* each of which has suffered far more than any of the others except perhaps *Merry Wives Q1*. Most of the important characters of *Contention* including Henry, Margaret, Humphry, Eleanor, Suffolk, Warwick, York and Cade indulge in the practice of repeating or anticipating a line or two. So also do the major characters of *Hamlet Q1,* with the one exception of the Queen. In *True Tragedy* the royal brothers, Edward and Richard, are the worst offenders. Warwick, who has the longest part, repeats one line only, and that a line of his own part, whilst neither Clifford, whose part most nearly corresponds verbally and in length to the same part in *3 Henry VI,* nor Margaret, whose part after the first act is the most mutilated and corrupt, repeats one line. Usually repetition occurs haphazardly and, except in *True Tragedy,* is not associated mainly with the speeches of one or two characters when the lengths of the parts are taken into account. Repeated lines may occur close together or in different scenes; when a few lines only separate the repeated lines it is usually the one character that speaks both, but when they are in different scenes each may be spoken by a different speaker.

REPEATED LINES OF THE BAD QUARTOS

Repeated lines of the bad quartos are divisible into two main groups:

A Those which are peculiar to the bad quartos, that is, are not in Shakespeare's corresponding plays.

B Those which are present in each pair of parallel texts, twice at least in the bad quarto, and also once at least in Shakespeare's parallel play. This group may be divided into two sub-groups:

(i) In some examples the first of the two or more repeated lines in the bad quarto is found, relatively to scene and context, in the corresponding portion of the authentic text; the second line merely repeats the first in a later quarto scene.

(ii) The first of the two bad quarto lines is an anticipation of the line in Shakespeare's play, to which the second line of the bad quarto usually corresponds in scene and context. These anticipatory lines of the bad quartos are important as evidence of the priority of Shakespeare's texts. They will be discussed later.

Below are some repeated lines present in each bad quarto, classified in the groups named above. Those in group A need no comment except that the second line usually adapts or echoes rather than repeats the first. In the second group, B, the line of the bad quarto appears first and is followed by the corresponding line of the parallel text; then comes the second quarto line. Sometimes the same two quarto lines correspond to two different lines of the parallel text; in such examples the second line of the parallel text is added.

A—Repetition of Lines Peculiar to Bad Quartos

Repeated lines unrepresented in the parallel authentic texts
are not very plentiful even in the more corrupt bad quartos. One
only occurs in *True Tragedy,* the opening lines of the tenth and
twelfth scenes being identical. *Henry V Q1* has none, and *Romeo
and Juliet Q1* three; two of these occur in the interpolated blank-
verse threnody in the last scene of the fourth Act. *Merry Wives Q1*
has eight examples at least, besides numerous half-lines and
phrases, but as the play is mostly in prose, repetition has less
significance. I find eight examples in *Contention,* viz., i.112,
iv.111; ii.74,v.136; iii.51,ix.8; vi.25-7,42-4; viii.15,81; x.171,195;
xxiii,34-5,47-8,56-7. Most noteworthy is the repetition in part of
the stage direction prefixed to scenes x and xi. The first is,

> Then the Curtaines being drawne, Duke Humphrey is dis-
> couered in his bed . . .

The second (scene xi) is:

> . . . and then the Curtaines be drawne, and the Cardinall
> is discouered in his bed, rauing and staring as if he were
> madde.

In the folio version this stage direction is,

> Enter the King, Salisbury, and Warwicke, to the Cardinal
> in bed.

The words 'rauing and staring as if he were madde' really repeat
one of Vaux's lines (x.185), which is not in the folio,

> Sometimes he raues and cryes as he were madde.

This line seems a vague recollection of *2 Henry VI* (3.2.370-1):

> For sodainly a greevous sicknesse tooke him,
> That makes him gaspe, and stare, and catch the aire.

Hamlet Q1 contains six repeated lines which are not derived from
Q2; half of them make their first appearance in the first act.
Below is a list; each line has prefixed the name of the speaker.

  (i) *Lear.* I in all loue and dutie take my leaue.   ii.25
       Guild. So in all duetie doe we take our leaue.   vi.16
  (ii) *King.* Spoke like a kinde and most louing sonne.   ii.51
      King. Why now you speake like a most louing sonne. xiii.65
 (iii) *Oph.* And withall, such earnest vowes.   iii.58
      Oph. And with them such earnest vowes of loue.   vi.158

(iv) *King.* That you will labour but to wring from him
     The cause and ground of his distemperancie.   vi.6-7
     Rosen.   and willingly if we might,
     Know the cause and ground of your discontent.   vii.53-4
     Cor. We cannot yet finde out the very ground
     of his distemperance.   viii.26-7
     Rosen. My good lord, let vs again intreate
     To know of you the ground and cause of your
                             distemperature.   ix.188-9

(v) *Gil.* My lord, we haue done all the best we could,
     To wring from him the cause of all his griefe.   viii.5-6
     Cor. There question you the cause of all his griefe.   viii.34

(vi) *King.* Now sonne Hamlet, where is this dead body?   xi.134
     King. But sonne Hamlet, where is this body?   xi.147

In addition some repeated phrases, not used in the parallel texts, are not uncommon in the bad quartos with the exception of *Henry V Q1.* Thus in *Contention* we find used twice 'with all my heart,' 'for to obey my (or your) will,' 'that ambitious Duke' and 'Iadie groom'; in *True Tragedy,* 'come let vs go' three times and 'in the thickest throngs' twice; in *Romeo and Juliet Q1,* 'as we past along' (twice) and 'a poxe on your houses' four times instead of 'a plague a' etc.' Such phrases peculiar to the bad quartos are most common in *Merry Wives Q1;* among them are 'Dinner staies for vs' and variants (three times), 'I lay my life' (twice), 'Let me alone' (passim), 'Ieshu blesse me' (four times). Locutions peculiar to *Hamlet Q1* are 'sonne Hamlet' (eight times), 'Prince Hamlet' (nine times), 'yong Ofelia' (three times), 'contents me not,' 'content your selfe,' etc.

Repeated Lines—Group B (i)

In this group of repeated lines common to a pair of parallel texts, the first spoken of two or more lines or passages of Q1 may be identical with a line or passage which occurs in the corresponding part of the same scene of Shakespeare's play, or is an unmistakable adaptation or echo of this line or passage. Usually the actor that first spoke the line or passage in Q1 repeats it in the same or a later scene; sometimes another actor, present on the stage when it was originally spoken, is the repeater. I shall discuss very briefly an example or two of this type chosen from

W

each bad quarto written in verse. Such repeated lines may each take their origin from the one line of the authentic text; occasionally the second or later line of Q1 may show certain changes most probably due to an imperfect recollection of the corresponding line of the authentic text. A good example of this peculiarity is found in *Contention;* Suffolk speaks both lines in each text. Addressing Duke Humphrey he says:

We do arrest thee of high treason here. (ix.39)

This corresponds to the folio line (3.1.97),

I doe arrest thee of High Treason here.

Later in the folio scene (3.1.136) he formally announces,

I doe arrest you in his Highnesse name,

but a trick or failure of memory causes the actor to repeat (ix.65), except for a slight change, the previous quarto line,

I do arrest thee on high treason here.

Another example of this contamination is to be found in *Contention* by comparing i.144-5 and ix.34-5 with 1.1.210-11 and 3.1.88-9 of the folio text.

Examples of this peculiar type of repetition occur in other bad quartos. One line (i.26) of *Henry V Q1*, repeated identically in l.38,

No female shall succeed in salicke land,

represents two folio variants, the first (i.2.41) being,

No Woman shall succeed in Salike Land,

and the second (1.2.52-3),

No Female
Should be Inheretrix in Salike Land.

Similarly in *Merry Wives Q1* the passages vi.134-5 and xi.85-6, are practically identical with the folio passage 2.2.238-9, whilst the second folio passage (3.5.119-20), which corresponds textually with the second quarto passage, takes an entirely different form.

There is no need for quoting many examples of straightforward repetition. Two in *Contention,* viz., vi.49 and xix.9, may be compared with 2.2.63, and xviii.118-120 and xix.13-15 with 4.8.63-4.

True Tragedy contains seven examples of more or less simple repetition. The folio line (1.1.49) spoken by Warwick,

Resolue thee Richard, clayme the English Crowne,

appears identically (i.44) in the corresponding speech in *True Tragedy*, and is echoed and amplified by Richard, once in the next scene:

Then noble father resolue your selfe,
And once more claime the crowne,   ii.20-1

and later before York town (xvi.42):

Resolue your selfe, and let vs claime the crowne.

Similarly Warwick's two lines (2.1.135-6):

But all in vaine, they had no heart to fight,
And we (in them) no hope to win the day,

are found verbatim in the corresponding speech of the quarto. Clarence echoes the second line (vi.11),

For yet theres hopes inough to win the daie,

and Oxford repeats (xx.19) Clarence's line without any change. Other examples may be studied in 2.3.3-4, vi.3-4, xx.25-6; 2.3.22, vi.25, xx.34; 2.3.103-4, viii.42,44; 4.1.47-8, xii.33-4, 36-8; v.2.40, xx.28,47.

Romeo and Juliet Q1 has not very many repeated lines of this type, but an important example occurs in the last, a very corrupt, act. Friar John explains (Q2. 5.2.4-11) why the letter to Romeo was not delivered:

Ioh. Going to find a barefoote brother out,
One of our order to associate me,
Here in this Citie visiting the sicke,
And finding him, the Searchers of the Towne
Suspecting that we both were in a house,
Where the infectious pestilence did raigne,
Seald vp the doores, and would not let vs forth.

This appears twice in Q1, mutilated and garbled. In the corresponding scene (xxi.4-9) we read:

Going to seeke a barefoote Brother out,
One of our order to associate mee,
Here in this Cittie visiting the sick,
Whereas the infectious pestilence remaind:
And being by the Searchers of the Towne
Found and examinde, we were both shut vp.

In Friar Laurence's final speech occurs another reference to this vagary of the goddess chance (xxii.179-182) :

> But he that had my Letters (Frier John)
> Seeking a brother to associate him,
> Whereas the sicke infection remaind,
> Was stayed by the Searchers of the Towne,

In Q2 the reference to this incident (5.3.250-2) is brief :

> But he which bore my letter, Frier Iohn,
> Was stayed by accident, and yesternight
> Returnd my letter back.

Evidently the pirate recollected only the first line of Shakespeare's text and the words 'was stayed' of the second; for the remainder he drew upon his memory.

Henry V Q1, apart from the example referred to above, does not exhibit any examples of repetition except in the comic or semi-comic scenes. Three examples may be cited, viz., 2.1.45-8, ii.40-1, x.57; 2.1.87-8, ii.71,79; 3.6.3-4, x.3,84. Nym's formula for concluding some speeches 'and that's the humor of it' appears in 2.1.55,66,92,111 and 2.3.58; in Q1 this has become 'and there's the humor of it,' found in ii.8,14,48,56,74,88; iv.44, vi.4, that is, it appears earlier and later in Q1 than in the folio version. Further it has been transferred to *Merry Wives Q1;* Nym uses it in i.50; iii.21,64,79; v.51,55, but it is not present in the authentic text.

Seven instances of repetition of the kind defined at the beginning of this section occur in *Hamlet Q1*. To each example the name of the speaker is prefixed.

(i) *King.* And now Laertes, whats the newes with you? 1.2.42
    King. And now Leartes, what's the news with you? ii.13
    Cor. How now Ofelia, what's the news with you? v.32

(ii) *Ham.* And what so poore a man as Hamlet is,
    May doe t'expresse his loue and frending to you
    God willing shall not lack. 1.5.185-7
    Ham. And what so poore a man as Hamlet may,
    To pleasure you, God willing shall not want. iv.228-9
    Queene. Thankes gentlemen, and what the Queene
                       of Denmarke
    May pleasure you, be sure you shall not want. viii.18-9

(iii) *Ham.* When he is drunke, a sleepe, or in his rage,
    Or in th'incestious pleasure of his bed,
    At game a swearing— 3.3.89-90

Ham. When hee's at game swaring, taking his
carowse, drinking drunke,
Or in the incestuous pleasure of his bed.   x.23-4
Ham. A! haue you eyes and can you looke on him
That slew my father, and your deere husband,
To liue in the incestuous pleasure of his bed?   xi.44-6

(iv) *Ghost.* If thou did'st euer thy deare father loue.   1.5.23
     Ghost. Hamlet, if euer thou didst thy deere
                         father loue.   iv.84
     Ham. O mother, if euer you did my deare father
                           loue.   xi.98

(v)   *Ham.* For I mine eyes will riuet to his face.   3.2.80
     Ham. For I mine eies will riuet to his face.   ix.61
     Hor. My Lord, mine eies shall still be on his face.   ix.65

(vi) *Clow.* A pickax and a spade a spade,
     for and a shrowding sheet
     O a pit of Clay for to be made
     for such a guest is meet.   v.1.89-92
     Clowne. A picke-axe and a spade,
     A spade for and a winding sheete,
     Most fit it is, for t'will be made,   *he throwes vp a shouel.*
     For such a ghest most meete.   xvi.32-5
     Clowne. A pick-axe and a spade, a spade,
     For and a winding sheete,
     Most fit it is for to be made,
     For such a ghest most meet.   xvi.40-3

(vii) *Pol.* The very cause of Hamlets lunacie.   2.2.49
     Cor. The very depth of Hamlets lunacie.   vi.28
     King. The cause of our sonne Hamlets lunacie.   viii.2

Among the phrases used once only in *Hamlet Q2* but more than
once in Q1 are 'My blessing with thee,' iii.25.42; 'your maiden
presence,' iii.50,62; 'what may this mean?' iv.29,35; 'still am I
called,' iv.48,58; 'Briefe let me be,' iv.95,110; 'Heauens secure
him,' iv.156, vi.176; 'Nay come letts go together,' iv.230,234; 'Goe
to a Nunnery goe' (and variants), vi.165,173,174,180,185,189,199,
200 compared with five instances in Q2; 'with all my heart,' ii.24;
vi.115, viii.13,18; xi.161; 'see where he comes,' vi.111, vii.5, xi.131.

REPETITION—GROUP B (ii)

For the purpose of this investigation, by far the most important
group of repeated lines is that in which the first-occurring of the
two identical lines of Q1 is found in an earlier scene than that

containing the corresponding line of the parallel text; usually Shakespeare's line matches in scene and context the second quarto line. This phenomenon is inconsistent with the theory that the copy for each bad quarto was obtained by note-takers in the theatre.

Notes, shorthand or longhand, at their worst must record in the order of hearing what the writer heard; he could not possibly introduce into his notes of the fifth scene a line spoken in the ninth, or set down in his records of the eleventh scene a distinctive phrase which the actor did not speak till the eighteenth scene. Two examples will present the problem that must be solved. The words 'that monstrous rebel' are found in the sixth, tenth, eighteenth, twentieth and twenty-first scenes of *Contention*. In *2 Henry VI* this phrase occurs once, viz., in the first scene of the fifth act which corresponds to the twenty-first scene of *Contention*. If this bad quarto is derived from a shorthand report of *2 Henry VI* how comes it that these unusual words appear in four different scenes, each earlier than the twenty-first to which they belong? Again the sentence 'Let vs march away' forms part of a line that concludes the second, fourth, twelfth and sixteenth scenes of *True Tragedy*. Reference to *3 Henry VI* proves that this half-line occurs only at the end of Act IV, sc. 7; this corresponds to the sixteenth scene of the derived play. Once more comes the query, how did this sentence get into the notes taken of the second, fourth and twelfth scenes, when theory insists that the note-taker did not hear it spoken until the end of the sixteenth scene?

If the report was taken in shorthand, it is impossible that such phrases could have been added by the stenographer during the process of transcription. He might make some corrections, based on memory, here and there, but no one would emend anything faulty in the sixth scene by reference to the twenty-first. Once his longhand transcription was in the hands of his employers, his work was done and that of the pirate began.

Modern stenographers, who had not read *Hamlet Q2,* would find it very difficult to take an accurate report of the speeches and dialogues of the ghost scenes, and probably would be satisfied if they succeeded in producing something equal to what we find in Q1. Elizabethan shorthand systems, such as Bright's *Characterie* or Bales's *Brachygraphy,* would have been useless for such intricate work. Bright's system involved learning by heart 570 symbols corresponding to 570 words; each symbol represented not merely the word but its derivatives, inflexions and even synonyms. But could such inexact and loose-meaning symbols serve to set down correctly the 3,880 words of *Hamlet*? How could any one provide symbols of any such fashion for most of the 158 words which, according to the compilers of the *Oxford English Dictionary*, make their first entrance into our literature in *Hamlet*? My friend, the late Sir Ernest Scott, Professor of History in the University of Melbourne, was for many years a professional shorthand-writer on the staff of the Commonwealth Parliament. Being interested in Shakespearean research, he learnt *Characterie* sufficiently well to write it with some fluency. He informed me that any practiser, however expert, of this system, would be unable to take down even a short speech with any real approach to accuracy, and he declared that it was useless for reporting a play. I accept his testimony as decisive.

Other difficulties would lie in the path of the note-taker. Some critics with no shorthand but a retentive memory have suggested that by attending six or eight performances of a play it would be possible to provide a text as good as that of *True Tragedy*. This test may have been made at six or eight consecutive performances of a modern play, and may have been completed within a period of a week or ten days; notes could be taken at night without any hindrance or interruption, and filled in after each performance. In Elizabethan days six or eight performances of a play would be spread over a month or six weeks, and thus the continuity and concentration necessary to success would be impaired; moreover, copious and continuous note-taking in broad daylight would be soon discovered and most vigorously discouraged by actors who had suffered from piracy.

I propose to discuss briefly some examples of 'anticipation' in the bad quartos of lines that in the authentic parallel texts appear either in a later part of the same scene or in a later scene. Usually the line or passage occurs a second time in a part of the bad quarto which exactly corresponds in scene and context to the position of the line in the authentic text. On the other hand anticipation in the bad quarto of a line in the authentic text may occur without any subsequent repetition in the quarto.

CONTENTION and 2 HENRY VI

(i) Suffolk explains to the King's Council the terms of the marriage treaty, and the King ratifies it:

> Heere are the Articles of contracted peace,
> Betweene our Soueraigne, and the French King Charles,
> For eighteene moneths concluded by consent.   1.1.40-2

These lines appear (1.37-9) as follows in *Contention*:

> Here are the articles confirmde of peace,
> Betweene our Soueraigne and the French King Charles,
> Till terme of eighteene months be full expirde.

Lines 37-8 are identical, except for one word, with those of the folio version; the third line in the passage from *Contention* anticipates a later folio line of the same scene:

> *King.*   Cosin of Yorke,
> We heere discharge your Grace from being Regent
> I'th parts of France, till terme of eighteene Moneths
> Be full expyr'd.   1.1.60-3

This last line is found *literatim* a second time in *Contention* 1.59-62. Singularly enough, the quarto version correctly preserves the words after 'Item'—'it is further agreed betweene them' when first Humphrey and then the Cardinal read the second condition of the treaty; in the folio version Humphrey omits them though the Cardinal must be reading from the same document.

(ii) One curious example of anticipation occurs in the seventh scene of *Contention* when *Dame Elnor Cobham, led with the Officers,* appears before the King's Council to receive from the King (vii.4-6) her sentence for sorcery:

> 'First for thy hainous crimes, thou shalt two daies in
> London do penance barefoot in the streets, with a white
> sheete about thy bodie, and a waxe Taper burning in thy
> hand.'

These details, except for the words 'after three days open Penance done,' are not in the folio version of the King's sentence, but are portion of a stage direction found after the sixteenth line of *2 Henry VI*, 2.4 (sc. viii of *Contention*):

> *Enter the Duchesse in a white Sheet, and a Taper burning in her hand, with the Sherife and Officers.*

In the corresponding stage direction of *Contention* she has *a waxe candle* in her hand, but in a subsequent speech refers to herself (viii.31),

> And thus with burning Tapor in my hand,

a line not in the corresponding speech of *3 Henry VI*. Into King Henry's sentence, pronounced at the beginning of the seventh scene of *Contention,* the reporter has foisted details of the penance as exhibited on the stage in the eighth scene.

(iii) My next example illustrates anticipation in which the words spoken out of place in *Contention* are found in a later scene of *2 Henry VI*. Duchess Elinor has been condemned to do public penance in London streets, and Duke Humphrey addresses the Sheriff:

> and Master Sherife,
> Let not her Penance exceede the Kings Commission. 2.4.74-5

In the version of *Contention* this passage is:

> Maister Sheriffe, I pray proceede no further against
> my Lady, then the course of law extendes. viii.57-8

Later Humphrey is arrested and the King commands that his uncle, who had been murdered, shall be given a fair trial:

> Lords take your places: and I pray you all
> Proceed no straiter 'gainst our Vnckle Gloster,
> Then from true euidence, of good esteeme,
> He be approu'd in practise culpable. 3.2.19-22

This is cut down in *Contention* (x.12-13):

> And good my Lords proceed no further against
> Our vnckle Gloster, then by iust proofe you can affirme,

Here Gloster's speech to the sheriff in the eighth scene anticipates the words used by the king of his uncle when the latter was dead.

(iv) Another instance of anticipation affects only one line of text; the king speaks of Gloster:

> My Conscience tells me you are innocent 3.1.141
> My mind doth tell me thou art innocent v.170
> My conscience tels me thou art innocent. ix.70

Other examples may be studied, e.g., 1.1.164,i.103,111; 1.1.209, i.111,132; ii.5-6,viii.35,2.4.43, etc.

Two widely-separated lines of *Contention* show in each of them changes due to both anticipation and recollection of the two corresponding lines of Shakespeare. The folio lines are,

> Suffolke, the new made Duke that rules the rost.   1.1.104
> For Suffolke he that can doe all in all.   2.4.51

The result is an amalgam of the two early parts of these lines,

> For Suffolke he, the new made Duke that rules the roast. 1.76
>   For Suffolk he,
> The new made Duke, that may do all in all.   viii.46-7

Some phrases occur in *Contention* earlier than in the original. Thus 'who is within there?' is found in ii.47,iii.30,iv.51, and ix.97; the same folio phrase occurs at 1.4.82. I have already referred to the use in the quarto of the phrase 'that monstrous rebel' four times prior to its occurrence in *2 Henry VI*. So also nine scenes of *Contention* close with the formula 'Come let vs go' or 'Come . . . let vs go,' whilst Shakespeare employs it once only towards the end of his play.

Anticipation in *Contention* of a line spoken in *2 Henry VI* occurs without any subsequent repetition. Thus Margaret's line (iii.49),

> But still must be protected like a childe,

precedes its original, the folio line (2.3.29), by four scenes:

> Should be to be protected like a Child.

Transposition in the contrary sense is noticeable when Warwick's line (vi.55) recalls the line (1.1.249) in the first scene of the authentic text spoken by York. Similarly, the two lines (xi.14-15) represent the earlier folio passage (3.1.169-171).

True Tragedy and 3 Henry VI

This play has a number of lines each of which anticipates an original line in a later scene of *3 Henry VI*.

(i) Many lines of the corrupt sixth scene echo lines of the twentieth:

> *Somer.* And said commend me to my valiant Brother. 5.2.42
> *Rich.*   and cride aloud:
> Richard, commend me to my valiant sonne.   vi.22
> *Somer.* And saie commend me to my valiant brother. xx.30

Here in the anticipation (vi.22) we should have 'brother' not 'sonne' because Salisbury, Warwick's father, was killed at or after the battle of Wakefield, and his half-brother at Towton.

(ii) In Richard's long soliloquy which concludes the tenth scene of *True Tragedy* is a line (x.107),

> For I am not yet lookt on in the world,

which is borrowed verbatim from an aside (5.7.22, xxiii.22) spoken by him in both versions of the last scene of the play:

> For yet I am not look'd on in the world.

Another interesting example may be studied by comparing the two passages of *True Tragedy* (i.102-3, v.143-4) which represent the folio versions (1.1.107-8,2.2.150-1). In each piece of text the second lines of the two quarto passages are modelled on the second line of the second folio passage. Other examples of anticipation are 1.1.171-3, i.165-7, 1.2.15, ii.9-10; 3.1.23,69, ix.12,37; 3.2.84, x.64, 4.6.71, xvii.19.

Among the repeated phrases of *True Tragedy*, the first-occurring of which is anticipatory of the same phrase in the folio, are 'the accursed Duke,' 1.3.4, i.227, iii.5; 'let vs march away,' referred to above; 'no way to flie,' 2.6.24, iii.62, viii.87; 'wilt thou yeeld the crowne,' 2.2.101, v.79,97; 'I will not hear them (him) speake,' 5.5.4, xviii.3, xxi.50. In each instance the quotation from the folio text corresponds to the second example quoted from *True Tragedy*.

Lines and passages, each used once only in each text, but which are found in *True Tragedy* earlier than in *3 Henry VI* are not uncommon. An excellent instance is Oxford's line (5.4.66) before the battle of Tewkesbury,

> Here pitch our Battaile, hence we will not budge.

This line, slightly altered, was spoken by Clifford (v.78) before the battle of Towton,

> Pitch we our battell heere, for hence we will not moue,

Other examples are 2.5.95, viii.7; 5.3.1-2, viii.94-5. Transposition in the reverse sense, i.e., from a scene of *3 Henry VI* to a later scene of *True Tragedy* is found in 1.2.33-4, v.52-3; 4.8.60-1, xx.64-5.

ROMEO AND JULIET Q1 and ROMEO AND JULIET Q2

I have found but one example of repetition of the anticipated line. Paris finds the banished Romeo near the tomb of the Capulets and says (Q2, 5.3.69), after denouncing him,

And apprehend thee for a Fellon here.

This line is slightly altered in Q1 (xxii.43),

I doe attach thee as a fellon heere,

a line which reappears nine lines later (xxii.52), and corresponds to the line of Q2:

And doe attach thee as a fellon heere.

Several lines of Q1 anticipate by scenes and even by acts the corresponding lines of Q2, but are not repeated. Romeo's line (vii.25):

Good morrow to my Ghostly Confessor,

was substantially spoken by Juliet (2.6.21), three scenes later,

Good euen to my ghostly confessor,

on her marriage day. Apart from its value as evidence of a reporter's activity, it proves the existence of this scene of Q2 at a time when the copy for the first quarto was being prepared, and suggests that we have in this scene as in the threnody at the end of scene xviii in Q1, a portion of an older play on the same story. Another interesting piece of joinery is to be found in Q1 (ix.5-6) Juliet says (Q2, 2.5.4-6).

           loues heraulds should be thoughts,
Which ten times faster glides then the Suns beames,
Driuing backe shadowes ouer lowring hills.

In Q1 this (ix.4-6) runs,

           Loues heralds should be thoughts,
And runne more swift, than hastie powder fierd,
Doth hurrie from the fearfull Cannons mouth.

This simile is rather grotesque—comparison of the speed of thought to the rapidity of the explosion when powder is fired from a cannon is incongruously inapposite. This figure appears later (5.1.64-5) when Romeo insists that the apothecary shall sell him a dram of poison—that will kill,

As violently, as hastie powder fierd
Doth hurry from the fatall Canons wombe.

This appears in Q1 (xx.44-5) thus,

> As suddenly as powder being fierd
> From forth a Cannons mouth.

Very noticeable is that the anticipatory interpolation in the ninth scene of Q1 is far nearer to the text of Q2 than what is kept in the twentieth scene which corresponds to Shakespeare's Act V, sc.i. Of equal significance is the transfer backwards of Capulet's bed-time message, i.e., 3.4.6-7 to v.100-102, and of the nurse's request for 'aqua-vitae' from 3.2.88 to ix.10-11. Two other such 'antici-pations' are 5.3.212, xii.20; and 4.5.140, xv.167.

Transposition of lines from the second quarto to a later scene of Q1 is not frequent except in a few phrases, Benvolio's line (Q2,1.1.111) describing part of the brawl between the rival partisans,

> While we were enterchanging thrusts and blowes,

is found in Q1,xi.116 as portion of Benvolio's account of the duel between Tybalt and Mercutio. Omitted in the first scene of Q1, its presence in the eleventh scene proves that it was spoken on the stage, and suggests that this cut was made by the pirate.

Henry V Q1 and Henry V Fo.

Much disorder exists in the conversation between Bardolph and Nym before the entrance of Pistol at the beginning of the second act, but this is due not to anticipation but to defect of memory. Some examples of anticipating the folio text do, however, occur. Fluellen in the tenth scene of Q1 (ll.79-80) remarks to Gower after Pistol has paid him a visit to help his fellow-rogue Bardolph,

> But when time shall serue, I shall tell him a
> litle of my desires.

In the last scene but one of the play before Pistol receives his long over-due cudgelling, Fluellen tells (5.1.11-13) his friends that he will wear his leek,

> in my Cap till I see him once againe, and then I will
> tell him a little piece of my desires.

Q1 has this passage (xx.11-12) a little abbreviated:

> But if I can see him, I shall tell him, a litle
> of my desires.

Another example not so good, is to be found in 1.2.213-4, i.134-5, 140-1; and perhaps 4.1.63-4, xi.61-2 though this probably involves some adaptation.

MERRY WIVES Q1 and MERRY WIVES Fo.

So much confusion exists in this very short bad quarto that no good purpose will be served by repeating what Dr. W. W. Greg has already done so well.

HAMLET Q1 and HAMLET Q2

On being compared with Q2, *Hamlet Q1* exhibits changes in the order of certain episodes. Hamlet's third soliloquy, beginning 'To be or not to be,' and his subsequent interview with Ophelia are found earlier in Q1, viz., in the sixth scene, and it thus precedes what in Q2 is his second soliloquy. In Q2 it follows 3.1.55; in Q1 it begins after the line corresponding to 2.2.169 in Q2, or more than five hundred lines earlier. Again that part of Hamlet's conversation with the courtier-spies in which he compares them to a sponge, i.e., Q2, 4.2.12-23, is in Q1 a tag to his previous conversation, following his question, 'wil you play vpon this pipe' (Q2, 3.2.334-5); it forms part of the ninth scene instead of the eleventh. These two long pieces of 'anticipation' differ essentially from those examples discussed above in that they point to a difference in staging Q1. For the change made in the position of the first episode in Q1 we have the full authority of Q2.

After Ophelia has informed her father of Hamlet's odd behaviour, Polonius says (2.1.101) to her,

Come, goe with mee, I will goe seeke the King,

continues moralising for a minute more, repeats himself 'Come, goe we to the King' (2.1.117) and ends with a peremptory 'Come,' which is followed by *Exeunt*. In the next scene Claudius gives his instructions to Rosencrantz and Guildenstern, and at line 39 they leave the stage. The stage direction, *Exeunt Ros. and Guyld.*, is followed immediately by *Enter Polonius*—without Ophelia—who announces the return of the ambassadors from Norway. In Q1 Corambis says to 'Ofelia,' much as does Polonius in Q2, 'Lets to the King,' and when the spies depart the entry is, 'Enter Corambis and Ofelia.' After the departure of the ambassadors, Corambis relates much as does Polonius in Q2 the story told him by his daughter, reads Hamlet's doggerel verses, suggests thwarted love as the origin of the hero's madness, and outlines to the King and Queen his plan of using Ophelia as a decoy. Hamlet enters, 'poring vppon a booke,' speaks a travesty of the soliloquy, and has his interview with Ophelia, King and father being hidden behind the arras. Subsequent staging of the next scene found in Q1 must have been difficult. Hamlet leaves the stage, Ophelia laments her lover's madness and makes her exit, her father and Claudius enter and discuss what they have seen, the king retires, and Hamlet re-enters and begins to banter Corambis—enough and to spare of exits and entrances, of opening and shutting of doors for eleven lines of text. Shakespeare has been careless in plotting this portion of his tragedy; he does not explain Ophelia's absence, and delays her entry for more than twenty minutes if the play ran its full course.

(i) Outside of these episodes *Hamlet Q1* has a number of identical lines of which the second or the third corresponds in scene and context to a folio line. Corambis sends his son this message (v.3) by Montano,

> And bid him ply his learning, Montano.

This is repeated (v.30) with a slight variation:

> And bid him ply his Musicke,

a line found substantially (2.1.73) in Q2,

> And let him ply his musique.

(ii) Another piece of anticipation occurs (xi.4-6) at the beginning of the scene between Hamlet and his mother:

> *Ham.* Mother, mother, O are you here?
> How i'st with you mother?
> *Queene.* How i'st with you?

In a modified form this recurs (xi.78-9) in Q1 later in the same scene:

> *Ham.* How i'st with you Lady?
> *Queene.* Nay, how i'st with you.

This second example is found in Q2 in the scene with his mother.

After the visitation of the ghost Hamlet turns to his mother saying (3.4.115-6),

> *Ham.* How is it with you Lady?

She replies:

> *Queene.* Alas how i'st with you?

Q1 has this phrase elsewhere.

> *Rosen.* Now my lord, how i'st with you?   ix.184
> *King.* How i'st with you sweete Ofelia?   xiii.26

(iii) Anticipation occurs in the sixteenth scene in which Hamlet speaks the following lines at intervals:

> I prithee tell me Horatio.   xvi.54
> I prethee tell mee one thing (to Clowne).   xvi.75
> Horatio, I prethee tell me one thing.   xvi.112-3

The third line (5.1.184) is in Q2,

> Prethee Horatio tell me one thing.

Other examples are 1.2.174, ii.85,91; 1.5.106, iv.144-5, 2.2.554-5, vii.224-5; 5.1.58, xvi.18,31; 5.1.55-6, xiii.93-4, xvi.29-30. Hamlet's 'Why I want preferment' (vii.55), spoken at his first interview with the two spies, echoes 'Sir I lacke advancement' spoken by him at his second interview with them; his first line (ii.33) in Q1

> My lord, ti's not the sable sute I weare,

is perhaps an anticipation of 'for Ile haue a sute of sables' in Q2, 3.2.121-2. Transposition of passages occur in Hamlet Q1 as in the other bad quartos; the most notable is of two lines of the ghost's speech (1.5.49-50) which are missing in the version of Q1, but reappear (xi.34-5) in the scene between Hamlet and his mother as part of Hamlet's speech:

> Whose heart went hand in hand euen with that vow,
> He made to you in marriage.

Some phrases of no special importance are transposed.

Much dislocation of the first and the third of Hamlet's soliloquies is apparent in Q1; this would be impossible in any report made by shorthand or longhand. His first soliloquy (1.2.129-159):

> O that this too too sallied flesh would melt etc.,

runs to 31 lines in Q2, and is reduced to 21 lines in Q1. Two lines are interpolated and a dozen omitted; the order in Q1 of the lines present in Q2 is ll.129,151,146 (part), 153-6,149,146 (part), 143-4,

156-8,147-9,158,159. Probably the omission of ll.131-7 and ll.139-142 represents cuts made by the play-adapter, but nearly two-thirds of the original are retained in hopeless confusion. His third soliloquy (the second in Q1) 'To be or not to be' etc. (3.1.56-90) is in even worse state. Two cuts (3.1.57-64,84-88) account for thirteen lines, seven lines are interpolated in place of an equal number of Shakespeare's, and fifteen much tattered lines of the original remain in the following disorder, ll.56,65-6,77,78,70,69, 77,75,76,78,80-3,89-90.

Precisely the same type of disarrangement occurs in portion of the scene between Suffolk and the pirates in *Contention,* in the earlier part of the brisk dialogue between Lady Elizabeth Gray and the three royal brothers in the tenth scene of *True Tragedy,* in the opening exchanges between Bardolph and Nym at the beginning of the second act of *Henry V Q1,* and throughout much of *Merry Wives Q1.*

I have shown that each bad quarto contains some lines each of which anticipates the occurrence of the corresponding line in the parallel text; usually this line recurs in the surreptitious text. What is the explanation of a phenomenon common to these six plays and present in *Orlando Furioso Q1?* Reports made by stenographers or note-takers in longhand could not possibly account for the presence in the first scene of a line or passage not spoken on the stage before the sixth scene. Elizabethan shorthand, in the opinion of a competent professional shorthand writer and scholar such as the late Professor Sir Ernest Scott, was totally unequal to the literal reproduction of a speech, to say nothing of a whole play.

Further, no contemporary makes any claim prior to 1612, or nine years later than the date of *Hamlet Q1,* that a play could be reported accurately by means of stenography. The passage so frequently quoted from the prologue spoken upon the revival at the Cockpit—and certainly not before 1617—of Heywood's play. *If you know not me, you know no Bodie Part 1* (printed 1605) does not, in my opinion, warrant the inference many writers have drawn. Heywood declares:

> Some by Stenography drew
> The plot: put it in print: (scarce one word trew).

x

He expressly states that the plot, not the play, was taken down in shorthand. He prefixed to the prologue the following comment: 'The Author taxeth the most corrupted copy now imprinted, which was published without his consent.' Part 1 of this play is by far Heywood's shortest, being over a thousand lines shorter than his average play; actually it is about as long as *Orlando Furioso Q1, A Shrew* or Peele's *Battle of Alcazar*, which it resembles in having many short and unmetrical lines. It is a hodge-podge of prose and verse with many rhyming couplets intermixed, and contains three dumb-shows. Probably a student of 'Characterie,' a regular theatre-goer, one who knew the names and parts of the various actors, would be equal to the task of making such a plot or skeleton outline of the play as that of *1 Tamar Cam;* he could insert the appropriate stage directions, exits and entrances, and describe the three dumb shows. One stage direction, *Exeunt omnes praeter Gage & const.* suggests that the writer knew a little more Latin than the rank and file of play-thieves.

Dr. Greg's investigations have made it almost certain that such repetitions, anticipations and recollections as are found in *Orlando Furioso Q1* and *Merry Wives Q1* may be put down to the account of actors and reporters who had a working knowledge of these plays as a whole; and a similar explanation is applicable to the similar phenomena so plentiful in the bad quartos.

Chapter XIX

PLAY-REPORTING AND REPORTERS

M ANY of the better preserved passages of these texts offer
good examples of the various types of error that a teacher
would expect to find in the work of his pupils, if he asked them
to write out from memory a long narrative poem or scene of a
play learnt by heart some months previously, and had given them
no opportunity of refreshing their recollections. Lines would be
omitted or misplaced, verse would be mislined or wanting a foot
or two, half-lines would abound, the sense would suffer, mis-
understood words would be mis-spelt or replaced by synonyms, and
some anticipations and recollections would be noticeable. If we
assume that two or more actors agreed to compile a play-book
from months-old memories of their own parts and those of others,
such misplacement of lines, passages and even scenes would be
almost inevitable.

Current criticism favours one actor as the 'only begetter' of
each bad quarto. There seems no good reason why any actor who
had no part in a scene should be excluded from the stage during its
rehearsal. Furthermore, anyone who possessed a quick and retentive memory and who had rehearsed and played in a scene a dozen
times, might learn without much effort all the parts played by the
other actors in this scene. Chetwood says of Richard Wilks, the
successor of Betterton,

that Wilks was not only perfect in every part he acted but in those
that were concerned with him in every scene—and the author of
the Laureat assures us, that he has known Wilks lay a wager and
win it, that he would repeat the part of Truewit in the *Silent
Woman,* which consists of 30 lengths, without misplacing a single
word.[1]

Certainly no such paragon as Wilks provided the copy for any of
the bad quartos, but in *True Tragedy* the two best actors have made
manifest their influence both in the comparative excellence of their
own parts and in the improved work of their fellows in all the

1. Genest, *History of the Drama and Stage in England,* Vol. II, p. 147. N.B.—A 'length'
was about 40 lines.

scenes in which the two took part. Given time and opportunity, two competent actors, especially if each doubled parts, might, if they made it their business to get some knowledge of the whole play and had some stage-craft, prepare the copy of such plays as *Romeo and Juliet Q1* and *True Tragedy*. From the 'plot,' usually hung on the stage for the prompter's use during rehearsals and public performances, they might obtain, as occasion offered, sufficient knowledge of the outline of scenes in which they had no parts. Important members of the company such as the sharers would not, in their own interest, stoop to piracy, but two or more of the hired men might be ready to earn a few shillings if there was a market for their stolen goods.

Most modern critics accept, with variations and additions, Dr. Greg's suggestion that the actor who played the part of the Host was responsible for the very short text—mainly prose—of *Merry Wives Q1*. He appears in eight of the twenty-three folio scenes and eight of the eighteen scenes of Q1, and was on the stage when 366 of the 2,634 folio lines or 285 of the 1,419 quarto lines were spoken. Thus the Host retained rather well eighty per cent. of the lines spoken when he was on the boards, whilst the other characters were unable to remember more than a half of theirs. These figures may be somewhat misleading, because Q1 is obviously a very corrupt abridgment of some acting version made from the folio text, and cuts will probably account for some of the loss in the Host's eight quarto scenes. Moreover we must keep in mind the vital fact that the Host was *not* on the stage while the greater portion, four-fifths, of the extant Q1 was being enacted. How did he get his copy for this remaining four-fifths, representing 1,134 lines of Q1, and comprising ten scenes in which he had no part and those portions of the other eight scenes spoken when he was absent from the stage? His reporting of the scenes in which he had played varies in quality, and is at its worst in the fifteenth and sixteenth scenes which correspond respectively to scenes five and six of the fourth act of Shakespeare's play. Some of the first scene after the entry of Falstaff and his rascally retinue, and much of the third scene after the Host leaves the stage, are almost as well preserved as those in which he speaks, and this estimate is, with some reservations, true of the main portions retained of

Falstaff's interviews with Mistress Quickly and the disguised Ford. Allowance must be made for losses of the folio text due to official and unofficial cuts. If the Host was the sole pirate, he must have attended assiduously all rehearsals of the full acting version or whatever reduced version was the parent of Q1; otherwise he must have had help from one or two other actors.

Contention disputes with *Hamlet Q1* the demerit of being the most corrupt of the bad quartos written mainly in verse. In his book, *Henry VI and Richard III*, Professor Alexander suggests (p. 75) that 'the Quarto text' of *Contention* 'is very largely due to the amicable collaboration of these opposites,' i.e., of Suffolk and Warwick. Again he asserts (p. 89) that in *True Tragedy* the impress of Warwick or Clifford can again be distinguished amid the confusion whenever each makes his entry.

Reference to my tables setting out the state of the text of each bad Quarto in relation to the corresponding parallel text of Shakespeare's play shows that *Contention* preserves 1,232 of 2,641 lines of verse in *2 Henry VI* or less than a half. Of those retained only 484 consist of lines which occur verbatim in the folio text or of lines differing from those of this text by one word only in a line. These two kinds of line in the bad quarto I propose to term lines identical with those of the parallel text corresponding in context and sense; in reality only twelve per cent. of the lines of verse in *Contention* are the same as the corresponding lines of *2 Henry VI*. Over half of these identical lines occur in the first, tenth, twenty-second and twenty-third scenes, which together average less than sixty per cent. of lines identical with those of corresponding scenes in *2 Henry VI;* not one of the remaining nineteen scenes of *Contention* has even half of its verse verbatim.

Suffolk and Warwick remember the best of a forgetful crew. Professor Alexander quotes (pp. 76-81) the parting between Suffolk and Margaret as 'a favourable example' of his work as a reporter; in the tenth scene Suffolk speaks 80 lines common to the two texts of which 61 are identical with the corresponding lines of *2 Henry VI*. He does even better in the first scene, 17 of his 20 lines being identical in both versions. In each of his six other scenes he is much less successful and speaks in them only 31 identical lines of 107 common to the two texts. If he helped to report the play, he was on the stage when the portion of the acting version made from 1,466 lines of Shakespeare's play was being represented; his own share of the verse was 284 lines. His report would run to 970 lines of which Suffolk spoke 207 lines, or only 18 lines more than should be spoken proportionately; 109 of his lines, or 53 per cent., are identical with folio lines. Suffolk's part represents a smaller percentage of his folio part than do Elinor's and Warwick's parts in *Contention* of their respective folio parts. Proportionally Cade keeps as much as Suffolk, Henry and Humphrey a little less. Suffolk's report of his own folio part retains identically only 53 per cent. of the lines common to the two texts, and his report of the speeches made by the other actors in the same scenes would certainly be much inferior to this.

Though the facts do not suggest that the text of *Contention* owes much to Warwick, his own part is, upon the whole, reported well enough to make him possible as a reporter of the play. He is a character of secondary importance, ranking well below Humphrey, Suffolk, York, Henry, Margaret and Cade. He appears in six quarto scenes, though he is provided with entries in eight, and speaks 107 lines of which 96 are derived from the folio text; of these 61, or 64 per cent., are identical with lines in *2 Henry VI*. He has little to do and not much to say in the first half of the play, and alternates muddle in the order and interpolation with patches of the original. In the all-important sixth scene he is the only character with a firm grip of the material facts; he speaks 19 lines, 5 being identical with those of the folio, but spoils his report by interpolating a ten-line speech of nonsense. After the murder of Humphrey he assumes the leadership of the party resolved on the overthrow of Suffolk and during this portion of the play his speeches in *Contention* deserve Professor Alexander's praise. Probably he took the part of Cade, but he was not, as in *2 Henry VI,* present at the death of Cardinal Beaufort.

Undoubtedly the parts of Suffolk and Warwick are the best reported of *Contention;* together they retain identically 58 per cent. of their lines common to the two texts. This is a very low proportion, and no surprise should be felt that such reporters failed to record more than a third of their fellow actors' parts identically. That *Contention* represents a report of an acting version of *2 Henry VI* is, in my opinion, demonstrably true—that Warwick and/or Suffolk were the reporters must remain a probable guess. Perhaps, as Professor Alexander suggests, *Contention* 'is occasionally based on transcription.' I accept his explanation. My only suggestion is that after Suffolk has concluded his four-line speech (1.1.39-42) of which the second line is,

Heere are the Articles of contracted peace,

he formally presents to the Protector, Duke Humphrey, an elaborately engrossed document of state from which the latter reads the terms of the marriage treaty. When Pembroke's men went on their disastrous tour with a copy of the acting version, they would probably be provided with a written copy of these articles, and perhaps a copy of the questions put to the spirit and the replies.

My table for *3 Henry VI* and *True Tragedy* shows that *3 Henry VI* contains 2,902 lines, of which *True Tragedy* has 1,896. If the full play was acted, 1,496 folio lines would be spoken while Warwick and Clifford were on the stage—this is reduced in *True Tragedy* by official and unofficial abridgment to 1,109 lines or 74 per cent. of the original. Consequently, 1,406 lines of *3 Henry VI* would be spoken when neither of these characters was present; of these *True Tragedy* retains 787 or not quite 56 per cent. Such a large difference as 17 per cent. in the proportions retained in *True Tragedy* of two arbitrarily chosen and approximately equal divisions of the folio play cannot depend on some difference in the amount of official abridgment. Warwick and Clifford reported their own parts exceedingly well, and were able from memory to report satisfactorily the parts of those actors who had played in various scenes with them. This lower percentage of 56 per cent. measures the ability of these two reporters to record the speeches of their fellow-actors for that part of the play in which neither of them took part, or represents the reporting efforts of actors other than these two.

Even better evidence may be drawn from the figures given above. Of the 1,496 lines of *3 Henry VI* spoken while Warwick or Clifford was on the stage, they speak 575 of which 494 or 86 per cent. are found in *True Tragedy;* there remain 921 folio lines spoken by characters other than these two actors, and of these the derived play keeps 615 or not quite 67 per cent. Once again the large difference between the two results cannot arise from official abridgment, but depends rather on the fact that an actor will always remember his own part better than those of the actors who played in the same scene with him.

Another method of illustrating the difference between the reports of the parts taken by these actors and those of the parts of the others is well worth discussion. Reference to the table for this pair of parallel texts shows, as said above, that *True Tragedy* has 1,896 lines in common with *3 Henry VI*. This total includes 854 lines literally the same in each text and 389 lines that differ from those of the folio version by not more than one word in each line. These two groups, numbering in all 1,243 lines, form what I have termed 'identical' lines. Warwick and Clifford between them have 494 lines common to their parts in both plays; of these 433 or nearly 88 per cent. are substantially identical with the corresponding folio lines; consequently the remaining 1,402 common to the two parallel texts must contain 810 identical lines or 58 per cent. of the total. Such a great superiority as thirty per cent. in favour of the parts of Clifford and Warwick suggests that if the actors of these parts reported this play, they reported much more of their own parts and this in a better state of preservation than the parts of their fellow actors.

In nine scenes and parts of scenes up to the end of the fourth act, Edward, Richard, Clarence, Henry and Margaret play the principal parts and Clifford and Warwick are absent; these nine scenes contain only 40 per cent. of the lines common to the two texts substantially identical with folio lines. Yet the same five characters play the principal parts in the final three scenes of the *True Tragedy,* and the percentage of the lines common to the two texts which are identical rises to 69 per cent. Of this anomalous fact I can find no explanation; *True Tragedy* is the one bad quarto which has the last act retained almost as well as the first.

Romeo and Juliet Q1 is an abridgment made by actors or reporters from an acting version of Q2, but evidence is wanting to justify the selection of any actor of an important part as reporter in preference to the actor of any other. Q2 has 2,585 lines of verse of which Q1 keeps 1,752 in some form or other—this percentage of 67·7 per cent. is the highest in the bad quartos; on the other hand the proportion of the verse-lines substantially identical in the two quartos is a little lower than in *True Tragedy*. Of the important characters Mercutio keeps the highest percentage of the verse-lines written for him by Shakespeare, and also the largest proportion of those retained substantially identical with the corresponding lines of Q2; then follow in order Romeo, Benvolio, Capulet and Friar Laurence. Each of these characters except Capulet has certain disabilities that disqualify him for the thievish office of reporter. Mercutio and Benvolio disappear after the first scene of the third act, and there are no new parts for them to double and thus keep them on the stage. Romeo is absent from the stage during half the third and all the fourth act, and Friar Laurence does not appear before the seventh scene. Perhaps these facts explain why certain critics favour the actor who played the part of Capulet as a likely reporter.

As is usual in the bad quartos, the boys who played the feminine characters retain less of their parts than the adult actors, and their lines in Q1 are more corrupt. Despite her excellent start in the third scene the nurse fails badly afterwards and retains less of her part than any other prominent character except Juliet. I must reject the actor of the nurse's part—man or boy—as a possible reporter, because an actor who knew his own part so badly must blunder much more if he tried to recollect the parts of others.

Henry V Q1 is admitted by nearly all critics to be a reported text, and differs from the five other bad quartos in having nothing in it but Shakespeare's text, largely perverted. Exeter, Fluellen and Pistol, in the order named, retain far higher percentages of the parts written for them in the folio than any of the other important characters do of theirs, but the abridgment, official and unofficial, is very heavy and apparently capricious. No reliable evidence is available to help us in deciding which of the actors played the reporter.

Hamlet Q1 keeps in some form 1,161 of the 2,715 verse-lines present in the received text; of the verse thus retained 591 lines are substantially identical with the corresponding lines of *Hamlet Q2*. While most critics agree that the first quartos of *Romeo and Juliet,*

Henry V and *Merry Wives* are reported texts, they differ widely on the interrelations of the first two quartos of *Hamlet*. Except for the far greater measure of corruption, which has changed the order in the surreptitious play of certain episodes, the relation of *Hamlet Q1* to *Hamlet Q2* does not, in my opinion, differ in any essential feature from that of the first quarto of *Romeo and Juliet* to the second quarto or from that of *True Tragedy* to *3 Henry VI*. Q1 bears every mark of being a reported text and differs from Q2 very much as *Orlando Furioso Q1* from the Dulwich MS. Who was the reporter? Sir E. K. Chambers[2] has hinted that:

the reporter might have been the Queen, as a boy, in the old play, and helped himself out with memories of that.

Women's parts in all the bad quartos are more drastically abridged, and the remainder worse reported than the parts of the men actors; the queen is not present in the best reported scenes of the first act, and does not speak a dozen lines of her part accurately. Most of her speeches are bungled paraphrases of Shakespeare's lines or are very poor specimens of interpolated verse. She appears in ten scenes of Q2 and has 136 lines provided for her by Shakespeare; no less than 70 of these are found in the scene with her son or in her description of Ophelia's death. Half of the verse in these two scenes of Q1 consists of interpolation, and only 16 lines are identical with lines of Q2. It is most improbable, in my opinion, that such an incompetent bungler could have reported the ghost scenes.

Professor Wilson's theory of the double revision of *Hamlet Q1* is discussed elsewhere. He thinks that the copy for the printer came from an actor who had played eight minor parts, taking in succession the parts of Marcellus, Voltimand, Reynaldo or Montano, a Player, a captain, the second grave-digger, a priest and an English ambassador. This multiplicity of parts is possible. The 'Plot' of *1 Tamar Cam* (acted 1602) shows that Dick Juby and Thos. Marbeck each took seven parts; in fact 10 of 30 named actors had at least two parts, while 12 of 26 actors named in the cast of *Battle of Alcazar* (acted 1598?) had from two to four parts. Marcellus must have changed his costume with almost incredible speed. He speaks the last two lines of the first scene as

2. *William Shakespeare*, Vol. i, p. 421.

a sentinel, and in less than thirty seconds must make his exit, doff his attire and appear in the royal procession dressed as a Danish ambassador. This difficulty recurs between the fourth and fifth scene when Marcellus, the sentinel, must instantly convert himself into Montano, a lord's servant dressed for travelling. Moreover, this many-parted pirate seems to have had a memory as variable as his parts. If he was the player who reported Hamlet's advice to the players, how came he to forget entirely the first and second speeches in the play before the king and fill the gap with inter-polations including a snippet from *Spanish Tragedy?* Again, those portions of the play should be most poorly reported which the pirate did not speak himself or hear others speak. Actually the larger portion of Hamlet's second soliloquy in Q1, Ophelia's songs and her rambling chatter in the mad scene, and the dialogue between Hamlet and the First Grave-Digger after his assistant had left the stage to fetch his master's beer, are as well reported as most of the scenes in which this stage Proteus played his parts.

Proof that the text of any bad quarto represents a report made by one, two or more actors from a stage version of Shakespeare's parallel text may be adequate or even almost complete, and yet this evidence may be insufficient to furnish more than a presumption upon such questions as who the reporter or reporters were, and, if they were actors in Shakespeare's play, what parts they played. Professor Alexander is justified, I think, in selecting the actors who played the parts of Clifford and Warwick as the reporters of *True Tragedy.* Dr. Greg has made a case, not quite so strong, in favour of the actor who played the Host in *Merry Wives Q1.* In the other bad quartos critics are much to seek, and at best must continue 'to hazard a wide solution' of the insolvable.

All the conditions precedent to the writing, buying, rehearsing, production and representation of plays in Elizabethan times did not make for even moderate accuracy of actors in the public repetition of their parts. Daily change of programme, the short acting life of the average play, the haphazard method of arranging the weekly acting list, and the uncertain supply of new and attractive dramas combined to impose a heavy burden of rehearsals upon the managers and players of each company. Each fortnight or three weeks the Admiral's men seem to have produced a new piece, and competition would compel the Chamberlain's men to provide similar novelties in equal abundance. Plays were frequently delivered by their authors to the company in two, three or more instalments. When terms were being made, an outline of the complete plot and a number of scenes amounting to about two acts were read to representatives of the company, and, if they were approved by them, a progress payment was made, and a date fixed for the delivery of the remainder of the play. With two acts in hand and a knowledge of the plot the company would be enabled to estimate the number of the cast required and to allot their parts to the actors best capable of playing them; the stage manager would probably make necessary cuts, and on receipt of the third act the company's scribe might prepare and distribute parts to the actors. Not much time elapsed after the author's manuscript had been delivered before the play was performed. Suitable costumes and the simple properties were bought a week to a month after the final payment had been made to the dramatist, and the first performance was given a few days later; for many plays costumes and properties already used in other plays would perhaps, after being remodelled, be available. I think it probable that the parts for the early acts were customarily in the actors' hands before the play was completed. Sir Henry Herbert's requirement that 'the players ought not to study their parts till I have allowed of the booke' was a disciplinary measure and belongs to the year 1633. Twenty years before, Daborne's letter (25/6/1613) to Henslowe, referring to his then unfinished tragedy *Machiavel and the Devil,* states that he has 'altered one other Scean in the third act which they have now in parts.' These three acts had been delivered to the company before 18 May, and the management, while waiting more than five weeks for the rest, had put the three acts into parts for the players; the playwright's changes in the third act would hinder rather than help them.

Dilatory dramatists such as Daborne made efficient working of a theatre difficult. His play was due for delivery on 31 May, and should have been staged in June. It was not completed on 25 June, and consequently the season's programme would be thrown into confusion. Probably the custom of giving the actors their parts for study as successive portions of the manuscript came from the author was an old one, and helps to an explanation of the fact, that the earlier acts of each bad quarto are closer to Shakespeare's text than the later acts. Nashe in *Summer's Last Will and Testament* (ll.1818-20) says:

But you will ne're haue any ward-robe wit while you liue. I pray you holde the booke well, we be not *non plus* in the latter end of the play.[3]

Evidently many actors made heavy demands on the prompter in the last acts. This early acknowledgment of the inferiority displayed by the actors in memorizing 'the latter end of the play' is confirmed by a glance at the results for each act given in the table for the parallel texts. Progressive falling-off from accuracy as the play proceeded is well marked in *Romeo and Juliet Q1, Henry V Q1* and the more corrupt *Hamlet Q1*. *True Tragedy* also exhibits a steady decline in the third and fourth acts, but improves considerably in the fifth act; the last two acts of *Merry Wives Q1* are the worst. *Contention* seems rather than is an exception. In Acts I-III one fifth of the verse is not Shakespeare's, a proportion that is doubled in the last two acts; in other words the loss of Shakespeare's text due to failure of memory was doubled proportionally in the fourth and fifth acts. Dr. Greg, writing of the parallel versions of Orlando's part, notes a gradual increase in the degeneration of the quarto text.[4]

3. *Works*, edited by R. B. McKerrow, Vol. iii, p. 290.
4. *Two Elizabethan Abridgments*, p. 291.

Chapter XX

INTER-PLAY BORROWINGS

The Pembroke Group of Plays

IN my tables setting out for each bad quarto the distribution of lines relatively to the corresponding parallel text is a column giving for each scene the number of non-Shakespearean lines. This heading is not strictly correct because the totals for each play except *Henry V Q1* contain some lines borrowed or echoed from other plays of Shakespeare. Genuine non-Shakespearean lines may be subdivided into two groups, one, consisting of lines borrowed from extant plays, and the second and larger, of lines manufactured by actors or pirates or, as some maintain, remnants of the old plays revised by the poet. Some lines of this second group may be taken from lost plays. This petty larceny is a well-marked characteristic of many corrupt plays, though some of our early dramas with sound texts contain such unacknowledged borrowings. Thus the verse of both *Locrine* and *Selimus* seems above suspicion except for lines and passages common to both; but as nothing is known of their date, authorship or stage history, critics like doctors disagree. Did the author of *Selimus* borrow from *Locrine* or vice versa? Or did one man write both plays and consciously or unconsciously repeat himself?

Modern research has shown that our early literary men, including dramatists such as Lyly, Lodge, Greene, Nashe, Jonson, etc., were unashamed and blushless plagiarists. The 'sugared' sonnets were too often stolen sweets. Sidney Lee has proved that of one hundred sonnets in Watson's *Passionate Century of Love* over a third were unavowed translations from the Italian. Sidney stole from Ronsard, Desportes and other French poets. Drayton, like Watson, a writer for the public stage, while declaring

My muse is rightly of the English strain,

affirms his originality in a line,

I am no pick-purse of another's wit,

which is stolen from Sidney. Where all are thieves, theft is no disgrace. Quotations from *Troublesome Raigne* of lines present in *2 Henry VI* and *3 Henry VI* suggest that the young Shakespeare fell, perhaps unconsciously, into the habit of many early Elizabethan authors, who seem to have treated whatever was in print, old or new, as a common upon which all writers might nibble at will.

I shall now investigate the inter-play borrowings common to a group of plays in which *Contention, True Tragedy* and *Edward II* are conspicuous, and shall offer what seems to me the most probable explanation of the various problems arising from these borrowings. Any explanation is liable, however, to valid objections, the result of our want of any exact knowledge concerning such matters as stage customs, the personnel of the various companies then in existence, the plays belonging to each company, the exact chronological order in which plays were written, staged and printed, their authorship, etc. Below is a list of lines and passages common to *Contention* and the plays named; wherever it is necessary the corresponding lines or passages of *2 Henry VI*, if such exist, are cited. Then follow similar lists for *True Tragedy* and *Edward II*. This group of plays and their inter-relations will be discussed in some detail.

References are to the Cambridge edition (1863-66) of *Contention* and *True Tragedy,* to Booth's facsimile text of the first folio for the texts of *2 Henry VI, 3 Henry VI* and *Titus Andronicus* (the verse-lining is that of the Cambridge edition named), to Professor Tucker Brooke's edition of Marlowe's works for *Edward II* and *Massacre at Paris,* and his edition of *The Shakespeare Apocrypha* for *Arden of Feversham,* to Professor Boas's edition of Kyd's works for *Spanish Tragedy* and *Soliman and Perseda,* to the Malone Society's reprints of *Battle of Alcazar* and *Edward I,* to the text of *A Shrew* printed by the Old Shakespeare Society and to W. Keller's text of *Thomas of Woodstock.* Acts, scenes and lines are given in English digits, e.g., 4.1.61 means fourth act, first scene, line sixty-one, whilst for plays not divided into acts, the number of the scene is given in Roman digits, thus, vi.91, means sixth scene, line ninety-one. E2. 1039 means *Edward II,* line 1,039.

INTER-PLAY BORROWINGS

I 2 HENRY VI and CONTENTION

(a) EDWARD II

(i) Farewell base stooping to the lordly peeres,
My knee shall bowe to none but to the king.   E2. 18-19
Suff.   No, rather let my head
Stoope to the blocke, then these knees bow to any,
Saue to the God of heauen, and to my King.   4.1.124-6
Suff. First let this necke stoupe to the axes edge,
Before this knee do bow to any,
Saue to the God of heauen and to my King.   xii.64-6

(ii) Yet dare you braue the king vnto his face.   E2. 116
Marg. But beard and braue him proudly to his face. xxi.71

(iii) And leuie armes against your lawfull king.   E2. 1516
King. To leauy Armes against his lawful King.   xxii.8

(iv) Liue where thou wilt, ile send thee gould enough,
And long thou shalt not stay.   E2. 409-10
Marg. For wheresoere thou art in this worlds Globe,
Ile haue an Iris that shall finde thee out.   3.2.406-7
Marg. Or liue where thou wilt within this worldes globe,
Ile haue an Irish that shall finde thee out,
And long thou shalt not staie.   x.172-4

(v) The wilde Oneyle, with swarmes of Irish Kernes,
Liues vncontroulde within the English pale.   E2. 966-7
Mess. The wilde Onele my Lords, is vp in Armes,
With troupes of Irish Kernes that vncontrold,
Doth plant themselues within the English pale.   ix.133-5

(vi) I humblie thanke your maiestie.   E2. 1049
Somer. I humbly thanke your Royall Maiestie.   1.3.209
Somer. I humbly thanke your royall Maiestie.   iii.164

(vii) As though your highnes were a schoole boy still,
And must be awde and gouernd like a child.   E2. 1336-7
Marg. I see no reason, why a King of yeeres
Should be to be protected like a Child.   2.3.28-9
Marg. But still must be protected like a childe,
And gouerned by that ambitious Duke.   iii.49-50

(viii)   My lord, I take my leaue,
To make my preparation for Fraunce.   E2. 1396-7
Somer. And take my leaue to poste with speed to France
iii.165

(ix) Long liue king Edward, Englands lawful lord.   E2. 1460
   War. Long liue our Soueraigne Richard, Englands King.
                                    2.2.63
   War. Long liue Richard Englands royall King.   vi.49
   Cliff. Long liue King Henry, Englands lawfull King. xix.9

(x) Did you regard the honor of your name.   E2. 1323
   Marg. And nere regards the honour of his name.   iii.48

(xi) Long liue my soueraigne the noble Edward,
   In peace triumphant.   E2. 1339-40
   Iden. Long liue Henry in triumphant peace.   xxi.44

(xii) I arrest you of high treason here,
   Stand not on titles, but obay th'arrest.   E2. 1924-5
   Suff. I doe arrest thee of High Treason here.   3.1.97
   Suff. I do arrest thee on high treason here.
— — — — — — — — — — — — — — — — — — —
   King. Good vnkle obey to his arrest.   ix.65,68
   Suff. We do arrest thee on high treason here.   ix.39
   Somer. Proud Traitor, I arest thee on high treason. xxi.82

(xiii) O is he gone! is noble Edward gone.   E2. 1967
   Duch. Art thou gone to? all comfort goe with thee.   2.4.87
   Duch. Then is he gone, is noble Gloster gone,   viii.72

(xiv) He weares a lords reuenewe on his back.   E2. 704
   Marg. She beares a Dukes Reuenewes on her backe. 1.3.78

(xv) But hath your grace no other proofe then this?   E2. 2611
   Card. But haue you no greater proofes then these?   x.70

(xvi) Nay, to my death, for too long haue I liued.   E2. 2651
   Duch. Welcome is Banishment, welcome were my Death.
                                      2.3.14
   Duch. Euen to my death, for I have liued too long.   vii.11

(xvii) Sweete father heere, vnto thy murdered ghost,
   I offer vp this wicked traitors head.   E2. 2667-8
   Y. Cliff. Sweete father, to thy murthred ghoast I sweare.
                                      xxiii.48

(xviii) I, if words will serue, if not, I must.   E2. 289
   Edw. I Noble Father, if our words will serue.
   Rich. And if words will not, then our Weapons shal.
                                     5.1.139-40
   Edw. Yes noble father, if our words will serue.
   Rich. And if our words will not, our swords shall.
                                     xxii.13-14

Y

(b) The Massacre at Paris

    (i) For this I wake, when others think I sleepe.   M.P. 105
    York. Watch thou, and wake when others be asleepe.
                                        1.1.244
    York. Watch thou, and wake when others be a sleepe. i.156

    (ii) I humbly thank your royall Maiestie.   M.P. 277
    See *1 Edward II* (vi) under group for
    2 Henry VI.

    (iii) O fatall was this mariage to vs all.   M.P. 206
    Humph.
    O, Peeres of England .... Fatall this marriage.
                                         1.1.93-4
    Humph. Ah lords, fatall is this marriage.   i.79

    (iv) For he hath solemnely sworne thy death.   M.P. 783
    King. Lord Say, Iacke Cade hath sworne to
                           haue thy head.   4.4.19
    King. Lord Say, Iacke Cade hath solemnely
                           vowde to haue thy head.   xv.667

    (v) And he shall follow thy proud Chariot wheeles.   M.P. 991
    Humph. That erst did follow thy prowd Chariot-Wheeles.
                                         2.4.13
    Humph. That earst did follow thy proud Chariot wheeles.
                                         viii.9

(c) 3 Henry VI and True Tragedy

    (i) *King.* Welcome Queene Margaret to English Henries
                                    Court.   i.18
    Lewis. Welcome Queene Margaret to the Court of France.
                                      T.T. xi.1

    (ii) *Edw.*   George kneele downe.
    We here create thee Duke of Clarence, and girt
    thee with the sword.   T.T. viii.157-9
    King.   Lord Marques kneel down,
    We heere create thee the first Duke of Suffolke,
    And girt thee with the Sword.   2 HVI. i.58-60
    King.   Lord Marquesse kneele downe,
    We here create thee first Duke of Suffolke, &
    girt thee with the sword.   i.57-9

    (iii) *Cliff.* The common people swarme like summer flies.
                                        T.T. viii.72
    War. The common people by numbers swarme to vs.
                                        T.T. xiii.2

War. The common people by numbers swarme to vs.

3 HVI. 4.2.2

Card. The common people swarme about him straight. i.98

(iv) *War.* Shall for the Fault, make forfeit of his head.

3 HVI. 2.1.197

War. Shall for the offence make forfeit of his head.

T.T. iv.165

Duch. Shall for th'offence, make forfeit of his head. ii.22

(v) *Marg.* I humblie thanke your royall maiestie. T.T. xi.7

This line in *2 Henry VI*, 1.3.209 and iii.164.

(vi) *Rich.* I cannot rest,

Vntill the White Rose that I weare, be dy'de

Euen in the luke-warme blood of Henries heart.

3 HVI. 1.2.32-4

Rich. I cannot ioie till this white rose be dide,

Euen in the hart bloud of the house of Lancaster.

T.T. 4.52-3

York. But I am not your King, till I be Crown'd,

And that my Sword be stayn'd

With heart-blood of the House of Lancaster.

2 HVI. 2.2.64-6

York. But Lords I am not your King, vntill this

sword be sheathed euen in the hart blood of

the house of Lancaster. vi.50-2

(vii) *Marg.* As I bethinke me, you should not be King,

Till our King Henry had shooke hands with Death.

3 HVI. 1.4.101-2

Marg. As I bethinke me you should not be king,

Till our Henry had shooke hands with death. T.T. 3.135-6

Suff. If our King Henry had shooke hands with death,

Duke Humphrey then would looke to be our King. ix.117-8

(viii) *War.* That if King Lewis vouchsafe to furnish vs

With some few Bands of chosen Soldiours.

3 HVI. 3.3.203-4

War. That if King Lewes vouchsafe to furnish vs

With some few bands of chosen souldiers. T.T. xi.128-9

York. Well Madame sith your grace is so content,

Let me haue some bands of chosen soldiers. ix.153-4

(ix) *War.* Tell him from me, that he hath done me wrong,

And therefore Ile vn-Crowne him, er't be long.

3 HVI. 3.3.231-2

War. The same identically in   T.T. xi.142-3
Cade. Or otherwaies ile haue his Crowne tell
him, ere it be long.   xiii.123-4

(x) *Edw.* Oh Clifford, boy'strous Clifford, thou hast slaine
The flowre of Europe, for his Cheualrie.   3 HVI. 2.1.70-1
Cade. Oh villaine, thou hast slaine the floure
of Kent for chiualrie.   xx.27-8

(xi) *Son.* This man whom hand to hand I slew in fight,
May be possessed with some store of Crownes.
                     3 HVI. 2.5.56-7

Iden. Loe, I present your Grace a Traitors head,
The head of Cade, whom I in combat slew. 2 HVI. 5.1.66-7
Eyden. I here present the traitorous head of Cade,
That hand to hand in single fight I slue.   xxi.46-7

(xii) *Cliff.* And till I root out their accursed Line,
And leaue not one aliue, I liue in hell.   3 HVI. 1.3.32-3
Cliff. Therefore till I root out that curssed line
And leaue not one on earth, Ile liue in hell.   T.T. iii.31-2
Y. Cliff. And left not one of them to breath on earth.
                      xxiii.51

(xiii) *Exet.* Away: for vengeance comes along with them,
Nay, stay not to expostulate, make speed,
Or else come after, Ile away before.   3 HVI. 2.5.134-6
Exet. Awaie my Lord for vengeance comes along with him;
Nay stand not to expostulate make hast,
Or else come after, Ile awaie before.   T.T. viii.61-3
Marg. Away my Lord, and flie to London straight
Make hast, for vengeance comes along with them,
Come stand not to expostulate, lets go.   xxiii.62-4

(xiv) *Rich.* Now Clifford, I haue singled thee alone.
                   3 HVI. 2.4.1.

York. Now Clifford, since we are singled here alone.
                    xxiii.32

(xv) *King.* Your labour is but spent in vaine.   T.T. ix.17
Humph. And is all our labours then spent in vaine. i.75

(xvi) *Edw.* Call Edward King, and at his hands begge Mercy,
And he shall pardon thee these Outrages? 3 HVI. 5.1.123-4
Stafford. Wilt thou yeeld thy selfe vnto the Kings mercy,
And he will pardon thee and these, their outrages.
                   xiii.119-121

(xvii) *Yor.* Hold Warwick: seek thee out some other chace
For I my selfe must hunt this Deere to death.
                  2 HVI. 5.2.14-15

Yorke. Hold Warwicke, and seeke thee out some other chase,
My selfe will hunt this deare to death.   xxiii.27-8
Rich. Nay Warwicke, single out some other chace,
For I my selfe will hunt this Wolfe to death.
                                    3 HVI. 2.4.12-13

(d) Titus Andronicus

(i) Ransomlesse heere we set our Prisoners free. Tit. 1.1.275
Capt. And as for these whose ransome we haue set,
It is our pleasure one of them depart: 2 HVI. 4.1.141-2
Capt. And ransomelesse this prisoner shall go free. xii.76

(ii) Heere comes a parcell of our hopefull Booty,
Which dreads not yet their liues destruction. Tit. 2.3.49-50
Humph. And thousands more must follow after me,
That dreads not yet their liues destruction.   ix.75-6

(iii) This is the day of Doome for Bassianus.   Tit. 2.3.42
York. Be this the day of doom to one of vs.   xxiii.33

(e) Taming of a Shrew

(i) Hands off I say, and get you from this place;
Or I wil set my ten commandements in your face.
                                    A Shrew. 1.1.152-3
Duch. Could I come neare your Beautie with my Nayles
I could set my ten Commandements in your face.
                                    2 HVI. 1.3.139-140
Duch. Could I come neare your daintie vissage
                    with my nayles,
Ide set my ten commandments in your face.   iii.138-9

(ii) The fairest bride that euer Marchant had. A Shrew. 3.6.70
Suff. The fairest Queene that euer King possest.   i.16

(f) Arden of Feversham

(i) Hell fyre and wrathfull vengeance light on me. Ard. 1.i.338
Marg. Mischance and Sorrow goe along with you.
                                    2 HVI. 3.2.300
Marg. Hell fire and vengeance go along with you.   x.143

(ii) Yet all my labour is not spent in vaine.   Ard. 1.1.455
Humph. And is all our labours then spent in vaine.   i.75

(iii) Then fix his sad eis on the sollen earth.   Ard. 3.1.45
Duch. Why are thine eyes fixt to the sullen earth?
                                    2 HVI. 1.2.5

(iv) What a Clock ist, sirra? Almost ten.   Ard. 3.1.35-6
Humph. Sirs, what's a Clock? Tenne, my Lord.
                     2 HVI. 2.4.5
Humph. Sirra, whats a clocke? Almost ten my Lord.
                     viii.1-2

(v) It is the raylingest knaue in christendome.   Ard. 4.4.54
Glos. Then Saunder, sit there,
Thy lying'st Knaue in Christendome.   2 HVI. 2.1.125-6
Humph. Then Sander, sit there, the lyingest
knaue in Christendom.   v.99-100

(vi) Can any greefe be halfe so great as this?   Ard. 1.1.19
Marg. Can any griefe of mind be like to this?   iii.58

(vii) And boldly beard and braue him to his teeth.   Ard. 4.3.75
Marg. But beard and braue him proudly to his face. xxi.71

(viii) With mightye furrowes in his stormye browes. Ard. 2.1.53
King. Deepe trenched furrowes in his frowning brow.
                     xxi.53

(g) Thomas of Woodstock

    And would my death might end these miseries.   ix.73
    And would my death might end the misserys.   T.W. 3.2.106

(h) Battle of Alcazar

    If honor be the marke wherat thou aimst,
    Then followe me in holy christian warres,
    And leaue to seeke thy Countries overthrow.   Alcazar. 760-2
    Cliff. If honour be the marke whereat you aime,
    Then haste to France that our forefathers wonne,
    And winne againe that thing which now is lost,
    And leaue to seeke your Countries ouerthrow.   xviii.94-7

(i) Soliman and Perseda

    (i) Take the braginst knaue in Christendom with thee.
                     S.P. 1.3.211

        See *Arden of Feversham* for passages from
        2 Henry VI and *Contention.*

    (ii) Within forst furrowes of her clowding brow. S.P. 1.4.135
    King. Deepe trenched furrowes in his frowning brow.
                     xxi.53

    (iii) Therefore ile about it straight.   S.P. 4.12.82
        Buck. Content, Come then let vs about it straight.   i.112
        Yorke. Content. Away then, about it straight.   iv.48

(iv) Trouble me not, but let me passe in peace. S.P. 5.4.138
King. Disturbe him not, let him passe peaceably.
2 HVI. 3.3.25

(j) SPANISH TRAGEDY

Viluppo, follow us for thy reward. S.T. 1.3.92
King. Come fellow, follow vs for thy Reward. 2 HVI. 2.3.102
vii.78

II 3 HENRY VI and TRUE TRAGEDY

(a) EDWARD II

(i) Am I a king, and must be ouer rulde? E2. 135
Marg. Enforc't thee? Art thou King, and wilt be forc't?
3 HVI. 1.1.230
Marg. Art thou a king and wilt be forst to yeeld? i.206

(ii) Why then my lord, giue me but leaue to speak.
But nephew, do not play the sophister. E2. 551-2
Rich. Brother, though I bee youngest, giue mee leaue.
Edw. No, I can better play the Orator. 3 HVI. 1.2.1-2
Rich. Brother, and cosen Montague, giue mee
leaue to speake.
Edw. Nay, I can better plaie the Orator. T.T. ii.1-2

(iii) The hautie Dane commands the narrow seas. E2. 970
Marg. Sterne Falconbridge commands the Narrow Seas.
3 HVI. 1.1.239
Marg. Sterne Fawconbridge Commands the narrow seas.
i.210-11

(iv) My swelling heart for very anger breakes. E2. 1002
West. My heart for anger burnes, I cannot brooke it.
3 HVI. 1.1.60
West. My hart for anger breakes, I cannot speake. i.55

(v) I humblie thanke your maiestie. E2. 1049
Marg. I humblie thanke your royall maiestie. xi.7

(vi) I wonder how he scapt. E2. 1119
War. I wonder how the King escap'd our hands?
3 HVI. 1.1.1
War. I wonder how the king escapt our hands. i.1

(vii) Farre be it from the thoughts of Lancaster. E2. 1131
King. Farre be the thought of this from Henries heart.
3 HVI. 1.1.70
King. Far be it from the thoughtes of Henries hart. i.65

(viii) Would cast vp cappes, and clap their hands for ioy.
             E2. 1667
 War. And he that casts not vp his cap for ioie. iv.164
 War. And he that throwes not vp his cap for ioy.
          3 HVI. 2.i.196

(ix) Now lords, our louing friends and countrimen,
 Welcome to England all.   E2. 1748-9
 Marg. Welcome to England, my louing friends of France.
             xxi.1

(x) Madam, tis good to looke to him betimes. E2. 1825
 Oxf. Tis best to looke to this betimes. xvii.28

(xi) They stay your answer, will you yeeld your crowne?
            E2. 2036
 War. What say'st thou Henry, wilt thou yeeld the Crowne?
         3 HVI. 2.2.101
 War. What saiest thou Henry? wilt thou yeelde
      thy Crowne?   v.97

(xii) And thus, most humbly do we take our leaue. E2. 2115
 Mont. And thus most humbly I doe take my leaue.
         3 HVI. 1.2.61

(b) THE MASSACRE AT PARIS

 (i) Thankes my good freend, I wil requite thy loue. M.P. 78
 Edw. Stanley, I will requite thy forwardnesse.
         3 HVI. 4.5.23
 Edw. Hastings, and Stanlie, I will requite your loues.
          xiv.6-7

 (ii)   Come my Lords, and let vs
 Goe tell the King of this.   M.P. 202-3
 Cliff. Come Cousin, let vs tell the Queene these Newes.
       . 3 HVI. 1.1.182
 Cliff. Nor I, come cosen, lets go tell the Queene. i.175

(iii) O let me pray before I take my death. M.P. 356
 Rutland. Oh let me pray, before I take my death.
        3 HVI. 1.3.35
 Rutland. Oh let me praie, before I take my death. iii.33

(iv) I feare the Guisians haue past the bridge,
 And meane once more to menace me. M.P. 367-8
 Edw. Are landed, and meane once more to menace vs. xx.55

 (v) What art thou dead, sweet sonne? Speak to thy Mother.
          M.P. 556

Marg. Oh Ned, sweet Ned, speake to thy Mother Boy.

3 HVI. 5.5.51

Marg. Ah Ned, speak to thy mother boy?   xxi.87

(vi) And he nor heares, nor sees vs what we doe.   M.P. 558
War. And he nor sees, nor heares vs, what we say.

3 HVI. 2.6.63

War. And he nor sees nor heares vs what we saie. viii.120

(vii) Then may it please your Maiestie to giue me leaue.

M.P. 621

Rich. And if it please your grace to giue me leaue.   ii.11

(viii) But villaine he to whom these lines should goe
Shall buy her loue euen with his dearest bloud. M.P. 702-3
Rich. Thou and thy Brother both shall buy this Treason
Euen with the dearest blood your bodies beare.

3 HVI. 5.1.68-9

(ix) How now sirra, what newes?   M.P. 729
Edw. Now Messenger, what Letters, or what
                    Newes from France? 3 HVI. 4.1.84
Edw. Now sirra, What letters or what newes?   xii.58

(x) In Gods name, let them come.   M.P. 734
York. A Gods name, let them come.   ii.42

(xi) For he doth lurke within his drowsie couch,
And makes his footstoole on securitie.   M.P. 743-4
Edw. Thus haue we swept Suspition from our Seate,
And made our Footstoole of Security.   3 HVI. 5.7.13-14
Edw. Thus haue we swept suspition from our seat,
And made our footstoole of securitie.   xxiii.13-14

(xii) The Duke is slaine and all his power dispearst,
And we are grac'd with wreathes of victory.   M.P. 793-4
Edw. Thus farre our fortune keepes an vpward course,
And we are grac'd with wreaths of Victorie. 3 HVI. 5.3.1-2
Edw. Thus farre our fortunes keepes an vpward
Course, and we are grast with wreathes of
victorie.   viii.94-5

(xiii) Sweet Duke of Guise our prop to leane vpon,
Now thou art dead, heere is no stay for vs.   M.P. 1122-3
Edw. Sweet Duke of Yorke, our Prop to leane vpon,
Now thou art gone, wee haue no Staffe, no Stay.

3 HVI. 2.1.68-9

Edw. Sweet Duke of Yorke our prop to leane vpon,
Now thou art gone there is no hope for vs.   iv.45-6

(xiv) These words reuiue my thoughts and comforts me.

M.P. 1232

Marg. Those gracious words Reuiue my drooping thoughts.

3 HVI. 3.3.21

(c) 2 HENRY VI and CONTENTION
See I.

(d) TITUS ANDRONICUS

(i)　　　　　Was none in Rome to make a stale
But Saturnine?　　　　　　　　　　　Tit. 1.1.304-5
War. Had he none else to make a stale but me?

3 HVI. 3.3.260

War. Had he none else to make a stale but me?　　xi.164

(ii) And at my sute (sweet) pardon what is past.　Tit. 1.1.431
War. My Noble Queene, let former grudges passe.

3 HVI. 3.3.195

War. My gratious Queene pardon what is past.　　xi.121

(iii) O Tamora, thou bear'st a womans face.　　Tit. 2.3.136
York. And yet be seene to beare a Womans face?

3 HVI. 1.4.140

York. And yet be seene to beare a womans face?　　iii.174

(iv) I will not heare her speake, away with her.　Tit. 2.3.137
Edw. Awaie with him, I will not heare him speake.

xviii.3

(v) Two of thy whelpes, fell Curs of bloody kind,
Haue heere bereft my brother of his life.　Tit. 2.3.281-2
Father. O Boy! thy Father gaue thee life too soone,
And hath bereft of thy life too late.　　3 HVI. 2.5.92-3
Father. Poore boy thy father gaue thee lif too late,
And hath bereau'de thee of thy life too sone.　　viii.32-3

(vi) To send for Lucius thy thrice-valiant sonne.　Tit. 5.2.112
Rich. Cride still for Warwicke his thrise valiant son.　vi.17

(e) TAMING OF A SHREW

(i)　　　　　　　Ferando loues thee well
And will with wealth and ease maintaine thy state.

A Shrew. 1.1.172-3

War. You haue a father able to maintaine you.

3 HVI. 3.3.154

War. You haue a father able to mainetaine your state.

xi.93

(ii) Let fates and fortune doo the worst they can.

A Shrew. 3.6.59

Edw. Well Warwicke, let fortune doe her worst.   xiii.39

(iii) Ile thrust myselfe amongst the thickest throngs.

A Shrew. 3.6.54

Prince. But with my sword presse in the thickest thronges.

xxii.18

(f) ARDEN OF FEVERSHAM

(i) Yet all my labour is not spent in vaine.   Ard. 1.1.455
King. Your labour is but spent in vaine.   ix.17

(ii) And let our salt teares be his obsequies.   Ard. 5.1.346
York. These Teares are my sweet Rutlands
Obsequies.   3 HVI. 1.4.147
York. These teares are my sweet Rutlands obsequies. iii.181

(iii) Tush, I haue broken fiue hundred oathes.   Ard. 2.2.97
Edw. I would breake a thousand Oathes, to
reigne one yeere. 3 HVI. 1.2.14
Edw. But I would breake an hundred othes to
raigne one yeare.   ii.9-10

(iv) Yet Arden, I protest to thee by heauen.   Ard. 5.1.226

War. King Lewis, I heere protest in ⎫   3 HVI. 3.3.181
sight of heauen. ⎭   xi.110

(g) BATTLE OF ALCAZAR

(i)   sure friends by our great master sent
To gratifie and to remunerate,
Thy loue, thy loialtie, and forwardnes,
Thy seruice in his fathers dangerous warre. Alcazar. 93-6
Clar. And hiely promise to remunerate
Their trustie seruice, in these dangerous warres.   vi.38-9

(ii) After this sodaine shocke and haplesse warre. Alcazar. 982
Edw. After this dangerous fight and haplesse warre.   iv.i.

(iii) My horsse Zareo, O the goale is lost,
The goale is lost, thou king of Portugall
Thrice happy chance it is for thee and thine
That heauen abates my strength and calles me hence.

Alcazar. 1328-31

York. The goale is lost thou house of Lancaster,
Thrise happie chance is it for thee and thine,
That heauen abridgde my daies and cals me hence. iii.51-3

(iv) Retreat is sounded through our Camp.   Alcazar. 1507
Oxf. And cause retrait be sounded through the Campe.
xx.40

For the last line compare Peele's *Edward I*
(1.5.173):
And cause retreat be sounded through the Campe.

(v) And they that loue my honor follow me.   Alcazar. 1171
Clar. You that loue me, and Warwicke, follow me.
3 HVI. 4.1.123

Clar.   All you that loue me and Warwike
Follow me.   xii.87-8

(h) SOLIMAN AND PERSEDA

(i) And all my former loue is turnd to hate.   S.P. 2.1.152
Marg. These words haue turn'd my Hate, to Loue.
3 HVI. 3.3.199

(ii) I, marry, Sir, then the case is altered.   S.P. 2.1.292
War. I, but the case is alter'd.   3 HVI. 4.3.31
War. I, but the case is altred now.   xiii.30

(iii) Ah stay, no more: for I can heere no more.   S.P. 2.2.28
Edw. Oh speake no more, for I haue heard too much.
3 HVI. 2.1.48
Edw. Oh speake no more, for I can heare no more.   iv.27

(iv) Their horse, I deeme them fiftie thousand strong.
S.P. 3.1.48
War. Their power (I thinke) is thirty thousand strong.
3 HVI. 2.1.177
War. Their power I gesse them fifty thousand strong.
iv.145

(v) I heere protest by heauens vnto you all.   S.P. 5.2.26
War. King Lewis, I heere protest in sight of heauen.
3 HVI. 3.3.181
War. King Lewis, I heere protest in sight of heauen.
xi.110

(vi) I, saist thou so? why then it shall be so.   S.P. 4.1.242
Yorke. I, saist thou so boie? why then it shall be so.   ii.23

(vii) I kisse I graunt thee, though I hate thee deadlie. S.P. 5.4.67
Marg. Alas poore Yorke, But that I hate thee deadly.
3 HVI. 1.4.84
Marg. Alas poore Yorke? but that I hate thee much. iii.120

(viii) Nay, die thou shalt for thy presumption.   S.P. 5.4.73
     Rich. Thy Son I kill'd for his presumption.   3 HVI. 5.6.34
     Rich. Thy sonne I kild for his presumption.   xxii.25

(ix) Off with his head, and suffer him not to speake.
                                    S.P. 5.4.112
     Edw. For Somerset, off with his guiltie Head.
     Goe beare them hence, I will not heare them speake.
                                      3 HVI. 5.5.3-4
     Edw. For Summerset off with his guiltie head.
     Awaie I will not hear them speake.   xxi.49-50

LINES COMMON TO EDWARD II AND PLAYS NAMED

(a) 2 HENRY VI and CONTENTION. See lists.

(b) 3 HENRY VI and TRUE TRAGEDY. See lists.

(c) MASSACRE AT PARIS

     (i) I cannot brooke these hautie menaces.   E2. 134
        I cannot brook thy hauty insolence.   M.P. 869

     (ii) Will be the ruine of the realme and vs.   E2. 239
        Will be the ruine of the realme and you.   E2. 1011
        Will be the ruine of that famous Realme of France.
                                      M.P. 929

     (iii) My lord, will you take armes against the King?   E2. 246
        That the Guise hath taken armes against the king. M.P. 908

     (iv) Warwicke and Lancaster, weare you my crowne.   E2. 332
        Guise, weare our crowne, and be thou King of France.
                                      M.P. 866

     (v) Ile fire thy crased buildings, and enforce
        The papall towers to kisse the lowlie ground.   E2. 396-7
        Ile fire his crased buildings and incense
        The papall towers to kisse the holy earth.   M.P. 1214-5

     (vi) My gratious lord, I come to bring you newes.   E2. 617
        My Lord, I come to bring you newes.   M.P. 1134

     (vii) And still his minde runs on his minion.   E2. 806
        His minde you see runnes on his minions.   M.P. 638

     (viii) Come Edmund lets away, and leuie men,
        Tis warre that must abate these Barons pride.   E2. 900-1
        Com let vs away and leauy men,
        Tis warre that must asswage this tyrantes pride.
                                     M.P. 1139-40

(ix) I humblie thanke your Maiestie.   E2. 1049
I humblie thanke your Maiestie.   M.P. 171
I humbly thank your royall Maiestie.   M.P. 277

(d) Arden of Feversham

(i) I haue my wish, in that I ioy thy sight.   E2. 151
I haue my wishe in that I ioy thy sight.   Ard. 5.1.349

(ii) Is this the fruite your reconcilement beares?   E2. 833
Is this the fruite thy reconcilement buds?   Ard. 1.1.187

(iii) Because he loues me more then all the world.   E2. 372
I loued him more then all the world beside.   Ard. 5.1.423

(iv) Looke vp my lord. Baldock, this drowsines
Betides no good, here euen we are betraied.   E2. 1911-2
This drowsines in me bods little good.   Ard. 3.2.19

(v) And then let me alone to handle him.   E2. 2164
And then let me alone to handle him.   Ard. 3.2.63

(e) Soliman and Perseda

(i) Thy woorth sweet friend is far aboue my guifts,
Therefore to equall it receiue my hart.   E2. 161-2
And sweet Perseda, accept this ring
To equall it : receiue my hart to boote.   S.P. 1.2.39-40

(ii) And when this fauour Isabell forgets,
Then let her liue abandond and forlorne.   E2. 594-5
when Erastus doth forget this fauor,
Then let him liue abandond and forlorne.   S.P. 4.1.198-9

(iii) Father, thy face should harbor no deceit.   E2. 1875
This face of thine shuld harbour no deceit.   S.P. 3.1.72

(iv)   Oh my starres!
Why do you lowre vnkindly on a king?   E2. 1929-30
Ah heauens........................
Why doe you vnkindly lowre on Solyman?   S.P. 5.4.82-3

(v) I tell thee tis not meet, that one so false
Should come about the person of a prince.   E2. 2248-9
It is not meete that one so base as thou
Shouldst come about the person of a king.   S.P. 1.5.71-2

(vi) O day! the last of all my blisse on earth.   E2. 1928
This day shall be the peryod of my blisse.   S.P. 5.4.155

(vii) Brother, the least of these may well suffice
    For one of greater birth then Gaueston.   E2. 158-9
    The least of these surpasse my best desart.   S.P. 3.1.101

(f) Edward I

(i) As Caesar riding in the Romaine streete
    With captiue kings at his triumphant Carre.   E2. 173-4
    Not Caesar leading thro the streetes of Rome
    The captiue Kings of conquered nations.   E1. 5.1.90-1

(ii) Tis but temporall that thou canst inflict.   E2. 1550
    Tis but temporal that thou canst inflict.   E1. 1.5.55

(iii) These comforts that you giue our wofull queene
    Binde vs in kindenes all at your commaund.   E2. 1684-5
    This comfort that your grace doth giue
    Binds me in double duty whilst I liue.   E1. vi.59-60

(iv) Hence fained weeds, vnfained are my woes.   E2. 1964
    Hence fained weeds! vnfained is my grief.   E1. xxv.123

(g) Spanish Tragedy

(i) Because he loues me more then all the world.   E2. 372
    Because she loued me more then all the world.   S.T. 3.6.6

(ii) O is he gone! is noble Edward gone.   E2. 1967
    Then is he gone? and is my sonne gone too?   S.T. 2.5.42

(h) Thomas of Woodstock

(i) On that condition Lancaster will graunt,
    And so will Penbrooke and I.
    And I.   E2. 589-91
    On these conditions brother we agree.
    And I.
    And I.   T.W.

(ii) I dare not, for the people loue him well.   E2. 1036
    I dare not Greene. . . . .
    . . . . .he's so well beloued.   T.W.

(iii) In heauen wee may, in earth neuer shall we meete.
                         E2. 1947
    On earth, I feare, we neuer more shall meet.   T.W.

I shall make some notes on some of the examples quoted, in so far as they concern the bad quartos.

EDWARD II

Of 18 examples common to *Edward II* and *2 Henry VI* and/or *Contention,* only no. xiv is common to *Edward II* and *2 Henry VI.* Margaret's line,

> She beares a Dukes Reuenewes on her backe,

was inserted in *Contention Q3* (1619); it was almost a commonplace in Elizabethan times, and, variously phrased, is found in *King Leir* and *Thomas of Woodstock.* Five other examples, viz., nos. i, vi, vii, xviii and the first line of no. xii are common to *Edward II* and both *2 Henry VI* and *Contention.* Eight examples comprise lines common to *Edward II* and *Contention,* and we may assume that the compiler of *Contention* borrowed them to fill gaps in his recollections. In the remaining four examples the line of *Contention* is much closer than the corresponding line of *2 Henry VI* to what is present in the text of *Edward II.* In no. iv there is an interesting amalgam or contamination of the two texts; the compiler begins with half a line of *Edward II,* inserts a line and a half of *2 Henry VI,* and concludes with another half line of *Edward II.* Clifford's line in *Contention* xix.9 is a reminiscence of Spencer's line in *Edward II,* but the adjective 'lawful' does not fit the context of *Contention* because Henry's title was not publicly challenged till a later scene. Similarly the King's speech in no. xii does not come from *2 Henry VI* but echoes the line quoted from Marlowe's play. In examples nos. xiii and xvi the quotations from *2 Henry VI* are unnecessary because the lines in *Contention* are obviously derived from *Edward II.*

In general *True Tragedy* keeps textually much closer to *3 Henry VI* than does *Contention* to *2 Henry VI.* In one example only, viz., no. xii, does a line of *Edward II,* one of ceremonious leave-taking, recur in *3 Henry VI;* in nos. v, ix and x, lines of *True Tragedy* may be borrowed from *Edward II,* though no. v is a conventional form of thanks to royalty. Example no. vii shows the influence of both lines belonging to the good texts in the formation of the line found in the bad quarto.

MASSACRE AT PARIS

Four of the five lines common to *Massacre at Paris* and *Contention* are found almost identically in *2 Henry VI,* a fact which suggests that the compiler of Marlowe's play must at least have heard these lines spoken on the stage as they appear in the folio text, and inserted them in his own piratical version. In example no. ii this conventional speech takes the form which it has in *2 Henry VI* rather than that in *Edward II.*

Much the same conclusion may be drawn from an examination of the passages common to *Massacre at Paris* and the other pair of parallel texts. Eight of the fourteen passages quoted from *Massacre at Paris* are common to both *3 Henry VI* and *True Tragedy,* two are in *3 Henry VI* only, and four are found only in *True Tragedy.* I think that in no. iv the context and the use of the words 'once more' make it likely that the line of *Massacre at Paris,*

and meane once more to menace vs,

was borrowed from *True Tragedy* or from the same source; the speaker, Ramus, appears for the first time here, and thus 'once more' is meaningless. Example no. vii is a ceremonial form of speech infrequent in *Tamburlaine* and *Edward II* but common in both parts of *Henry VI.* Similarly Shakespeare in his early plays employs the phrase 'in Gods name' far more freely than Marlowe; again I suggest that the compiler of *Massacre at Paris* inserted these lines from recollections of Shakespeare's plays. Both context and diction of nos. v and xiii make it probable that they were interpolated from *3 Henry VI.* In no. v I suggest that Margaret's words 'sweet Ned' were changed to Catherine's 'sweet sonne' in *Massacre at Paris,* whilst in no. xiii the word 'stay' in the version of *Massacre at Paris* points to the version of *3 Henry VI,* though the rest of the line takes the form found in *True Tragedy.* Many complex inter-relations are possible between the four texts, *2 Henry VI, 3 Henry VI, Contention* and *True Tragedy;* I find practically no lines common to Shakespeare's two plays, and no borrowings from *2 Henry VI* in *True Tragedy.* The seventeen examples cited are divisible into five groups:

I Lines common to *2 Henry VI, Contention* and *True Tragedy,* nos. ii, v, and vi.

II Lines common to *3 Henry VI, Contention* and *True Tragedy,* nos. iii, iv, vii, viii, ix, xii and xiii.

III Lines common to *3 Henry VI* and *Contention,* nos. x, xi, xiv and xvi.

z

IV Lines common to 2 *Henry VI*, 3 *Henry VI* and *Contention*, no. xvii.

V Lines common to *Contention* and *True Tragedy*, nos. i and xv.

Four lines only of *Contention* are present in 3 *Henry VI* but not in *True Tragedy*. Jack Cade, mortally wounded by Iden, adapts rather inconsequentially in no. x two lines of a speech made by Edward on learning of his father's death. Thus we discover that these two lines of 3 *Henry VI* were spoken on the stage though omitted in *True Tragedy*. Another interesting example is no. xi, in which the second line of Iden's speech as it appears in *Contention* echoes a line as it is spoken in 3 *Henry VI*. Similarly in nos. xiv and xvii York before fighting with old Clifford uses in *Contention* practically the same words as Shakespeare puts into Richard's mouth before fighting with young Clifford. These examples have importance because they prove that the text of 3 *Henry VI* and not that of *True Tragedy* was spoken on the stage. More commonly the line of *Contention* is found in both versions but usually is closer to the version of *True Tragedy*. Thus Elinor's line in no. iv uses the word 'offence' which in *True Tragedy* replaces the poet's 'fault'; in the thirteenth example *Contention* adopts from *True Tragedy* the interpolated 'My Lord' in the first line and 'make hast' in the second line, neither of which is found in 3 *Henry VI*. Lines of *True Tragedy* come directly from 2 *Henry VI* and *Contention*. Thus in no. ii part of Edward's speech addressed in *True Tragedy* to his brother George is not in 3 *Henry VI*, but is adapted from what is found in 2 *Henry VI* and *Contention*. Apparently the ceremony of investiture in *True Tragedy* took place immediately on the battle-field; in Shakespeare's play Edward's words are:

> Richard, I will create thee Duke of Gloucester
> And George of Clarence;

they suggest a later ceremony elsewhere. Another simple example of such borrowing occurs in no. v. The second and third lines of Richard's speech in the version of no. vi in *True Tragedy* come identically from the line of *Contention* which is itself very close to that of 2 *Henry VI*; Clifford refers, however, to 'luke-warme blood' in the penultimate scene of *Contention*. Inclusion of the word 'king' in Suffolk's first line in no. vii suggests that it comes from 3 *Henry VI* rather than from *True Tragedy*. Only in the first and fifteenth examples of group (c) have we lines of *True Tragedy* derived from those of *Contention*.

Our ignorance of the chronological order in which the Pembroke plays were composed makes it difficult to decide whether certain examples quoted from *Titus Andronicus* were the source of lines found in *3 Henry VI* and *True Tragedy*, or were transferred from those plays to *Titus Andronicus*. *Contention* was entered five weeks after the last named play and may have been in print before it; if both plays were in the repertory of Pembroke's men we may reasonably assume that the lines common to these plays were originally part of *Titus Andronicus*. Six examples of lines common to this play and *3 Henry VI* and/or the corresponding bad quarto have been quoted, and are divisible into two groups of three each. Those which are common to *Titus Andronicus* and *True Tragedy* have probably their source in the former play; the other three examples are found in the three plays. If Shakespeare is repeating himself, the question of priority may be decided on the external evidence that *3 Henry VI* preceded *Titus Andronicus* in composition.

The Taming of a Shrew, the fourth play known to belong to Pembroke's men, has about a dozen passages borrowed from *Faustus* and the two parts of *Tamburlaine,* and a few lines common to it and *Orlando Furioso, Arden of Feversham* and *Alphonsus of Arragon.* I have not found any line of it in *Edward II* or *Titus Andronicus.* Links with the parallel texts are by no means plentiful; except for one line spoken by Elinor in *2 Henry VI* and *Contention,* they are limited to short phrases, half a line long, usually adapted to the characters and context of the play. The first example under II (e) suggests that the compiler of *True Tragedy* has avoided the feminine ending by making an Alexandrine of which the second half may be a recollection of a line in *A Shrew.*

Reference to the preceding lists proves that each of the plays, *Contention, True Tragedy, Edward II* and *Massacre at Paris,* has a considerable number of lines each of which is in one or more of the other three, and also a number found in one or more of *Arden, Soliman and Perseda, Battle of Alcazar, Titus Andronicus, A Shrew, Spanish Tragedy* and *Edward I.* All of these plays were entered on the Stationers' Register between April 1592 and 1595,

and only *Edward I* and those of Marlowe had the author's name
on the title-pages. Below are transcribed certain details of these
plays taken from Sir Edmund Chambers's *Elizabethan Stage,*
vol. iv, pp. 382-5.

TABLE XX

Date of Entry	Date of Print	Title	Source	Author
1592, Apr. 3	1592	Arden of Feversham		Anon.
1592, Oct. 6	n.d.	Spanish Tragedy	Strange's?	[Kyd]
1592, Nov. 20	n.d.	Soliman and Perseda		Anon.
1593, July 6	1594	Edward II	Pembroke's	Marlowe
1593, Oct. 8	1593	Edward I		Peele
1594, Feb. 6	1594	Titus Andronicus	⎰ Derby's ⎱ Pembroke's ⎰ Sussex's	[Shakespeare]
1594, Mar. 12	1594	Contention	Pembroke's?	Anon.
1594, May 2	1594	Taming of a Shrew	Pembroke's	Anon.
	1594	Battle of Alcazar	⎰ Strange's ⎱ Admiral's	[Peele]
	1595	True Tragedy of Richard Duke of York	Pembroke's	Anon.
	n.d.	Massacre at Paris	⎰ Strange's ⎱ Admiral's	Marlowe

The date of entry tells us no more than the latest possible limit
for the composition of the play; usually representation on the stage
would have preceded the entry by months or perhaps years. These
eleven plays may be divided into two groups; the first, ending with
Titus Andronicus, consists of plays with good or sound texts, while
all the plays in the second group, entered or not, are corrupt. The
title-pages of three plays do not give the names of the companies
by which they were performed. One of these, *Arden of Feversham,*
has the poorest text of the first group; much of the verse is harsh
or irregular, and not much better than that of *Romeo and Juliet Q1*
except that there are less twelve-syllable lines. Prose and verse are
so intermingled that it is difficult to determine with any degree of
certainty where verse begins or ends. From the epilogue we have
evidence that the play was acted on the stage, and this inference
receives some confirmation from the number of lines belonging to
this play which are found in other plays. *Soliman and Perseda* was
entered when all the London theatres were closed during the

plague; lines from it in other plays and the reference to the braggart Basilisco in *King John* make it almost certain that it was acted and was popular. *Edward I* has no stage history, but probably belonged as did *Battle of Alcazar* to the Admiral's men, and after some revision may have been *Longshanks* recorded by Henslowe as acted in 1595. It was in print before the first extant edition of *Edward II,* but was not even entered when Marlowe was killed.

The period from 1587 to 1594 was marked by the breaking up and reorganization of all the dramatic companies; too many of them were struggling to maintain a place in a London of about 150,000 people. Leicester's company had disbanded in 1588, and its dissolution and the gradual fall from court favour of the Queen's men combined to set a number of the best actors free to make fresh ties. Strange's and the Admiral's men seem to have combined about 1590 for acting purposes; this was perhaps a temporary amalgamation to reduce the severity of competition. When the theatres closed on 23 June, 1592, the two main companies, Strange's men and the Admiral's men, after waiting near London for some weeks, each went on a country tour till the end of the year; they both returned to London just before the New Year and played a short winter season at the Rose Theatre. Continuance of the plague drove them to travel again at the beginning of February, 1593. Some weeks or perhaps months before the end of 1592 there emerges a third company styled Pembroke's men. Its origin is obscure. Sharers belonging to either of the two important companies, Strange's men and the Admiral's men, would certainly not renounce permanent membership of such well-established companies to join one brought together by poverty and the plague, and, like the others, compelled to tour the provinces. Pembroke was a shrewd, trusted, wealthy and influential nobleman, President of Wales, one who kept aloof from parties and was well liked by the Queen. Several competent and popular actors must have joined the new venture, which must have started not later than the beginning of December, because on 26 December, 1592 and 6 January, 1593 'the seruantes of the Erle of Pembroke' gave two plays at Court; Strange's men acted on three days between the dates named. Their country tour was unsuccessful, and they were compelled to return to London almost penniless about the middle of August, 1593, and disappear from the records for more than two years. One sign of the disintegration of companies produced by the plague is the presence of the names of two or more companies on the title-pages of the numerous plays that came to the press in the years 1593-5. Of twenty-two plays entered or printed between 7 December, 1593, and the end of 1594 no less than seven, viz., *Orlando Furioso, Titus Andronicus, Looking Glass, Friar Bacon, King Leir, Four Prentices* and *Battle of Alcazar,* bear each of them on the title-page the statement that it had been acted by more than one company. Three of the above plays are included in the list of eleven tabulated above. Two others of Marlowe's plays, *Jew of Malta,* entered 17 May, 1594, and *Massacre at Paris* are known to have been acted by at least two companies. How jealously each company protected its own property appears from the fact that neither before nor after 1593-4 does the title-page of any play except *Satiromastix* and those acted by the two children's companies bear the name of more than one company.

Of the plays included in the list given above Pembroke's men had four, viz., *Edward II, Titus Andronicus, Taming of a Shrew* and *True Tragedy;* to these *Contention* may be added with some amount of confidence. *Edward II* is the mystery play of this period, and nothing is known of its history except what is found in the Stationers' Register and on the title-page; the latter reads:

As it was sundrie times publiquely acted in the honourable citie of London, by the right honourable the Earle of Pembrooke his seruants. Written by Chri. Marlow Gent. 1594.

There are also editions of 1598, 1612 and 1622. No London company would have dared to stage *Edward II* before Queen Elizabeth, and this cannot have been one of the two plays presented by Pembroke's men at Christmas, 1592. Nothing in *Richard II* would have given such mortal offence to the Queen as the scene in which the barons and archbishop combine to coerce King Edward. Below, two extracts (ll. 346-359 and ll. 379-385) give some notion of the plain words used:

> *Bish.* You know that I am legate to the Pope,
> On your allegeance to the sea of Rome,
> Subscribe as we haue done to his exile.

Mor.iu. Curse him, if he refuse, and then may we
Depose him and elect an other King.
Edw. I, there it goes, but yet I will not yeeld,
Curse me, depose me, doe the worst you can.
Lan. Then linger not my lord, but do it straight.
Bish. Remember how the Bishop was abusde,
Either banish him that was the cause thereof,
Or I will presentlie discharge these lords
Of dutie and allegeance due to thee.
Edw. It bootes me not to threat, I must speake faire,
The Legate of the Pope will be obayd.

Edward tries to bribe the barons to permit Gaveston to remain, but they are adamant.

Bish. Are you content to banish him the realme?
Edw. I see I must, and therefore am content.
In steede of inke, ile write it with my teares.
Mor.iu. The king is loue-sick for his minion.
Edw. Tis done, and now accursed hand fall off,
Lan. Giue it me, ile haue it published in the streetes.
Mor.iu. Ile see him presently dispatched away.
Bish. Now is my heart at ease.
Warw. And so is mine.
Pemb. This will be good newes to the common sort.

Elizabeth herself had been excommunicated, had survived the papal Bull of Deposition declaring her deposed and her subjects absolved from their allegiance, and had suppressed the rebellion of the Catholic earls of the north which preceded the issue of the Bull. In 1592-3 the excommunicated Elizabeth was helping the excommunicated King of France to fight against his own subjects, also absolved from their allegiance, and the Spaniards. Many plots had aimed at her life, and she could well prefigure her own fate in Marlowe's story of Edward's misgovernment, imprisonment, deposition and murder; she was Edward II and her Gaveston was the popular Earl of Essex. She would have almost choked with rage to hear such treason spoken by common players. Eight or nine years afterwards Sir Francis Hubert's long poem on Edward of Carnarvon was refused publication because the deposition of a king was in effect a denial of a king's divine right to rule. I do not believe that the Master of the Revels would have permitted *Edward II* to be acted in London at any time after the publication of Doleman's book, *A Conference about the Next Succession,* in 1594. Certainly it was the only one of Marlowe's plays that Henslowe or the Admiral's men did not own or produce.

Marlowe was stabbed at the end of May, 1593, and on 6 July *Edward II* was entered on the Stationers' Register and may possibly have been printed in the same year; if so, the entire edition must have disappeared, and only two copies of that of 1594 survive. Pembroke's men acted it 'publiquely' in London—a production that must have been before 22 June, 1592, or during the short winter season beginning 29 December, 1592, and ending 1 February, 1593, or during the next winter season between 27 December, 1593 and 6 February, 1594. So far no mention of Pembroke's men has been found before the closing of the theatres, and therefore any performance of *Edward II* in the first half of the year 1592 must be more than doubtful. We know they were in London for the short winter season of 1592-3, and probably within these five weeks must be placed the 'sundrie' performances of this play. Their country tour was a failure, and they were back in London five or six weeks after the entry of *Edward II.*

How *Titus Andronicus* came successively into the hands of Pembroke's, Derby's, Sussex's and finally the Chamberlain's men is a problem that invites every critic to hazard a guess. I cannot discover any reason for accepting the conjecture that the non-extant *Titus and Vespasian* was used by Shakespeare as his raw material for *Titus Andronicus,* except that we cannot be certain what *Titus and Vespasian* was about. Every dramatist of the period would know that portion of Roman history well enough to avoid such an absurd mixture as the Goths and Roman emperors of the first century of the Christian era. Arguments drawn from German and Dutch versions of *Titus Andronicus* have little cogency when we recall the strange travesty of *Hamlet* made in Germany; certainly Elizabethan or Jacobean actors were capable of combining the incongruous plots of these two plays merely because 'Titus' was a leading character in each. There are other objections besides our complete ignorance of *Titus and Vespasian.* This play was first acted on 11 April, 1592, and was successful, seven performances bringing Henslowe the high average of £2/8/- each. Two months afterwards the same companies staged a new

play entitled *A Knacke to Know a Knave,* which contains a number
of allusions to contemporary plays. There are two made to
Vespasian; the first occurs at the beginning (ll. 3-4) :

> And giues us leave to rule in this our land
> Like wise Vaspasian Romes rich Emperour ;

the second on B3 is longer,

> Or lyke Vaspasian Romes vertuous gouernour,
> Who for a blowe his sonne did giue a Swaine
> Did straight commaund that he should loose his hand.
> Then vertuous Edgar, be Vaspasian once
> In giuing sentence on a gracelesse childe.

Possibly these allusions to Vespasian and his Brutus-like severity
towards his son—Domitian was a vicious youth—may refer to
incidents which were part of the plot of *Titus and Vespasian.* Any
reader of *A Knacke* cannot but notice how the author has stuffed
the play with bits of heathen mythology, scraps of Roman and
Greek history, similes and abundant moralising.

Later in *A Knacke* a character named Osrick, in welcoming King
Edgar to his house, says :—

> My gracious Lord, as welcome shall you be
> To me, my Daughter, and my sonne in Law,
> As Titus was vnto the Roman Senators
> When he had made a conquest on the Goths,
> That in requitall of his seruice done
> Did offer him the imperiall Diademe.
> As they in Titus, we in your grace shall find
> The perfect figure of a Princesse mind.

There is also a short sketch of the plot of *Locrine,* and possibly a
reference to a play *'Abraham and Lot'* acted by Sussex's men
during the season when they produced *Titus Andronicus* as the one
novelty.

Whoever wrote *A Knacke* must have been busy with it when
Titus and Vespasian was acted for the first time, and no more than
seven performances could have been given before the complete
manuscript of *A Knacke* must have been in the hands of the actors.
Even in this primitive period not less than a month would elapse
before the allowance of the censor, preparation of the parts,
provision of costumes and properties and the necessary rehearsals
would enable a play to be staged. *Titus and Vespasian* was one of

the plays acted by the combined Strange's and Admiral's men
during the short winter season of 1592-3. I do not think the actors
would have paid Shakespeare or any one else to rewrite a proved
money-getting play so soon after its first production. Though it
did not make its appearance when the theatres reopened in June,
1594, the name of this play is found in a Revels' list dated 1919.
Certain of Shakespeare's plays had alternative names, e.g., Jacobean
references style the two parts of *Henry IV*, *Hotspur* and *Falstaff*,
but *Titus and Vespasian* could not then be an alternative title of
the extant *Titus Andronicus*. Perhaps the play referred to in
A Knacke may be some popular old play which Shakespeare
subsequently rewrote much as he did *A Shrew;* the existence of
such a play about 1589 would explain Jonson's casual reference in
1614 to 'fiue and twentie or thirty yeeres' in his Induction to
Bartholomew Fair. The extant *Titus Andronicus* was marked by
Henslowe as a new play when produced by Sussex's men on
23 January, 1594, and was a financial success. On 6 February it
was played for the third time, and the same day was entered by
John Danter in the Stationers' Register, having probably been sold
before it was acted. The title-page of the first edition of 1594 states,

As it was Plaide by the Right Honourable the Earle of Darbie,
Earle of Pembrooke, and Earle of Sussex their Seruants.

On the title-page of the edition of 1600 this list of companies reads:

As it hath sundry times beene playde by the Right Honourable the
Earle of Pembrooke, the Earle of Darbie, the Earle of Sussex,
and the Lorde Chamberlaine theyr Seruants.

Its subsequent stage history was short. Henslowe records the plays
acted during an eight-day season after Easter, 1594, of the Queen's
and Sussex's men together; the latter company instead of staging
their new and most successful play put on *Fair Maid of Italy* and
Jew of Malta twice. Perhaps their reason was that they no longer
owned it; the sale to Danter would not have prevented its revival.
However that may be, the combined Strange's and Admiral's men
presented it to very small houses at Newington Butts early in June.
Each of these companies went to its own theatre and *Titus
Andronicus* remained with the Chamberlain's men.

This play was probably revived in Jacobean days if the statement
'As it hath sundry times beene plaide by the Kings Maiesties

Seruants' on the title-page of the quarto dated 1611 has the meaning which the words imply. Perhaps, too, its popularity continued, because Jonson would not sneer at it and *Spanish Tragedy* without a cause. In this edition the names of the other companies are omitted. On issuing a new edition of an old play, publishers advertised it by stating on the title-page the name of the existing company which had most recently played it. Changes from 'Lord Chamberlaines Seruants' used during Elizabeth's reign to 'Kings Maiesties Seruants' were made in the quartos of *Richard III* (1612), but not in that of 1605, of *Love's Labour's Lost* (1631), *Romeo and Juliet* (1607), *Richard II* (1608, copies with cancel title-page); also in *Thomas Lord Cromwell* (1613), and corresponding changes in *Famous Victories* (Queen's in 1598, to Kings Maiesties Seruants in 1617), *Friar Bacon* (1594 and 1630) and *Edward II.*

Perhaps the simplest explanation of the successive changes of ownership may be that this play was the property of an actor and not of any company; we know that Edward Alleyn and Martin Slater, two actors, owned plays. Shakespeare may have been rewriting an old play upon the theme of *Titus Andronicus* when, without warning, the Privy Council on the 22 June, 1592, closed all the London theatres on account of recent riots; later an outbreak of the plague kept them closed. Companies about to pad the hoof on country roads would not be likely to spend money on new plays, and some prominent actor associated with Strange's men may have bought it. This actor may have been a member of Pembroke's men who were perhaps preparing to present *Titus Andronicus* at a London theatre during the short winter season in 1592-3; being prevented from doing this by the closing of the theatres on 1 February, 1593, they may have played it on their country tour. When the company returned to London bankrupt, the owner of this play and perhaps one or two more of Strange's men may have rejoined Derby's men and produced it in some of the larger country towns. Unable, perhaps, to endure the hardships of a winter tour he may have returned to London and have become a hired actor with Sussex's men, who produced this as the one new play of their London season; the owner sold a copy of the play to Danter who entered it in the Stationers' Register on the day when the theatres were shut down. Subsequently the actor rejoined the Chamberlain's men, and his play became portion of their repertory. This guess seems as good as any of the others.

A Shrew and *True Tragedy* are the other two plays known to have belonged to Pembroke's men or to some prominent actors of the company. Four plays would not be enough for a week's stay in York or Norwich, and *Contention* or *2 Henry VI* was almost certainly one of their plays. To these *Massacre at Paris* and perhaps two or three more may be added.

I have thought it better to discuss at this stage certain questions concerning the provenance of *Edward II* and *Titus Andronicus* before making any particular examination of lines common to any pair of plays. My interpretation of the known facts does not attempt more than some provisional explanation consistent with them and, like every theory on this dark period of Elizabethan stage history, resolves itself into a series of not too improbable guesses.

My lists of lines common to various pairs of plays are perhaps much too elaborate, but my purpose is to show how the concentration of most commentators in the past on the question of the authorship of *Contention* and *True Tragedy* has put aside as unimportant the fact that many texts of this period assumed to be free from corruption contain, each of them, a considerable number of verses present also in one or more other plays. How these verses found their way from one text to another provides critics with a problem which includes the interrelations of *Edward II, 2 Henry VI, 3 Henry VI, Contention, True Tragedy* and *Massacre at Paris* as a part and a part only; and many diverse solutions are inevitable. As a pre-requisite to any attempt to solve this problem, a study of the possible interconnection of all plays of this period in which identical or echoed lines are present is necessary.

In the following table I have set out in order the total number of lines or passages common to each pair of the plays named; in the final column are totals for the plays in their rows. For each pair of the parallel texts totals are given under three separate headings, one total for those in Shakespeare's play only, a second for those common to the play named and the two parallel texts, and the third for those present in the bad quarto only. In consequence the total for *2 Henry VI* will be obtained by adding together the total given in the final column for *2 Henry VI* only to that for *2 Henry VI* and *Contention;* similarly the totals for *3 Henry VI, Contention* and *True Tragedy* will be obtainable. It must be noted that certain passages of both *2 Henry VI* and *3 Henry VI* are quoted merely in order to illustrate the formation of passages in the bad quartos. This table includes also totals for plays for which no quotations are given in my lists; the latter consist entirely of pairs of lines or passages, one of which at least comes from *Edward II, 2 Henry VI, 3 Henry VI, Contention* or *True Tragedy;* I may add that lines common to *Troublesome Raigne* and any one of these five plays are omitted from the totals.

TABLE XXI

TOTALS OF LINES COMMON TO PAIRED PLAYS NAMED

Name of Play	Edward II	2 Henry VI	2 Henry VI and Contention	Contention	3 Henry VI	3 Henry VI and True Tragedy	True Tragedy	Massacre at Paris	Arden of Feversham	Soliman and Perseda	Titus Andronicus	A Shrew	Spanish Tragedy	Battle of Alcazar	Edward I	Totals
Edward II	–	1	6	11	1	8	3	9	5	7	–	–	2	–	4	57
2 Henry VI	1	–	–	–	–	–	–	–	1	1	–	–	–	–	–	3 ⎫
2 Henry VI and Contention	6	–	–	–	1	–	3	4	3	1	–	1	1	–	–	20 ⎬23 ⎫
Contention	11	–	–	–	3	7	2	1	4	2	3	1	–	1	–	35 ⎬55
3 Henry VI	1	–	–	4	–	–	–	2	–	1	–	–	–	–	–	8 ⎫
3 Henry VI and True Tragedy	8	–	–	7	–	–	–	8	2	7	3	–	–	1	–	36 ⎬44 ⎫
True Tragedy	3	–	3	2	–	–	–	4	2	1	3	3	–	4	1	26 ⎬62
Massacre at Paris	9	–	4	–	2	8	4	–	3	2	–	–	–	–	–	32
Arden of Feversham	5	1	3	4	–	2	2	3	–	5	3	2	2	–	–	32
Soliman & Perseda	7	1	1	2	1	7	1	2	5	–	2	–	8	–	–	37
Titus Andronicus	–	–	–	3	–	3	3	–	3	2	–	–	–	–	–	14

This list of totals does not pretend to be exhaustive or complete even for the two plays on Henry VI, the two bad quartos and *Edward II.* More than half of the so-called parallel passages have been omitted because the 'parallels' are too often limited to an unusual word or short phrase. In addition *Troublesome Raigne* has fourteen lines or passages found in Shakespeare's two plays, and numerous passages of *Thomas of Woodstock* echo lines belonging to the same plays, *Richard II* and *Edward II.*

If *Contention* and *True Tragedy* are regarded as independent plays, the table gives for each of nine named plays the number of lines or passages common to it and certain other named plays. *Edward II* has 59 lines or passages common to it and ten other plays if two lines in *A Knacke* are added to those in the table 2 *Henry VI* has 28 and 3 *Henry VI* 50 in 11 other plays if those common to *Troublesome Raigne* and these plays are added, *Contention* 55 in 11 other plays, *True Tragedy* 62 in 10 other plays, *Massacre at Paris* 32 in 7 other plays, *Arden* 32 in other plays and *Soliman and Perseda* 37 in other plays. *A Shrew* has no borrowings from *Edward II* and *Titus Andronicus*, yet I find in it 22 lines or passages borrowed from 8 other plays most of which are from the early plays of Marlowe and Greene; *Titus Andronicus* has none common to either *Edward II* or *A Shrew*. Possibly the latter was an old play and off the acting list of Pembroke's men when *Edward II* and *Titus Andronicus* became part of their repertory, and the last named play was not long enough on their acting list to become as contaminated as the others. I have already noted the fact that the text of *Arden* is poor; the verse exhibits many of the defects characteristic of a report and over a hundred lines are harsh or unmetrical. There are 63 lines of nine syllables of which 28 are defective in the first foot and 31 others in the interior of the line. Perhaps the best evidence of a reporter's presence is the large number of twelve-syllable lines, some of which have an extra initial syllable and a final unstressed syllable to make cacophony complete. In addition there are thirty unscannable lines of eleven syllables; in many of these the extra syllable is a monosyllabic enclitic such as 'but,' 'and,' 'for,' 'why,' etc., prefixed to an ordinary decasyllabon. Most of these defects are undoubtedly the work of actors.

Shakespeare's parallel texts enable us to examine the inflow and distribution of lines belonging to other plays with some particularity. Below is set out a list under four headings denominated A, B, C, D. Under the heading A are set out the totals of verse lines in 2 *Henry VI* and 3 *Henry VI* respectively, and beneath each of these totals is the number of lines and passages borrowed from or common to the plays named in the previous tables. Under the heading B are given the totals of such verse lines found in 2 *Henry VI* and

3 *Henry VI* respectively but not in the corresponding bad quartos, and beneath each of these totals is the number of the lines of this portion of Shakespeare's play found also in other plays named in the tables. Under the heading C will be found the totals of verse lines common to each pair of these parallel texts, and below each total the number of lines present also in one or other of the plays named. Under the heading D are the respective totals of non-Shakespearean lines in *Contention* and *True Tragedy* and beneath each of these totals is the number of these lines found also in the other plays named in the tables.

SUBDIVISION OF BORROWED LINES

	A	B	C	D
2 *Henry VI* and *Contention*	2,602	1,370	1,232	420
	23	3	20	35
3 *Henry VI* and *True Tragedy*	2,902	1,006	1,896	228
	43	8	35	26
Totals	5,504	2,376	3,128	628
	66	11	55	61

Some comments on these interesting results are worth while. Lines common to one or the other of Shakespeare's plays and to some of the other plays named, but not present in the bad quartos are few in number, and this small number is further reduced if five borrowed lines common to 3 *Henry VI,* the corrupt *Contention* and the equally corrupt *Massacre at Paris* are excluded from the total given for 3 *Henry VI.* On the other hand, the totals of verse lines under the heading C common to 2 *Henry VI* and *Contention* and 3 *Henry VI* and *True Tragedy* taken together and the other plays are, relatively to length, four times as numerous as those under heading B. If Shakespeare was responsible for inserting 66 lines or passages from other plays in 5,504 lines of his own verse we have a peculiar conundrum to explain. How did it come about that in 2,376 lines of his verse, most of them presumably not spoken on the stage by the actors, we find at most eleven lines common to his plays and those of other writers, whilst in the remaining 3,128 lines written by him and spoken on the stage more or less accurately there are at least 55 lines common to these portions of his plays and the other plays on the list? Such an unequal distribution cannot be an accident, for such a lopsided vagary of chance ought not to operate twice in the same direction, first in *2 Henry VI* and next in *3 Henry VI.* Possibly the play-adapter during the making of the stage versions may have contrived to reject or to retain portions of Shakespeare's text according as lines from other plays previously learnt by the actors were absent or present. That the actors helped themselves freely from the same group of plays is proved by the presence of 61 lines in *Contention* and *True Tragedy,* which were borrowed consciously or unconsciously by the compilers of these plays to fill the many gaps due to faulty memory. Such pilferings amount to nearly ten per cent. of the non-Shakespearean work present in these two bad quartos. Shakespeare was not responsible, in my opinion, for the insertion of many lines and passages from other plays, nor do I think that any play-adapter used or would have been permitted to use such an arbitrary method of making an acting version.

Such a great difference as that between the total of non-Shakespearean lines under heading B and the similar total under heading C in each of Shakespeare's plays points, in my opinion, to unsuspected and unexplained activities of the actors during those abnormal years, 1592-4. Compelled to tour the provinces during these plague years, certain actor-scribes may have meddled with the poet's manuscripts while they were preparing acting versions and may have inserted lines from other plays in what they thought were suitable parts of their texts. Thirty years later the original manuscripts or fair copies of them may have been sent to the press with these unauthorized additions. These acting versions may have been used as prompt copies when these plays were revived. On the other hand, if the folio text represents Shakespeare's manuscripts, a critic may reasonably claim that the poet in his prentice days followed the practice of the early playwrights and borrowed lines from the plays of others as he thought fit. Only two possibilities exist. Either Shakespeare borrowed these lines or some other persons—most probably actors—inserted them in the poet's manuscripts.

To the critics who believe that Shakespeare revised or rewrote *Contention* and *True Tragedy* I leave the task of explaining why he did his work in such an odd way. Of 55 lines common to *Contention* and other plays he rejected 35 and retained 20 in 1,232 lines of verse, whilst he was satisfied with the addition of only three such lines to 1,370 new lines of his own. Similarly of 61 lines common to *True Tragedy* and other plays he kept 35 and expunged 26; simultaneously he was content to insert eight lines only from other plays in over a thousand new lines of verse.

Perhaps the most important inference deducible from the results set out in this table is that no firm or decisive inference can be drawn from the presence in two plays of lines common to both unless at least one of the plays is corrupt. This problem involves an answer to the question, to which of the three plays does the line,

> Because he loues me more than all the world,

originally belong? To *Arden*? to *Spanish Tragedy*? or to *Edward II*? to arrange them in the order of entry on the Stationers' Register. Another question follows, which of the variants represents the original line? Critics have, in general, accepted as sound the texts of these plays and of *Soliman and Perseda, Titus Andronicus, 2 Henry VI* and *3 Henry VI;* that of *Edward I* is open to suspicion. Some editors have assumed that if a line or passage was common to two plays, it must belong to the earlier printed text, an assumption not invariably justifiable. Excluding *2 Henry VI* and *3 Henry VI*, we know the dates of entry on the Stationers' Register of all the other plays on the list above and the year of publication, but we do not know the respective dates of composition or of stage representation, the condition of the manuscripts sent to the printer, the circumstances in which and the reasons why they came to the press, or even the names of the companies by which three of them were acted. Our complete ignorance of the dates of composition and representation renders almost futile any discussion of such rhetorical questions as are put above; consequently the eleven plays in my earlier table cannot be arranged in chronological order.

In his monograph[1] on the parallel texts of *Henry VI* Professor Tucker Brooke has postulated a definite chronological order, viz., *Massacre at Paris, Contention, True Tragedy* and *Edward II*. Most critics identify the first of these four plays with the 'tragedy of the

---

1. Transactions of Connecticut Academy, *The Authorship of 2, 3 Henry VI*, Vol. xvii, p. 141, *et seq.*

gyves' acted as a new play on 26 January, 1593, and as Marlowe was dead on 1 June, 1593, obvious difficulties exist against the acceptance of such an order of composition or representation on the stage. Professor Brooke suggests that Marlowe was prone to the repetition of striking lines and phrases. I have already pointed out that in the two parts of *Tamburlaine* he adopts repetition as a literary or dramatic device very much as did Greene, Peele, and Kyd, but many of the lines repeated in *Massacre at Paris* and *Edward II* are not striking and do not subserve any literary or dramatic purpose. Professor Brooke suggests that in *Edward II* he used over again 37 lines or passages that are found in the three preceding plays; but he must also account for 22 lines and passages 'conveyed'—to use Pistol's term—from *Arden, Spanish Tragedy, Soliman and Perseda* and *A Knacke,* all of them acted or in print when he was writing his play, and *Edward I.* Marlowe's petty borrowings in *Edward II* total in all 65 lines or two and a half per cent. of the length of this play. This amount of plagiarism exceeds anything found in the most corrupt play of that period and must equal what is present in *Wily Beguiled.* Professor Brooke's suggested order of composition does not, I think, fit the facts. First, I do not believe that *Contention* and *True Tragedy* had any existence as independent plays except as current names given to debased and abridged versions of *2 Henry VI* and *3 Henry VI.* Secondly, *Massacre at Paris* was, in my opinion, written after and not before the three other plays, though the borrowings might be either way, from them to it or from it to them. Thirdly, certain considerations suggest that *Edward II* was written after and not before *2 Henry VI* and *3 Henry VI.* Marlowe seems to have been influenced by Shakespeare's work in several respects. *Edward II* is much the longest and dramatically the best of his plays, and is comparatively free from the spate of classical allusions and similes found so plentifully in *Tamburlaine* and *Faustus;* speeches are much shorter and more direct, dialogue more plentiful and to the point, the plot less diffuse, bombast more subdued and less in evidence, and characterization somewhat improved. Fourthly, if *Edward II* was unacted and perhaps unwritten by 26 January, 1593, how could it have been 'sundrie times publiquely acted in the honourable citie of London, by the right honourable the Earl of Pembroke his servants'? I have suggested that this company produced it not at the court, but when they were in London during the winter of 1592-3, but this suggestion tells against the chronological order favoured by Professor Brooke. I do not believe that London companies gave new plays their first airing in the country towns; if the extant *Massacre at Paris* was the new play acted just before the London theatres closed, then Pembroke's men produced three new plays, the revised *Contention,* the revised *True Tragedy* and *Edward II* during a country tour.

In his monograph Professor Brooke concentrated on proving his thesis that Marlowe had a hand in writing *2 Henry VI* and *3 Henry VI;* he treated *Massacre at Paris* as a textually sound abridgment and quoted passages from it, which are also found in *True Tragedy,* as if such parallels chosen from a play even more corrupt than *True Tragedy* had a decisive value as evidence for the truth of his theory. By confining his search for 'parallels' to this small group of plays he missed the vitally important fact that at least ten plays with texts assessed as of average soundness are inextricably linked together in a net-work of lines or passages common to two or more plays. If Elizabethan dramatists of this period neighbourly borrowed some lines from the plays of others, we have a simple explanation of the loan-lines we find in *Edward II;* as a guide to a critic in search of an author the presence of such lines may mean, and usually does mean, nothing at all except a side-track into a morass of difficulties. When corrupt plays are under examination, corruption cannot be ignored. Such plays are usually the result of two separate abridgments, the first made by order of the company, the second by the actors or reporter in their attempts to remember parts of this acting version which had been half learnt or partly forgotten. My table suggests that these factors cannot be neglected or undervalued when the borrowings of *Contention* and *True Tragedy* from other plays are being discussed; they equal three per cent. of each play, and represent ingatherings from at least ten extant plays and probably as many more plays no longer in existence.

To the four recognized plays in the Pembroke's repertory I suggest the addition of a second four, viz., *Contention, Arden,*

Soliman and Perseda and *Massacre at Paris*. Four plays, including a comedy and three sombre tragedies, would not offer much choice to the burghers of the larger towns situated within two days' tramp of the Welsh border. Pembroke was Lord President of Wales and its virtual ruler, and the scanty records show that his servants were far more highly rewarded by the civic dignitaries of such towns than companies under the patronage of other lords. Moreover a country nobleman would, like Sir Thomas More in the play bearing his name as title, assume the right of commanding the actors to present a play which he had not seen during his rare visits to London, and eight plays would provide greater variety of choice than four.

Chapter XXI

INTER-PLAY BORROWINGS OF THE LATER
BAD QUARTOS

THIS group consists of four plays printed between 1597 and 1603, and includes the first quartos of *Romeo and Juliet, Henry V, Merry Wives* and *Hamlet*. Of these *Henry V Q1* has some repeated and transposed lines but none from other plays, a fact which suggests that the reporter knew the text of the original well enough to know what was not in it. Each of the other three quartos has some borrowed lines; in *Romeo and Juliet Q1* and *Merry Wives Q1* these come as far as is known exclusively from other plays of the poet's. The reporter of *Hamlet Q1* took in far more lines from a greater variety of plays including some from those not written by Shakespeare. Henslowe records the production of 38 new plays in 90 playing weeks during the two years that may have preceded the representation of *Romeo and Juliet*. Most probably the public love of novelty compelled the Chamberlain's men to stage during this period about thirty new plays or one every three weeks; Shakespeare's contribution would not exceed seven or eight or not a fourth of the total number requisite. Not one of the remaining twenty-two plays is now extant. Probably some lines borrowed from one or more of these plays are represented in the non-Shakespearean lines of Q1, for we cannot assume that the dramatic fare provided by the company for their audiences was entirely Shakespearean.

Six years elapsed between the printing of *Romeo and Juliet Q1* and of *Hamlet Q1,* and our knowledge of the repertory of the Chamberlain's men is scanty in the extreme; omitting the plays of Shakespeare and Jonson, we know of five only, viz., *Warning for Fair Women, A Larum for London, Satiromastix, Thomas Lord Cromwell,* a lost morality, *Cloth Breeches and Velvet Hose,* and perhaps *Mucedorus.* It is not surprising, therefore, that very few lines from the plays of other dramatists are discoverable in *Hamlet Q1* which contains lines or echoes of lines belonging to fifteen plays of Shakespeare. Some lines may have been carried

391

over from the so-called *Ur-Hamlet*, the old play which Shakespeare
may have rewritten and which we know was acted in 1594
and may have been again on the acting list in 1596 or even
later. Possibly the company may have revived the perennially
popular *Spanish Tragedy* shortly before or after *Hamlet Q2* had
been staged. Nashe's allusion suggests that *Ur-Hamlet* dated as
early as 1589, and thus it may well have gathered some snippets
from *Arden, Soliman and Perseda* and *Spanish Tragedy* as did
Edward II. Some echoes of phrases or unusual words found in
Every Man out of His Humour, Antonio's Revenge and *Thomas
Lord Cromwell* together with borrowings from *Twelfth Night,
Pericles* and *Othello* suggest that the reporter did not neglect
popular plays acted c. 1601-2.

III Romeo and Juliet Q1

Except for the omission of numerous short and long passages,
few of which are of much importance to the plot, the text of the
first two acts of *Romeo and Juliet Q1* does not differ from the
corresponding portions of Q2 more than the better preserved
portion of Orlando's part in *Orlando Furioso Q1* differs from
what appears in the Dulwich MS. This surreptitious quarto
contains some borrowings from earlier plays of Shakespeare
notably from *2 Henry VI, 3 Henry VI, Richard III, Titus
Andronicus* and *Two Gentlemen*. Most of the examples below
consist of a half line of Q2 to which has been added a half line
from another play of Shakespeare's; a few are adaptations of
alien lines.

(i) *Prince*. Your liues shall pay the forfeit of the peace.
Q2. 1.1.95

   Prince. Your liues shall pay the ransome of your fault.
Q1. 1.1.50

   And lowly words were Ransome for their fault,
2HVI. 3.1.127

   And that shall be the ransome for their fault.   *Tit*. 3.1.156

(ii) *Rom*. O blessed blessed night, I am afeard
   Being in night, all this is but a dreame.   Q2. 2.2.139-40
   Rom. O blessed blessed night, I fear being night,
   All this is but a dreame I heare and see.   Q1. vi.162-3
   How like a dreame is this? I see, and heare.   *T.G*. 5.4.26

(iii) *Iul.* How doth her latter words reuiue my hart.   Q1. ix.42
King. Oh Clifford, how thy words reuiue my heart.
3HVI. 1.1.163

(iv) *Cap.* Nurse prouide all things in a readines.   Q1. xiii.127
All things are in readinesse.   *R3.* 5.3.52

(v) *Friar.* Peace ho for shame, confusions care liues not,
In these confusions.   Q2. 4.5.65-6
Friar. O peace for shame, if not for charity.   Q1. xix.71
Peace, peace for shame: If not, for Charity.   *R3.* 1.3.273

(vi) *Paris.* Accept this latest fauour at my hands.   Q1. xxii.11
But beg one fauour at thy gracious hand.   *R3.* 1.2.208

(vii) *Paris.* With funerall praises doo adorne thy Tombe.
Q1. xxii.13
Till we with Trophees do adorne thy Tombe.   *Tit.* 1.i.388

(viii) *Rom.* So get thee gone and trouble me no more. Q1. xxii.22
And then be gone, and trouble you no more.   *R2.* 4.1.303

IV HENRY V Q1

No borrowings.

V MERRY WIVES OF WINDSOR Q1

(a) ROMEO AND JULIET Q2

Quick. And, as they say, she is not the first
Hath bene led in a fooles paradice.   Q1. vi.39-40
Nurse. If ye should leade her in a fooles
paradise, as they say, it were a very grosse
kinde of behauior.   *R.J.* Q2. 2.4.155-6

(b) MERCHANT OF VENICE

(i) *Fal.* Ha, ha, misteris Ford, and misteris Page,
haue I caught you a the hip? go too.   Q1. vi.74-5
If I can catch him once vpon the hip.   *M.V.* 1.3.41

(ii) *Fenton.* Then thus my host. Tis not vnknown to you.
Q1. xvi.6
Tis not vnknowne to you Anthonio.   *M.V.* 1.1.122

(c) 2 HENRY IV

Pist. When Pistoll lies do this.   Q1. v.44
Pist. When Pistol lyes, do this.   *2HIV.* 5.3.117

(d) HENRY V Fo.

   (i) *Pist.*   I do retort the lie,
     Euen in thy gorge, thy gorge, thy gorge.   Q1. i.46-7
     Pist. I do retort the solus in thy bowels.   *HenV*. 2.1.48

   (ii) *Nym.* But if you run bace humors of me.   Q1. i.50
     Nym. I will run no base humor.   *M.W.Fo*. 1.3.71
     Nym. The King hath run bad humors on the knight.
                            HenV. 2.1.116

   (iii) *Nym.* And there's the humor of it.   Q1. i.51; iii,21,64,79.
                                           v.55
     Nym. And that's the humor of it.   *HenV*.(Fo) 2.1.66
     Nym. And there's the humor of it.   *HenV*.(Q1) iii.50

   (iv) *Evans.* He is an arant lowsie beggerly knaue:
     and he is a coward beside.   Q1. viii.35-6
     Evans. Now you are an honest man, and a
     scuruy beggerly lowsie knaue beside.   Q1. xv.58-9
     Flucl. Your Maiestie heare now, sauing your
     Maiesties Manhood, what an arrant rascally,
     beggerly Knaue it is.   *HenV*. 4.8.31-3
     Fluel. The rascally, scauld, beggerly, lowsie
     pragging Knaue Pistoll.   *HenV*. 5.1.5
     Fluel. Aunchient Pistoll: you scuruie lowsie Knaue.
                              HenV. 5.1.15-6

(e) HAMLET Q1

   Mrs. Ford. What is the reason that you vse me thus?
                             Q1. xii.102
   What is the reason that you vse me thus? *Ham Q2*. 5.1.277
   What is the reason, sir, that you wrong mee thus?
                              Ham Q1. xvi.163

VI HAMLET Q1

(a) SPANISH TRAGEDY

   (i) *Dutchesse.* Thou maist (perchance) haue a more noble
     mate.   Q1. ix.111
     I, but perhaps she hopes some nobler mate.   *S.T*. 2.1.26

   (ii) *Lear.* Therefore I will not drowne thee in my teares.
                               Q1. xv.53
     To drowne thee with an ocean of my teares.   *S.T*. 2.5.23

   (iii) *Lear.* Reuenge it is must yeeld this heart releefe.
                               Q1. xv.54
     For in reuenge my hart would find releife.   *S.T*. 2.5.41

(iv) *Queen.* I will conceale, consent and doe my best,
What stratagem soe're thou shalt deuise.   Q1. xi.106-7
Hieronimo, I will consent, conceale
And ought that may effect for thine auaile.   *S.T.* 4.1.46-7

(v) *Ham.* I neuer gaue you cause.   Q1. xvi.164
Hieronimo, I neuer gaue you cause.   *S.T.* 3.14.148

(vi) *Ham.* For if the King like not the Comedie,
Why then belike he likes it not perdy.   Q2. 3.2.281-2
Ham. And if the King like not the tragedy,
Why then belike he likes it not perdy.   Q1. ix.185-6
Hier. And if the world like not this Tragedie,
Hard is the hap of olde Hieronimo.   *S.T.* 4.1.196-7

(b) 2 HENRY VI and CONTENTION

(i) *King.* Being the chiefest piller of our state.   Q1. xiii.59
Braue Peeres of England, Pillars of the State.
    2HVI. 1.1.75

(ii) *Hor.*   he hath appoynted me
To meete him on the east side of the Cittie } Q1. xiv.15-16
To morrow morning.
This Euening, on the East side of the Groue. *2HVI.* 2.1.43

(iii) *Ham.* Farewel Horatio, heauen receiue my soule.
    Q1. xviii.108
King. Ah vnkle Gloster, heauen receive thy soule.
    Cont. x.50

(iv) *Lear.* Now that the funerall rites are all performed.
    Q1. ii.16
King. Go take him hence, and see his funerals
              be performde.   *Cont.* xi.21

(v) *King.* As milde and gentle as a Doue.   Q1. xvi.161
Suff. As milde and gentle as the Cradle-babe.
    2HVI. 3.2.392

(c) 3 HENRY VI and TRUE TRAGEDY

(i) *King.* O these are sinnes that are vnpardonable.   Q1. x.7
Marg. Oh 'tis a fault too too vnpardonable. *3HVI.* 1.4.106

(ii) *King.* Therefore Leartes be in readynes.   Q1. xvii.6
Gent. And desires you to be in readinesse.   Q1. xviii.27
Mess. Royall Commanders, be in readinesse.
    3HVI. 2.1.208

(iii) *King.* And not the deerest friend that Hamlet lov'de
Will euer haue Leartes in suspect.   Q1. xv.26-7
Edw. Giue me assurance with some friendly Vow,
That I may neuer haue you in suspect.   *3HVI.* 4.1.141-2

(iv) *Lear.* For woe begets woe, and griefe hangs on griefe.
Q1. xv.55

Wo aboue wo : greefe more then common greefe.
3HVI. 2.5.94

(d) RICHARD III
(i) *Ghost.* Yea, murder in the highest degree.   Q1. iv.88
Murther, sterne murther, in the dyr'st degree. *R3.* 5.3.196

(ii) *Rosen.* Bound By loue, by duetie, and obedience.
Q1. vi.11-12

And put meeknes in thy breast,
Loue Charity, Obedience, and true Dutie.   *R3.* 2.2.107-8

(iii) *Ham.* And diue into the secreet of my soule.   Q1. ix.207
Diue thoughts downe to my soule, here Clarence comes.
R3. 1.1.41

(iv) *King.* How now Gertred, why looke you heauily?
Q1. xv.39

Why lookes your Grace so heauily to day?   *R3.* 1.4.1

(e) TITUS ANDRONICUS
(i) *Ham.* A looke fit for a murder and a rape.   Q1. xi.39
By nature made for murthers and for rapes.   *Tit.* iv.1.59

(ii) *Coram.* Into this frensie, which now possesseth him.
Q1. vi.94

Vnlesse some fit or frenzie doe possesse her,   *Tit.* 4.1.17

(f) COMEDY OF ERRORS
(i) *Lear.* Therefore I will not drowne thee in my teares.
Q1. xv.53

Oh traine me not sweet Mermaide with thy note,
To drowne me in thy sister floud of teares.   *C.E.* 3.2.45-6

(ii) *Ham.* Treason, ho, keepe the gates.   Q1. xviii.85
Dromio keepe the gate.   *C.E.* 2.2.205

(g) ROMEO AND JULIET
(i) *Gild.* My lord, your mother craues to speake with you.
Q1. ix.190
Madam your mother craues a word with you. *R.J.* 1.5.109

(ii) *Queen.* I had thought to adorne thy bridale
                          bed, faire maide,
And not to follow thee vnto thy graue.   Q1. xvi.139-42
                          Euery one prepare
To follow this faire Coarse vnto her graue.   *R.J.* 4.5.95-6

(iii) *King.* None liues on earth, but hee is borne to die. Q1. ii.47
Well, we were borne to die.   *R.J.* 3.4.4

(h) MERCHANT OF VENICE

(i) *Coram.* For louers lines are snares to intrap the heart.
                                              Q1. iii.66
The Painter plaies the Spider, and hath wouen
A golden mesh to intrap the hearts of men *M.V.* 3.2.121-2

(ii) *Coram.* Mary wel thought on, t'is giuen me to vnderstand.
                                              Q1. iii.49
But there the Duke was giuen to vnderstand.   *M.V.* 2.8.7

(i) 1 HENRY IV

(i) *King.* How now son Hamlet, how fare you, shall‘
we haue a play?   Q1. ix.69
Shall we haue a Play extempory?   *1HIV.* 2.4.268-9

(ii) *Ham.*   i'le take the Ghosts word
For more then all the coyne in Denmarke.   Q1. ix.182-3
Ile not beare mine owne flesh so far afoot again,
for all the coine in thy Fathers Exchequer. *1HIV.* 2.2.33-4

(j) HENRY V

(i) *King.* Well sonne Hamlet, we in care of you;
but specially in tender preseruation of your health.
                                              Q1. xi.155-6
                          in their deere care
and tender preseruation of our person.   *HenV.* 2.2.58-9

(ii) *King.* The winde sits faire, you shall aboorde to night.
                                              Q1. xi.159
Now sits the winde faire, and we will aboord:
                                              HenV. 2.2.12
We will aboord to night   *HenV.* 2.2.71

(k) TWELFTH NIGHT

(i) *Coram.*   Such men often proue,
Great in their wordes, but little in their loue. Q1. iii.69-70
                          for still we proue
Much in our vowes, but little in our loue.   *T.N.* 2.4.117-8

(ii) *Queen.* Whenas he came, I first bespake him faire.

Q1. xi.114

But I bespake you faire, and hurt you not.   *T.N.* 5.1.181

(iii) *King.*   wee'le put on you
Such a report of singularitie.   Q1. xv.30-1
Put thy selfe into the tricke of singularitie. *T.N.* 2.5.134-5

(1) OTHELLO

(i) *Ghost.* Nay pitty me not, but to my vnfolding
Lend thy listning eare.   Q1. iv.74-5
Oth.   Most Gracious Duke,
To my vnfolding, lend your prosperous eare.

Oth. 1.3.242-3

(ii) *Ham.* Vpon my loue I charge thee let it goe.   Q1. xviii.102
Oth. Speake: who began this? On my loue I
charge thee?   *Oth.* 2.3.168

(iii) *Ham.* I neuer gaue you cause: but stand away. Q1. xvi.164
Des. Alas the day, I neuer gaue him cause.   *Oth.* 3.4.159

(iv) *Coram.* My Lord, content you a while.   Q1. vii.3
Iago. Content thy selfe, a-while.   *Oth.* 2.3.361

(v) *King.* Although I know your griefe is as a floud,
Brimme full of sorrow.   Q1. xiii.118-9
Brab.   For my perticular griefe
Is of so flood-gate, and ore-bearing Nature.   *Oth.* 1.3.55-6

(vi) *Ham.* Ile no more of it.   Q1. vi.196
Cass. Let's haue no more of this.   *Oth.* 2.3.101

(m) PERICLES

(i) *King.* The cause and ground of his distemperancie.

Q1. vi.7

Coram. We cannot yet finde out the very ground
Of his distemperance.   Q1. viii.26-7
Rosen. My good lord, let vs again intreate
To know of you the ground and cause of your
distemperature.   Q1. ix.188-9
Vpon what ground is his distemperature?   *Per.* 5.1.27

(ii) *Lear.* Yet something is there whispers in my hart. Q1. ii.19
But there is something glows vpon my cheek,
And whispers in mine ear, Go not till he speake.

Per. 5.1.94-5

(n) TAMING OF THE SHREW

> *King.* Therefore let mee intreat you stay in Court.
>
> Q1. ii.31
>
> Let vs intreat you stay till after dinner.   *T.S.* 3.2.192

(o) MUCH ADO

> *Lear.* And now his tongue, Speakes from his heart.
>
> Q1. iii.5-6
>
> For what his heart thinkes, his tongue speakes. *M.A.* 3.2.14

(p) 1 HENRY VI

> (i) *Queene.* God grant it may, heau'ns keep my Hamlet safe.
>
> Q1. xiii.5
>
> *Talb.* Then be it so: Heauens keepe old Bedford safe.
>
> *1HVI.* 3.2.100

> (ii) *Ham.* To affright children and amaze the world.   Q1. xi.41
>
> *Talb.* The Scar-crow that affrights our Children so.
>
> *1HVI.* 1.4.21

(q) CROMWELL

> (i) *King.* Meane while be patient, and content your selfe.
>
> Q1. xiii.68
>
> Father, be patient, and content your selfe.   *Crom.* 1.2.47

> (ii) *Queene.*   lest that he
> Faile in that he goes about.   Q1. xiv.20-1
> Heauen prosper you in that you goe about.   *Crom.* 3.1.97

(r) ANTONIO'S REVENGE

> *Ghost.* Speake to her Hamlet, for her sex is weake.
>
> Q1. xi.76
>
> I pardon thee, poore soule! O shed no teares;
> Thy sex is weake.   *A.R.* 3.5.7-8

> (Spoken by ghost of Andrugio to his ex-wife).

My list above does not exhaust the borrowed phrases and the echoes of lines with which the reporter filled *Hamlet Q1;* they are scattered throughout the play, especially in those scenes where Claudius, Laertes and the two courtiers play the chief parts. Their speeches are frequently a patchwork of such fragments and at times degenerate into nonsense. Examples could be quoted of phrases drawn from most of the plays which have furnished lines to Q1 ; I shall refer more particularly to those derived from *Othello, Romeo and Juliet* and *Merry Wives*. The phrase 'loue and dutie,' found three times in *Hamlet Q1* but not in the second quarto, was used for the first time by Shakespeare in *Othello*. Iago declares (1.1.60-1) that he follows Othello,

> Heauen is my Iudge, not I for loue and dutie,
> But seeming so, for my peculiar end.

More significant of direct borrowing is the use in *Hamlet Q1* of the compound adjective 'Olympus-high,' used in *Othello* (2.1.184-5) :

> And let the labouring Barke climbe hills of Seas
> Olympus high.

As Laertes leaps into the grave he cries (Q1. xvi.142),

> Now powre your earth on, Olympus hie.

Another word 'splintered' used in *Richard III* and *Othello* in the then current surgical sense of 'bound up with a splint' or 'splinter' is used by Ophelia (Q1. vi.203) in the ordinary sense of 'broken into splinters.'

Romeo and Juliet Q2 contributed several scraps to this garbled text. Claudius refers to mad Ophelia as 'A pretty wretch !' (Q1. xiii.41), a phrase used by the nurse of baby Juliet, and his command to his courtiers 'Spare for no cost' (Q1.viii.15) is almost identical with Capulet's instructions to his servants 'Spare not for cost' (*Romeo and Juliet Q2.*4.4.6) ; similarly the phrase 'noble parentage' has been transferred rather grotesquely to Q1 from the same play. Shakespeare's attempts to vary the stale gags with which the low comedian prefaced his mocking comments on the answers given by his butts to his riddles were doomed to failure. In *Romeo and Juliet Q2* he sets down 'Prates' and 'Prates to' as Peter's successive retorts to the blundering replies given by the two musicians (Q2. 4.5.129,132). Will Kemp seems to have altered these, as the corresponding retorts in Q1, which probably gives us what was spoken on the stage, are 'Pretie' and 'Prettie too' (Q1. xix.99,101). Most modern authors have followed Pope in his unwarranted preference for the reading of the bad quarto; throughout this scene Peter is purposely uncomplimentary. In *Hamlet Q2* the first gravedigger's gags are 'too't againe, come,' and afterwards 'Too't' (Q2. 5.1.47,52). In Q1 the reporter combined the gags in *Hamlet Q2* and *Romeo and Juliet Q1,* and the grave-digger encourages his assistant with 'That's prety, too't agen, too't agen,' and later 'Prety agen.'

One line (Q1. xii.102) found in the bad quarto of *Merry Wives* but not in the folio version,

> What is the reason that you vse me thus?

is found identically in *Hamlet Q2* (5.1.277), but in Q1 (xvi.163) becomes unmetrical,

> What is the reason sir that you wrong mee thus?

Similarly Desdemona's line (1.3.243) in *Othello,*

> To my vnfolding lend your prosperous eare,

is found (iv.74-5) in *Hamlet Q1* as follows,

> > but to my vnfolding
> Lend thy listning eare,

but is not in *Hamlet Q2.*

Sir E. K. Chambers thinks that *Merry Wives* must be later than *Hamlet,*[1] but the presence of the line in *Merry Wives Q1* proves nothing. These plays were entered on the Stationers' Register, *Merry Wives* on 18 January 1602, and *Hamlet Q1* on 26 July 1602, an entry which seems to have provided for the printing of *Hamlet Q2* in 1604. Few critics will believe that Shakespeare deliberately inserted in *Hamlet Q2* a line borrowed from *Merry Wives Q1* though not in the folio version, or inserted in *Othello* a line belonging to *Hamlet Q1* but not in Q2. Obviously if *Merry Wives* and *Hamlet* had been on the acting list for some months before 18 January 1602, the borrowing might have been either way; similarly if *Hamlet* and *Othello* had been on the same acting list for some time prior to 26 July 1602, transfer of a line from one play to the other would be possible. The balance of probabilities, however, tells very heavily against the possibility that the Shakespeare of *Hamlet* and *Othello* borrowed lines from the pirated editions of his own plays. My assumption that the reporter responsible for the issue of *Hamlet Q1* inserted in it lines and phrases borrowed from *Othello* implies that the latter play had been produced not later than the early months of the year 1602.

1. *William Shakespeare*, Vol. i, p. 423.

There are snippets such as Polonius's 'changde his colour' (vii.180) and Ophelia's 'his shooes untide' (v.44) from *As You Like It,* reminiscences of *King John* in Ophelia's 'gripes me by the wrist' (v.47) and the King's 'princely sonne' (ii.27); cant sayings which had seen much service in other plays, such as 'But what remedy' and 'have a care of,' and identical borrowings from *Two Gentlemen,* e.g. Laertes' phrase, 'You haue preuail'd my Lord' (xiii.122) and the King's 'forbear awhile' (xiii.119). The remark of Claudius to Polonius 'see where hee comes poring vppon a booke' (vi.111) seems an echo of the phrase in *Love's Labour's Lost;* Polonius's 'vemencie of loue' (vii.28) recalls Falstaff's words to the disguised Ford, and his declaration 'I my selfe will stand behind the arras' (viii.33) is almost identical with a stage direction in *Merry Wives Q1.* Gertrude's simile 'as raging as the sea' (xi.113) reminds us of a similar phrase in *Troilus and Cressida,* and to this play may be referred Polonius's line 'as deepe as the centre of the earth' (vi.102).

Study of the many borrowings from Shakespeare's other plays provides evidence almost sufficient in itself to refute the theory that *Hamlet Q1* is an independent play, the work of some unknown dramatist. No educated thief would have been so stupidly impudent as to steal so much, and then misuse and misplace most of what he had stolen. Some speeches are a composite of pilfered lines and phrases unskilfully joined together, and almost every passage which is not represented in the second quarto or the folio text, lacks thought, expression and, at times, meaning.

CHAPTER XXII

STAGE DIRECTIONS

I N the *Oxford English Dictionary* the term 'stage direction' is defined as the direction 'inserted in a written or printed play where it is thought necessary to indicate the appropriate actions, etc.'; this will be taken to include entrances and exits. Study of the variations found in the respective stage directions of each pair of parallel texts adds considerably to the evidence in favour of the priority of Shakespeare's plays.

In general the stage directions found in the first editions of this group of Shakespeare's plays are, if not those of the author, the work of some other competent man of the theatre. Occasionally an entry and some exits are omitted, 'exit' may be written where 'exeunt' is necessary, but few difficulties of interpretation or staging result from such small defects. One play, the folio version of *Merry Wives,* stands apart from the others. It is the only play of the six divided completely into acts and scenes, and also the only play unprovided with stage directions. At the head of each scene, except I. iii, iv; II. i, iii; III. i, ii, there appears a list of the characters that take part in it arranged in order of their appearance; only one entry, *Enter Fairies,* occurs in the last scene elsewhere than at the beginning. Exits of characters who leave the stage during the progress of the scene are unmarked; the final 'exeunt' should sometimes be 'exit.'

Professor Dover Wilson suggests that the author's manuscript was lost, and that the folio text was made up from the actors' parts; perhaps this could be done, though the reconstruction of long scenes in which a number of characters appear would be many times more difficult than any cross-word puzzle. Two remarks on this suggestion occur to me. Whoever did this job of 'assembling' the text should have been able, without giving himself much trouble, to supply from the parts themselves the necessary exits and entrances and insert them in the order of their occurrence in each scene. Again, Professor Wilson assumes that the parts

403

between them contained the full text, and ignores the fact that, in a play so full of action and stage 'business,' the company would not need at most more than the 2,200-2,300 lines which could be acted in the two hours allotted for representation. A text prepared from actors' parts, that is, the acting version, would have been nearly four hundred lines shorter than the extant folio text. Perhaps the copy for the folio was obtained by Heminge and Condell from one of the poet's admirers, one who had often seen the play acted and had paid a scribe to provide him with the full text. If the Dulwich MS. of Orlando's part is accepted as typical of Elizabethan stage practice, entrances and exits would be indicated in each part by lines ruled across the sheet of paper; only two 'exits' and one 'exeunt' occur in the manuscript.

Exclusive of entrances and exits the directions of the other five authentic texts are sufficient, and not much more than are necessary for staging the plays; they are more numerous and fuller in detail in the two parts of *Henry VI* and *Romeo and Juliet* than in the three later plays. As the plot, characters and scenes of each bad quarto and of Shakespeare's parallel text are largely identical, the entrances and the exits found in the bad quarto will ordinarily correspond with those of the authentic text in number and relative position. Yet the rest of the directions may be different in each text. It is important to keep in mind that each of these plays of Shakespeare was abridged before being acted, and practically all the actors would know nothing of the text beyond what was in their parts or was spoken on the boards. Official abridgment might omit some unimportant characters, but, however drastic the 'cuts' may have been, the stage directions would not necessarily be much shorter than those of the full text. If a printed play was a corrupt abridgment of the official acting version, the stage directions might differ entirely from those written for this acting version; those inserted by the author or the play-adapter may disappear, and those of the actors and reporter take their place.

Stage directions originate in the theatre not in the study. Good sense prescribes that the author of a drama in the vernacular should give his instructions to the actors in their native tongue. Our early popular drama exhibits the paradox of an English text garnished with stage directions in Latin. If we compare the Dulwich MS.

with *Orlando Furioso Q1,* we perceive that Greene's crisp Latin
directions in MS. have disappeared in Q1, or have been translated
into English, or have been expunged together with some lines of
the original text, and the sense of both condensed into a side-note
or a line of description. *Currunt* (MS. 301) has been lost with
the six lines of text that preceded it. *Decumbit* (MS. 323) is
translated *He lies downe againe* (Q1. 1274); 'againe' refers to an
earlier and interpolated direction *lies downe to sleepe* (Q1. 1253).
Three consecutive Latin directions *pugnant* (MS. 445), *N. victus*
(MS. 446) and *Oliver victus* (MS. 453) together with MS. 446-56
are omitted and compressed into a centred stage direction, *He
fighteth first with one, and then with another, and ouercomes them
both* (Q1. 1526-7). Later in the same scene two other Latin
directions, *pugnant* (MS. 464) and *O. Victus* (MS. 468) and five
lines of text are replaced by a short description, *They fight a good
while and then breath* (Q1. 1536).

From these changes which we know were made by the actors and
inserted by them in *Orlando Furioso Q1,* we learn that the actors
disliked Latin, and all Latin words except 'exit,' 'exeunt,' 'manet'
and 'manent' disappeared from the majority of plays shortly after
Shakespeare began to write for the stage. Marlowe inserted a
number of Latin stage directions in *Edward II,* perhaps his latest
play; Chapman and Jonson used them in their tragedies, but good
sense triumphed ultimately over pedantry.

Other changes made in the text of *Orlando Furioso Q1* by the
reporter are not so commendable. He wrote notes, usually centred,
descriptive of what was taking place on the stage; he gave at
times a brief summary of Greene's text which had been struck out
or poorly memorized, and he inserted directions unnecessary for
competent actors who knew how to use action suitable to whatever
the author had written. Excellent examples of such superfluous
notes and instructions, characteristic of reported texts, occur in an
interpolated comic scene of *Orlando Furioso Q1* in ll. 1192-1233.
Argalio hires a fiddler to play 'a fit of mirth' to cheer up his mad
master, Orlando, who is then asleep. He asks him twice to play
some music, yet the reporting pirate, when the fiddler begins a
tune, instead of putting a direction, *he plays,* at the right hand

side of the page, inserts in the body of the text the following centred note (ll. 1213-4) :

> *He plays and sings any odde toy, and*
> *Orlanáo wakes.*

Being out of his senses, Orlando thinks that 'Shan Cuttelero' has brought him his sword, takes the fiddle from its owner, tests the bow-string which he thinks is the edge of his sword, beats the musician with his own instrument, and finally breaks the fiddle over the owner's head. Though the dialogue tells the story well enough, the pirate inserted between each four or five lines of text a running account of Orlando's actions. We have:

> *He takes away his fiddle.*   (Q1. 1220)
> *He strikes and beates him with his fiddle.*   (Q1. 1225)
> *He breakes it about his head.*   (Q1. 1232)

Quite naturally the scene ends with *Exit Fidler.*

Dr. Greg has proved that the pirate and his assistants, the actors, are responsible for the insertion of these inept descriptions of stage 'business' in *Orlando Furioso Q1;* we scarcely need the partial check supplied by the Dulwich M.S. to accept this statement. Texts above suspicion provide few examples of this type of stage direction; accordingly we may reasonably infer the handiwork of the actors whenever such directions are found in a play otherwise corrupt.

Differences between the stage directions of Shakespeare's authentic plays and those of the corresponding bad quartos are to be expected. He wrote them for the public theatre, and added to the text such instructions as would enable the manager to stage and the actors to play to the best advantage; publication was entirely secondary and an after-thought. Each bad quarto is based on the abridged version of a play which had been cut down before it was acted, and was a composite of actors' recollections eked out perhaps by some actors' parts and memories of the 'plot.' After some kind of a text had been compiled, the pirate added such directions and notes as he thought necessary for readers; usually the bad quarto was intended for publication and not for staging the play. Such a difference of purpose might in our day result in a considerable difference between the running commentary written by the dramatist for the players, and the first aids to understanding thought necessary for

the general body of readers. In Elizabethan times the pirate
would most probably model his instructions to the readers on
what was customarily found in printed texts, and would do the
best that his memory, inexperience and want of education permitted. As far as is known, the most careful editors, such as
Chapman, Jonson or Marston, did not increase the instructions and
notes inserted for the actors; buyers of their printed plays would
know that they might read hundreds of lines omitted in representation in addition to those spoken on the stage.

One peculiarity of the stage directions of the bad quartos is the
almost complete lack of any instructions for music. Of twenty-five
such directions in *3 Henry VI* only one remains in *True Tragedy,*
and *Henry V Q1* omits all those in the folio version. Flourishes,
sennets, marches, drum-beating, in fact all varieties of military
music, were seemingly looked upon as such an invariable portion
of a 'drum-and-trumpet' play that the pirate did not trouble himself
to append instructions for them. Grammar, syntax and diction of
the stage directions written by the compilers of the bad quartos
suffer the same eclipse as much of the text, and suggest the
derivative character associated with inability to write ordinary
English correctly.

Contention and 2 Henry VI

Contention is nearly eleven hundred lines shorter than *2 Henry VI*
yet has more and longer stage directions, though Shakespeare's
play is more bountifully provided with such aids to the actors than
most of his other plays. Few directions for the playing of music
are inserted except an imperative *Sound Trumpets* after the newly-
crowned Margaret has taken her seat by her husband; this corresponds to a *Florish* in the folio. Saunder Simpcox comes upon the
stage (v.54) *with Musicke,* and *a flourish* proclaims (xxiii.67) the
victory of the Yorkists at St. Albans. Another centred direction,
'*Now sound vp the Drumme*' after the knighting of Dick Butcher,
may be a part of Cade's speech (xiii.78); if not, it may be a piece
of clownish burlesque added to grace Cade's accolade. This
episode and the stage direction are additions due to the reporter.

His Latin is most barbarous. *Exet* replaces both *exit* and
exeunt; twice he writes *exet omnis,* and once (ix.168), in his '*Exet
omnis manit Yorke,*' achieves four blunders in writing three words.

Of five Latin words, only 'imprimis' and 'item' are correct, being probably part of a document read on the stage by Gloster; of eight phrases and sentences only three remain, two imperfectly transcribed.

Another singularity of *Contention* is that on each occasion that a person of rank enters, the stage directions give the full title of this character. Thus the folio play opens with:

> *Flourish of Trumpets: Then Hoboyes.*
> *Enter King, Duke Humfrey, Salisbury, Warwicke, and Beauford*
> *on the one side.*
> *The Queene, Suffolke, Yorke, Somerset, and Buckingham,*
> *on the other.*

In *Contention* the corresponding stage direction is:

> *Enter at one doore, King Henry the sixt, and Humphrey Duke of Gloster, the Duke of Sommerset, the Duke of Buckingham, Cardinall Bewford, and others.*
> *Enter at the other doore, the Duke of Yorke, and the Marquesse of Suffolke, and Queene Margaret, and the Earle of Salisbury and Warwicke.*

Another pair of stage directions is worth citing. Act two, scene three of *2 Henry VI* opens thus:

> *Sound Trumpets. Enter the King and State*
> *with Guard, to banish the Duchesse.*

Compare this crisp entry with the opening of the seventh scene of *Contention*:

> *Enter King Henry, and the Queene, Duke Humphrey, the Duke of Suffolke, and the Duke of Buckingham, the Cardinall, and Dame Elnor Cobham, led with the Officers, and then enter to them the Duke of Yorke, and the Earles of Salsbury and Warwicke.*

Except that Duke Humphrey, at this time heir to the throne, usually keeps his title, and is twice styled *Protector* and once *Gloster*, and that Beaufort is referred to as *Cardinall*, nearly all the entries and all the exits of *2 Henry VI* refer to the characters without naming their titles. Order of precedence in entries and the grouping on the stage vary in each text. Speech-prefixes are haphazard and inconsistent in the abbreviations used. Thus Humphrey is termed *Glo., Glost., Gloster, Hum.,* and *Humf.* in *2 Henry VI;* in *Contention* he is variously *Hum., Hump., Humph.,*

Humphr., and at times *Humphrey.* In *Pinner of Wakefield* the reporter adopted the same habit of giving nobles and knights their full titles upon each entry. As will be noticed in these directions, traces of the language used in contemporary 'plots' are present in *Contention.* Thus the simultaneous entrance involved in *Enter at one doore . . . Enter at the other doore* at the beginning of the play recurs also in the seventh, twentieth and twenty-first scenes; *to them* is found in three entries.

Another marked peculiarity of *Contention* concerns the language used by characters about to leave the stage. Shakespeare knew that the dull actor always found it difficult to make a natural exit at the end of a scene, and devised many ingenious methods and varied forms of words to help him to get 'within' gracefully. In a surreptitious quarto such as *Contention* the actors reduced his diversity of formulas to two, viz., 'and so farewell' and 'come lets go,' and variants of these. Wherever one of these two occurs in the last line of a scene, corruption may be suspected, because Shakespeare usually provided the actors with a different method of talking themselves off the stage on each occasion. One humorous incident occurs at the end of the sixth scene of *Contention.* The Duke of York has invited the Earl of Salisbury and his son, the Earl of Warwick, to sup with him at the ducal palace. Their 'simple supper ended,' their host explains to his guests his pedigree and his just title to the crown. They accept his statement and acknowledge his title by doing him homage. York thanks them, and closes the scene with the words 'come lets goe'! These stupid mummers did not understand that during this scene the stage represents the palace of a prince, and that by using the words 'come lets goe' their host was asking his important guests to leave his house. Shakespeare's dramatic ingenuity had provided for the difficulty of getting the three nobles off the stage. Six lines before the end Salisbury rises from his seat and says (2.2.77) to York:

My Lord, breake we off; we know your minde at full.

All rise and as they walk to the stage door, Warwick promises his help; and the Duke of York concludes the scene, as they leave the stage together, with a promise (2.2.81-2):

to make the Earle of Warwick
The greatest man in England, but the King.

This quarto has several stage directions which give unnecessary details of stage 'business.' After a long conversation between the queen and Suffolk the latter remarks (iii.69) to her,

> But staie Madame, here comes the King.

Then follows a long entry:

> *Enter King Henry, and the Duke of Yorke and the Duke of Somerset on both sides of the King, whispering with him, and enter Duke Humphrey, Dame Elnor, the Duke of Buckingham, the Earle of Salsbury, the Earle of Warwicke, and the Cardinall of Winchester.*

Then follows this dialogue (iii.70-5):

> *King*. My Lords I care not who be Regent in France,
> or York, or Somerset, alls wonne to me.
> *Yorke*. My Lord, if Yorke haue ill demeande himselfe,
> Let Somerset enioy his place and go to France.
> *Somerset*. Then whom your grace thinke worthie, let him go,
> And there be made the Regent ouer the French.

In the folio the entry gives the names of the characters, omitting Somerset; the sense of the dialogue is substantially the same. Henry's first speech makes it clear that the two candidates for the regency of France had previously been pressing their claims upon him; actors of intelligence would not need the instruction given in the quarto direction in order to play their parts.

In the quarto version of the quarrel between the queen and the Duchess the incident is first described and then acted. Humphrey has left the stage and we read (iii.133-7):

> *The Queene lets fall her gloue, and hits the Duches of Gloster, a boxe on the eare.*
> *Queene*. Giue me my gloue. Why Minion can you not see?
> > *She strikes her.*
> I cry you mercy Madame, I did mistake,
> I did not thinke it had bene you.
> *Elnor*. Did you not proud French-woman.

One stage direction is all that is necessary, and only one is found in the folio.

In the following example the stage-notes are taken from the text. The Witch is directing the conjuring of the spirits and says (iv.9-13):

Then Roger Bullinbrooke about thy taske,
And frame a Cirkle here vpon the earth,
Whilst I thereon all prostrate on my face,
Do talke and whisper with the diuels be low,
And coniure them for to obey my will

She lies downe vpon her face.
Bullenbrooke makes a cirkle.

Both of these notes are unnecessary. In the folio version, Bullin-brooke is director of ceremonies, and tells the Witch 'be you prostrate and grouell on the Earth'; there is no stage note.

Several stage directions give interesting but unnecessary details. Thus the fifth scene opens with,

Enter the King and Queene with her Hawke on her fist,
and Duke Humphrey and Suffolke, and the Cardinall, as if
they came from hawking.

In *2 Henry VI* the only addition to the list of characters is *with Faulkners hallowing.*

In the eighth scene Humphrey's wife does penance for committing the sin of sorcery.

Enter Dame Elnor Cobham, bare-foote, and a white sheete about
her, with a waxe candle in her hand, and verses written on
her backe and pind on, and accompanied with the Sheriffes
of London, and Sir Iohn Standly, and Officers, with billes
and holbards.

The folio version has much less detail, because the text supplies it:

Enter the Duchesse in a white Sheet, and a Taper burning in her
hand, with the Sherife and Officers.

Certain stage directions are practically identical in both versions and probably have a common source. In the fifth scene Gloster exposes the tricks of an impostor, who had been shamming blindness and lameness, and pretends that his sight had been miraculously restored at the shrine of Saint Albans. The scene begins with a stage direction,

Enter one crying, A miracle (a miracle).

Then comes a procession of the townsmen,

Enter the Maior of Saint Albones and his brethren (with
Musicke), bearing the man (that had bene blind), between two in
a chaire.

Gloster cross-examines him, convicts him of imposture, and orders the beadle to whip him to cure his lameness with the result described below:

> *After the Beadle hath hit him one girke, he leapes ouer the stoole and runnes away, and they run after him, crying, A miracle, (a miracle).*

Brackets enclose words not in the folio version; in the third direction *once* replaces *one girke*, and the words *follow and cry* are used instead of *run after him, crying*.

In the seventh scene, an elaborate stage-direction provides the setting for the trial by battle between the armourer Horner and his man Peter.

> *Enter at one doore, the Armourer and his neighbours, drinking to him so much that he is drunken, and he enters with a drum before him, and his staffe with a sand-bag fastened to it, and at the other doore, his man with a drum and sand-bagge, and Prentises drinking to him.*

This is identical in both versions except for some variations in spelling and punctuation.

So the stage directions at the beginning of the sixteenth, seventeenth and eighteenth scenes are identical except for minor deviations. They are:

> *sc. xvi. Enter (the) Lord Skayles vpon the Tower (Walles) walking. Enter (three or foure) Citizens below.*

In the folio *three or foure* of *Contention* is *two or three*.

> *sc. xvii. Enter Iack Cade and the rest, and strikes his (sword) vpon London Stone.*

In the folio *sword* is changed to *staffe;* the *Contention* version agrees with the sentence used in Halle.

he strooke his sword on London stone saieng, Now is Mortimer Lord of this citie,

a line which Cade speaks at the beginning of this scene.

> *sc. xviii. Alarmes, (and then) Matthew Goffe is slaine, and all the rest (with him). Then enter Iacke Cade (again), and his company.*

This identity of certain long stage directions in these two parallel plays is closely related to an almost line-for-line correspondence of the two texts preceding or following the direction. Professor Alexander suggests[1] that:

---

1. *Shakespeare's Henry VI and Richard III*, Cambridge, 1929, p. 82.

the copy for the Quarto does not everywhere consist of reported matter; it is occasionally based on transcription.

He discusses two or three such passages of considerable length and comes to the conclusion:

The sudden appearance and equally sudden cessation of transcription of this kind in the course of the Quarto Text can only be explained on the hypothesis that the compilers had at their disposal not only what they could remember of their own parts but a fragmentary transcript of the play.[2]

This explanation seems reasonable and adequate, and the facts are sufficient to support the hypothesis. I suggest that the number of lines identically common to *Contention* and *2 Henry VI* in the examples cited by Professor Alexander could be considerably increased, if it is remembered that any transcript for a country tour would be made from the acting version and would not include much more than three-fourths of the text of *2 Henry VI*. In addition, at least two pages of the transcript used in compiling *Contention* differ textually from what is found in the folio in such a haphazard and puzzling way as to indicate defects in the pages. They may have suffered badly from the wear and tear incident to continuous use and the rough life of a country tour mostly on foot; and the interpolations present may represent attempts of the actors to restore broken or missing lines of text.

Abridgment is a factor of the first importance, one that cannot be disregarded in discussing the origin of such a corrupt text as *Contention*. The official play-cutter must excise a fourth of *2 Henry VI* to make an acting version that can be played in about two hours. York's long soliloquy (1.1.209-254) is so written that the first twenty-two lines can be removed without leaving a trace of their existence; all that is essential to the plot and characterization is in ll. 231-254, and this portion is, except for a word, almost literatim in *Contention,* in which it is preceded by four lines spoken by Warwick and followed by two lines spoken by Eleanor, all practically word perfect. Warwick's speech (1.1.204-8) has lost a line in *Contention;* this omission rather improves the passage. Then follow the last twenty-four lines of York's soliloquy, and the first scene ends; the second scene opens with a stage direction:

Enter Duke Humphrey and Dame Ellanor, Cobham his wife,

2. *Op. cit.*, p. 86.

which is slightly varied in *2 Henry VI*. Eleanor speaks two lines
perfectly and then begins to mangle her lines. Thus this page of
transcript would extend to 34 lines if the two exits are counted,
and it more closely corresponds to the text of the folio than any
other piece of transcription, equal to it in length.

There is the usual disorder in the earlier portion of the dialogue
that gives us Duke Humphrey's cross-examination of the impostor
in the first scene of the second act, but from Suffolk's line (v.86),

> And yet I thinke Ieat he did neuer see,

the agreement of the two texts is very good. Professor Alexander
thinks that transcription begins here with Suffolk's line and ends
with the stage direction after l. 122. I agree with this view because,
though the same characters speak throughout this episode (v.49-
132), lines 49-85 are in hopeless disorder, lines 86-122 except at
the beginning are exceedingly close to the folio text, and lines
123-133 are clearly a poor report. Dialogue is difficult to speak
and even more difficult to report, and the variation cannot be
explained except as Professor Alexander has done.

I am not so confident that the episode of the trial by combat
(vii.40-78) came from a transcript of *2 Henry VI* (2.3.59-102),
unless it had lost patches of script, represented an abridgment of
the text, and had undergone some considerable amount of interpolation. Certainly this transcript was neither as complete nor as
accurate as the previous two. Both of York's speeches (2.3.90-1,
93-4) are missing as are two lines of the armourer's speech
referring to him; these omissions may be cuts, but one of his lines,

> Sound Trumpets, Alarum to the Combattants,

seems necessary. It is replaced in *Contention* by *Alarmes* as part
of a stage direction more descriptive than that in the folio. In both
versions three of Horner's neighbours accompany him, and each
speaks the same speech in both, and drinks to the armourer in
turn; the third neighbour adds to his part 'and be merry' taken from
the speech of the second prentice. It is curious that in each text
the names of the three prentices, Robin, Will and Tom, are the
names of three of Cade's followers in *Contention;* the three speak
in this play but two only in the folio version. Thus we have:

> *1. Prentise.* Here Peter I drinke to thee, and be not affeard.
> (*2. Pren.* Here Peter, heres a pinte of Claret-wine for thee.)

3. Pren. (And heres a quart for me, and) be merry Peter,
And feare not thy maister, fight for credit of the Prentises.
Peter. I thanke you all, ∧ (but Ile drinke no more).

In these five lines the interpolations, enclosed in brackets, about
equal in length an omission in Peter's folio speech, marked by a
caret. Robin gets the hammer and Will the apron; it is vice versa
in *2 Henry VI.* Just before the duel begins Peter exclaims,

Law you now, I told you hees in his fence alreadie.   (vii.69)

This interpolated line is interesting because it introduces the
expletive 'law' to our language. After the victory he omits the
two lines of pious thanks written for him by Shakespeare, and
contents himself with a simple,

O God I giue thee praise.   (*He kneeles downe.*

His master protests his innocence, but omits, as said above, two
lines about the Duke of York and his own loyalty; he replaces
them with two muddled lines including an order to 'fill all the pots
again,' and varies the order of the clauses in,

to proue him a Knaue, and my selfe an honest man.

His quarto speech closes with an interpolated line,

as Beuys of South-hampton fell vpon Askapart.

Bevis may be the name of an actor in Pembroke's company; he
enters at the opening of Act four, scene two with John Holland,
an actor (c. 1590-2). The armourer's dying words are a variant
of the line in the folio. Henry's six lines are word perfect, but
Contention omits the direction, *Sound a flourish.*

Professor Alexander adds:

as before the manuscript available did not contain merely the scene
itself, it also included the opening stage direction for the following
scene:

Enter Duke Humphrey and his men, in
mourning cloakes

This direction is also given in the Folio.[3]

I accept this as correct, and I suggest that to this direction should
be appended the ten following lines of the eighth scene of *Contention.* If the folio version (2.4.1-16) be examined, it will, I
think, be agreed that Gloster's first four lines (2.1.1-4):

3. *Shakespeare's Henry VI and Richard III*, p. 84.

Thus sometimes hath the brightest day a Cloud:
And after Summer, euermore succeedes
Barren Winter, with his wrathfull nipping Cold;
So Cares and Ioyes abound, as Seasons fleet.

are prosy platitudes that any play-cutter who knew his job would at once mark for omission. There would be left a typically Shakespearean scene-opening as in *Contention*:

Humph. Sirra, whats a clocke?
Seruing. (Almost) ten my Lord.

The next four lines of the folio are omitted and have been replaced by three of the pirate's own; the five lines following them are almost letter-perfect. Lines 15-16 of the folio are not represented in *Contention,* and were probably an official cut; after the last two lines common to both versions,

That erst did follow thy prowd Chariot-Wheeles,
When thou didst ride in triumph through the streets,

the stage direction of either version gives an admirably dramatic contrast in the spectacle afforded by the entry of Duchess Eleanor.

Professor Alexander has, in my opinion proved that a transcript was the source of scenes xvi and xvii and the opening lines of scene xviii of *Contention.* There are some small changes in words, an interpolation, a puzzling inversion of order in two lines (xvii. 3 and 4) and an omission of two lines (4.6.9-10), very probably an original cut.

Acceptance of Professor Alexander's hypothesis becomes almost a logical deduction when 'the fragmentary transcript' includes an authentic stage direction that the pirate could not have inserted in his copy for the printer unless he had a page of official manuscript containing it. Yet passages of the poet's text have been omitted in a page that should retain them, and this disappearance can be explained satisfactorily only on the assumption that the play-adapter struck them out before making the acting version; consequently the transcript derived from this acting version could not have in it the passages of the original marked for omission. No hypothesis, however, can be accepted as valid unless it is completely in accord with all the known facts. Professor Alexander's remark on the episode of the Armourer and his man:

The dialogue that follows this direction is given in the Folio and Quarto almost word for word; each version has a few phrases not found in the other,[4]

understates the defects and peculiarities of the quarto text here. About eight lines of the folio text are missing, and the equivalent of more than eight lines has been added. York has no share in the dialogue or action, and the parts of the prentices are increased; two inversions of order occur, and one stage direction is changed and two more inserted. Official abridgment will explain the loss of Shakespeare's text, and possibly continuous thumbing, hard usage and accidents of flood and field may have worn out and obliterated parts of the few salvaged pages of manuscript. Semi-conscientious interpolation will account for the rest of the changes made. Unless the actors tinkered with the text of their transcript, I cannot account for a proportion of interpolated lines in it equal to the average for the whole play; many reported passages of *True Tragedy* and *Romeo and Juliet Q1* and even some of *Hamlet Q1* are closer to the authentic text than this account in *Contention* of the trial by battle.

In the last scene of Cade's eventful history the folio version, after a direction, *Enter Cade,* gives him a soliloquy, in the course of which he explains (4.10.7-9) that he has climbed over a brick wall,

> into this Garden, to see if I can eate Grass, or picke a Sallet another while, which is not amisse to coole a mans stomache this hot weather.

All of this soliloquy is omitted in *Contention;* in its place is inserted a descriptive account of his actions at the opening of the twentieth scene:

> *Enter Iacke Cade at one doore, and at the other, maister Alexander Eyden and his men, and Iack Cade lies downe picking of hearbes and eating them.*

He catches sight of Iden, abuses and challenges him as in *2 Henry VI,* and finally declares (xx.16-17):

> and I doe not leaue thee and thy fiue men as dead as a doore nayle, I pray God I may neuer eate grasse more.

What could any audience that had not heard the relevant part of Cade's soliloquy quoted above make of his meaningless chatter about eating grass? The stage direction of *Contention* was for the

---

4. *Shakespeare's Henry VI and Richard III,* p. 84.

actors and did not help the audience. It would seem that the reporter remembered nothing of the soliloquy, and replaced it with a description of what he had seen on the stage; apparently, as Cade spoke some lines at least of the soliloquy, he had gone through the farce of pretending to pick 'hearbes' from the bare boards and of eating them on the stage. Here the stage direction of *Contention* provides definite evidence that part of the soliloquy in *2 Henry VI* omitted in *Contention* was spoken on the stage before the latter play was compiled.

I have discussed elsewhere (pp. 205-7) certain of the stage directions in the twenty-first scene of *Contention,* and their relation to portions of the folio text necessary to the sense of passages in the corresponding portions of the quarto.

3 Henry VI and True Tragedy

Practically all the stage directions of *True Tragedy* are without any evidential value for the purpose of deciding whether it was the source or the derivative of *3 Henry VI;* such errors, defects and variants as exist are not uncommon in many of Shakespeare's undoubted plays. There are scenes in both *True Tragedy* and *3 Henry VI* in which characters who have no entries and no part in the dialogue nor share in the action are present on the stage; a satisfactory explanation is that pairs of richly attired noblemen formed the stage retinue or 'state' of a king. In five scenes of *True Tragedy* the stage directions omit the names of characters requisite for staging the play; among them are George and Richard. George in the eighth scene has no entry, yet not only speaks but is created Duke of Clarence on the battle-field, and Richard, omitted from the characters in the last scene, speaks (xxiii.21-5, 33-4) malevolently and publicly bestows Judas-like kisses on his baby nephew, heir to the throne. Reduction of the number of characters present in the folio scenes occurs in some quarto scenes. For example the 'Lord Maire' of York city appears 'vpon the wals' but not in company with his 'Brethren' as in the folio. A centred stage-note in the same scene of *True Tragedy* states:

The Maire opens the dore, and brings the keies in his hand.

The words 'opens the dore,' i.e., the stage-door, smack of the reporter with his eye on stage 'business' rather than on what the

Mayor said, 'The Gates shall be opened.' In the folio *the Maior and two aldermen* enter, and Edward demands and, as a side-note states, *Takes his Keyes.*

Later the nineteenth scene opens with the direction,

Enter Warwicke on the walles

of Coventry. This is much longer in *3 Henry VI* (Act V. Sc. i):

Enter Warwicke, the Maior of Couentry, two Messengers, and others vpon the Walls.

Except as a stage ornament and a mummer's tribute to the species, the speechless Mayor was unnecessary, but the two messengers or 'posts' take part in the dialogue; and almost immediately Somerville has an entry and talks in the folio, whilst a person styled Summerfield appears from nowhere in *True Tragedy* to speak the same lines as in the folio. These messengers and Somerville could not have been 'within' because they spoke, and to be in sight of the audience ought to have been 'on the walls.'

In the first entry of the play the reporter gives, as did his fellow-pirate of *Contention,* his full title to each nobleman present, including the 'yong Earle of Rutland,' not in the folio cast, and concludes the roll of Yorkists present with the descriptive words 'with White Roses in their hats' and the list of Lancastrians 'with red Roses in their hats.' These details help us to understand a passage in the first scene of the last act of *3 Henry VI.* Warwick has watched Oxford, Montague and Somerset, each 'with Drumme and Colours,' enter Coventry and sees his son-in-law, Clarence, approach; he welcomes him and concludes (5.1.80),

Come Clarence, come: thou wilt, if Warwicke call.

To this 'false, fleeting, perjur'd Clarence' replies (5.1.81-2):

Father of Warwick, know you what this meanes?
Looke here, I throw my infamie at thee:

and renounces the cause of Lancaster. In *True Tragedy* there are helpful changes. Clarence approaches Coventry shouting (xix.52) a similar refrain to the others,

Clarence, Clarence, for Lancaster,

to which his brother Edward replies (xix.53-4);

Et tu Brute, wilt thou stab Caesar too?
A parlie sirra to George of Clarence.

CC

Then follows a descriptive stage-note:

> *Sound a Parlie, and Richard and Clarence whispers togither, and then Clarence takes his red Rose out of his hat, and throwes it at Warwike.*

As the dialogue proceeds exactly as above in the folio text, Clarence's action should proceed simultaneously with his speech quoted above.

One change in a folio direction, *Enter Edward running* (2.3.5), to *Enter Richard running* (vi.14) is remarkable, because it is not consistent with what Richard says of himself (xii.91-4):

> For why hath Nature
> Made me halt downe right, but that I
> Should be valiant and stand to it, for if
> I would, I cannot runne awaie.

An entry at the head of the ninth scene,

> *Enter Clifford wounded, with an arrow in his necke,*

gives some detail not in the folio. He had removed his armour, and literally got it in the neck; this happening may, or may not, be satirized in the last scene of *Knight of the Burning Pestle,* but did not prevent Ralph or Clifford from speaking a long soliloquy. A very long description of the battle of Barnet occurs after xxi.46, which has very little to do with the plot.

> *Alarmes to the battell, Yorke flies, then the chambers be discharged. Then enter the King, Cla. & Glo. and the rest, & make a great shout, and crie, for Yorke, for Yorke, and then the Queene is taken, & the prince, & Oxf. and Sum. and then sound and enter all againe.*

In style this direction reminds us of those at the head of the seventh, twelfth, thirteenth and eighteenth scenes, but has even more resemblance to several directions of *Contention.* Certain commentators point out that this description follows the account given in the chronicles of what happened in this battle, viz., a pretended retreat of the Yorkists, a Lancastrian pursuit followed by the surrounding and destruction of Margaret's forces, and the capture of the leaders. This may have been the customary method of staging this battle, but Shakespeare could not adopt it because he had already used it earlier in this play as a scene in the battle of Towton.

Several unusual features occur in the stage directions of this quarto. First some are put imperatively. Thus when York is captured, we read *Fight and take him* (iii.97) ; afterwards comes, *Sound for a post within* (xi.94), *Sound a Parlie* (xix.80) and *Stab him againe* (xxii.55). Secondly, not only are *exit, exeunt, manet* employed accurately, but we find *Yorke solus* (iii.49) *Henry solus* (viii.i) and *ex. ambo* (xx.44). Edward also quotes *Et tu Brute* to his brother Clarence. None of these bits of Latin are in the folio text. Another peculiarity is an entry, *Enter Gloster to King Henry in the Tower,* which reminds us of the language used in extant 'plots.'

Romeo and Juliet Q1

Q1 is full of side-notes and descriptions more suited to a novel or modern play than to Shakespearean drama. Many of the stage directions in the last three acts are interesting and throw some light upon contemporary methods of staging and acting; they are written with more intelligence and in better style than those in the other bad quartos. In the opening of the first scene occurs a description of certain episodes that are part of the text of Q2. Perhaps the play-adapter struck out more than twenty lines of speeches after Gregory's remark to Sampson (1.1.56-7) :

Say better, here comes one of my maisters kinsmen,

to the first line of the Prince's speech (i.i.79) :

Rebellious subiects enemies to peace.

Instead of these twenty-two lines the reporter gives us a description of the successive happenings (i.42) :

They draw, to them enters Tybalt, they fight, to them the Prince, old Mountague, and his wife, old Capulet and his wife, and other Citizens and part them.

After the entrance of Tybalt the characters are named in the order of rank and not of their appearance on the stage. Shakespeare's words present a vivid scene full of sharp contrasts and vigour, but in a brawl action is better than dialogue. Use of the words, *to them,* twice, suggests that the reporter was familiar with the technical language of the 'plot' of the play ; he may have used it here.

When Capulet begs the 'gate-crashing' maskers to wait for 'a trifling foolish banquet,' the next line runs (1.5.121) :

Is it ene so? Why then I thanke you all.

In Q1 (v.97-9) the passage is:

> We haue a trifling foolish banquet towards.
>
> *They whisper in his eare.*
>
> I pray let me intreat you Is it so?
>
> Well then I thanke you honest Gentlemen.

This unneeded side-note describes a piece of stage 'business,' similar to the whispering in the King's ear, already referred to in my remarks on the stage directions of *Contention*. Here, too, is an admirable example of how the pirate made two lines out of one of Shakespeare's.

Two other notes descriptive of stage business occur in the eighth scene. Mercutio has been making fun of the nurse and sings an indecent song. Q1 inserts (viii.114) a note:

> *He walkes by them and sings.*

As Burbage would play Mercutio or Romeo and Kemp played Peter, I do not think that Shakespeare would be at pains to tell these famous actors how to play their parts. In the third part of *Return from Parnassus* Kemp scoffingly says of the University actors:

The slaues are somewhat proud; and besides, it's a good sport in a part to see them neuer speak in their walk, but at the end of the stage: just as though in walking with a fellow, we should neuer speak but at a stile, a gate, or a ditch, where a man can go no further.[5]

Upon the departure of Mercutio the nurse asks Romeo (2.4.136-7)

> What sawcie merchant was this that was so full of his roperie?

and after freely expressing her indignation, turns to her man Peter and scolds him roundly (2.4.145-6):

> and thou must stand by too and suffer euery knaue
> to vse me at his pleasure.

In Q1 this rebuke is preceded by an unnecessary stage direction,

> *She turnes to Peter her man.*

In Q1 the language of the marriage scene differs entirely from what we read in Q2. In both versions the bridegroom is the first to arrive, and a little later we have *Enter Iuliet* in Q2, but in Q1 this becomes (x.10):

> *Enter Iuliet somewhat fast, and embraceth Romeo,*

a record of stage 'business' rather than a stage direction.

---

5. Hawkins, *Origin of the English Drama*, Vol. iii, p. 270.

After the fatal duel between Tybalt and Mercutio, the stage direction of Q2 is *Away Tybalt;* in Q1 we find (xi.54):

> *Tibalt vnder Romeos arme thrusts Mer-*
> *cutio, in and flyes.*

Mercutio and Benvolio both explain how Tybalt managed to stab his opponent; the audience would see the fight, so the description given is unnecessary.

One ridiculous entry (xii.4) in Q1,

> *Enter Nurse wringing her hands, with the ladder*
> *of cordes in her lap.*

follows hard upon the most drastic 'cut' in the play—Juliet speaks in Q1 only six of the thirty-five lines set down for her. This laughable absurdity is probably due to an association of ideas suggested subconsciously from the reporter's imperfect recollection of the following bit of Shakespeare's dialogue (Q2, 3.2.34-7):

> *Iu.* Now Nurse, what newes, what hast thou there,
> The cords that Romeo bid thee fetch?
> *Nur.* I, I, the cords.
> *Iu.* Ay me, what news? why dost thou wring thy hands?

Three of the longer stage-notes in the thirteenth and fourteenth scenes of Q1 describe the manner in which the actor suited his action to the lines he was declaiming, and are not stage directions in the Elizabethan sense. Thus of Romeo the reporter writes (xiii.103):

> *He offers to stab himselfe, and Nurse snatches*
> *the dagger away.*

As Romeo had previously declared metaphorically but definitely that he would stab himself, and Friar Laurence says to him later,

> Has thou slaine Tybalt? wilt thou slay thy selfe?

this note is superfluous. Juliet has charged her Nurse to give her husband a ring and ask him to visit her. Romeo promises to see his bride and says, 'Farwell good Nurse' (xiii.135). Then follows a note,

> *Nurse offers to goe in and turnes againe,*

with the words,

> Heere is a Ring Sir, that she bad me giuc you.

This is an actor's trick, which Paris plays on Capulet in the next scene. He says to Lady Capulet (xiv.7-8):

> These times of woe afford no time to wooe,
> Maddam farwell, commend me to your daughter.

Then comes the description of what Paris did:

> *Paris offers to goe in, and Capolet*
> *calles him againe.*

Not one of the preceding three notes are in Q2 or Fo. Throughout the fifteenth scene the trail of the reporter is visible in his side-notes. Romeo leaves Juliet (xv.37):

> Farewell my Loue, one kisse and Ile descend,

and *He goeth downe* tells us that he has used the ladder of cords. Shortly afterwards the nurse enters *hastely,* a superfluous adverb considering the context. Capulet sternly rebukes his daughter for her refusal to marry Paris; she says (3.5.158):

> Good Father, I beseech you on my knees,

and Q1 takes up two lines' space to insert a centred direction *She kneeles downe.* Later in scene xvii.21 she tells him that her confessor has 'enjoynd' her 'to fall prostrate here' and ask pardon; once more a superfluous *She kneeles downe* mars the page. Another piece of 'business' occurs at the end of this scene. Before leaving Juliet her nurse has advised her to forget the banished Romeo and marry Paris. Amazed at this time-serving duplicity, Juliet exclaims (xv.186):

> Auncient damnation, O most cursed fiend etc.

Our pirate gravely tells us that before Juliet spoke,

> *She lookes after Nurse.*

One entry in the last scene of the fourth act (Q2) is the famous *Enter Will Kemp;* this was repeated in the third quarto (1609) but excised from the text of the folio version. He is called *Seruing-man* in Q1. Singularly enough, what seems a definite reference to the same actor occurs earlier in Q1, which treats the fourth and fifth scenes of the fourth act as continuous. Preparations are being made for the wedding-feast, and the pirate gives us the centred stage direction (xix.10):

> *Enter Seruingman with Logs & Coales.*

Capulet, who has been making a nuisance of himself, fussily asks,

> How now sirra?
> What haue you there?

and the following dialogue ensues:

> *Ser.* Forsooth Logs.
> *Cap.* Goe, goe choose dryer. Will will tell thee where
> thou shalt fetch them.
> *Ser.* Nay I warrant let me alone, I haue a heade I troe to
> choose a Log.

In the second quarto Capulet says (4.4.15-18):

> *Cap.* Make haste, make haste sirra, fetch drier logs.
> Call Peter, he will shew thee where they are.
> *Fel.* I haue a head sir that will find out logs,
>   And neuer trouble Peter for the matter.

We know that Will Kemp played Peter; Capulet refers to Peter in
Q2, and it is reasonable to explain 'Will' in Q1 as the Christian
name of the actor who impersonated Peter.

After Juliet has drunk the sleeping draught, Q1 concludes the
scene with a dramatic note,

> *She fals vpon her bed within the Curtaines,*

very much in the manner of a Victorian novelist. Such details as
within the Curtaines, and the consequential one afterwards (Q1,
xix.79), *shutting the Curtens,* help us to understand Elizabethan
stage methods, but were unnecessary for spectators or contemporary readers. When the supposed death of Juliet is discovered, the compiler of Q1 writes of the mourning family,

> *All at once cry out and wring their hands,*

an emotional display of stage sorrow which the Friar subdues with
his speech beginning 'Peace ho for shame' (4.5.65).

Exits and entrances in Q2 following the end of the Friar's last
speech in this scene are inextricably muddled. We have first after
line 95, *Exeunt manet.* The dialogue (4.5.96-9) is:

> *Musi.* Faith we may put vp our pipes and be gone.
> *Nur.* Honest good fellowes, ah put vp, put vp,
> For well you know, this is a pitifull case.
> *Fid.* I by my troath, the case may be amended.
>   *Exit omnes.*
>   *Enter Will Kemp.*

He at once begins to bait the musicians who according to the stage
direction should not be there. Q1 explains the *Exeunt manet* of Q2
but characteristically adds details of stage 'business':

> *They all but the Nurse go forth, casting Rosemary on*
> *her and shutting the Curtens.*

Then follows *Enter Musitions,* and the dialogue proceeds:

> *Nur.* Put vp, put vp, this is a wofull case.   *Exit.*
> *1.* I by my troth Mistresse is it, it had need be mended.
>   *Enter Seruingman.*

In Q1 the pirate's description explains that the nurse stayed behind;
if after *manet* we write 'Nurse' the main difficulty associated with
the meaningless *Exeunt manet* of Q2 is solved. Q1 also gives an
entry for the musicians who may have been 'within' from the time
when they played after line 20 in this scene. *Exit Omnes* blunders
in two respects; the musicians did not leave the stage but the nurse
did; *exit* or *exit nurse* would make sense.

Scene twenty-two of Q1 has prefixed this stage direction:

> *Enter Countie Paris and his Page with flowers*
> *and sweete water.*

instead of *Enter Paris and his Page* as in Q2 and Fo. Paris
informs us (5.3.12-17) why he brings 'flowers and sweete water':

> Sweet flower, with flowers thy Bridal bed I strew
> O woe, thy Canapie is dust and stones,
> Which with sweete water nightly I will dewe,
> Or wanting that, with teares distild by mones,
> The obsequies that I for thee will keepe:
> Nightly shall be, to strew thy graue and weepe.
>   *Whistle Boy.*

In Q1 another stage direction precedes the text that corresponds to
the above rhymed lines of Q2:

> *Paris strewes the Tomb with flowers.*
> Sweete Flower, with flowers I strew thy Bridale bed:
> Sweete Tombe that in thy circuite dost containe,
> The perfect modell of eternitie:
> Faire Iuliet that with Angells dost remaine,
> Accept this latest favour at my hands,
> That liuing honourd thee, and being dead
> With funerall praises doo adorne thy Tombe.
>   *Boy whistles and calls.*   My Lord.

Both versions explain what was done with the flowers carried by the page but no mention is made in Q1 of the 'sweete water' which Paris brought. For an explanation of the use made of it the text of Q2 must be consulted. Thus the presence of these words in the stage direction of Q1, which are meaningless unless the text of Q2 was available, furnishes proof that this part of Q2 was in its present form before the copy for Q1 was compiled. Paris had instructed his page to whistle if he heard any one approach; in Q2 he obeys orders, in Q1 he calls as well and informs Romeo and Peter (Balthasar in Q1) that two others are in the church-yard.

During the remainder of this scene the stage directions of Q1 usually have something superfluous. Thus the entry (xxii.15):

> *Enter Romeo and Balthasar, with a torch, a*
> *mattocke, and a crow of yron.*

is followed by Romeo's line (xxii.19):

> Giue mee this mattocke, and this wrentching Iron.

This line with 'that' instead of 'this' occurs in Q2 and Fo without any mention of these tools in the respective entries. Next follows the note,

> *Romeo opens the tombe.*

followed by a speech declaring that he has forced it open. The Friar enters later *with Lanthorne, Crowe* and *Spade,* meets Romeo's man and approaches the Capulets' vault. We read in Q1:

> *Fryer stoops and lookes on the blood and weapons.*

and he begins to speak of what he has seen (xxii.97):

> What bloud is this that staines the entrance
> Of this marble stony monument?
> What meanes these maisterles and goory weapons?

Such a stage direction is without any value; it is descriptive of an action with which the dullest actor would preface and illustrate the words of the author.

HENRY V Q1

Except for a discharge of stage cannon and the use of scaling-ladders at the siege of Harfleur, 'properties' are unmentioned in the folio version; there are no accounts given of costumes, stage-groupings except at the end of the play, no descriptive touches and no information about the relationship existing between the characters. In both the quarto and the folio versions *exit* is used very frequently when more than one leave the stage, and in Q1 *exit omnes* is the usual indication that the stage is ready for a new scene. Several characters in various scenes of Q1, viz., Constable (sc. v), Fluellen (sc. x) and Burgundy (sc. xx) speak though there is no entry at the head of the scene; on the other hand several characters are named as present who do not speak and are not named by other speakers. I have discussed elsewhere the bungling in sc. xiii which results from abridgment and absurd stage directions. Another such difficulty recurs in the eighteenth scene which opens with a conversation between Gower and Fluellen; the latter remains on the stage till almost the end of the scene when he is asked to bring Gower to the royal tent. Neither Shakespeare nor the compiler of Q1 took the trouble of giving Gower an exit, and thus two men, first Williams and next Fluellen, are sent to find a man who should by convention be on the stage. Worse blunders follow. Immediately Fluellen leaves—he has no exit in Q1—the king asks Warwick and Gloster (unnamed in Q1) to

Follow Flewellen closely at the heeles,

to prevent the mischief that may result from the King's practical joke; in Q1 there is no exit marked for any character present in the scene. A change of scene must take place because Williams in Gower's presence strikes Fluellen who insists on his assailant's arrest for treason; the entry of King Henry, Warwick, Clarence and Exeter proves that they had left the stage. In the folio version Gower has no exit provided, but the other stage directions are definite and would permit actors to play the scene as the author intended.

Another sign of the pirate's presence is manifest in the inclusion of Pistol in the dramatis personae of the seventeenth scene of Q1 which concludes with the line,

Bid euery soldier kill his prisoner.

Up to this point Pistol has not given tongue, but now draws his hand across his throat, and 'swelling like a Turky-cock' gobbles out 'Couple gorge,' a favourite phrase of his, and one of the actors' gags censured in *Hamlet*.

In *Henry V Q1* there are heavier reductions of the cast requisite for the authentic version than in any other bad quarto. Thirteen speaking characters disappear, and with them most of the lines written for them. In some instances, as in the other quartos, lines spoken by one character in folio are spoken by another in Q1. On the other hand Clarence and a certain mysterious Gebon figure in Q1 though unnamed in the folio version.

MERRY WIVES Q1

In the absence of any stage directions for the folio version of *Merry Wives* except a list of the entries, not always in the order of appearance, at the head of each scene and a general 'exit' or 'exeunt' at the end, we may assume that the stage directions found in Q1 represent the work of the pirate and his assistants. Q1 has a sufficiency of such stage directions as are necessary for representation. Entries and exits are unusually complete though the defects characteristic of reported texts are noticeable. Thus *exit omnes* replaces 'exeunt' of the folio, and certain characters appear on the stage and disappear from it without any notice. Those present in the opening scene include Bardolph who has no lines to speak and to whom no one refers; apparently the reporter knew that he was among those present but could not remember anything that he said or did. Dr. Greg has given good reasons for believing that the Host was the pirate; if so, he took little notice of the comings and goings of his tapster. Bardolph opens the eleventh scene in company with his old master Falstaff, leaves the stage to bring the customary quart of sack, returns with it and carries a message from Mistress Quickly—all this without an entrance or exit. Slender fares as badly. He has, with Shallow, Page and the Host, an entry in the seventh scene, but his salutation, 'Give you good morrow, sir' is cut out in Q1. Perhaps this explains why the reply of Caius to their greetings in the folio version (2.3.21):

Vat be all you one, two, tree, fowre, come for?

has been cut down in Q1 (vii.10) to

Vat be all you, van to tree come for, a?

Yet Slender was present as 'cauellira Slender' was bidden to go 'ouer the fields to Frogmore.' Here we have proof of the pre-existence of the folio version, because the word 'fowre' necessary to the sense of Q1 is missing though present in the folio. He has an entry in the next scene, but neither speaks nor is spoken to nor takes any part in the action; in the corresponding portion of Shakespeare's play he inconsequentially ejaculates 'O sweet Anne Page' at irregular intervals. His inclusion in the quarto entries suggests as does that given to Bardolph in the first scene that the reporter remembered that Slender was on the stage but forgot what he contributed to the dialogue. Such unnecessary entries in Q1 of characters necessary only in the folio version are an argument for the priority of the latter.

Several stage directions of Q1 have the needless particularity and descriptive style so characteristic of corrupt texts. As in *Contention* and *Hamlet Q1* a fondness for mouthing titles has crept into the entries, though usually non-existent in the exits. On the title-page of Q1 parson Hugh Evans has become 'Syr Hugh the Welch Knight,' a ludicrous blunder eliminated in the second quarto of 1619. Throughout Q1 he is styled 'Syr Hugh' except in scenes x and xii where he is termed 'Priest'; in speech-prefixes he is *Syr Hu* or *Syr Hugh,* rarely *Hu*, and is so addressed throughout the play. In entries the pirate writes 'Sir John Falstaff' or 'Sir John,' but *Fal.* in speech-prefixes and exits. He signs his letter to the wives 'Syr Iohn Falstaffe,' just as Hamlet signs his love-letter to Ophelia in *Hamlet Q1* 'unhappy Prince Hamlet.' Mistress Quickly bids Simple 'step into the counting-House,' and therefore the stage-note a line later,

He steps into the Counting-house.

is superfluous, as is another side-note *'And she opens the doore'* after saying to Simple 'I go to see whose at doore.' Another such piece of superfluity occurs immediately after. Mistress Page says (xii.70) to Falstaff,

Step behind the arras good Sir John.

Pat comes the side-note,

He steps behind the arras.

Ford asks the Host for 'A word with you sir,' and the stupid pirate records (v.99) the piece of stage business,

Ford and the Host talkes.

Such a long description as we find after x.55 :

Sir Iohn goes into the basket, they put cloathes ouer him,
the two men carries it away: Foord meetes it, and all
the rest, Page, Doctor, Priest, Slender, Shallow,

is not necessary in the folio text because each petty detail has been previously arranged by the wives. Later when the women play a trick upon Ford by carrying out the buck-basket just as the men enter the house to search for Falstaff, the larger portion of the previous stage-note was repeated in almost the same words. The very long descriptive note after xvii.65 is needed in Q1 and Folio; it is the basis of what is found in modern texts.

HAMLET Q1

In Q2 the stage directions of several scenes are insufficient for even the modest needs of an Elizabethan play; in Q1 entries are occasionally omitted and exits often unnoted as in other bad quartos, but otherwise the stage directions of Q1 are as good as those in Q2, or even better. The first entry in the second scene of Q1 is:

Enter King, Queene, Hamlet, Leartes, Corambis,
and the two Ambassadors, with Attendants.

The corresponding entry in Q2 runs:

Florish. Enter Claudius, King of Denmarke, Gertrad the Queene,
Counsaile: as Polonius, and his Sonne Laertes,
Hamlet Cum Alijs.

This entry is unusual; the two ambassadors, who speak immediately after the King, are not named and must be included in the 'others.' In the folio version Ophelia has an entry, probably as companion to the queen, and the two ambassadors enter after line 25 of the King's speech; upon their entry while the King was speaking, Professor Dover Wilson has based in part his theory of the double revision of Q1.

Shakespeare wrote thirty-nine lines for the new King's first speech to his council; in Q1 it is reduced to ten badly garbled lines, begins in the middle of the twenty-seventh line, and omits mention of the hostile acts and grievances of which the Danish envoys are to complain. What has become of the omitted two-thirds of the royal speech? Professor Wilson notes the coincidence that in the folio version Cornelius and Voltimand enter at that line of the speech which is the starting point of the scene in the first quarto. He assumes that the actor who played the part of Marcellus and spoke the last lines of the first scene was cast for the part of Voltimand in the next; probably if the royal procession entered leisurely and Claudius spoke his lines after the fashion of some modern kings, Marcellus might change his costume and face and become Voltimand. Professor Wilson is compelled to assume that Claudius spoke all the speech set down for him and to insist that the second quarto omitted to give the ambassadors an entry after the twenty-fifth line. Unless the great-coat and scarf of the sentinel completely covered the rich garb and trappings of the ambassador underneath, Marcellus could not take his place as Voltimand and enter 'Cum Alijs' as in Q2. In his pamphlet, The Copy for Hamlet, 1603, the author makes his meaning clear,

The omission of the first half of the speech proves that the memoriser was one of the ambassadors, who were not on the stage while it was spoken.[6]

I agree with him that what is left in Q1 of the King's speech 'is clearly a piece of bad memorization,' and I think it possible that he may be right in his choice of the pirate, but I do not believe that the omission of the preceding twenty-six lines was due to the pirate's absence from the stage.

There is another and, to my mind, better explanation of this omission. Is it not possible that the stage-adapter struck out all or nearly all this portion of the king's speech to his council because it could be spared without any loss to the acted play? What do these omitted lines tell the audience? First, that King Hamlet is dead, secondly, that Claudius has married his brother's widow, and thirdly, that Fortinbras is intriguing to recover lands lost by his father. The audience has learnt already that King Hamlet is dead and that preparations are being made against hostile inroads on the part of Fortinbras, and of the king's incestuous marriage with his brother's wife Hamlet's first soliloquy will supply details to spare. Every critic must admit that Fortinbras and his activities have very little to do with the story of Hamlet; by the end of the eighteenth century every trace of him and his affairs had been removed by the actors from the tragedy. If I might hazard a wide solution of Shakespeare's reason for his inclusion, it would be that the

6. *The Copy for Hamlet*, 1603, p. 4.

deaths of Claudius and Hamlet left Denmark without an heir to the throne—'a most lame and impotent conclusion' to a semi-historical play in Elizabethan times.

Shakespeare's plays were not represented exactly as he wrote them. For the stage acting versions were prepared, and the length of these in my opinion would not usually exceed 2,300 lines. Hence it follows that official abridgment is responsible for most of the loss of the poet's text in the bad quartos. *Hamlet* is by far the longest of the six authentic plays corresponding to these quartos, and therefore was the most severely abridged, if it was to be acted within the usual time limit. However much modern Shakespearolatry may grieve, an Elizabethan play-adapter, faced with the drudgery of reducing 3,760 lines to an acting version of 2,300 lines would groan, utter some of the poet's most vigorous objurgations, begin abridging and keep on abridging till over 1,400 lines were excised. Long speeches were invariably cut down in preference to dialogue. Of 850 lines in the first act of the received text Q1 retains 633 lines—many half lines of Q2 are counted as full lines of Q1; thus nearly three-fourths remain, a proportion that must be heavily decreased in the other acts. No less than 508 lines of the 586 lines in the popular ghost scenes, or nearly seven-eighths, are found in Q1; in consequence only 125 lines, or less than half, could be retained of the remaining 264 lines. Ghost scenes, and a murder mystery were then, and still are, more entertaining than a meeting of platitudinous statesmen or the domestic affairs of such a humorless household as that of Polonius. I think that the play-abridger struck out the sixteen lines on the king's marriage, and left three or four of those relating to Fortinbras in order to make intelligible to the audience the instructions given to the ambassadors.

After Hamlet has finished his muddled soliloquy in Q1, Horatio and Marcellus enter; Barnardo was certainly with them though without an entry in Q1. Professor Wilson says:

If Barnardo figured at all in the original, he appeared in the first scene only, and had not more than a line or two to say. Voltemar has been at some pains to fit him in, but it is not difficult to detect the joinery-work, one of the clues being that, while he is referred to as present in 1.2.76-188, no provision for his entry is made at the head of the scene.[7]

7. Dover Wilson, *The Copy for Hamlet*, 1603, p. 20.

'Original' I take to mean *Ur-Hamlet* before the suggested first revision. Hamlet has the politeness of princes. Horatio, accompanied by Marcellus and Barnardo, visits Hamlet. Horatio enters first and Hamlet greets his friend affectionately; the dialogue proceeds (Q1, ii.81-4):

> *Ham.* But what make you from Wittenberg Horatio?
> Marcellus.
> *Marc.* My good Lord.
> *Ham.* I am very glad to see you, good euen sirs:

In Q2 the last line goes:

> I am very glad to see you (good euen sir).

After asking Horatio the question quoted above he notices for the first time the presence of two others; Marcellus he knows, the other is a stranger. Before Horatio has time to answer, Hamlet addresses Marcellus by name and welcomes him; then as the brackets indicate the prince's tone changes to the more formal 'good euen sir' spoken to Barnardo. In Q1 'sirs' replaces 'sir' and includes Marcellus and Barnardo.

Horatio, in recounting to Hamlet the appearance of the apparition, refers in both texts to his companions as 'these gentlemen, Marcellus and Barnardo,' implying that both are present. Later (ii.147-152) we read:

> *Ham.* Hold you the watch to night?
> *All.* We do my Lord.
> *Ham.* Armed say ye?
> *All.* Armed my good Lord.
> *Ham.* From top to toe?
> *All.* My good Lord, from head to foote.

Later the three visitors take leave of Hamlet with the words (ii.182):

> *All.* Our duties to your honor.

That the speech-prefix *All* does not mean *Both* either here or elsewhere is certain, because in the fourth scene when Horatio and Marcellus speak together three times, the speech-prefix on each occasion is *Both*. These pieces of dialogue are practically identical in both texts; I cannot 'detect the joinery work' to which Professor Wilson refers. Nearly all the speeches and dialogue are not badly preserved except that lines of Q2 with a metre-marring enclitic prefixed, a couple of composite lines, mislineation due to a dropped phrase and the usual limping verse all testify to the presence of the pirate. Nor can it be said that the style carries the reader back to 1593. Freed from the pirate's garbling, both the dialogue and verse of this scene belong to Shakespeare's mature middle period.

Professor Wilson makes too much of the absence of Barnardo's name at the head of the scene in Q1. There are later omissions of entries of far more importance. I have discussed elsewhere the pirate's blunder in omitting an entry for Horatio when Hamlet is about to explain to him why

the play's the thing
Wherein Ile catch the conscience of the King.

Again when the royal party enters to hear the play bespoken from the players by Hamlet, no entry is provided for Ophelia; so too, after the play is over and Hamlet must visit his mother, Q1 has no entry for him. I can find no other reason for these lapses from bibliographical grace than the pirate's neglect.

Q2 provides a particularly detailed account of the 'Dumbe Show.' What we find in Q1 is not derived from the authentic text, and explains what an inattentive spectator would see, in language reminiscent of words used by the ghost. One essential fact is omitted, that the king was asleep when he was murdered. Perhaps the most famous stage direction (xi.61) ever written,

Enter the ghost in his night gowne,

occurs during the scene between Hamlet and his mother. Stage custom seems to have prescribed that a stage ghost was entitled to a change of costume. On the battlements the apparition revisits 'the glimses of the Moone' clad 'in compleat steele'; when it pays a midnight call upon its ex-family, its garb assumes the semblance of the familiar night attire, and it 'steales away' unseen by the queen. Another longer stage direction (xiii.14) in Q1,

Enter Ofelia playing on a Lute, and her haire
downe singing

may be contrasted with the entry given in Q2, *Enter Ophelia;* a side-note, *shee sings,* is opposite the beginning of her song.

In the sixteenth and eighteenth scenes of Q1, there are several notes either unnecessary or too long. Thus the grave-digger is singing as he digs, and there appears (xvi.34),

he throwes up a shouel,

DD

of clay we may suppose; perhaps this is an error for 'scull.' After line 134 of this scene we have,

> *Enter King and Queene, Leartes, and other lordes,*
> *with a Priest after the coffin.*

In Q2 the side-entry (xvi.205) is:

> *Enter K. Q. Laertes and the corse.*

Neither Q2 nor Fo gives the priest an entry; in Q2 the speech-prefix is *Doct.,* in Q1 and Fo it is *Priest.*

Details of the stage-quarrel at the grave-side vary in Q1, Q2 and F. In Q1 there is a centred note,

> *Leartes leapes into the graue,*

after xvi.141, and opposite to line 143 a side-note, *Hamlet leapes in after Laertes;* in Q2 nothing, and in Fo the first of the two directions in Q1. Much the same occurs in the respective accounts of the duel and the sequence of tragedies that follow; Q1 has too much, Q2 too little and Fo all that are necessary. Thus, when the Queen says (xviii.75),

> Here Hamlet, thy mother drinkes to thee,

it is unnecessary to take up space for a line with *Shee drinkes.* On the other hand the text of the second quarto does not explain how Hamlet came to kill Laertes, and the stage notes and directions are insufficient. Q1 after line 82 has a long description of what took place, culminating in a piece of absurd nonsense:

> *They catch one anothers Rapiers, and both are wounded,*
> *Laertes falles downe, the Queene falles downe and dies.*

Then follow two lines (xviii.83-4) of dialogue:

> *King.* Looke to the Queene.
> *Queene.* O the drinke, the drinke, Hamlet, the drinke.

Q1 thus represents the dead queen as warning her son against drinking from the poisoned cup! Q2 has nothing; the folio has a side-note, *Play,* as the third bout begins and three lines later, a centred stage direction:

> *In scuffling they change Rapiers.*

This suggests that Hamlet, being wounded, attacked Laertes, seized the buttonless weapon and inflicted a mortal wound on his opponent.

CHAPTER XXIII

SUMMARY

I this inferre,
That many things hauing full reference
To one consent, may worke contrariously,
As many Arrowes loosed seuerall wayes
Come to one marke: as many wayes meet in one towne,
As many fresh streames meet in one salt sea;
As many Lynes close in the Dials center;
So may a thousand actions once a-foote,
End in one purpose, and be all well borne
Without defeat.

Henry V, 1.2.204-13.

SO many and so varied have been the topics discussed in this volume that a brief summary is necessary. My endeavour now must be to twist and splice all the threads and strands of evidence into one strong cable of proof. My thesis is to prove that each bad quarto is a garbled abridgment of an acting version made officially by the play adapter of the company from Shakespeare's manuscript; my aim throughout has been to make even destructive criticism lend some support to this central truth.

All the external evidence points the one way, to the theory that each bad quarto is a derivative of the parallel play written by Shakespeare. Since the appearance of Professor A. W. Pollard's *Shakespeare Folios and Quartos* and his clear proof that the quartos issued prior to the publication of the first folio are divisible into 'good' quartos and 'bad' quartos, the declaration of Heminge and Condell:

As where (before) you were abus'd with diuerse stolne, and surreptitious copies, maimed, and deformed, by the frauds and stealthes of iniurious impostors, that expos'd them: even those are now offer'd to your view cur'd, and perfect of their limbes,

has taken a definite meaning. These words inform us that the first folio contains the true texts of *2 Henry VI, 3 Henry VI, Henry V* and *Merry Wives,* plays previously known to readers only in the form of bad quartos. Three 'good' quartos of *Romeo and Juliet,* each said to be 'Newly corrected, augmented, and amended,' and

437

two 'good' quartos of *Hamlet,* each affirming that it was 'Newly imprinted and enlarged to almost as much againe as it was, according to the true and perfect Coppie,' had been in the hands of readers many years before the publication of the first folio; the censure of the two editors would revive memories of these two early thefts. Every detail relating to the bibliographical history of *Contention* and *True Tragedy* (see Appendix) confirms the identification of these two plays as two 'stolne and surreptitious copies' of *2 Henry VI* and *3 Henry VI.* On the title-pages of *Merry Wives Q1* and *Hamlet Q1* appears the name of William Shakespeare as author. Absence of his name on any of the quartos printed in the last decade of Elizabeth's reign does not necessarily imply doubts of his authorship; nearly seventy per cent. of the plays printed from 1590 to 1600 have no author's name on the title-page.

Four of the bad quartos are each long enough to occupy almost the two hours allotted by the actors for the representation of a play; their average length is not two hundred lines under that of all the plays (Jonson's and Shakespeare's excepted) which have sound texts and were acted or printed between 1590 and 1603. It is remarkable that the bad quartos of *3 Henry VI* and *Hamlet,* which differ by 860 lines in length, themselves differ by only thirty lines. From these facts I draw the conclusion that these four bad quartos are corrupt abridgments of acting versions that conformed well enough to the standard length of 2,300 lines in existence not later than 1594.

In the *Times Literary Supplement* for 25 January, 1936, a reviewer referred to my tests based on vocabulary as a 'new weapon in the armoury of the textual critic.' Such tests are new, and, being unfamiliar and not easily understood, may displease readers who prefer their literary fare free from digits, arithmetic and tables. They may reasonably ask why any new critical weapon is necessary. My answer to this query is that certain literary critics have for thirty years been employing methods practised in the dark ages, and, to use an expressive Americanism, have been 'getting away with it.' One favourite device of these self-styled 'scientific' critics of literature was to select arbitrarily a few dozen words from a play of Shakespeare, christen them 'clues,' and then bolster up unsound theories, usually pre-formed, by 'discovering' these 'clues' in the plays or poems of another dramatist. I think any ingenious person could so choose his 'clues' as to 'prove' that Shakespeare wrote *Hero and Leander* and Marlowe *Venus and Adonis*. Essentially my tests, based on vocabulary and word-groups, depend on a simple principle, understood and accepted by everybody. If two imaginative dramatists each wrote a play in verse of about 20,000 words on the same theme, we should expect and would find complete difference in the choice of incidents, in treatment, in characterization, in thought and imagery, in versification, etc., and, as the expression of each dramatist's individuality, equally complete difference of diction. Difference of diction implies in its turn, difference in the less commonly used words, compound words and other words peculiar to each dramatist. Totals of the words peculiar to each play of six pairs are to be found in column F of Table I.

It was my purpose to investigate the statement that Shakespeare re-wrote the bad quartos wholly or in part. I had collected the vocabularies of all Shakespeare's and Marlowe's plays and poems, of Kyd's plays, and of some anonymous plays, and found that, when the vocabularies of two plays, 2,000 lines at least in length and with sound texts, were compared,

(i)   each play contained a large proportion, varying from 40 to 60 per cent. of its vocabulary, in common with the other;
(ii) each play had a large number of words peculiar to it equal to not less than 40 per cent. of its vocabulary; and
(iii) almost all the rarer words, those new to literature and the compound words present in one play are not in the other, i.e., are in group (ii) above.

Every critic agrees that Shakespeare's *King John* represents his rewriting of *Troublesome Raigne,* and, when I compared the two vocabularies, I obtained results precisely similar to those for any pair of plays not so related; the same result held for *King Leir* and *King Lear* and for *A Shrew* and *The Shrew*. As the source plays are not Shakespeare's, each contains a number of words not in the concordance; there are 136 in *Troublesome Raigne,* 82 in *King Leir* and 61 in *A Shrew*. All the other 'peculiar' words of the three source-plays are in the concordance. Here are certain definite

criteria, which may be applied to test the suggestion that Shake-
speare rewrote the bad quartos. I compared the vocabularies of
Contention and *2 Henry VI, True Tragedy* and *3 Henry VI* and
Hamlet Q1 and *Hamlet* (received text) and my results were:

  (i) The number of words common to each pair of the parallel
       texts ranged from 87 to 93 per cent. of the vocabulary of
       the bad quarto.
 (ii) Each bad quarto had a very small number of words
       peculiar to it, equal to from 7 to 13 per cent. of the
       vocabulary. For the genuine source-plays it ranged from
       34 to about 50 per cent. of the vocabularies.
(iii) Three-quarters of the less common and seven-eighths of
       the compound words of each bad quarto were present in the
       parallel text.
 (iv) Each bad quarto had a very small number of words not in
       the concordance; some of these words were perversions of
       words in the authentic texts.

In other words the vocabulary of Shakespeare's play contains
all but a very small percentage of the words in the corresponding
bad quarto, and hence follows the inevitable conclusion that Shakespeare did not re-write the bad quartos. Tests depending on large
groups of words, e.g., the less common words and the compounds,
were made in exactly the same way and with the same results.

Professor Dover Wilson's theory of double or partial revision
was tested much in the same way; the results obtained would apply
to any revision-theory. No objection can be taken to the removal
of small portions of the supposedly unrevised texts of *Romeo and
Juliet Q1* and of *Hamlet Q1,* and with the removal of these portions
go the 'alien' words named in the lists. Table XI (p. 59) sets out
the changes made, and on comparison with the distribution given in
Table X (p. 56) the theory has no visible means of support.
Editors of Shakespeare's text in their endeavour to discover what
the poet wrote must meticulously collate and weigh in the balance
the smallest textual difference between successive quartos and the
folio version, but this continuous absorption in the infinitely little
seems to have disabled in some measure the judgment of otherwise
acute critics when they studied the omnipresent ravages of illiteracy
in such an abridged text as that of *True Tragedy* They are wont to
stress the difference and neglect the resemblance between this play
and *3 Henry VI;* hence has arisen the first sketch theory. My

series of tables exhibiting the state of the quarto texts relatively to Shakespeare's plays is designed to give quantitative expression to both likeness and difference, but I stress in both this chapter and the next likeness rather than difference. My totals prove that *True Tragedy* has nearly two-thirds of *3 Henry VI* in recognizable form, and nearly a half of the poet's play is preserved identically or with very small alterations. An even larger proportion of the verse and prose of *Romeo and Juliet Q1* is almost identical with the corresponding portions of Q2.

My chapters on 'The Style of the Bad Quartos' and 'Non-Shakespearean Verse' illustrate the infinite variety of the garbling, petty larceny, solecisms, anacolutha, irrelevance, vulgarity, fustian and nonsense so plentiful in these texts, and for these no dramatist but rather the persons who vamped up the copy for the printer must be responsible. To a critic capable of maintaining that Shakespeare rewrote the version of Hamlet's first soliloquy found in Q1, one may say with Touchstone 'thou art in a parlous state'; on the other hand, if the reporter did make such 'pell-mell hauocke and confusion' of what Shakespeare wrote, why look elsewhere for the cause of every other defect in Q1?

Perhaps the most remarkable feature of the many essays written on the origin of the bad quartos is the complete absence of any but the most casual reference to the custom of abridging plays prevalent in our early theatre. Though the writers knew that Shakespeare lived by and for the theatre, and must have read the numerous allusions made by actors and dramatists to the two hours' traffic of the stage, most of them tacitly assume or explicitly state in their critical remarks that even his longest plays were originally acted without any shortening except a few 'cuts' here and there. Many of these essayists were habitual theatre-goers, and whether they lived in the eighteenth, nineteenth or twentieth century knew that in representation *Romeo and Juliet, Henry V* and *Hamlet* were cut down to 2,400 lines or less. This persistent ignoring of official abridgment as the main factor in the reduction in length of these plays, each of them too long to be acted in its entirety, contributed very largely, in my opinion, to the general acceptance of the erroneous belief that Shakespeare revised or rewrote the bad quartos.

In general, most of the actors would know no more of any play than what was in the acting version of about 2,200-2,400 lines made by the play-adapter from the manuscript of the author. I have described in some detail the making of the acting version of a little known play such as *Edmund Ironside,* partly because it shows that even a short play was liable to be cut down if there were passages unsuitable for the public stage, but mainly because the number of passages excised and the nature of their subject-matter remind me of the numerous cuts which turned scenes of *3 Henry VI* and *Romeo and Juliet Q2* into the better-kept scenes of *True Tragedy* and *Romeo and Juliet Q1.* My review of the omissions in those parallel texts of Shakespeare for which two good texts, the quarto and the folio, are extant shows that, after the excision of a passage, the usual method was to bring the broken ends together; only rarely was any attempt made to mend an injury done to sense or verse. I assume that abridgment of an over-long play was the reason for making these cuts, but maintain that the Elizabethan acting version of *Hamlet* would more closely resemble the version in which Richard Wilks played the hero in 1715. Probably about 250 passages containing 1,400 lines would necessarily be excised to reduce it to a two-hour play.

Disproof of the First Sketch Theory or of any theory which postulates that Shakespeare rewrote the bad quartos depends in final analysis partly on disproof of the conjecture that Shakespeare began dramatic work as a play-cobbler, and was busy cobbling *Hamlet Q1* between writing *Twelfth Night* and *Othello.* Not a scrap of evidence is obtainable in support of this hoary conjecture. That it is in the highest degree improbable, that no dramatist of his own or any other century professed such a calling, and that no dramatist writing for the public stage is known to have added to the length of plays already long enough in the manner suggested, —all these facts do not deter editors and critics from repeating this absurd nonsense.

Most of my long chapter on the verse-structure of these quartos breaks new ground. It is amazing that so many learned critics have written on them, and yet have paid little or no attention to the ubiquitous corruption which affects on the average three of every ten lines of verse. I have compared each line of the quarto texts with the corresponding line (if it exists) of the parallel texts, and my considered judgment is that the Protean deviations from normal verse constitute in their totality an unanswerable argument against the priority of the bad quartos. Of especial significance as evidence of corruption are the numerous octosyllabic lines many of which are reduced lines of Shakespeare's blank verse, nine-syllable lines with a syllable wanting at the end or in the middle of the verse, hendecasyllabic lines with the extra syllable (usually an enclitic) at the beginning, and the excessively large number of twelve-syllable lines. All these abnormal types of verse are almost unknown in the blank verse written by any dramatist of repute. My brief study of the corrupt verse in *Orlando Furioso Q1* offers proof that all the defective verse is the work of the actors. My gorge rises at the suggestion that the Shakespeare of *Romeo and Juliet* and *Hamlet* honoured with his corrections so many hundreds of jolting unmusical lines and fragments of lines, and, pupil-like, paid slavish deference to the rubbish in which too often these lines were imbedded by hand-picking the words retained. If thus he sank into the pedant, the less Shakespeare he. Even more convincing evidence in favour of the pre-existence of the canonical plays may be culled from my chapter on Rhymed Lines. The pirate of *Hamlet Q1* seems to have been able to hammer out rude rhyming couplets of his own that were metrically correct, yet his memory linked in rhyming discord tetrameter and pentameter, dimeter and hexameter, and other such misfits. My discussion of what I term 'composite' lines gives the first account of an unofficial compression of two lines into one, usually at the expense of the metre.

Of especial importance in determining the priority of Shakespeare's plays is the chapter on those blunders or omissions in the bad quartos which may be explained only after the corresponding passages of the authentic text have been consulted. Two important examples relating to the genealogy of the French kings I owe to Daniel, and two others of a similar character to Professor Alexander; one or two more may have been 'conveyed' from sources which I cannot now name, but most of the blunders were systematically collected in the course of my collation of each pair of texts line by line. Each omission or blunder occurs in a portion of Q1 which otherwise almost duplicates the corresponding part of

Shakespeare's play, and bears strong witness to the pre-existence of the latter. So numerous are the examples and so evenly spread throughout the scenes of each bad quarto that the cumulative evidence so provided is sufficient in itself to determine the main question in favour of Shakespeare's play.

In my next chapter I seem to turn a somersault backwards, and use the text of the bad quarto to make good the sense of Shakespeare's parallel play. This fact stresses the closeness of the relation between each pair of parallel texts, and would seem to suggest the priority of the bad quartos, but my explanation of this seeming paradox is, I think, satisfactory. According to my theory, the text of a bad quarto rests on the oral transmission of what an actor could recollect of a part written out by a scribe from the acting version made officially from the author's manuscript. On the other hand, the authentic text was generally printed from the same manuscript or some transcript of it. There is nothing surprising in the fact that the reported text serves at times to correct slips in the manuscript or printer's errors found in the authentic text.

In my treatment of repetition I have discarded many of those parallel passages which have been used by two generations of critics in search of an author. I have nothing to add to the judicious words of Sir E. K. Chambers on the critical value of such 'echoes.'[1] When a line common to a pair of parallel texts appears in the bad quarto earlier than its place in the authentic text warrants, this fact furnishes first, almost conclusive evidence against the employment of stenography by a reporter of Shakespeare's play, and secondly, a strong presumption against the theory that he revised the bad quartos. Shakespeare may have set down in his tables or his memory a word or a phrase that took his fancy, but does any critic seriously contend that he would remove a line from one part of *True Tragedy*, his supposed source-play, and save it for future use in a later portion of *3 Henry VI*?

Of reporting and reporters I have little to say that is new. Chetwood's story of Richard Wilks and the facts recorded of Macaulay's powers of memory prove that reporting a play almost perfectly is not an impossible feat. The actors who played the

1. *William Shakespeare*, Vol. i, pp. 222-3.

parts of Clifford and Warwick were probably the reporters of *True Tragedy*. Dr. Greg has made out a good case for the Host as the pirate of *Merry Wives;* but the evidence for Suffolk and Warwick as the reporter of *Contention* is rather weak.

Borrowings from other plays are in a different category from repetition. My chapter on the inter-play borrowings characteristic of certain early plays, including those acted by Pembroke's men, suggests the thought that many essayists, engrossed in problems of authorship, have stressed unduly the value as evidence of borrowings which are scattered indiscriminately between any pair of plays chosen from *Contention, True Tragedy, 2 Henry VI, 3 Henry VI, Massacre at Paris* and *Edward II,* and have entirely neglected the significance of the borrowings between each of these plays and *Spanish Tragedy, Soliman and Perseda* and *Arden of Feversham; Titus Andronicus* also must be taken into account. I do not offer any explanation other than a hesitant conjecture of a wide-spread peculiarity which affects the textual purity not merely of five corrupt quartos but of seven plays with sound texts. I must insist, however, that the arbitrary choice and use of certain portions only of these borrowings, and the equally arbitrary neglect of the significance attaching to those left unused, nullify the validity of all the conclusions drawn from the chosen and used borrowings. This method of using facts cannot be defended. I shall go farther, and assert that no conclusion concerning priority of composition can be drawn with any approach to certitude from such borrowings as are in my lists, except that such as are in *Massacre at Paris* and *A Shrew* and those in *Contention* and *True Tragedy,* but not in *2 Henry VI* and *3 Henry VI,* were almost certainly introduced by the pirates. Sir E. K. Chambers has given a very useful list of printed plays in Appendix L (pp. 379-397) of the fourth volume of his *Elizabethan Stage,* but he would be the last man to suggest that the order of these plays is the order of composition.

Borrowed lines and phrases in *Hamlet Q1* include some of small importance, but my list is certainly far from being complete. Most of them come from other plays of Shakespeare, but, except for the plays of Jonson and Shakespeare, we know so little of the repertoire of the Chamberlain's men before 1602, that unknown borrowings from lost plays may exceed those from the poet's own plays.

Obviously these borrowed lines cannot be part of a source-play and are excellent evidence that Q1 is a reported text. Some echoes of words, phrases and a line of *Othello* throw back the date of that play to not later than the early months of 1602.

Stage directions assume some importance in this investigation because those of the bad quartos must be the work of the reporter and not of a dramatist. Except for entries and exits, they differ from those of the authentic versions in style, scope and content. Professor Alexander has shown that where a stage direction of *Contention* is identical with one in *2 Henry VI* the text preceding and following it in each version is also identical. This identity, he considers, makes it almost certain that the reporter possessed a fragmentary transcript of this portion of Shakespeare's play.[2] I think he has proved his case; the transcript, in my opinion, would be from the acting version, and I have given reasons for extending the transcript to cover a little more of the text of *Contention*. Apart from this direct evidence furnished from the very corrupt text of *Contention,* descriptions of what took place on the stage and directions for stage 'business,' which Elizabethan playwrights properly left to the judgment of the actors, are found in all the bad quartos. In *Contention, Romeo and Juliet Q1* and *Henry V Q1* stage directions take the place of lines of the authentic text, a phenomenon noticeable in *Orlando Furioso Q1*. At times, also, entries and exits are given to characters who are unnecessary to the action; reference to the authentic text proves that these characters were on the stage and spoke. Here is evidence that the reporter remembered their presence on the stage but forgot their words. Twice in *Henry V Q1* a stage manager who followed the stage directions would make a muddle of the scenes.

In an appendix to my main thesis I have set out my reasons for rejecting the prevalent belief that Marlowe was, solely or in collaboration, the author of *2 Henry VI* and *3 Henry VI*. Some writers have suggested Kyd as the author of the *Ur-Hamlet*. They may be right, but unless fragments of this lost play are imbedded in *Hamlet Q1*, this conjecture is valueless. I have made a careful examination of Kyd's writings and vocabulary, and cannot find the smallest scrap of evidence that would justify me in fathering the

2. *Shakespeare's Henry VI and Richard III*, pp. 82-9.

non-Shakespearean parts of Q1 on Kyd or any other contemporary dramatist. Whatever is not Shakespeare in shabby rags is too bad for any scribbler of the time. Other essayists have suggested that *Romeo and Juliet Q1* is not debased Shakespeare; such conjectures are the froth and bubble generated during the turbid workings of the iconoclastic mind.

Much more might have been written on transposition of lines and phrases, inversions of order, the use of expletives and oaths, equalization of actors' parts, the disappearance of unusual words, etc., but those who decide doubtful questions on facts and, where facts are scarce, on the balance of probability, will have enough and to spare. My essays on play abridgment were designed originally to form part of this book, but since my conclusions applied to every extant play written between 1587 and 1642, I decided to give these essays earlier publicity. Though my facts have been gathered for the purpose of proving my main thesis, they have the merit of helping critics to disprove my conclusions.

Every scholar fashions for himself, I suppose, a mental picture of the master-poet at work, and to it subconsciously refers all that he thinks or reads of him and his plays. My own conception of Shakespeare and his genius squares with the sayings of those who knew and loved him, Heminge, Condell, Jonson, Drayton, Webster, Heywood, and with the many unsolicited commendations of admirers such as Meres, Weever, Barnfield, Davies and Freeman. I cannot reconcile what they tell of him with painstaking revision of another man's work. Whether he was conscious of his own genius is hard to say; his play once written, he seems to have left the rest of his fellows. We have no evidence that he ever revised a line of his own work; certainly the man who neglected to edit the second quartos of *Romeo and Juliet* and *Hamlet* had in him little or nothing of 'that last infirmity of Noble mind.'

Perhaps the poet has described his manner of writing in the famous lines put into the mouth of Theseus:

> The Poets eye in a fine frenzy rolling, doth glance
> From heauen to earth, from earth to heauen.
> And as imagination bodies forth the forms of things
> Vnknowne; the Poets pen turnes them to shapes,
> And giues to aire nothing, a locall habitation,
> And a name.

Such would be the man who 'never blotted out line.' Jonson's generous eulogy rings sincere, and springs from genuine love of the man and admiration of 'what he hath left vs.' He was not alone in this; his prophecy contained in the line,

> He was not of an age, but for all time!

had been anticipated in a rhyming letter sent to Jonson by another great poet and dramatist, Francis Beaumont:

> heere I would let slippe
> (If I had any in mee) schollershippe,
> And from all Learninge keepe these lines as (cl)eere
> as Shakespeares best are, which our heires shall heare
> Preachers apte to their auditors to showe
> how farr sometimes a mortall man may goe
> by the dimme light of Nature.

In that age of rapid writing Beaumont wrote, probably alone, our first burlesque, *The Knight of the Burning Pestle,* in eight days, and tradition says that Shakespeare composed the *Merry Wives* in a fortnight. Dozens of small slips compel me to believe that what Shakespeare wrote in haste, he did not revise at leisure.

APPENDIX

DID MARLOWE WRITE THE PLAYS ON HENRY VI?

AT this point I shall offer my reasons for rejecting the wide-spread opinion that Marlowe had a main hand in writing *2 Henry VI* and *3 Henry VI*. Complete proof that *Contention* and *True Tragedy* are debased and abridged reports of official acting versions made by the company's play-adapter from the original manuscripts of the corresponding plays on Henry VI involves no reference to authorship. Whether that author is Shakespeare or Marlowe or Greene or Kyd, individually or in collaboration, is a separate question upon which a critic may pass judgment according to his knowledge of contemporary plays and poetry, his ability to appreciate dramatic literature and differences of style where and if such differences exist, and his capacity for estimating and weighing the worth of evidence, three qualities that do not always co-exist.

EXTERNAL EVIDENCE

All the external evidence is entirely in favour of Shakespeare's authorship. Heminge, who had known Shakespeare for nearly a quarter of a century and had probably acted with Condell, his co-editor, in the plays on Henry VI, included them in the first folio. I prefer his opinion to that of Malone who nearly two centuries after the first production of these plays wrote a thesis in favour of Marlowe's authorship. Greene's reference in his last pamphlet points to a direct connection between *3 Henry VI* and 'Shake-scene,' obviously a nick-name for Shakespeare, and we may reasonably assume that *3 Henry VI* or the acting version that is the original of *True Tragedy* had been acted in 1592 or earlier. Francis Meres does not include either play in his list printed in 1598; six tragedies are named to balance the six comedies, i.e., all that Shakespeare had written by that date. This omission may be deliberate or due to ignorance, but Shakespeare's direct reference to the plays on Henry VI in the epilogue to

Henry V makes it certain that they had been acted not long before. Moreover the passage below covers the three parts.

> Henry the Sixt, in Infant Bands crown'd King
> Of France and England, did this King succeed:
> Whose State so many had the managing,
> That they lost France, and made his England bleed:
> Which oft our Stage hath showne; and for their sake,
> In your faire minds let this acceptance take.

This virtual acknowledgment of the poet's authorship more than offsets the contemporary silence of Meres. Then follows an entry on the Stationers' Register in 1602:

19 Aprilis ... Thomas Pavier. Entred for his copies by assignement from Thomas Millington these bookes folowinge, Saluo Jure cuiuscunque viz. . . . The firste and Second parte of Henry the vjt ij bookes xijd. Entred by warrant vnder master Setons hand.

Millington owned *Contention* and *True Tragedy* which in 1602 Pavier bought and accepted as two parts of *Henry VI*. Next follows Pavier's issue in 1619 of *Contention* and *True Tragedy;* the title-pages declare them to be 'newly corrected and enlarged. Written by William Shakespeare, Gent.' These are two of those 'stolne and surreptitious copies' against which Heminge and Condell inveigh in their address 'To the great Variety of Readers'; the false ascription of these to their 'worthy' fellow, 'our Shakespeare' induced his friends to insert the authentic text in the first folio.

However scanty and insufficient this evidence may seem to critics who have resolved to disregard it, we have in it a chain of facts which stretch over the years from 1592 to 1623. I have read most of the essays on the authorship of these plays from the days of Malone to those of J. M. Robertson, and prefer the contemporary knowledge of his lifelong friends and even of Pavier to the subjective impressions of a wilderness of critics two or three hundred years after the poet's death.

Vocabulary

From the beginning of his poetic and dramatic career Shakespeare's vocabulary was fuller, more varied and expressive of finer shades of meaning than that of any of his early contemporaries. I have discussed this statement with special reference to the plays on Henry VI at some length in an essay on the 'Vocabulary of *Edward III*,'[1] and shall make only a short summary.

Shakespeare uses 6,032 words in the 12,253 lines of the York and Lancaster tetralogy, Marlowe 6,051 words in the 14,805 lines of his seven plays. These totals indicate that Marlowe was prone to repeating in one play words used in earlier plays, while Shakespeare introduced into each new play a much larger proportion of fresh words. His plays average five hundred words more than Marlowe's, but where equality of length permits just comparison his predecessor's inferiority in vocabulary is manifest. Thus *Edward II* has six hundred words fewer than *1 Henry VI* though the two plays are of the same length. Moreover, the size of the vocabularies of Marlowe's plays show a steady decline despite increase of length and greater variety of theme. Thus,

> *1 Tamburlaine* has 2,316 lines and 2,507 words
> *2 Tamburlaine* ,, 2,330 ,, ,, 2,371 ,,
> *Jew of Malta* ,, 2,410 ,, ,, 2,204 ,,
> *Edward II* ,, 2,670 ,, ,, 2,391 ,,

My comparison of these two authors' vocabularies refers mainly to plays of Shakespeare written in Marlowe's lifetime; if we form the composite vocabulary of *Hamlet* and *Troilus and Cressida*, two plays not half the length of Marlowe's seven, we find it contains within five hundred words of the combined vocabulary of Marlowe's plays.

I shall now examine some large groups of words in certain plays of each author.

(i) My first group contains all the words beginning with the important prefixes *ad-, be-, con-, de-, dis-, en-, ex-, for-, in-, out-, over-, per-, pre-, pro-, re-, sub-, un-*, and variants of these. Shakespeare has 1,556 in the 8,653 lines of the plays on Henry VI, Marlowe 1,432 in the 9,052 lines of *Tamburlaine I* and *II*, *Edward II* and *Dido*, the four plays of his which have sound texts. After making an adjustment for difference in length, I find that Shakespeare has 15 per cent. more of these words in equal length of text.

(ii) My second group consists of adjectives ending in suffixes *-ant, -ary, -ate, -ble, -ent, -ful, -ish, -ive, -less, -ous*, and *-y*, nouns

1. *Shakespeare and the Homilies*, pp. 219-241.
EE

ending in suffixes *-ance, -ence, -er, -ment, -or* and *-tion,* and adverbs ending in *-ly.* Shakespeare's three plays have 1,148 such words, and Marlowe's four 1,045. Here the difference in favour of Shakespeare equals 17 per cent. for equal length of text.

(iii) Of adjectival compound words Shakespeare's four early plays on English History and *Titus Andronicus* together contain 292 compared with 159 in the seven extant plays of Marlowe—a difference of more than 45 per cent. for equal length of text.

(iv) Of the so-called parasynthetic compounds, and those ending in a present or past participle Shakespeare has 167 in these five early plays, and Marlowe 77 in an equal length of play-text, or a difference of 54 per cent. In his poems and translations Marlowe uses these types of compound adjective very freely; but any one who imposes on himself the task of making line-for-line translations of Latin hexameters or elegiac distichs cannot use the words he would, but such as he must.

VERSE

Comparison of the details given in my table for the versification of *1 Tamburlaine* and *Edward II* with those set out in the Metrical Tables of *William Shakespeare*[2] reveals points of difference, the most important being the different proportion of the so-called double or feminine endings present. *1 Tamburlaine* has 2·6 per cent. and *Edward II* 4·5 per cent. of feminine endings in the respective totals of blank verse. Compare with these low results, typical of this period, the 14 per cent. of such endings recorded in *Metrical Tables* for the second and third parts of *Henry VI.* Reference to my table entitled *Abnormal Verse of bad Quartos* gives the percentage of feminine endings in the blank verse of *Contention* as 4·5 per cent., of the Shakespearean portion of *True Tragedy* as 9·3 per cent., and of the non-Shakespearean portion of this quarto as 4·3 per cent. This high percentage in *True Tragedy* is the more significant because many lines of *3 Henry VI* with feminine endings have been reduced by the actors to normal decasyllables or nine-syllable lines, whilst many more have been turned into alexandrines.

Shakespeare was making a metrical innovation, not popular with the actors, at a time when Peele, Greene, Marlowe, Lodge

2. Sir E. K. Chambers, *op. cit.,* vol. ii, appendix H, pp. 398-402.

Kyd etc. were maintaining the vogue of the normal decasyllabic line, usually end-stopped; their plays contained from one to a little more than four per cent. of feminine endings. I have previously discussed their use of feminine endings. J. M. Robertson has built storey upon storey of his baseless fabric, the 'unsigned' plays of Marlowe, upon the single fact that this poet used fourteen per cent. of such endings in his line-for-line translation of Lucan's *Pharsalia, Book I,* and entirely disregarded what the evidence obtained from his seven acknowledged plays proved, viz., that Marlowe did not like a line with an unstressed syllable at the end unless it coincided with a natural pause. Seven plays should provide enough facts for a considered judgment on his usual versification, and no amount of special pleading can alter the conclusion that Marlowe could not have written *True Tragedy* or the plays on Henry VI or *Edward III.* Robertson's verbal 'clues,' his parade of parallel passages, his dogmatic assertions, his mediaeval disdain of inconvenient facts cannot affect a result that any person can obtain from an examination of Marlowe's known plays.

CLASSICAL ALLUSIONS

Shakespeare's learning and its extent and quality were much debated topics in the second half of the eighteenth century; however little or much it may have been, he used it to better purpose than his early contemporaries. Malone in his *Dissertation on Henry VI*[3] says of *1 Henry VI*:

There are more allusions to classical authors and to ancient and modern history than, I believe, are to be found in any one piece of our author's written on an English story.

Malone has made a bad mistake—there are more in *2 Henry VI, 3 Henry VI, Henry V, Titus Andronicus, Merchant of Venice, As You Like It* and *Hamlet,* and this mis-statement has misled and still misleads each generation of commentators. Literary errors have an enduring vitality and fade away as slowly as popular beliefs. As late as 1910 we find Oliphant Smeaton[4] writing of the 'numberless classical allusions' in *1 Henry VI* and the 'frequency of classical allusions' in *2 Henry VI;* it is amusing to read of

3. Variorium Edition (1821), vol. xviii, p. 553 *et seq.*
4. Oliphant Smeaton, *Life and Works of Shakespeare,* pp. 63, 67, 195.

Merchant of Venice, 'Classical allusions . . . are now disappearing
slowly and steadily from the Shakespearean dramas.' Actually
there are more in *Merchant of Venice* than in any one of the plays
on Henry VI. Even such a model of documented accuracy as the
author of *William Shakespeare*[5] notes the 'many classical allusions'
found in the second and third parts of *Henry VI;* they are less
in number than those in *Merchant of Venice* and *As You Like It*
or in *Henry V* and *Hamlet.* Shakespeare's two long poems are on
classical themes and might seem to invite him to make a display of
classical erudition, yet in *Venus and Adonis* there are only seven,
and in *Lucrece* eight, except for those necessary to the heroine's
description (ll. 1362-1561) of a picture,

> a piece
> Of skilful painting made for Priams Troy.

Contrast these small totals with 86 classical allusions in *Hero and
Leander* which is nearly a thousand lines shorter than *Lucrece,* and
with the 32 such allusions in Peele's *Honour of the Garter,* a poem
less than a fourth of the length of *Lucrece.*

I have already stated that each of his predecessors used far
more classical allusions than Shakespeare; the 2,316 lines of
1 Tamburlaine have more than the 8,653 lines of the plays on
Henry VI, and *Edward II* has as many as the 'numberless' allusions
in *1 Henry VI* and *2 Henry VI* put together. Marlowe, Greene
and Peele move rather uneasily under their cumbrous trappings of
classical finery. As Malone says, many of their mythological
similes do not spring naturally from the context and are apt to
obscure rather than illuminate the main thought of the passage;
they are padded with unnecessarily informative detail and seemingly
are dragged in to parade the author's erudition. Shakespeare pads
his plays at times in the same way as in two examples already
quoted, but in general his allusions are fewer, shorter, more direct
and apposite. Some examples will help to make this difference
of treatment clear.

(i) Tamburlaine predicts his future fame:

> My name and honor shall be spread,
> As far as Boreas claps his brazen wings,
> Or fair Bootes sends his cheerefull light.   *1 Tamb.* 400-2

5. *William Shakespeare,* vol. i, p. 287.

(ii) The Soldan of Egypt and King of Arabia march to war:

> Me thinks we martch as Meliager did,
> Enuironed with braue Argolian knightes:
> To chace the sauage Cal(i)donian Boare,
> Or Cephalus with lustie Thebane youths
> Against the Woolfe that angrie Themis sent,
> To waste and spoile the sweet Aonian fieldes.
>
> *1 Tamb.* 1571-6

(iii) Callapine offers his gaoler, Almeda, Grecian virgins

> As faire as was Pigmalions Iuory gyrle,
> Or lovely Io metamorphosed.   *2 Tamb.* 213-4

(iv) Tamburlaine mourns for Zenocrate and demands:

> Flieng Dragons, lightning, fearful thunderclaps,
> Singde these fair plaines, and make them seeme as black
> As is the Island where the Furies maske
> Compast with Lethe, Styk and Plegeton.   *2 Tamb.* 884-7

(v) Tamburlaine stabs his son and threatens Jove:

> Thou hast procur'd a greater enemie,
> Than he that darted mountaines at thy head,
> Shaking the burthen mighty Atlas beares *2 Tamb.* 1,485-7

(vi) Faustus rhapsodizes on Helen's beauty:

> Brighter art thou then flaming Iupiter,
> When he appeard to haplesse Semele,
> More lovely then the monarke of the skie
> In wanton Arethusaes azurde armes.   *Faustus.* 1,343-6

(vii) Barabbas prepares poisoned pottage for his daughter and wishes:

> In few, the blood of Hydra, Lerna's bane;
> The iouyce of Hebon, and Cocitus breath,
> And all the poysons of the Stygian poole
> Breake from the fiery kingdome; and in this
> Vomit your venome, and inuenome her.
>
> *Jew of Malta.* 1,403-7

(viii) King Edward is eager for Gaveston's return:

> Beamont flie,
> As fast as Iris, or Ioues Mercurie.   *Edward II.* 657-8

(ix) Edward wishes his crown may destroy Mortimer:

> Heauens turne it to a blaze of quenchelesse fier,
> Or like the snakie wreathe of Tisiphon,
> Engirt the temples of his hatefull head. *Edward II.* 2,030-2

It is worth remark that 205 of Marlowe's classical allusions occur in the 7,322 lines of *Tamburlaine I* and *II* and *Edward II*, three plays with sound texts, whilst only 65 occur in the 5,753 lines of *Faustus, Jew of Malta* and *Massacre at Paris,* three plays whose extant texts are corrupt and full of interpolations. I have already stated in table XIV that *Contention* and *True Tragedy* retain 25 only of the 54 classical allusions in *2 Henry VI* and *3 Henry VI.* I suggest that the 65 allusions present in Marlowe's three corrupt plays are all that the actors permitted to be spoken of a much larger number in the author's manuscripts.

Of the 54 classical allusions in the two plays on Henry VI, two, viz., *2 Henry VI,* 1.1.227-30 and *3 Henry VI,* 4.2.19-21, have already been quoted (pp. 153-4). Here follows some others:

(x) Clifford vows vengeance on the house of York:

> Meet I an infant of the house of Yorke,
> Into as many gobbits will I cut it
> As wilde Medea yong Absirtis did.   *2 Henry VI.* 5.2.57-9

(xi) Edward reproaches Queen Margaret with infidelity:

> Helen of Greece was fayrer farre then thou,
> Although thy Husband may be Menelaus;
> And ne're was Agamemnons Brother wrong'd
> By that false Woman, as this King by thee.
>   *3 Henry VI.* 2.2.146-9

(xii) Young Richard betrays his ambition and hidden thoughts:

> Ile play the Orator as well as Nestor
> Deceiue more slyly then Vlysses could,
> And like a Synon, take another Troy.
>   *2 Henry VI.* 3.2.188-190

In such examples as these Shakespeare was playing the upstart crow and was beautifying his verses with the fine feathers so popular with his predecessors, but he soon devised another and better method of making allusions to the myths and famous men of Greece and Rome. Three examples are quoted (p. 153); I give a few others.

(xiii) Queen Margaret tells her lover Suffolk not to despair:

> Ile haue an Iris that shall finde thee out.
>   *2 Henry VI.* 3.2.407

(xiv) Clifford jeers York who had claimed the Crown:

Now Phaeton hath tumbled from his Carre,
And made an Euening at the Noone-tide Prick.
                                        3 Henry VI. 1.4.33-4

(xv) Henry addresses Gloster who comes to murder him:

What Scene of death hath Roscius now to Acte?
                                        3 Henry VI. 5.6.10

(xvi) Richard tells King Edward why his reprieve of Clarence came too late:

But he (poore man) by your first order dyed,
And that a winged Mercurie did beare.
                                        Richard III. 2.1.87-8

Many of Marlowe's classical allusions are conceived fancifully rather than imaginatively; the central thought tends to become lost in a maze of melodious imagery and fails to impress itself on our minds. His comparisons decorate rather than illuminate what he wishes to say. He too frequently illustrates the known by comparing it with the unknown, and so loses touch with the reality which drama demands. Would many members of his audience know who Bootes, Meleager and Arethusa were, or understand the reference to 'Pigmalions Iuory gyrle'? Tamburlaine the Scythian shepherd, Ithamore the Turkish slave of Barabbas, and the dairy-maid in Greene's *Friar Bacon,* are all classical scholars; had Marlowe written *2 Henry VI* Cade and Dick Butcher would have babbled of Boreas, Hercules and Hydra's heads. Shakespeare usually keeps the sense of a passage uppermost in his mind, and rarely permits an overlay of ornament to obscure his meaning. He knew his public and fellow-actors and did not overwork his small Latin and less Greek; most of his classical allusions refer to the major gods and goddesses of heathendom, the story of Troy and the more famous demi-gods and heroes of antiquity. Even our latin-less age does not boggle at them. Shakespeare's device of allusively identifying a character with some god or hero of whom theatre-goers would often have heard is rarely used by Marlowe; I find no example in the 47 allusions to ancient history or mythology in *Edward II.* This method of using classical imagery is a marked characteristic of Shakespeare's work; it begins in *1 Henry VI* and continues throughout the canonical plays.

SIMILES

Shakespeare commenced playwright by following the current fashion. The 'vpstart Crow' saw no reason why English kings and nobles should not speak in classical parables and indulge themselves in similes, if the public was content to endure the Scythian Tamburlaine's mouthings of mythology and to stomach a surfeit of comparisons five to ten lines long. Being an actor, he must, however, have heard some mutterings of discontent at this abandonment of plain English and have resolved to tread somewhat cautiously in the steps of Marlowe and Greene. He reduced the dosage of mythology and increased the infusion of similes, tempering these as he thought best to the taste of a mixed audience. He probably recognized that redundant and prolix comparisons, however beautiful, delayed the action and retarded the development of the play, but, by referring his similes to the life about him, thought to make them more palatable. He failed, and realized that similes may suit such a poem as *The Faery Queene,* and that metaphors or condensed similes give life to drama.

I have provided some evidence that the actors disliked too much talk of Jupiter and Proserpine, but they seem to have objected even more strongly to a plethora of similes; of 96 in Shakespeare's two plays on Henry VI the corresponding bad quartos have only 29, a difference more than double of what might have been expected from the loss in length of these pairs of parallel texts. Marlowe has 24 classical similes in *1 Tamburlaine* or almost as many as are found in the three parts of *Henry VI*; in *Hero and Leander* there are 15 compared with 2 in *Lucrece* and none in *Venus and Adonis*. *Edward II* exhibits the same profusion as *Tamburlaine,* and the comparative paucity of this type of decorative ornament in the plays on Henry VI and in *Titus Andronicus* suggests the absence rather than the presence of Marlowe.

Apart from similes based on mythology and ancient history, Marlowe has comparatively few in *Tamburlaine* and *Edward II,* and the total number in these three plays does not much exceed what we find in *3 Henry VI*. Shakespeare did not draw them from books, from the study of Ovid, Virgil or Lucan or from the recollections of his reading, but from what he saw about him. They have the reality and vigour of everyday life, and the most lively and striking are inspired by rural sights and sounds. His imagination was fired by familiar things; field sports such as coursing, falconry, hunting the deer and birding; displays of skill in running, wrestling, archery and fencing; rural labours such as thrashing corn, forestry, felling trees and harvesting; rough pastimes such as bear or bull baiting; natural phenomena such as clouds, wind, lightning, storms on land or at sea, and sunrise; animals, birds or insects, ships at sea, the tides, the stage, actors, etc. Whatever he had seen or had taken part in was expressed so vividly and naturally that his similes light up the context wherever they appear. Yet most of them seem to have been struck out by the actors, probably because they were compelled to reduce what he wrote by some hundreds of lines; poetic ornament was not necessary to their ideal play—a good tale well told in two hours.

Most of the non-classical similes in the second and third parts of *Henry VI* are as like those in *Venus and Adonis* and *Lucrece* as peas in a pod; they suggest Shakespeare rather than Marlowe or Greene. Marlowe's longer non-classical similes often trail super-fluous lines at the end which would tend to confuse rather than illuminate the minds of his audience; the connection of ideas between the person or thing compared and the simile is frequently very slight, at times grotesque, and occasionally almost meaningless.

NATURAL HISTORY

Another peculiarity of Shakespeare's early work is the large number of allusions to insects, birds, reptiles, animals, fish, etc. They abound in each of his long poems and early plays and are almost as numerous in some later plays. *Venus and Adonis, Lucrece, 2 Henry VI, 3 Henry VI* and *Titus Andronicus* each contain as many allusions to natural history as are to be found in both parts of *Tamburlaine, Edward II* and *Massacre at Paris* taken together. Marlowe's fauna is scanty and narrow in its range; a home-keeping bookish poet cannot have seen some of the animals alluded to, e.g., camels, tigers, serpents, wolves, crocodiles, flying-fish, etc., alive and at large, and would depend, as would Shake-speare, for their description, nature and habits, on such ponderous folios as Gesner's and especially Pliny's. Many of his allusions to the more common animals suggest that he lacked the seeing eye of a nature-lover.

Tradition associates Shakespeare's departure from Stratford with poaching exploits, and no one but an out-of-doors man, interested in the wild life of the fields, woods and streams, could have penned his many similes and references to field-sports. Many critics have remarked on the number and variety of his allusions to the animal world; one of them, Furnival I think, rhetorically demanded to know who is this bird and beast man. Certainly not Marlowe nor Greene nor Peele, each of whom displays little interest in or knowledge of natural history; the only answer is Shakespeare.

So far I have been discussing facts concerning *2 Henry VI* and *3 Henry VI,* and Marlowe's plays which are capable of being evaluated numerically to some extent. External evidence, vocabulary and verse tests, the number and type of classical allusions and similes and the methods used by each of these authors, and the references to natural history have each been proved to favour the authorship of Shakespeare and to tell strongly against the still prevalent acceptance of Malone's opinion that Marlowe was the author of these plays or of the main portions of them. My conclusions on each of the topics mentioned rest on a careful examination of the relevant facts, which are in themselves enough in number and sufficiently definite to justify the judgment that Marlowe had no hand in writing the plays on Henry VI.

Upon the more strictly dramatic qualities of these plays and those of Marlowe and Greene, e.g., characterisation, comic power, dialogue, plot and dramatic technique, different opinions have been expressed by critics from the days of Malone. All admit that Shakespeare excelled every dramatist of his time in character-drawing, a superiority which becomes manifest even in his earliest work. Let any one read the scenes in which King Edward's gaolers, Matrevis and Gurney, contrive the murder of their prisoner, and afterwards peruse the famous scene of *Richard III* describing how two hired, unnamed assassins dispatch Clarence. Matrevis and Gurney seem to me twin automata, as alike as two tennis balls and as equally incapable of independent action. Martrevis might speak all or any of Gurney's lines, or Gurney some or all of those of Matrevis without affecting the dialogue or

action of the play; Marlowe has failed to differentiate these two
puppets of Mortimer. From their entrance to the Tower Shakespeare's two murderers talk and act as differently as two such
men in real life would in similar circumstances. After each has
uttered a dozen lines we know them, and their speeches could not be
interchanged because the art of the dramatist has made a sharp distinction between the surly, discourteous, brutal, conscienceless
bravo who makes murder a trade, and the more mannerly,
irresolute, conscience-stricken ruffian who wishes his crime undone.
I do not think Marlowe was much interested in his minor
characters; no other dramatist of this period than Shakespeare
would or could have written this interesting scene.

Marlowe does not mix comedy and tragedy, or comedy and
history as did Peele and Greene; we have no comic scenes from
his pen unless we are content to father upon him some anonymous
plays or those usually ascribed to other authors. Cade, Richard
and Queen Margaret are outstanding characters in the second and
third parts of *Henry VI*; of these Richard alone might have
attracted Marlowe, but I think many scenes of the three plays in
which the royal criminal figures were beyond this writer's powers.
In the character of Cade Shakespeare brought into our drama a
new, fresh and higher type of humour. Previously the clown had
dominated our comedy; Greene had the contemporary reputation
of being the 'only maker of comedies'; the extant specimens of his
work in this kind are farcical rather than humorous, and rarely
rise above the level of the low comedian. Miles, the doltish servant
of Friar Bacon rides on the back of the devil to Hell, and puts on
spurs to prevent his satanic majesty from trotting. Adam, the
blacksmith's man in *A Looking Glass,* lifts up the foot of the
self-styled devil, discovers that the cloven hoof is missing, and
conjures him with a cudgel. Both of these clowns and Slipper, the
rascally valet of the scoundrel Ateuken in *James IV,* seem to have
been conceived with no deeper purpose than to raise a laugh from
the groundlings. Greene's clowns all suffer from a chronic thirst
and are always either coming from or going to the alehouse; they
drain pints or quarts of ale in full view of an equally thirsty
audience, and are but one remove, in that they have a name, from
personators of the Vice and the Devil in the old moralities.

In Greene's play the amusement springs from some incongruous or absurd stage situation, or from the grimaces, caperings, posturing or practical jokes of some motley-coated fool; it is centred on externals, eating, drinking, obscenity, beating and being beaten, mock conjuring, etc., and the appeal is to the grotesque side of life and rarely touches the emotions, pleasures or griefs. In *A Looking Glass* the smith discovers that his apprentice, the clown of the play, is making successful love to his wife and proposes to beat him; his man proves by some parody of logic that the master ought to be corrected by the servant, and clenches his proof by soundly cudgelling his master, doubtless to the intense delight of the prentices in the audience. Argalio is ordered by his master, the mad Orlando, to bring to his presence the false Angelica; she is missing, so he engages a red-faced bearded clown fresh from drinking ale to personate her. The fun arises from the absurd spectacle of Orlando's paying high-flown compliments to the eyes, cheeks and complexion of this bloated guzzler of beer, and from the apt comments of this odd 'unexpressive she.' The scene concludes with the customary cudgelling of the mock Angelica. Such is still the comedy of our pantomime, circus, music-hall, and comic opera; such a scene would still raise a laugh in the modern cinema.

In *2 Henry VI* we are in another world, the world in which men live, where we meet Jack Cade and his misled troop of vagabonds. In these scenes Shakespeare paints a masterly portrait of the mob-orator, the dictator in the shell, with his Fortunatus' cap, a trifle greasy, filled with promises of benefits to come if they support the semi-deluded leader of credulous dupes,

> moody Beggars, staruing for a time
> Of pell-mell hauocke, and confusion.

How familiar to our ears sounds the programme (*2 Henry VI*, 4.2.59-69) of the 'Reformation' he 'vowes':

> *Cade.* Be braue then, for your Captaine is Braue, and Vowes
> Reformation. There shall be in England, seuen halfe peny
> Loaues sold for a peny; the three hoop'd pot, shall haue
> ten hoopes, and I wil make it Fellony to drink small Beere.
> All the Realme shall be in Common, and in Cheapside shall
> my Palfrey go to grasse: and when I am King, as King I will
> be.
> *All.* God saue your Maiesty.

Cade. I thanke you good people. There shall be no mony,
all shall eate and drinke on my score, and I will apparrell
them all in one Liuery, that they may agree like Brothers,
and worship me their Lord.

In substance these words spoken on the stage three hundred and
fifty years ago will be heard triennially or quinquennially in every
English-speaking democracy; modern Jack Cades would perhaps
hesitate to declare 'there shall bee no mony.'

This self-elected leader of the proletariat follows the customary
procedure of reform in every century:

> All Schollers, Lawyers, Courtiers, Gentlemen,

he condemns to death, and bids his followers follow their instincts:

> go and set London Bridge on fire,
> And if you can, burne downe the Tower too;

adding,

> Burne all the Records of the Realme, my mouth shall be
> the Parliament of England.

His speech to Lord Say is a masterpiece of political satire, the more
effective because it is simple and forthright:

> Thou hast most traiterously corrupted the youth of the
> Realme, in erecting a Grammar Schoole: and whereas before,
> our Fore-fathers had no other Bookes but the Score and the
> Tally, thou hast caused printing to be vs'd, and contrary to
> the King, his Crowne, and Dignity, thou hast built a Paper-
> Mill. It will be prooued to thy Face, that thou hast men about
> thee, that vsually talke of a Nowne and a Verbe, and such
> abhominable wordes, as no Christian eare can endure to heare.
> Thou hast appointed Iustices of Peace, to call poore men
> before them, about matters they were not able to answer.

Robbery, pillage, outrage and murder attend his progress, and he
falls only when Clifford outbids him by promising his rabble the
invasion, conquest and spoils of France.

These brilliant scenes, so unfortunately true to past and present
history, have a grim sardonic humour touched with a practical
wisdom beyond the known powers of Marlowe, Greene or Peele.
They were probably written, and postdated from what happened
in the days of Wat Tyler and Jack Straw, as a warning to the
turbulent prentices and artisans of London, who had for some

years been so disturbing the peace of the city streets with their riots that the theatres were closed in June, 1592. Like wise men of every age Shakespeare hated mobs and mob-rule, and these pen-pictures of the chaos and anarchy that ever follow hard upon

> base and abiect Routs
> Led on by bloodie Youth, guarded with rags,
> And countenanc'd by Boyes, and Beggerie,

may well describe many a recent scene of mob-violence enacted in half a dozen lands. These scenes foreshadow the mob-scene in *Julius Caesar* where another mob-orator, the aristocratic Antony,

> Rides in the whirlwind and directs the storm,

that overwhelms Brutus, and another in *Coriolanus* where the plebeians break the unbending pride of the great patrician. Shakespeare, not Marlowe or another, drew Cade.

Another remarkable and well-sustained character, Queen Margaret, the 'she-wolf of France,' shares with her husband the distinction of playing a part in each of the three plays on Henry VI; Shakespeare, greatly daring, has in *Richard III* extended her dramatic life beyond the grave. She is the first of a long line of Shakespeare's wicked queens, a group that includes Tamora, Eleanor, Gertrude, Lady Macbeth, Regan, Goneril and the unnamed wife of Cymbeline. Endued with none of the softer graces and little feminine charm, she holds the stage by sheer force of passion and character. Prisoner of Suffolk, they fall in love, and she is depicted in *2 Henry VI* as the unfaithful wife and intriguing politician who combines with her lover, Beaufort and York to ruin and murder the Protector, Duke Humphrey, and plunge the realm into civil war. In *3 Henry VI* she vies with Clifford and Richard in ruthless savagery and pitiless hatred of her enemies. Several of the most dramatic scenes of these two plays, e.g., the parting between her and Suffolk, the death of York, the meeting of the rival partisans before the battle of Towton, and the scene after Tewkesbury when her son was murdered in her presence, bear witness to her tenacity of purpose, courage and devotion to the cause of the Lancastrians and the rights of her son. Of her Milton's description of Satan seems true:

> What though the field be lost?
> All is not lost; th' unconquerable will,
> And study of revenge, immortal hate
> And courage never to submit or yield,
> And what is else not to be overcome.

Returning to England from banishment, the bereaved wife and mother confounds and terrifies the victorious Yorkists with her curses and sinister prophecies, and dauntlessly confronts Richard in the royal palace. Her portrait owes little to history and is essentially Shakespeare's alone.

Marlowe had in the chronicles of Fabian and Holinshed enough details of the events of Edward the Second's reign to have made an equally striking and tragic figure of Queen Isabel, the guilty contriver of her husband's ruin and death, without distorting historic facts as Shakespeare did. His Isabel is little more than a paste-board queen without any fixity of character or purpose. This 'shallow-changing woman' wrings her hands, weeps and bewails her woes, protests her love to her husband, yet consents to urge the repeal of Gaveston who had charged her with infidelity in presence of the king. She is meek where she should justly be angry and seems incapable of any deeply felt emotion. At the end of one scene she plays the constant wife and says of Edward who has called Mortimer her 'lover,'

> Heauens can witnesse I loue none but you,
>   (*Exit Edward*)
> From my imbracements thus he breakes away.
> O that mine armes could close this Ile about,
> That I might pull him to me where I would,
> Or that these teares that drissell from mine eyes
> Had power to mollifie his stonie heart,
> That when I had him we might neuer part.   ll. 1112-18

Less than forty lines after this voluntary declaration of constancy she has betrayed her husband's plans and purpose to Mortimer, who leaves her with these words,

> But thinke of Mortimer as he deserues.   l. 1156

To this her answer is,

> So well hast thou deseru'de sweete Mortimer,
> As Isabell could liue with thee for euer.   ll. 1157-8

When Edward has been deposed, and Mortimer suggests to her the coronation of her son, she replies,

> Sweet Mortimer, the life of Isabell,
> Be thou perswaded, that I loue thee well,
> And therefore so the prince my sonne be safe,
> Whome I esteeme as deare as these mine eyes,
> Conclude against his father what thou wilt,
> And I my selfe will willinglie subscribe.   ll. 2157-62

We are not surprised that this shallow hypocrite suggests that her husband shall be murdered 'so 'twere not by my meane.' Such is Marlowe's conception of a woman in whose life-story was mingled every element of soul-searching tragedy; she excites neither terror nor pity but rather indifference, contempt and disgust. Like Abigail and Zenocrate, she is a shadow of passionless womanhood, a dim, vague simulacrum, a marionette moving as chance or events dictate. If we are to judge, as we must, by the portraits of women in his plays he did not contribute a line to the powerful, if crude, sketch of that valiant, formidable, ruthless fury, Queen Margaret.

Another important difference between the plays of Marlowe and Shakespeare has to do with the quality of the dialogue. Marlowe has not given any proof in his known plays that he was capable of writing either the lively and telling cross-examination in 2 *Henry VI* of the impostor Saunders Simpcox by Duke Humphrey, or the brisk and entertaining duel of wits between King Edward and Lady Grey in Act III, Scene ii of 3 *Henry VI*. In this scene Gloster and Clarence are present and their satirical comments on what they hear and notice strike the first note of discord between the young leaders of the victorious Yorkists. Lady Grey petitions King Edward for the restoration of the lands forfeited by her dead husband, and Edward, attracted by her beauty, tells his brothers that he wishes to 'trye this Widowes wit.' Her skilful parrying of the King's more than doubtful suggestions, her short-lived gratitude for a boon withdrawn almost in the granting, her indignation at his offer to sell the royal justice at the price of her honour, his unexpected proposal of marriage, her modest diffidence in accep-tance and the cross-fire of asides by the two brothers combine into a rapid and agreeable piece of natural and well-sustained dialogue such as might occur in real life. Nothing of such good quality is to be found in any other play of this period.

Dramatically both parts of *Henry VI* are too well constructed, too sane and broad-based, and have too sound a grip of the essentials and lessons of history to have come from the pens of the authors of *James IV* or *Edward I*. These plays are little more than a sequence of disconnected episodes and lack any basic principle of unity. *Edward I* is an incoherent travesty of historical facts mixed with fable and dull comedy. Queen Eleanor, the heroic wife of King Edward, is depicted as a vain wayward monster, guilty of purposeless pranks and atrocities that smack of criminal lunacy, and the play ends in a muddle of infamy, dishonour and death. Perhaps the actors may have interpolated certain episodes in what is undoubtedly a corrupt text, but Peele's plot wants form, coherence and sense.

James IV has an equally improbable plot and abounds in fable and fiction. It purports to relate part of the history of James IV, King of Scotland, the husband of Margaret, sister of Henry the Eighth. Greene's play begins in 1520 and his James is married to Dorothea, daughter of the King of England. James IV had been killed at Flodden seven years before the year when the action of the play begins. Dramatic licence might seem to have gone beyond reason in presenting on the stage a dead king married to an imaginary daughter of a living English king, but Greene brings together as presenters Oberon, King of the fairies, and Bohan, a discontented Scot turned hermit, who keeps up a running commentary on the action and characters in an atrocious dialect. All Greene's plays contain characters that meddle in magic, and *James IV* is fiction rather than history. Several of the female characters are pleasingly drawn, but *The Scottish History of James the Fourth* is entirely lacking in any element of historic credibility.

I shall briefly summarize what has been written above. The external evidence is cumulative, unusually abundant, dated and definite; it interconnects both sets of the parallel texts and covers the thirty years between the composition of the plays on Henry VI and their publication in the folio; those of his contemporaries who knew the facts make no mention of Marlowe. Such portions of the internal evidence as are capable of being to some extent tabulated, e.g., various texts based on vocabulary and verse, the paucity of

FF

and method of using classical imagery and allusions, the numerous similes drawn from life and the references to natural history, all proclaim the authorship of Shakespeare. Moreover, the superior characterisation, especially of minor characters and of women, the humour and truth of the Cade scenes, the quality of the dialogue, the construction of the plots, and the observance of such dramatic unity as chronicle plays permitted, compel me to reject the authorship of Marlowe or of any other contemporary playwright.

Against Shakespeare's authorship critics have offered nothing except flat rejection or ignoring of all external evidence and silence on internal evidence expressible in tabular form. Mediæval methods of handling inconvenient facts are still rampant. I have already shown that parallel passages and inter-play borrowings are not confined solely to Marlowe's plays and those of Shakespeare, and that *Contention* and *True Tragedy* link together at least a dozen plays of this period as in a maze or net. This phenomenon, whether it originated with the authors or their friends, the actor-owners or private buyers of plays, the scribes or the reporters, has not yet been explained, and may involve some principle or cause, as yet imperfectly known. Until the causes underlying these widely spread inter-play borrowings are discovered, the arbitrary detachment of four or five plays from this group cannot logically be justified; why should lines common to *Edward II* and the plays on Henry VI concern the authorship of the latter plays any more or any less than the lines common to them and *Arden* or *Soliman and Perseda?*

Those who favour Marlowe's authorship of *2 Henry VI* and *3 Henry VI* cannot but renounce, as an argument, the use of facts that would prove him the author of at least eleven other plays in my list; they must therefore base their opinion almost solely on aesthetic or subjective impressions. Unfortunately these impressions have led to such diversity of disagreement that a student must conclude that in the multitude of critics is not safety, but confusion. In a final analysis their judgment rests upon an unexpressed article of their literary faith which is implicit in all they write on this subject. Their Shakespeare was never beginner, novice or imitator, but sprang, like Athena from the head of Zeus, miraculously endowed with all the artistic panoply of poet and dramatist. That this opinion is at complete variance with all that we know of the development of every great poet or artist is not taken into account. I prefer Lowell's dictum that the first runnings of the Pierian spring are apt to be turbid or a little muddy, and am content to compare *2 Henry VI* and *3 Henry VI* with *Richard III,* his *Venus* and *Lucrece* and the plays of his contemporaries. His growth to maturity may be traced in *Midsummer Night's Dream, Romeo and Juliet, Henry IV, Twelfth Night, Hamlet, Othello, Macbeth, Antony and Cleopatra* and *Tempest;* but much of his early work is not much superior to these two plays of his nonage.

INDEX

This index is selective, not exhaustive. Titles of all plays and of other literary works are printed in italics. Titles of non-extant plays and some technical terms are in inverted commas. Cross references are given if necessary.

Brown, Prior, Anderson Pty. Ltd.

DATE DUE

MY 08 85			
GAYLORD			PRINTED IN U.S.A.